STEP-BY-STEP MEDICAL CODING

Carol J. Buck

STEP-BY-STEP MEDICAL CODING

THIRD EDITION

Carol J. Buck, BS, MS
Program Director
Medical Secretary Program
Northwest Technical College
East Grand Forks, Minnesota

Technical Collaborators

Karla R. Lovaasen, RRA, CCS
Director of Patient Information Services
(Health Information and Business Office)
St. Francis Medical Center/Home
Breckenridge, Minnesota

Michelle A. Green, MPS, RRA, CMA
Associate Professor
Physical and Life Sciences Department
Alfred State College
Alfred, New York

W.B. SAUNDERS COMPANY
A Harcourt Health Sciences Company
Philadelphia London New York St. Louis Sydney Toronto

W.B. Saunders Company
A Harcourt Health Sciences Company
The Curtis Center
Independence Square West
Philadelphia, Pennsylvania 19106

Library of Congress Cataloging in Publication Data

Buck, Carol J.
Step-by-step medical coding / Carol J. Buck ; technical collaborators, Karla R. Lovaasen.—3rd ed.
p. ; cm.
Includes bibliographical references and index.
ISBN 0-7216-8458-0
1. Nosology—Code numbers. I. Lovaasen, Karla R. II. Title.
[DNLM: 1. Classification. 2. Terminology. WB 15 B922s 2000]
RB115.B83 2000
616'.001'48—dc21
99-049761

Editor-in-Chief: Andrew Allen
Senior Acquisitions Editor: Adrianne Williams
Senior Developmental Editor: Helaine Barron
Senior Illustrator: Karen Giacomucci

STEP-BY-STEP MEDICAL CODING ISBN 0-7216-8458-0

Printed in the United States of America

Last digit is the print number: 9 8 7 6 5 4

To the students,
whose drive and determination to learn
serve as my endless source of inspiration and enrichment.

To teachers,
whose contributions are immense and workloads daunting.
May this work make your preparation for class a little easier.

To DJ,
for sharing the vision.

This book is dedicated in loving memory to my mother,
Gladys E. Swen.

Acknowledgments

This book developed from collaboration by educators and employers in their attempt to meet the needs of students preparing for a career in the medical coding allied health profession. Obtaining employers' input about the knowledge, skills, and abilities desired of entry-level coding employees benefits educators tremendously. This text is an endeavor to use this information to better prepare our students.

There are several other people who deserve special thanks for their efforts in making this text possible:

Karla R. Lovaasen and Michelle A. Green, Technical Collaborators, for their immense technical knowledge and constant willingness to share that knowledge in the education of others.

Adrianne C. Willliams, Senior Acquisitions Editor, Health Related Professions, W.B. Saunders Company, for her enthusiasm and encouragement. Helaine A. Barron, Senior Developmental Editor, W.B. Saunders Company, for her creativity and patience.

Dorith Brown, Department of Coding of Nomenclature, American Medical Association, Chicago, Illinois, for her assistance during the development of the text.

Linda Krechlau, Professional Relations Representative, BCBS, St. Paul, Minnesota, for translating the *Federal Register* into "ordinary words."

Introduction

The number of people seeking health care services has increased as a result of an aging population, technologic advances, and better access to health care. At the same time, there is an increase in the use of outpatient facilities. This increase is due, in part, to the government's introduction of tighter controls over inpatient services. The government continues to increase its involvement in, and control over, health care through reimbursement of services for Medicare patients. Other insurance companies are following the government's lead and adopting reimbursement systems that have proven effective in reducing third-party-payer costs.

Health care in America has undergone tremendous change in the recent past, and more changes are promised for the future. The outcome of these changes has resulted in an ever-increasing demand for qualified medical coders. The government predicts a growth in demand for medical coders of 51% during the 1996–2006 time period.[1] The national shortage has increased the salary for the coding occupation, and salaries in general show a solid upward trend.

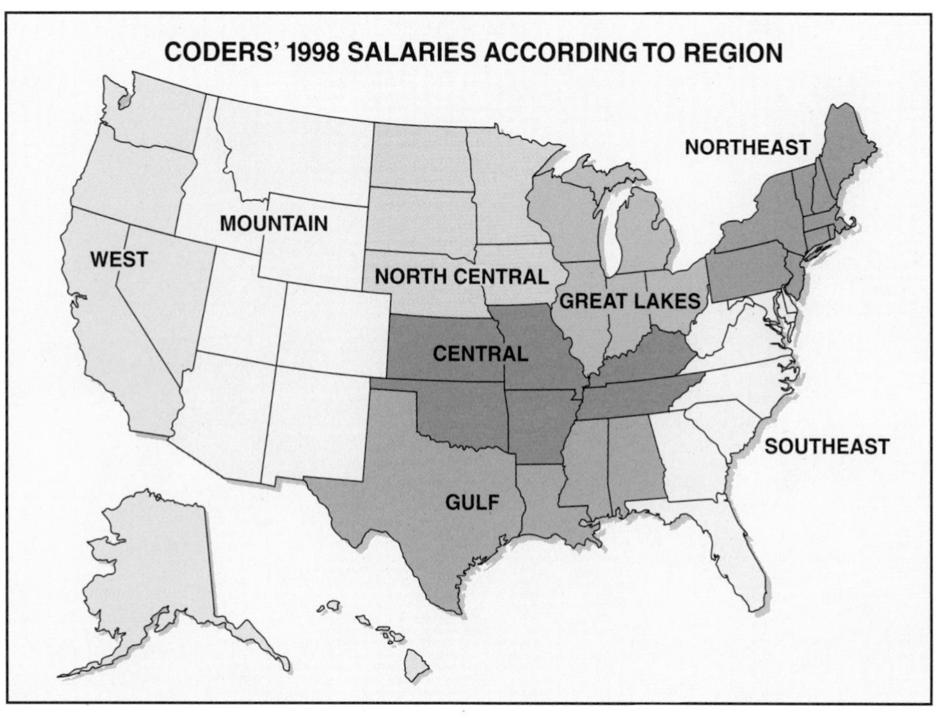

The regional averages for certified procedural coders from the 1998 Salary Survey[2] by the American Academy of Procedural Corders (AAPC) are as follows:*

West	$29,623
Mountain	$27,665
North Central	$24,414
Great Lakes	$27,743
Central	$26,064
Gulf	$24,187
Southeast	$31,262
Northeast	$30,545
All regions	$27,687

Opportunity for career advancement exists with certified managerial positions averaging $40,721 annually.[2]

Medical coding is far more than assigning numbers to services and diagnoses. Coders abstract information from the patient record and combine it with their knowledge of reimbursement and coding guidelines to optimize physician payment. Coders have been called the "fraud squad" because they optimize, never maximize, and code only for services provided to the patient that are documented in the medical record.

There is a demand for skilled coders, and you can be one of those in demand. Put your best efforts into building the foundation of your career and you will be rewarded for a lifetime.

References

1. America's Career InfoNet: Fastest Growing Careers, Bureau of Labor Statistics, 1996. (http://www.acinet.org/acinet/oview1.htm?Level=Overall)
2. 1998 Salary Survey. AAPC News 9(5), 1998. Salt Lake City, American Academy of Procedural Coders.

---

*American Academy of Procedural Coders, published by permission.

Reviewers

Kay Appenfeldt
Moraine Park Technical College
Fond du Lac, Wisconsin

Cynthia Brunette, BA, Ed
Business Institute of Pennsylvania
Sharon, Pennsylvania

Paul E. Miller, Jr., MS
Peirce Junior College
Philadelphia, Pennsylvania

Barbara Steinbeck, ART
Manager, Clinical Research Department
3M Health Information System
Wallingford, Connecticut

Kimberly S. Wilson, MEd
Greene County Career College
Xenia, Ohio

Roberta J. Yankovich, ART
AHIMA-AOE
Chicago, Illinois

Contents

UNIT 1

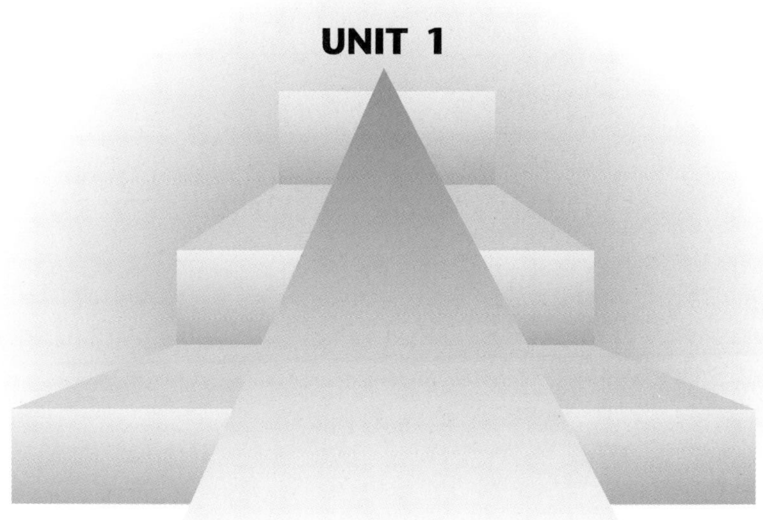

Current Procedural Terminology–4 (CPT–4)

1 Let's Look at the CPT Manual

CHAPTER TOPICS

Learning Objectives

After completing this chapter, you should be able to

1. Identify the purpose of the CPT manual.
2. State the importance of using the current-year CPT manual.
3. Recognize the symbols used in the CPT manual.
4. List the major sections found in the CPT manual.
5. Identify information in appendices of the CPT manual.
6. Interpret the information contained in section Guidelines.
7. Identify elements of the CPT manual format.
8. Assign modifiers.
9. Determine what is meant by unlisted procedures/services.
10. State the purposes of a special report.
11. Locate terms in the CPT manual index.
12. Define chapter terminology.

PURPOSE OF THE CPT MANUAL

Current Procedural Terminology (CPT) is a coding system developed by the American Medical Association (AMA) to convert widely accepted, uniform descriptions of medical, surgical, and diagnostic services rendered by health care providers into five-digit numeric codes. The CPT codes are presented in manual format in *Current Procedural Terminology.* The use of the CPT codes enables health care providers to communicate both effectively and efficiently to third-party payers (ie, insurance companies, Medicare, Medicaid) about the procedures and services provided to the patient.

Health care providers are reimbursed based on the codes submitted for the procedures and services rendered. For an example of placement of the CPT codes on a claim form refer to Figure 1–1. Assignment of the correct code is essential because incorrect coding can result in a provider's being reimbursed incorrectly. The CPT coding system is used by clinics, outpatient hospital departments, ambulatory surgery centers, and third-party payers to describe health care services. Although there are differences in the rules governing coding in various health

PLEASE DO NOT STAPLE IN THIS AREA

APPROVED OMB-0938-0008

CARRIER

PICA **HEALTH INSURANCE CLAIM FORM** PICA

1. MEDICARE (Medicare #) MEDICAID (Medicaid #) CHAMPUS (Sponsor's SSN) CHAMPVA (VA File #) GROUP HEALTH PLAN (SSN or ID) FECA BLK LUNG (SSN) OTHER (ID)

1a. INSURED'S I.D. NUMBER (FOR PROGRAM IN ITEM 1)

2. PATIENT'S NAME (Last Name, First Name, Middle Initial)

3. PATIENT'S BIRTH DATE MM DD YY SEX M F

4. INSURED'S NAME (Last Name, First Name, Middle Initial)

5. PATIENT'S ADDRESS (No., Street)

6. PATIENT RELATIONSHIP TO INSURED Self Spouse Child Other

7. INSURED'S ADDRESS (No., Street)

CITY STATE

8. PATIENT STATUS Single Married Other

CITY STATE

ZIP CODE TELEPHONE (Include Area Code) ( )

Employed Full-Time Student Part-Time Student

ZIP CODE TELEPHONE (INCLUDE AREA CODE) ( )

9. OTHER INSURED'S NAME (Last Name, First Name, Middle Initial)

10. IS PATIENT'S CONDITION RELATED TO:

11. INSURED'S POLICY GROUP OR FECA NUMBER

a. OTHER INSURED'S POLICY OR GROUP NUMBER

a. EMPLOYMENT? (CURRENT OR PREVIOUS) YES NO

a. INSURED'S DATE OF BIRTH MM DD YY SEX M F

b. OTHER INSURED'S DATE OF BIRTH MM DD YY SEX M F

b. AUTO ACCIDENT? PLACE (State) YES NO

b. EMPLOYER'S NAME OR SCHOOL NAME

c. EMPLOYER'S NAME OR SCHOOL NAME

c. OTHER ACCIDENT? YES NO

c. INSURANCE PLAN NAME OR PROGRAM NAME

d. INSURANCE PLAN NAME OR PROGRAM NAME

10d. RESERVED FOR LOCAL USE

d. IS THERE ANOTHER HEALTH BENEFIT PLAN? YES NO ***If yes,*** return to and complete item 9 a-d.

READ BACK OF FORM BEFORE COMPLETING & SIGNING THIS FORM.

12. PATIENT'S OR AUTHORIZED PERSON'S SIGNATURE I authorize the release of any medical or other information necessary to process this claim. I also request payment of government benefits either to myself or to the party who accepts assignment below.

SIGNED ______ DATE ______

13. INSURED'S OR AUTHORIZED PERSON'S SIGNATURE I authorize payment of medical benefits to the undersigned physician or supplier for services described below.

SIGNED ______

PATIENT AND INSURED INFORMATION

14. DATE OF CURRENT: MM DD YY ILLNESS (First symptom) OR INJURY (Accident) OR PREGNANCY(LMP)

15. IF PATIENT HAS HAD SAME OR SIMILAR ILLNESS. GIVE FIRST DATE MM DD YY

16. DATES PATIENT UNABLE TO WORK IN CURRENT OCCUPATION FROM MM DD YY TO MM DD YY

17. NAME OF REFERRING PHYSICIAN OR OTHER SOURCE

17a. I.D. NUMBER OF REFERRING PHYSICIAN

18. HOSPITALIZATION DATES RELATED TO CURRENT SERVICES FROM MM DD YY TO MM DD YY

19. RESERVED FOR LOCAL USE

20. OUTSIDE LAB? YES NO $ CHARGES

21. DIAGNOSIS OR NATURE OF ILLNESS OR INJURY. (RELATE ITEMS 1,2,3 OR 4 TO ITEM 24E BY LINE)

1. ___ . __ 3. ___ . __

2. ___ . __ 4. ___ . __

22. MEDICAID RESUBMISSION CODE ORIGINAL REF. NO.

23. PRIOR AUTHORIZATION NUMBER

24. A DATE(S) OF SERVICE From MM DD YY To MM DD YY	B Place of Service	C Type of Service	D PROCEDURES, SERVICES, OR SUPPLIES (Explain Unusual Circumstances) CPT/HCPCS MODIFIER	E DIAGNOSIS CODE	F $ CHARGES	G DAYS OR UNITS	H EPSDT Family Plan	I EMG	J COB	K RESERVED FOR LOCAL USE
1										
2										
3										
4										
5										
6										

25. FEDERAL TAX I.D. NUMBER SSN EIN

26. PATIENT'S ACCOUNT NO.

27. ACCEPT ASSIGNMENT? (For govt. claims, see back) YES NO

28. TOTAL CHARGE $

29. AMOUNT PAID $

30. BALANCE DUE $

31. SIGNATURE OF PHYSICIAN OR SUPPLIER INCLUDING DEGREES OR CREDENTIALS (I certify that the statements on the reverse apply to this bill and are made a part thereof.)

SIGNED DATE

32. NAME AND ADDRESS OF FACILITY WHERE SERVICES WERE RENDERED (If other than home or office)

33. PHYSICIAN'S, SUPPLIER'S BILLING NAME, ADDRESS, ZIP CODE & PHONE #

PIN# GRP#

PHYSICIAN OR SUPPLIER INFORMATION

(APPROVED BY AMA COUNCIL ON MEDICAL SERVICE 8/88) ***PLEASE PRINT OR TYPE*** FORM HCFA-1500 (12-90) FORM OWCP-1500 FORM RRB-1500

Form 1240LM

Figure 1–1

HCFA-1500 Health Insurance Claim Form, also known as the "universal claim form," used by outpatient facilities for claims submission. (Courtesy of U.S. Department of Health and Human Services, Health Care Financing Administration.)

care settings, CPT codes offer increased compatibility and comparability of data among users and providers, allowing for comparative analysis, research, and reimbursement.

The CPT coding system was developed by the AMA in 1966 as a method of billing for medical and surgical procedures and services using standard terminology. Three editions of *Current Procedural Terminology* were published in the 1970s, and updates and revisions reflected changes in the technology and practices of health care. Use of the CPT manual was increased in 1983 when the Health Care Financing Administration (HCFA) incorporated the CPT codes with HCFA's Common Procedure Coding System (HCPCS). Level II national codes (HCPCS) are used by providers to code for services, supplies, and equipment provided to Medicare patients for which no CPT codes exist. Level II codes are discussed in more detail later in this text.

Updating the CPT Manual

Because the practice of medicine is ever changing, the CPT manual is ever changing. It is updated annually to reflect technologic advances and editorial revisions. It is very important to use the most current CPT manual available to provide quality data and ensure appropriate reimbursement. Updated editions of the CPT manual are available for purchase in November for use beginning the following January 1. The CPT manual may be ordered by writing to Order Department, American Medical Association, P.O. Box 7046, Dover, DE 19903-7046 or by calling 1-800-621-8335.

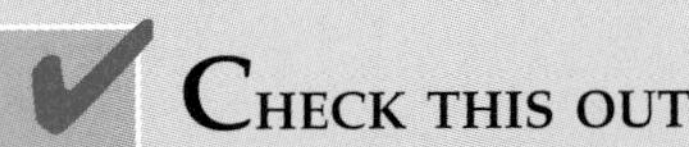

The American Medical Association (AMA) has a Web page located at http://www.ama-assn.org.

THE CPT MANUAL FORMAT

Five Important Symbols

In the CPT manual, *new* codes for procedures and services are identified by the bullet (●) symbol that is placed in front of the code number. Note the location of this symbol in Figure 1–2.

A triangle (▲) placed in front of a code indicates that the description for the code has been *changed* or modified since the previous edition. Changes may be additions, deletions, or revisions in code descriptions (Fig. 1–3).

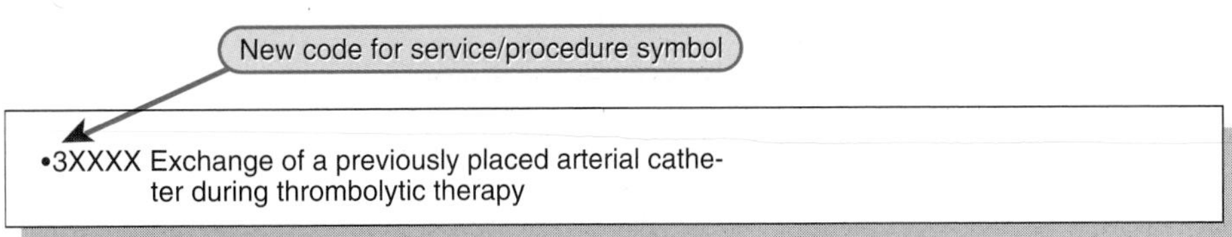

Figure 1–2
New code symbol.

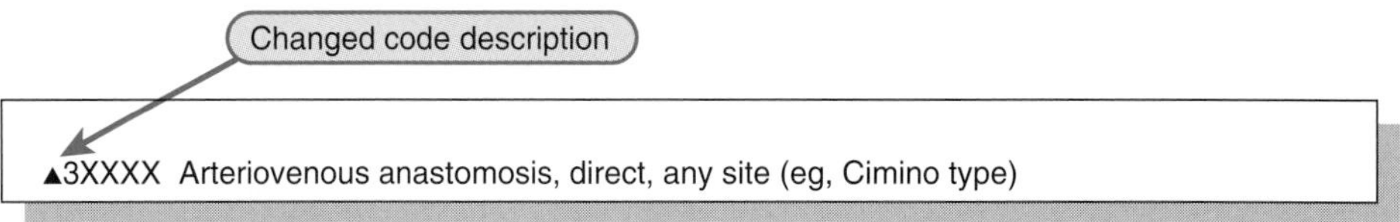

Figure 1–3
Changed code symbol.

The plus symbol (+) placed in front of a code indicates an **add-on code** (Fig. 1–4). Add-on codes are never used alone; rather, they are used with another primary procedure or service code. For example, code 11000 describes a debridement (removal of contaminated tissue) of up to 10 percent of the body surface. Add-on code 11001 is used for each additional 10 percent of the body surface debrided. Code 11001 cannot be used unless code 11000 is used first. Also notice in Figure 1–4 that there is a note in parentheses that indicates code 11001 can be used only in conjunction with code 11000. **Appendix E** in the CPT manual lists all add-on codes.

The circle with a line through it (⃠) identifies a **modifier -51 exempt code** (Fig. 1–5). This symbol warns you to check the primary procedure code to see what is included in the primary procedure code before using the modifier -51 exempt code. For example, when coding procedures in which a graft or implant is used, you will usually find that the primary procedure code includes the graft or implant done during the procedure, making a separate graft code unnecessary. Also note in Figure 1–5 that the category notes for "Grafts (or Implants)" indicate that

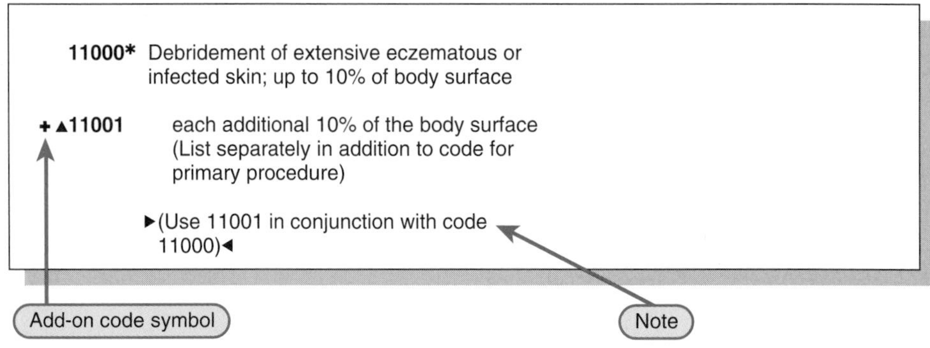

Figure 1–4
Add-on code symbol.

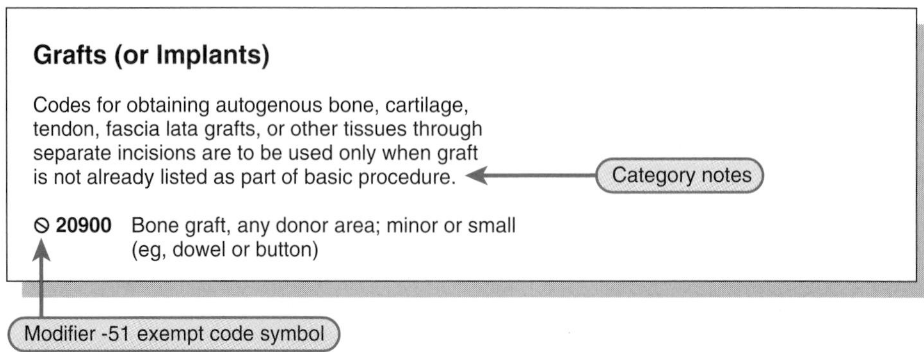

Figure 1–5
Modifier -51 exempt code symbol.

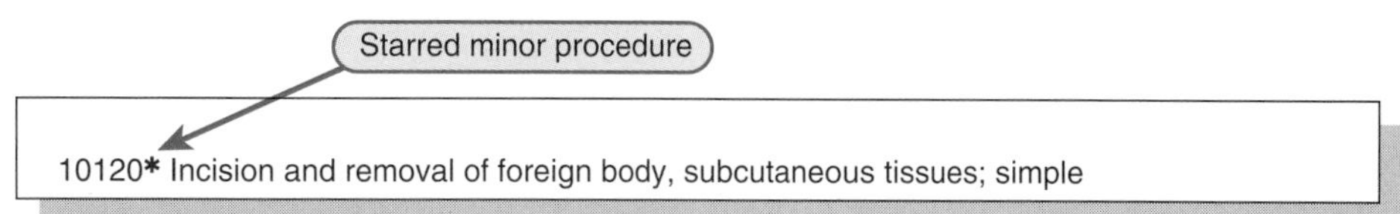

Figure 1–6
Minor procedure symbol.

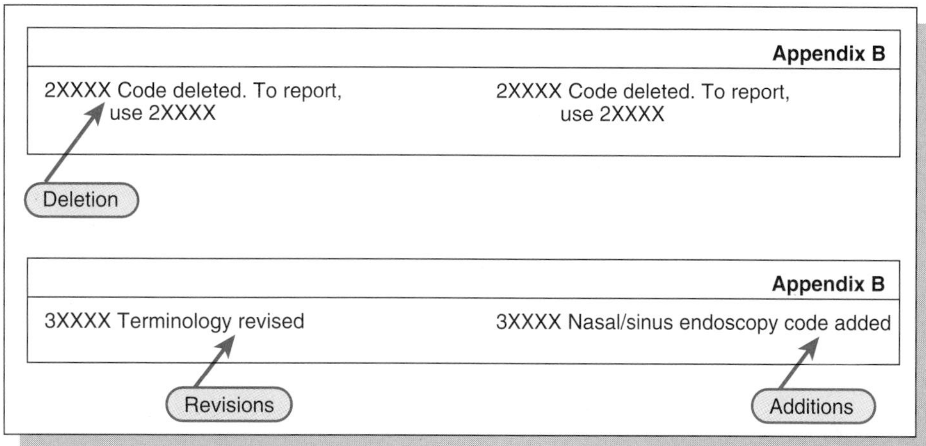

Figure 1–7
CPT manual Appendix B showing types of changes.

the codes in the category are used only when the graft is not a part of the basic procedure. **Appendix F** in the CPT manual contains the complete list of modifier -51 exempt codes.

A star (✱) placed after a code number indicates that the service includes the *surgical procedure only* (Fig. 1–6). The starred minor procedure is discussed in Chapter 3 along with the modifier -51 exempt code and the add-on code.

Appendix B of the CPT manual contains a complete list of the additions, deletions, and revisions from the previous edition of the CPT manual. When a code is listed in Appendix B, the type of change is listed beside the code number (Fig. 1–7). For example, if the procedure or service is still available but is to be reported with a different code, the deleted code is listed, followed by the new code to be used.

EXERCISE A Symbols

When you are finished with the following exercise, ask your instructor for the Chapter Exercise Answers.

Match the following code symbols with the correct definition:

1. ▲ ____
2. ✱ ____
3. ● ____
4. ⃠ ____
5. + ____

a. surgical procedure only
b. modifier -51 exempt
c. changed
d. add-on
e. new

6. Where is a complete list of additions, deletions, and revisions located in the CPT manual?

____

7. Which CPT manual appendix contains a complete list of all modifier -51 exempt codes?

____

8. Which CPT manual appendix contains a complete list of add-on codes?

____

The Six Sections

The CPT manual is composed of six divisions into which all codes and descriptions are categorized. These divisions are called sections.

The Divisions of the CPT Manual

CPT Sections

- Evaluation and Management
- Anesthesia
- Surgery
- Radiology
- Pathology and Laboratory
- Medicine

The sections are further divided into subsections, subheadings, categories, and subcategories. A section is a chapter that covers one of the six topics covered in the CPT manual: Evaluation/Management (E/M), Anesthesia, Surgery, Radiology, Pathology/Laboratory, and Medicine. The CPT codes are arranged in numerical order in each section.

Sections are divided into subsections. For example, the Surgery section includes subsections of Integumentary, Musculoskeletal, Respiratory, Cardiovascular, and so forth.

Subsections, subheadings, categories, and subcategories are divisions of sections that are based on anatomy, procedure, condition, description, or approach.

EXAMPLE

Section:	Surgery
Subsection:	Cardiovascular System
Subheading:	Arteries and Veins
Category:	Embolectomy/Thrombectomy
Subcategory:	Arterial, With or Without Catheter

Section:	Surgery
Subsection:	Nervous System
Subheading:	Skull, Meninges, and Brain
Category:	Approach Procedures
Subcategory:	Anterior Cranial Fossa

EXERCISE B *Section, Subsection, Subheading, and Category*

To see an example of section, subsection, subheading, and category, locate the code "19000 Puncture aspiration of cyst of breast" in the CPT manual in the Surgery section.

With a CPT manual beside you and opened to the page on which CPT code 19000 is located, or referring to Figure 1–8, find the following information on the CPT manual page:

Section: At the top of the page, the word "Surgery" indicates the section. Note that this word is followed by a range of numbers, which is a list of all the code numbers located on that page.

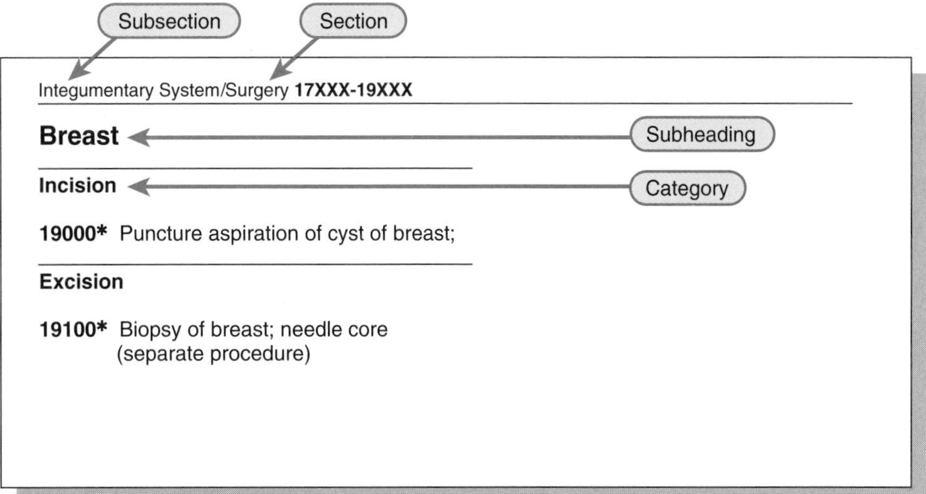

Figure 1–8
Section, subsection, subheading, and category.

Subsection: Also at the top of the page, just before the word "Surgery," the phrase "Integumentary System" indicates the subsection.

Subheading: The word "Breast" indicates the subheading.

Category: The word "Incision" indicates the category. In summary, the divisions for the previous example are

Section:	Surgery
Subsection:	Integumentary System
Subheading:	Breast
Category:	Incision

Now you try one.

With a CPT manual open to the page that contains code 30100, locate the following information for the 30100 code:

1. Section: ______________________
2. Subsection: ______________________
3. Subheading: ______________________
4. Category: ______________________

Using the section, subsection, subheading, and category information makes it much faster and easier to get around within the CPT manual.

What's in the Guidelines?

Each section in the CPT manual includes "Guidelines." Guidelines provide specific information about coding in that section and contain valuable information for the coder. Guidelines that are applicable to all codes in the section are found at the beginning of each section (Fig. 1–9). Notes pertaining to specific codes or

Section Guidelines applicable to all Surgery codes

Surgery Guidelines

Items used by all physicians in reporting their services are presented in the **Introduction**. Some of the commonalities are repeated here for the convenience of those physicians referring to this section on **Surgery**. Other definitions and items unique to Surgery are also listed.

Figure 1–9
Section guidelines.

Specific notes applicable to a group of codes

> **SURGERY OF SKULL BASE**
> The surgical management of lesions involving the skull base (base of anterior, middle, and posterior cranial fossae) often requires the skills of several surgeons of different surgical specialties working together or in tandem during the operative session. These operations are usually…

Figure 1–10
Specific notes.

groups of codes are listed before or after the codes (Fig. 1–10). The Guidelines and notes may contain definitions of terms, applicable modifiers, subsection information, unlisted services, special reports information, or clinical examples. Always read the Guidelines and notes before coding to help ensure accurate assignment of the CPT codes.

EXERCISE C *Sections*

Using the Guidelines for each of the sections, answer the following questions:

1. Write the definition of a chief complaint using the E/M Guidelines. ________
   ____
   ____
   ____
2. According to the Surgery Guidelines, is surgical destruction usually considered part of a surgical procedure? ______________________________
3. Who must sign a written report to have the report considered part of the radiologic procedure? ______________________________
4. Under whose supervision are Pathology and Laboratory services provided? ______________________________
5. What is the code listed in the Medicine Guidelines that is to be used to identify materials supplied by the physician that are beyond those ordinarily included in the service provided? ______________________________

Code Format

Procedure descriptions are located after the code number (Fig. 1–11). These descriptions are commonly accepted descriptions of services or procedures that are provided to patients.

There are two types of codes: **stand-alone codes** and **indented codes** (Fig. 1–12). Only the stand-alone codes have the full description. It is understood that descriptions for indented codes include the portion of the stand-alone code description that precedes the semicolon. The purpose of the semicolon is to save space.

You may not have realized it, but you just got a critical clue to coding—the semicolon. The following information will help you understand why the semicolon is so important.

In Figure 1–12 the code 26011 is an indented code—the indentation serves to represent the words "Drainage of finger abscess" which appear before the semicolon in CPT code 26010. The semicolon is a powerful tool in the CPT manual; when you see it, be sure to read the words before it carefully.

The words following the semicolon can indicate alternative anatomic sites, alternative procedures, or a description of the extent of the service.

EXAMPLE

Alternative Anatomic Site:

27705	Osteotomy; tibia
27707	fibula
27709	tibia and fibula

Alternative Procedure:

31505	Laryngoscopy, indirect (separate procedure); diagnostic
31510	with biopsy
31511	with removal of foreign body
31512	with removal of lesion

Description of Extent of the Service:

20520*	Removal of foreign body in muscle or tendon sheath; simple
20525	deep or complicated

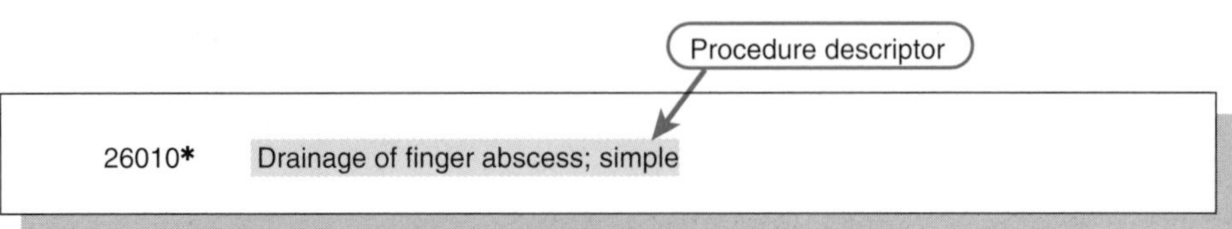

Figure 1–11
Code and description format.

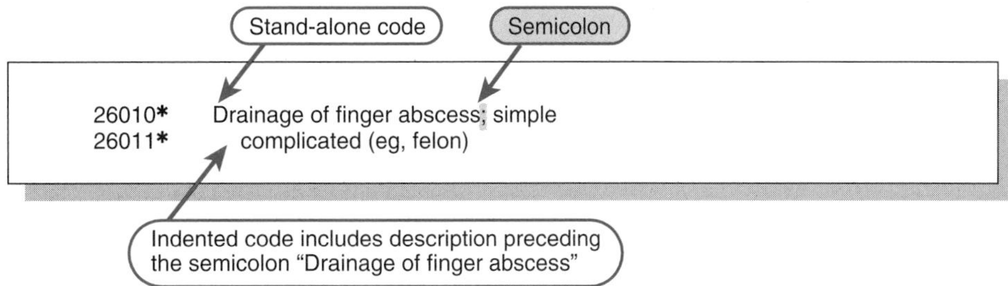

Figure 1–12
Stand-alone codes and indented codes.

Before assigning an indented code, make sure you refer to the stand-alone code and read the words that precede the semicolon. That is the only way to ensure a full description and select a correct code.

EXERCISE D CPT Manual Format

1. Describe a stand-alone code. ______________________________

____

____

2. Describe an indented code. ______________________________

____

____

3. Words following the semicolon in stand-alone codes can indicate the following three things:

   a. ______________________________

   b. ______________________________

   c. ______________________________

The Many Uses of Modifiers

Modifiers provide additional information to the third-party payer about services provided to a patient. At times, the five-digit CPT code may not totally reflect the service or procedure provided. Because numeric codes, not written procedure descriptions, are required by third-party payers, additional numbers or letters may be added to the basic five-digit code to modify the CPT code to give further specificity. These additional modifiers may be two-number or two-letter modifiers that are appended, or "tacked on," to the basic five-digit CPT code, or they may be five-digit numbers that are listed together with the basic code. In the Health Care Procedure Coding System (HCPCS), two-letter modifiers (eg, -RC and -QN) are used. You will learn about the specific use of these two-letter modifiers in later chapters of this text.

In the CPT system, a modifier can be either an appended two-digit number or an additional five-digit number.

EXAMPLE

-62

or

09962

The two-digit modifier is added onto the five-digit CPT code.

EXAMPLE

Code 43820 is the CPT procedure code for a gastrojejunostomy, without vagotomy. If two surgeons with different surgical skills participated in the surgery, the procedure code 43820 could be altered by the addition of the modifier -62 to indicate two co-surgeons (Fig. 1–13). The code would be 43820-62 for a gastrojejunostomy, without vagotomy, in which two surgeons participated. Each physician would submit his or her own bill indicating code 43820-62.

The five-digit modifiers are used for electronic billing and in the hospital outpatient setting. As illustrated in Figure 1–14, the five-digit modifier is composed of the prefix 099 plus the two-digit modifier.

EXAMPLE

The two-digit modifier -22 is used to indicate a more extensive or unusual procedure. The five-digit modifier is 09922. The code 27332 for an arthrotomy of the knee with complex excision of cartilage can be stated two ways:

27332-22 Arthrotomy, knee, complex

or

27332 and 09922 Arthrotomy, knee, complex

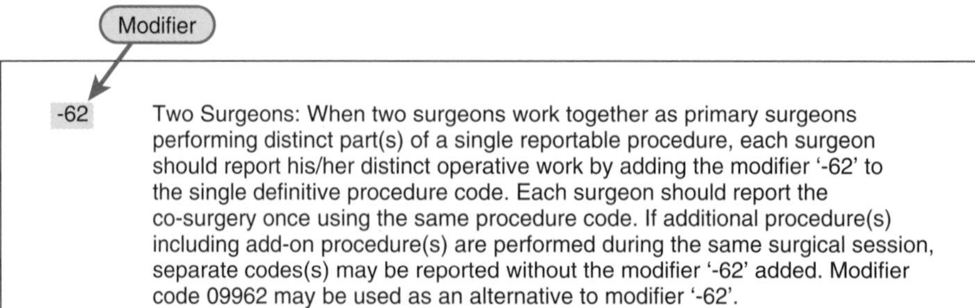

Figure 1–13
Two-digit modifier.

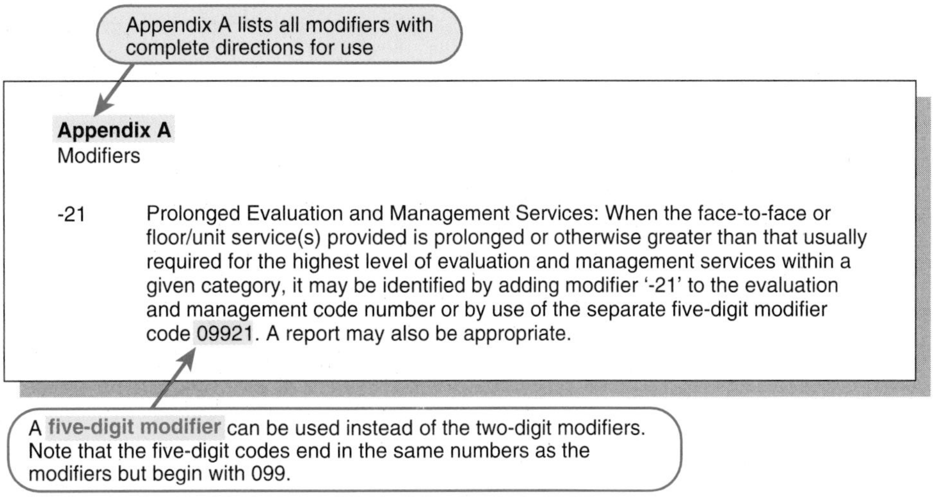

Appendix A lists all modifiers with complete directions for use

Appendix A
Modifiers

-21 Prolonged Evaluation and Management Services: When the face-to-face or floor/unit service(s) provided is prolonged or otherwise greater than that usually required for the highest level of evaluation and management services within a given category, it may be identified by adding modifier '-21' to the evaluation and management code number or by use of the separate five-digit modifier code 09921. A report may also be appropriate.

A five-digit modifier can be used instead of the two-digit modifiers. Note that the five-digit codes end in the same numbers as the modifiers but begin with 099.

Figure 1–14
Modifiers in Appendix A.

Refer to Figure 1–14 for an example of **Appendix A.** For a complete listing of all modifiers, see Appendix A in the CPT manual. Further information regarding modifiers is presented throughout the following chapters of this text.

EXERCISE E *Two- and Five-Digit Modifiers*

Using Appendix A of the CPT manual and the information you just learned, fill in the blank with the correct number:

1. What is the five-digit modifier to indicate two primary surgeons?

   Code(s): ____________

2. If the CPT code is 43820 (gastrojejunostomy without vagotomy) and two primary surgeons performed the service, the service could be stated two ways:

   ____________ or ____________

   and ____________.

Use Appendix A of the CPT manual to list the correct two- and five-digit modifiers in the following examples. You do not have to supply the five-digit CPT procedure code, only the two- and five-digit modifiers.

3. Bilateral inguinal herniorrhaphy: ____________ and ____________.

4. A postoperative ureterotomy patient needs to be returned to the operating room for a related procedure during the postoperative period:

   ____________ and ____________.

5. Regional or general anesthesia was used in a procedure in which only local anesthesia is standard: ____________ and ____________.

6. There is a need for multiple procedures during the same surgical session:

    ______________________ and ______________________.

7. A surgical team is required: ______________ and ______________.

8. Physician A assists physician B: ______________ and ______________.

WATCH FOR SPECIAL CIRCUMSTANCES

When to Use Unlisted Procedures

When developing the CPT manual, the AMA realized that not every surgical or diagnostic procedure could be listed. There may not be a code for many procedures that are considered experimental, newly approved, or seldom used. In addition, medical advancements often create a variation of procedures currently performed. A procedure or service not found in the CPT manual can be coded as an "unlisted procedure." For example, when the first heart transplant was done, there was no code to use to report the new surgical procedure. Until a code was available, the unlisted code for cardiac surgery was used to report this procedure (Fig. 1–15). The Surgery Guidelines have unlisted procedure codes by body site or type of procedure. Individually unlisted procedure codes are also at the end of the subsection or subheading to which they refer. For example, at the end of the Cardiovascular System subsection is the unlisted cardiac procedure code 33999, and at the end of the Respiratory System is the unlisted lungs/pleura code 32999.

EXERCISE F ***Unlisted Procedure Codes***

Using the unlisted procedure Guidelines in the front of the sections indicated below, locate the five-digit unlisted procedure code for the following:

1. Surgery

    Unlisted procedure; middle ear: Code(s): ______________

    arthroscopy: Code(s): ______________

    esophagus: Code(s): ______________

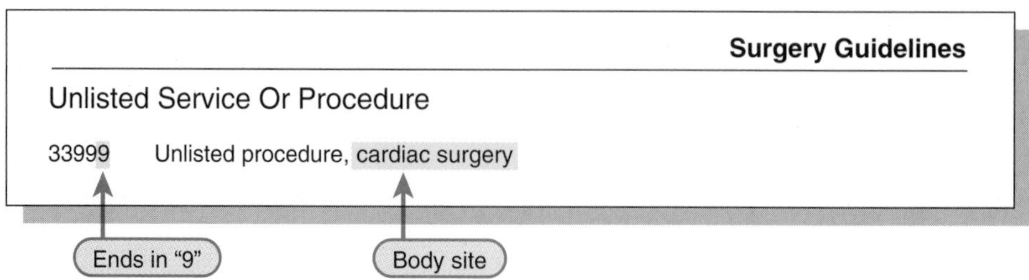

Figure 1–15
Unlisted service or procedure.

2. Pathology and Laboratory

   Unlisted procedure; cytogenetic study: Code(s): ________________

   urinalysis procedure: Code(s): ________________

   chemistry procedure: Code(s): ________________

3. Medicine

   Unlisted procedure; special service, procedure, or report: Code(s): ________________

4. Radiology

   Unlisted procedure; clinical brachytherapy: Code(s): ________________

   Unlisted miscellaneous procedures; diagnostic nuclear medicine: Code(s): ________________

When to Use Special Reports

Special reports must accompany claims when an unusual, new, seldom used, or unlisted procedure is performed. The special report should include an adequate definition or description of the *nature, extent,* and *need* for the procedure and the *time, effort,* and *equipment* necessary to provide the service. The special report helps the third-party payer determine the appropriateness of the care and the medical necessity of the service provided.

STARTING WITH THE INDEX

Locating the Terms

The CPT index is located at the back of the CPT manual and is arranged alphabetically. Index headings located at the top right and left corners of the index pages direct the coder to the entries that are included on that page, much like a dictionary. Use of index headings will speed location of the term (Fig. 1–16).

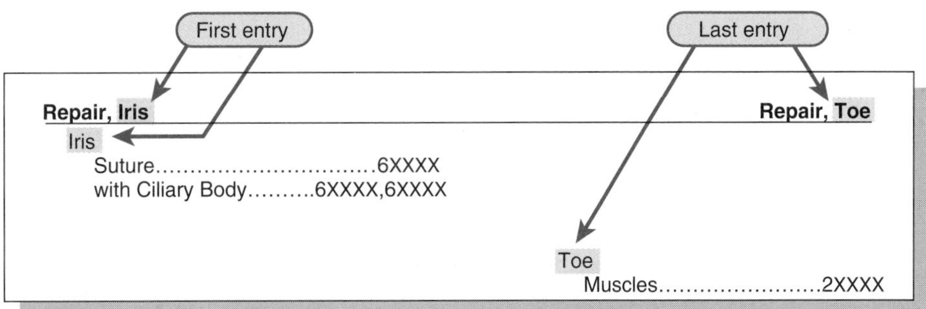

Figure 1–16
CPT manual index headings.

Code numbers are displayed in the CPT index in one of the three following ways.

EXAMPLE

single code: 38115

multiple codes: 26645, 26650

range: 22305–22325

See Figure 1–17 for an example of the display in the index using the single, multiple, and range formats.

Single Code

When only one code number is stated, you should verify the code in the main portion of the CPT manual to ensure its accuracy.

Multiple Codes

The use of a *comma* between code numbers indicates the existence of only those numbers displayed. If more than one code number is listed, then all codes must be referenced to make an accurate choice.

Range of Codes

A range is indicated by a *hyphen*. When a range is given in the index, you must look at each code in the main portion of the CPT manual to select the appropriate code from the range.

Never code directly from the index. You can't be sure you have the right code until you have located the code in the main portion of the CPT manual and read information presented there regarding the specifics of the code.

The index is in alphabetical order by main terms and further divided by subterms. Figure 1–18 illustrates the main term and subterm as used in the index. Having identified the main term of the service or procedure, you can locate the

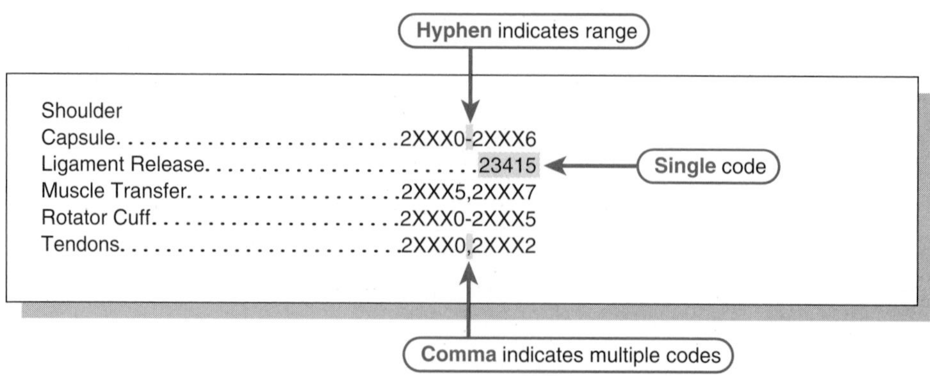

Figure 1–17
Code display.

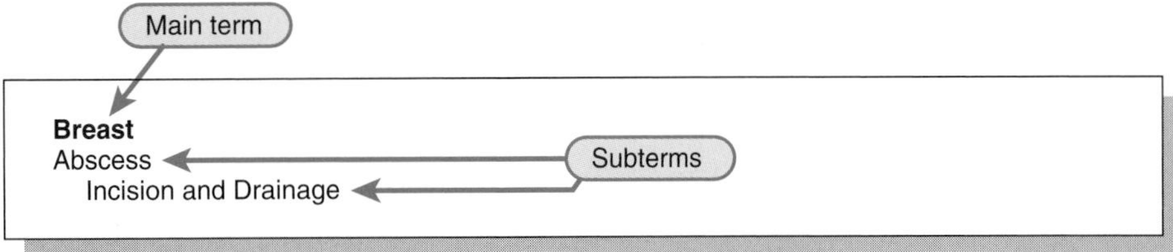

Figure 1–18
CPT manual index indicating main terms and subterms.

term in the index. When you are just beginning to use the CPT manual, it may be difficult to locate the main term. Not being able to locate a term in the index can be very frustrating, but don't be discouraged if you don't identify the main term on the first try. This is a skill that is learned from practice, and part of the practice is making mistakes. Soon you'll be locating those main terms quickly. Just keep thinking about the service or procedure and looking up the words in the index.

Some basic location methods will help you locate these main terms.

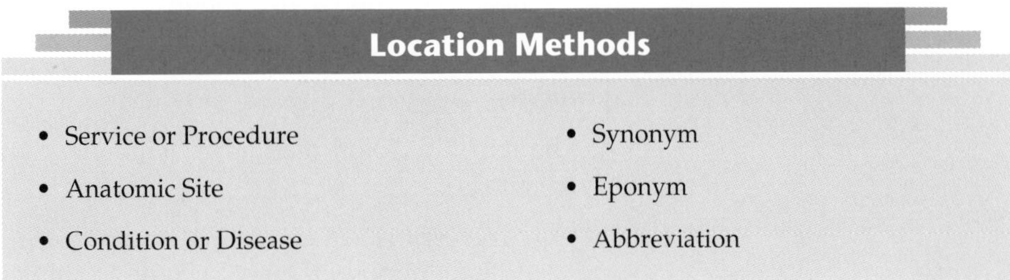

Let's take these location methods and apply each one to locating a "repair of a fracture of a femur."

EXERCISE G Term Practice

Service or Procedure

1. With the service or procedure location method, "repair" would be the main term in "*repair* of a fracture of a femur."
   a. Locate "Repair" in the index of the CPT manual. Using this location method, "Repair" is the main term and the subterms are "Fracture" and "Femur."
   b. Under the main term "Repair," locate the subterm "Femur." If you were to look under "Repair" and then for the term "Fracture," you wouldn't find "Fracture," because listed under "Repair" are the anatomic divisions that can be repaired. Since "Fracture" isn't an anatomic division, it isn't located under "Repair." It can be just as difficult to locate the correct subterm as it is to find the main term.

Right now, don't be concerned with looking up the codes in the main part of the CPT manual; we will come to that in subsequent chapters. For now, concentrate on learning how to locate the main term and subterms in the index.

Anatomic Site

2. The second location method of anatomic site uses the word "femur" as the main term, and the subterms are "fracture" and "repair."
   a. Locate "Femur" in the index of the CPT manual.
   b. Under the main term "Femur," locate the subterm "Fracture."
   c. Notice that the entry "Fracture" is further divided based on repair type or anatomic location.

Condition or Disease

3. The third location method is the condition or disease. In this instance you would use the main term "fracture" as a condition.
   a. Locate the main term "Fracture" in the index.
   b. Locate the subterm "Femur."

The use of the first three location methods will usually get you to the applicable codes in the index. If you try each of the first three methods and still can't locate the codes in the index, don't despair; try one of the other location methods: synonym, eponym, and abbreviation.

Synonym

4. The fourth location method is synonym. Synonyms are words with similar meanings.
   a. Toe joint is a synonym for interphalangeal joint or metatarsophalangeal joint. Suppose, then, you couldn't think of the correct medical term, but you could think of the word "toe." In that case, you could look up "Toe" in the CPT manual index, and that entry would direct you to:

      See also Interphalangeal Joint, Toe; and Metatarsophalangeal Joint, Phalanx

Eponym

5. The fifth location method is eponym. Eponyms are things that are named for people. For example, the Barr Procedure—a tendon-transfer procedure—was named after the person who developed it.
   a. Locate "Barr Procedure" in the CPT manual index. You are directed to "*See* Tendon Transfer, Leg, Lower."

Abbreviation

6. The sixth location method is abbreviation. Abbreviations are common in medicine for names of drugs, diseases, and procedures.
   a. Locate the abbreviation "INH" in the index of the CPT manual. You are directed to "*See* Drug Assay."

Medicine uses many synonyms, eponyms, and abbreviations. A good medical dictionary that contains the more common synonyms, eponyms, and abbreviations will be a necessity for you.

Locate each of the following main terms in the CPT manual index, and then locate the subterms and sub-subterms:

	Main Term	Subterm	Sub-Subterm
1.	Repair	Abdomen	Suture
2.	Femur	Abscess	Incision
3.	Fracture	Ankle	Lateral

Never code directly from the index. The index does not include information necessary for appropriate code selection.

Locate the code in the index and then verify the code in the main part of the CPT manual to ensure the code is correct for assignment.

Don't rely on memory.

Always follow the steps outlined for coding.

You are now ready to put term location skills to work with this next exercise.

EXERCISE H Main Term Location

Identify main terms in the following examples and write the main term on the line provided. Then, locate main terms and any subterms in the CPT manual index. Write the code listed in the index for that service or procedure on the line provided.

1. Description: Emergency Department Services, Physician Direction of Advanced Life Support
   a. Main term: ______________________________
   b. Locate the code available in the index of the CPT manual for Emergency Department Services, Physician Direction of Advanced Life Support

      Code(s): ______________
2. Condition/Disease: intertrochanteric femoral fracture (closed treatment)
   a. Main term: ______________________________
   b. Locate the code available in the index of the CPT manual for intertrochanteric femoral fracture (closed treatment)

      Code(s): ______________

3. Procedure: removal of gallbladder calculi

   a. Main term: ______________________

   b. Locate the code available in the index of the CPT manual for removal of gallbladder calculi

      Code(s): __________

4. Anatomic site: lung, bullae excision

   a. Main term: ______________________

   b. Locate the code available in the index of the CPT manual for excision of bullae of lung

      Code(s): __________

STOP!

As you can probably see from this exercise, there are often many ways to locate an item in the index. The same word often serves as a main term or a subterm depending on the location method you are using. In addition, the annual updating of the CPT results in numerous changes within the index.

You will be locating terms in the CPT manual index throughout the chapters of this text. For your ready reference, there is a guideline at the beginning of the index in the CPT manual that contains directions on the use of the CPT manual index. Beginning with Chapter 2 of this text, the key will list not only the correct code answer, but also one index location for that code. For example, if the correct answer was 99203, the following would appear in the key after the code: (Office and/or Other, Outpatient Visit, New Patient). It is difficult to locate items in the CPT index when you begin coding, so, if you get stuck and just cannot locate the index entry, you will be able to find one location in the key for this text.

"See" or "See also"

"See" and *"See also"* are cross-reference terms found in the index of the CPT manual. These terms direct you to another term or other terms.

"See" indicates that the correct code will be found elsewhere.

EXAMPLE

Anticoagulant *See* Clotting inhibitors

"See also" indicates that a more specific code may be found in a different location.

EXAMPLE

Biopsy *See also* Brush Biopsy; Needle Biopsy

The coder must follow the instructions given in the index.

EXERCISE 1 ***"See" or "See also"***

Complete the following:

1. Locate "Renal Disease Services" in the CPT index. You are directed to ______ ______________________________.

2. Locate the abbreviation "ANA" in the CPT index. The entry you find is ______ ______________________________.

3. Locate "Arm" in the CPT index. You are directed to ______________ ______________________________.

Never code directly from the index. To ensure correct coding, the code number must be located in the main portion of the CPT manual.

Two More CPT Appendices

The CPT is available on computer diskettes. **Appendix C** of the CPT manual contains a listing of the updates to the electronic data file to reflect all the additions, revisions, and deletions that were made to the manual since the last edition (see Fig. 1–19). With these updates, the data files can be updated without having to purchase a new set of diskettes. Although the electronic version saves the coder time, it is not a replacement for the skill and knowledge of the coder—it is only a tool to be used by a skillful and knowledgeable coder.

Update to Short Descriptors

This listing includes changes necessary to update the short descriptors on the *CPT 2000* data file.

The descriptors have been changed to reflect additions, revisions, or deletions to the *CPT 2000* codes, or to enhance or correct the data file.

The descriptors which have been enhanced, but do not necessarily reflect a change to the *CPT 2000* codes, are indicated with an asterisk.

00100 Revise: ANESTH, SALIVARY GLAND

Data file update

Figure 1–19
Appendix C of the CPT manual contains electronic updating information.

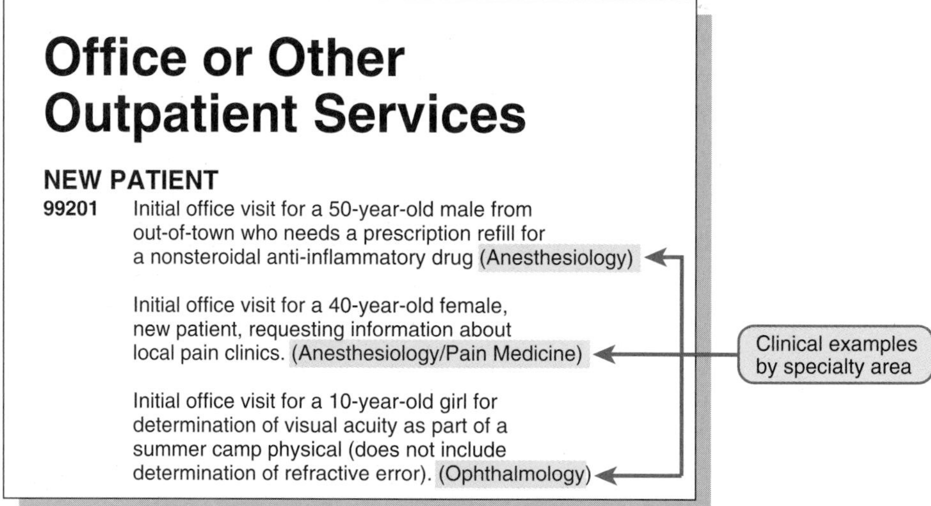

Figure 1–20
Appendix D of the CPT manual contains clinical examples in the use of E/M codes.

Appendix D of the CPT manual contains clinical examples of the Evaluation and Management (E/M) service codes (see Fig. 1–20). The examples are those meant to give the beginning coder a broad idea of the type of services that each code could represent. But, a word of caution: only the patient record and the particular services rendered by the physician to a particular patient can determine the level of service provided. Appendix D is not meant to be an exhaustive list of E/M services.

CHAPTER GLOSSARY

Appendix A: located near the back of the CPT manual; lists all modifiers with complete explanations for use

Appendix B: located near the back of the CPT manual; contains a complete list of additions, deletions, and revisions from previous editions

Appendix C: located near the back of the CPT manual; contains the list of updates to the electronic version of the CPT

Appendix D: located near the back of the CPT manual; presents clinical examples of Evaluation and Medical (E/M) Procedures

Appendix E: located near the back of the CPT manual; contains a listing of the CPT add-on codes

Appendix F: located near the back of the CPT manual; contains a list of modifier -51 exempt codes

CPT (Current Procedural Terminology): a coding system developed by the American Medical Association (AMA) to convert widely accepted, uniform descriptions of medical, surgical, and diagnostic services rendered by health care providers into five-digit numerical codes

Guidelines: provide specific instructions about coding for each section; the Guidelines contain definitions of terms, applicable modifiers, explanation of notes, subsection information, unlisted services, special reports information, and clinical examples

modifiers: two- or five-digit numbers added to CPT codes to supply more specific information about the services provided to the patient

sections: the six major areas into which all CPT codes and descriptions are categorized

"See" or **"See also":** a cross-reference system within the index of the CPT manual used to direct the coder to another term or other terms. The *"See"* indicates that the correct code will be found elsewhere. The *"See also"* indicates that a more specific code may be found in a different location.

special reports: detailed reports that include adequate definitions or descriptions of the nature, extent, and need for the procedure and the time, effort, and equipment necessary to provide the services

subsections: the further division of sections into smaller units, usually by body systems

symbols: special guides that help the coder compare codes and descriptors with the previous edition. A bullet (●) is used to indicate a new procedure or service code added from the last edition of the CPT manual. A solid triangle (▲) placed in front of a code number indicates that the code has been changed or modified since the last edition. A star (✱) placed after a code number indicates a minor procedure. A plus (+) is used to indicate an add-on code. A circle with a line through it (⃠) is used to identify a modifier -51 exempt code.

term location methods: service/procedure, anatomic site/body organ, condition/disease, synonym, eponym, and abbreviation

unlisted procedures: procedures that are considered unusual, experimental, or new and do not have a specific code number assigned; unlisted procedure codes are located at the end of the subsections or subheadings and may be used to identify any procedure without a specific code

CHAPTER REVIEW Chapter 1, Part I, Theory

Do not use your CPT manual for this part of the review.

1. CPT stands for ______________________________.
2. The CPT manual often reflects the technologic advances made in medicine with ______________________________.
3. The CPT manual is divided into how many sections? ______________
4. What type of five-digit code begins with 099? ______________
5. Coding information that applies to the entire section is located where? ______________________________
6. Procedures that include variable preoperative or postoperative services are noted in the CPT manual with what symbol? ______________
7. What is the name of the two-digit code number that is located after the CPT code number and provides more detail about the code? ______________
8. Where is a list of all the modifiers located? ______________
9. When using an unlisted procedure, third-party payers will usually require submission of what? ______________
10. Additions, deletions, and revisions are listed in what Appendix? __________

    A listing of all add-on codes is located in what Appendix? __________
11. The symbol used between two code numbers to indicate a range is available is a ______________________________.

There were six location methods presented in Chapter 1. List any four of the methods:

12. ____________________

13. ____________________

14. ____________________

15. ____________________

A special report should contain a description of what six things about the services provided?

16. ____________________

17. ____________________

18. ____________________

19. ____________________

20. ____________________

21. ____________________

22. What association publishes the CPT? ____________________

23. When you see the symbol ▲ placed in front of a code, you know what about the code? ____________________

24. What type of code has the full code description? ____________________

25. What type of code has only a portion of the code description? ____________________

Using Figure 1–21 identify the category, section, subheading, and subsection.

26. ____________________

27. ____________________

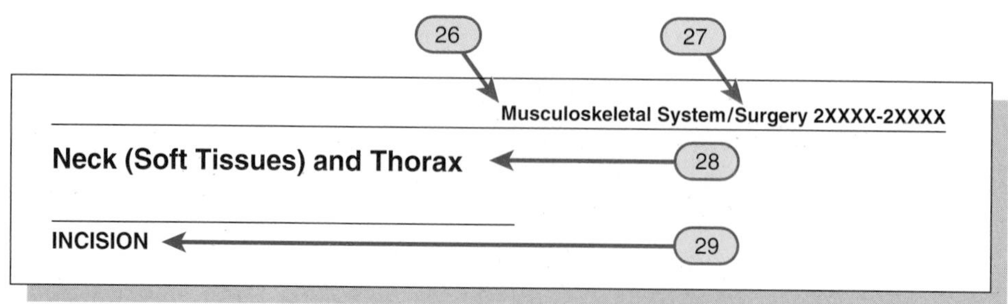

Figure 1–21
Identify the section, subsection, subheading, and category.

28. ______________________________

29. ______________________________

Chapter 1, Part II, Practical

Use your CPT manual for this part of the review. Using Appendix A of the CPT manual, list the correct two- and five-digit modifiers for the following services:

30. Repeat procedure by the same physician: __________ or __________

31. Surgical care only: __________ or __________

32. Anesthesia by the surgeon: __________ or __________

33. Bilateral procedure: __________ or __________

Locate the following unlisted procedure codes:

Surgery

34. orbit __________ Code(s): __________

35. rectum __________ Code(s): __________

36. lips __________ Code(s): __________

37. general musculoskeletal __________ Code(s): __________

Radiology

38. clinical brachytherapy __________ Code(s): __________

39. miscellaneous procedures, diagnostic nuclear medicine __________ Code(s): __________

40. therapeutic radiology treatment management __________ Code(s): __________

Pathology

41. chemistry procedure __________ Code(s): __________

42. quantitation of drug __________ Code(s): __________

Medicine

43. allergy/clinical immunologic service __________ Code(s): __________

44. special dermatological service __________ Code(s): __________

45. special service, procedure, or report __________ Code(s): __________

Using the index of the CPT manual, locate an example for each of the following types of code display:

46. single code ______________________________

47. multiple code ______________________________

48. range ______________________________

Using the index of the CPT manual, locate the following terms and write what the index note directs you to do:

49. Td Shots ______________________________

50. SHBG ______________________________

51. Radius ______________________________

52. Physical Therapy ______________________________

Using the index of the CPT manual, locate the code(s) for the following:

53. Repair, abdomen ______________________________

54. Bypass graft, excision, abdomen ______________________________

55. Catheterization, arteriovenous shunt ______________________________

56. Cystotomy, with drainage ______________________________

57. Fracture, femur, intertrochanteric, closed treatment ______________________________

58. Alveoloplasty ______________________________

59. Duodenotomy ______________________________

Learning About the Evaluation and Management (E/M) Section

CHAPTER TOPICS

Contents of E/M Section
Three Factors of E/M Codes
Various Levels of E/M Service
An E/M Code Example
Using the E/M Codes
HCFA Documentation Guidelines
Chapter Glossary
Chapter Review

Learning Objectives

After completing this chapter, you should be able to

1. Identify and explain the three factors of E/M code assignment.
2. Analyze the key components.
3. Explain the levels of E/M service.
4. List contributing factors.
5. Analyze code information.
6. Assign E/M codes.
7. Understand HCFA Documentation Guidelines.
8. Define chapter terminology.

CONTENTS OF E/M SECTION

The information in Chapter 1 provided you with the basic format of the CPT manual. The information and exercises in this chapter will familiarize you with the first section of the CPT manual, Evaluation and Management (E/M). The E/M section has 17 subsections.

E/M Subsections

1. Office or Other Outpatient
2. Hospital Observation
3. Hospital Inpatient
4. Consultations
5. Emergency Department
6. Critical Care
7. Neonatal Intensive Care
8. Nursing Facility
9. Domiciliary, Rest Home, or Custodial Care
10. Home Services
11. Prolonged Services
12. Case Management
13. Care Plan Oversight
14. Preventive Medicine
15. Newborn Care
16. Special Evaluation and Management Services
17. Other Evaluation and Management Services

THREE FACTORS OF E/M CODES

Code assignment in the E/M section varies depending on three factors.

Factors

1. Place of Service
2. Type of Service
3. Patient Status

Place of Service

The first factor the coder must consider in code assignment is the place of service (Fig. 2–1). Place of service explains the setting where the services were provided to the patient. Codes vary depending on the place of the service. Places of service can be the physician's office, hospital, emergency department, nursing home, and so on.

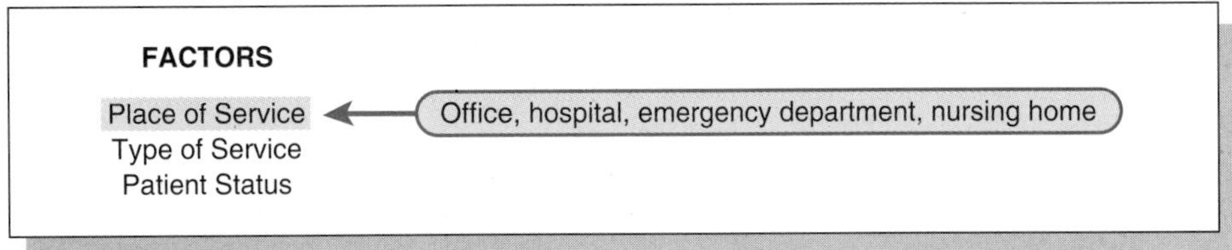

Figure 2–1
Place of service.

Type of Service

The second factor in code assignment is the type of service (Fig. 2–2). Type of service is the reason the service is requested or performed. Examples of types of service are consultation, admission, newborn care, and office visit.

- *Consultations* are requested to obtain the opinion, or advice on a diagnosis or management option, from another physician.
- *Admission* is a request for immediate attention to an acute illness or injury, resulting in an admission to a hospital.
- *Newborn care* is a request for evaluation and determination of care management of a newly born infant.
- *Office visit* request is a face-to-face encounter of a physician and patient to allow for primary management of a patient's health care status.

The type of service may also indicate whether the visit is for a new or established patient.

Patient Status

The third factor in code assignment is the patient status (Fig. 2–3). The four types of patient status are new patient, established patient, outpatient, or inpatient. Codes are often grouped in the CPT manual according to the type of patient.

- *New patient* is one who has not received professional services from the physician or another physician of the same specialty in the same group within the past 3 years.
- *Established patient* is one who has received professional services from the physician or another physician of the same specialty in the same group within the past 3 years.
- *Outpatient* is one who has not been formally admitted to a health care facility.
- *Inpatient* is one who has been formally admitted to a health care facility.

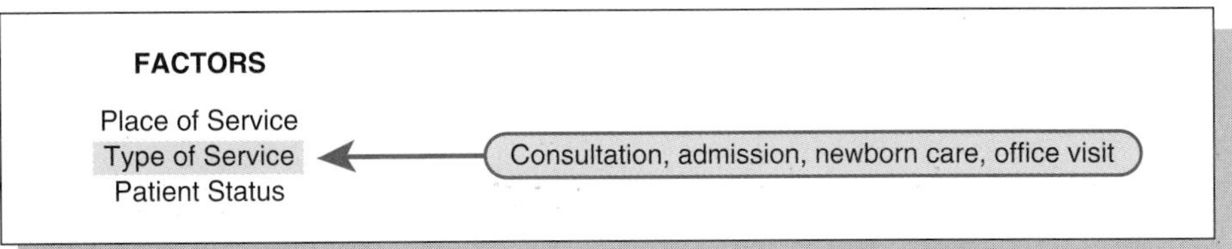

Figure 2–2
Type of service.

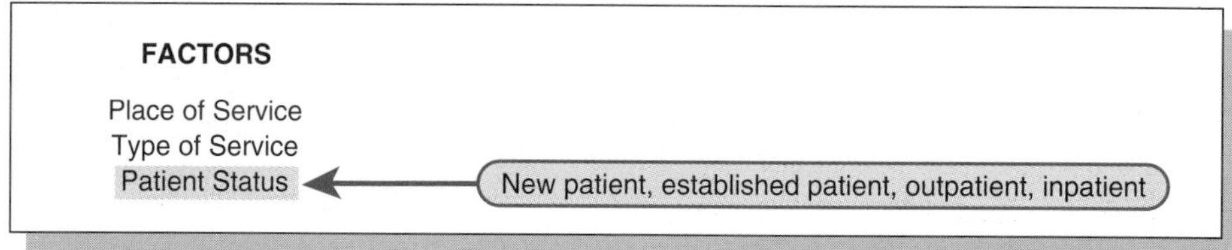

Figure 2–3
Patient status.

EXERCISE A *Factors of E/M Codes*

Using a CPT manual, locate the subsection "Office and Other Outpatient Services" and then the category "New Patient" in the E/M section to answer the following questions:

1. Where is the place of service? ____________________
2. What is the type of service? ____________________
3. What is the patient status? ____________________
4. What is the first code number listed under "New Patient"?

   Code(s): ____________
5. Each code represents a different level of service. How many codes are listed under "Office or Other Outpatient Services" for a new patient? ________
6. How many codes are listed for the established patient in the "Office or Other Outpatient Services" category? ____________________

VARIOUS LEVELS OF E/M SERVICE

The levels of E/M service are based on documentation located in the patient record supporting various amounts of skill, effort, time, responsibility, and medical knowledge used by the physician to provide the service to the patient. The levels of service are based on **key components** (history, examination, and medical decision-making complexity) and **contributing factors** (counseling, coordination of care, nature of presenting problem, and time). The components contain a great deal of information that you need to know before you learn about factors. Let's look at each of these components and factors individually.

Key Components

Key Components

- History
- Examination
- Medical Decision-Making

The key components of history, examination, and medical decision-making reflect the clinical information that is recorded by the physician in the patient's record. Key components are present in every patient case except counseling encounters, which are discussed later in the chapter. Key components enable you to choose the appropriate level of service. New patient encounters, consultations, emergency department visits, and admissions require documentation of all three components. Subsequent visits such as daily hospital visits or outpatient visits for an established patient require that only two of the three key components be present for assignment to a given code.

History

The history is the *subjective* information the patient tells the physician based on the four elements of a history—chief complaint (CC); history of present illness (HPI); review of systems (ROS); and past, family, and/or social history (PFSH). The history contains the information the physician needs to appropriately assess the patient's condition. Not all histories have all elements. The inclusion of each of the elements and the extent to which each of the elements is contained in a history are determined by the physician based on the need for more or less subjective information and will determine the history level. The documentation of the history is found in the patient's chart and is recorded by the physician.

Four Elements of a History

- Chief Complaint (CC)
- History of Present Illness (HPI)
- Review of Systems (ROS)
- Past, Family, and/or Social History (PFSH)

History Elements

You need to be able to identify the various elements and levels of a history by reading the notes entered into the medical record by the physician.

1. **Chief Complaint (CC)** is a concise statement describing the symptom, problem, condition, diagnosis, physician recommended return, or other factor that is the reason for the encounter, usually stated in the patient's words.

2. **History of Present Illness (HPI)** is a chronological description of the development of the patient's present illness from the first sign and/or symptom or from the previous encounter to the present. It includes the following elements:
   - Location
   - Quality
   - Severity
   - Duration
   - Timing
   - Context
   - Modifying factors
   - Associated signs and symptoms
3. **Review of Systems (ROS)** is an inventory of body systems obtained through a series of questions seeking to identify signs and/or symptoms which the patient may be experiencing or has experienced. According to Huffman's *Health Information Management,** the "ROS is an inventory of systems to reveal subjective symptoms that the patient either forgot to describe or which at the time seemed relatively unimportant. In general, an analysis of the subjective findings will indicate the nature and extent of the examination required." For purposes of ROS, the following systems are recognized:
   - Constitutional symptoms

     Usual weight, recent weight changes, fever, weakness, fatigue
   - Eyes

     Glasses or contact lenses, last eye examination, visual glaucoma, cataracts, eyestrain, pain, diplopia, redness, lacrimation, inflammation, blurring
   - Ears, Nose, Mouth, Throat

     Ears: hearing, discharge, tinnitus, dizziness, pain
     Nose: head colds, epistaxis, discharges, obstruction, postnasal drip, sinus pain
     Mouth and Throat: condition of teeth and gums, last dental examination, soreness, redness, hoarseness, difficulty in swallowing
   - Cardiovascular

     Chest pain, rheumatic fever, tachycardia, palpitation, high blood pressure, edema, vertigo, faintness, varicose veins, thrombophlebitis
   - Respiratory

     Chest pain, wheezing, cough, dyspnea, sputum (color and quantity), hemoptysis, asthma, bronchitis, emphysema, pneumonia, tuberculosis, pleurisy, last chest radiograph
   - Gastrointestinal

     Appetite, thirst, nausea, vomiting, hematemesis, rectal bleeding, change in bowel habits, diarrhea, constipation, indigestion, food intolerance, flatus, hemorrhoids, jaundice

---

*Definitions from Huffman E: Health Information Management, 10th ed. Revised by the American Medical Record Association. Berwyn, IL, Physician's Record Company, 1994, pp 57–62.

- Genitourinary

  Urinary: frequent or painful urination, nocturia, pyuria, hematuria, incontinence, urinary infection
  Gastroreproductive: male—venereal disease, sores, discharge from penis, hernias, testicular pain or masses; female—age at menarche and menstruation (frequency, type, duration, dysmenorrhea, menorrhagia; symptoms of menopause), contraception, pregnancies, deliveries, abortions, last Papanicolaou smear

- Musculoskeletal

  Joint pain or stiffness, arthritis, gout, backache, muscle pain, cramps, swelling redness, limitation in motor activity

- Integumentary (skin and/or breast)

  Rashes, eruptions, dryness, cyanosis, jaundice, changes in skin, hair, or nails

- Neurological

  Faintness, blackouts, seizures, paralysis, tingling, tremors, memory loss

- Psychiatric

  Personality type, nervousness, mood, insomnia, headache, nightmares, depression

- Endocrine

  Thyroid trouble, heat or cold intolerance, excessive sweating, thirst, hunger, or urination

- Hematologic/Lymphatic

  Anemia, easy bruising or bleeding, past transfusions

- Allergic/Immunologic

4. **Past, Family, and/or Social History (PFSH)***

   - *Past history* is the patient's past experience with illnesses, operations, injuries, and treatments; specifically:

     "Prior major illnesses and injuries
     Prior operations
     Prior hospitalizations
     Current medications
     Allergies (eg, drug, food)
     Age appropriate immunization status
     Age appropriate feeding/dietary status."

   - *Social history* is an age appropriate review of past and current activities that includes significant information about:

     "Marital status and/or living arrangements
     Current employment
     Occupational history
     Use of drugs, alcohol, and tobacco
     Level of education

---

*Definitions from 1999 CPT, Evaluation and Management Guidelines, pp 2–3.

Sexual history
Other relevant social factors."

- *Family history* is a review of medical events in the patient's family that includes significant information about:
  "The health status or cause of death of parents, siblings, and children
  Specific diseases related to problems identified in the Chief Complaint or History of the Present Illness, and/or System Review
  Diseases of family members which may be hereditary or place the patient at risk."

Three of the elements of a history (HPI, ROS, and PFSH) are included to varying degrees in all patient encounters. The degree or level of history is determined by the chief complaint or presenting problem of the patient.

History Levels

Now that you have reviewed the elements of a history you are prepared to choose a history level. There are four history levels based on the extent of the history during the history-taking portion of a physician/patient encounter.

History Levels

- Problem Focused
- Expanded Problem Focused
- Detailed
- Comprehensive

1. **Problem focused:** The physician focuses on the chief complaint and a brief history of the present problem of a patient.

   A *brief* history would include a review of the history regarding pertinent information about the present problem or chief complaint. Brief history information would center around the severity, duration, and symptoms of the problem or complaint. The brief history does not have to include the past, family, or social history or review of systems.

2. **Expanded problem focused:** The physician focuses on a chief complaint, obtains a *brief* history of the present problem, and also performs a *problem pertinent* review of systems. The expanded problem focused history does not have to include the past, family, or social history.

   This history would center around specific questions regarding the system involved in the presenting problem or chief complaint. The review of systems for this history would cover the organ system most closely related to the chief complaint or presenting problem and any related or associated body system. For example, if the presenting problem or chief complaint was a red, swollen knee, the system reviewed would be the musculoskeletal system.

3. **Detailed:** The physician focuses on a chief complaint, obtains an *extended* history of the present problem, *extended* review of systems, and a *pertinent* PFSH.

TABLE 2–1 Elements Required for Each Level of History

Level of History	HPI	ROS	PFSH
Problem Focused	Brief	N/A	N/A
Expanded Problem Focused	Brief	Problem pertinent	N/A
Detailed	Extended	Extended	Pertinent
Comprehensive	Extended	Complete	Complete

The system review in this history is "extended," which means positive responses and pertinent negative responses for multiple organ systems should be documented.

4. **Comprehensive:** This is the most complex of the history types in which the physician documents the chief complaint, obtains an *extended* history of the present problem, does a *complete* review of systems, and obtains a *complete* PFSH.

For a summary of the elements required for each level of history, see Table 2–1.

EXERCISE B ***History Levels***

Using the CPT manual, locate the Office or Other Outpatient Services subsection, New Patient category, to identify the history level on each of the following codes:

Code	History Level
1. 99201	____________
2. 99202	____________
3. 99203	____________
4. 99204	____________
5. 99205	____________

Examination

The patient has presented the physician with the *subjective* information regarding a complaint or problem in the history portion of the encounter; now the physician will do an examination of the patient to provide *objective* information (those findings observed by the physician) about the complaint or problem. The physician then documents the objective findings in the patient record.

Examination Levels

The examination levels have the same titles as the history levels. The four levels are used to indicate the extent and complexity of the patient examination.

Examination Levels

- Problem Focused
- Expanded Problem Focused
- Detailed
- Comprehensive

1. **Problem focused:** Examination is limited to the affected body area or organ system identified by the chief complaint.
2. **Expanded problem focused:** Examination is limited to the affected body area or organ system and other related body area(s)/organ system(s).
3. **Detailed:** An extended examination of the affected body area(s) or related organ system(s).
4. **Comprehensive:** This is the most extensive examination that encompasses a complete single specialty examination or complete multisystem examination.

Table 2–2 summarizes the elements required for each level of examination. These elements include different body areas (BAs) and organ systems (OSs). They also include an assessment of a patient's general condition, which is indicated by the patient's general appearance, vital signs, and the like. These three elements—BA, OS, and general—are as follows:

Body Areas

- Head (including the face)
- Neck
- Chest (including breasts and axilla)
- Abdomen
- Genitalia, groin, buttocks
- Back
- Each extremity

Organ Systems

- Eyes
- Ears, nose, mouth, throat
- Respiratory

TABLE 2–2 Elements Required for Each Level of Examination

Level of Examination	Body Area(s)/Organ System(s)
Problem Focused	Affected BA and OS
Expanded Problem Focused	Affected BA and other BA/OS
Detailed	Extensive affected BA(s) or related OS
Comprehensive	Complete BA(s) and complete OS(s)

- Cardiovascular
- Genitourinary
- Hematological/lymphatic/immunologic
- Musculoskeletal
- Skin
- Neurological
- Psychiatric
- Gastrointestinal

General

- Constitutional (vital signs, general appearance)

EXERCISE C *Examination Levels*

Using the CPT manual, locate the Office or Other Outpatient Services subsection, New Patient category, to identify the examination levels for each of the following codes:

Code	Examination Levels
1. 99201	____________
2. 99202	____________
3. 99203	____________
4. 99204	____________
5. 99205	____________

The patient record will reflect the number of systems examined by a brief statement as to the findings. The examination would include the examination elements in the number and extent required for the physician to arrive at the diagnosis. For example, if a patient came to the physician with a complaint of a small foreign object lodged in the eye, the physician would not need to do a cardiologic examination. The extent of the examination is based on what needs to be done to treat the patient.

Now, you need to pull all the information on history and examination together so that it is usable information. What better way to do that than to use the information in the practical application of an exercise?

EXERCISE D *Examination Elements*

Label each of the following as body area (BA) or organ system (OS):

1. Skin ____________
2. Head ____________
3. Eyes ____________

4. Ears ___________

5. Nose ___________

6. Mouth ___________

7. Throat ___________

8. Neck ___________

9. Thorax, anterior and posterior ___________

10. Breasts ___________

11. Lungs ___________

12. Heart ___________

13. Abdomen ___________

14. Genitourinary ___________

15. Vaginal ___________

16. Arm ___________

17. Musculoskeletal ___________

18. Lymphatics ___________

19. Blood vessels ___________

20. Neurologic ___________

Read the following patient record:

21. A new patient, 8-year-old female, is brought into the office by her mother, who states that the child has an earache in the right ear. Mother reports that the child has been complaining of aching and ringing in right ear of increasing severity for the past 2 days. Child appears to be in only minor distress. Temperature, 101°F. Examination: ears, eyes, and nose. Tympanic membrane red, fluid noted in right ear. Diagnosis: Otitis media.

From the patient record, we can identify the history elements—chief complaint (CC), history of present illness (HPI), past, family, and/or social history (PFSH), and review of symptoms (ROS), as in the following list:

History Elements	Patient Record
CC:	*earache in the right ear*
HPI:	*aching and ringing in right ear of increasing severity for the past 2 days*
PFSH:	*Review of child's health history* (The patient information form completed by the mother contains the information that the physician reviewed, along with questions to the patient.)

ROS: *ears, eyes, and nose* (one organ system)

head (The complaint involves only one body area.)

In this case, the physician focused on the chief complaint and did a brief history centered on gathering information about the present illness. Referring to the description of history levels summarized in Table 2–1 or discussed in the E/M Guidelines, answer the following question:

a. What is the history level for this case? ______________________________

Now let's establish the level of the examination:

Examination	**Patient Record**
General Survey:	*Child appears in minor distress*
Vital Signs:	*Temperature is 101°F*
Body Areas/ Organ Systems:	*head* (one body area) *ears, eyes, and nose* (one organ system)

In this case, the physician focused on one affected body area and one organ system. Referring to the description of examination levels summarized in Table 2–2 or discussed in the E/M Guidelines, answer the following question:

b. What is the examination level for this case? ______________________________

That wasn't so difficult, was it? Okay, now you do one.

Read the following patient record:

22. A 68-year-old female established patient presents to the office with a "cold" of 9 days' duration. Patient reports that she has had a dry, hacking cough and nasal congestion for the past 6 days and a fever for the last 3 days. She states she is unable to sleep due to the cough, fever, and aching. She appears in minor distress. Personal and family history negative for respiratory problems. Temperature is 100°F; blood pressure 150/90; pulse 93 and regular. Lungs clear to percussion and auscultation. Examination of head and ears, normal; nose, mucous membranes inflamed with postnasal phlegm. Diagnosis: Sinusitis. Plan: Patient was advised to drink fluids, take aspirin as needed for pain, obtain bed rest, and to return if symptoms are not improved in 5 days.

Locate the information in the patient record that matches the history element and place the information on the line provided:

History Elements	**Patient Record**
CC:	______________________________
	______________________________
	______________________________
HPI:	______________________________
	______________________________
	______________________________

PFSH: ______________________

____

____

ROS: ______________________

____

____

With the information you placed on the preceding lines, choose the correct history level:

a. What is the history level for this case? ______________________

Locate the information in the patient record that matches the examination and place the information on the line provided:

Examination	**Patient Record**
General Survey:	______________________
Vital Signs:	______________________
	______________________
	______________________
	______________________
Body Areas/ Organ Systems:	______________________

With the information you placed on the preceding lines, choose the correct examination level:

b. What is the examination level for this case? ______________________

Medical Decision-Making

The key component of decision-making is based on the complexity of the decision the physician must make about the patient's diagnosis and care. Complexity of decision-making is based on three elements:

1. Number of diagnoses or management options. The options can be minimal, limited, multiple, or extensive.
2. Amount or complexity of data to review. The data can be minimal to none, limited, moderate, or extensive.
3. Risk of complication or death if the condition goes untreated. Risk can be minimal, low, moderate, or high.

The extent to which each of these elements is considered results in the levels of medical decision-making complexity.

Medical Decision-Making Complexity Levels

- Straightforward
- Low
- Moderate
- High

1. **Straightforward decision-making:** *minimal* diagnosis and management options, *minimal or none* for the amount and complexity of data to be reviewed, and *minimal* risk to the patient of complications or death if untreated.
2. **Low-complexity decision-making:** *limited* number of diagnoses or management options, *limited* data to be reviewed, and *low* risk to the patient of complications or death if untreated.
3. **Moderate-complexity decision-making:** *multiple* diagnoses and management options, *moderate* amount and complexity of data to be reviewed, and *moderate* risk to the patient of complications or death if untreated.
4. **High-complexity decision-making:** *extensive* diagnoses and management options, *extensive* amount and complexity of data to be reviewed, and *high* risk to the patient for complications or death if the problem is untreated.

Some basic guidelines for documentation of *management options* in the medical record are as follows:

1. For each encounter, an assessment, clinical impression, or diagnosis should be documented. It may be explicitly stated or implied in documented decisions regarding management plans or further evaluation.
   - For a presenting problem with an established diagnosis the record should reflect whether the problem is: (a) improved, well controlled, resolving, or resolved; or (b) inadequately controlled, worsening, or failing to change as expected.
   - For a presenting problem without an established diagnosis, the assessment or clinical impression may be stated in the form of differential diagnoses or as a "possible," "probable," or "rule out" (R/O) diagnosis.
2. The initiation of, or changes in, treatment should be documented. Treatment includes a wide range of management options, including patient instructions, nursing instructions, therapies, and medications.
3. If referrals are made, consultations requested, or advice sought, the record should indicate to whom or where the referral or consultation is made or from whom the advice is requested.

The following are some basic documentation guidelines for the amount and complexity of *data* to be reviewed:

1. If a diagnostic service (test or procedure) is ordered, planned, scheduled, or performed at the time of the E/M encounter, the type of service (eg, laboratory or radiologic) should be documented.
2. The review of laboratory, radiology, or other diagnostic tests should be documented. An entry in a progress note such as "WBC elevated" or "chest

x-ray unremarkable" is acceptable. Alternatively, the review may be documented by initialing and dating the report containing the test results.

3. A decision to obtain old records or to obtain additional history from the family, caregiver, or other source to supplement that obtained from the patient should be documented.
4. Relevant findings from the review of old records or the receipt of additional history from the family, caregiver, or other source should be documented. If there is no relevant information beyond that already obtained, that fact should be documented. A notation of "old records reviewed" or "additional history obtained from family" without elaboration is insufficient.
5. The results of discussion of laboratory, radiology, or other diagnostic tests with the physician who performed or interpreted the study should be documented.
6. The direct visualization and independent interpretation of an image, tracing, or specimen previously interpreted by another physician should be documented.

Some basic documentation guidelines for *risk* of significant complications, morbidity, or mortality include the following:

1. Comorbidities underlying diseases or other factors that increase the complexity of medical decision-making by increasing the risk of complications, morbidity, or mortality should be documented.
2. If a surgical or invasive diagnostic procedure is ordered, planned, or scheduled at the time of the E/M encounter, the type of procedure (eg, laparoscopy) should be documented.
3. If a surgical or invasive diagnostic procedure is performed at the time of the E/M encounter, the specific procedure should be documented.
4. The referral for or decision to perform a surgical or invasive diagnostic procedure on an urgent basis should be documented or implied.

The following are examples of the levels of risk:

Level of Risk	Presenting Problem or Problems
Minimal	One self-limited or minor problem (eg, insect bite, tinea corporis)
Low	Two or more self-limited or minor problems
	One stable chronic illness (eg, well-controlled hypertension or non-insulin dependent diabetes, cataract, benign prostatic hypertrophy)
	Acute uncomplicated illness or injury (eg, cystitis, allergic rhinitis, simple sprain)
Moderate	One or more chronic illnesses with mild exacerbation, progression, or side effects of treatment
	Two or more stable chronic illnesses
	Undiagnosed new problem with uncertain prognosis (eg, lump in breast)
	Acute illness with systemic symptoms (eg, pyelonephritis, pneumonitis, colitis)
High	One or more chronic illnesses with severe exacerbation, progression, or side effects of treatment
	Acute or chronic illnesses or injuries that pose a threat to life or body function (eg, multiple trauma, acute myocardial infarction, pulmonary embolus, severe respiratory distress, progressive severe rheumatoid arthritis, psychiatric illness with potential threat to self or others, peritonitis, acute renal failure)
	An abrupt change in neurologic status (eg, seizure, transient ischemic attack, weakness, or sensory loss)

TABLE 2–3 Elements Required for Each Level of Medical Decision-Making

Level of Decision-Making	Diagnoses and Management Options	Amount and Complexity of Data	Risk
Straightforward	Minimal	Minimal or none	Minimal
Low Complexity	Limited	Limited	Low
Moderate Complexity	Moderate	Moderate	Moderate
High Complexity	Extensive	Extensive	High

When you select one of the four types of complexity of medical decision-making—straightforward, low, moderate, or high—the documentation in the medical record must support the selection in terms of the number of diagnoses or management options, amount and/or complexity of data to be reviewed, and risks.

Refer to Table 2–3 for an overview of medical decision-making. Given the information in the patient record, you would consider the information in the context of the complexity of the diagnosis and management options, data to be reviewed, and risks to the patient to choose the complexity of medical decision-making. Let's look at an example of choosing the medical decision-making level.

EXAMPLE 1

An established patient's office medical record states the following: Female patient fell and scraped arm; problem focused history and examination were done. The patient states that she slipped on the ice on the walk outside her home approximately 3 hours ago. The area of abrasion appears to be relatively clean, with no noted foreign materials imbedded. There appears to be only minimal cutaneous damage. The area was washed and a dressing applied.

1. Diagnosis and management options for an abrasion (clean and dress). (Options can be minimal, limited, multiple, or extensive.)
   How many various options are open to the physician to diagnose the problem and decide how to manage this patient's care—minimal, multiple, extensive? The management of an abrasion is fairly clear—clean and dress the wound; therefore, the diagnosis and management options are minimal.
2. Data to review to provide service. (Data can be minimal/none, limited, moderate, or extensive.)
   How much and how complex would the information (data) be that the physician must obtain, review, and analyze to care for this patient—minimal/none, limited, moderate, or extensive? The amount of data to review would be minimal/none for the abrasion.
3. Risks of infection if not treated. (Risk can be minimal, low, moderate, or high.)
   How great a risk is there that the patient would die or encounter severe complications if the abrasion were not treated—low, moderate, or high? The risk of death or of complications is low.

The diagnosis and management options are minimal, data are minimal/none, and risk is low. Consideration of these three elements has placed this patient's care into straightforward medical decision-making complexity.

The history level would be problem focused and the examination level problem focused. The patient was an established patient seen as an outpatient. CPT code 99212 is where this service to the patient fits. Carefully look at each of the boldface type items in code 99212 set below. The place of service, type of service, patient status, type of history, type of examination, and the complexity of the medical decision-making are identified in the description of the code.

99212 **Office or other outpatient** visit for the evaluation and management of an **established patient,** which requires at least two of these three key components:

- **a problem focused history**
- **a problem focused examination**
- **a straightforward medical decision-making**

Now let's establish the medical decision-making level for a more complex case.

EXAMPLE 2

The patient record states: Unknown (new) patient presenting in the office with severe chest pain. A comprehensive history and an examination were done.

Again, the medical decision-making complexity must be chosen:

1. Diagnosis and management options for cardiac origin of possible myocardial infarction, angina, or heart block. Gastrointestinal origin could be reflux or an ulcer. Respiratory origin could be a pulmonary embolism or pleuritis. (Options can be minimal, multiple, or extensive.)
   What do you think it would take for the physician to decide on the diagnosis or management options of this patient—minimal, multiple, or extensive? There are many possibilities of origin for the chest pain; therefore, the diagnosis and management options are extensive.
2. Data to review to provide service. (Data can be minimal/none, limited, moderate, or extensive.) How much data would the physician have to obtain through current tests on the patient and review and analysis of previous records to provide services to the patient—minimal/none, limited, moderate, extensive? In this case, the patient's care will require moderate data review.
3. Risks if left untreated. (Risk can be low, moderate, or high.) If the patient's condition was untreated, what would you think the risk of death or serious complication would be—low, moderate, or high? This patient would have a high risk of death or of severe complications if untreated.

The extensive diagnosis and management options and high risk to the patient if this condition is not treated meet the necessary two of three elements to qualify this patient's care for a high level of medical decision-making complexity. A new patient with a comprehensive history and examination together with a high medical decision-making complexity places this case as a 99205.

EXERCISE E *Medical Decision-Making Complexity*

A patient's record states that an initial office visit was made for the evaluation and management of a 48-year-old male with recurrent low back pain from a herniated disk, with pain radiating to the leg. A detailed history and physical examination were done on this new patient.

Using this patient information, identify the following about the case:

1. Diagnosis and management options for recurrent low back pain radiating to the leg. (Options can be minimal, limited, multiple, or extensive.)

   Diagnosis and management options: ______________________

2. Data to review to provide service. (Data can be minimal/none, limited, moderate, or extensive.) Data to review: Current record available.

   Data: ______________________

3. Risks if left untreated. (Risk can be minimal, low, moderate, or high.)

   Risks: ______________________

4. Two of the three elements have been met to qualify this patient for what level of decision-making complexity? (straightforward, low, moderate, high)

   ____

5. The patient record indicates a detailed history and examination were done. When this is combined with the level of decision-making complexity you arrived at for this patient, what is the correct CPT code for the case?

   Code(s): ____________

Analyze another case in which the patient record states: 40-year-old male patient (new) is evaluated for contusion of finger. The history and examination were problem focused.

6. Diagnosis and management options for contusion of finger. (Options can be minimal, limited, multiple, or extensive.)

   Diagnosis and management options: ______________________

7. Data to review to provide service. (Data can be minimal/none, limited, moderate, or extensive.) Data to review: only data available are current information obtained during the visit.

   Data: ______________________

8. Risks if left untreated. (Risk can be minimal, low, moderate, or high.)

   Risks: ______________________

9. All three of the elements have been met to qualify this patient for what level of decision-making complexity?

   ____

10. The patient record indicates that a problem focused history and examination were done. When this is combined with the level of decision-making complexity you arrived at for this patient, what is the correct CPT code for the case?

    Code(s): ______________

Now, let's look again at two cases you previously established the history and examination levels for:

11. A new patient, 8-year-old female, is brought into the office by her mother, who states that the child has an earache in the right ear. Mother reports that the child has complained of aching and ringing in right ear of increasing severity for the past 2 days. Child appears in only minor distress. Temperature, 101°F. Examination: ears, eyes, and nose. Tympanic membranes red, fluid noted in right ear. Diagnosis: Otitis media.

    What is the medical decision-making level for this patient? ______________

12. A 68-year-old female, established patient, presents to the office today with a complaint of "flu-like" symptoms of 9 days' duration. Patient reports that she has had a dry, hacking cough for the past 6 days and a fever for the last 3 days. She states that she aches all over and is unable to sleep due to the cough, fever, and aching. She appears well nourished and in minor distress. Personal and family history negative for respiratory problems. Temperature is 100°F; blood pressure 150/90; pulse 93 and regular. Lungs clear to percussion and auscultation. Examination of head and ears, normal; nose, mucous membranes inflamed with postnasal phlegm. Diagnosis: Sinusitis. Plan: Patient was advised to drink fluids, take aspirin as needed for pain, obtain bed rest, and return if symptoms are not improved in 5 days.

    What is the medical decision-making level for this patient? ______________

You have examined each of the three key components and seen how they apply to the assignment of a code. You will be referring to the information as you are presented with further cases. Make note of the important points and remember that the information about the key components is in the E/M Guidelines at the beginning of the section in the CPT manual.

Now that you are familiar with the key components of history, examination, and medical decision-making, let's review the contributing factors.

What Are the Contributing Factors?

There are four contributing factors: counseling, coordination of care, nature of the presenting problem, and time. Contributing factors are those conditions that help the physician determine the extent of history, examination, and decision-making (key components) necessary to treat the patient. Contributing factors may or may not be considered in every patient case.

Contributing Factors

- Counseling
- Coordination of Care
- Nature of Presenting Problem
- Time

Counseling

Counseling is a service that physicians provide to patients and their families that involves discussion of diagnostic results, impressions, and recommended diagnostic studies; prognosis; risks and benefits of treatment; instructions for treatment; importance of compliance with treatment; risk factor reduction; and patient and family education. Some form of counseling usually takes place with all physician and patient encounters, and this was factored into the codes when they were developed by the AMA. Only when counseling is the reason for the encounter or consumes most of the visit time is counseling considered a component for level assignment. The following statement is made often within the codes in the E/M section.

> *Counseling* and/or coordination of care with other providers or agencies are provided consistent with the nature of the problem(s) and the patient's and/or family's needs.

Coordination of Care

Coordination of care with other health care providers may be necessary for the care of a patient. In coordination of care, a physician might arrange for other services to be provided to the patient, such as arrangements for admittance to a long-term nursing facility.

Nature of Presenting Problem

A presenting problem is the patient's chief complaint or situation that leads the physician into determining the level of care necessary to diagnose and treat the patient. There are five types of presenting problems.

Types of Presenting Problems

- Minimal
- Self-limiting
- Low Severity
- Moderate Severity
- High Severity

1. **Minimal:** A problem may not require the presence of the physician but service is provided under the physician's care. A minimal problem is a blood pressure reading, dressing change, or a service that can be performed without the physician's being immediately present.
2. **Self-limiting:** Also called a minor presenting problem, a self-limiting problem runs a definite and prescribed course, is transient, and is not likely to permanently alter health status or has a good prognosis with management and compliance.
3. **Low severity:** The risk of complete sickness (morbidity) without treatment is low, there is little to no risk of death without treatment, and full recovery without impairment is expected.
4. **Moderate severity:** The risk of complete sickness (morbidity) without treatment is moderate, there is moderate risk of death without treatment, and uncertain prognosis or increased probability of impairment is expected.
5. **High severity:** The risk of complete sickness (morbidity) without treatment is high to extreme, there is a moderate to high risk of death without treatment, or high probability of severe, prolonged functional impairment is expected.

The patient's record should contain the physician's observation of the complexity of the presenting problem(s) of the patient. Your responsibility is to identify the words that correctly indicate the type of presenting problem.

Time

Time was not included in the CPT manual before 1992 but was incorporated to assist with the selection of the most appropriate level of E/M services. The times indicated with the codes are only averages and represent only an average of the possible duration of a service.

Direct face-to-face and *unit/floor* time are two measures of time. Outpatient visits are measured as direct face-to-face time. Direct face-to-face time is the time a physician spends directly with a patient during an office visit obtaining the history, performing an examination, and discussing the results. Inpatient time is measured as unit/floor time and is used to describe the time a physician spends in the hospital care setting dealing with the patient's care. Unit/floor time includes care given to the patient at the bedside as well as at other settings on the unit or floor (eg, the nursing station). It is an often heard comment that physicians get paid a great deal of money to stop in to see a hospitalized patient. However, what is not realized is that the physician spends time reviewing the patient's records and writing orders for the patient's care.

Time in the E/M section is referred to in statements such as this one that is located with code 99203:

> Usually, the presenting problem(s) is (are) of moderate severity. Physicians typically spend 30 minutes face-to-face with the patient and/or family.

AN E/M CODE EXAMPLE

With the CPT manual open to the first page of the E/M section, locate the paragraphs above the 99201 code. These paragraphs highlight the incidents when codes in that particular category are appropriate for assignment. The notes above

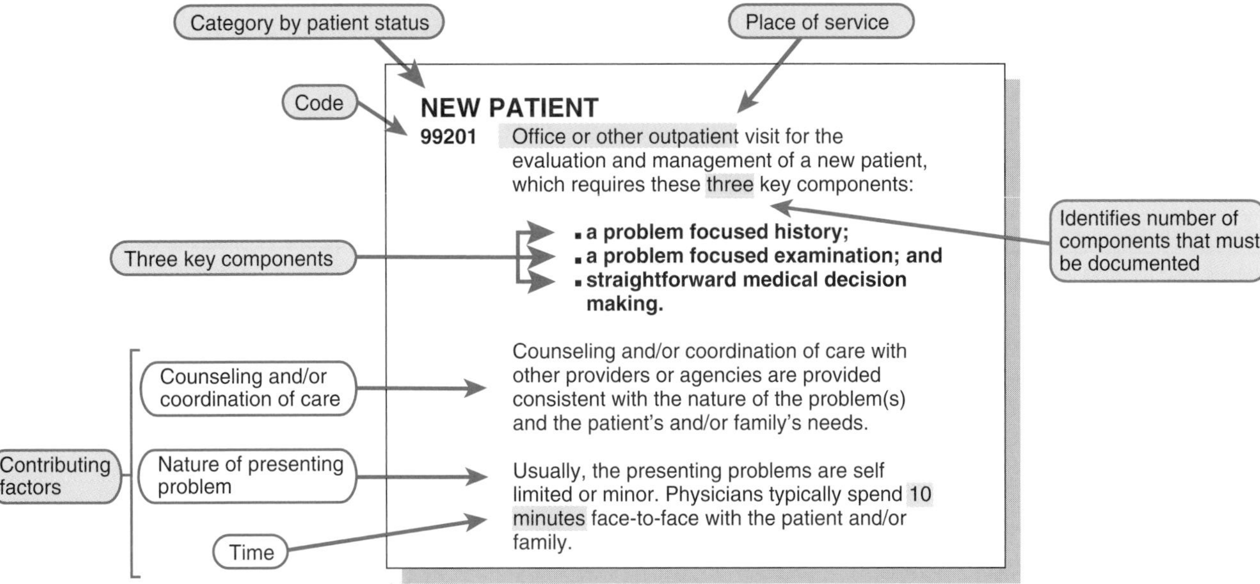

Figure 2–4
Code information.

99201 indicate that the codes that follow the notes are appropriate for use in the places of service of outpatient settings, ambulatory facilities, and physicians' offices.

The information also directs you to other code subsections if the patient classification is not correct. As an example of this directional feature, the notes above 99201 indicate that "Office or Other Outpatient Services" is not appropriate when identifying services provided in the emergency department. You are directed to see codes in the Emergency Department subsection.

Figure 2–4 shows the first code for a new patient under the category "New Patient" under subsection "Office or Other Outpatient Services." Review Figure 2–4 carefully before continuing. Note the location of each important piece of information.

Locate the following items in Figure 2–4:

1. three contributing factors
2. three key components
3. number of key components required
4. place of service
5. category of the code

USING THE E/M CODES

Now you are going to use the information you have learned about codes in the E/M services section as you continue to identify the differences among the code numbers.

Office and Other Outpatient Services

New Patient

The first subsection in the E/M section is for Office and Other Outpatient Services, New Patient category.

EXERCISE F ***Office and Other Outpatient Services***

Using the CPT manual, fill in the blanks with the correct word:

1. For code 99203 the history level is _________, the examination is _________, and the medical decision-making is of _________ complexity.
2. Code 99204 has a history level of ______________, an examination that is ____________, and a medical decision-making complexity of ____________.
3. Code 99205 has a history level of ______________, an examination that is ____________, and a medical decision-making complexity of ____________.

Code the following cases:

4. A 53-year-old patient presents for an initial office visit for surgical vasectomy for sterilization. The history and examination are detailed.

   Code(s): ________________

5. A 4-year-old new patient presents for the removal of sutures for an appendectomy 10 days ago in another city.

   Code(s): ________________

6. A 23-year-old man has an initial office visit for severe depression that has led to frequent thoughts of suicide in the past several weeks. Over an hour is spent discussing the patient's problems and options. Past medical history is negative. Social history indicates sleeplessness; smokes 2 to 2 1/2 packs of unfiltered cigarettes a day, drinks 10 to 12 cups of coffee; denies current use of drugs. (The actual patient record continues and indicates that a comprehensive examination was done.)

   Code(s): ________________

7. A 10-year-old boy is brought in by his father for a knee injury sustained in a hockey game. The knee is swollen and the patient is in apparent pain. A detailed history and examination are obtained. A diagnosis of probable meniscus tear is made.

   Code(s): ________________

8. A 41-year-old woman complains of headache and rhinitis of 4 days' duration. The patient states that she has previously had a problem with her allergies

during this season for years. An expanded problem focused history and examination are done.

Code(s): ____________________

STOP! *The second category of codes in subsection "Office or Other Outpatient Services" is for the established patient in an outpatient setting.*

Established Patient

EXERCISE G *Established Patients*

Fill in the blanks with information from codes in the Established Patient category:

1. 99211
   This minimal service level does not exist in the New Patient category because a new patient is usually seen by the physician. The established patient may or may not be seen by the physician. Read the description and information for code 99211 in the CPT manual. Would an established patient returning for a simple suture removal be appropriately reported as 99211? ________________

2. A 42-year-old established patient presents for an office visit with complaints of severe vaginal itching and moderate pain. The patient states that several weeks ago she noted a slight itching, which has increased in severity. Yesterday, she noted a lesion on her genitalia. Burning and painful urination have increased over the last 5 days accompanied by rectal itching. She has tried a variety of over-the-counter ointments and creams with no improvement. The patient states that she has had several yeast infections in the past that were successfully treated by her previous physician. Personal history indicates several prior urinary infections. No discharge noted. Examination revealed a lesion, which had previously ruptured, located on the vulva. Rectal, negative. Bacterial and viral smears were done. The patient was advised that the smears would be back in 24 hours and that a treatment plan would be developed based on the reports.

   Code(s): ____________________

3. The history level is expanded problem focused, the examination is expanded problem focused, and the medical decision-making is of low complexity.

   Code(s): ____________________

4. The history level is detailed, the examination is detailed, and the medical decision-making is of moderate complexity.

   Code(s): ____________________

5. The history level is comprehensive, the examination is comprehensive, and the medical decision-making is of high complexity.

   Code(s): ____________________

6. A 17-year-old football player comes to the clinic for a urinalysis for suspected cocaine use. The nurse saw this established patient. (Code only the E/M service.)

   Code(s): ____________________

7. A 53-year-old patient complains of frequent fainting. The history and examination were comprehensive and the decision-making was of high complexity.

   Code(s): ____________________

8. A 61-year-old established patient is seen for medication management of fatigue produced by hypertensive medication. An expanded problem focused history and examination were done, and the medical decision-making was of low complexity.

   Code(s): ____________________

9. An established 31-year-old patient presents with an irritated skin tag. A problem focused history and examination were done.

   Code(s): ____________________

10. A 48-year-old woman has had diarrhea for the past 5 days. Her temperature is 101°F. An expanded problem focused history and examination were done.

    Code(s): ____________________

Hospital Observation Services

The codes in the Hospital Observation subsection are used to identify initial observation care or for observation discharge services. The services in the observation subsection are for patients who are in a hospital on observation status.

Observation is a status used for the classification of the patient who does not have an illness severe enough to meet acute inpatient criteria and does not require resources as intensive as an inpatient but does require hospitalization for a short period of time. In some parts of the country, observation status is conducted in the TCU (temporary care unit).

The observation codes are for new or established patients. There are no time components with observation codes.

If a patient is admitted to the hospital as an inpatient after having been admitted earlier the same day as an observation patient, you do not report the observation status separately. The services provided on the observation status become part of (bundled into) the initial inpatient hospital admission code.

Observation Care Discharge Services

Observation Care Discharge Services include the final examination of the patient upon discharge from observation status. Discussion of the hospital stay, instructions for continued care, and preparation of discharge records are also included in (bundled into) the Observation Care Discharge Services codes.

Initial Observation Care

Initial Observation Care codes are used to designate the beginning of observation status in a hospital. The hospital does not need to have a formal observation area, since the designation of observation status is dependent on the severity of illness of the patient. These codes also include development of a care plan for the patient while on observation status and periodic reassessment.

Services performed in sites other than the observation area (eg, clinic, nursing home, emergency department) preceding admission to observation status are included in (bundled into) the Initial Observation Care codes and are not to be coded separately.

If a patient is admitted to observation status and then becomes ill enough to be admitted to the hospital, an initial hospital care code, not an observation code, is used to bill services.

EXERCISE H *Hospital Observation Services*

Using the CPT manual, locate the correct information about the Hospital Observation codes:

1. A 60-year-old man is transferred from the emergency department to the observation unit. His private physician visits and notes the patient's chief complaint of vague, nonexertional chest and back pain. The patient is able to describe the location, severity, duration, and timing of his chest pain and its accompanying shortness of breath and mild sweating. The doctor notes these elements in his history of present illness. A complete review of systems is taken, addressing 12 organ systems. The physician reviews the patient's past, family, and social history with the patient and documents all of these aspects in the record. The physician then performs a general multisystem physical examination addressing all 12 organ systems. The physician has a variety of provisional diagnoses to consider including angina, myocardial infarction, dissecting aneurysm, or another thrombotic event. Multiple tests had been ordered in the emergency room, and the physician considered all of the results. Old records were requested, and the physician noted the multiple admissions the patient had had in the past. The physician acknowledged that while the patient's symptoms were vague, they were distressing to the patient; and taken together, the patient's signs and symptoms could herald a major, impending serious illness. The physician requested a cardiovascular consultation immediately and requested that the patient stay in the observation unit under cardiac monitoring and direct nursing supervision.

   Indicate the medical decision-making complexity of this case:

   ____

2. A patient who was on observation status for 48 hours is discharged from the hospital.

   Within which subheading would you locate a code to report this service?

   ____

3. Initial observation of a patient for lower right quadrant pain, accompanied by nausea, vomiting, and a low-grade fever, was done. Surgical consultation

was obtained, and it was suggested to keep the patient overnight to rule out the possibility of a ruptured appendix.

Indicate the medical decision-making complexity of this case:

____

4. A patient was in an automobile accident and is complaining of a minor headache and no other apparent injuries. History from bystanders states that patient was not wearing a seat belt and hit his head on the windshield. Fifteen-minute loss of consciousness was noted. The patient is now admitted for 24-hour observation to rule out head injury. (*Note:* For a condition such as this, the medical decision-making would have moderate complexity.)

Code(s): _______________

Hospital Inpatient Services

Hospital Inpatient Services codes are used to indicate a patient status as an inpatient in a hospital or partial hospital setting, and, therefore, to identify the hospital setting as the place the physician renders service to the patient. An **inpatient** is one who has been formally admitted to a health care facility. The subsection of Hospital Inpatient Services is divided into three subheadings.

Hospital Inpatient Services Subheadings

1. Initial Hospital Care
2. Subsequent Hospital Care
3. Hospital Discharge Services

Initial Hospital Care

Initial Hospital Care codes are used to code for the service of admission to the hospital by the admitting physician. These codes reflect services in any setting (office, emergency department, nursing home) that are provided in conjunction with the admission to the hospital. If the patient is seen in the office and subsequently admitted to the hospital, the office visit is considered part of (bundled into) the initial hospital care service.

EXERCISE I *Initial Hospital Care*

Fill in the missing words or codes for the following:

1. Which Initial Hospital Care code has a comprehensive history with a low complexity of medical decision-making?

Code(s): _______________

2. Which code has a time component of 70 minutes?

   Code(s): ____________________

3. Code 99222 has a __________ history and examination level and a __________

   medical decision-making complexity.

4. An 80-year-old woman has inflammation of the kidneys and renal pelvic area. She is complaining of hematuria, dysuria, and pyuria. She is in good general health other than this condition. She has had some previous workup for this condition as an outpatient but is now being admitted for a cystoscopy. In the patient's history, the physician noted the patient's chief complaints and described the bright red nature of the hematuria, the severe discomfort associated with the dysuria including burning and itching, and her other symptoms of frequency and urgency. The patient had stated that her symptoms began gradually over the past 2 weeks but became more intense in the last 48 hours. The physician documented the patient's positive responses and pertinent negative responses in his review of her cardiovascular, respiratory, genitourinary, musculoskeletal, neurologic, and endocrine systems. Her past history related to urinary and renal problems was reviewed. The physical examination noted the complete findings relative to her reproductive system as well as the urinary system. An examination of her back and related musculoskeletal structures was included because she complained of mild back pain as well. After completing the history and examination, the physician concluded with provisional diagnoses of cystitis and pyelitis, possibly associated with endometritis. The patient was reassured and told to expect a short length of stay once the exact problem was pinpointed. (*Note:* This is a detailed history and examination.)

   Code(s): ____________________

5. A 58-year-old male heart-transplant patient is admitted with shortness of breath with physical activity and occasionally at rest. He has had several incidents of waking in the night unable to breathe. The night-waking incidents were accompanied by coughing and wheezing. He is immunosuppressed owing to the transplant. The patient's multiple chief complaints were noted. In the history of present illness, the physician noted the intensity and duration of the patient's shortness of breath and how frequently it occurred. Also noted were the accompanying persistent cough and wheezing, which the physician documented in terms of its context to the shortness of breath experienced during the night. The physician's lengthy review of systems addressed 14 body systems. The patient's complete past, family, and social history noted his extensive number of hospitalizations in the past, his extensive history relative to his transplant and subsequent follow-up care, and his inability to return to work since the operation. A complete multisystem physical examination was performed. (Due to the patient's immunosuppression, the patient was at risk for a multitude of problems.) Extensive consultations were requested including infectious disease, cardiothoracic, pulmonary medicine, and immunology/allergy.

   Code(s): ____________________

6. A 48-year-old patient with chronic renal failure is admitted with an infection of the hemodialysis access site. Antibiotics will be given intravenously, and consultation will be requested to assess the necessity of changing access sites.

The physician's history included the patient's chief complaint of pain, swelling, and drainage at the access site, noting how long the patient had experienced the pain and how much swelling had occurred. The patient's chronic renal failure appeared to be under control with the dialysis. The physician's review of systems documented positive and negative findings related to 12 body systems. The patient's extensive past medical and surgical history was reviewed. The prevalence of hypertension and kidney disease in his family was noted. The patient was found to be on a disability pension due to his kidney disease. The physical examination noted positive and negative findings related to the head, neck, chest, abdomen, genitalia, back, and extremities. The physician reviewed the extensive past medical records and considered the series of complications that could occur owing to this patient's renal failure and current inability to withstand hemodialysis due to the infection at the access site. Appropriate surgical and medical consultations were requested.

Code(s): ________________

Subsequent Hospital Care

Subsequent Hospital Care codes are the second subheading of codes in the Hospital Inpatient Services subsection. The Subsequent Hospital Care codes are used by physicians to bill for daily hospital visits while the patient is hospitalized.

The first Subsequent Hospital Care code is 99231. Typically, the 99231 level implies a patient in stable condition and responding well to treatment. Subsequent codes in the subsection indicate (in the "Usually, the patient . . ." area) the status of the patient, such as stable/unstable or recovering/unresponding. Be certain to read the contributing factors area for each code in this subsection.

More than one physician can use the subsequent care codes on the same day. This is called concurrent care. **Concurrent care** is the provision of services to the same patient by more than one physician on the same day for different conditions. An example of concurrent care is when physician A, a cardiologist, treats the patient for a heart condition and at the same time physician B, an oncologist, treats the patient for a cancer condition. The patient's attending physician maintains the primary responsibility for the overall care of the patient.

An **attending physician** is a doctor of medicine or a doctor of osteopathy who, by virtue of education, training, and experience, is granted medical staff membership and clinical privileges by a health care organization to perform specified diagnostic or therapeutic procedures.* An attending physician is legally responsible for the care and treatment provided to a given patient. The attending may be a patient's private or personal physician or a physician assigned to the patient who is admitted to a hospital through an emergency room. While the attending physician is usually a person who provides primary care, such as a family practitioner, internist, or pediatrician, an attending physician may be a surgeon or another type of specialist. In an academic medical center, the attending physician is a member of the academic or medical school staff who is responsible for the supervision of medical residents, interns, and medical school students and oversees the care the residents, interns, or students provide to the patients.

---

*O'Leary M, et al: Lexikon: Dictionary of Health Care Terms, Organizations, and Acronyms for the Era of Reform. Oakbrook Terrace, IL, Joint Commission on Accreditation of Healthcare Organizations, 1994, pp 551–552. Reprinted by permission.

EXAMPLE J

Subsequent Hospital Care

Fill in the codes for the following:

1. A 72-year-old man, who had been admitted yesterday through the emergency room, was found to have suffered a cerebrovascular accident. At the time of admission, he was fairly alert and conversant. However, today the nurses told the physician the patient had become much more lethargic and feverish and had become aphasic. Based on computed tomography (CT) of the brain and other diagnostic test findings, the physician suspected that the patient had a second cerebrovascular accident or some other type of thrombotic or embolic episode. This appeared to be a significant complication for the patient. The patient's history since the physician's previous visit was reviewed with the nurses. The patient was unable to respond to a review of systems, but the physician was able to elicit positive signs and symptoms related to his eyes, ears, nose and throat, cardiovascular, musculoskeletal, neurologic, and hematological systems. The physician essentially performed another multisystem examination based on the dramatic change in the patient over the past 24 hours. The physician noted the patient to be acutely ill with multiple problems surfacing. Appropriate consultations were requested with neurology, cardiology, and infectious disease specialists.

   Indicate the level of the following:

   History: ______________________________

   Examination: ______________________________

   Medical decision-making complexity: ______________________________

2. A patient was seen on her third postoperative day after an open reduction with internal fixation of a fracture of her left ankle. She appeared to be stable and was tolerating more progressive physical therapy, which led the physician to believe she could be discharged within the next 2 days. What type of decision-making do you expect the physician would be performing during this subsequent hospital visit?

   ____

3. A 2-year-old boy with bacterial pneumonia has had 5 days of antibiotic therapy. Today the child developed a fever of 101°F with a mild rash on his torso. What type of medical decision-making would the physician like to be performing for this type of subsequent hospital visit?

   ____

4. A 70-year-old woman who fell 2 days previously and fractured her hip underwent open reduction with internal fixation yesterday. She is a diabetic and requires follow-up in the hospital by her family practitioner for diabetes management. Her family practice physician will evaluate her daily to assess her glucose and insulin levels. What level of medical decision-making is the daily hospital visit?

   ____

5. The 80-year-old patient admitted yesterday for hematuria, dysuria, and pyuria is now spiking a fever and urine cultures are growing *Escherichia coli.* The patient was started on antibiotic therapy but is still responding inadequately. The physician conducted an extended HPI and ROS. The examination reviewed the affected body areas and several related organ systems. Results of sensitivity studies are pending. A change in antibiotic will be considered when the studies are completed and if the patient's temperature does not come down.

   Indicate the level of the following:

   History: ____________________

   Examination: ____________________

   Medical decision-making complexity: ____________________

6. A 35-year-old man with known prostate cancer was admitted 2 days ago with debilitating back pain and joint pain. The patient has been on chemotherapy for 1 week and is also experiencing severe nausea with vomiting, resulting in dehydration. The patient was admitted to rule out bone metastases and had developed severe anemia. The patient was subsequently transferred to the intensive care unit, where his condition is rapidly deteriorating.

   Indicate the level of the following:

   History: ____________________

   Examination: ____________________

   Medical decision-making complexity: ____________________

Hospital Discharge Services

Inpatient Hospital Discharge Services are billed on the final day of services for a multiple-day stay in a hospital setting. The service reflects the final examination of the patient, follow-up instructions to the patient, and arrangements for discharge, including completion of discharge records. The codes are based on the time spent by the physician for final discharge of the patient.

The Hospital Discharge Services codes are not used if the physician is a consultant. If a consulting physician is following the patient for a separate condition, he or she would bill using a subsequent hospital care code. Only the attending physician, not the consultant, is responsible for completion of the final examination, follow-up instructions, and arrangements for discharge and discharge records. Since these additional services are included in the Hospital Discharge codes, only the attending physician can bill using the codes.

EXERCISE K *Hospital Discharge Services*

Fill in the blanks:

1. What are the times indicated for each of the Hospital Discharge Services codes? ____________________

2. According to the category notes in Hospital Discharge Services, does the time spent by the physician for the final hospital discharge of the patient need to be continuous? ________________

Consultation Services

We all need advice once in a while—maybe for a problem or situation that we cannot find a solution to. Perhaps we think we are doing the right thing, but want another person's advice or view to make certain we are following the best course of action. Physicians need opinions and advice, too, and when they do, they ask another physician for an opinion or advice on the treatment, diagnosis, or management of a patient. The physician asking for the advice or opinion is making a *referral* and is the referring physician. The physician giving the advice is providing a consultation and is the *consultant*. Consultations can be done for both outpatients and inpatients. The CPT manual has different codes for each of the three patient consultation types—outpatient, inpatient, and confirmatory.

In the Consultation subsection, there are four subheadings of consultations.

Four Consultation Subheadings

1. Office or Other Outpatient
2. Initial Inpatient
3. Follow-up Inpatient
4. Confirmatory

The first three subheadings define the location in which the service is rendered, either outpatient or inpatient. The fourth subheading—Confirmatory—can be provided either on an outpatient or inpatient basis. All the subheadings are for new or established patients, except the Follow-up Inpatient subheading. Only one initial consultation is reported by a consultant for the patient on each admission, and any subsequent service is reported with codes from the Follow-up Inpatient subheading.

A *consultation* is a service provided by a physician whose opinion or advice regarding the management or diagnosis of a specific problem has been requested. The consultant provides the opinion or advice requested to the attending physician, documents the opinion and services provided in the medical record, and has then completed the care of the patient. Sometimes the attending physician will request the consultant to assume responsibility for a specific area of the patient's care. For example, a consultant is asked by the attending physician to see an inpatient regarding the care of the patient's diabetes while the patient is hospitalized for gallbladder surgery. After the initial consultation, the attending physician asks the consultant to continue to monitor the patient's diabetic condition. The consultant assumes responsibility for management of the patient in the specific area of the patient's diabetes. Subsequent visits made by the consultant would be coded using the subheading "Follow-up Inpatient Consultations," category "Established Patient."

Documentation in the medical record for a consultation must show a request from the attending physician for an opinion or advice of a consultant on a specific condition. Findings and treatments rendered during the consultation must be documented in the medical record by the consultant and communicated to the attending physician. A consultant can order tests and services for an inpatient, but the medical necessity of all tests and services must be indicated in the medical record.

Office or Other Outpatient Consultations

The Office or Other Outpatient consultation codes are used to code consultative services provided to a patient in an office or other ambulatory patient setting. Outpatient consultations include consultations provided in the emergency department, since the patient is considered an outpatient in the emergency department setting. The codes are for both new and established patients. The codes in this subsection are of increasing complexity based on the three key components and any contributing factors.

EXERCISE L *Office or Other Outpatient Consultations*

Using the CPT manual, answer the following:

1. A 56-year-old female was referred to the oncologist for his opinion regarding the treatment options. The patient had had a right breast carcinoma 6 years ago but over the past 4 months has developed progressively more painful back pain. In the physician's history of present illness it was noted that the pain was in the mid-back with the patient rating it an 8 on a scale of 1 to 10 in intensity. However, when the pain started, she thought it was about a 4 on the same scale. The pain has caused her to have neck and leg pains as well, as she has adjusted her walking stance in order to alleviate the pain. She responded to the physician's questions in the review of seven of her body systems. Her past medical and surgical history was noted, including the fact that her mother and one sister also had breast cancer. She had worked as a legal secretary up until 2 weeks ago but was on sick leave now. The physical examination performed by the physician was a complete multisystem review of 12 organ systems. The physician ordered a series of radiographic and laboratory tests and reviewed her recent spine x-ray series, which revealed multiple vertebral compression fractures.

   Code(s): ____________________

2. A 45-year-old man was referred to an orthopedic surgeon's office for acute pain and stiffness in his right elbow. In his history, the physician noted that the man was a farmer and used his right hand and arm repeatedly, lifting heavy objects. The patient had no other complaints and reported to be in otherwise excellent health. The farmer described the pain as severe and unrelenting, and it prevented him from using the arm. The physical examination noted the man's slightly swollen right elbow with marked pain on movement. No other problems were noted with his right upper extremity. The physician diagnosed the problem as elbow tendinitis and bursitis, recommended warm compresses, and gave the patient an anti-inflammatory prescription.

   Code(s): ____________________

3. A 47-year-old female was sent for an office consultation to a gynecologist by her family practice physician. The patient had been suffering with moderate pelvic pain, a heavy sensation in her lower pelvis, and marked discomfort during sexual intercourse. The gynecologist noted the location, severity, and duration of her pelvic pain and related symptoms. In the review of systems, the patient had positive findings related to her gastrointestinal, genitourinary, and endocrine body systems. The physician noted that her past medical history was noncontributory to the present problem. The physical examination centered on her gastrointestinal and genitourinary systems with a complete pelvic examination. The physician ordered laboratory tests and a pelvic ultrasound in order to consider uterine fibroids, endometritis, or other internal gynecologic pathology.

   Indicate the level of the following:

   History: ____________________

   Examination: ____________________

   Medical decision-making complexity: ____________________

4. A female teenager with a recent dramatic change in her personality including loss of interest in her schoolwork and sports activities and overall withdrawal from friends and family is referred to a psychiatrist for evaluation in her office. The psychiatrist performs a complete psychiatric examination with multiple psychological tests. The patient is complaining about completing a very extensive questionnaire about her life and activities that the physician reviews and discusses with her. After spending more than 2 hours with the patient, the psychiatrist recommends admission to the hospital but the patient refuses. With 24-hour monitoring by her family, the physician agrees to let her go home for the weekend, with another appointment scheduled for Monday at 10 AM. The physician considers multiple scenarios including major depression, situational anxiety, adjustment disorder, and possible bipolar disorder.

   Indicate the level of the following:

   History: ____________________

   Examination: ____________________

   Medical decision-making complexity: ____________________

5. A 72-year-old man is seen in the internal medicine clinic as an outpatient for medical clearance prior to his right knee replacement. The patient has a history of essential hypertension and mild coronary artery disease. The internist notes that the patient has no complaints relative to his hypertension or heart disease. His blood pressure appears to be controlled with his medication and low-salt diet. The patient denies any chest pain or discomfort either while working or at rest. The physician's review of his cardiovascular and respiratory systems appears to be unremarkable. The physician performs a physical examination of his head, neck, chest, and abdomen but finds no major problems related to his cardiovascular or respiratory systems. The internist confirms the diagnoses previously established with no change in the management of either condition.

   Code(s): ____________________

6. A 52-year-old patient is sent to a surgeon for an office consultation for hemorrhoids. A problem focused history and examination are performed. The consultant recommends treating with medication.

   Code(s): ____________________

7. An office consultation is done for a 62-year-old postmenopausal woman who complains of slight occasional spotting in the past 6 months with right lower quadrant tenderness. Detailed history and physical examination are performed.

   Indicate the level of medical decision-making complexity: ____________________

8. A 50-year-old woman is asked to see a general surgeon for evaluation of a breast lump found by her family practitioner during her annual gynecologic examination. The patient has a family history positive for breast cancer. She has had one abnormal mammogram in the past 2 years with diagnosis of probable fibrocystic disease, to be watched closely. The consultant notes the patient's chief complaint and the location, duration, and quality of the breast lump and the associated signs and symptoms in her axilla. The patient had negative responses to the physician's inquiry in 11 of 12 of her body systems. The physician notes that the woman's grandmother, mother, and two aunts have been diagnosed with breast cancer over the past 30 years. A complete physical examination of her head, neck, chest, abdomen, genitalia, spine, and four extremities is negative except for her breast and axilla on the right side. Multiple diagnoses including metastatic disease have to be considered given her positive family history, past positive mammogram, and physical findings to date.

   Indicate the level of the following:

   History: ____________________

   Examination: ____________________

   Medical decision-making complexity: ____________________

9. A 60-year-old man is seen in consultation by a cardiologist for complaints of dyspnea, fatigue, and lightheadedness. He has a prior history of pacemaker insertion 6 years ago. He also has a history of mitral regurgitation. The cardiologist performs a complete cardiology physical examination including cardiac monitoring, pacemaker evaluation, and review of his associated respiratory status. Noted in his history is the variety of complaints the patient has now along with his past pacemaker insertion and mitral valve regurgitation diagnosed by cardiac catheterization. The physician reviews the patient's past medical history from his first signs of problems 6 years ago until today. His review of systems elicits positive findings in the cardiovascular, respiratory, gastrointestinal, genitourinary, musculoskeletal, and neurologic systems. The other systems had negative responses. The physician had multiple management options concerning the pacemaker function but also had to consider new valvular problems that may be present as well as related gastrointestinal symptoms. Extensive tests that had been performed recently were reviewed, and additional testing was ordered.

   Code(s): ____________________

Initial Inpatient Consultations

The codes in the Initial Inpatient Consultations subheading are used to report services by physicians in an inpatient setting. This subheading is for both new and established patients and can be reported only one time per patient admission per consulting physician.

After the initial consultation report, the subsequent hospital visit codes would be used to report services, unless documentation meets the criteria for a follow-up consultation (discussed later in this chapter).

EXERCISE M *Initial Inpatient Consultations*

Fill in the codes for the following:

1. An inpatient consultation is performed for a 32-year-old female who recently had an elective abortion performed on an outpatient basis. The woman has been admitted with a high fever, pelvic pain, and dysuria. The urologist noted in the history of present illness that the patient's symptoms began about 2 days after the abortion and progressed to the acute phase she is in at the present time. The location of the pain is in the lower abdomen and rated 9 on a scale of 1 to 10. She reports the quality of the pain to be sharp and stabbing. In the review of systems, the doctor notes positive responses in 5 out of the 12 body systems investigated. The urologist notes a negative past medical history related to urinary symptoms other than a mild cystitis about 10 years ago. The physical examination performed by the urologist centers on the genitourinary system and gastrointestinal system in significant detail. Given the patient's past surgical procedure and physical findings at the present, the consultant considers the diagnoses of pyelonephritis, cystitis, pyelitis, and endometritis.

   Indicate the level of the following:

   History: ______________________________

   Examination: ______________________________

   Medical decision-making complexity: ______________________________

2. A 65-year-old man recently underwent a prostatectomy for prostate cancer. Since his surgery, his previously controlled atrial fibrillation has become a problem again. A cardiologist is called in for consultation and reviews the patient's present status including the duration and severity of his symptoms. His review of systems relates strictly to the cardiovascular system. The physical examination is focused on the man's neck, chest, and abdomen and attempts to elicit all cardiovascular pathology. The consultant suggests that the atrial fibrillation can be controlled better with a newer medication.

   Code(s): ______________

3. A 23-year-old man has been hospitalized because of progressive respiratory insufficiency due to his cystic fibrosis. A pulmonary disease specialist is asked to see the patient in consultation. Shortly before the consultant arrives, the patient experiences an anoxic episode and subsequently is intubated and placed on a ventilator. The consultant finds the patient unresponsive but

talks to the family, attending physician, and nurses to gather the details of the history of the present illness. A complete review of systems is performed based on physical findings and conversations with others. The consultant reviews the patient's extensive medical history back to age 6, including his family history, which includes a cousin with cystic fibrosis as well. A complete cardiorespiratory physical examination is performed. The patient does not have a living will. Multiple respiratory, neurologic, and cardiovascular conditions begin to be investigated.

Indicate the level of the following:

History: ______________________________

Examination: ______________________________

Medical decision-making complexity: ______________________________

4. A dermatologist was asked to see a 75-year-old man who was in the hospital for treatment of cholecystitis. The man had several skin lesions on his face. After taking a brief history, the dermatologist examined the patient's lesions and concluded that the lesions were seborrheic keratoses. The physician was able to make a straightforward decision based on the characteristic appearance of the lesions. The patient was advised to make an appointment to have the lesions removed as an outpatient at the dermatologist's office.

   Code(s): ________________

5. An internist requested an inpatient consultation from an orthopedic surgeon to evaluate and manage a 35-year-old female who had been in a motor vehicle accident. After reviewing the multiple x-ray reports and the documentation generated by the emergency room physicians, paramedics' progress notes from the scene of the accident, and history and physical examination produced by the internist, the orthopedist performed a complete review of systems; complete past, family, and social history; and extended details of the history of present illness. The physical examination was a complete musculoskeletal and neurologic examination with a review of all other body systems. Based on the patient's multiple fractures and internal injuries, the orthopedist concluded that the patient needed immediate surgery to repair and control the life-threatening conditions that existed. A neurosurgeon and a general surgeon were also asked to see the patient immediately and possibly assist in surgery. (Code only the orthopedic consultation.)

   Code(s): ________________

6. A 55-year-old patient was injured at work when he fell from a house roof and struck his head. He was admitted for a right frontal parietal craniotomy with removal of a subdural hematoma. He was recovering rapidly from surgery 5 days ago. Consultation was requested regarding a drug reaction that produced a rash on the upper torso. The physician conducted a brief HPI with a ROS focused on the patient's condition. The examination included three body areas and one organ system.

   Code(s): ________________

7. An initial inpatient surgical consultation was requested for a patient with pancreatitis to rule out a biliary obstruction as the cause. A detailed history and physical examination were performed.

   Indicate the level of medical decision-making complexity:

   ____

8. A 10-year-old was admitted 4 days ago for tympanotomy. Postsurgically the child developed fever and seizures of unknown origin. A pediatric consultation was requested. The HPI was extended with a complete ROS. A complete PFSH was elicited from the mother. A complete examination was conducted on all body areas and organ systems. A moderate amount of data was reviewed.

   Code(s): ____________________

Follow-up Inpatient Consultations

The follow-up inpatient consultation is used only for inpatients. These codes are used only if the consultant must subsequently see the patient to complete the initial consultation or if the attending physician requests another evaluation and the consultant has not already assumed responsibility for part of the patient's care.

EXERCISE N *Follow-up Inpatient Consultations*

Fill in the information for the following:

1. A follow-up consultation was performed by an infectious disease specialist for a 25-year-old female with resolving bacterial pneumonia. The patient had undergone an extended course of intravenous antibiotic therapy. The consultant wrote an interval history note focusing on her respiratory status and performed another, but briefer, physical examination. After reviewing laboratory reports and nurses' notes, the specialist concluded the patient's pneumonia was resolved and antibiotic therapy was no longer needed.

   Indicate the level of the following:

   History: ____________________

   Examination: ____________________

   Medical decision-making complexity: ____________________

2. A cardiologist was asked by a family practitioner to see an 80-year-old male patient again. One week prior, the patient, who has multiple other medical problems, suffered an anterior wall myocardial infarction. Despite following the medical management suggested by the cardiologist, the patient continued to have angina and ventricular arrhythmias. The cardiologist closely examined all of the documentation and test results that had been generated in the past week and performed a complete review of systems and an extended history of the present illness. The physical examination performed was a complete cardiovascular system examination. Based on the subjective and objective findings, the cardiologist concluded that more aggressive medical management was in

order. Given the patient's multiple problems coupled with the new threat of cardiorespiratory failure, the patient was immediately transferred to the ICU.

Code(s): ___________________

3. A physical medicine and rehabilitation specialist was asked to re-evaluate a patient for rehabilitation. The specialist had seen the patient 10 days earlier when the patient first was diagnosed with a cerebrovascular accident. An in-depth history was performed focusing on the patient's recovery to date. The physical examination focused on the patient's neurologic, cardiovascular, and musculoskeletal systems. After considering multiple management options, the physician concluded that the patient was now ready for active rehabilitation of her aphasia and her left-sided paralysis. The physician asked the patient's internist to continue to closely monitor the patient, who had multiple medical problems that required ongoing management.

   Indicate the level of the following:

   History: ___________________

   Examination: ___________________

   Medical decision-making complexity: ___________________

4. The attending physician requests a follow-up inpatient consultation on the 55-year-old patient injured at work when he fell from a house roof and struck his head. The patient had a right frontal parietal craniotomy 6 days previously and is recovering rapidly. An initial consultation was requested regarding a drug reaction that produced a rash on the upper torso. The consultant recommended a medication change, but after 48 hours the patient had no improvement. The consultant was asked to re-evaluate for other possible causes of the rash. An expanded problem focused interval history and a physical examination were performed.

   Indicate the level of medical decision-making complexity:

   ____

5. The attending physician had requested an inpatient consultation on a 10-year-old admitted 7 days earlier for tympanotomy. Postsurgically, the patient developed fever and seizures. An initial consultation diagnosis was febrile seizure. Now, on day 7, the child's temperature has returned to normal but the child has had a recurrence of seizures of increased severity. A follow-up consultation is requested. The consultant performs a detailed history and physical examination.

   Code(s): ___________________

Confirmatory Consultations

Various persons request consultations. Patients may request a confirmation of a diagnosis or recommended treatment, such as surgery. Insurance companies and other third-party payers may request a consultation for confirmation of a diagnosis, prognosis, or treatment plan for a patient. These consultations are *confirmatory consultations.* Patients and third-party payers will often seek more than one confirmatory consultation. The consultant should document that he or she is providing a second or third opinion. The "Confirmatory Consultations" codes for "New or Established Patient" are used to report services provided when the consulting physician is aware of the confirmatory nature of the opinion sought. Confirmatory consultations can be for inpatients or outpatients. Services after the initial confirmatory consultation are coded using the appropriate level of office visit, established patient, or subsequent hospital care. If the confirmatory consultation is required, the Mandated Service modifier (-32) is used with the correct five-digit code.

EXERCISE O Confirmatory Consultations

Using the CPT manual, fill in the codes for the following:

1. Dr. Jones asked Dr. Williams to confirm the diagnosis of tetralogy of Fallot for a 6-day-old male infant prior to cardiovascular surgery. Dr. Williams performed a comprehensive history and physical examination on the infant and reviewed the results from the extensive tests already performed. The consultant concluded that the child's problem was of moderate to high severity and recommended immediate surgery.

   Code(s): ____________________

2. The 45-year-old female's insurance company required a second opinion regarding the degenerative disk disease of her lumbar spine. One orthopedic surgeon had recommended a laminectomy. A second orthopedic surgeon was consulted and performed an expanded problem focused history and physical examination, particularly of her musculoskeletal and neurologic systems. Based on his findings and the conclusive findings of a recent myelogram, the second orthopedic surgeon was quick to conclude that the laminectomy was a reasonable course to follow.

   Code(s): ____________________

3. A 14-year-old male had been injured in an ice hockey game and received a severe gash to his left cheek. The original surgeon involved in suturing the wound did not think any further repair was needed. However, the young man's family practitioner thought more cosmetic surgery might be indicated and asked a second surgeon to evaluate the patient. The second surgeon focused his attention on the healed facial wound and face muscles. A brief history of the present illness was documented, and the physical examination described the patient's face and neck. However, the second surgeon agreed with the family practitioner and recommended that a plastic surgeon see the patient to prevent significant scar disfiguration.

   Indicate the level of the following:

   History: ____________________

   Examination: ____________________

   Medical decision-making complexity: ____________________

4. A 50-year-old man was referred by his internist to a second gastroenterologist to determine if the man's chronic duodenal ulcer could be managed differently. The patient had been following the advice of another gastrointestinal specialist but continued to complain of symptoms. The gastroenterologist completed an extended history of the patient, including an extended past, family, and social history, as well as a physical examination of his gastrointestinal system and related organ systems. The consultant concluded that the patient's ulcer was moderately severe and that more aggressive treatment was in order.

   Indicate the level of the following:

   History: ______________________________

   Examination: ______________________________

   Medical decision-making complexity: ______________________________

5. A 35-year-old female was admitted to the substance abuse treatment center for management of her drug addiction. Her addictive medicine physician had asked a gynecologist to evaluate her complaints of severe pelvic pain. The gynecologist could not identify any specific pathology that might be causing the problem. The patient continued to complain of worsening pelvic and rectal pain, and a second consultation was sought. The second gynecologist performed a complete head-to-toe physical examination and talked to the patient at great length to gather her medical history of present illness, including her complete past medical, family, and social history. The second gynecologist recommended an immediate laparoscopic examination to rule out multiple conditions such as endometriosis and other uterine and ovarian pathology. The physician indicates the patient is in a high risk category.

   Indicate the level of the following:

   History: ______________________________

   Examination: ______________________________

   Medical decision-making complexity: ______________________________

6. A patient seeks confirmatory consultation regarding his own physician's recommendation for surgical repair of a hernia. A brief history of present illness and an examination of the affected body area and organ system are performed.

   Indicate the level of the following:

   History: ______________________________

   Examination: ______________________________

   Medical decision-making complexity: ______________________________

7. A third-party payer seeks confirmatory consultation for an opinion on a patient's ability to return to work after the removal of a subdural hematoma 2 months previously. The patient states that he continues to have severe and incapacitating headaches and is unable to return to work. Comprehensive

history and physical examination are performed. Medical decision-making is of high complexity based on physician findings.

Code(s): ____________________

8. A physician seeks confirmatory consultation for a 63-year-old man who underwent triple bypass surgery a year ago. Subsequently, the patient has developed severe chest pain of 4 weeks' duration. The attending physician has recommended another bypass procedure, and the patient is hesitant to have the surgery. The patient's condition has deteriorated in the past 2 weeks and the patient is experiencing angina. An extended HPI and a complete ROS and PFSH were performed. The examination encompassed all body areas and organ systems.

   What is the examination level?

   ____

9. Office consultation is requested by Workers' Compensation for a 32-year-old man on workers' compensation who is unable to work because of a dislocated vertebra. Two previous surgical repairs have been unsuccessful in relieving the patient's pain. The patient has been unable to return to his employment as a bricklayer. He complains of radiating pain throughout the buttocks and leg with numbness throughout the leg and foot. Reflexes are minimal to nonexistent. A second opinion is being asked of the neurosurgeon to confirm or refute previous treatment plans. A comprehensive history and physical examination are performed. (Medical decision-making complexity is increased due to the prior surgeries and continued complaints.)

   Indicate the level of medical decision-making complexity:

   ____

Emergency Department Services

Emergency Department Services codes are used for new or established patients when services are provided in an emergency department that is a part of a hospital and available 24 hours a day. These patients are presenting for immediate attention. The codes are used for patients without appointments. Emergency Department Services codes are not used for patients at the hospital on observation status.

The codes in the Emergency Department Services are based on the type of service the physician performs in terms of the history, examination, and the complexity of medical decision making. In addition to this information within each code, note that the paragraph at the end of each code that begins with "Usually, the presenting problem(s) are of . . ." identifies the immediacy of the care. For example, 99283 indicates the presenting problem is of "moderate severity," whereas 99285 indicates that the presenting problem is of "high severity and poses an immediate significant threat to life. . . ." Sometimes the patient's clinical condition poses an immediate threat to life, making it possible for the physician to use the higher level code even if it may not be possible to perform the required history and physical examination.

Critical care provided to the patient in the emergency department is reported using additional codes from the Critical Care Service codes. More information will be presented later on the use of these Critical Care Service codes.

EXERCISE P *Emergency Department Services*

Use the information contained in the code descriptions from the Emergency Department Services subsection to answer the questions in this exercise.

1. Key components: problem focused history, problem focused examination, straightforward medical decision-making complexity. The severity of the presenting problem would usually be: ______________________

2. Key components: detailed history, detailed examination, and moderate medical decision-making complexity. The severity of the presenting problem would usually be: ______________________

3. Key components: expanded problem focused history, expanded problem focused examination, low medical decision-making complexity. The severity of the presenting problem would usually be: ______________________

4. Key components: expanded problem focused history, expanded problem focused examination, moderate medical decision-making complexity. The severity of the presenting problem would usually be: ______________________

Fill in the information for the following:

5. A patient in the emergency department has extreme acute chest pains and goes into cardiac arrest. The emergency department physician is unable to obtain a history or perform a physical examination because the patient's condition is critical.

   Code(s): ______________

6. A patient in the emergency department has a temperature of 105°F and is in acute respiratory distress. Symptoms include shortness of breath, chest pain, cyanosis, and gasping. The physician is unable to obtain a history or perform a physical examination because the patient's condition is critical.

   Code(s): ______________

7. A child presents to the emergency department with his parents after being bitten by a dog. The child is in extreme pain and bleeding from a wound on the forearm. The animal has not been located to quarantine for rabies. An expanded problem focused history is obtained and a physical examination is performed. (Medical decision-making complexity would be increased because of the possibility of rabies.)

   Code(s): ______________

8. A patient presents to the emergency department after being involved in a motor vehicle accident. The patient was not wearing a seat belt and com-

plains of neck, back, and shoulder pain. The abdomen is also tender. The patient's condition is of moderate severity. A brief HPI and ROS were done centered on the current problem. The examination was done on several body areas and organ systems. Moderate data were reviewed by the physician as he considered multiple diagnoses options.

Indicate the level of the following:

History: ____________________

Examination: ____________________

Medical decision-making complexity: ____________________

9. A patient presents to the emergency department with a wrist sprain sustained in a softball game when the patient slid into home. The patient is in apparent pain with a swollen wrist that he is unable to flex. An expanded problem focused history and physical examination are done. Radiographs show fracture of distal radius.

   Indicate the level of medical decision-making complexity:

   ____

Other Emergency Department Service

There is one Other Emergency Department Service code number at the end of the Emergency Department Services subsection used to report the services of a physician based at the hospital who provides two-way communication with the ambulance or rescue team. This physician provides direction and advice to the team as they attend the patient en route to the emergency department.

The notes preceding the code contain examples of the types of medical services the physician might direct. Be certain to read these notes, so you understand the types of services the code refers to.

EXERCISE Q ***Other Emergency Department Service***

Fill in the codes for the following:

1. The physician directs the emergency medical technicians via two-way communications with an ambulance en route to the emergency room with a patient in apparent cardiac arrest.

   Code(s): ____________________

Critical Care Services

Critical Care Services codes are used to identify services that are provided during medical emergencies to patients who are either critically ill or injured. These service codes require the physician to be constantly available to the patient and providing services. For example, a patient who is in shock or cardiac arrest would require the physician to be providing bedside critical care services. Critical care is often, but not required to be, provided in an acute care setting of a hospital. Acute care settings are intensive care units, coronary care units, emergency departments, or similar critical care units of a hospital. Codes in this subsection are listed according to the time the physician spends immediately available to or with the patient.

The total critical care time, per day, the physician spends in care of the patient is stated in one amount of time, even if the time was not concurrent. Code 99291 is used only once a day. As an example, if a physician sees a critical care patient for 74 minutes and then leaves and returns for 30 minutes of critical care at a later time in the same day, the coding would be for 104 minutes of care. The coding for 104 minutes would be:

99291 for the 74 minutes
99292 for the second 30 minutes

Code 99291 is reported for the first 30–74 minutes of critical care. If the critical care is less than 30 minutes, an E/M code would be used to report the service.

There are procedure codes that are bundled into the Critical Care Services codes. These services are normally provided to stabilize the patient. As an example of this bundling, a physician starts ventilation management (94656) while providing critical care services to a patient in the intensive care unit of a hospital. The ventilator management would not be reported separately but, instead, is considered to be bundled into the Critical Care Services code. The notes preceding the critical care codes in the CPT manual list the services and procedures bundled into the codes. If the physician provided a service at the same time as critical care and that service was not bundled into the code, the service could be reported separately. You will know what is bundled into the codes because this information is listed either with the description of the code or in the information preceding the code. Be certain to read the notes preceding the Critical Care Services codes before coding in this subsection, as the notes contain many exclusions and inclusions for these codes.

If the patient is in a critcal care unit but is stable, you report the services using codes from the Hospital Inpatient Services subsection, Subsequent Hospital Care subsection, or from the Consultation subsection, Initial Inpatient or Follow-up Inpatient subheadings.

EXERCISE R *Critical Care*

Fill in the information for the following:

1. Critical care is provided to the patient for 70 minutes.

   Code(s): ____________________

2. Can code 99292 be reported without code 99291? ____________________

3. A physician is called to the intensive care unit to provide care for a patient who has received second-degree burns over 50 percent of his body. The physician provides support for 2 hours. After leaving the unit, the physician returns later that day to provide an additional hour of critical care support to the patient.

   Code(s): ____________________

Neonatal Intensive Care Services

Neonatal Intensive Care Services are provided by the physician in a neonatal intensive care unit. The codes here are based on initial or subsequent visits and whether the infant is critically ill *though* stable or critically ill *and* unstable. For example, code 99295 states "critically ill," the second code in the subsection states "critically ill and unstable," and the third code in the subsection states "critically ill though stable." The notes preceding the subsection include a list of services that are bundled into the Neonatal Intensive Care Services codes for which separate payment is not allowed.

EXERCISE S Neonatal Intensive Care Services

Answer the following:

1. What does the abbreviation VLBW mean? ______________________
2. Once a neonate is no longer considered to be critcally ill and has attained a birth weight of 1500 grams, the codes from what subheading would be used to report services? ______________________
3. Which code is the only code in the Neonatal Intensive Care subsection for reporting services on the admission date? ______________________
4. Can you report a code from the subheading Physician Standby Services with a Neonatal Intensive Care code? ______________________
5. A neonate is admitted to Neonatal Intensive Care in critical condition and requires respiratory support which includes ventilation. The physician directs the health care team in an attempt to stabilize the infant.

   Code(s): ______________

Nursing Facility Services

A **nursing facility*** is a nonhospital health care organization with inpatient beds and an organized professional staff that provides continuous nursing and other health-related, psychosocial, and personal services to patients who are not in an acute phase of illness, but who require continued care. Nursing facilities provide a broad range of services and levels of care ranging from skilled nursing care to custodial care.

A **skilled nursing facility*** has an organized professional staff, including medical and nursing professionals, rehabilitation specialists, social workers, activities therapists, and others required to meet established standards. Professional and

---

*Definitions reprinted with permission from O'Leary M, et al: Lexikon: Dictionary of Health Care Terms, Organizations, and Acronyms for the Era of Reform. Oakbrook Terrace, IL, Joint Commission on Accreditation of Healthcare Organizations, 1994, pp 551–552.

practical nursing services are available 24 hours a day. Rehabilitation services, such as occupational therapy, physical therapy, and speech therapy, are available on a daily basis. A skilled nursing facility previously may have been called an extended care facility. Patients may stay several weeks in a skilled nursing facility before returning home or being transferred to an intermediate care facility for long-term care. Skilled nursing facilities provide care for individuals of all ages even though the majority of services are provided to geriatric patients.

An **intermediate care facility*** provides regular, basic health services to individuals who do not need the degree of care or treatment provided in a hospital or a skilled nursing facility. Residents, because of their mental or physical conditions, require assistance with their activities of daily living, such as bathing, dressing, eating, and ambulating. Intermediate care facilities generally provide long-term care, usually over several years. Professional and practical nursing services are available on a 24-hour basis. Activities, social service, dietary, and other restorative therapies are available on a daily basis. The majority of residents of intermediate care facilities are geriatric individuals or individuals of any age with mental retardation or developmental disabilities.

The phrase **long-term care facility*** is a broad term describing health and personal services provided to the chronically ill, aged, disabled, or retarded individual for an extended period of time. Different types of facilities are better described as skilled and intermediate care facilities.

These codes are also used for a psychiatric residential treatment center where individuals are provided 24-hour-a-day care with a professional staff engaging in a systematic treatment process. Two subheadings of nursing facility services are available: Comprehensive Nursing Facility and Subsequent Nursing Facility Care.

Comprehensive Nursing Facility Assessment

Comprehensive nursing facility assessment codes do not distinguish between new and established patients. These codes are used to report services provided by the physician at the time of admission or at a time during the resident's stay when his or her condition substantially changes and a reassessment is warranted. These assessments by physicians play a central role in the development of the resident's individualized care plan. The care plan is developed by an interdisciplinary care team using the Resident Assessment Instrument (RAI) and the Minimum Data Set (MDS).

EXERCISE T *Nursing Facility Services*

Answer the following:

1. What is the time indicated in code 99303 as a possible contributing factor?

 ____

2. A 72-year-old male patient is transferred to a nursing facility from a hospital after suffering a cerebrovascular accident. The patient needs a comprehensive assessment before his active rehabilitation plan can be started. A thorough history is gathered by the internist including the patient's chief complaint of

---

*Definitions reprinted with permission from O'Leary M, et al: Lexikon: Dictionary of Health Care Terms, Organizations, and Acronyms for the Era of Reform. Oakbrook Terrace, IL, Joint Commission on Accreditation of Healthcare Organizations, 1994, pp 551–552.

paralysis and weakness, an extended history of his present illness, and a complete review of systems. Details of the patient's past, family, and social history add information to the care planning process. The internist performed a complete multisystem physical examination. After much deliberation with the multidisciplinary rehabilitation team, the physician determined that the patient was ready for active rehabilitation. The physician also wrote orders to continue treatment of the patient's other medical conditions, including hypertension and diabetes.

Code(s): ____________________

3. The 88-year-old female's family physician comes to the nursing facility to perform the resident's annual assessment. An interval history is taken with some information from the patient, but due to her limited cognitive abilities, the majority of the detailed information is gathered from the nurses and past records. A complete multisystem physical examination is performed, which includes extensive body areas and related organ systems. Multiple diagnoses must be considered for this patient, who has senile dementia, diabetes, hypertension, hypothyroidism, and recurrent transient ischemic attacks. The creation of a new treatment plan is required because some of the patient's conditions have worsened.

   Indicate the level of the following:

   History: ____________________

   Examination: ____________________

   Medical decision-making complexity: ____________________

4. An 82-year-old male with advanced Alzheimer's disease has developed urinary and fecal incontinence along with a number of other medical problems that appear to have worsened. The resident's physician gathers an extended history from family members, nurses, and the documentation in the long-term care record provides the necessary information for the extended ROS. A head-to-toe physical examination is performed to assess all body systems. The physician writes all new orders as the patient has had a dramatic change in his physical and mental condition. A new treatment plan is created.

   Indicate the level of the following:

   History: ____________________

   Examination: ____________________

   Medical decision-making complexity: ____________________

Subsequent Nursing Facility Care

Subsequent nursing facility care codes do not distinguish between new and established patients. These codes reflect services provided by physicians on a periodic basis when the resident does not need a comprehensive assessment performed. Typically these residents have not had a major change in their condition since the previous physician visit but require ongoing management of chronic conditions or treatment of acute short-term problems.

EXERCISE U *Subsequent Nursing Facility Care*

Using the information within the code descriptions in the Subsequent Nursing Facility Care subheading, match the time in the description of the code with the stated current status of the patient:

Status		Time
1. inadequate response to therapy	_____	a. 35
2. stable, recovering, improving	_____	b. 25
3. significant new complication	_____	c. 15

Fill in the information for the following:

4. Subsequent follow-up care is provided for the 82-year-old man with Alzheimer's disease. The resident has responded well to some new medications and appears to have recovered some of his cognitive abilities. The physician performs a problem focused history and physical examination of his neurologic problem and orders that current treatments should be continued.

   Indicate the level of medical decision-making complexity:

   ____

5. Subsequent follow-up care is provided for the comatose patient transferred to the long-term care center from the hospital. The resident shows no signs of consciousness on examination but appears to have developed a minor upper respiratory tract infection with a fever and cough. The physician performs an expanded problem focused interval history and physical examination including neurologic status, respiratory status, and other related organ systems. Because the physician is concerned that the respiratory infection could progress to pneumonia, appropriate treatment is ordered.

   Code(s): ____________________

6. Subsequent follow-up care is provided for the patient who was transferred to a nursing facility from an acute care hospital after partial recovery from a stroke. The patient has developed periods of extreme dizziness and mental confusion. A detailed interval history is gathered and a detailed physical examination of the affected body systems is performed. Given the possibility that a new stroke could have occurred or that other neurologic problems have developed, new orders are written, and the physician plans to return the next day to evaluate the patient's condition again.

   Indicate the level of medical decision-making complexity:

   ____

Domiciliary, Rest Home (eg, Boarding Home), or Custodial Care Services

These codes are divided by new and established patient status. The codes are arranged in levels based on documentation in the patient record. There are no time estimates established for codes in this category.

These codes are used for the evaluation and management of residents who reside in a domiciliary, rest home, or custodial care center. Generally, health services are not available on site. These facilities provide residential care including lodging, meals, supervision, personal care, and leisure activities. These facilities provide live-in care to persons who, because of their physical, mental, or emotional condition, are not able to live independently. Such facilities might include alternative living residences, retirement centers, community-based living units, group homes, or residential treatment centers. These facilities provide custodial care for residents of all ages.

Separate codes are available for the evaluation and management of new patients and established patients based on the level of service provided. There are no time estimates established for these codes.

EXERCISE V *Domiciliary, Rest Home, or Custodial Care Services*

Complete the following:

1. The physician provides services to a new resident of a rest home for an ulcerative sore on the foot. Given the fact that the patient is in reasonably good health and is not a diabetic, the physician focuses his attention on the right lower extremity during the physical examination. The physician knows the resident well and is able to perform the brief HPI and ROS easily. The resident thinks the sore is from new shoes recently purchased, and the physician agrees with that conclusion. Topical antibiotic cream is ordered, and the new shoes are sent to the cobbler to be stretched.

   Indicate the level of the following:

   History: ______________________________

   Examination: ______________________________

   Medical decision-making complexity: ______________________________

2. A physician provides services to a new patient who is in a custodial care center. The patient is a 34-year-old quadriplegic who has pneumonia. The physician's notes indicate that the patient's pneumonia is of moderate severity. The physician performs a brief review of the history of present illness and a problem-pertinent review of systems. The physical examination looks at the respiratory, musculoskeletal, and neurologic systems as part of the extended review.

   Indicate the level of the following:

   History: ______________________________

   Examination: ______________________________

   Medical decision-making complexity: ______________________________

3. The physician provides care to a 94-year-old established patient who has the late effects of a stroke and is not responding to therapy. A brief HPI and ROS are performed. The physical examination focuses on the affected body areas and other symptomatic organ systems.

   Indicate the level of the following:

   History: ________________________________

   Examination: ________________________________

   Medical decision-making complexity: ________________________________

Home Services

Health care services can also be provided to patients in their homes. Times have not been established for this category of services. These services are also divided into new and established patient codes.

EXERCISE W *Home Services*

Answer the following:

1. A 44-year-old woman (new patient) has severe back pain after lifting a heavy washing machine to retrieve her daughter's crayon. The woman is unable to get out of bed and is very upset about not being able to care for her young daughter as well as the rest of her family. The history included a detailed history of the present illness, an extended review of systems, and pertinent past, family, and social history. The physical examination reviews the affected body area and other related organ systems. The physician has to consider multiple diagnoses including a possible herniated lumbar disk with myelopathy. Given the potentially debilitating nature of the condition, the patient is advised to be hospitalized immediately.

   Indicate the level of the following:

   History: ________________________________

   Examination: ________________________________

   Medical decision-making complexity: ________________________________

2. The physician sees an 84-year-old established male patient with advanced macular degeneration at the patient's home. The family members state that the patient is unable to care for himself at home. He is not responding to any treatment and will not allow health care workers to care for him at home. The physician does an interval history that includes a brief HPI and ROS. The physical examination concentrates on his eyes, ears, nose, and throat but also considers other symptomatic organ systems. The physician advises the patient and the family that long-term care placement is the only other option if the patient continues to refuse treatment in his home.

Indicate the level of the following:

History: ______________________________

Examination: ______________________________

Medical decision-making complexity: ______________________________

3. A 64-year-old established female patient has diabetes mellitus and has been having problems adjusting her insulin doses. She has had an onset of dizziness and sensitivity to light. The physician gathers a brief history of the present illness and a problem-pertinent review of systems. The physical examination focuses on the body systems now affected by the diabetes. The physician finds the patient's condition to be moderately severe.

   Code(s): ____________________

Prolonged Services

In the Prolonged Services subsection there are two subheadings—Prolonged Physician Service *With* Direct Patient Contact (ie, face-to-face encounters between physician and patient) and Prolonged Physician Service *Without* Direct Patient Contact (ie, non–face-to-face encounters between physician and patient). The assignment of codes depends on the kind of contact (face-to-face or non–face-to-face) the physician has with the patient, the amount of time spent in that encounter, and the site (outpatient or inpatient setting) where the service is performed. There is a code for the first hour and a code for each additional 30 minutes of time. For face-to-face encounters, there are different codes for outpatient and inpatient health care settings. However, for encounters that do not involve direct patient contact, there are no separate codes for outpatient and inpatient settings.

Physician Standby Services

The codes for Physician Standby Services are used by a physician who, at the request of the attending physician, is "standing by" in case his or her services are needed. The "standby" physician cannot be rendering services to another patient during this time. The standby codes are reported in increments of 30 minutes.

An important note for the standby codes is that these codes are used only when no service is performed. These codes are not used when the standby status ends in a physician's providing a service to the patient. The services that the physician provided would be billed as any other service even though the service began as a physician standby.

EXERCISE X *Prolonged and Physician Standby Services*

Using the notes in the subsections, answer the following:

1. Does the time the physician spends with the patient in prolonged, direct contact need to be continuous? ______________________________

2. Can a code from the Prolonged Service subsection be reported alone? _______

3. If the prolonged contact with the patient is less than 30 mintues, is the time reported separately? ______

4. The codes in the Prolonged Physician Service With Direct Patient Contact subheading are based not only on the time the physician spends with the patient, but also on another factor. What is that other factor? ______

5. Are the codes in the subheading Prolonged Physician Service Without Direct Patient Contact categorized based on the place of service? ______

6. According to the notes in the Physician Standby Services subsection, can a physician report the time spent in proctoring (monitoring) another physician?

   ______

7. If the physician who is standing by does so for 25 minutes, can he/she round the time up to 30 minutes for reporting purposes? ______

8. Prolonged direct patient contact of 1 hour and 50 minutes in an office or other outpatient setting.

   Code(s): ______

9. A 44-year-old asthmatic patient is scheduled for a routine Papanicolaou smear, but when she is in the office she develops severe breathing complications, and the physician spends the next hour and 30 minutes administering treatment.

   Code(s): ______

Case Management Services

The Case Management Services subsection of codes consists of codes used by physicians to report coordination of care services with other health care professionals. These services may include team conferences and telephone calls for the purpose of coordinating medical care of a patient. Telephone calls are based on complexity of service but are not usually paid by most third-party payers.

EXERCISE Y *Case Management Services*

Complete the following:

1. What are the two time components specified in the Team Conference codes from the Case Management Services subsection? ______

2. Telephone call codes are based on the complexity of service. What are the three measurements? ______________________________

3. An internist who practices medicine in a small city surrounded by mountainous terrain telephones an established patient to report on test results instead of having the patient drive 45 miles to his office. The 45-year-old man had a cardiovascular stress test that was normal, as were his cholesterol and other chemistry tests. The tests were done as part of a yearly physical examination. The patient was given the test results and the doctor was able to clarify some instructions given to the patient at the time of the stress test.

   Would you classify this telephone call as simple, intermediate, or complex?

   ____

4. A 15-year-old girl is hospitalized with bacterial meningitis while her father is away from home on business in England. The father naturally is very distraught over his daughter's sudden illness and has many questions when the girl's physician telephones him to discuss treatment options. The girl's mother is also very upset and does not want to make any decisions about the daughter's care without the father talking to the physician. The physician has a prolonged conversation with the father concerning the girl's deteriorating condition. Afterward, the father decides to return home immediately, which the physician agrees is a good idea.

   Would you classify this telephone call as simple, intermediate, or complex?

   ____

Care Plan Oversight Services

At times, physicians are asked to manage complex cases, such as hospice patients, who are homebound and receive the majority of their health care from visiting nurses. When regular communication is necessary between the nurse and the physician concerning revisions of care plans, coordinating treatment plans with other professionals, or adjustments of therapies, codes from the Care Plan Oversight Services subsection may be used to bill for these additional services. Billing is by time over a month's period.

Preventive Medicine Services

Use Preventive Medicine Services codes to report the routine evaluation and management of a patient when the patient is healthy and has no complaint or when the patient has a chronic condition/disease that is controlled but has planned, yearly routine physicals. The codes in this subsection would be used to report a routine physical examination done at the request of the patient, such as a well-baby check-up. Preventive Medicine codes are intended to be used to identify comprehensive services, not a single system examination, such as a yearly gynecologic examination. There are two subcategories of codes—new or established patients—and each subcategory is further divided based on the age of the patient.

EXERCISE Z Preventive Medicine Services

Complete the following:

1. According to the notes in the Preventive Medicine Services subsection, the extent and focus of the services provided will largely depend upon what factor?

   ____

2. If, during the preventive medicine evaluation, a problem is encountered that requires the physician to perform a problem focused E/M service, from what subsection would a code be selected to report the service and what modifier would be appended to the code? ____________________

3. A 39-year-old man, new to the area, obtains a referral from a local hospital to Dr. Tanner, an internist. The man reports that he feels well, exercises regularly, and has no particular complaints, but wants to establish himself with a physician for ongoing medical care. The physician performs a comprehensive history and physical examination, discusses risk factor reduction with the patient, and orders a series of laboratory and electrocardiographic tests as appropriate for the man's age. All test results are returned with normal findings, and the patient is advised to return in 1 year for another annual examination or earlier if any problems arise.

   Under what category in the Preventive Medicine Services subsection and within what age range does this patient fit?

   ____

4. A 70-year-old woman who is an established patient of the family practitioner is seen in the office for her annual physical examination. The patient has complaints of some aches and pain, usually when getting out of bed in the morning, but no other significant problems have limited her rather active lifestyle. During the course of her comprehensive history and physical examination, the physician notes several new senile keratoses that have appeared on the woman's face and hands. The physician does not believe these lesions are malignant but advises the patient to use a sunblock on her skin every day. Various laboratory and other tests are ordered on a preventive basis and for comparison purposes since her last examination. The negative test results are later reported to the patient.

   Under what category in the Preventive Medicine Services subsection and within what age range does this patient fit?

   ____

Counseling and/or Risk Factor Reduction Intervention

Counseling and/or Risk Factor Reduction Intervention codes are for both new and established healthy patients. The services are based on whether there is individual or group counseling provided to the patient. These codes can be used in conjunction with preventive medicine services. Codes in this category would be used to report a physician's services to a patient for risk factor interventional counseling, such as diet and exercise program, smoking cessation, or contraceptive management.

Besides preventive counseling for individuals or groups, there are also two additional codes under the category for Other Preventive Medicine Services that include unlisted preventive procedures and administration and interpretation of a health risk assessment.

Newborn Care Services

The Newborn Care Services subsection has codes used to identify services provided to normal or high-risk newborns. The codes are for services provided to a newborn in several settings. Note that there are two history and examination codes; one is specifically for a newborn assessment and discharge from a hospital or birthing room on the same date, and one is for birthing room deliveries.

If the physician provides a discharge service to a newborn who is discharged subsequent to the admission date, you would choose a code from the Hospital Inpatient Services subsection, Hospital Discharge Services category.

Special Evaluation and Management Services

The codes in this subsection are used to report evaluations for life or disability insurance baseline information. The services can be performed in any setting for either a new or an established patient. The codes vary, based on whether the code is being used for an examination for life or disability insurance and whether the examination is done by the treating physician or by someone other than the treating physician.

EXERCISE AA *Special Evaluation and Management Services*

Answer the following:

1. An insurance examination was conducted by the physician for a new patient for a term life insurance policy. From what category would you select a code to report this service? ________________________

2. A 50-year-old man is referred for a disability examination. The patient was injured when he slipped off a ladder and fell from a height of 10 feet, landing on his back. He has not returned to work since that time 6 months ago. The patient has been under the care of a physician from another state and has been referred by the insurance company for the assessment of the patient's ability to return to work. His primary physician has stated that this patient will be unable to return to his previous work as a bricklayer.

   From what category would you select a code to report this service?

   ____

3. What is the difference between the two codes in the Work Related or Medical Disability Evaluation Services codes? ________________________

4. A 58-year-old man was seen by his private physician for an examination as part of his claim for long-term medical disability. The patient has chronic obstructive lung disease with severe emphysema and has been unable to work over the past year. The physician completed all the necessary documentation required from the insurance company, including his opinion that the patient would be unable to work in the future as his pulmonary function is markedly impaired, in spite of continual respiratory and pharmacologic therapy.

   Code(s): ________________

Other Evaluation and Management Services

Other Evaluation and Management Services is the last subsection in the E/M section. It is used to report unlisted services. Use of this code indicates that there is *no* code in the E/M section that accurately represents the services provided to the patient. A special report would accompany the unlisted E/M service code.

Coding Practice

Good job! You have been through all of the E/M codes and are now familiar with the basics of CPT code arrangement. Can you imagine how well you would know your favorite novel if you read it several times a month? Well, coders use their CPT manuals every day and become very familiar with the information in the guidelines, notes, and descriptions of the codes. Please be sure to locate the code in the CPT manual and read all notes, guidelines, and descriptions about each code you work with. In this way, you will build a solid knowledge foundation.

Now let's begin to do some coding that will require you to combine all the information you have learned in Chapters 1 and 2 as you begin to code patient cases.

EXERCISE BB *Coding Practice*

Code the following:

1. A new patient is seen in the office for an earache (otalgia). The history is problem focused, the examination is problem focused, and the medical decision-making complexity is straightforward.

   Code(s): ________________

2. An established patient was seen in the office of an ENT specialist with a chief complaint of ear pain or otalgia. The physician completed a history and physical examination of the head, eyes, ears, nose, and throat. To the physician, this was a straightforward case of acute otitis media, and prescription medications were ordered.

   Code(s): ________________

3. An established patient is seen in the office for suture removal, which is done by the physician's nurse.

   Code(s): ________________

4. A new patient is seen in the office for a variety of medical problems. The patient has insulin dependent diabetes mellitus with complicating eye and renal problems. She also has hypertensive heart disease with episodes of congestive heart failure. Her peripheral vascular disease has worsened, and she can only walk a block before she is crippled with extreme leg pain. The patient reports that a new problem has surfaced, throbbing headaches with radiating neck pain. In order to manage and investigate the multiplicity of problems, the physician performs a comprehensive history and physical examination. A complete review of systems is performed, as is an update to her complete past medical, family, and social history. The physician has to take a multitude of factors into consideration, as this patient's problems are highly complex.

   Code(s): ___________________

5. A new patient is seen in the office with complaints of a cough, fever, excessive sputum production, and difficulty in breathing. The patient had been reasonably well up until now. Because the physician did not know the patient, she performed an extended examination of the respiratory system as well as a review of the patient's cardiovascular and gastrointestinal systems. An extended history of the present illness and an extended review of systems were performed. The physician's impression was that the patient possibly had pneumonia, and she referred the patient for a chest x-ray with a follow-up visit scheduled the next day.

   Code(s): ___________________

6. A new patient is admitted to the hospital on an observation status after a moderately severe fall from a height of about 8 feet. The patient has complaints of pain in multiple areas, and numerous x-rays were ordered. The physician performs a comprehensive history and physical examination. Given the possibility that multiple fractures have occurred, the physician's medical decision-making is moderately complex.

   Code(s): ___________________

7. The pediatrician admits a 20-month-old infant to the hospital after confirming pneumonia on a chest x-ray. The initial hospital care includes a detailed history and detailed physical examination with an extended problem-pertinent review of systems completed with the child's mother. The course of treatment envisioned by the physician is fairly straightforward, as the child's condition is of low severity.

   Code(s): ___________________

8. A family practice physician, who is treating a 20-year-old man for bronchitis, calls in a urologist to examine him because he has requested a circumcision. The consultant performs a problem focused history and problem focused physical examination and determines that there is no urgency for the surgical procedure. The physician's decision-making is fairly straightforward, and he recommends that the patient have the procedure done as an outpatient at a later date.

   Code(s): ___________________

9. A 75-year-old woman is visited by her physician in the extended nursing facility as part of her annual assessment. The physician completes a detailed interval history with a comprehensive, head-to-toe, physical examination. The physician reviewed and affirmed the medical plan of care developed by the multidisciplinary care team at the nursing facility. The patient's condition is stable; her hypertension and diabetes (type II) are in good control and she has no new problems. The physician has minimal data to review and few diagnoses to consider.

   Indicate the level of medical decision-making complexity:

   ____

How did you do? Did you get most of the answers correct? If you had more than three wrong, take the time now to review the first nine questions. If you got fewer than three wrong, continue on with the following cases, which will become increasingly more difficult.

10. Lilly Wilson, a new patient, is seen by the physician in the skilled nursing facility for an initial nursing facility assessment. Mrs. Wilson recently suffered a cerebral thrombosis with residual dysphagia and paresis of the left extremities. She was transferred from the acute care hospital to the skilled nursing facility for concentrated rehabilitation. Mrs. Wilson also has arteriosclerotic heart disease with a permanent pacemaker in place, rheumatoid arthritis, urinary incontinence, and macular degeneration in her right eye. The physician, who did not know Mrs. Wilson prior to her transfer, performs a comprehensive history and comprehensive physical examination. Given the patient's multiple diagnoses and the moderate amount of data the physician has to review, the decision-making is of a moderate to high level of complexity.

    Code(s): ____________________

11. Jeff Johnson, an established patient, is seen in the hospital on day two of his hospital stay. Mr. Johnson had been admitted through the Emergency Room with status asthmaticus and has been undergoing extensive respiratory therapy over the past 24 to 30 hours. The physician performs a detailed interval history and physical examination and reviews an extensive amount of documentation and laboratory and other test results that have been added to the record. The possibility of pneumonia complicating the asthma must be considered. The patient's respiratory condition is still unstable.

    From what subsection and subheading would you select a code to assign to this case?

    Subsection: ____________________

    Subheading: ____________________

    Indicate the level of medical decision-making complexity:

    ____

12. John Taylor is a 16-year-old outpatient who is a new patient to your office. John complains of severe facial acne. The history is problem focused with an

expanded problem focused physical examination, as the physician must consider related organ systems in addition to the integumentary system in order to properly treat the condition. With the minimal number of diagnoses to consider and the minimal amount of data to review, the physician's decision-making is straightforward with regard to the plan of care.

Code(s): ____________________

13. Jan Sharp, an established patient, had an office appointment because she needed a new dressing on the laceration on her arm. The physician's nurse changes the dressing.

    Code(s): ____________________

14. Gladys Swain stepped off a street curb and twisted her ankle. Because of the severe pain she was suffering and the inability to bear weight on the foot, she sought treatment at her neighborhood hospital emergency department. The triage nurse and the treating physician were fairly confident that Ms. Swain had an ankle injury and sent her immediately to Radiology for an x-ray. The physician completed a history focusing on her injury and limited her physical examination to her right foot and ankle. The radiologist confirmed that this was a simple closed fracture of the medial malleolus. The physician immobilized the ankle and referred the patient to an orthopedic surgeon.

    From what subsection and category would you select a code to assign to this case?

    Subsection: ____

    Category: ____

    Indicate the level of medical decision-making complexity:

    ____

15. Anna Rall was seen in the emergency department complaining of pressure in her chest and the feeling that her heart was racing. After her vital signs were taken, an immediate electrocardiogram was performed, and her heart rate was in excess of 160 beats per minute, with increased activity at the atrioventricular junction. After performing a comprehensive history and comprehensive physical examination, the physician continued to evaluate the patient, who had been placed on continuous electrocardiographic monitoring. The emergency department physician considered the diagnosis of paroxysmal nodal tachycardia and called a cardiologist for a consultation and possible admission to the hospital. Given the uncertainty of the diagnosis and the various other possible options, the physician's decision-making was at a highly complex level.

    Code(s): ____________________

16. The physician was called to the intensive care unit at the local hospital to care for Joe West, a patient in coronary crisis. The physician spent an hour at the patient's bedside stabilizing the patient.

    Code(s): ____________________

17. The physician was preparing to leave the hospital after he saw Joe West but was called back to the intensive care unit to see and stabilize another patient, Ted Keel. The service to the patient took 1½ hours.

    Code(s): ________________

18. George White, an established longstanding patient of Dr. York, needed to be seen for follow-up care after his recent inguinal hernia repair. Mr. White's wife was also ill and no one else was available to bring Mr. White to the doctor's office, so the doctor decided to visit Mr. White at home. After performing a problem focused interval history and problem focused physical examination, Dr. York concluded that Mr. White was improving but should remain at home for the next 2 weeks.

    From what subsection and category would you select a code to assign to this case?

    Subsection: ________________________________

    Category: ________________________________

    Indicate the level of medical decision-making complexity:

    ____

19. Henry Green, an established patient, came into the office for his yearly physical examination. Henry is 72 and in good health.

    From what subsection and category would you select a code to assign to this case?

    Subsection: ________________________________

    Category: ________________________________

20. An established patient, Harriet Turner, came into the office for a follow-up visit. She had been prescribed medication for her recent onset of depression, but since her last visit, when the dosage had been increased, she felt as if the medication was making her sleepy and lethargic. Considering the other factors such as other medical problems and drug interactions, the physician spent 25 minutes with the patient performing a detailed history and a detailed physical examination. After reviewing the details as well as recent laboratory work, the physician concluded that a different medication should be prescribed. The physician's decision-making was moderately complex given the possible medical complications that could arise.

    Code(s): ________________

21. Dr. Welton called Dr. Stouffer to perform a consultation on Carol Jones for advice on the management of her diabetes. Mrs. Jones had been hospitalized for a hysterectomy, which had been an uncomplicated procedure, but was having a slow recovery. Her abdominal wound did not appear to be healing well and her blood sugar was fluctuating each day. Dr. Stouffer, who had never met Mrs. Jones before, performed a comprehensive, multisystem physical examination as well as completing a comprehensive history with a com-

plete review of systems and extensive past medical history review. Dr. Stouffer recommended a new insulin regimen in addition to other medications to manage what might be a postoperative wound infection. Dr. Stouffer's medical decision-making had to consider multiple diagnoses, a moderate amount of data, and the moderate risk of complications that Mrs. Jones could develop.

Code(s): ___________________

Now you're coding! Be sure to check your answers as you complete each activity. If you identify a code incorrectly, go back and read the CPT manual information again.

HCFA DOCUMENTATION GUIDELINES

Medicare recipients account for a majority of patients receiving services in the American health care system. Thus, any change by the third-party payer, Medicare, has dramatic effects on the health care system. One such change that currently is in development is the documentation necessary when submitting a claim for Evaluation and Management services provided to a Medicare patient. The Medicare program is the responsibility of the Health Care Financing Administration (HCFA). Several years ago, HCFA determined that there should be a nationally uniform requirement for documentation contained in the patient record when submitting charges for E/M services. HCFA developed a set of standards for documentation for E/M services. The standards are informational items that must be in the patient record to substantiate a given level of service. The standards are called the **Documentation Guidelines.** These guidelines apply only to E/M services and only to patients covered by Medicare. The importance of the guidelines cannot be underestimated. Whatever the guidelines HCFA institutes for Medicare patients, they have a dramatic effect on the systems in health care and will soon spread to other third-party payers who will then begin to require the same or similar documentation.

The Documentation Guidelines specify the information that must be documented in the medical record for an E/M service to qualify for a given level of service. For example, Figure 2–5 illustrates the examination requirements for a general multisystem examination. Note that for an examination to qualify as an expanded problem focused examination the medical record must document that the physician performed at least six of the elements identified by a bullet (•) in Figure 2–6. If the medical record only documented that five of the elements identified by a bullet were performed, the examination would have to be reported at the lower problem focused examination level.

HCFA published the first set of documentation guidelines in 1994, but did not require compliance for payment of Medicare claims. A new set of guidelines was published in July 1997 for implementation January 1, 1998. The 1998 set of guidelines would be the standard used when reviewing claims for payment. If the physician did not have the documentation required in the guidelines, payment would be adjusted based on what was actually in the medical record. The guidelines were so complex and required such extensive revision of medical record keeping practices, that the AMA (American Medical Association) on behalf of its physician members requested an extension of the implementation date to allow

GENERAL MULTISYSTEM EXAMINATIONS

To qualify for a given level of multisystem examination, the following content and documentation requirements should be met:

- ***Problem Focused Examination***—should include performance and documentation of one to five elements identified by a bullet (•) in one or more organ system(s) or body area(s).
- ***Expanded Problem Focused Examination***—should include performance and documentation of at least six elements identified by a bullet (•) in one or more organ system(s) or body area(s).
- ***Detailed Examination***—should include at least six organ systems or body areas. For each system/area selected, performance and documentation of at least two elements identified by a bullet (•) is expected. Alternatively, a detailed examination may include performance and documentation of at least twelve elements identified by a bullet (•) in two or more organ systems or body areas.
- ***Comprehensive Examination***—should include at least nine organ systems or body areas. For each system/area selected, all elements of the examination identified by a bullet (•) should be performed, unless specific directions limit the content of the examination. For each area/system, documentation of at least two elements identified by a bullet is expected.

Figure 2–5
Documentation Guidelines for general multisystem examination requirements. (Courtesy of U.S. Department of Health and Human Services, Health Care Financing Administration.)

time for education about the guidelines and for HCFA to meet with representatives of the AMA to reconsider the guidelines. Although HCFA rescinded the requirement for strict compliance with the guidelines, they continue random review of claims based on whichever set of guidelines (1994 or 1997) the provider has elected to use.

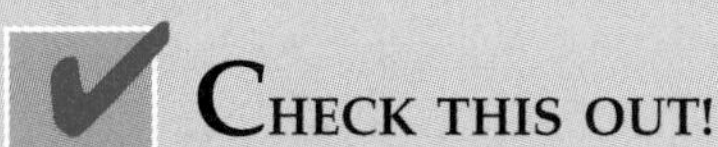

CHECK THIS OUT!

The HCFA has its own website:
http://www.hcfa.gov
You'll find the HCFA Documentation Guidelines under the Medicare information, Professional/Technical option.

Although the guidelines will change before implementation and will continue to be revised, guidelines will be a part of the standard for the medical record now and in the future for Medicare patients. You can anticipate that, as a coder, you will be required to learn about Medicare Documentation Guidelines. The most current Documentation Guidelines are provided in Appendix B of this text for your review.

General Multisystem Examination

System/Body Area	Elements of Examination
Constitutional	• Measurement of **any three of the following seven** vital signs: 1) sitting or standing blood pressure, 2) supine blood pressure, 3) pulse rate and regularity, 4) respiration, 5) temperature, 6) height, 7) weight (may be measured and recorded by ancillary staff) • General appearance of the patient (eg, development, nutrition, body habitus, deformities, attention to grooming)
Eyes	• Inspection of conjunctivae and lids • Examination of pupils and irises (eg, reaction to light and accommodation, size and symmetry) • Ophthalmoscopic examination of optic disks (eg, size, C/D ratio, appearance) and posterior segments (eg, vessel changes, exudates, hemorrhages)
Ears, Nose, Mouth, and Throat	• External inspection of ears and nose (eg, overall appearance, scars, lesions, masses) • Otoscopic examination of external auditory canals and tympanic membranes • Assessment of hearing (eg, whispered voice, finger rub, tuning fork) • Inspection of nasal mucosa, septum, and turbinates • Inspection of lips, teeth, and gums • Examination of oropharynx: oral mucosa, salivary glands, hard and soft palates, tongue, tonsils, and posterior pharynx
Neck	• Examination of neck (eg, masses, overall appearance, symmetry, tracheal position, crepitus) • Examination of thyroid (eg, enlargement, tenderness, mass)

Figure 2–6
Documentation Guidelines of the general multisystem elements. (Courtesy of U.S. Department of Health and Human Services, Health Care Financing Administration.)

CHAPTER GLOSSARY

attending physician: the physician with the primary responsibility for care of the patient

concurrent care: the provision of similar services (eg, hospital visits) to the same patient by more than one physician on the same day. Each physician provides services for a separate condition, not reasonably expected to be managed by the attending physician. When concurrent care is provided, the diagnosis must reflect the medical necessity of different specialties

consultation: includes those services rendered by a physician whose opinion or advice is requested by another physician or agency concerning the evaluation and/or treatment of a patient; a consultant is not an attending physician

counseling: a discussion with a patient and/or family concerning one or more of the following areas: diagnostic results, impressions, and/or recommended diagnostic studies; prognosis; risks and benefits of treatment; instructions for treatment; importance of compliance with treatment; risk factor reduction; and patient and family education

critical care: the care of critically ill patients in medical emergencies that requires the constant attendance of the physician (eg, cardiac arrest, shock, bleeding, respiratory failure); critical care is usually, but not always, given in a critical care area, such as the coronary care unit (CCU) or the intensive care unit (ICU)

emergency care services: services that are provided by the physician in the emergency department for unplanned patient encounters; no distinction is made between new and established patients who are seen in the emergency department

established patient: a patient who has received professional services from the physician or another physician of the same specialty in the same group within the past 3 years

new patient: a patient who has not received any professional services from the physician or another physician of the same specialty in the same group within the past 3 years

outpatient: a patient who receives services in an ambulatory health care facility and is currently not an inpatient

referral: the transfer of the total or a specific portion of care of a patient from one physician to another that does not constitute a consultation

systemic: affecting the entire body

CHAPTER REVIEW Chapter 2, Part I, Theory

Without the use of the CPT manual, complete the following:

1. How many subsections are there in the E/M section? ____________________

2. The four types of patient status are ______________________________,

   ______________________________, ______________________________,

   and ______________________________.

3. The first visit is called the __________ visit, and the second visit is called the

   __________ visit.

4. The first three factors a coder must consider when coding are __________

   ______________________________, ______________________________,

   and ______________________________.

5. How many types of histories are there? ____________________

6. Which history is more complex: the problem focused history or the expanded problem focused history? ____________________

7. The four types of examination components in order of difficulty (from least difficult to most difficult) are as follows:

   a. ______________________________

   b. ______________________________

   c. ______________________________

   d. ______________________________

8. The examination that is limited to the affected body area is the

____.

9. What does VLBW stand for? ______________________________

10. What medical decision-making involves a situation in which the diagnosis and management options are minimal, data amount and complexity that must be reviewed are minimal/none, and there is a minimal risk to the patient of complications or death? ______________________________

11. What term is used to describe a patient who has been formally admitted to a hospital? ______________________________

12. The four types of medical decision-making, in the order of complexity from most to least complex, are as follows:

    a. ______________________________

    b. ______________________________

    c. ______________________________

    d. ______________________________

13. Complexity of medical decision-making is based on three

____.

14. List the five types of presenting problems from the most risk and least recovery to the least risk and most recovery:

    a. ______________________________

    b. ______________________________

    c. ______________________________

    d. ______________________________

    e. ______________________________

15. Counseling and coordination of care are what kind of factors in most cases?

____

16. Time that is used as a guide for outpatient services is what kind of time?

____

Inpatient time spent at the bedside or nursing station during or after the visit is what kind of time? ______________________________

17. List three of the five types of presenting problems:

    a. ______________________________

    b. ______________________________

    c. ______________________________

18. A patient who is defined as one who has not received any professional services from the physician or another physician of the same specialty in the same group within the past 3 years is a(n) __________________ patient.

19. A discussion with a patient and/or family concerning one or more of the following areas: diagnostic results, impressions, and/or recommended diagnostic studies; prognosis; risks and benefits of treatment; instructions for treatment; importance of compliance with treatment; risk factor reduction; and patient and family education is ______________________________.

20. What type of patient has been admitted to a health care facility?

    ____

21. There is no distinction made between new and established patients in this service department of a hospital: ______________________________

22. Those services rendered by a physician whose opinion or advice is requested by another physician or agency in the evaluation and/or treatment of a patient is a _______________, whereas the physician who has primary responsibility for the patient in the hospital is called a(n) __________________.

23. When critically ill patients in medical emergencies require the constant attendance of the physician (eg, cardiac arrest, shock, bleeding, respiratory failure) to stabilize them, what kind of care is needed? __________________

24. When care is the provision of similar services (eg, hospital visits) to the same patient by more than one physician on the same day for different conditions, the care is ______________________________.

25. What is the name for the transfer of the total or specific care of a patient from one physician to another that does not constitute a consultation?

    ____

26. What type of patient has received professional services from the physician or another physician of the same specialty in the same group within the past 3 years? ______________________________

Chapter 2, Part II, Practical

Using the CPT manual, identify the codes for the following cases:

27. The physician provides initial intensive care service for the evaluation and management of a critically ill newborn.

    Code(s): ________________

28. A 55-year-old man was seen by the dermatologist for the first time and complained of two cystic lesions on his back. Considering that the patient was otherwise healthy and had a primary care physician caring for him, the dermatologist focused the history of the present illness on the skin lesions and focused the physical examination on the patient's trunk. The physician concluded with straightforward decision-making that the lesions were sebaceous cysts. The physician advised the patient that the lesions should be monitored for any changes but that no surgical intervention was warranted at this time.

    Code(s): ________________

29. A 68-year-old woman visited her internist again complaining of angina that seemed to have worsened over the past 3 days. The patient had had an acute anterior wall myocardial infarction (MI) 2 months ago. One month after the acute MI, she began to have angina pectoris. The patient also stated that she thought the medications were causing her to have gastrointestinal problems while not relieving her symptoms. She had refused a cardiac catheterization after her MI to evaluate the extent of her coronary artery disease. The physician performed a detailed history and detailed physical examination of her cardiovascular, respiratory, and gastrointestinal systems. The physician thought his decision-making process was moderately complex given the number of conditions he had to consider and the moderate to high risk this patient's problems created.

    Code(s): ________________

30. A 22-year-old woman visits the gynecologist for the first time since relocating from another state last year. The patient wanted a gynecologic examination and wanted to discuss contraceptive options with the physician. The physician collected pertinent past and social history related to the patient's reproductive system and performed a pertinent systems review extended to a limited number of additional systems. The physician completed the history with an extended history of her present physical state. A physical examination included her cardiovascular and respiratory systems with an extended review of her genitourinary system. Given the patient's history of not tolerating certain types of oral contraceptives in the past, the physician's decision-making involved a limited number of management options, all with low risk of morbidity to the patient.

    Code(s): ________________

31. An established patient is admitted on observation status for influenza symptoms and extreme nausea and vomiting. The patient is severely dehydrated and has been experiencing dizziness and mental confusion the past 2 days.

Prior to this episode the patient had been well but became acutely ill overnight with these symptoms. Given the abrupt onset of these symptoms, the physician had to consider multiple possible causes and ordered a variety of laboratory tests to be performed. The patient was at risk for a moderate number of complications. A comprehensive history was collected and a complete head-to-toe physical examination was performed.

Code(s): ________________

32. The physician (in Question 31) returned to the hospital the following day to visit the patient on observation status with severe influenza. The decision is made to admit the patient, whose condition had worsened and who was not responding to the therapy initiated on the observation unit. The physician performed a detailed history and detailed physical examination to reflect the patient's current status. The patient's problem was of low severity but required ongoing active management with possible surgical consultation.

Code(s): ________________

33. A 2-year-old child is presented for a routine vaccination for mumps. The child is a new patient. No history and physical examination were noted. (The mumps immunization would also be coded 90704.)

Code(s): ________________

34. A 33-year-old man was brought to his private physician's office by his wife. The man, who was an established patient, had experienced severe leg pain of 2 weeks' duration. In the past 2 days, the patient had experienced fainting spells, nausea, and vomiting. The patient had multiple other vague complaints over the past month that he dismissed as unimportant, but his wife was not so sure, and she described his general health as deteriorating. The physician performed a complete multisystem physical examination after performing a complete review of systems and a complete past medical, family, and social history with an extended history of the present illness. The physician had to consider an extensive number of diagnoses and ordered a variety of tests to be performed immediately.

Code(s): ________________

35. A 42-year-old woman, who was an established patient, visited her family practitioner with the chief complaint of a self-discovered breast lump. She described a feeling of fullness and tenderness over the mass that had become more pronounced in the past 2 weeks. Because the patient was otherwise healthy and had had a physical within the past 6 months, the physician focused his attention on the breast lump during the taking of the history and performance of the physical examination. The physician ordered an immediate mammography to be performed and a follow-up appointment in 5 days. The physician gave the patient no other options.

Code(s): ________________

36. An 82-year-old man visited his family practitioner again concerning his diabetes mellitus. The man performed daily glucose monitoring and had a blood glucose test performed every week at the local hospital. It was becoming evident that the man had to be switched from an oral medication to insulin. In

order to be certain, the physician performed an expanded problem focused history and an expanded problem focused physical examination. At this time, there were a limited number of diagnoses and treatment options for the physician to consider, and he had limited new data to review.

Code(s): ________________

37. A 74-year-old patient is referred by a third-party payer for a second opinion regarding osteoarthritis in the right knee. Her family physician has recommended a total knee replacement and wanted to refer the patient to an orthopedic surgeon. The consultant seeing the patient at the insurance company's request had never met the patient before. He performed an extended history of the present illness and a complete review of systems with a complete past, family, and social history. His physical examination was a comprehensive musculoskeletal review. The physician reviewed x-ray films brought by the patient and numerous records from the family practitioner. The consultant agreed with the diagnosis and thought that the osteoarthritis would progress, leaving the patient with more disability in the near future.

    Code(s): ________________

38. A cardiac arrest patient is in the intensive care unit of the hospital. The patient is in respiratory failure, and the physician spends 2 hours and 30 minutes in the care of the patient.

    Code(s): ________________

39. The physician returns to the hospital to care for a patient who was admitted several days ago for resection of the colon. The patient is stable and recovering.

    Code(s): ________________

40. An attending physician has requested a consultation for a patient who is an alcoholic and was admitted to the hospital for gastrointestinal bleeding. The consultant included a brief history of the present illness and a problem pertinent systems review in his history. The physical examination concentrated on the patient's gastrointestinal and hematological and lymphatic systems. The consultant was fairly confident that the active bleeding was from a chronic gastric ulcer that was confirmed by radiologic studies. The consultant recommended that an esophagogastroduodenoscopy be performed as soon as possible.

    Code(s): ________________

41. The physician directs the emergency medical support team on a two-way radio from the emergency department to an ambulance that is en route to the hospital with a third-degree burn patient in critical condition.

    Code(s): ________________

42. In the emergency department, the physician is required to care for a 62-year-old man who presents with rapid heart beat and profuse sweating. The condition presents an immediate threat to the patient's life.

    Code(s): ________________

43. A follow-up consultation is requested by the attending physician for the patient who is an alcoholic and was admitted to the hospital for gastrointestinal bleeding in a previous case. The patient is not responding to conventional treatment. His condition has deteriorated to unstable.

    Code(s): ___________________

44. The physician is requested to provide standby service to another physician. The physician provides an hour of standby service without any direct contact with the patient.

    Code(s): ___________________

3 Understanding the Anesthesia and Surgery Sections

CHAPTER TOPICS

Part I: Learning About the Anesthesia Section

Part II: Learning About the Surgery Section

Integumentary System

Musculoskeletal System

Respiratory System

Cardiovascular System

Hemic and Lymphatic Systems

Mediastinum and Diaphragm

Digestive System

Urinary System

Male Genital System

Intersex Surgery

Laparoscopy

Female Genital System

Maternity Care and Delivery

Endocrine System

Nervous System

Eye and Ocular Adnexa

Auditory System

Chapter Glossary

Chapter Review

Learning Objectives

After completing this chapter, you should be able to

1. Explain the Anesthesia section and subsection format.
2. Recognize the elements of the anesthesia formula.
3. Identify the modifiers used in the Anesthesia section.
4. Accurately report unlisted anesthesia procedures.
5. Calculate anesthesia service payment.
6. Analyze cases and apply the correct CPT codes.
7. Understand Surgery section and subsection formats.
8. Define Surgery section and subsection terminology.
9. Analyze unique Surgery subsection characteristics.
10. Code using each of the Surgery subsections.

Part I: Learning About the Anesthesia Section

The Anesthesia section is a specialized section that is used by an anesthesiologist, anesthetist, or other physician to report the provision of anesthesia services, usually during surgery. *Anesthesia* means induction or administration of a drug to obtain partial or complete loss of sensation. *Analgesia* (absence of pain) is achieved so that a patient may have surgery or a procedure performed without pain. Types of anesthesia may be general, regional, or local.

The practice of anesthesiology is not limited to administration of anesthesia for the surgical patient. The American Society of Anesthesiologists (ASA) defines the practice of anesthesiology as follows:

- The management of procedures for rendering a patient insensible to pain and emotional stress during surgical, obstetrical, and certain medical procedures.
- The evaluation of management of life functions under the stress of anesthetic and surgical manipulations.
- The clinical management of the patient unconscious from whatever cause.
- The evaluation and management of problems in pain relief.
- The management of problems in cardiac and respiratory resuscitation.
- The application of specific methods of respiratory therapy.
- The clinical management of various fluid, electrolyte, and metabolic disturbances.*

The Section Format

Anesthesia procedure codes are divided first by anatomic site and then by specific type of procedure, as shown in Figure 3–1.

The last two subsections in Anesthesia—Radiologic Procedures and Other Procedures—are *not* by anatomic division. The CPT codes from the Radiologic Procedures subsection are used to report anesthesia service when radiologic services are provided to the patient for diagnostic or therapeutic reasons.

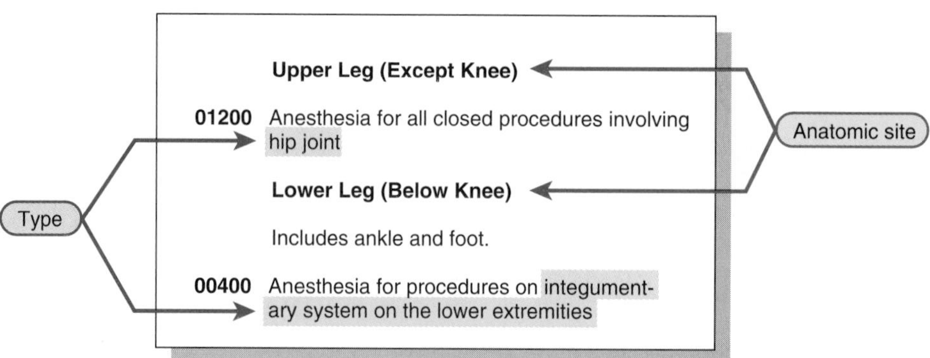

Figure 3–1
Anatomic divisions in Anesthesia section.

*Definitions excerpted from the *1998 Relative Value Guide,* American Society of Anesthesiologists, p. iii. A copy of the full text can be obtained from ASA, 520 N. Northwest Highway, Park Ridge, IL 60068-2573.

EXAMPLE

Therapeutic reason:	01921	Anesthesia for angioplasty
Diagnostic reason:	01922	Anesthesia for noninvasive imaging or radiation therapy

EXERCISE A Anesthesia Format

Complete the following exercise:

1. Using the CPT manual, list each subsection in the Anesthesia section.

____

____

____

____

____

____

____

____

____

____

____

____

____

____

____

____

____

2. Which two subsections are *not* divided by anatomic site? _______________

   and _______________

3. What is analgesia? _______________

4. What is anesthesia? ______________________________

5. Name the three types of anesthesia: ______________________,

______________________, and ______________________

Formula for Anesthesia Payment

What makes anesthesia coding different from any other coding is the way in which anesthesia services are billed. There is a standard formula for payment of anesthesia services that is, for the most part, nationally accepted. The formula is basic units + time units + modifying units (B + T + M). Let's look at each of these elements in more detail.

What Is a Basic Unit?

The American Society of Anesthesiologists (ASA) publishes a *Relative Value Guide* (RVG), which contains codes for anesthesia services. The CPT manual contains most of these anesthesia service codes in the Anesthesia section. The RVG includes about 20 anesthesia service codes that are not included in the CPT manual (see Fig. 3–2) and several codes that have components of the service that vary from the CPT description for the code (see Fig. 3–3).

The RVG lists a modifier that is not included in the CPT manual: -75. Modifier -75 is for Concurrent Care: "Services rendered by more than one physician: When the patient's condition requires the additional services of more than one physician, each physician may identify his or her services by adding the modifier '-75' to the basic service performed or the service may be reported by use of the five-digit modifier code 09975."*

The ASA Relative Value is not a fee schedule (a list of the charges for services) but instead is intended as a comparison of anesthesia services to each other. For example, anesthesia services provided for a biopsy of a sinus is less complicated than services provided for a radical sinus surgery. A team of physicians with expertise in anesthesiology developed the comparison and assigned numerical values to each service, termed the **basic unit value** (see Fig. 3–4). The ASA's basic unit is accepted as the standard in the United States.

One coding circumstance unique to anesthesia coding occurs when multiple surgical procedures are performed during the same session. In this case the procedure with the highest unit value is the basic unit value. For example, during the

Figure 3–2
RVG codes not included in the CPT manual. (Based on the *1998 Relative Value Guide* of the American Society of Anesthesiologists. A copy of the full text can be obtained from ASA, 520 N. Northwest Highway, Park Ridge, IL 60068-2573.)

**01216 Revision of total hip arthroplasty........................10 + TM

**01997 Daily hospital management of intravenous patient-controlled analgesia..............................2

**This code is not included in CPT-4

*Excerpted from *1998 Relative Value Guide,* The American Society of Anesthesiologists, p. viii. ASA, 520 N. Northwest Highway, Park Ridge, IL 60068-2573.

*00918	Anesthesia for transurethral procedures (including urethrocystoscopy); with fragmentation, manipulation and/or removal of ureteral calculus.......................................6 + TM

*In CPT, "manipulation" was not included in this code until the 2000 CPT.

Figure 3–3
RVG code whose description differs from that in the CPT manual. (Based on the *1998 Relative Value Guide* of the American Society of Anesthesiologists. A copy of the full text can be obtained from ASA, 520 N. Northwest Highway, Park Ridge, IL 60068-2573.)

same surgical procedure session, a clavicle biopsy (basic unit value of 3) and a radical mastectomy (basic unit value of 5) are done, the basic unit value for both procedures becomes 5.

Another coding circumstance unique to anesthesia coding applies when there is a second attending anesthesiologist (one who performs the same types services as the first attending physician). In this case a basic value of 5 units is added. A special report must accompany the submission to the third-party payer explaining why the procedure required the services of two anesthesiologists. The time for both anesthesiologists is also reported.

T Is for Time

Anesthesia services are provided based on the time anesthesia was administered in hours and minutes. The time is started when the anesthesiologist begins preparing the patient to receive anesthesia, continues through the procedure, and ends when the patient is no longer under the personal care of the anesthesiologist. The hours and minutes anesthesia was administered are recorded in the patient record. Carriers independently determine the amount of time in a unit. Usually, 15 minutes equals a unit.

M Is for Modifying Unit

As the name implies, modifying units reflect circumstances or conditions that change or modify the environment in which the anesthesia service is provided. There are two basic modifying characteristics: qualifying circumstances and physical status modifiers.

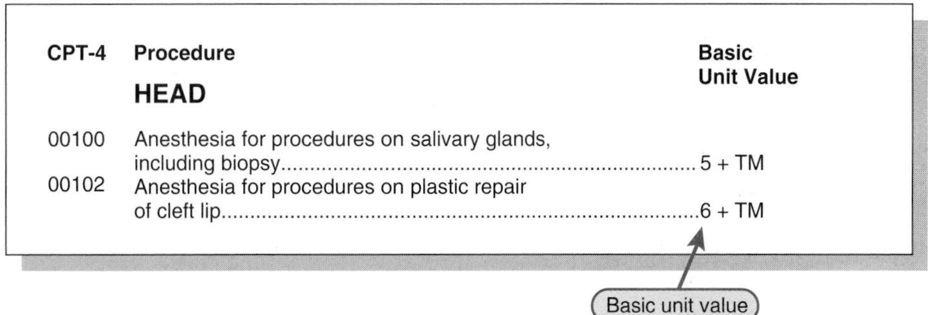

CPT-4	Procedure	Basic Unit Value
	HEAD	
00100	Anesthesia for procedures on salivary glands, including biopsy..	5 + TM
00102	Anesthesia for procedures on plastic repair of cleft lip..	6 + TM

Figure 3–4
Base unit value. (Based on the *1998 Relative Value Guide* of the American Society of Anesthesiologists, p. 1. A copy of the full text can be obtained from ASA, 520 N. Northwest Highway, Park Ridge, IL 60068-2573.)

Qualifying Circumstances

At times, anesthesia is provided during situations that make the administration of the anesthesia more difficult. These types of cases include those that are performed in emergancy situations and those dealing with patients of extreme age; they also include services performed during the use of controlled hypotension or the use of hypothermia. The codes begin with the number 99 and are considered **adjunct codes,** which means that the codes cannot be used alone but must be used in addition to another code and are used to provide additional information only. The qualifying circumstances code is used in addition to the anesthesia procedure code. There is a plus (+) symbol next to the qualifying circumstances codes in both the Anesthesia Guidelines and the Medicine section of the CPT manual.

You were just presented with some very important information about the use of certain codes within the CPT manual. The plus (+) symbol next to any CPT code—not just to Qualifying Circumstances codes—indicates that that code cannot be used alone. Throughout the remaining sections of the CPT manual, the plus symbol will appear to caution you to use the code only as an adjunct code.

When used, the qualifying circumstances code is listed separately in addition to the primary anesthesia procedure code. For example, if the anesthesia was provided for an 80-year-old patient during a corrective lens procedure, the coding would be:

00142 Anesthesia for procedure on eye; lens surgery

99100 Anesthesia for 80-year-old patient

The *Relative Value Guide* lists the qualifying circumstances along with the relative value for each code (see Fig. 3–5). The CPT index lists the qualifying circumstances coded under Anesthesia, Special Circumstances.

Physical Status Modifiers

The second type of modifying unit used in the Anesthesia section is the physical status modifier. These modifiers are used to indicate the patient's condition at the time anesthesia was administered. The physical status modifier not only indicates the patient's condition at the time of anesthesia but also serves to identify the level of complexity of services provided to the patient. For instance, anesthesia service to a gravely ill patient is much more complex than the same type of service to a normal healthy patient. The physical status modifier is not assigned by the coder but is determined by the anesthesiologist and documented in the anes-

Figure 3–5
Qualifying circumstances with relative value. (Based on the *1998 Relative Value Guide* of the American Society of Anesthesiologists, p. ix. A copy of the full text can be obtained from ASA, 520 N. Northwest Highway, Park Ridge, IL 60068-2573.)

Qualifying Circumstances

Code	Description	Relative Value
+99100	Anesthesia for patient of extreme age, under one year and over seventy	1
+99116	Anesthesia complicated by utilization of total hypothermia	5
+99135	Anesthesia complicated by utilization of controlled hypotension	5
+99140	Anesthesia complicated by emergency conditions (specify)	2

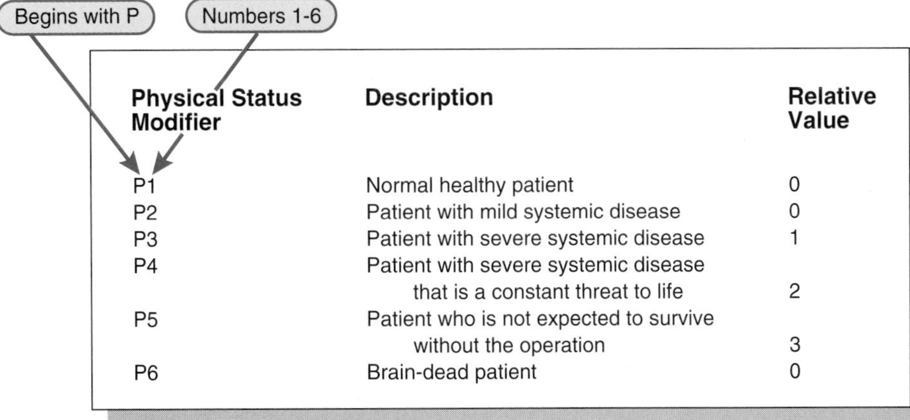

Physical Status Modifier	Description	Relative Value
P1	Normal healthy patient	0
P2	Patient with mild systemic disease	0
P3	Patient with severe systemic disease	1
P4	Patient with severe systemic disease that is a constant threat to life	2
P5	Patient who is not expected to survive without the operation	3
P6	Brain-dead patient	0

Figure 3–6
Physical status modifiers. (Based on the *1998 Relative Value Guide* of the American Society of Anesthesiologists. A copy of the full text can be obtained from ASA, 520 N. Northwest Highway, Park Ridge, IL 60068-2573.)

thesia record. The physical status modifier begins with the letter "P" and contains a number from 1 to 6 (Fig. 3–6). Note that the relative value for P1, P2, and P6 is zero, since these conditions are considered not to affect the service provided. A physical status modifier is used after the five-digit CPT code and is illustrated in Figure 3–7.

Summing It Up!

Let's put the elements of the equation to practical use by applying the equation to a patient case.

An 84-year-old female (qualifying circumstance for extreme age, value 1) with severe hypertension has a 4-cm malignant lesion removed from her right knee (basic value of 3). The total time of anesthesia service was 60 minutes (4 units). The anesthesiologist indicates in the medical record that the patient's physical status at the time of the procedure was P3 (relative value of 1).

3	basic value
4	time units
2	modifiers: physical status = 1; exteme age = 1
11	total units

The coding would be:

00400-P3	Anesthesia for procedure of integumentary system of knee
99100	Anesthesia for an 84-year-old patient
11	Units at the third-party payer established rate per unit

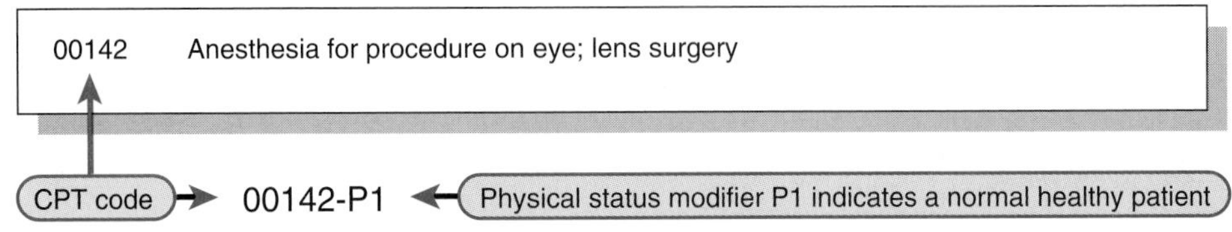

Figure 3–7
Anesthesia code and modifier.

Locality Name	Anesthesia Conversion Factor
Manhattan, NY	20.48
NYC suburbs/Long I., NY	20.01
Queens, NY	19.79
Rest of state	16.84
North Carolina	16.01
North Dakota	15.77

Figure 3–8
1999 HCFA Anesthesia Conversion Factors.

Conversion Factors

A conversion factor is the dollar value of each unit. Each third-party payer issues a list of conversion factors. The lists vary based on geographic location since the cost of practicing medicine varies from one location to another. See Figure 3–8 for an example of a third-party payer's anesthesia conversion factors. Note that North Dakota is $15.77 per unit and Manhattan, NY, is $20.48 per unit as it is much less expensive to provide anesthesia services in Grand Forks, ND, than it would be to provide the same services in Manhattan, NY.

The conversion factor for your locale is multiplied by the number of units in the procedure. For example, the case above has 11 units. If the anesthesiologist were located in Manhattan, NY, which has a conversion factor of $20.48, the total for the procedure would be $225.28 (11 × $20.48). If the same services were provided in North Dakota, with the conversion factor of $15.77, the total for the procedure would be $173.47 (11 × $15.77).

Standard Modifiers

The CPT two-digit modifiers are used with anesthesia service codes. Modifier -51, multiple procedures, is not usually used with anesthesia codes because when multiple services are provided during the same anesthesia session the value assigned to the highest valued service is used to report all services. If a service for a value of 10 and 5 were done during the same session, the value of 10 would report all services for that session. In coding within other sections of the CPT, the modifier -51 is added to the second procedure and usually the third-party payer would pay that second service at a reduced rate, but this is not the case in anesthesia.

EXERCISE B ***Standard Modifiers***

Using Appendix A of the CPT manual, identify the following CPT modifiers:

1. Unusual Procedural Services ______________________

2. Unusual Anesthesia ______________________

Using the descriptions for the preceding modifiers, answer the following. Which modifier would be used to identify:

3. A service greater than that usually provided? ______________

4. A service that required general anesthesia when usually local would be used?

____

The preceding modifiers you identified are the most commonly used modifiers in the Anesthesia section.

5. In addition to modifier -51, Appendix A of the CPT manual identifies one modifier that is not to be used with anesthesia procedures. Identify this "not-to-be-used" modifier.

____

Concurrent Care Modifiers

Some third-party payers require additional modifiers to indicate how many cases an anesthesiologist is performing or supervising at one time. Certified registered nurse anesthetists (CRNAs) may administer anesthesia to patients under the direction of a licensed physician, or they may work independently. When an anesthesiologist is directing the provision of anesthesia on more than one case at a time, modifiers are used to indicate the context and number of cases that are concurrently being billed. The following modifiers are examples of those commonly used:

- AA Anesthesia services performed personally by anesthesiologist
- AB Medical direction of own emlpoyee(s) by anesthesiologist (not more than four employees)
- AC Medical direction of other than own employees by anesthesiologist (not more than four individuals)
- AD Medical supervision by a physician: more than four concurrent anesthesia procedures
- AE Direction of residents in furnishing not more than two concurrent anesthesia services—attending physician relationship met
- AF Anesthesia complicated by total body hypothermia
- QX Certified registered nurse anesthetist (CRNA) service, with medical direction by a physician
- QZ CRNA service, without medical direction by a physician

These modifiers are not CPT modifiers but third-party payer modifiers. These modifiers further define the services provided. As a coder, you will need to become familiar with numerous coding systems that are used in addition to the CPT codes.

EXERCISE C *Anesthesia Modifiers*

Complete the following:

1. If the anesthesia service was provided to a patient who had mild systemic disease, what would the physical status modifier be likely to be?

____

2. If the same service was provided to a patient who had severe systemic disease, what would the physical status modifier be likely to be?

____

3. Anesthesia complicated by utilization of total body hypothermia

   Code(s): ____________________

4. Anesthesia complicated by emergency conditions (specify)

   Code(s): ____________________

5. Anesthesia for patient of extreme age, under 1 year or over 70

   Code(s): ____________________

6. Anesthesia complicated by utilization of controlled hypotension

   Code(s): ____________________

Complete the following terminology questions:

7. Which of the words used in the previous questions means abnormally low blood pressure?

   ____

8. Which of the words used in the previous questions means low body temperature?

   ____

The Unlisted Anesthesia Code

Anesthesia has an unlisted procedure code number available. The unlisted procedure code is located under the Other Procedures subsection in the Anesthesia section.

EXERCISE D *Anesthesia Codes*

Complete the following:

1. What is the unlisted anesthesia procedure code number?

   Code(s): ____________________

Locate anesthesia procedures in the CPT manual index under the entry "Anesthesia" and then subtermed by the anatomic site. Write the CPT index location on the line provided (eg, Anesthesia, Thyroid). Then locate the code(s) identified in the Anesthesia section of the CPT manual. Choose the correct code(s) and write the code(s) on the line provided.

2. Needle biopsy of the thyroid (neck)

   Index location: ____

   Code(s): ____________________

3. Cesarean section

   Index location: ______________________________

   Code(s): ______________

4. Transurethral resection of the prostate

   Index location: ______________________________

   Code(s): ______________

5. Repair of cleft palate

   Index location: ______________________________

   Code(s): ______________

6. Repair of ruptured Achilles tendon without graft

   Index location: ______________________________

   Code(s): ______________

7. Arthroscopic procedure of knee joint

   Index location: ______________________________

   Code(s): ______________

8. Biopsy of the clavicle

   Index location: ______________________________

   Code(s): ______________

9. Corneal transplant

   Index location: ______________________________

   Code(s): ______________

10. Total cystectomy

    Index location: ______________________________

    Code(s): ______________

Using the following information and the B+T+M formula, calculate the payment for the anesthesia services.

For the following questions a time unit will be 15 minutes. Basic unit value for each case is provided within the questions. Refer to Figure 3–8 for the conversion factors used in these questions, Figure 3–5 for the value of the Qualifying Circumstances, and Figure 3–6 for value of the Physical Status Modifiers.

11. A needle biopsy, lasting 15 minutes, was conducted in North Dakota on a normal healthy 75-year-old patient. The basic unit value for the service is 3.*

    Anesthesia payment: ____________________

12. A patient with diabetes mellitus, controlled by diet and exercise, undergoes a 60-minute anesthesia time period for a transurethral resection of the prostate (basic unit value of 5).* Calculate the anesthesia rate if the procedure was performed in the following cities:

    a. Manhattan ____________________

    b. North Carolina ____________________

13. A cesarean section was conducted in Alfred, NY, on a patient with preeclampsia. The basic unit value for the service is 7.* Calculate the anesthesia rate for two different length of procedures:

    a. 30-minute procedure ____________________

    b. 45-minute procedure ____________________

The Anesthesia section is a very specialized section used to code services provided to patients. The next section, Surgery, is the largest of the CPT manual sections, and you will most certainly encounter coding from this section in your allied health career.

Part II: Learning About the Surgery Section

The Section Format

The Surgery section is the largest in the CPT manual. The codes range from the 1000s to the 6000s. Surgery is divided into 17 subsections. Most Surgery subsections are divided based on anatomic site (eg, integumentary or respiratory).

EXERCISE E *The Surgery Section Format*

To help you become familiar with the format of the Surgery section, write the names of the Surgery subsections on the lines provided in the order in which they are found in the CPT manual.

---

*Excerpted from *1998 Relative Value Guide,* American Society of Anesthesiologists, 520 N. Northwest Highway, Park Ridge, IL 60068-2753.

List the Surgery subsections:

1. ______________________
2. ______________________
3. ______________________
4. ______________________
5. ______________________
6. ______________________
7. ______________________
8. ______________________
9. ______________________
10. ______________________
11. ______________________
12. ______________________
13. ______________________
14. ______________________
15. ______________________
16. ______________________

Within the Surgery section, some of the more complex subsections are Integumentary, Musculoskeletal, Respiratory, Cardiovascular, Digestive, and Female Genital. These subsections have extensive notes, and each is covered in this chapter. Before we get into the details of the subsections, let's look at the general information that is pertinent to the entire Surgery section.

Notes and Guidelines

Guidelines are found at the beginning of each of the six CPT sections. The section Guidelines define items that are necessary to appropriately interpret and report the procedures and services contained in that section. For example, the Surgery Guidelines contain the following information:

- *Physicians' Services:* when to use an E/M code with surgery codes
- *Listed Surgical Procedures:* what is included in a procedure
- *Follow-up Care for Diagnostic Procedures:* how to list services when procedures such as an endoscopy are done

- *Follow-up Care for Therapeutic Surgical Procedures:* what is included in therapeutic services
- *Materials Supplied by Physician:* when code 99070 is used
- *Reporting More Than One Procedure/Service:* how to report same-day, same-procedure services
- *Add-on Codes:* what an add-on code is and how it is used
- *Separate Procedure:* how to use codes with this designation
- *Subsection Information:* titles and code ranges for each Surgery subsection
- *Unlisted Service or Procedure:* all unlisted service codes from the section
- *Special Reports:* when to submit this report
- *Starred Procedures or Items:* what a star next to a procedure means and how to use starred codes
- *Surgical Destruction:* when destruction is part of a surgery

The Guidelines contain information that you will need to know in order to correctly code in the section, and most of the information is not repeated elsewhere in the section. So, always review the Guidelines before coding in the section. Remember that with each new edition of the CPT manual, you will need to review the Guidelines for any changes. The changes are indicated with the "New or Revised Text" symbols used throughout the CPT manual (Fig. 3–9).

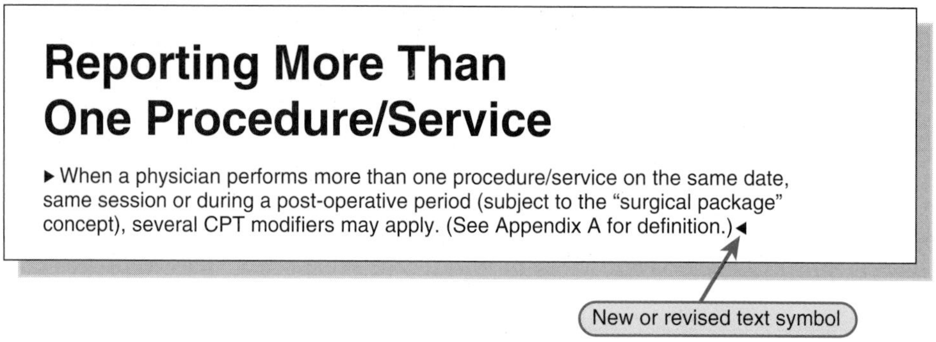

Figure 3–9
New or revised text symbol.

Reporting More Than One Procedure/Service

▸ When a physician performs more than one procedure/service on the same date, same session or during a post-operative period (subject to the "surgical package" concept), several CPT modifiers may apply. (See Appendix A for definition.)◂

New or revised text symbol

Figure 3–10
Subsection notes.

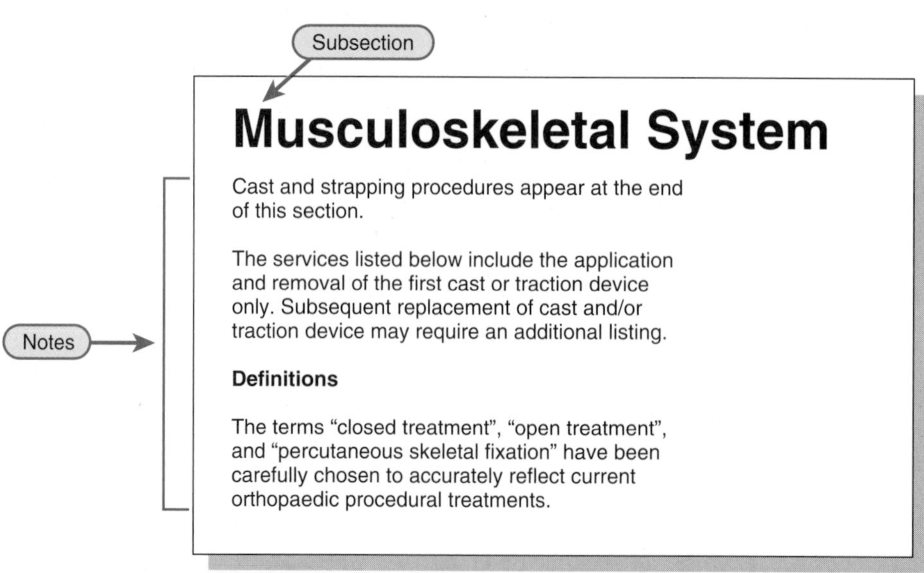

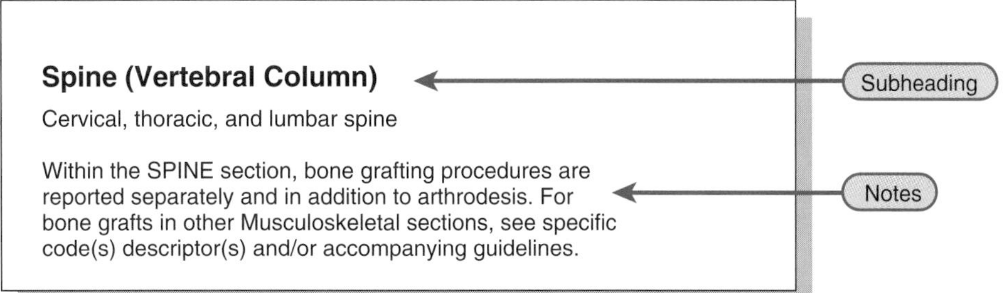

Figure 3–11
Subheading notes.

Common throughout the CPT manual are "notes." Notes may appear before subsections (Fig. 3–10), subheadings (Fig. 3–11), categories (Fig. 3–12), and subcategories (Fig. 3–13). The information in the notes indicates the special instructions unique to particular codes or unique to particular subheadings. The notes are extremely important because the information contained in them is not usually available elsewhere in the CPT manual. Always make it a practice to read any notes available before coding. If notes are present, they must be followed for accurate coding.

The additional information is enclosed in parentheses (called parenthetical phrases) and sometimes follows the code or group of codes and gives further information about codes that may be applicable. For example, 42120 for the resection of the palate or extensive resection of a lesion is followed by information about the codes you would use if reconstruction of the palate followed the resection (see Fig. 3–14). Deleted codes are also indicated within the CPT manual enclosed in parentheses. Often the code that is to be used in place of the deleted code will be listed (see Fig. 3–15). Also note in Fig. 3–15 that the arrows at the beginning and end of the information indicate that the information is new or revised for the current edition. New to the edition is that code 16040 was deleted.

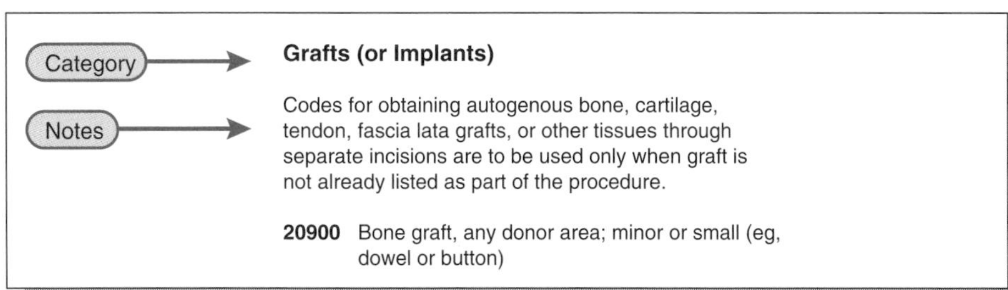

Figure 3–12
Category notes.

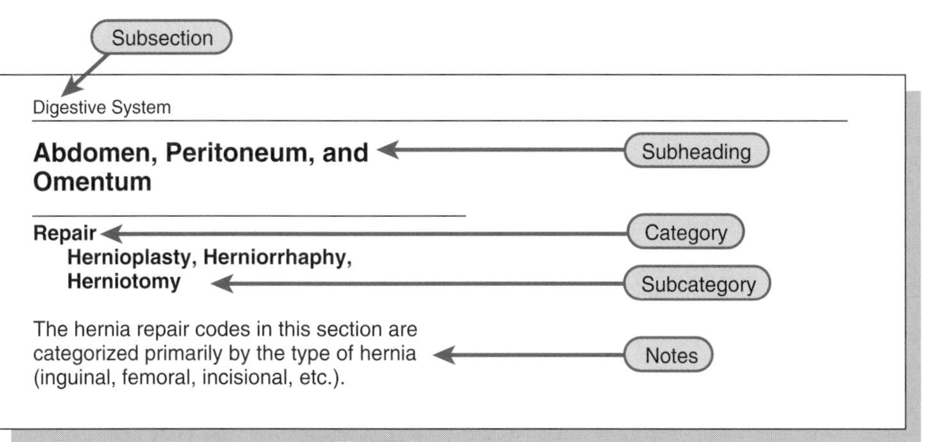

Figure 3–13
Subcategory notes.

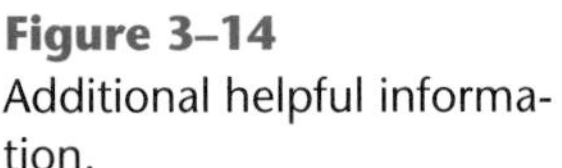

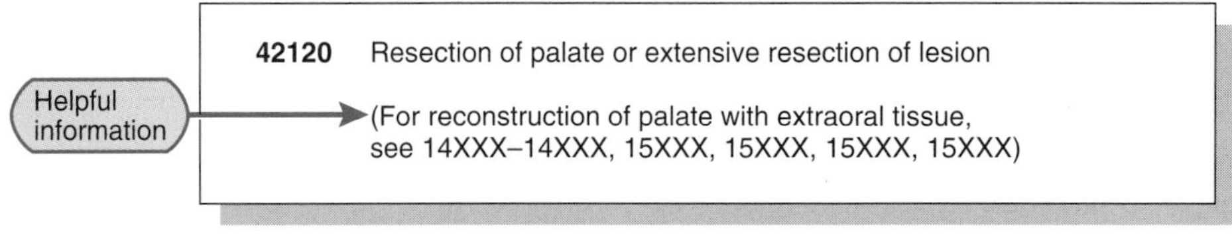

Figure 3–14
Additional helpful information.

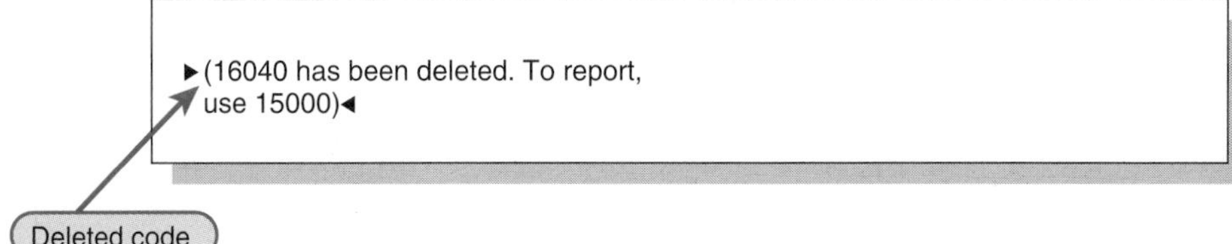

Figure 3–15
Deleted codes.

Watch for Special Circumstances

Using the Unlisted Procedure Codes

The Surgery Guidelines contain many unlisted procedure codes presented by anatomic site. These unlisted codes are not presented in alphabetical order but in the order of their location in the Surgery section—by body system. The unlisted codes are used to identify procedures or services throughout the Surgery section for which there is no CPT code.

EXERCISE F *Using the Unlisted Procedure Codes*

Using the CPT manual, locate the unlisted procedure codes in the Surgical Guidelines, and identify the unlisted procedure codes for the following anatomic areas:

1. Musculoskeleton system

   Code(s): ____________________

2. Inner ear

   Code(s): ____________________

3. Skin, mucous membrane, and subcutaneous tissue

   Code(s): ____________________

4. Leg or ankle

   Code(s): ____________________

5. Nervous system

   Code(s): ____________________

6. Eyelids

   Code(s): ____________________

Special Reports

When using an unlisted procedure code for surgery, a special report describing the procedure must accompany the claim. According to the CPT manual, "Pertinent information [in the special report] should include an adequate definition or description of the nature, extent, and need for the procedure, and the time, effort, and equipment necessary to provide the service." Unlisted codes are used only after thorough research fails to reveal an existing code.

Watch for Separate Procedures

Some procedure codes will have the words "separate procedure" after the descriptor. "Separate procedure" does not mean that the procedure was the only procedure that was performed; rather, it is an indication of how the code can be used. Locate code 19100 in the CPT manual. The breast biopsy code 19100 has the words "separate procedure" after the description. Procedures followed by the words "separate procedure" (in parentheses) are minor procedures that are coded only when they are the only service performed or when the procedure is on a different body area. Modifier -59 is used with the procedure code to indicate that the procedure was not a part of another procedure or service. When the same minor procedure is performed in conjunction with a related major procedure, the minor procedure is considered incidental and bundled into the code with the major procedure.

EXAMPLE

Separate procedure bundled into the major procedure: Breast biopsy (19100) has "separate procedure" after it. If a breast biopsy was performed in conjunction with a modified radical mastectomy (19240), only the mastectomy would be coded. Because the breast biopsy and the mastectomy were conducted on the same body area, the breast biopsy would be considered a minor procedure that was incidental and would be bundled into the major procedure of the mastectomy.

EXAMPLE

Two separate procedures: If a breast biopsy (19100—separate procedure) was performed in conjunction with an esophagoscopy (43200), both the breast biopsy and esophagoscopy would be coded. Because the breast biopsy and the esophagoscopy were conducted on different body areas, the breast biopsy is considered a separate procedure and not a minor procedure incidental to a major procedure.

EXAMPLE

Separate procedure bundled into the major procedure: Salpingo-oophorectomy (58720—removal of tubes and ovaries) has "separate procedure" after it. If a salpingo-oophorectomy was performed in conjunction with an abdominal hysterectomy (58150), only the hysterectomy would be coded. Because the salpingo-oophorectomy and the abdominal hysterectomy were conducted on the same body area, the salpingo-oophorectomy would be considered a minor procedure that was incidental and would be bundled into the major procedure of the hysterectomy.

EXAMPLE

Two separate procedures: If a salpingo-oophorectomy (58720—separate procedure) was performed in conjunction with an esophagoscopy (43200), both the salpingo-oophorectomy and the esophagoscopy would be coded. Because the salpingo-oophorectomy and the esophagoscopy were conducted on different body areas, the salpingo-oophorectomy is considered as a separate procedure and not a minor procedure incidental to a major procedure.

Watch for Starred Procedures

The CPT manual includes many procedures that are considered minor surgical procedures requiring a varying amount of preoperative or postoperative services or both.

Figure 3–16 illustrates a CPT code with a star after the code, which indicates the code is subject only to the starred procedure guidelines. If the 10080 code procedure ("Incision and drainage of pilonidal cyst; simple") was done at the time of an initial visit of a new patient, the procedure would be coded along with a code to indicate an office visit for a new patient. In comparison, procedure code 10081 is for a more complicated procedure and does not have a star after it. Code 10081 would typically include the office visit, and a separate office visit would not be coded.

What Is a Surgery Package?

Often, the time, effort, and services rendered when accomplishing a procedure are "bundled" together to form a "surgery package." Payment is made for a package of services and not for each individual service provided within the package. The CPT manual describes the surgery package as including the operation itself, local anesthesia, and the "normal, uncomplicated follow-up care." Local anesthesia is defined as local infiltration, metacarpal/digital block, or topical anesthesia. The CPT manual further states that follow-up care for complications, exacerbations, recurrence, and the presence of other diseases that require additional services is not included in the surgery package. General anesthesia for surgical procedures is not part of the surgery package and general anesthesia services are billed separately by the anesthesiologist.

Third-party payers have varying definitions of what constitutes a surgery package and varying policies about what is to be included in the surgery package. Surgery packages also define the services for which you can or cannot sub-

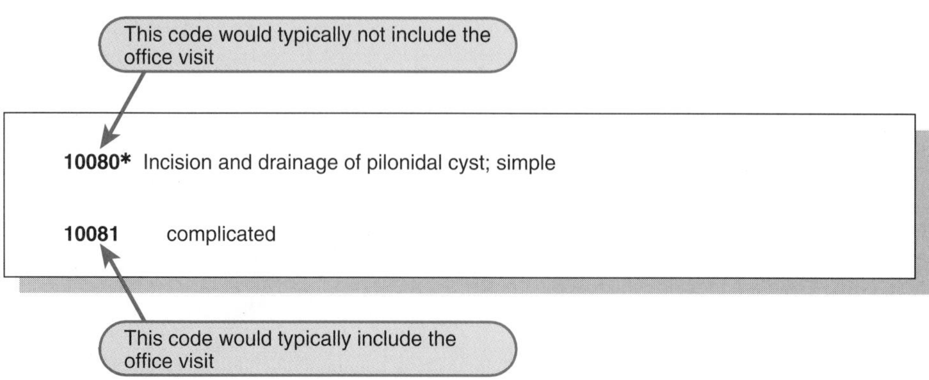

Figure 3–16 Starred and unstarred procedures.

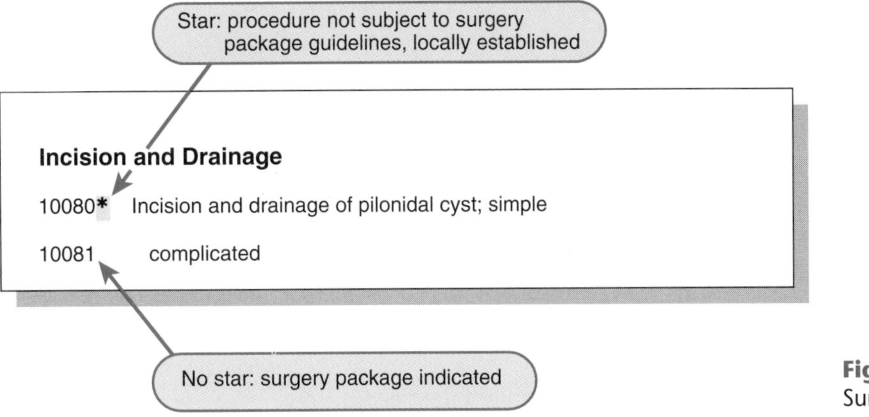

Figure 3–17
Surgery package.

mit additional charges because the surgery package rules define what is or is not included in addition to the surgical procedure. Included in the definition for the surgery package are usually the preoperative care and postoperative care—including complications—up to a predefined number of days before and after the surgery. The period of time following each surgery is established by the third-party payer and is referred to as the global surgery period. The global surgery period is usually 90 days.

Not all procedures include a surgery package. Many of those procedures that do not have a surgery package are identified by a star (*) after the code number.

When materials or supplies are used over and above those used in an office visit, you code and charge for these materials and supplies in addition to the charge for the office visit. For example, when a physician does a wound repair during an office visit and uses a surgical tray, the surgical tray is identified by code 99070. Code 99070 is listed in the Medicine section, Special Services and Reports subsection, Miscellaneous Services category.

The surgery package is a very important concept for billing purposes. Follow-up care or care for complications after a starred surgical procedure can usually be billed. Starred procedures have varying degrees of preoperative and postoperative services included with the operative procedure itself.

Figure 3–17 shows CPT codes 10080 and 10081 for incision and drainage of a cyst. Code 10080 is starred and has no surgery package. This means you would usually charge for any additional services provided after the initial incision and drainage. But CPT code 10081 is not starred and would usually have a surgery package. Code 10081 would include routine follow-up care as services (such as removal of sutures) at no charge because suture removal would be part of the surgery package.

There are four major guidelines relating to the surgical package located in the Surgery section.

1. Unstarred surgical procedures usually include the preoperative service, procedure, and postoperative service.

EXAMPLE

An established patient, Mary Smith, has her annual mammography examination, which reveals a right breast mass. Mary's physician refers her to Dr. Green, a general surgeon, who subsequently examines Mary and discusses diagnosis, prognosis, and risks involved with each treatment option available to her. Dr. Green recommends that Mary be admitted to the hospital the next day for a breast biopsy, and if indicated, recommends that a mastectomy be performed at that time. Mary is admitted and the biopsy specimen proves to be malignant. A simple, complete mastectomy (19180) is performed during the same surgery at which the biopsy was taken. Mary's recovery is uneventful, and she is discharged 4 days postoperatively. Dr. Green sees Mary in the office for the routine follow-up care.

The office visit with Dr. Green (preoperative service), biopsy/mastectomy (procedure), and follow-up care (postoperative service) are all bundled into the surgical package for code 19180.

2. If the surgical procedure is starred, preoperative and postoperative services are usually billed separately.

EXAMPLE

Jane, an established patient with a history of breast cysts (fibrocystic breasts), comes into the office for a visit for a breast lump found during self-examination. Because of her past history, Dr. Green performs a needle biopsy (19100*) in the office surgical suite, and the specimen is sent to the lab for analysis. The results are benign. The office visit for an established patient (99214) and the needle biopsy (19100*) are billed separately. Code 19100, breast biopsy, has a "(separate procedure)" statement following the code, which means that the biopsy would be billed if it is a major component of the service at the time of the visit. In a previous example, Mary Smith's physician performed a breast biopsy, but the biopsy was not a major component of the service. Instead, Mary's biopsy was bundled into the major service of the mastectomy. With Jane, the breast biopsy was the major service provided during the office visit and therefore would be billed. The billing for Jane would be:

99214	Office visit, established patient	$xx.xx
19100	Needle biopsy, right breast	$xx.xx
99070	Surgical tray	$xx.xx

3. When a surgical procedure is starred, services for preoperative and postoperative care, in addition to complications, are added on a service-by-service basis. When the procedure is not starred, preoperative and postoperative care and care for the usual complications are usually included in the surgical package. Have you noticed how the words "usual" and "usually" keep appearing in the sentences about surgical packages? That is because third-party payers vary greatly in what is or is not included in each surgical package for each code.

   When a procedure is starred, the preoperative services are considered as one of the following:

   a. The starred procedure is carried out at the time of the initial visit for a new patient, and the starred procedure is the *major service* provided at the visit. Instead of the E/M code for an office visit for a new patient, the Medicine code 99025 is used in addition to the procedure code. The description for 99025 is "Initial (new patient) visit when starred (*) surgical procedure constitutes major service at that visit." Note that the phrase "new patient" is specified for use of code 99025; therefore, the code cannot be used with an established patient service.

EXAMPLE

Sally, a new patient, sees the physician at an office visit and has a breast biopsy of the right breast. The coding would be:

19100	Needle biopsy, right breast (starred procedure)	$xx.xx
99025	New patient, office visit	No Charge
99070	Surgical tray	$xx.xx

b. The starred procedure is carried out at the time of the visit for a new or established patient, and the starred procedure is a *significant service* for the office visit. The office visit, procedure, and any follow-up care are billed separately.

EXAMPLE

Deb, a 42-year-old established patient, sees her physician for a physical. During the examination, the physician notes a mass in the right breast and does a needle biopsy. Deb returns for a follow-up visit a week later. The billing would be:

99396	Routine physical examination	$xx.xx
19100	Needle biopsy, right breast (starred procedure)	$xx.xx
99070	Surgical tray	$xx.xx
99213	Office visit, established	$xx.xx

c. The starred procedure is carried out at the time of the follow-up visit of an established patient and the starred procedure is the major service. Therefore, only the procedure is coded. No E/M code is assigned.

EXAMPLE

19100	Needle biopsy, right breast (starred procedure)	$xx.xx
99070	Surgical tray	$xx.xx

d. When the starred procedure requires hospitalization, the hospital visit(s), procedure, and follow-up are billed.

EXAMPLE

Adele (new patient) is admitted to the hospital for a biopsy of a breast lump in the left breast after an office visit with Dr. Green. Adele is taken into surgery, Dr. Green does a needle biopsy, and the pathology report is negative. No further procedure needs to be done. Adele remains overnight in the hospital because she is experiencing severe nausea and vomiting after administration of the anesthesia. By morning, her condition has improved, and after Dr. Green talks with Adele the next morning, the decision is made that she is well enough to be released. She returns to Dr. Green's office a week later for a follow-up visit. The billing would be:

99204	Office visit, new patient	$xx.xx
19100	Breast biopsy, left breast (starred procedure)	$xx.xx
99231	Hospital visit, subsequent	$xx.xx
99202	Office visit, established patient	$xx.xx

4. For starred procedures, preoperative services are added on a service-by-service basis. For example, in the case above, the initial office visit for the established patient was billed.
5. Complications are added on a service-by-service basis.

Even though the routine follow-up care service is not billed for, the service is still coded to indicate the service was provided. The CPT code 99024 ("Postoperative follow-up visit, included in global service") alerts the third-party payer that the services were rendered to the patient but were included in a surgery package and not charged.

EXAMPLE

A patient had a wound repair that was coded 12014 (unstarred code) and shortly after saw the physician for routine follow-up care. The fee statement for the office visit at which the routine follow-up care was provided would be

99024	Postoperative follow-up visit	No Charge

But if a patient had repair of a 7.9-cm wound that was coded 12004 (starred code) and saw the physician a few days later for routine follow-up care, the service is coded and charged for.

12004	Wound repair, 7.9 cm	$xx.xx
99212	Office visit	$xx.xx
99070	Surgical tray	$xx.xx

The code 99025 is used to identify the patient visit when a surgical procedure is the major service of a visit.

EXAMPLE

If a new patient visits the physician for a simple repair of a scalp wound (2.4 cm) coded 12001 (starred code), only the wound repair is charged for.

99025	Office visit, new patient	No Charge
12001	Wound repair, 2.4 cm	$xx.xx
99070	Surgical tray	$xx.xx

Inclusion or exclusion of a procedure in the CPT manual does not imply any health insurance coverage or reimbursement policy. Although the CPT manual includes guidelines on usage, third-party payers may interpret and accept the use of CPT codes and the guidelines in any manner they choose.

EXERCISE G What Is a Surgery Package?

Answer the following:

1. What are the three things bundled into a surgery package?

   a. ______

   b. ______

   c. ______

2. Is general anesthesia included in the surgery package? ______

3. Do all third-party payers follow the same reimbursement guidelines for the global packages? ______

Code the following:

4. Jack, a new patient, visits the office for the first time to have a simple repair of a 3.3-cm wound on his right foot. A surgical tray was used.

   Code(s): ______

5. John, an established patient, has a simple repair of a 12-cm wound to his right calf. A surgical tray was used.

   Code(s): ______

6. Josephine, an established patient, has a breast needle biopsy of the right breast done in Dr. Green's office. A surgical tray was used.

   Code(s): ______

If the global surgery package includes services provided the day before surgery through 90 days after surgery, based on the following case, answer the following questions:

On July 4, Mr. Jones sees Dr. Brown for abdominal pain. Dr. Brown has never seen Mr. Jones before. The pain is very severe, and Dr. Brown believes that admission to the hospital for further study is warranted. After admission, the pain becomes increasingly more severe, and Dr. Brown asks Dr. Green, a surgeon, to evaluate Mr. Jones and give an opinion as to what the problem might be. Dr. Green determines that exploratory surgery is necessary and takes Mr. Jones to the operating room later that night. Mr. Jones is found to have a ruptured appendix and has his appendix removed. He is released from the hospital 3 days later and sees Dr. Green for a follow-up visit 2 weeks later.

7. Can Dr. Brown charge a fee (bill) for the services of July 4? ______

8. If Dr. Brown could charge a fee for the services, what section of the CPT manual would be used to locate the code and what category of code would be used?

____

9. Can Dr. Green bill for seeing Mr. Jones before surgery? _______________

10. If yes, what category of code would be used? _______________

11. What modifier applies and why?

____

12. What code would be used to bill Mr. Jones' visit to Dr. Green 2 weeks after surgery?

Code(s): _______________

Using Modifiers in the Surgery Section

Modifiers are used throughout the Surgery section to apprise the third-party payer of circumstances that may affect the way payment is made. Remember that a modifier may be a two-digit code added to the five-digit code or may be listed as its own five-digit modifier number. CPT manual Appendix A lists all modifiers and gives their circumstance of use. You will first learn about and work with modifiers for procedures that are multiple (-51), reduced (-52), unusual procedure services (-22), and bilateral (-50).

Modifier -51

During any given operative session, more than one procedure may be performed. This is referred to as "multiple procedures." But you have to be careful when coding multiple procedures because CPT codes include many different procedures bundled together as one code. For example, code 58200 is a total abdominal hysterectomy but also includes a partial vaginectomy (removal of the vagina) with para-aortic and pelvic lymph node sampling, with or without removal of tube(s), and with or without removal of ovary(ies). It would be incorrect to code separately for each service because they are included (bundled) in the description for code 58200. Listing the subsequent procedures separately (unbundling) may be considered fraud by a third-party payer. **Unbundling** is assigning multiple codes when one code will fully describe the service or procedure. Assigning of multiple codes results in increased reimbursement.

However, if one code does not describe all of the procedures performed, and the secondary procedure is not considered a minor procedure that is incidental to the major procedure, each procedure may be billed by using the "multiple procedure" modifier (-51). For example, if a patient had a laminectomy with lumbar disk removal (for a herniated disk)—code 63030—and also had an arthrodesis (stabilization of the area where the disk was removed)—code 22612—these are multiple procedures. Both services would be coded and modifier -51 would be used after the lesser of the two codes (services).

Modifier -51 is not used with add-on codes that specify "each additional. . . ." For example, 19290 is for placement of one wire *into a breast lesion. If two wires were placed, the first wire would be coded 19290 from the subheading Breast and category Introduction, and the second wire would be coded with an additional code from the Introduction category.*

Modifiers -53, -52, and -22

Whenever a procedure is performed, circumstances may occur that prolong the surgery or cut it short. In cases in which the surgery is terminated before its expected completion, modifier -53 (discontinued procedure) is placed after the surgical code to indicate that the service was discontinued. When less than expected services were rendered, modifier -52 is placed after the surgical code to indicate a reduced service. In extremely difficult or prolonged cases, modifier -22 is used to indicate an unusual procedural service. Use of modifier -22 necessitates a special report to the third-party payer to explain the circumstances that occurred. Modifier -22 indicates that a service was provided that was greater than usual, and the special report explains exactly in which ways the services were greater.

Modifier -50

If the same procedure is performed on a mirror image part of the body, modifier -50 indicating a bilateral procedure would be billed. For example, an arthroplasty (total knee replacement, 27447 and 27447-50) for both left and right knees at the same operative session would be coded using the -50 modifier.

Another example in which the same services may be performed on different sides would be a bilateral breast procedure (ie, bilateral, simple complete mastectomy, 19180 and 19180-50).

Be sure to know if your third-party payer wants the surgical code used once with the modifier (code plus modifier -50) or used twice (code alone and code plus modifier -50), or whether the procedure should be listed twice. For hospital outpatient coding, the code is usually listed twice. New, as of 1999, some modifiers are allowed for hospital outpatient coding. Appendix A of the CPT manual contains a section that lists all modifiers approved for hospital outpatient coding.

Some CPT codes are for bilateral procedures and do not require a bilateral modifier. For example, 27395 is for a bilateral lengthening of the hamstring tendon, and it would be incorrect to place a bilateral modifier on the code.

EXERCISE H Modifiers -50, -51, -52, -53, and -22

Fill in the missing modifiers and codes for the following:

1. What is the code for a single arthroplasty, knee (total knee replacement)?

   Code(s): ____________________

2. What modifier indicates that a bilateral procedure was performed?

   Code(s): ____________________

3. What are the codes for a bilateral arthroplasty of the knees?

   Code(s): ____________________

4. The code for a radical mastectomy is 19200. List two ways the bilateral modifier could be used to indicate a bilateral procedure was done, depending on the third-party payer preferences.

   Code(s): ________________

5. What modifier indicates that the surgery was not completed as expected?

   Code(s): ________________

6. What modifier indicates that a procedure was prolonged? ____________

7. If a patient had multiple procedures, what modifier would be added to the lesser of the two codes (used on the additional procedure codes)?

   ____

Modifiers -54, -56, -55, -57, and -25

You will now learn about and work with modifiers to identify:

- surgical care only, -54
- preoperative management only, -56
- postoperative management only, -55
- decision for surgery, -57
- separate E/M service, -25

There may be times when the surgeon performs the surgery only (modifier -54) and asks another physician to perform the preoperative evaluation (modifier -56) and/or the postoperative care (modifier -55). When billing for his or her own individual services, each physician would use the same procedure code for the surgery, letting the modifier indicate to the third-party payer the part of the surgical package that each personally performed.

EXAMPLE

19180	Mastectomy, simple, complete
19180-54	Mastectomy, simple, complete, surgery only
19180-56	Mastectomy, simple, complete, preoperative evaluation only
19180-55	Mastectomy, simple, complete, postoperative care only

At the present time, not all modifiers are recognized by all third-party payers. Some third-party payers have agreed to pay the physician separately from the surgical package for the initial evaluation of a condition during which the decision to perform surgery was made. Under the conditions of a global package, this visit would have become part of the preoperative care if performed the day of or day before major surgery. When this initial visit occurs within the time requirements of the preoperative portion of the global surgical package, modifier -57 is used to let the payers know that payment for this initial evaluation should be paid in addition to the payment for surgery. E/M services provided the day before, or on the day of a major surgery or on the day of a minor procedure, are included in the global package unless it is the initial visit to the physician. To receive payment for these initial visits, modifier -57 is added to the E/M services with major procedures and -25 to the E/M services with minor procedures.

EXAMPLE

99215-57 Office visit for established patient at which a decision for surgery was made

EXERCISE 1 ***Modifiers -54, -56, -55, -57, and -25***

Code the following:

1. The surgical care only for a total esophagectomy without reconstruction

   Code(s): ____________________

2. The postoperative care only for a radical mastectomy including pectoral muscles, axillary, and internal mammary lymph nodes

   Code(s): ____________________

3. The procedure in Question 2, above, when the preoperative service only is provided

   Code(s): ____________________

Modifiers -58, -78, and -79

You will now learn about and work with modifiers to identify procedures that were:

- staged or related, -58
- during a postoperative period, -78
- unrelated, -79

Sometimes additional surgery must be performed after the patient has already had one operation. When a patient has another procedure within the postoperative recovery period of a first operation, a modifier explaining the reason for the subsequent surgery must be used on the subsequent surgery code. If modifiers are not used, there is no payment made for the subsequent services because the third-party payer would identify the subsequent surgery as a part of a surgery package from the previous surgery. There are three modifiers that will alert the third-party payer to the special circumstances of the subsequent service: -58, -78, and -79.

Modifier -58 explains that the subsequent surgery was planned or staged at the time of the first surgery. For example, multiple skin grafts are often done in stages to allow adequate healing time between procedures. The -58 can also be used if a therapeutic procedure is done because of the findings of a diagnostic procedure. For example, a patient may have a surgical breast biopsy, and if the pathology report indicates the specimen was malignant, the patient may elect to have an immediate radical mastectomy. The mastectomy may be performed during the postoperative period of the biopsy. Modifier -58 indicates to the third-party payer that the second surgery was therapeutic treatment after the diagnostic procedure and full payment would be made for the mastectomy procedure. A new postoperative period would start for the mastectomy, and any postoperative care provided to the patient would come under the surgical package for the mastectomy.

Modifier -78 is used to explain the circumstance when a patient is taken back to the operative room for surgical treatment of a complication of the first procedure. Modifier -78 is placed after the subsequent procedure code to indicate to the third-party payer that the second surgery was necessary because of complications from the first operation. For many third-party payers, only the surgery portion (intraoperative) of the surgical package is paid when the -78 modifier is used. The patient remains within the postoperative period of the first operation for any further preoperative or postoperative care.

Modifier -79 is used to explain a patient requiring surgery for a condition totally unrelated to the first operation. For example, the patient may have an appendectomy and 2 weeks later has a gallbladder episode that necessitates removal of the gallbladder. The -79 would be placed on the cholecystectomy (gallbladder removal) code, indicating that the subsequent procedure was unrelated to the first operation.

EXERCISE J Modifiers -58, -78, and -79

Fill in the blanks:

1. If Mr. Smith has an appendectomy done June 8 and then has a cholecystectomy done August 16, what modifier would be placed on the cholecystectomy code?

   Code(s): ____________________

2. Mrs. Knight has a diagnostic surgical biopsy of deep cervical lymph nodes on May 8, and the pathology report comes back showing malignancy. Mrs. Knight elects to have a lymphadenectomy on May 11. What modifier would be used with the lymphadenectomy code?

   Code(s): ____________________

3. Mr. Williams has an appendectomy done on March 4 and is taken back to surgery on March 6 for evacuation of a hematoma of the wound site. What modifier would be used?

   Code(s): ____________________

Modifier -80

You will now learn about and work with the modifier to identify an assistant surgeon (-80).

A commonly used modifier for surgical procedures is -80, which indicates that there was a physician assisting the primary surgeon with the surgical procedure. The assisting physician uses the same surgical code as the attending surgeon, but places a modifier -80 after the code to indicate the capacity of assistant.

For example, Dr. Blue assisted Dr. Smith in a radical mastectomy. The code and modifier for Dr. Blue would be:

19220-80 Radical mastectomy

Review of Modifiers

Let's review the key modifiers as they apply to the Surgery section:

Multiple Procedures	-51
Reduced Services	-52
Unusual Procedural Services (extremely difficult)	-22
Bilateral Procedure	-50
Surgical Care Only	-54
Staged or Related Procedures	-58
Return to Operating Room for a Related Procedure During the Postoperative Period	-78
Unrelated Procedure	-79
Preoperative Management Only	-56
Postoperative Management Only	-55
Significant, Separate Identifiable E/M Service by the Same Physician on the Same Day of the Procedure or Other Service	-25
Decision for Surgery	-57
Assistant Surgeon	-80
Discontinued Procedure	-53

EXERCISE K *Review of Modifiers*

Without looking back at the text, see how many modifiers you can identify:

1. Surgery only ______________________
2. Preoperative care only ______________________
3. Postoperative care only ______________________
4. Initial evaluation for minor procedure ______________________
5. Initial evaluation for major procedure ______________________
6. Planned subsequent surgery ______________________
7. Surgery for complication of a prior surgery ______________________

Using code 58200 (total abdominal hysterectomy), attach a modifier to indicate the following:

8. Surgery only ______________________

9. Performed to correct complication of prior surgery ______________________

10. Postoperative care only ______________________

Multiple Procedures

Now that you know about modifier -51, let's look more closely at the use of this important modifier. There are three significant times when multiple procedures are coded:

1. Same Operation, Different Site
2. Multiple Operation(s), Same Operative Session
3. Procedure Performed Multiple Times

Same Operation, Different Site

Multiple procedures are coded using modifier -51 when the same procedure is performed on different sites. For example, a patient has an excision of a 1.5-cm benign lesion from the forearm and at the same time has an excision of a 3-cm benign lesion from the neck. In this case the coding would be 11423 for the 3-cm lesion and 11402-51 for the 1.5-cm lesion. The third-party payer would usually pay for the second procedure at 50% of the usual full cost of the procedure. Therefore, the code after which you place the -51 modifier is very important. Always list the most resource-intensive procedure first, without a modifier.

Multiple Operation(s), Same Operative Session

Multiple procedures (-51) are also coded when more than one procedure is performed during the same operative session.

The primary procedure during the surgical session would be paid at the full fee, the second procedure during the same session would usually be paid at 50% of the fee, and the third procedure would usually be paid at 25% of the fee. Therefore, when you are coding procedures for payment, it is important that you put the most resource-intensive procedure first, without a modifier, then list the subsequent procedures in order of complexity, remembering to use the -51 modifier on all subsequent procedures. This process of assigning the -51 modifier will help ensure that optimal reimbursement occurs. For example, an abdominal hysterectomy (58150) may be done with a posterior (rectocele) repair (57250-51). The hysterectomy is the most resource-intensive procedure, so it is listed first, without the modifier, to be paid at the full fee. The posterior repair is less resource-intensive, so it is listed second, with the modifier, to be paid at 50% of the fee.

Procedure Performed Multiple Times

Multiple procedures are also coded when the same procedure code is used to identify a service done more than once during the operative session. There are two ways for billing procedures performed multiple times, depending on the requirements of the third-party payer. The code number may be used only once, but the number of times it is performed (number of units) is listed. For example, if a patient needs a repair of two flexor tendons of the leg, you would use 27658 × 2 units. Units are identified because the code description states "each" tendon, and two tendons were repaired. The other way to code this would be to list 27658 once without a modifier and again with modifier -51 (ie, 27658-51). Remember, check with the payers on the preferred method of billing.

EXERCISE L *Multiple Procedures*

Using the CPT manual, code the following:

1. Destruction of malignant lesion of neck (most resource intensive), 4 cm in diameter, with destruction of malignant lesion of arm, 4 cm in diameter

   Code(s): ____________________

2. Abdominal hysterectomy with posterior (rectocele) repair

   Code(s): ____________________

3. Treatment of two tarsal bone fractures, without manipulation

   Code(s): ____________________

The surgery and global packages, modifiers, terminology, and multiple procedures are general information that apply to the entire Surgery section. Now, it is time to take a closer look at the subsections and the specific important points in each. Take the time necessary to look up any terminology of which you are not sure. The extra time you spend on the terminology review will make the subsection much easier for you to conquer.

General Surgical Medical Terminology

Throughout the Surgery section, some words, prefixes, and suffixes occur over and over, changing only according to the anatomic site. The terms that are used throughout the section will be presented first and terms specific to a particular subsection will be presented at the beginning of the subsection for which the terms apply. The following exercise will help you to learn these common terms.

EXERCISE M *General Surgical Medical Terminology*

Match the following terms to the correct definitions:

1. abscess _______
2. benign _______
3. cyst _______
4. lesion _______

a. abnormal or altered tissue (ie, wound, cyst, abscess, or boil)

b. term used to describe a cancerous tumor that grows worse over time

c. swelling or enlargement; a spontaneous growth of tissue that forms an abnormal mass

5. malignant _______
6. tumor _______

d. localized collection of pus that will result in the disintegration of tissue over time
e. closed sac containing matter or fluid
f. not progressive or recurrent; usually used to describe a growth that does not spread to another location in the body

Match the following ways to obtain a biopsy specimen to the correct definitions:

7. aspiration _______
8. punch _______
9. incisional _______
10. excisional _______

a. surgically cutting into
b. removal of an entire lesion for biopsy
c. use of a needle and a syringe to withdraw fluid
d. use of small hollow instrument to puncture a lesion

Match the following common procedures and suffixes to the correct definitions:

11. biopsy _______
12. curettage _______
13. drainage _______
14. endoscopy _______
15. excision _______
16. incision _______
17. injection _______
18. ligation _______
19. repair _______
20. suture _______
21. -centesis _______
22. -ectomy _______
23. -otomy _______
24. -plasty _______
25. -rrhaphy _______

a. to remedy, replace, or heal
b. suffix meaning technique involving molding or surgically forming
c. free flow or withdrawal of fluids from a wound or cavity
d. cutting or taking away
e. to unite parts by stitching them together
f. inspection of body organs or cavities by the use of a lighted scope that may be placed through an existing opening or through a small incision
g. scraping of a cavity using a spoon-shaped instrument
h. forcing of a fluid into a vessel or cavity
i. suffix meaning suturing
j. suffix meaning puncture of a cavity
k. suffix meaning removal of part or all of an organ of the body
l. removal of a small piece of living tissue for diagnostic purposes
m. surgically cutting into
n. binding or tying off, as in constricting blood flow of a vessel or binding fallopian tubes for sterilization
o. suffix meaning incision into

INTEGUMENTARY SYSTEM

The Integumentary System subsection of the Surgery section includes codes used by many different physician specialties. There is no restriction on who uses the codes from this or any subsection. You may find a family practitioner using the incision and drainage, debridement, or repair codes; a dermatologist using excision and destruction codes; a plastic surgeon using skin graft codes; or a surgeon using breast procedure codes.

You will learn about the Integumentary System subsection by first reviewing the subsection format, then completing a review of the subsection terminology, and finally learning about coding the services and procedures within the subsection.

Format

The subsection is formatted by anatomic site and category of procedure. For example, an anatomic site is "neck" and a category of procedure is "repair."

The subsection Integumentary contains the subheadings Skin, Subcutaneous, and Accessory Structures; Nails; Repair; Destruction; and Breast. Each subheading is further divided by category. For example, the subheading Skin, Subcutaneous, and Accessory Structures is divided into the following categories:

- Incision and Drainage
- Excision—Debridement
- Paring or Curettement
- Biopsy
- Removal of Skin Tags
- Shaving
- Excision—Benign Lesions
- Excision—Malignant Lesions

Terminology

EXERCISE N ***Integumentary System Terminology***

Match the following terms to the correct definitions:

1. dermis _______
2. epidermis _______
3. subcutaneous _______
4. incision and drainage _______
5. abscess _______
6. cyst _______
7. debridement _______
8. paring _______
9. biopsy _______
10. shaving _______

a. full-thickness removal of a lesion that may include simple closure
b. prefix meaning breast
c. localized collection of pus that will result in the disintegration of tissue over time
d. second layer of skin holding blood vessels, nerve endings, sweat glands, and hair follicles
e. removal of a small piece of living tissue for diagnostic purposes
f. transplantation of tissue to repair a defect
g. not progressive or recurrent
h. killing of tissue, possibly by electrocautery, laser, chemical, or other means
i. destruction of lesions using extreme cold

11. excision _______
12. benign _______
13. malignant _______
14. repair _______
15. skin graft _______
16. tissue transfer _______
17. destruction _______
18. mast- _______
19. cryosurgery _______

j. outer layer of skin
k. horizontal or transverse removal of dermal or epidermal lesions, without full-thickness excision
l. pertains to suturing a wound
m. cleansing of or removing dead tissue from a wound
n. to cut and withdraw fluid
o. removal of thin layers of skin by peeling or scraping
p. tissue below dermis, primarily fat cells that insulate the body
q. piece of skin for grafting that is still partially attached to the original blood supply and is used to cover an adjacent wound area
r. used to describe a cancerous tumor that grows worse over time
s. closed sac containing matter or fluid

Identify the split-thickness and full-thickness skin grafts on Diagram 3–1.

Diagram 3–1
Cross section of skin.

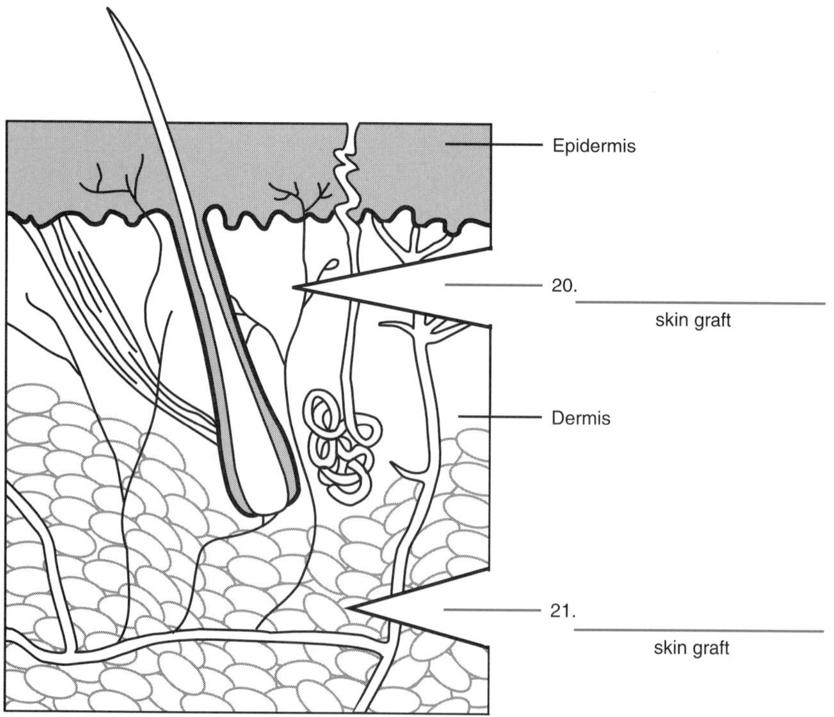

Congratulations! This terminology will be very useful as you begin your review of coding in the Integumentary System subsection.

Integumentary System Coding Highlights

Lesion Excision and Destruction

There are many types of lesions of the skin (Fig. 3–18) and many types of treatments of lesions. Types of treatment of lesions include paring, shaving, excision, and destruction. To properly code these procedures, you must know the *site, number,* and *size* of the lesion(s), as well as if the lesion is malignant or benign. *The size of the lesion must be taken from the physician's notes, not the pathology report.* The

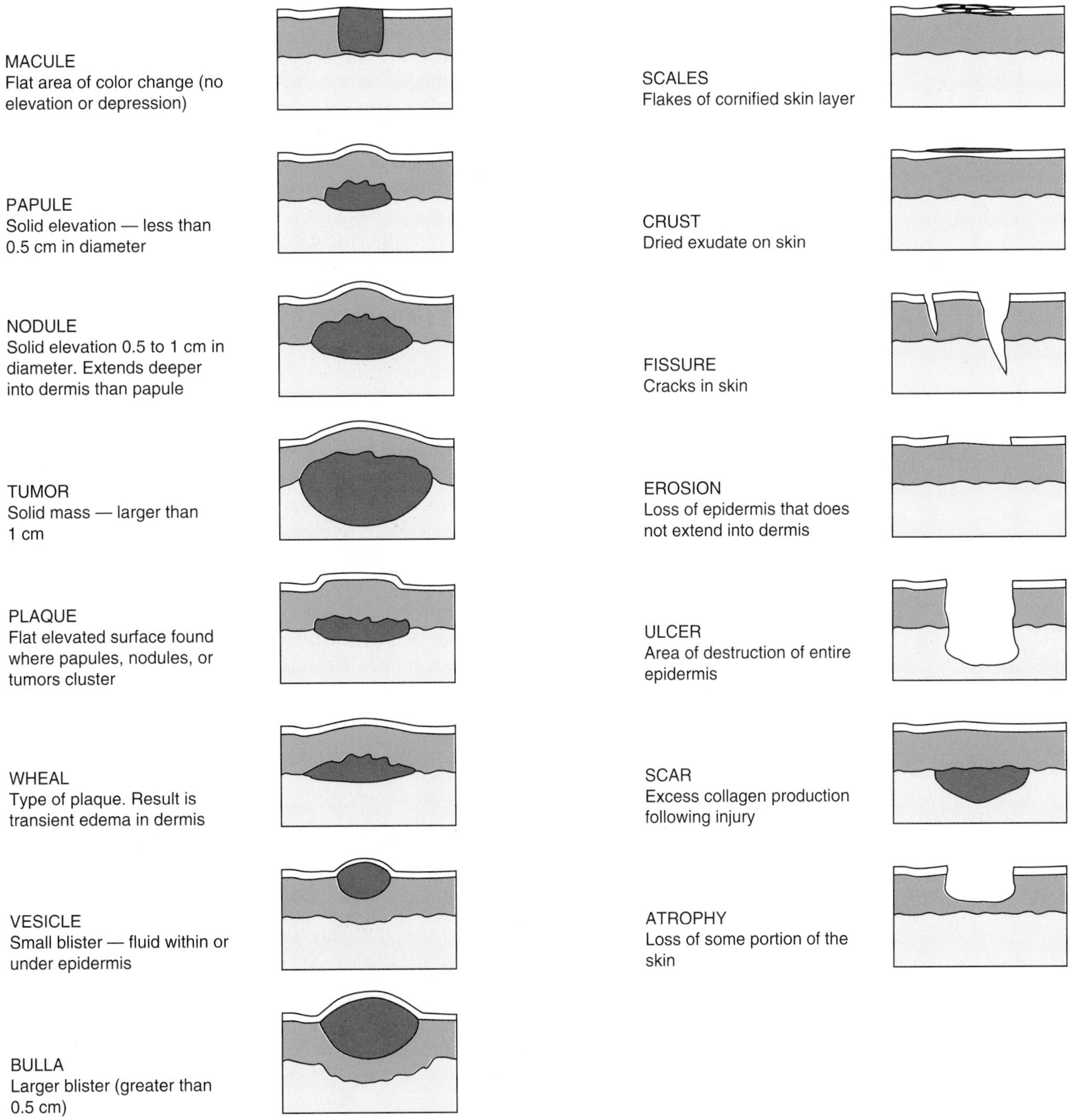

MACULE
Flat area of color change (no elevation or depression)

PAPULE
Solid elevation — less than 0.5 cm in diameter

NODULE
Solid elevation 0.5 to 1 cm in diameter. Extends deeper into dermis than papule

TUMOR
Solid mass — larger than 1 cm

PLAQUE
Flat elevated surface found where papules, nodules, or tumors cluster

WHEAL
Type of plaque. Result is transient edema in dermis

VESICLE
Small blister — fluid within or under epidermis

BULLA
Larger blister (greater than 0.5 cm)

SCALES
Flakes of cornified skin layer

CRUST
Dried exudate on skin

FISSURE
Cracks in skin

EROSION
Loss of epidermis that does not extend into dermis

ULCER
Area of destruction of entire epidermis

SCAR
Excess collagen production following injury

ATROPHY
Loss of some portion of the skin

Figure 3–18
Lesions of the skin.

pathology report will include margins (extra skin) taken from around the lesion, thus giving an inaccurate size for coding. Also, the preserving fluids in which the specimen is placed for processing may shrink the tissue sample so the pathology report is only used to identify the size of the lesion if no other record of the size can be documented. The malignant lesion codes are the same whether the lesion is malignant melanoma or basal cell carcinoma. The codes reflect only the size of the lesion. All lesions that are excised will have a pathology report for diagnosing the removed tissue as malignant or benign; and since the codes are divided based on if the excised lesion is malignant or benign, the billing for the excision is not submitted to the third-party payer until the pathology report has been completed.

Destruction of lesions destroys all tissue, leaving none available for biopsy; therefore, there will be no pathology report for lesion destruction by laser, chemical, electrocautery, or other destruction methods. In this case you will need to take the size of the destroyed lesion from the medical record.

Codes in the Integumentary System subsection differ greatly in their descriptions. Some codes indicate only one lesion per code, others are for the second and third lesions only, and still others indicate a certain number of lesions (eg, up to 15 lesions). When coding multiple lesions, you must read the description carefully to prevent incorrect billing.

If multiple lesions are treated, code the most complex lesion procedure first and the others with modifier -51 to indicate multiple procedures were performed. Remember that the third-party payer will usually reduce the payment for the services identified with modifier -51; so you want to be certain you place the highest dollar cost service first without the modifier. If the code description includes multiple lesions (a stated number of lesions), the -51 is not necessary.

Lesion Closure

Included in the codes for lesion excision is the direct, primary, or simple closure of the operative site. The notes following the category for the excision of the benign lesion defines a simple excision as full-thickness (through the dermis) and a simple closure as one that is non-layered (Fig. 3–19). Closures can also be intermediate (layered; see Fig. 3–20) or complex (greater than layered). The codes in the Excision—Benign Lesions category are based on the size and location of the lesion excised. The local anesthesia is also included in the excision codes. Any closure other than a simple closure can be billed separately.

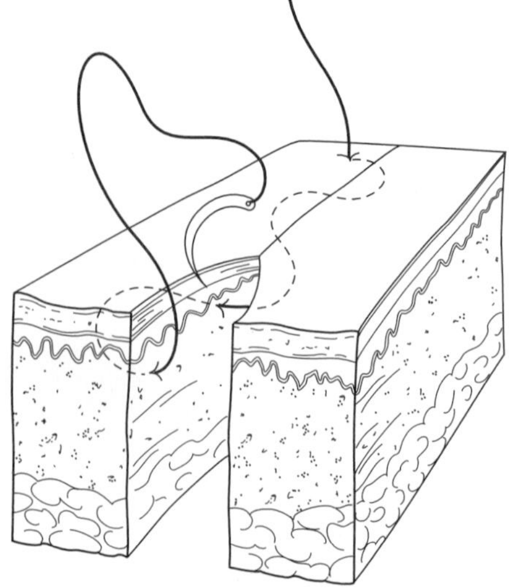

Figure 3–19
Simple subcuticular closure.

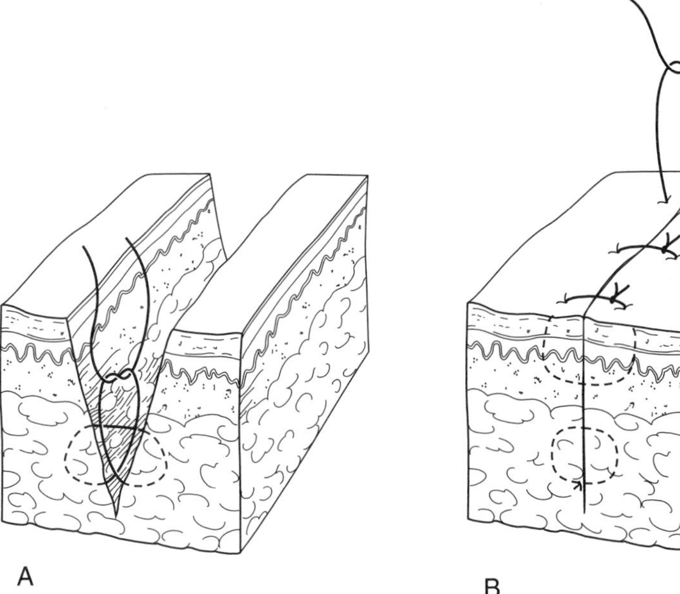

Figure 3–20
Intermediate two-layer closure.

There are several codes at the end of the category for excision of the skin and subcutaneous tissue or hidradenitis, which is the chronic abscessing and subsequent infection of the sweat gland. The abscess is excised and left open to heal. The hidradenitis codes are based on the abscess location (axillary, inguinal, perianal, perineal, or umbilical) and the complexity of the repair (simple, intermediate, or complex).

Three final notes on treatment of lesion(s):

1. Shaving of lesions requires no closure because no incision has been made.
2. Excision includes simple closure and may require more complex closure. If more complex closure is required, follow the notes in the CPT manual to appropriately code for these services.
3. Destruction may be by any method, including freezing, burning, chemical, and so on.

EXERCISE O *Lesion Destruction*

Apply the information for lesion procedures by coding the following:

1. Paring of three warts

   Code(s): ____________________

2. Removal of 15 skin tags

   Code(s): ____________________

3. Shaving of 1-cm lesion of face

   Code(s): ____________________

4. Excision of 4-cm benign lesion of face (most resource-intensive) and excision of 3-cm benign lesion of neck

   Code(s): ___________________

5. Excision of a 2.5-cm malignant lip lesion and two malignant lesions of the chest, each 1.5 cm in diameter

   Code(s): ___________________

6. Destruction of three benign facial lesions

   Code(s): ___________________

7. Destruction of 4.5-cm malignant lesion of hand

   Code(s): ___________________

Repair (Closure)

When coding wound repair the following three factors must be considered:

1. Length of the wound in centimeters
2. Complexity of repair
3. Site of wound repair

Remember *length, complexity,* and *site.* Figure 3–21 illustrates an example from the CPT manual of these three factors in the wound repair codes.

There are many different types of wounds (Fig. 3–22). Wound repair is classified by the type of repair necessary to repair the wound. There are three types of repair.

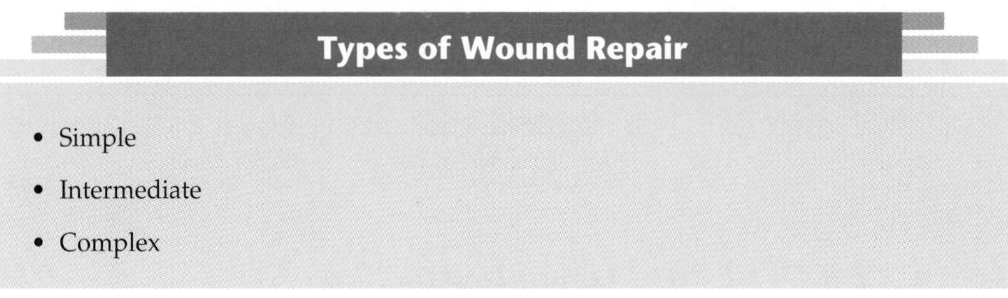

Types of Wound Repair

- Simple
- Intermediate
- Complex

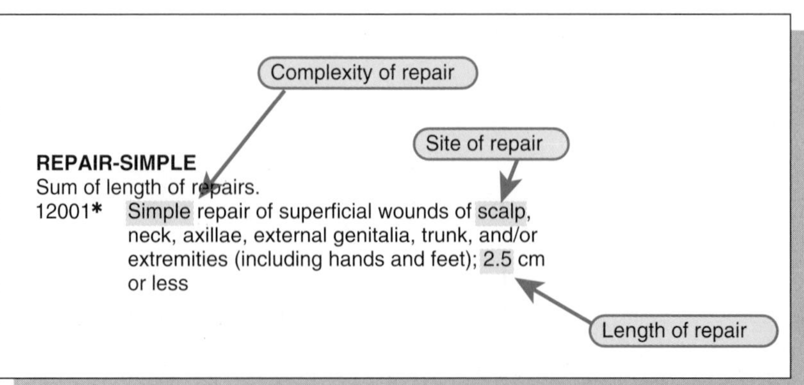

Figure 3–21
Wound repair. Note that metric measure is used throughout the CPT.

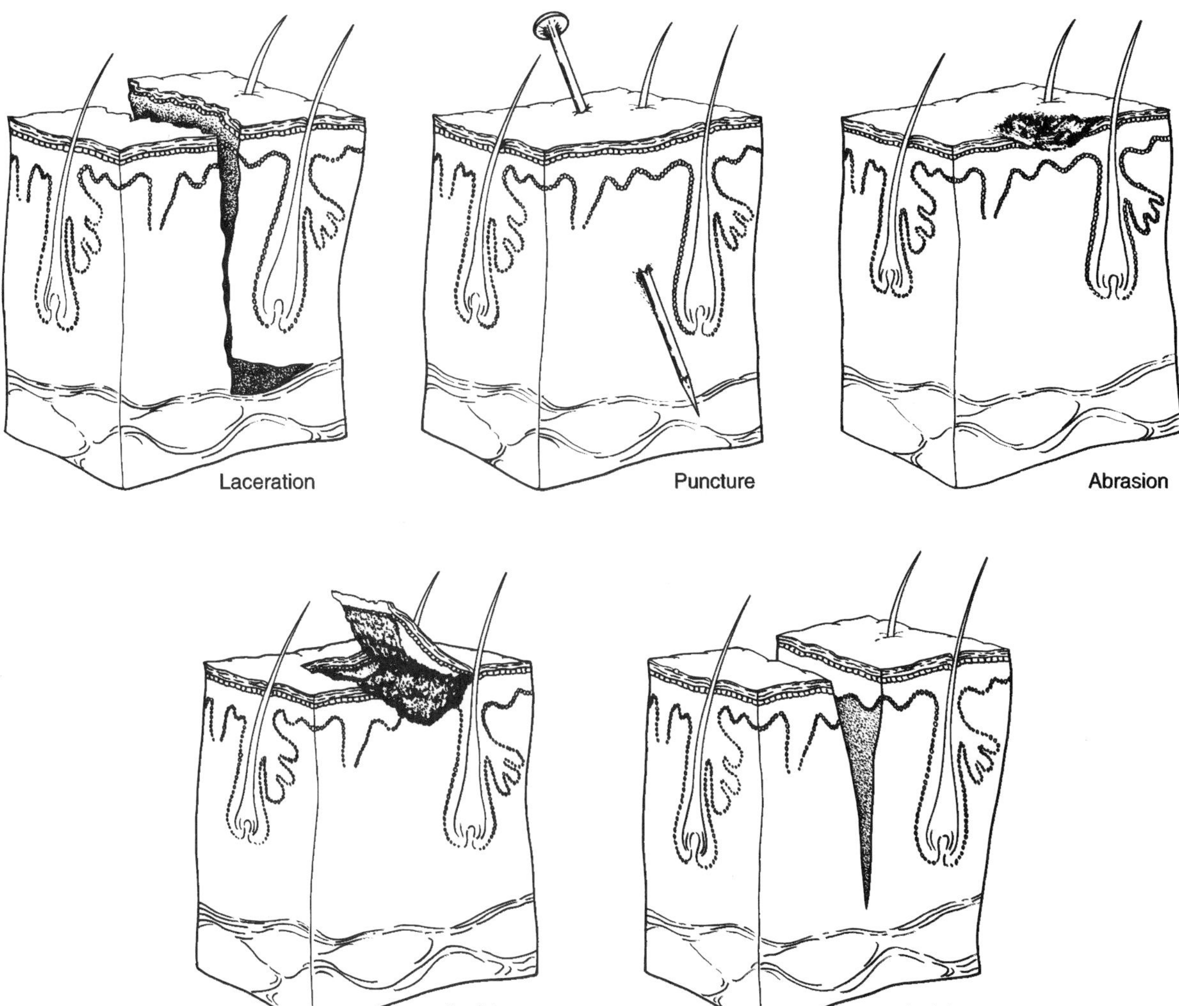

Figure 3–22
Types of wounds.

1. *Simple:* superficial wound repair, involving epidermis, dermis, and subcutaneous tissue, requiring only simple one-layer suturing. If the simple wound repair is accomplished with tape or adhesive strips, the charge for the closure is included in the E/M service code and would not be coded separately with a "Repair" code. The repair codes are for suture closure.
2. *Intermediate:* requires closure of one or more subcutaneous tissue and superficial fascia, in addition to the skin closure. You can use the codes for intermediate closure when the wound has to be extensively cleaned, even if the closure was a single-layer closure.
3. *Complex:* involves complicated wound closure including revision, debridement, extensive undermining, stents or retention sutures, and more than layered closure.

The lengths of wounds are totaled together by complexity and group (ie, all the simple wounds of the same group are added together; all the intermediate wounds of the same group added together; and all the complex wounds of the same group added together). The codes group together sites that require similar techniques to repair. For example, 12001 groups superficial scalp, neck, axillae, external genitalia, trunk, and extremities. Wound repair is totaled by type (simple, intermediate, and complex) and anatomic site. When there is more than one repair type, the *most* complex type is listed as the first or primary procedure. The secondary procedure is then reported using modifier -51 (multiple procedure). Remember that the placement of the -51 will determine the percentage of reimbursement received.

The CPT manual notes under the subheading "Repair" include extensive definitions of each of these levels of repair. These notes must be read carefully before you code repairs.

There are three things that are considered part of wound repair:

Wound Repair

- Ligation
- Exploration
- Debridement

1. Simple *ligation* (tying) *of vessels* is considered part of the wound repair and not listed separately.
2. Simple *exploration* of surrounding tissue, nerves, vessels, and tendons is considered part of the wound repair process and is not listed separately.
3. Normal *debridement* (cleaning and removing skin or tissue from the wound until normal, healthy tissue is exposed) is not listed separately.

If the wound is grossly contaminated and requires extensive debridement, a separate debridement procedure may be coded. (CPT codes in the category Excision—Debridement are used for extensive debridement.) Figure 3–23 illustrates a nonsurgical type of debridement.

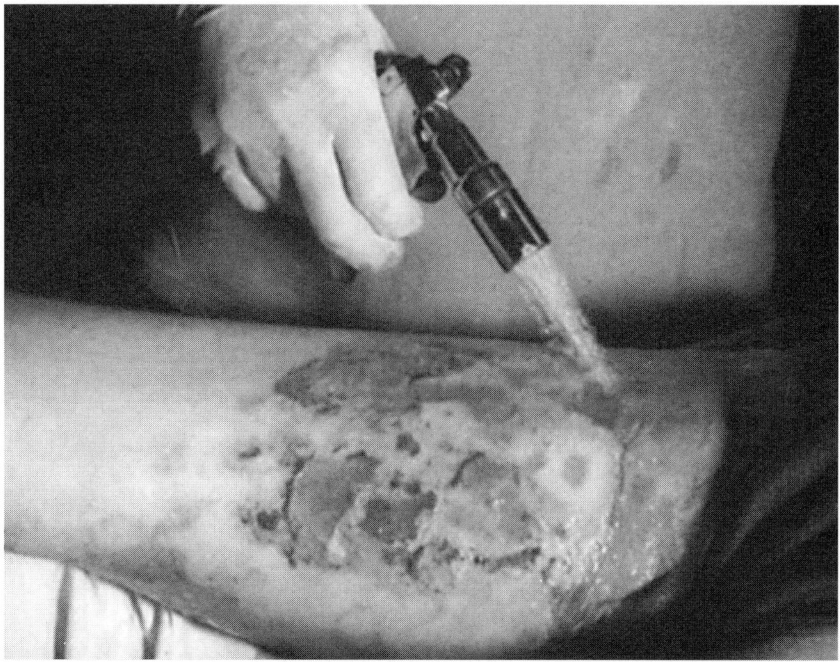

Figure 3–23
Burn debridement. (From Converse JM [ed]: Reconstructive Plastic Surgery: Principles and Procedures in Correction, Reconstruction and Transplantation. Philadelphia, WB Saunders, 1964, vol 1, p 241.)

You have learned about some commonly used categories in the Integumentary System subsection, especially the wound repair categories. There is always something new to learn about coding. It is never boring, because every case is a new coding challenge. Now you are going to put your knowledge of wound repair to work in the following exercise.

EXERCISE P Repair (Closure)

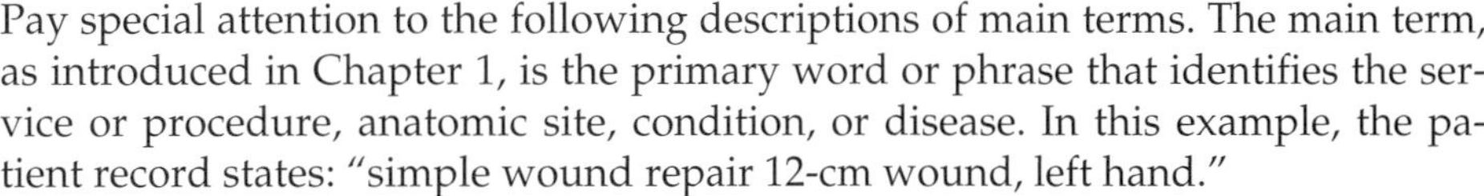

Pay special attention to the following descriptions of main terms. The main term, as introduced in Chapter 1, is the primary word or phrase that identifies the service or procedure, anatomic site, condition, or disease. In this example, the patient record states: "simple wound repair 12-cm wound, left hand."

To locate the code for the repair in the CPT manual index using the *condition method,* you first locate the main term "Wound" and then the subterm "repair." "Wound" is the condition and "Repair" is the procedure. Finally, you identify the type (ie, complex, simple).

To locate the code using the *service or procedure method,* you would first locate the main term "Repair." Repair is the service or procedure. The subterm "wound" is to be located next, and finally the type (ie, complex, simple). These are just two of the ways to locate this service in the index.

From the main term, "Wound," subterm of "simple," you are directed to a range of codes beginning with 12001. Locate this range in the CPT manual. The notes under the subheading "Repair (Closure)" are "must" reading. Also, read the description of the first code in the category (12001*). The description specifies that the code includes "hands," which is what you are looking for. Now locate the correct length (12 cm), and you will have the correct code of 12004.

Now you do one:

The patient record states: "complex wound repair on leg, 3.1 cm."

1. What is the correct code?

   Code(s): ____________________

2. After an assault with a knife, a patient requires simple repair of a 3-cm laceration of the neck, simple repair of a 4-cm laceration of the back, simple repair of a 5-cm laceration of the forearm, and complex repair of a 3-cm laceration of the abdomen.

   Code(s): ____________________

3. Harry Torgerson, a 42-year-old construction worker, was injured at work today when a box containing wood scraps and shingles fell from a second-story scaffolding and struck him on the left forearm, resulting in multiple lacerations. Forearm repairs: 5.1-cm repair of the subcutaneous tissues and a 5.6-cm laceration with particles of shingles and wood materials deeply embedded, requiring closure of single layer. There is also a superficial wound of the scalp of 3.1 cm.

   Code(s): ____________________

4. Suzanne Osterland, a 4-year-old, is brought to the office by her father. Suzanne was playing on the swing set in the back yard when she fell from the

top step of the play set, approximately 5 feet. When she fell, she struck her leg on a bird bath rim and then on a pail with several garden tools protruding over the rim, sustaining 12.9-cm, 3.1-cm, and 2.1-cm lacerations of right leg. There was extensive deep-layer involvement, and deep-layered closure was accomplished after extensive debridement.

Code(s): ____________________

Skin Grafts

There are many types of grafting procedures that can be performed to correct a defect (eg, adjacent tissue transfers or rearrangements, free skin grafts, flaps). To understand skin grafting, the coder must know that the **recipient site** is the area of defect that receives the graft, and the **donor site** is the area from which the healthy skin has been taken for grafting. (If a skin graft is required to close the donor site, the closure is coded as an additional procedure.) Below is a brief description of some different types of skin grafting and coding guidelines specific to their use.

Adjacent Tissue Transfer or Rearrangement

There are many types of adjacent tissue transfers. Some of them are Z-plasty (Fig. 3–24), W-plasty, V-Y plasty, rotation flaps (Fig. 3–25), and advancement flaps. Each procedure describes variations of methods of moving segments of skin from one area to an adjacent area, while leaving at least one side of the flap (moved skin) intact. At least one side of the flap is left connected to retain some measure of blood supply to the graft. Incisions are made, and the skin is undermined and moved over to cover the defect area, leaving the base or connected portion intact. The flap is then sutured into place.

Adjacent tissue transfers are coded according to the size of the recipient site. The size is measured in square centimeters. Simple repair of the donor site is included in the tissue transfer code and not coded separately. If there is a complex closure, or grafting of the donor site, this could be coded separately. Adjacent Tissue Transfer or Rearrangement in the CPT manual is subdivided based on location of the defect (trunk or arm) and size of the defect. In addition, there are codes at the end of the category for coding defects that are extremely complicated.

Figure 3–24
Z-plasty is named for the shape of the incision.

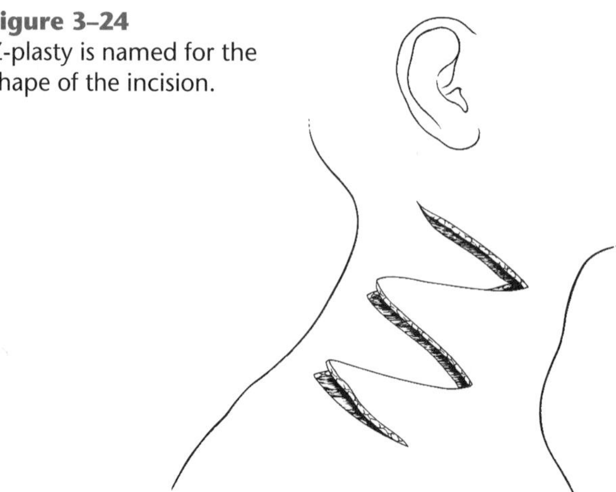

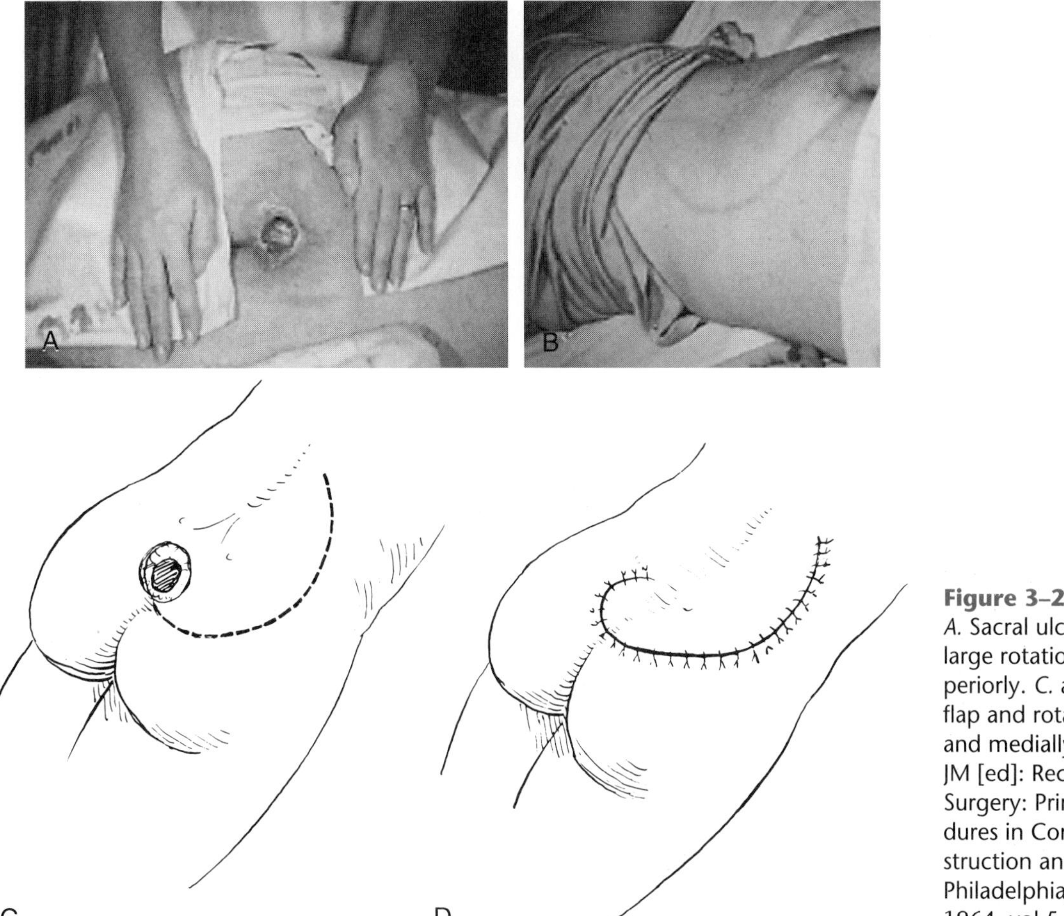

Figure 3–25
A. Sacral ulcer. *B.* Closure by a large rotation flap based superiorly. *C.* and *D.* Outline of flap and rotation downward and medially. (From Converse JM [ed]: Reconstructive Plastic Surgery: Principles and Procedures in Correction, Reconstruction and Transplantation. Philadelphia, WB Saunders, 1964, vol 5, p 1988.)

Any excision of a lesion that is repaired by adjacent tissue transfer is included in the tissue transfer code. If the coder tried to bill for the excision in addition to the transfer, it would be considered unbundling.

Adjacent tissue transfer codes can be located in the CPT manual index under the term "Skin."

Free Skin Grafts

Free skin grafts are pieces of skin that are either split thickness, which consists of epidermis and part of the dermis, or full thickness, which consists of the epidermis and all of the dermis. The grafts are completely freed from the donor site and placed over the recipient site. There is no connection left of the graft to the donor site (Fig. 3–26).

Free skin grafts are coded by recipient site, size of defect, and type of repair. The size is measured in square centimeters. If the donor site requires repair by grafting, an additional graft code is used. Simple repair (closure) of the donor site is included in the graft code.

The category of Free Skin Grafts contains several different types of repair: *pinch graft,* a small split-thickness repair; *split graft,* a repair that involves the epidermis and some of the dermis; and a *full-thickness graft,* which involves the epidermis and all of the dermis. Often the split-thickness graft is referred to in the patient record as STSG and the full-thickness skin graft as FTSG. There are also several codes for grafts that include application of grafts from other persons (allografts)

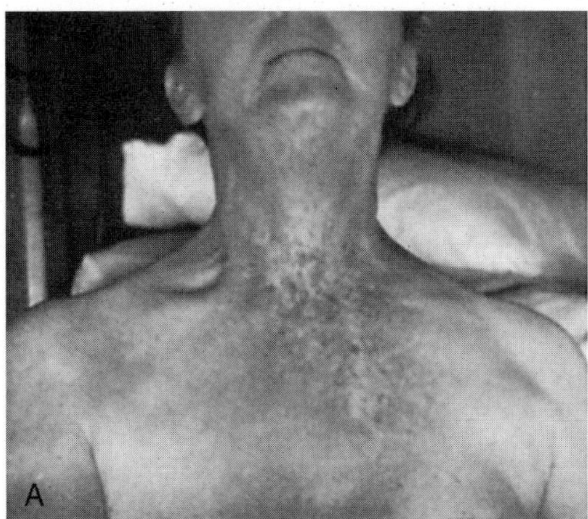

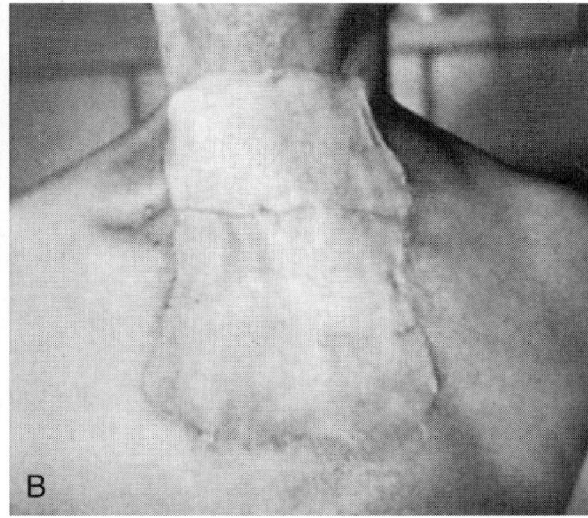

Figure 3–26
A. Chronic radiodermatitis of skin of the neck and sternal area following radiation treatment for hyperthyroidism 25 years previously. *B.* The irradiated skin was excised and covered with split-thickness skin grafts. (From Converse JM [ed]: Reconstructive Plastic Surgery: Principles and Procedures in Correction, Reconstruction and Transplantation. Philadelphia, WB Saunders, 1964, vol 1, p 321.)

or other species (xenografts), such as pigskin grafts to humans. These grafts are used as temporary grafts to help protect defect sites while healing is taking place (Figs. 3–27 and 3–28). A permanent graft may be placed over the site at a later date to complete the repair process.

CPT code 15000 is to be used to identify the additional procedure of preparing the recipient for grafting. The 15000 code does not need the -51 modifier because the description states: "list as a separate service in addition to the skin graft." Preparation of the site would also include removing or excising scar tissue or lesions.

Free skin grafts can be located in the CPT manual index under "Skin Grafts and Flaps" or "Grafts."

Flaps

The physician may decide to develop a donor site at a location far away from the recipient site. The graft may have to be accomplished in stages. The graft code can be assigned more than once when the surgery is done in stages. Notes specific to this group of codes state that when coding transfer flaps (in stages), the donor site is used when the *tube graft* (Fig. 3–29) is formed for later or when a *de-*

Figure 3–27
Three sheets of cultured epithelial autograft are in place on the left anterior thigh, which 3 weeks before was excised to muscle fascia and covered with cadaver allograft. (From Gallico GG, O'Connor NE: Cultured epithelium as a skin substitute. Clin Plast Surg 12[2]:155, 1985.)

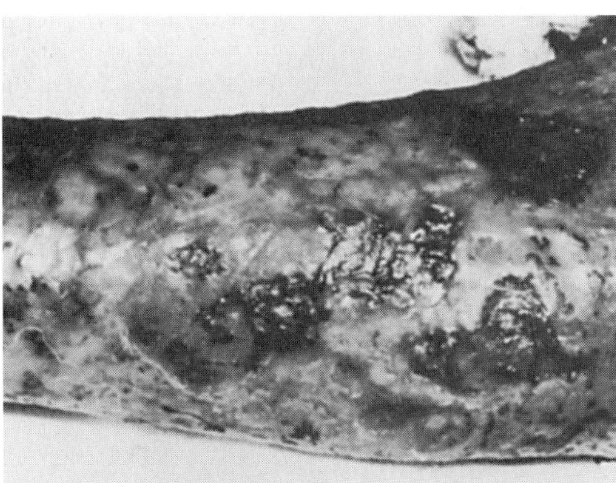

Figure 3–28
The same area of left anterior thigh as in Figure 3–27, 1 month after grafting. (From Gallico GG, O'Connor NE: Cultured epithelium as a skin substitute. Clin Plast Surg 12[2]:155, 1985.)

layed flap is formed before transfer (Fig. 3–30). The recipient site is used for coding when the graft is attached to its final site.

Delayed graft means that a portion of the skin is lifted and separated from tissue below, but it still stays connected to blood vessels at one end of the graft. This keeps the skin viable while moving it from one area to another, while also getting the graft used to living on a small blood supply. It is hoped that living on a small blood supply will help the graft have a better chance of survival when it is inset into the recipient site.

There are two categories of codes for flaps. The first category, Flaps (Skin and/or Deep Tissues) is subdivided based on the type of flap (ie, pedicle, cross finger, delayed, or muscle flaps) and then by the location of the flap (scalp, trunk, or lips). The second category, Other Flaps and Grafts, is subdivided based on the type of flap (free muscle, free skin, fascial, or hair transplant).

Other Procedures

Two other categories within the Repair subheading are Other Procedures and Pressure Ulcers. The Other Procedures category contains codes for a wide variety of repair services, such as abrasions, chemical peel, or blepharoplasty. The codes are divided based often on site or extent of repair. Pressure ulcers are repaired with excision of the ulcer and repair of the site (see Fig. 3–25). Read the code descriptions carefully when coding from the ulcer repair category as the codes are divided based on location, type, and extent of closure needed.

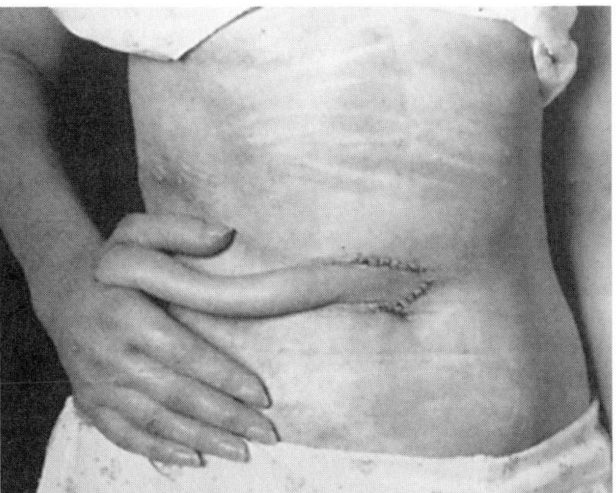

Figure 3–29
Transfer of an upper abdominal tube flap that was later used to reconstruct a nose. (From Converse JM [ed]: Reconstructive Plastic Surgery: Principles and Procedures in Correction, Reconstruction and Transplantation. Philadelphia: WB Saunders, 1964, vol 5, p 1956.)

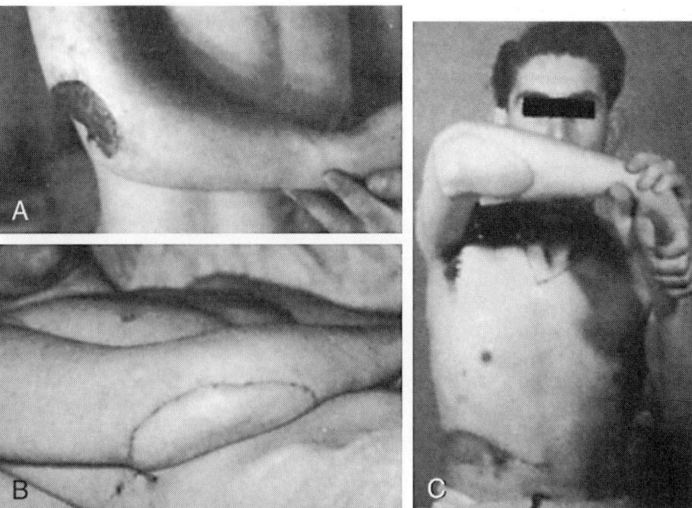

Figure 3–30
A. Compound fracture of the elbow. A resection of the joint is necessary. Adequate soft tissue covering must be provided. *B.* A direct abdominal flap has been applied after complete excision of the scarred and infected tissues. Note the generous size of the flap and also the position of the upper extremity against the trunk. *C.* The flap after healing. The donor area on the abdomen has been partly closed by direct approximation. The remainder of the defect has been skin grafted. (From Converse JM [ed]: Reconstructive Plastic Surgery: Principles and Procedures in Correction, Reconstruction and Transplantation. Philadelphia, WB Saunders, 1964, vol 1, p 66.)

EXERCISE Q *Grafts and Flaps*

Code the following:

1. A patient with multiple healed scars requests that these be removed and repaired for cosmetic purposes. The defects include a 100-cm^2 scar of the right cheek and a 200-cm^2 defect of the left upper chest. Several split-thickness skin grafts totaling 300 cm^2 are harvested from the left and right thighs. The scar tissue is cut away, and the sites prepared for grafting.

   Code(s): ____________________

2. The patient had a 20-cm^2 defect of the right cheek that was repaired with a rotation flap.

   Code(s): ____________________

3. The patient had a 10-cm^2 malignant neoplasm removed from the forehead. Z-plasty was used to repair this site. How would the excision and repair be coded?

   Code(s): ____________________

4. A patient has had a portion of his mandible removed due to excision of a malignant tumor. Repair of the site is now planned by use of a myocutaneous flap graft.

   Code(s): ________________

Burn Treatment

Burn treatment is unique in that it is common to have multiple dressing changes or debridements (see Fig. 3–23) during the healing period. Dressing and debridement codes are either initial or subsequent treatments. Burn dressing and/or debridement codes are divided based on whether the dressing or debridement was accomplished with or without anesthesia and on the percent of body surface involved. The CPT codes are divided based on small, medium, and large body surface areas. Although not stated, an approximation is as follows: small is less than 4½%; medium, 4½% to 9%; large, over 9%. The Rule of Nines is used to estimate the percentage of body surface (Fig. 3–31). For example, 4½% to 9% surface is the whole face and one extremity.

Excision of burns using **alloplastic dressings** is listed by percentage of body surface area. These dressings are manmade coverings used in the healing process and are not skin grafts.

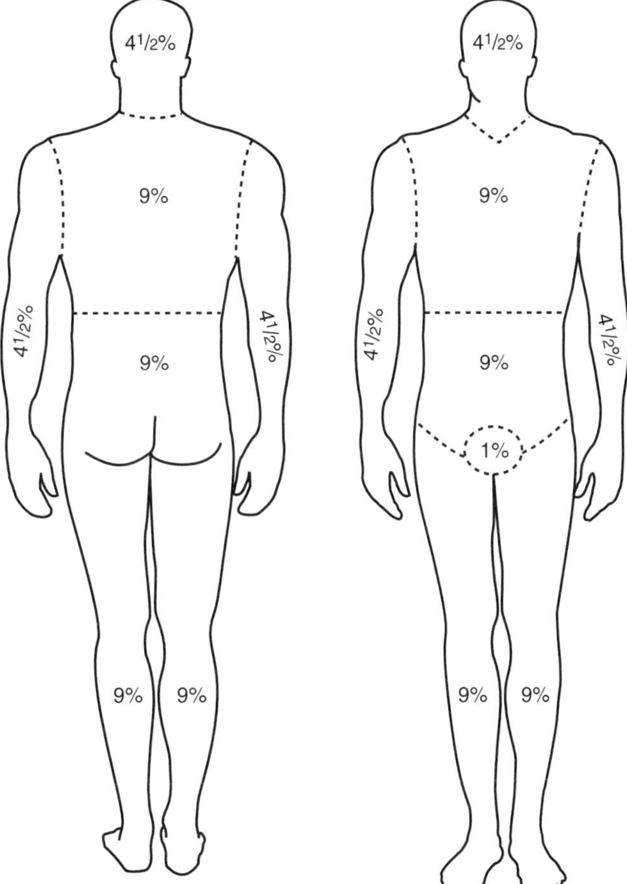

Figure 3–31
Rule of Nines.

EXERCISE R Burn Treatment

Code the following:

1. A patient incurred second- and third-degree burns of the abdomen and thigh when she pulled a pan of boiling water off the stove. She will require daily debridements or dressing changes for the first week (Monday through Friday). She is in severe pain and will require anesthesia during these treatments. The following 2 weeks she will be receiving dressing changes every other day (Monday, Wednesday, Friday), and it is expected that enough healing will take place that anesthesia will not be necessary.

   Code(s): ____________________

Destruction by Other Methods

The next subheading in the subsection of the Integumentary System is Destruction. The codes are for destruction of lesions by means other than excision. The codes in this subsection are for benign, premalignant, or malignant lesions destroyed using electrosurgery (use of various forms of electrical current to destroy the lesion), cryosurgery (use of extreme cold), laser (**l**ight **a**mplification by **s**timulation **e**mission of **r**adiation), or chemicals (acids). Read the notes under the Destruction subsection heading, which contains a list of types of lesions.

The codes are usually divided based on method of destruction, although there are some codes that can be used no matter what the method. Further divisions are based on number of lesions destroyed or size of area destroyed. The malignant lesions are divided based on location (nose, ear, etc.) and size (0.6 cm to 1.0 cm, etc.), regardless of the method.

One sophisticated destruction procedure is Mohs' micrographic surgery. The **Mohs' microscope** is used by the surgeon during the surgical procedure to view the lesion and assess its pathology. If the lesion is malignant, the lesion is immediately removed. The surgeon acts as both the pathologist and the surgeon. The codes in the category include the removal of the lesion(s) and pathologic evaluation of the lesion(s). These codes are also divided based on the stage (first, second, third) of the surgery and the number of specimens the surgeon takes during the surgery for pathologic examination.

Breast Procedures

Breast procedures are divided according to category of procedure (eg, incision, excision, introduction, repair). You must read documentation to identify the procedure used, such as incisional versus excisional biopsies. An incisional biopsy is an incision into the lesion with a small portion of the lesion taken out. Excisional biopsy means the entire lesion has been removed for biopsy. In some cases it may be necessary to mark the lesion preoperatively by placing a thin wire (radiologic marker) down to the lesion to identify its exact location (Fig. 3–32). The placement of the wire is coded and the excision of the lesion identified by the marker is coded.

There are multiple codes used to identify mastectomies. You should carefully review the operative report to confirm if pectoral muscles, axillary lymph nodes, or internal mammary lymph nodes were also removed. This information will be necessary to determine the correct type of mastectomy code.

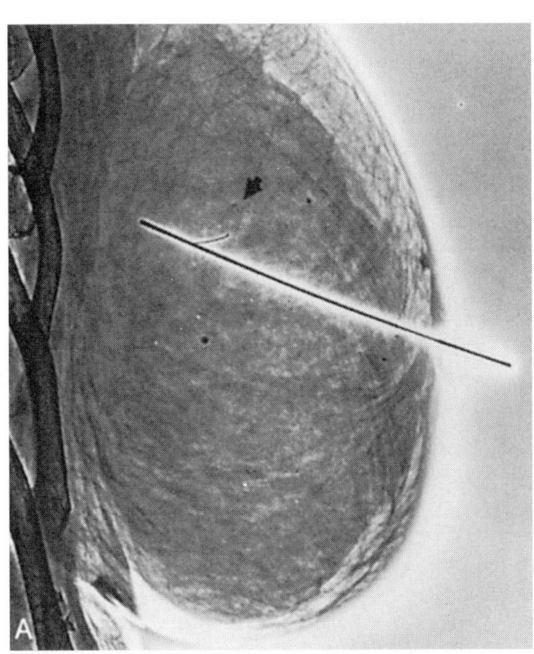

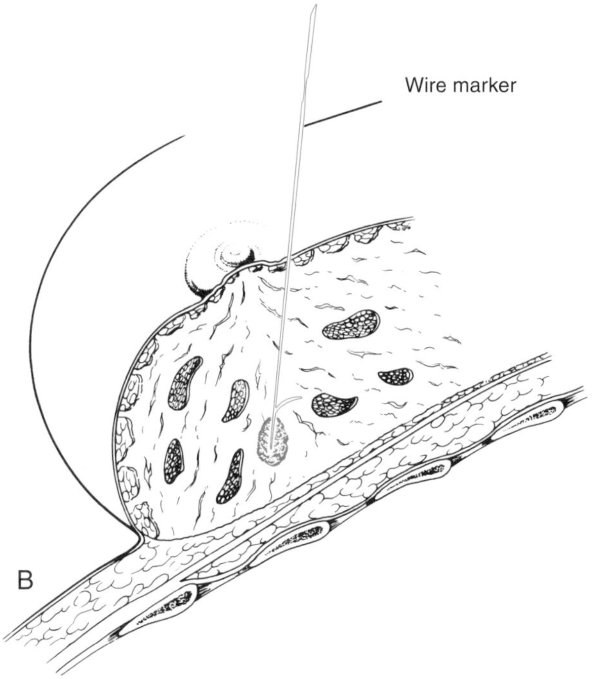

Figure 3–32
Wire marker used to mark breast lesion. *A.* Mammography is used to place a preoperative needle used to mark a lesion. (From Bland KI [ed]: The Breast: Comprehensive Management of Benign and Malignant Diseases. Philadelphia, WB Saunders, 1991.) *B.* The wire marker serves as a guide for the surgeon to perform the biopsy. (Redrawn from Bland KI [ed]: The Breast: Comprehensive Management of Benign and Malignant Diseases. Philadelphia, WB Saunders, 1991.)

Remember, any breast procedure done on **both** *breasts must be coded as a bilateral procedure (modifier -50).*

EXERCISE 5 Breast Procedures

Locate the correct code for the following procedures. Be sure to read all notes in the CPT manual and the description of the code before applying the code:

1. Aspiration of one cyst, breast

   Code(s): ____________________

2. Simple, complete bilateral mastectomies

   Code(s): ____________________

3. Right modified radical mastectomy, including axillary lymph nodes without any muscles

   Code(s): ____________________

4. Preoperative placement of one breast wire, left breast

   Code(s): ________________

5. Reconstruction of nipple/areola

   Code(s): ________________

Congratulations! You made it through the entire Integumentary System subsection! The subsection is quite complicated and you have done a great job if you understand the basics of these codes. As you use them here and on the job, your knowledge will continue to grow.

MUSCULOSKELETAL SYSTEM

Format

The Musculoskeletal System subsection is formatted by anatomic site. The first subheading in the subsection is "General" and contains procedures that are applicable to many different anatomic sites. Subsequent subheadings use anatomic sites for identification and then are further divided by category of procedure to include incision, excision, introduction/removal, repair/revision/construction, fracture/dislocation, arthrodesis, amputation, and unlisted procedures. Any or all of the categories of procedures may be found under each subheading. For example, under the subheading of Head and Finger there are category codes for incision, excision, introduction/removal, repair/revision/construction, etc.

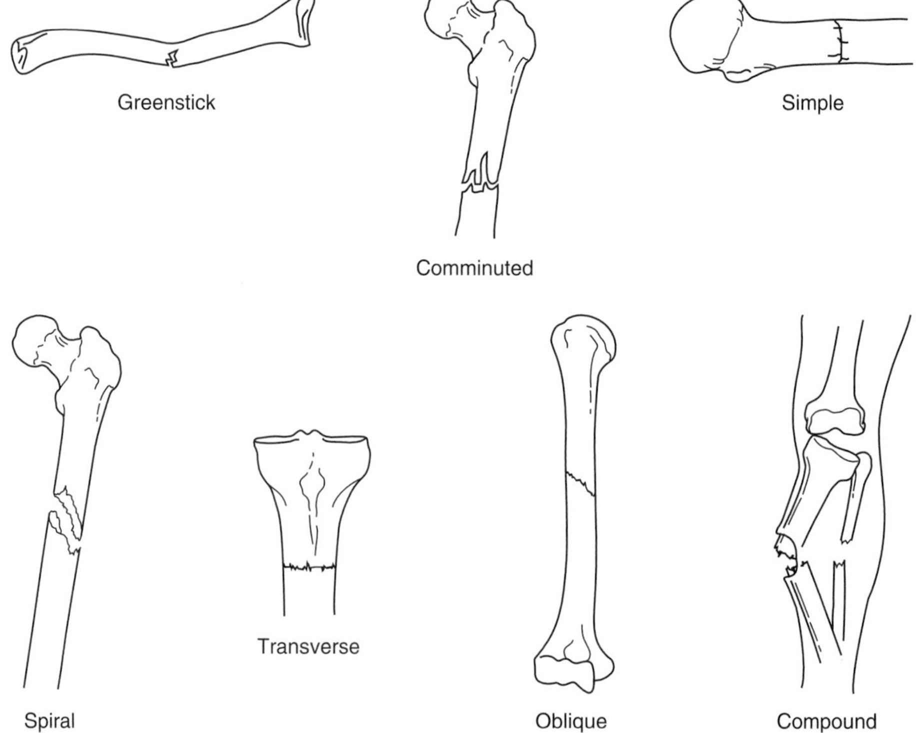

Figure 3–33
Types of fractures.

Terminology

Orthopedic procedures are reported according to the treatment method. Take special care to code by type of treatment. For example, *open* treatment occurs when the fracture site is surgically opened to allow for repair. *Closed* treatment occurs when the fracture is not opened, but is repaired by methods such as traction or manipulation. A simple or greenstick fracture (Fig. 3–33) may receive a closed treatment, whereas a more complicated comminuted fracture may need an open treatment to provide internal fixation (eg, wires, pins, screws). The treatment method will depend on the type of damage being repaired. There will be more information regarding fractures later in the section. The following terminology exercise will help you identify the most common treatment methods that you will need to know to code within the subsection Musculoskeletal System.

EXERCISE T Musculoskeletal Terminology

Match the following terms to the correct definitions:

Hint: Check out the notes in the CPT manual at the beginning of the Musculoskeletal System subsection for treatment definitions.

1. closed treatment _______
2. open treatment _______
3. percutaneous skeletal fixation _______
4. fracture _______
5. dislocation _______
6. manipulation or reduction _______
7. internal/external fixation _______
8. skeletal traction _______
9. soft tissue _______
10. arthroplasty _______
11. arthrodesis _______

a. application of force to a limb with the use of a pin, screw, wire, or clamp attached to the bone

b. placement in a location other than the original location

c. application of pins, wires, screws, and so on to immobilize; these can be placed externally or internally

d. fracture site that is not surgically opened and visualized

e. words used interchangeably to mean the attempted restoration of a fracture or joint dislocation to its normal anatomic position

f. fracture site that is surgically opened and visualized

g. surgical immobilization of a joint

h. tissues (fascia, connective tissue, muscle, etc.) surrounding a bone

i. break in a bone

j. considered neither open nor closed; the fracture is not visualized, but fixation is placed across the fracture site under x-ray imaging

k. reshaping or reconstructing a joint

Musculoskeletal Coding Highlights

Thorough review of the health record will help identify key information necessary for coding. The following tips will help you choose the most correct code from this subsection:

1. Identify whether the procedure is being performed on soft tissue or bone.
2. Determine if treatment is for a traumatic injury or medical condition.
3. Identify the most specific anatomic site. For example, when coding vertebral procedures it is necessary to know if the condition was for cervical, thoracic, or lumbar vertebrae.
4. Determine if the code description includes grafting or fixation. If grafting or fixation is not listed within the major procedure code description, each may be coded as additional procedures.
5. Read the code carefully to determine if it describes a procedure done on a single site (eg, each finger). If the same procedure is performed on multiple sites (eg, multiple fingers), you must indicate the number of units done or list the code multiple times.

Fractures

Fractures are coded by treatment—open, closed, or percutaneous. *Open repair* of a fracture is when a surgery is performed in which the fracture is exposed by an incision made over the fracture. *Closed repair* is when the physician repairs the fracture through the skin without opening the skin. The repair method used—open or closed—depends on the type and severity of the fracture. Fractures are coded to the specific anatomic site and then according to whether manipulation was performed. All fractures and dislocations are coded based on the reason for the treatment. For instance, if a hip replacement (arthroplasty) is done for medical reasons such as osteoarthritis, it is coded to 27125, located under the subheading "Repair, Revision, and/or Reconstruction." The repair was the reason for the treatment. If the hip replacement was done for a fracture, it is coded 27236, located under the subheading "Fracture and/or Dislocation." The fracture was the reason for the treatment.

The CPT manual definitions of open, closed, and percutaneous treatments are as follows:

Closed treatment means that the fracture site is not surgically opened (exposed to the external environment and directly visualized). This terminology is used to describe procedures that treat fractures by three methods: (1) without manipulation, (2) with manipulation, and (3) with or without traction.

Open treatment is used when the fracture is surgically opened (exposed to the external environment). In this instance, the fracture (bone) is visualized and internal fixation (pins, screws, etc.) may be used.

Percutaneous skeletal fixation describes fracture treatment that is neither open nor closed. In this procedure, the fracture fragments are not visualized, but fixation (eg, pins) is placed across the fracture site, usually under x-ray imaging.

Before continuing with the coding highlights of the Musculoskeletal System, be certain that you have a firm understanding of the definitions of treatments such as closed, open, and percutaneous as these terms are used throughout the subsection to differentiate between codes.

General Subheading

The first subheading in the Musculoskeletal subsection is General. As the name implies, this subheading includes a wide variety of codes. The first code, 20000, is for the incision of a *soft tissue abscess.* There are codes in the Integumentary System for incisions that are for tissue only. What makes the 20000 code different from those in the Integumentary System is that this code is used when the abscess is associated with the bone that underlies the area of abscess. The physician would make an incision into the abscess, explore the abscess, clean the abscess, and debride (remove dead tissue). If the underlying bone is affected, the physician would usually remove the bone, irrigate the area, place a drain into the area, and pack the area. This is a much different procedure than what you would find in the Integumentary System codes for incision of an abscess.

The *Wound Exploration* codes are for traumatic wounds that result from a penetrating trauma, eg, gunshot, knife wound. Wound Exploration codes include basic exploration and repair of the area of trauma. These codes are used specifically when the repair requires enlargement of the existing wound for cleaning and repair. If the wound does not need to be enlarged, you would use a code from the Integumentary System, Skin Repair codes. If, however, the wound is more severe than what a Wound Exploration code would indicate, the repair code would come from the specific repair area codes. For example, if a stab wound to the chest penetrated the lung, the treatment might be a thoracotomy with control of the hemorrhage and repair of the tear of the lung. The thoracotomy code would come from the subsection Respiratory System under the subheading Lungs. As you can see from this wound example, you have to assess the extent of the procedure carefully, reading the medical record to ensure you are in the correct area to choose the correct service code.

Note that under the *Excision* category there are codes for biopsies of the muscles and bones. It is within the Introduction/Removal category that you will find the codes for the placement of skeletal traction. You reviewed the codes for grafts that involve the skin in the Integumentary System, but there are graft codes in this general area of the Musculoskeletal System, too. Beginning with 20900, the category codes are for *bone grafts* of various sites and using various repair methods. There are also more extensive bone graft codes in the Other Procedures category.

The anatomic subheadings that follow the General subheading (eg, head, neck, back, spine) each contain codes divided based on the procedure, ie, incision, excision, fracture. There are extensive notes throughout the Musculoskeletal System subsection that give the specifics for reporting services using the codes. Many of the notes even tell you what specific anatomic areas the codes cover. For example, notes under the subheading Shoulder indicate that the areas covered are clavicle, scapula, humerus, head and neck, sternoclavicular joint, acromioclavicular joint, and shoulder joint. So, be certain to read any notes carefully before using the codes.

As you use the codes, you will begin to know this background information and the coding process will become faster for you. But, at the beginning, reading the notes is how you gain the knowledge that you are seeking. Now is not the time to take shortcuts.

Cast/Strapping

The first application of a cast or strapping is included in the initial procedure code (ie, fracture care code). Refer to the notes preceding the casting and strapping codes for all the details on codes in this subheading. Strapping is taping of

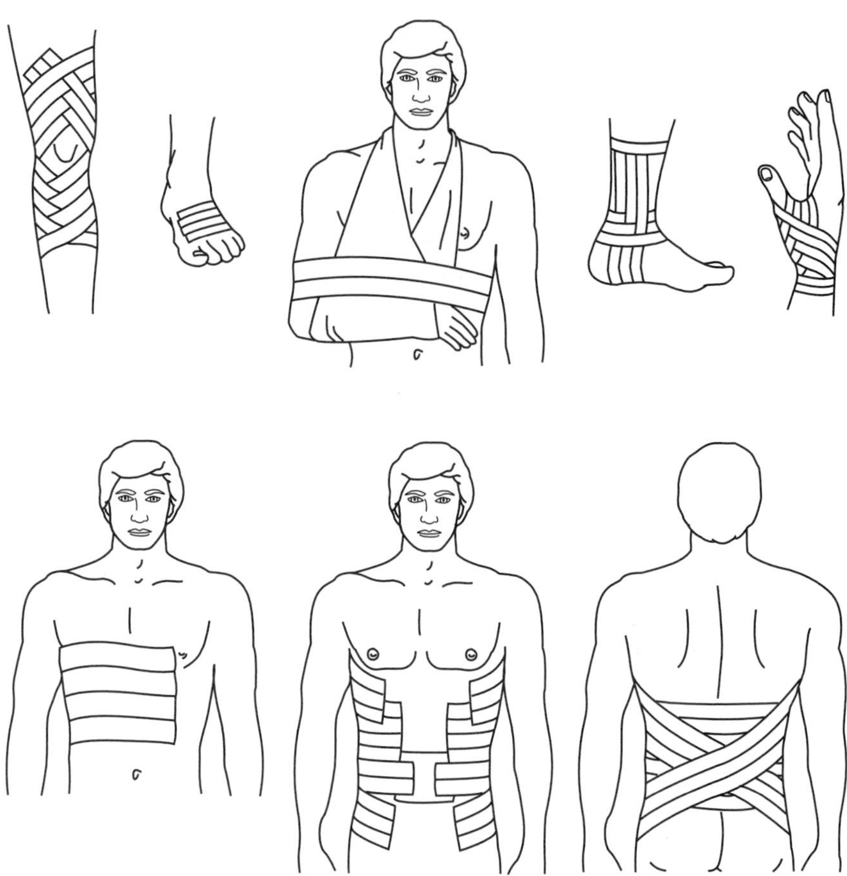

Figure 3–34
Types of strapping.

the body as illustrated in Figure 3–34. If reapplication of a cast/splint or strapping is necessary, a code from the subheading Application of Casts/Strapping, categories Body/Upper Extremity or Lower Extremity, is reported depending on the type of device (eg, cast) and the anatomic site. Codes in the category Removal/Repair are for the removal or repair of casts.

Arthroscopic Procedures

Arthroscopy is fast becoming the treatment of choice for many surgical procedures. The incisions are smaller, which decreases the risk of infection and speeds recovery time. Several small incisions are made through which lights, mirrors, and instruments are placed. The arthroscopy codes are located separately at the end of the Musculoskeletal subsection. If multiple procedures are performed through a scope, they are reported with modifier -51. Bundled into all arthroscopic procedure codes are both the diagnostic arthroscopy and the surgical arthroscopy. You must not unbundle and code a diagnostic arthroscopy and surgical arthroscopy, even if both were performed during the same encounter.

EXERCISE U *Musculoskeletal Procedures*

Code the following:

1. George Adams fell off a wagon and fractured his right fibula and tibia. He had an open treatment of his shaft fractures with multiple screws placed.

   Code(s): ___________________

2. Ryan Jones stubbed his foot on a chair last night. His toes kept hurting and the next day he decided to see a physician. After radiographs were taken, it was found that he had fractured his great toe and second toe. Ryan had his toes strapped and went on his way. How would the fracture be coded?

   Code(s): ________________

3. Doris Smith had a total hip replacement done 4 years ago. When she was getting out of a chair today, she noticed a severe pain in her hip and was unable to move well. Examination in the emergency department revealed that Doris had dislocated her prosthetic hip. An orthopedic surgeon was called in. The hip was manipulated back into place. How would the manipulation be coded?

   Code(s): ________________

4. Jaime Martinez at 3 weeks after repair of a fracture is returning to the physician to have a short-leg walking cast applied.

   Code(s): ________________

5. Julie Mason is coming in today to have her long-arm cast removed and replaced with a short-arm cast.

   Code(s): ________________

6. Jack Johnson jumped over a candlestick and twisted his knee when he fell. The orthopedist believed it was necessary to do a diagnostic arthroscopy of the knee to ensure permanent damage had not occurred. On exploration of the knee, it was found that Jack had torn his medial meniscus. A meniscal repair was then performed.

   Code(s): ________________

RESPIRATORY SYSTEM

Format

The Respiratory System subsection is arranged by anatomic site (ie, nose, sinus, larynx) and then by procedure (ie, incision, excision, introduction). Again, your knowledge of the respiratory terminology is important (Fig. 3–35). The Musculoskeletal section had the arthroscopy codes at the end of the subsection, but the Respiratory subsection has the endoscopy codes listed throughout by anatomic site. Fracture repair, such as of the nose or sternum, is listed in the Musculoskeletal subsection, not the Respiratory subsection.

The Respiratory subsection contains some codes that may be considered cosmetic. It is important to note the extent of the cosmetic repair indicated in the patient's record. The extent is important so that you do not report the same service more than once and unbundle a code. For example, under the subheading Nose and the category Repair is code 30420 for a rhinoplasty. The rhinoplasty can be

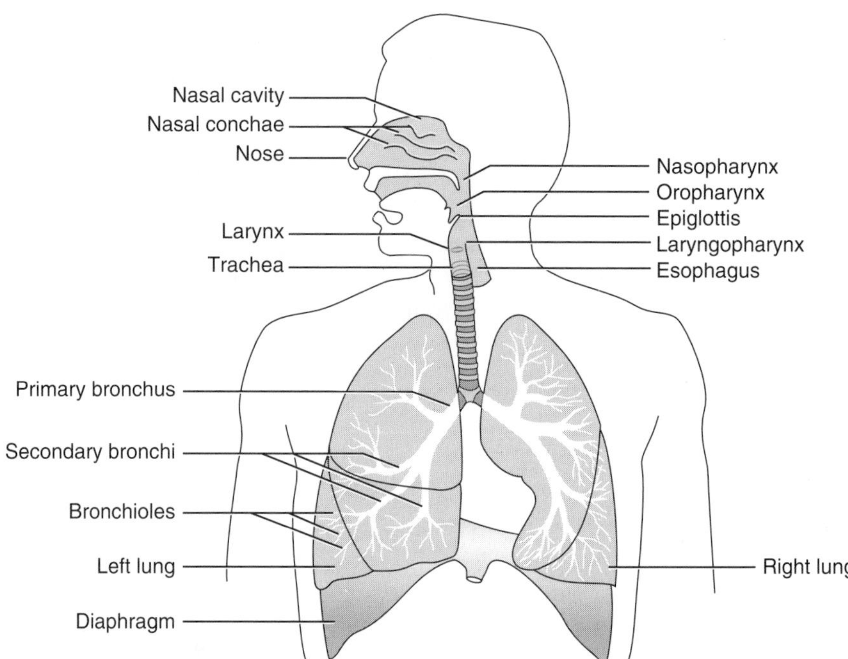

Figure 3–35
Respiratory system.

performed either through external skin incisions (open) or through intranasal incisions (closed), and both approaches can be coded to 30420. The extent of the procedure varies based on the desired outcome, but it can include fracturing the deformed septum, repositioning of the septum, reshaping and/or augmenting the nasal cartilage, removal of fat from the area and layered closure, and application of splint or cast. If all of these components of a rhinoplasty were done, they would all be bundled into code 30420. You have to read all of the notes and the code information carefully to ensure that each service provided to the patient is reported only once.

Terminology

EXERCISE V *Respiratory Terminology*

Match the following terms and prefixes to the correct definitions:

1. polyp _______
2. rhino- _______
3. endoscopy _______
4. sinuses _______
5. antrum _______
6. antrotomy _______
7. laryngo- _______
8. bronchoscopy _______

a. excision of a lobe of the lung
b. maxillary sinus
c. prefix meaning larynx
d. tumor on a pedicle that bleeds easily and may become malignant
e. prefix meaning lung or air
f. surgical puncture of the thoracic cavity, usually using a needle, to remove fluids
g. inspection of the bronchial tree using a bronchoscope
h. prefix meaning nose

9. thoracentesis _______
10. thoracotomy _______
11. thoracostomy _______
12. thoracoscopy _______
13. lobectomy _______
14. pleura _______
15. pneumo- _______
16. embolectomy _______

i. use of a lighted endoscope to view the pleural spaces and thoracic cavity or perform surgical procedures
j. removal of blockage (embolism) from vessels
k. inspection of body organs or cavities using a lighted scope that may be placed through an existing opening or through a small incision
l. covering of the lungs and thoracic cavity that is moistened with serous fluid to reduce friction during respiratory movements of the lungs
m. cutting into the thoracic cavity to allow for enlargement of the heart or for drainage
n. cutting through the antrum wall to make an opening in the sinus
o. cavities within the nasal bones
p. surgical incision into the thoracic cavity

Label Diagram 3–2 with the paranasal sinuses.

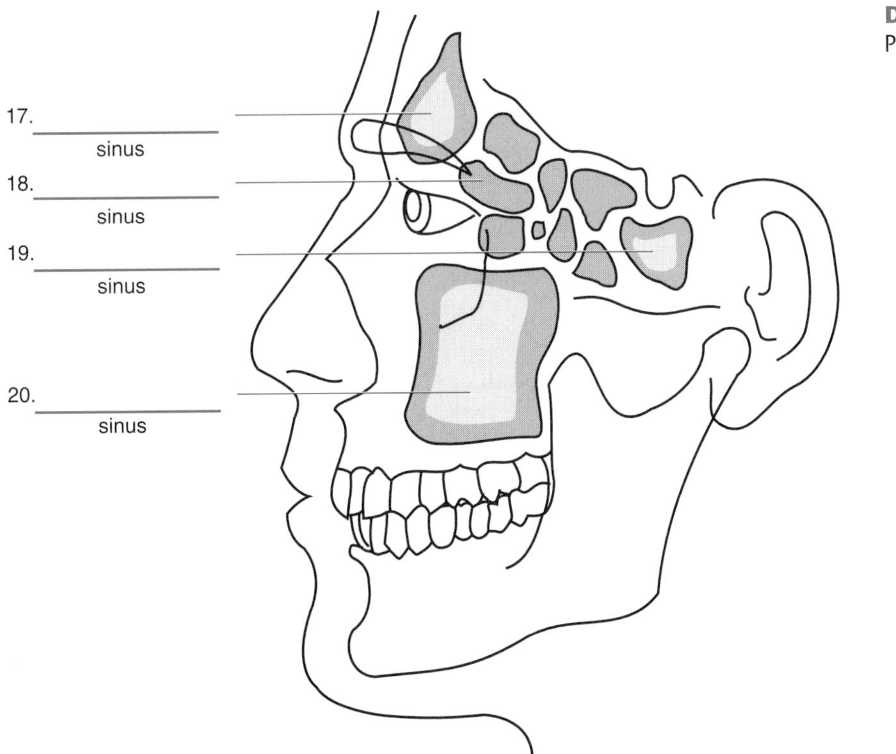

Diagram 3–2
Paranasal sinuses.

Respiratory Coding Highlights

Endoscopy

In endoscopic procedures, a scope is placed through an existing body orifice (opening) or a small incision is made into the cavity for scope placement.

When sinus endoscopies are done, a scope is placed through the nose into the nasal cavity. Codes for sinuses are used to report unilateral procedures unless otherwise specified. Multiple procedures may be done within different sinuses (anterior and posterior sinuses, ethmoidal sinuses, sphenoidal sinuses, and frontal sinuses) during the same operative session. The CPT manual has combined into a single code some multiple sinus procedures commonly done at the same operative session.

EXAMPLE

31276	Nasal/sinus endoscopy, surgical with frontal sinus exploration with or without removal of tissue from frontal sinus

Also, endoscopic procedures may start at one site (such as the nose) and follow through to another site (such as the larynx or bronchial tubes). It is important to choose the code that most appropriately reflects the full extent of the procedure. For example, if a direct laryngoscopy (31515) is performed, the scope is progressed past the larynx and can include examination of the trachea. The 31515 code description states either with or without tracheoscopy. However, if it is necessary to continue the procedure to the bronchial tubes, the only code used would be 31622 (bronchoscopy). The larynx and trachea must be passed to get to the bronchial tubes and can be visualized while progressing to the farthest point (bronchial tubes).

Code to the full extent of the procedure.

The same surgical procedure may be performed using different approaches. For example, code 32141 describes a thoracotomy with "excision-plication (removal/shortening) of bullae (blister); with or without any pleural procedure." Code 32655 describes a surgical thoracoscopy with excision-plication of bullae, including any pleural procedures. Code 32655 describes the same procedure as 32141, except that 32655 is a procedure done through very minute incisions utilizing a thorascope, whereas code 32141 describes an open incision through the thorax, opening the full operative site to the surgeon.

Code the correct approach for the procedure.

Multiple endoscopic procedures may be performed through the scope during the same operative session. When this occurs, each procedure should be coded with modifier -51 placed on subsequent procedure(s). Suppose, for example, bronchoscopy with biopsy is performed as well as a bronchoscopy with removal of foreign body. Not only would you code a bronchoscopy, but you would also code the removal of a foreign body. The multiple procedure modifier -51 would need to be placed after the lesser priced (least resource-intensive) procedure.

The exception to this is when the CPT manual offers a code that includes all the elements of the procedure bundled into one code.

Locating Endoscopy Codes

Endoscopy codes can be located in the CPT manual index under "Endoscopy" and then under the anatomic subterm of the site. You can also locate an endoscopic procedure by the anatomic endoscopy title. For example, a bronchial biopsy using an endoscopy would be under "Bronchoscopy," and then under the subterm "Biopsy."

EXERCISE W ***Respiratory System***

Code only the physician services in this exercise. Do not code the laboratory or radiology services.

Code the following:

1. Jack Rogers developed chest pain and difficulty breathing. He had also been coughing up thick, blood-tinged sputum. A chest radiograph showed an ill-defined mass. A diagnostic bronchoscopy was done, with a specimen taken of the mass. The pathology report came back positive for cancer. One week later, a lobectomy was performed.

   Code(s): ____________________

2. James Wilson has been having difficulty breathing and has had continual sinusitis. Dr. Adams takes James to the operating room to perform a sinus endoscopy with anterior and posterior ethmoidectomy with removal of polyps.

   Code(s): ____________________

3. Mary Bronson has a nosebleed that she can't get stopped. She goes to the emergency department, where anterior packing is done to control the nasal hemorrhage.

   a. Code(s): ____________________

   b. Would an E/M code be used with this case? ____________________

CARDIOVASCULAR SYSTEM

Format

The Cardiovascular System subsection is divided into subheadings by the anatomic sites of Heart/Pericardium and Arteries/Veins. The subheadings are then divided by codes for various procedures, ie, pacemaker, defibrillator, valve procedures, coronary bypass grafting, and cardiac anomalies. The subsection is further divided into artery and vein codes, beginning with embolectomies or thrombectomies, then aneurysm or occlusive disease procedures, repairs, angioplasty, vascular bypass, injections, intravascular shunting, and ligations or other procedures.

Terminology

EXERCISE X Cardiovascular Terminology

Match the following terms to the correct definitions:

1. pericardium _______
2. cardiopulmonary _______
3. bypass _______
4. pacemaker _______
5. single-chamber pacemaker _______
6. dual-chamber pacemaker _______
7. electrode _______
8. ventricle _______
9. atrium _______
10. cardioverter-defibrillator _______
11. artery _______
12. vein _______
13. aneurysm _______
14. embolism _______
15. thrombosis _______
16. endarterectomy _______
17. angioplasty _______
18. injection _______
19. catheter _______
20. arteriovenous fistula _______
21. anomaly _______
22. ischemia _______

a. forcing of fluid into a vessel or cavity

b. blood bypasses the heart through a heart-lung machine during open heart surgery

c. lead attached to a generator that carries the electric current from the generator to the atria or ventricles

d. vessel that carries unoxygenated blood to the heart from the body tissues

e. blood clot

f. abnormal opening from one area to another area or to outside the body

g. to go around

h. surgically placed device that directs an electric current shock to the heart to restore rhythm

i. blockage of a blood vessel by a blood clot or other matter that has moved from another area of the body through the circulatory system

j. direct communication (passage) between an artery and vein

k. tube placed into the body to put fluid in or take fluid out

l. surgical or percutaneous procedure on a vessel to dilate the vessel opening; used in treatment of atherosclerotic disease

m. electrode of the pacemaker is placed only in the atrium or only in the ventricle, but not in both places

n. membranous sac enclosing the heart and ends of the great vessels

o. vessel that carries oxygenated blood from the heart to the body tissues

p. sac of clotted blood or fluid formed in the circulatory system, ie, vein or artery

q. incision into an artery to remove the inner lining to remove disease or blockage

r. divert or make an artificial passage

s. refers to the heart and lungs

23. cardiopulmonary bypass _______
24. fistula _______
25. shunt _______

t. electrodes of the pacemaker are placed in both the atria and the ventricles of the heart
u. deficient blood supply due to obstruction of the circulatory system
v. chamber in the upper part of the heart
w. electrical device that controls the beating of the heart by electrical impulses
x. chamber in the lower part of the heart
y. abnormality

Cardiovascular Coding Highlights

Pacemakers

A pacemaker and a cardioverter-defibrillator are devices that are inserted into the body to electrically shock the heart into regular rhythm. When a pacemaker is inserted, a pocket is made and a generator and lead(s) are placed inside the chest (Fig. 3–36). Sometimes, only components of the pacemaker are reinserted, repaired, or replaced. You need to know three things about the service provided to correctly code the pacemaker.

1. If an electrode (lead) is inserted into the atrium, ventricle, or both
2. Whether the procedure involves initial placement, replacement, or repair of all components or separate components of the pacemaker
3. The approach used to place the pacemaker (epicardial or transvenous)

Approaches

The two approaches used in insertion of a pacemaker are epicardial and transvenous and the codes are divided based on the surgical approach.

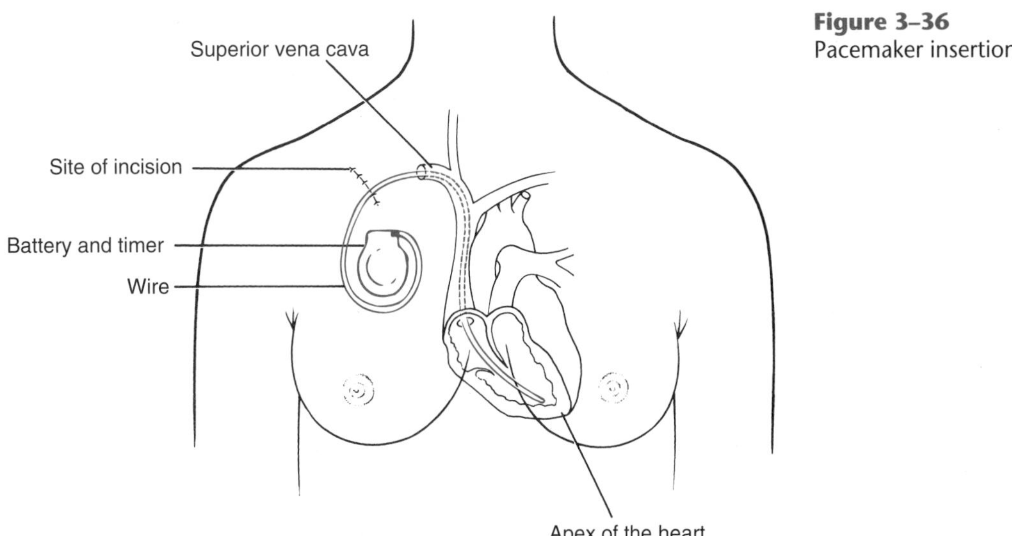

Figure 3–36
Pacemaker insertion.

1. **Transvenous** involves access to a vein (subclavian or jugular) and inserting a needle with a wire into the vein. A fluoroscope is then passed into the heart and the pacemaker affixed by creating a pocket into which the pacemaker generator is placed. The fluoroscopic portion of the procedure is coded separately because it is not bundled into the pacemaker codes. Transvenous codes are further divided based on the area of the heart into which the pacemaker is inserted. For example, 33207 is reported for transvenous placement of a pacemaker into the ventricle of the heart. If the pacemaker components were placed in both the atrium and the ventricle, 33208 is reported.
2. **Epicardial** involves opening the chest cavity and placing the pacemaker on the heart. A pocket is formed on the surface of the heart and the pacemaker generator is placed into the pocket. A tunnel is made into the heart into which the wires are fed. The wires are then connected to the pacemaker generator and the chest area is closed. Codes for the epicardial process are further divided based on the approach to the chest wall (thoracotomy) or upper abdominal (xiphoid region).

The patient record will indicate whether a pacemaker or the cardioverter-defibrillator is totally inserted or replaced.

The same set of criteria applies to the cardioverter-defibrillator codes:

1. Revision or replacement of lead(s)
2. Replacement, repair, removal of components
3. Approach used for insertion or repair

EXERCISE Y *Pacemakers*

Code the following:

1. Allen Jackson gets very tired walking up and down stairs. He has a hard time catching his breath and will have instances when his heart feels as if it is beating fast. His physician has told him that he will require a pacemaker implantation. Allen goes to surgery and has a single-chamber pacemaker implanted into the ventricle.

   Code(s): ________________

2. Five days after the pacemaker is implanted, Allen feels very dizzy and his electrocardiogram is showing some abnormalities. His physician takes him back to the operating room and discovers that the pacemaker lead is malfunctioning. The pacemaker is replaced, and Allen recovers nicely.

   Code(s): ________________

3. Five years later, Allen is found to have battery depletion of his pacemaker. He is also having some other symptoms that his physician believes necessitate not only a replacement pacemaker but also an upgrade to a dual-chamber device.

   Code(s): ________________

Cardiac Valves

The category Cardiac Valves has subcategory codes of aortic, mitral, tricuspid, or pulmonary. The procedures are about the same for each valve; some are a little more extensive than others. Code descriptions vary depending on whether a cardiopulmonary bypass (heart-lung) machine is used during the procedure. The cardiopulmonary bypass is a resource-intensive procedure that requires a heart-lung machine to assume the patient's heart and lung functions during surgery.

The procedures are located in the CPT manual index under the valve type or under what was done, such as repair or replacement. For example, the replacement of an aortic valve is located in the CPT index under "Aorta," subterm "Valve," subterm "Replacement."

EXERCISE Z *Cardiac Valves*

Label the cardiac valves in Diagram 3–3.

Code the following:

1. Mary Black's echocardiogram and cardiac catheterization show severe mitral stenosis with regurgitation. Her physician believes that because she is symptomatic, she should have her mitral valve replaced. The mitral valve replacement includes cardiopulmonary bypass.

   Code(s): ____________________

2. Andrew Nelson has a loud heart murmur and, after study, is found to have severe aortic stenosis. He elects to have an aortic valve replacement. He is taken to the operating room and placed on a heart-lung machine. He then has his aortic valve replaced with a prosthetic valve.

   Code(s): ____________________

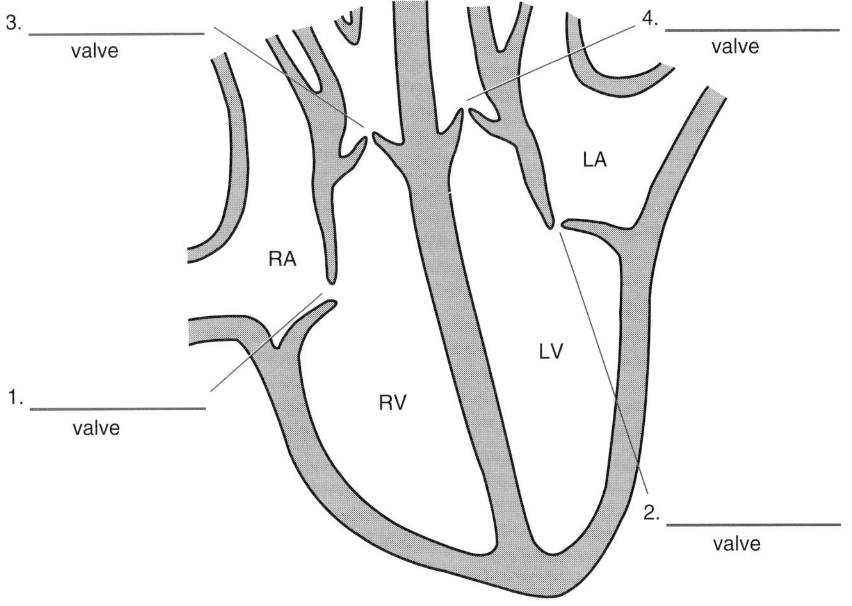

Diagram 3–3
Cardiovascular valves.

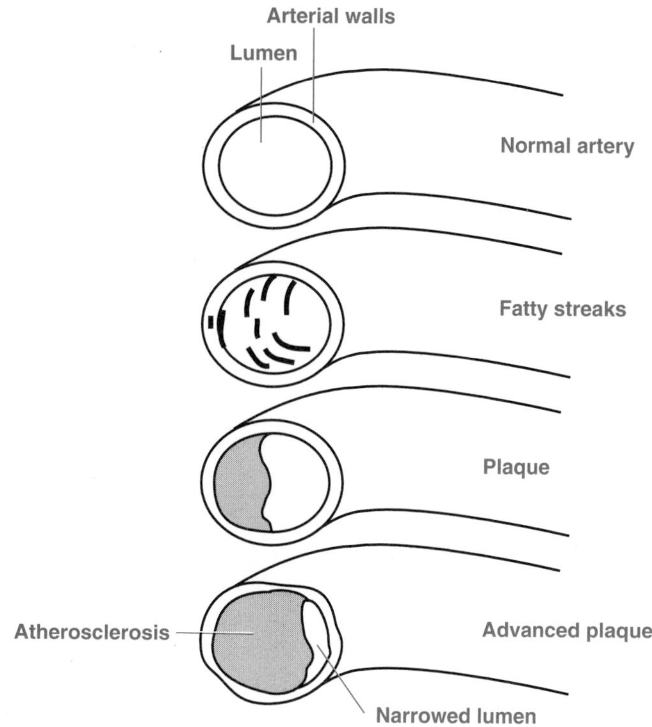

Figure 3–37
Atherosclerosis.

Coronary Artery Bypass

Arteries deliver oxygenated blood to all areas of the body, and veins return blood full of waste products. The pulmonary vessels, however, are not included in this cycle. The pulmonary vein carries oxygenated blood and the pulmonary artery carries waste products. The heart muscle is fed by coronary arteries that encircle the heart. When these arteries clog with plaque (known as arteriosclerotic coronary artery disease) (Fig. 3–37), the flow of blood lessens. Sometimes the arteries

Figure 3–38
Coronary artery bypass.

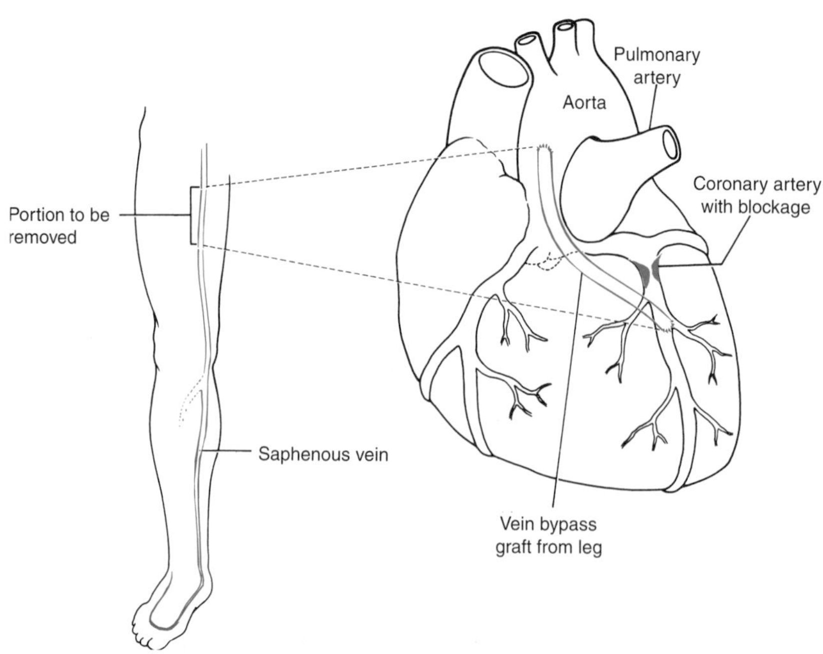

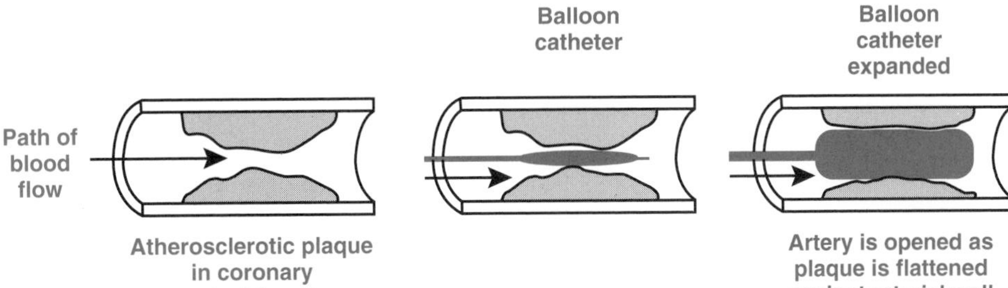

Figure 3–39 Percutaneous transluminal coronary angioplasty.

clog to the point that the heart muscle begins to perform at low levels due to lack of blood (*reversible ischemia*) or to actually die (*irreversible ischemia*). Reversible ischemia means that if the blood flow is increased to the heart muscle, the heart muscle may again begin to function at normal or near-normal levels. Coronary artery bypass grafting is one way to increase the flow of blood. The diseased portion of the artery is "bypassed" by attaching a healthy vessel above and below the diseased area and allowing the healthy vessel to then become the conduit of the blood, thus bypassing the blockage (Fig. 3–38). Blockage can also be pushed to the side of the coronary arterial walls by a procedure in which a balloon is expanded inside the artery. This procedure is known as a percutaneous transluminal coronary angioplasty (Fig. 3–39).

To correctly code coronary bypass grafts, you must know if an artery, vein, or both are being used as the bypass graft. You must also know how many bypass grafts are being done. There may be more than one blockage to be bypassed and, therefore, more than one graft. If only a vein is used for the graft (most often the saphenous vein from the leg is harvested and used for this purpose; see Fig. 3–38), the code reflecting the number of grafts would be chosen from the category Venous Grafting Only for Coronary Artery Bypass.

The following exercise will help you learn the differences in coding bypass grafts using arteries, veins, or both.

EXERCISE AA Coronary Artery Bypass

Code the following:

1. Two coronary bypass grafts using veins only

   Code(s): ____________________

The code for Question 1 came from the category Venous Grafting Only for Coronary Artery Bypass because the bypass was accomplished using a venous graft. If the bypass was accomplished using an arterial graft, the codes in the category Arterial Grafting for Coronary Artery Bypass would be used to report the service. If both veins and arteries were used to accomplish the bypass, you would report the service by using an artery bypass code and a code from the category Combined Arterial-Venous Grafting for Coronary Bypass. Because the title of the category contains "arterial-venous," you might think that the codes in the category report both the artery and the vein; but this is not the case. The category codes for "arterial-venous" are only for venous grafts used in addition to the arterial grafts codes.

For example, a patient has had a five-vessel coronary artery bypass graft, for which two bypasses were accomplished using internal mammary arteries and three bypasses were accomplished using veins:

2. Coronary artery bypass using two arterial grafts

   Code(s): ________________

3. Coronary artery bypass using three venous grafts

   Code(s): ________________

Modifier -51 would not be used with the code for the venous grafts because a note preceding the code states "list separately **in addition to** *code for arterial graft." This means that the venous code is never used alone, but always follows an arterial code.*

Code groupings for arteries and veins vary according to procedures such as thrombectomies, aneurysm repair, bypass grafting, repair, angioplasties, arthrectomies, and all other procedures. A good vascular book will be an invaluable tool to you as you begin coding in the cardiovascular subsection and as you begin your career as a coder.

Thrombectomy/Embolectomy

An *embolus* is a mass of undissolved matter present in blood that is transported by the blood current. A *thrombus* is a blood clot that occludes or shuts off a vessel. When a thrombus is dislodged, it becomes an embolus. Thrombectomies or embolectomies are performed to remove the unwanted debris or clot from the vessel and allow unrestricted blood flow. Thrombus or embolus may be removed by opening the vessel and scraping out the debris or by percutaneously placing a

Figure 3–40
Embolectomy.

balloon within the vessel to push the material to the sides and out of the vessel (see Fig. 3–39). A catheter may also be used to draw the thrombus or embolus out of the vessel, as illustrated in Figure 3–40. Embolectomy/Thrombectomy codes begin with 34001 and are divided based on the artery or vein in which the clot or thrombus is located (eg, radial artery, femoropopliteal vein) with site of incision for catheter specified (eg, arm, leg, abdominal incision). You can locate these codes in the CPT manual index under embolectomy or thrombectomy, subdivided by arteries and veins (eg, carotid artery, axillary vein).

When more involved procedures, such as grafts, are performed, inflow and outflow establishment is included in the major procedure codes. This means that if a thrombus is present and a bypass graft is performed, the removal of the thrombus is bundled into the grafting procedure if done on the same vessel. Also bundled into the aortic procedures is any sympathectomy (interruption of the sympathetic nervous system) or angiogram (radiographic view of the blood vessels).

EXERCISE BB *Thrombectomy/Embolectomy*

Code the following:

1. Thrombectomy of the femoropopliteal aortoiliac artery, by leg incision

   Code(s): ________________

2. Embolectomy, carotid artery, by neck incision

   Code(s): ________________

3. Thrombectomy of venous bypass graft

   Code(s): ________________

Cardiovascular Repairs

The category of Venous Reconstruction contains codes for the various repairs made to the valves of the heart, vena cava, and saphenous vein. The *valve repairs* are done by opening the site and clamping off the vessels that lead to the valve. The surgeon then tacks down excess material of the valve with sutures (plication). If there is a defect in the valve, the surgeon will repair the defect with a graft, usually harvested from elsewhere in the body. *Vein repairs* are done by locating the defective vessel, clamping the vessel off, and bypassing or grafting the defect.

The category Direct Repair of Aneurysm or Excision (Partial or Total) and Graft Insertion for Aneurysm, False Aneurysm, Ruptured Aneurysm, and Associated Occlusive Disease contains *aneurysm repair* codes that are divided by the type of aneurysm (eg, false, ruptured) and the vessel the aneurysm is located in (subclavian artery, popliteal artery). The aneurysm, which is a sac of clotted blood, is located and clamps are placed above and below the aneurysm. The section containing the aneurysm is then removed or bypassed. The aneurysm codes often refer to a *false aneurysm,* which is an aneurysm in which the vessel is completely destroyed and the aneurysm is being contained by the tissue that surrounded the vessel.

Repair, Arteriovenous Fistula category codes are for *fistula repair* and are divided based on if the fistula (abnormal passage) is congenital or if it is acquired or traumatic. An arteriovenous fistula is when blood flows between an artery and a vein. An example of an acquired arteriovenous fistula is the creation of an

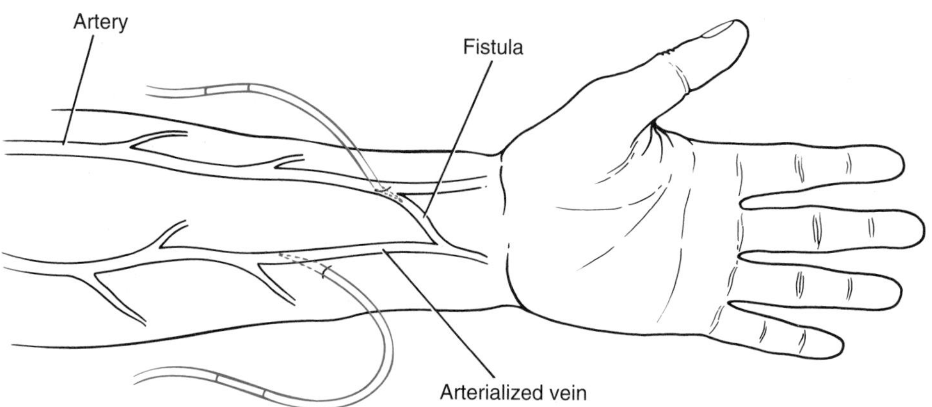

Figure 3–41
Hemodialysis.

arteriovenous connect that is used for a hemodialysis site (Fig. 3–41). The repair of a fistula involves the surgeon separating the artery and vein and then patching the area of separation either with sutures or a graft.

If an *angioscopy* is done of the vessel or graft area during a therapeutic procedure, code 35400 is listed in addition to the procedure code. For example, suppose the surgeon performed the repair of an arteriovenous fistula (of the neck, 35188) and then placed a scope into the artery to visually determine if the repair was complete. Code 35188 would describe the primary therapeutic procedure of repair of the arteriovenous fistula and code 35400 would describe the angioscopy. Note that 35400 is an add-on code and cannot be used alone, but only in conjunction with a therapeutic procedure code.

A *transluminal angioplasty* is when a vessel is punctured and a catheter is passed into the vessel for the purposes of stretching the vessel. The category codes are divided based on the catheter being passed into the vessel by incising the skin to expose the vessel (open) or by passing the catheter through the skin (percutaneous) into the vessel. Further divisions of the codes are based on the vessel into which the catheter is placed (eg, iliac, aortic).

A *transluminal atherectomy* is when the vessel is punctured and a guidewire is threaded into the vessel. The surgeon then inserts a device called an atherectomy catheter into the vessel containing a device that can destroy the materials clogging the vessel. This procedure can be done either by an open or percutaneous method and the codes are divided based on the method and the vessel into which the catheter is passed.

Bypass Grafts, Veins

As with coronary artery bypass grafting, you must know the type of grafting material being used for vascular bypass grafts. Grafts can use vessels harvested from other areas of the body or may be made from artificial material. Codes are chosen by the type of graft and the specific vessel(s) that the graft is being bypassed from and to. For example, code 35506 describes a graft that is placed to bypass a portion of the subclavian artery. During this procedure the surgeon would sew a harvested vein to the side of the carotid artery and attach the other end of the vein to the subclavian artery below the damaged area, creating a bypass around the defect.

One way to locate the graft codes in the CPT manual index is under "Bypass Graft" and then under the subterm type (eg, carotid, subclavian, vertebral).

Vascular Families

A vascular family can be compared to a tree with branches. The tree has a main trunk from which large branches and then smaller branches grow. The same is true with vascular families. A main vessel is present, and then other vessels branch off from the main vessel. Vessels that are connected in this manner are considered families. Catheters may have to be placed in vessels for monitoring, removal of blood, injection of contrast material, or infusion. It is necessary to know the vessel into which the catheter is being placed and the reason for its placement. Some codes vary according to the type of catheter (eg, central venous lines, or whether the catheter is placed selectively or nonselectively). A *nonselective catheter placement* means the catheter or needle is placed directly into an artery or vein (and not manipulated farther) or is placed only into the aorta from any approach. *Selective catheter placement* means the catheter must be moved, manipulated, or guided into a part of the arterial system other than the aorta or the vessel punctured (into the branches), generally under fluoroscopic guidance. Codes also vary based on the vascular family into which the catheter is placed.

Some treatments are given through the blood by means of vascular access. For instance, patients receiving hemodialysis may have arteriovenous fistulas created for dialysis treatments (see Fig. 3–41). This means that an artificial connection is made between a vein and an artery, allowing blood to flow from the vein through the graft for dialysis (cleansing of waste products) and then returned to the artery.

EXERCISE CC Graft Codes

Code the following:

1. Bypass graft, with vein; carotid-subclavian

   Code(s): ____________________

2. Bypass graft, with vein; femoral-popliteal

   Code(s): ____________________

3. Bypass graft, using Gore-Tex; axillary-axillary

   Code(s): ____________________

4. Excision of and application of a patch graft for an aneurysm, common femoral artery

   Code(s): ____________________

5. Venous bypass graft for occlusive disease, femoral-popliteal

   Code(s): ____________________

6. The patient has a diagnosis of end-stage renal disease and requires an arteriovenous fistula (shunt) using Gore-Tex graft for hemodialysis.

   Code(s): ____________________

7. The patient in Question 6 continued to have occlusions of the shunt and of the fistula, and a revision with thrombectomy was necessary.

   Code(s): ____________________

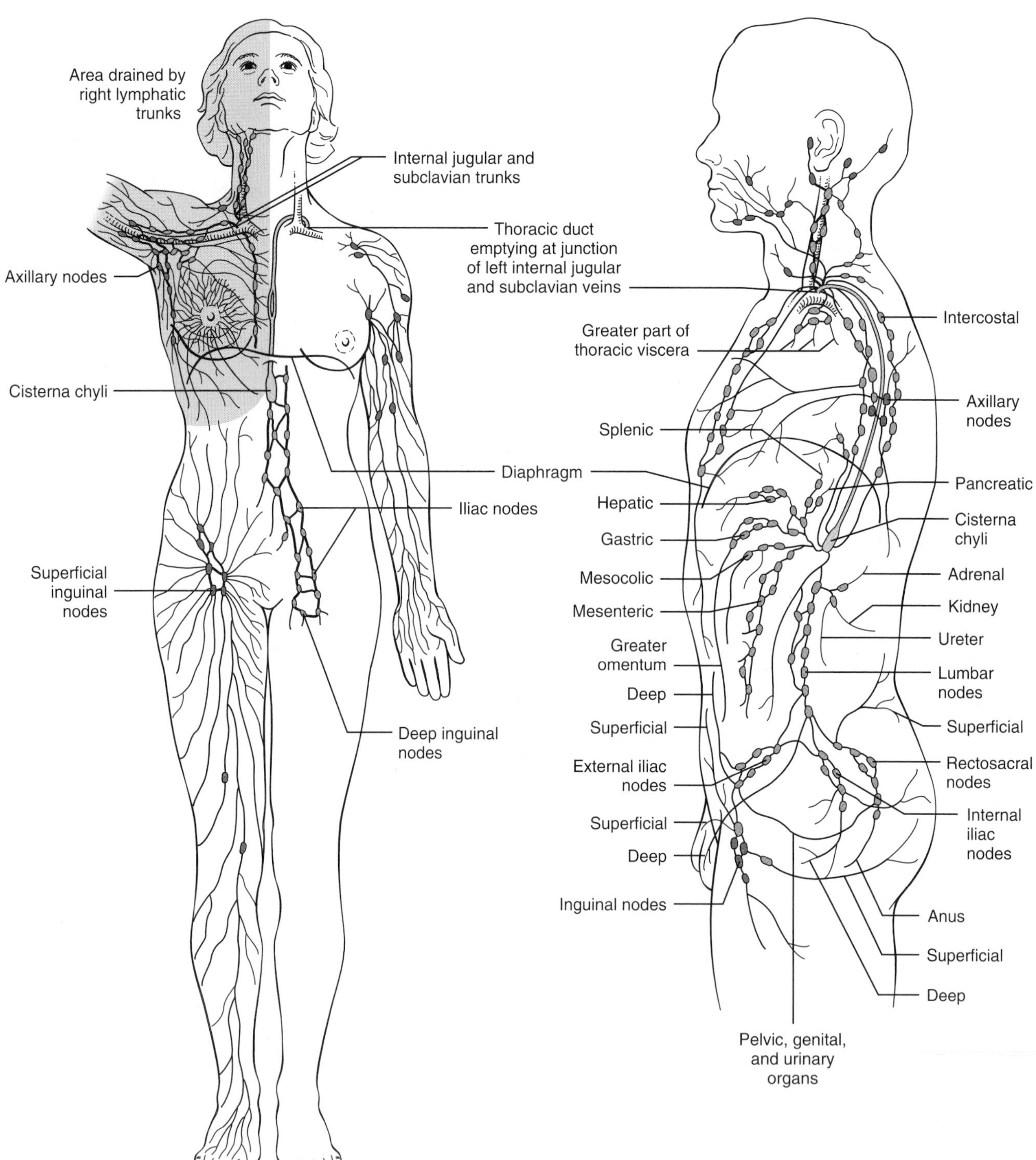

Figure 3–42
Lymphatic system.

HEMIC AND LYMPHATIC SYSTEMS

Format

The format of the Hemic and Lymphatic Systems subsection is divided by spleen, bone marrow, and lymph nodes/channels (Fig. 3–42). Further division is based on type of procedure (ie, excision, incision, repair). The codes for spleen, bone marrow, and lymph nodes are located in the CPT manual index under spleen, bone marrow, and so forth.

Terminology

EXERCISE DD *Hemic and Lymphatic Terminology*

Match the following terms to the correct definitions:

1. axillary nodes _______
2. splenectomy _______
3. splenoportography _______
4. allogenic _______
5. autologous, autogenous _______
6. aspiration _______
7. stem cell _______
8. transplantation _______
9. lymph node _______
10. lymphadenitis _______
11. lymphangiotomy _______
12. thoracic duct _______
13. lymphadenectomy _______
14. retroperitoneal _______
15. jugular nodes _______
16. cystic hygroma _______
17. Cloquet's node _______

a. behind the sac holding the abdominal organs and viscera (peritoneum)
b. grafting of tissue from one source to another
c. excision of the spleen
d. immature blood cells
e. incision into a lymphatic vessel
f. insertion of a tube into a duct or cavity
g. lymph nodes located next to the large vein in the neck
h. radiographic procedure to allow visualization of the splenic and portal veins of the spleen
i. of the same species, but genetically different
j. inflammation of a lymph node
k. collection and distribution point for lymph, and the largest lymph vessel located in the chest
l. excision of a lymph node (or nodes)
m. from one's self
n. congenital deformity of benign tumor of the lymphatic system
o. also called a gland; it is the highest of the deep groin lymph nodes
p. use of a needle and syringe to withdraw fluid
q. station along the lymphatic system
r. term that refers to the groin and thigh

18. inguinofemoral _______
19. cannulation _______
20. abscess _______

s. lymph nodes located in the armpit
t. localization of pus

Hemic and Lymphatic Coding Highlights

Spleen

The spleen is composed of lymph tissue and is located in the left upper quadrant of the abdomen. The spleen is easily ruptured and can cause massive hemorrhage. A splenectomy is the surgical removal of the spleen; removal can be partial or total. You can live with your spleen removed because the bone marrow, liver, and lymph nodes take over the work of the spleen after a total splenectomy.

Codes in the subheading Spleen are further divided into three categories for excision, repair, and introduction. Codes in the Excision category are based on the type of splenectomy: total, partial, or total with extensive disease. The splenectomy, total and partial, has the designation "(separate procedure)" behind the code description. This means that if the splenectomy is an integral part of another procedure, it is bundled into the main procedure code and not reported separately. For example, if a repair of a ruptured spleen was performed and the surgeon removed a portion of the spleen as a part of the repair, you would report only the repair code (38115).

Bone Marrow

Bone marrow is the inner core of bones that manufactures most blood cells. Immature blood cells, called stem cells, originate in the marrow of bones. Leukemia is a malignant disease of the bone marrow in which excessive white blood cells are produced. Treatment often includes total-body irradiation or aggressive chemotherapy followed by transplantation of normal bone marrow. The bone marrow is harvested by aspiration. The immature stem cells are obtained through withdrawing of blood in which the immature, stem cells reside.

Allogenic bone marrow is from a close relative, so there is a genetic similarity. Autologous bone marrow is collected from the patient and later transplanted or reinfused.

Note that there are harvesting codes for collection of bone marrow from the donor as well as codes for transplantation of bone marrow into the recipient.

Lymph Nodes

The lymphatic system is a transportation system to take fluids, proteins, and fats through the lymphatic channels back to the bloodstream. Stations along the lymphatic system are called lymph nodes. The nodes fight disease when lymphocytes from the nodes produce antibodies. The subheading on the lymph nodes is divided by the various procedures (ie, incision, excision, resection, and introduction).

Within the Lymph Node and Lymphatic Channels subheading are two categories of codes for lymphadenectomies based on whether the lymphadenectomy is limited or radical. A *limited lymphadenectomy* is the removal of the lymph nodes only; a *radical lymphadenectomy* is the removal of the lymph nodes, submandibular gland, and surrounding tissue. Sometimes, a limited lymphadenectomy will be bundled into a larger procedure, such as prostatectomy. If this is the case, you would not report the lymphadenectomy separately. Rather, you would report only the main procedure, such as the prostatectomy code from the Male Genital System subsection of the Surgery section.

EXERCISE EE Hemic and Lymphatic Systems

Code the following:

1. Excision of an axillary cystic hygroma, which the patient record indicates involved no deep neurovascular dissection

   Code(s): ____________________

2. Total removal of the spleen

   Code(s): ____________________

3. Injection procedure for a radiographic view of the portal vein of the spleen

   Code(s): ____________________

4. Injection procedure for a radiographic view of the lymphatic system

   Code(s): ____________________

5. Radical cervical lymphadenectomy

   Code(s): ____________________

6. Incision and drainage of a simple lymph node abscess

   Code(s): ____________________

7. Harvesting of bone marrow from a donor

   Code(s): ____________________

MEDIASTINUM AND DIAPHRAGM

Format

The mediastinum is the area between the lungs (Fig. 3–43). The Mediastinum subsection of the CPT manual is divided by procedures and includes incision, excision, and endoscopy. The difference between the mediastinum incision codes is the surgical approach. The approach can be either cervical (neck area) or across the thoracic area (transthoracic) or sternum. The excision codes vary based on whether a cyst or tumor was excised. Codes for the mediastinum procedures are usually located in the CPT manual index under "Mediastinum."

The diaphragm is the wall of muscle that separates the thoracic and abdominal cavities. The codes in the diaphragm subsection are repair codes. Repairs are usually to a hernia or laceration. Diaphragm codes are usually located in the CPT manual index under "Diaphragm."

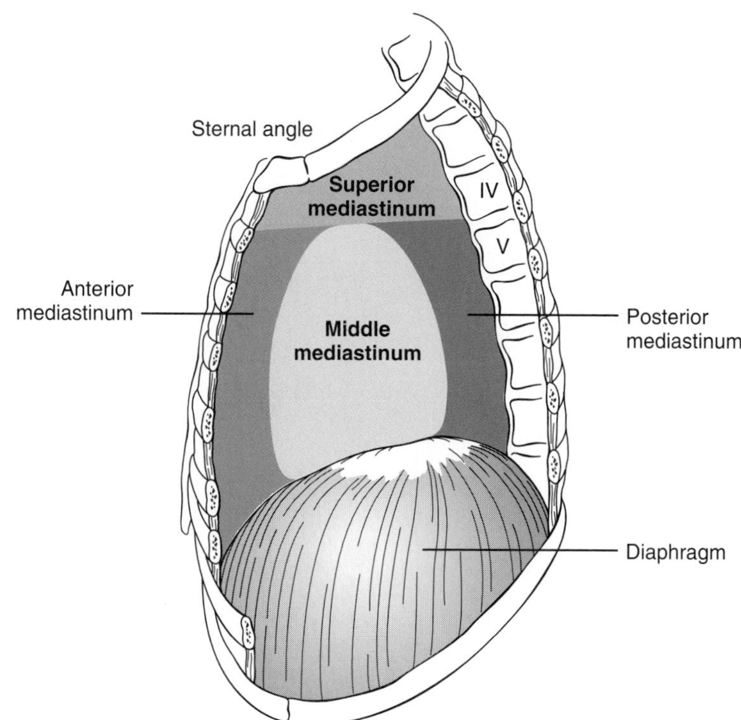

Figure 3–43
Mediastinum and diaphragm.

Terminology

EXERCISE FF *Mediastinum and Diaphragm Terminology*

Match the following terms to the correct definitions:

1. mediastinum _______
2. diaphragm _______
3. mediastinotomy _______
4. fundoplasty _______
5. pyloroplasty _______
6. diaphragmatic hernia _______
7. mediastinoscopy _______
8. imbrication _______
9. transthoracic _______
10. transabdominal _______
11. paraesophageal hiatus hernia _______

a. overlapping
b. surgical separation of the vagus nerve
c. muscular wall that separates the thoracic and abdominal cavities
d. incision and repair of the pyloric channel
e. operation on the stomach for repair or reconfiguration
f. repair of the bottom on an organ or muscle
g. hernia that is near the esophagus
h. hernia of the diaphragm
i. across the abdomen
j. cutting into the mediastinum
k. across the thorax
l. use of an endoscope inserted through a small incision to view the mediastinum

12. gastroplasty _______	m. that area between the lungs that contains the heart, aorta, trachea, lymph nodes, thymus gland, esophagus, and bronchial tubes
13. vagotomy _______	

Mediastinum and Diaphragm Coding Highlights

Mediastinum

The mediastinum incision category of codes is based on the approach for the mediastinotomy. A cervical or anterior mediastinotomy is a surgical procedure in which an incision is made in the lower portion of the front of the neck for exploration, drainage, biopsy, or removal of a foreign body. Codes for removal of a foreign body are located in the Incision category. You would think removal of a foreign body would be in the Excision codes; but the Excision codes are only for cysts or tumors. The codes for Excision also use a surgical approach in which the surgeon makes the operative incision just below the nipple line, pulls back the rib cage, retracts the muscles, and has exposure of the thoracic cavity. The cyst or tumor is removed and the incision closed.

Diaphragm

Other than one code for unlisted diaphragm procedures, all diaphragm codes are for repair of the diaphragm. The repairs are for lacerations or hernias, with one code for imbrication of the diaphragm. An imbrication of the diaphragm may be performed for eventration, which is when the diaphragm moves up, usually because of the paralysis of the diaphragmatic nerve (phrenic nerve). In this case the surgeon sutures the diaphragm back into place.

EXERCISE GG *Mediastinum and Diaphragm*

Code the following:

1. Paraesophageal repair of hiatus hernia, abdominal approach with limited fundoplasty

   Code(s): ____________________

2. Exploratory mediastinotomy with biopsy accomplished with approach through the neck

   Code(s): ____________________

3. Excision of benign tumor of the mediastinum

   Code(s): ____________________

4. Repair of an esophageal hiatal hernia accomplished with approach across the thoracic area

   Code(s): ____________________

DIGESTIVE SYSTEM

Format

The format of the Digestive System subsection is divided by anatomic site (Fig. 3–44) and procedure. Included in this subsection are codes for sites beginning with the mouth and ending with the anus. Also included are those internal organs that aid in the digestive process, including the pancreas, liver, and gallbladder. This subsection includes codes for abdomen, peritoneum, omentum, and all types of hernias. Endoscopic codes can be found throughout the subsection depending on the anatomic site at which they are performed.

Separate procedures are common in this subsection. Procedures such as gastrostomies and colostomies are always bundled into the major procedure unless the code specifically states to code separately. For example, code 44141 is a colectomy (removal of part or all of the colon) with colostomy (creation of an artificial opening). Included in the description for 44141 is the establishment of the colostomy; thus, it would not be correct to report 44320, which is a separate code for the establishment of a colostomy. However, if only a colostomy was developed, it would be appropriate to code it 44320.

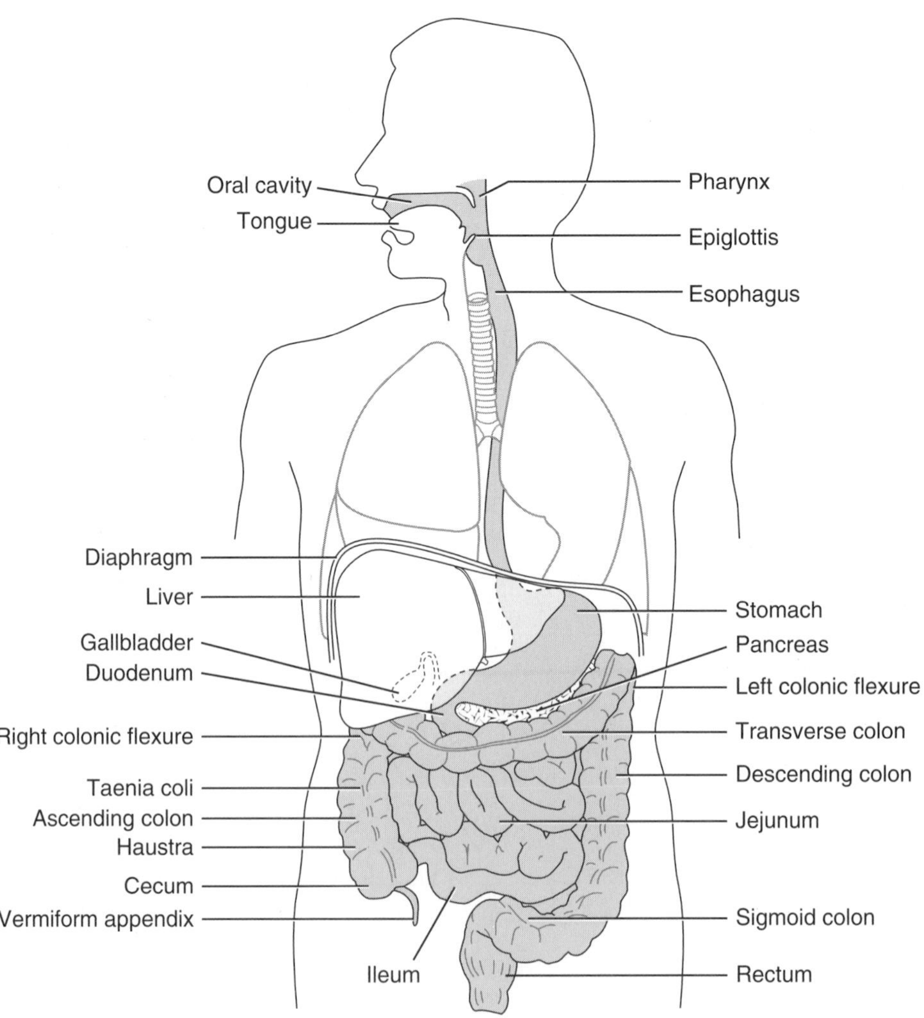

Figure 3–44
Digestive system.

Terminology

EXERCISE HH Digestive Terminology

Match the following terms to the correct definitions:

1. gloss- _______
2. gastro- _______
3. anastomosis _______
4. hernia _______
5. gastrointestinal _______
6. ostomy _______
7. colostomy _______
8. ileostomy _______
9. jejunostomy _______
10. gastrostomy _______
11. proctosigmoid-oscopy _______
12. sigmoidoscopy _______
13. colonoscopy _______
14. cholangi-ography _______
15. chole- _______
16. hepat- _______
17. incarcerated _______
18. reducible _______

a. regarding hernias, a constricted, irreducible hernia that may cause obstruction of an intestine

b. artificial opening between the colon and the abdominal wall

c. prefix meaning tongue

d. artificial opening between the stomach and the abdominal wall

e. radiographic recording of the bile ducts

f. able to be corrected or put back into a normal position

g. organ or tissue protruding through the wall or cavity that usually contains it

h. prefix meaning stomach

i. artificial opening between the ileum and the abdominal wall

j. partial excision of an organ or structure

k. fiberscopic examination of the entire colon that may include part of the terminal ileum

l. prefix meaning liver

m. surgical connection of two tubular structures, such as two pieces of the intestine

n. pertaining to the stomach and intestine

o. fiberscopic examination of the entire rectum and sigmoid colon that may include a portion of the descending colon

p. artificial opening

q. artificial opening between the jejunum and the abdominal wall

r. prefix meaning bile

s. fiberscopic examination of the sigmoid colon and rectum

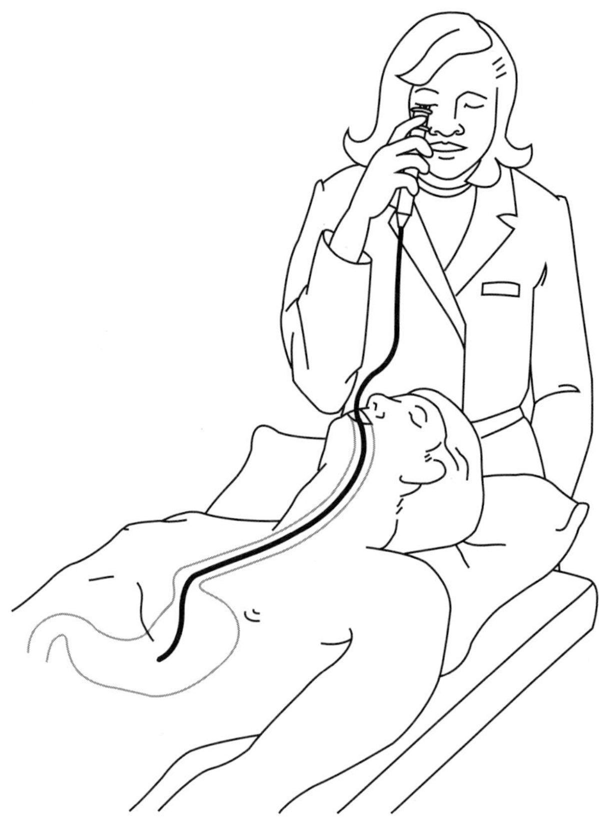

Figure 3–45
Endoscopy.

Digestive Coding Highlights

Endoscopic Procedures

Many procedures are done through endoscopes (such as the gastroscopy in Fig. 3–45). Endoscope codes are available for procedures throughout the digestive system depending on how far down (through the mouth) or up (through the anus) the scope is passed. The code selection varies according to the procedure(s) performed and includes the sites the scope passed through to accomplish the procedure. To choose the proper code, the *extent* of the procedure must be determined. For example, if a scope is passed to the esophagus only, the code would be chosen from the endoscopy codes beginning with 43200. If the scoping process is continued through the esophagus to the stomach, duodenum, and/or jejunum, the code selection would be from the endoscopy codes, such as 43239, which specify the extent of the scopy was to the duodenum or jejunum. Once the anatomic site of the endoscope procedure is correctly identified, the surgical procedure(s) performed would be listed. A surgical endoscopy always includes a diagnostic endoscopy, so don't unbundle and code for both. Remember to use modifier -51 if more than one procedure is performed.

EXERCISE 11 *Endoscopic Procedures*

Code the following:

1. Esophagogastroduodenoscopy with biopsy and control of bleeding

   Code(s): ____________________

2. Flexible sigmoidoscopy with three biopsies

   Code(s): ____________________

3. Colonoscopy with removal of polyp by a snare

   Code(s): ____________________

Resections

Resection of the intestine means taking out a diseased portion of the intestine and either joining the remaining ends (anastomosis) directly or developing an artificial opening (exteriorizing) through the abdominal wall. Figure 3–46 illustrates three types of anastomoses. The artificial opening (stoma) allows for the removal of body waste products (Fig. 3–47) as with the colostomy. The type of anastomosis or exteriorization depends on the medical condition of the patient and on the amount of intestine (large or small) that needs to be removed. Some patients have temporary exteriorization for the length of time it takes the remaining small or large intestine to heal itself to perform necessary functions. Other patients will have permanent exteriorization because too much of the intestine has been removed to allow for adequate functioning. Openings to the outside of the body are named for the part of the intestine from which they are formed—colostomy is an artificial opening from the colon, ileostomy from the ileum, gastrostomy from the stomach, and so forth (Fig. 3–48). Therefore, it is critical that you identify the correct anatomic site from which the ostomy originated as well as the procedure used to establish the ostomy.

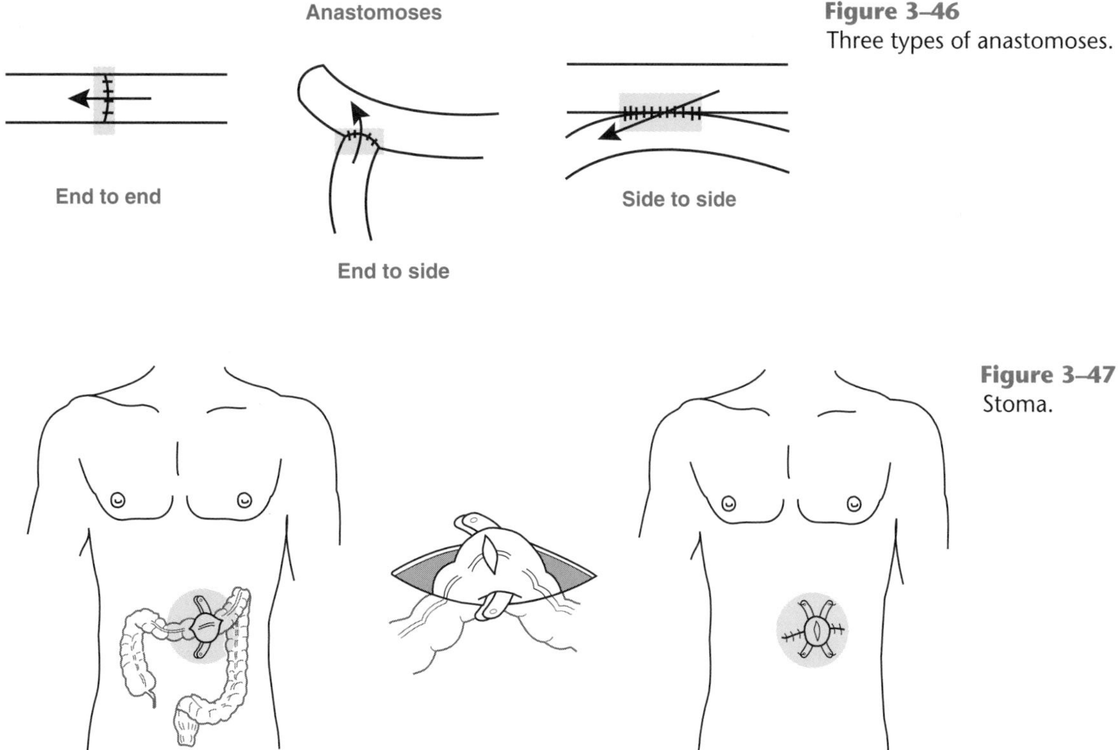

Figure 3–46 Three types of anastomoses.

Figure 3–47 Stoma.

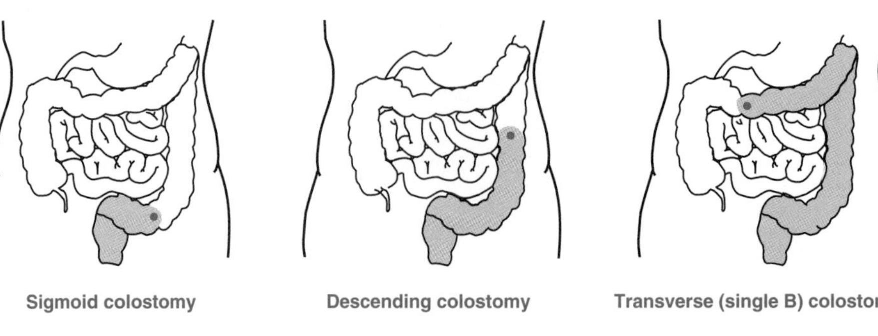

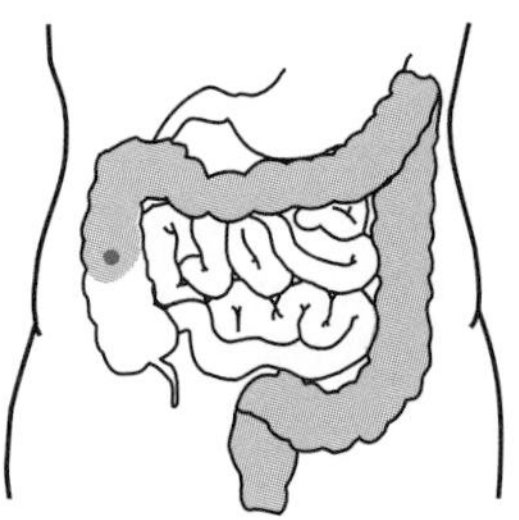
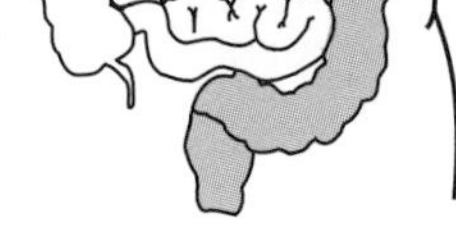

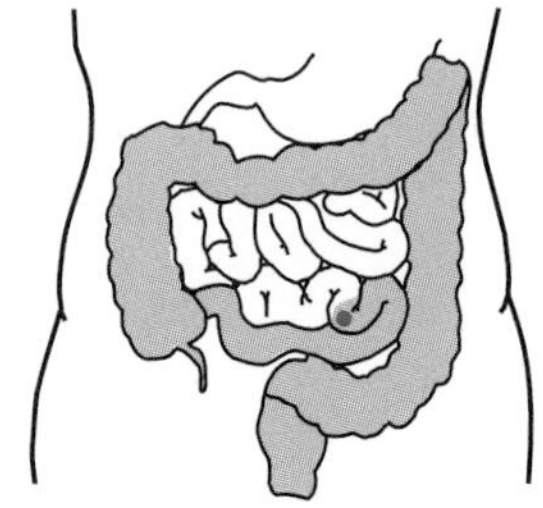

Figure 3–48
Various ostomies.

EXERCISE JJ Resections

Using your knowledge of medical terminology, identify what the following procedures surgically accomplish:

1. coloproctostomy ______________________________

____

2. ileostomy ______________________________

____

3. colostomy ______________________________

4. enteroenterostomy ______________________________

____

Code the following:

5. Partial bowel resection with colostomy

   Code(s): ______________

6. Resection of small intestine, single resection, with anastomosis

   Code(s): ______________

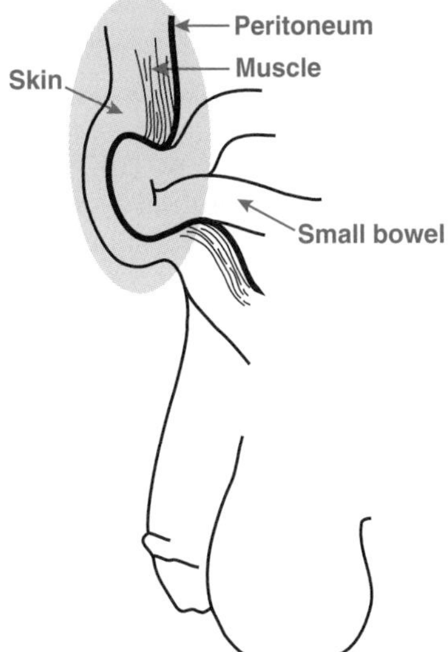

Figure 3–49
Hernia.

Laparotomy

A laparotomy is a surgical opening into the abdomen. Sometimes, a laparotomy is used as an approach in digestive system surgery. When it is used as an approach, a laparotomy is never coded separately. An exploratory laparotomy may be done to investigate the cause of a patient's illness. If only the exploratory laparotomy is performed, it is appropriate to report it with an exploratory laparotomy code, such as 49002. However, if the exploratory procedure progresses to a more definitive surgical treatment (such as an appendectomy), only the definitive treatment (appendectomy) is reported.

Hernia

Hernia codes are listed by type of hernia. Figure 3–49 is an illustration of an inguinal hernia that would be surgically repaired by a herniorrhaphy. The defect would be closed with sutures. Other factors in coding hernias are whether the hernia is *strangulated* (the blood supply is cut off) or *incarcerated* (can't be returned to the abdominal cavity); if the repair is an initial or subsequent repair; if the hernia is reducible (can be returned to the abdominal cavity); and the age of the patient. The hernia codes are located in the index under the main term "Hernia."

EXERCISE KK ***Miscellaneous Digestive Coding***

Code the following:

1. Exploratory laparotomy with cholecystectomy

   Code(s): ____________________

2. Cholecystotomy with exploration and removal of calculus

   Code(s): ________________

3. Repair of recurrent reducible incisional hernia, with implantation of a mesh graft, abdominal approach

   Code(s): ________________

4. Repair of an initial incarcerated inguinal hernia in a 5½-year-old

   Code(s): ________________

5. Biopsy of lip

   Code(s): ________________

6. Palate, abscess drainage

   Code(s): ________________

7. Dilation of salivary duct

   Code(s): ________________

8. Direct ligation of esophageal varices

   Code(s): ________________

9. Duodenotomy with biopsy

   Code(s): ________________

10. Colostomy formation

    Code(s): ________________

URINARY SYSTEM

Format

The Urinary System subsection of the CPT manual is arranged anatomically by the subheadings of kidney, ureter, bladder, and urethra, with category codes arranged by procedure (ie, incision, excision, introduction, repair). A wide range of terminology is used in the subsection because of the four major subheadings of the urinary system, and each subheading has its own terminology (Fig. 3–50). The Glossary in this chapter has many of the terms that you will encounter in the CPT manual. Always be certain you know the meaning of all the words in the code description before you assign a code.

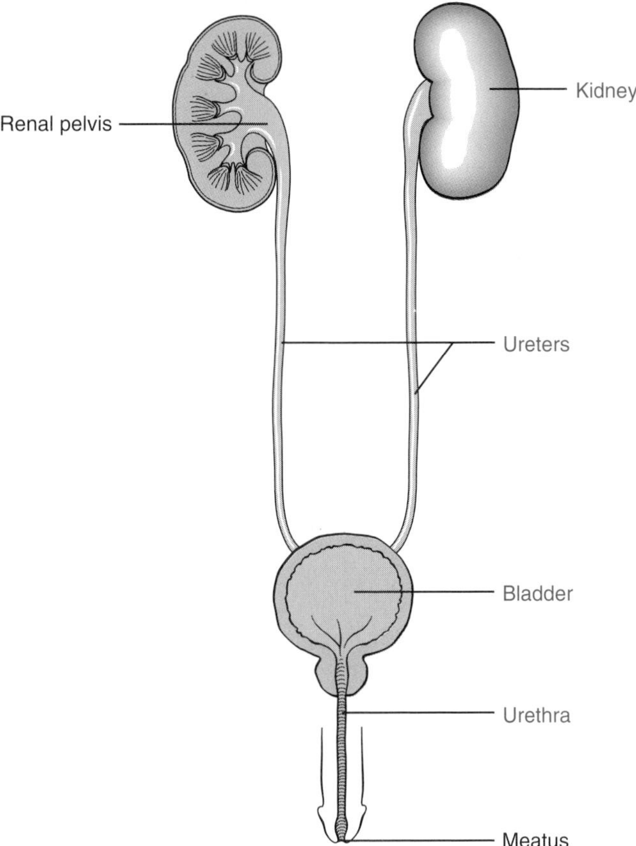

Figure 3–50
The four subheadings of the Urinary System subsection in the CPT manual are: Kidney, Ureters, Bladder, and Urethra.

Terminology

EXERCISE LL *Urinary System Terminology*

Match the following terms to the correct definitions:

1. calculus/calculi _______
2. cystolithectomy _______
3. cystometrogram (CMG) _______
4. endopyelotomy _______
5. exstrophy _______
6. nephrectomy, paraperitoneal _______
7. fulguration _______
8. Kock pouch _______
9. lithotripsy _______

a. procedure of the bladder and ureters with insertion of a stent
b. kidney transplant
c. crushing of a gallbladder or urinary bladder stone followed by irrigation to wash the fragment out
d. prefix meaning renal pelvis
e. concretion of mineral salts, also called a stone
f. removal of a stone from the ureter
g. surgical connection of one ureter to the other ureter
h. surgical creation of a temporary diversion around the ureter
i. surgical creation of a urinary bladder from a segment of the ileum

10. marsupialization _______
11. nephro- _______
12. nephrostomy _______
13. perivesical _______
14. perirenal _______
15. pyelo- _______
16. pyeloplasty _______
17. pyelostomy _______
18. renal pelvis _______
19. retroperitoneal _______
20. transuretero-ureterostomy _______
21. uretero-lithotomy _______
22. ureterotomy _______
23. urethro-cystography _______
24. urethrorrhaphy _______

j. condition in which an organ is turned inside out
k. measurement of the pressures and capacity of the urinary bladder
l. suturing of the urethra
m. behind the sac holding the abdominal organs and viscera (peritoneum)
n. around the kidney
o. creation of a channel into the renal pelvis of the kidney
p. surgical procedure that creates an exterior pouch from an internal abscess
q. radiography of the bladder and urethra
r. removal of a calculus from the urinary bladder
s. use of electrical current to destroy tissue
t. around the bladder
u. kidney
v. funnel-shaped sac in the kidney where urine is received
w. surgical reconstruction of the renal pelvis
x. incision into the ureter

Urinary Coding Highlights

Kidney

The first subheading in the Urinary subsection is Kidney, which contains the category Endoscopy. The endoscopy codes identify procedures (ie, biopsy, removal, insertion, repair) for the patient who already has an established stoma. The procedure to create the stoma is the nephrostomy. The stoma is created by placing a catheter through the skin and into the kidney (percutaneous nephrostomy, 50395). Once a stoma has been created, the endoscopy codes can be used to indicate procedures performed using the stoma as the entry point. When coding procedures, you must identify the entry method before choosing the correct code. For example, a kidney stone (calculus) can be removed by endoscopy through a stoma or surgically by opening the kidney to view and subsequently to remove the stone. The codes for removal of calculus would be:

skin incision	50060 (nephrolithotomy)
stoma	50561 (renal endoscopy)

There are Excision codes for biopsy, nephrectomy (removal of the kidney), or removal of a cyst. The biopsy codes are based on the approach, either percutaneous (through the skin) or through surgical exposure of the kidney. The nephrectomy codes are based on complexity and extent of the procedure (ie, partial or total removal of the kidney, or the removal of surrounding tissues such as the bladder cuff in addition to partial or total removal of the kidney).

"Introduction" category codes in the Kidney subheading are for aspiration, catheters, injections for radiography, guides, and tube changes. There are extensive notes with the category codes, so you must be certain to read all notes when coding in this area.

"Repair" category codes include plastic surgery (pyeloplasty), suturing (nephrorrhaphy), and closure of fistula (created channels).

You will locate the kidney codes in the CPT manual index under "Kidney" and subtermed primarily by category (ie, insertion, excision, repair). Another location method in the CPT manual index for kidney codes is under the medical term for the procedure (eg, nephrostomy or nephrotomy). Again, there are other index location methods; these are just a couple to help you get started locating the codes.

Ureter

The next subheading in the Urinary system subsection is Ureter. The category codes are based on procedure (ie, incision, excision, introduction, repair, endoscopy). The endoscopy codes in this subheading are procedures conducted using an established stoma (ureterostomy). The procedures conducted through the ureterostomy are similar to the types of procedures conducted through the nephrostomy (ie, biopsy, catheterization, irrigation, instillation, etc). Excellent medical terminology skills are essential for working within this subheading because the words can be intimidating: transureteroureterostomy, ureteroneocystostomy, ureterosigmoidostomy. So be sure to spend adequate time on the terminology practice exercise for the Urinary system and keep your medical dictionary close by to look up any words you are not absolutely sure about. You can also refer to the Glossary at the end of this chapter or at the back of the book. The time you spend now increasing the depth and breadth of your medical terminology vocabulary is an excellent investment and will greatly increase your coding accuracy.

Bladder

The Bladder subheading is next and contains category codes not only for the usual procedures, such as incision and excision, but also for urodynamics. *Urodynamics* pertains to the motion and flow of urine. Urinary tract flow can be obstructed by renal calculi, narrowing (stricture) of the ureter, cysts, etc. The procedures in the subheading are to be conducted by or under the direct supervision of a physician, and all the instruments, equipment, supplies, and technical assistance necessary to conduct the procedure are bundled into the codes. If the physician conducts only a portion of the service (eg, interpretation of the results), modifier -26 (professional component) is used with the procedure code to identify that not all the services bundled into the code were provided by the physician. For example, if a physician provides only the interpretation (-26) of urethral pressure profile (UPP) (51772), you would report it as 51772-26.

In the Bladder subheading, there are category codes for bundled endoscopy procedures (ie, cystoscopy, urethroscopy, cystourethroscopy). The codes contain the primary procedure of a cystourethroscopy (endoscopic procedure to view the bladder and urethra) and minor related procedures or functions performed at the same time. For example, a cystourethroscopy was done for biopsy of the ureter with radiography. Bundled into the code for the procedure (52007) is the catheterization, endoscopic procedure, and biopsy(ies). To unbundle individual components of the procedure would not be correct. If the secondary procedure(s) required significant additional time or effort, the procedure can be identified using modifier -22 (unusual procedure).

Pelvis

Cystourethroscopy codes are found not only in the subheading Endoscopy but also in the subheading Ureter and Pelvis. The Ureter and Pelvis cystourethroscopy codes include the establishment of a stent or nephrostomy, or cystourethroscopy with ureteroscopy and/or pyeloscopy (fluoroscopic examination of the renal pelvis). The notes preceding these codes indicate when certain modifiers (-50, -51, -58) should be used.

Urethra

The subheading Urethra contains codes for the usual procedures of incision, excision, and repair. There is a category for Manipulation with codes that are a bit different from those you encountered in the Urinary system subsection. *Manipulation* is performed on the urethra (eg, dilatation or catheterization). *Dilatation* stretches or dilates a passage that has narrowed. The codes are based on initial or subsequent dilatation of male or female. The catheterization codes are for either a simple or complicated procedure.

Congratulations! You have finished the Urinary system subsection, and, as promised, the terminology was extensive. Now, you will have an opportunity to put all this great information to work by actually coding some procedures.

EXERCISE MM

Urinary System

Code the following:

1. Needle aspiration of bladder

   Code(s): ____________________

2. Endoscopy for establishment of a Gibbon ureteral stent

   Code(s): ____________________

3. Repeat nephrolithotomy

   Code(s): ____________________

4. Closure of a urethrostomy in a 54-year-old man

   Code(s): ____________________

5. Second stage, Johannsen type, surgical reconstruction of the urethra

   Code(s): ____________________

6. Cystourethroscopic biopsy (brush) with irrigation, radiography, and catheterization of ureter

   Code(s): ____________________

7. Endoscopy for renal biopsy through established stoma

   Code(s): ____________________

8. Introduction of catheter for drainage of renal pelvis

   Code(s): ____________________

9. Ureteroneocystostomy of single ureter

   Code(s): ____________________

10. Transurethral electrosurgical vasectomy, complete

    Code(s): ____________________

MALE GENITAL SYSTEM

Format

The Male Genital System subsection of the CPT manual is divided into anatomic subheadings (penis, testis, epididymis, tunica vaginalis, vas deferens, spermatic cord, seminal vesicles, and prostate) (Fig. 3–51). The category codes are divided by procedure. The greatest number of category codes fall under the penis

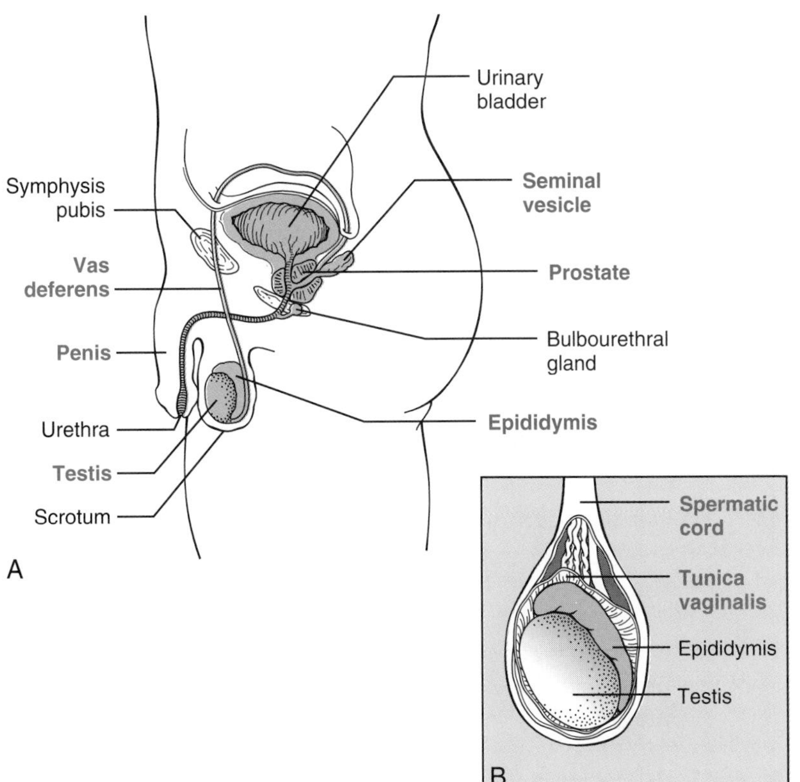

Figure 3–51
A. Male genital system.
B. Testis.

subheading because there are many repair codes in this subheading. The other subheadings are mainly for incision and excision, with only few repair codes for the remaining subheadings.

Terminology

EXERCISE NN Male Genital Terminology

Match the following terms to the correct definitions:

1. electro-desiccation _______
2. lymph-adenectomy _______
3. corpora cavernosa _______
4. epididymis _______
5. priapism _______
6. cavernos-ography _______
7. cavernos-ometry _______
8. plethys-mography _______
9. tumescence _______
10. chordee _______
11. urethroplasty _______
12. hypospadias _______
13. penoscrotal _______
14. cavernosa–saphenous vein shunt _______
15. cavernosa–corpus spongiosum shunt _______
16. cavernosa–glans penis fistuliza-tion _______
17. orchiectomy _______

a. tube that carries sperm from the epididymis to the urethra
b. swelling of a scrotal vein
c. creation of a connection between the cavity of the penis and a vein
d. castration
e. sac of fluid
f. recording of the flow in the vas deferens
g. surgical repair of the urethra
h. referring to the penis and scrotum
i. painful condition in which the penis is consistently erect
j. excision of a lymph node(s)
k. condition resulting in the penis being bent downward
l. cyst filled with spermatozoa
m. creation of a new connection between the vas deferens and epididymis
n. creation of an opening in the vas deferens
o. covering of the testes
p. incision into the seminal vesicle
q. gland that secretes fluid into the vas deferens
r. surgical removal of the epididymis
s. creation of a connection between a cavity of the penis and the urethra
t. creation of a connection between a cavity of the penis and the glans penis, which overlaps the penis cavity
u. reversal of a vasectomy
v. surgical procedure to release undescended testis
w. suturing of the vas deferens

18. orchiopexy _______
19. spermatocele _______
20. epididy-mectomy _______
21. epididymovas-ostomy _______
22. hydrocele _______
23. vasotomy _______
24. vasogram _______
25. vasovas-ostomy _______
26. vasovas-orrhaphy _______
27. varicocele _______
28. vesiculotomy _______
29. vesiculectomy _______
30. prostatotomy _______
31. vas deferens _______
32. seminal vesicle _______
33. tunica vaginalis _______

x. state of being swollen
y. excision of the seminal vesicle
z. determining the changes in volume of an organ part or body
aa. incision into the prostate
bb. destruction of a lesion by the use of electrical current radiated through a needle
cc. tube located on the top of the testes that stores sperm
dd. measurement of the pressure in a cavity, ie, penis
ee. two cavities of the penis
ff. radiographic measurement of a cavity, ie, the main part of the penis
gg. congenital deformity of the urethra in which the urethral opening is on the underside of the penis rather than the end

Male Genital Coding Highlights

Penis Incisions and Destruction

Under the Incision category of the subheading Penis, there is an incision and drainage code (54015). Recall that under the Integumentary System section there are incision and drainage codes. The code from the Penis subheadng is for a deep incision, not just an abscess of the skin. For the deep abscess described in 54015, the area is anesthetized, the abscess is opened and cleaned, and often a drain is placed to maintain adequate drainage. Under the Destruction category of the Penis subheading there are also destruction codes for lesions of the penis. These lesion destruction codes are divided based on whether the destruction is simple or extensive. The simple destruction is further divided based on the method of destruction (ie, chemical, cryosurgery, laser). The code for extensive lesion destruction can be used for any method.

EXERCISE 00 *Male Genital System*

Code the following:

1. Radical orchiectomy with insertion of prosthesis using scrotal approach

   Code(s): ____________________

2. Epididymis exploration without biopsy

   Code(s): ____________________

3. Aspiration of fluid sac on the testicular covering

   Code(s): ____________________

4. Extensive electrodesiccation of a condyloma on the penis

   Code(s): ____________________

5. Reversal of previously completed vasectomy

   Code(s): ____________________

INTERSEX SURGERY

The Intersex Surgery subsection is located after the Male Genital Surgery subsection and contains only two codes: one for a surgical procedure to change the sex organs of a male into a female and one for changing the sex organs of a female into a male. These procedures are very specialized and are performed by physicians who have special skills and training in the procedures.

The intersex surgeries include a series of procedures that take place over an extended period of time. The procedure for changing the male genitalia to female genitalia involves removing the penis, keeping the nerves and vessels intact. These tissues are used to form a clitoris and a vagina. The urethral opening is shifted to be in the position of a female.

The surgical procedure to change the female genitalia to male genitalia involves a series of procedures that uses the genitalia and surrounding skin to form a penis and testicle structures into which prosthetics are inserted.

LAPAROSCOPY

Format

Prior to the 2000 edition of the CPT manual, many endoscopic procedures were located in a separate subsection, Laparoscopy/Hysteroscopy, of the Surgery section. The codes in this subsection were used to report digestive, female/male genital, endocrine, and lymphatic endoscopic procedures. In the CPT 2000, the Laparoscopy/Hysteroscopy subsection was disbanded and the codes were placed in the subsection to which they referred. For example, all digestive endoscopic procedure codes are relocated into the Digestive System subsection of the Surgery section.

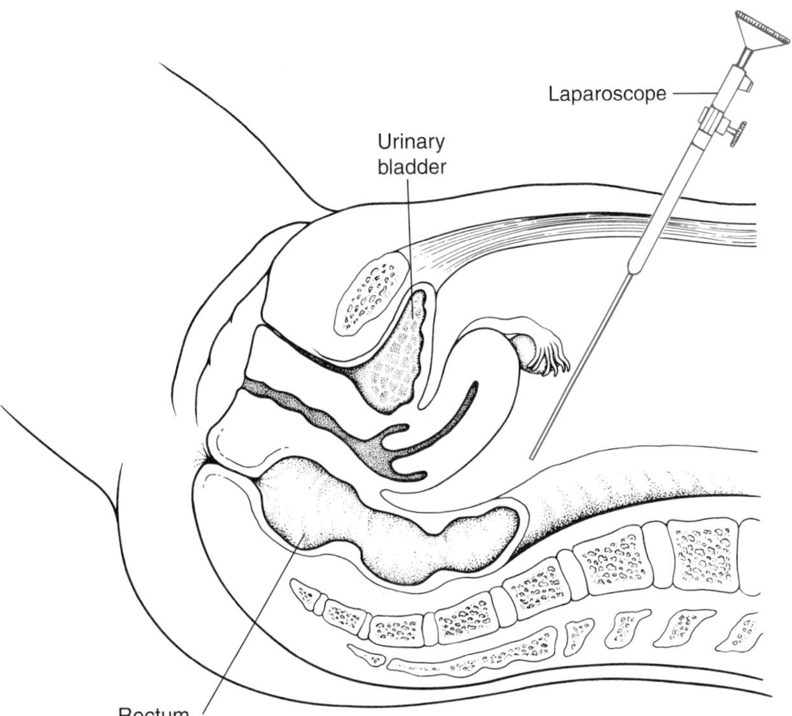

Figure 3–52
Laparoscopy.

More and more procedures are being performed through use of an endoscope, instead of opening the area to complete view with a large incision. With an endoscopic procedure, usually two to three small incisions are made through which lights, cameras, and instruments may be passed. Since endoscopic procedures are a less invasive type of procedure, the endoscopic approach is often the one chosen by the physician. Figure 3–52 illustrates a laparoscopy procedure. Figure 3–53 shows a

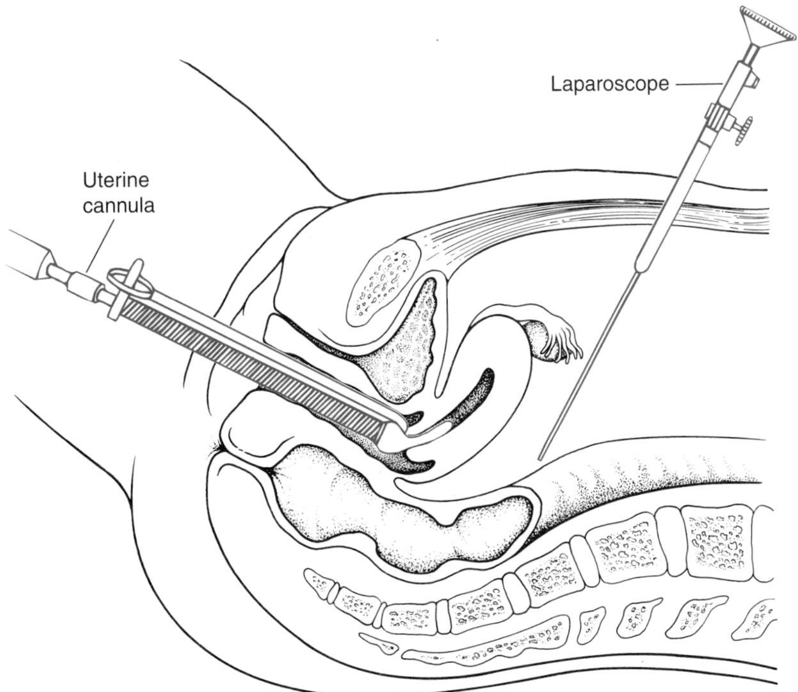

Figure 3–53
Peritoneoscopy.

peritonoscopy procedure, which has a scope passed through the abdomen as well as the vagina. Laparoscopy is not only used for gynecologic procedures; it has become standard for various general surgical procedures (eg, laparoscopic cholecystectomy, laparoscopic general hernia repair).

Surgical endoscopic procedures always include diagnostic endoscopy. It would be considered unbundling if you were to code both a surgical endoscopy and a diagnostic endoscopy during the same procedure. The diagnostic endoscopy codes always have "(separate procedure)" following the code description. Only if a diagnostic endoscopy was the only procedure performed would it be correct to code for the service.

Laparoscopy codes are located in the index of the CPT manual under the procedure Laparoscopy and further subdivided by the procedure performed (ie, gastrostomy, diagnostic, ureterolithotomy).

EXERCISE PP *Laparoscopy Terminology*

Match the following terms to the correct definitions:

1. hysteroscopy _______
2. peritoneoscopy _______
3. laparoscopy _______
4. lysis _______
5. oophorectomy _______
6. cholecystoenterostomy _______
7. cholecystectomy _______
8. salpingostomy _______
9. fimbrioplasty _______
10. transhepatic _______
11. cholangiography _______

a. exploration of the abdomen and pelvic cavities using a scope placed through a small incision in the abdominal wall

b. visualization of the abdominal cavity using one scope placed through a small incision in the abdominal wall and another scope placed in the vagina

c. visualization of the canal of the uterine cervix and cavity of the uterus using a scope placed through the vagina

d. surgical repair of the fringe of the uterine tube

e. creation of a connection between the gallbladder and intestine

f. surgical removal of the ovary(ies)

g. across the liver

h. radiographic recording of the bile ducts

i. surgical removal of the gallbladder

j. releasing

k. creation of a fistula into the uterine tube

EXERCISE QQ *Laparoscopy*

Code the following:

1. Laparoscopic tubal fulguration

   Code(s): ____________________

2. Laparoscopic cholecystectomy

   Code(s): ____________________

3. Laparoscopy with vaginal hysterectomy

   Code(s): ____________________

FEMALE GENITAL SYSTEM

Format

The Female Genital System subsection is divided by anatomic site from the vulva up to the ovaries (see Fig. 3–54). The anatomic sites are then divided by category of procedure (ie, incision, excision, destruction).

The anatomy in this subsection will start at the vulva and progress upward to the ovary. Codes for in vitro fertilization are found at the end of the subsection. The subsection has a wide variety of codes for minor procedures performed in a physician's office as well as major procedures performed in a hospital. It is important to read the descriptions for codes as well as the notes to avoid unbundling in this subsection. For example, if a total abdominal hysterectomy was

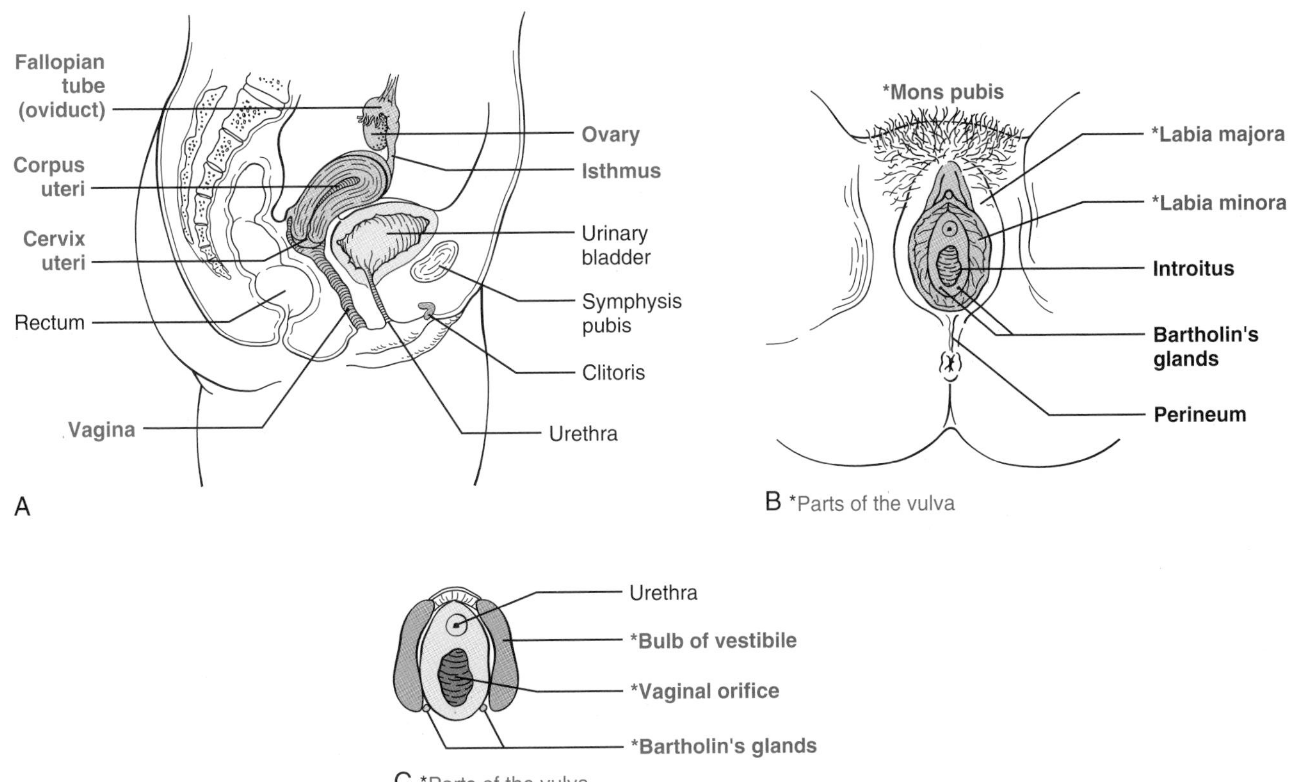

Figure 3–54
A. Female genital system. *B.* External female genital system. *C.* Parts of the vulva.

performed as well as a bilateral oophorectomy (removal of ovaries), only CPT code 58150 would be used. CPT code 58150 includes in the description the statement: "with or without removal of ovary(s)." Bundled into the code are both the abdominal hysterectomy and the bilateral oophorectomy.

The codes in this subsection often refer to the vulva. The vulva includes the following: mons pubis, labia majora, labia minora, bulb of vestibule, vaginal orifice or vestibule of the vagina, and greater (Bartholin's gland) and lesser vestibular glands (see Fig. 3–54B and C). When the code indicates, for example, the incision and drainage of an abscess of the vulva, the code covers an abscess of any of the anatomic areas previously listed.

Terminology

EXERCISE RR *Female Genital Terminology*

Match the following terms to the correct definitions:

1. vulva _______
2. perineum _______
3. introitus _______
4. vagina _______
5. cervix uteri _______
6. corpus uteri _______
7. oviduct _______
8. salpingo- _______
9. oophor- _______
10. curettage _______
11. dilation _______
12. cystocele _______
13. rectocele _______

a. herniation of the bladder into the vagina
b. rounded, cone-shaped neck of the uterus, part of which protrudes into the vagina
c. prefix meaning ovary
d. external female genitalia including labia majora, labia minora, clitoris, and vaginal opening
e. uterus
f. herniation of the rectal wall through the posterior wall of the vagina
g. prefix meaning tube
h. opening or entrance to the vagina from the uterus
i. scraping of a cavity using a spoon-shaped instrument
j. expansion
k. area between the vulva and anus; also known as the pelvic floor
l. canal from the external female genitalia to the uterus
m. fallopian tube

Female Genital Coding Highlights

Incision and Drainage

Definitions of vulvectomy codes (simple, radical, partial, complete) are found in the notes above CPT code 56405 in the CPT manual. The extent of the procedures is located in these notes and in the definitions of the codes. Be sure to read these notes before coding in the subsection. This subsection contains many lesion codes that you may think would be in the Integumentary subsection but that are located in the Female Genital subsection.

Dilation and Curettage

Many third-party payers will not reimburse for a dilation and curettage (D&C) (58120) if performed with any other pelvic surgery because it is thought to be integral to the procedure. The CPT manual does not list dilation and curettage as a separate procedure; therefore, you need to be familiar with reimbursement policies in your area.

EXERCISE SS *Female Genital Coding*

Code the following cases:

1. Simple destruction of one lesion of vaginal vestibule

   Code(s): ________________

2. Biopsy of three lesions of the vulva

   Code(s): ________________

3. Closure of rectovaginal fistula, abdominal approach

   Code(s): ________________

4. Cone biopsy of cervix with dilation and curettage

   Code(s): ________________

5. Unilateral salpingectomy with oophorectomy

   Code(s): ________________

Using the vulvectomy notes in the CPT manual, match the following procedures with the correct definition:

Procedure	The removal of:
6. simple _______	a. greater than 80 percent of the vulvar area
7. radical _______	b. skin and deep subcutaneous tissue
8. partial _______	c. skin and superficial subcutaneous tissues
9. complete _______	d. less than 80 percent of the vulvar area

MATERNITY CARE AND DELIVERY

Format

The Maternity Care and Delivery subsection is divided by type of procedure. As a general rule, the subsection progresses from antepartum procedures through delivery procedures. The guidelines are very detailed as to the procedures included in antepartum and delivery care, not only to facilitate coding but also to help guard against unbundling. Notes found at the beginning of this subsection describe, in depth, the services listed in obstetric care. Abortion codes, whether spontaneous abortion, missed abortions, or induction of abortion, are found at the end of the subsection. Abortion codes indicate treatment of a spontaneous abortion or missed abortion, including additional division for trimester or induction of abortion by method. You must be aware of the gestational age of the fetus to determine whether a delivery code or abortion code would be appropriate.

Treatment for ectopic pregnancies is based on the site of the pregnancy, extent of the surgery, and whether the approach was by means of laparoscopy or laparotomy.

Terminology

EXERCISE TT Maternity Care and Delivery Terminology

Match the following terms to the correct definitions:

1. antepartum _______
2. postpartum _______
3. abortion _______
4. delivery _______
5. cesarean _______
6. ectopic _______
7. version _______
8. amniocentesis _______
9. cordocentesis _______
10. chorionic villus (CVS) sampling _______
11. hysterotomy _______
12. salpingectomy _______
13. oophorectomy _______
14. hysterectomy _______
15. hysterorrhaphy _______
16. tocolysis _______
17. VBAC _______

a. turning of the fetus from a presentation other than cephalic (head down) to cephalic for ease of birth
b. termination of pregnancy
c. surgical opening through abdominal wall for delivery
d. before childbirth
e. after childbirth
f. pregnancy outside the uterus (ie, in the fallopian tube)
g. childbirth
h. incision into the uterus
i. surgical removal of the uterus
j. percutaneous aspiration of amniotic fluid
k. surgical removal of the ovary(ies).
l. biopsy of the outermost part of the placenta
m. suturing of the uterus
n. repression of uterine contractions
o. surgical removal of the uterine tube
p. vaginal delivery after a previous cesarean delivery
q. procedure to obtain a fetal blood sample, also called a percutaneous umbilical blood sampling

Maternity Care and Delivery Coding Highlights

Maternity and Delivery

When the maternity case is uncomplicated, the service codes normally include the antepartum care, delivery, and postpartum care. *Antepartum care* is considered to include both the initial and subsequent history and physical examinations, blood pressures, patient's weight, routine urinalysis, fetal heart tones, and monthly visits to 28 weeks of gestation, biweekly visit from gestation week 29 through 36, and weekly visit from week 37 to delivery when these services are provided by the same physician. If the patient is seen by the same physician for a service other than those identified as part of antepartum care, you would report that service separately. For example, if a patient in week 32 came to the office for cold symptoms, an E/M service code would be billed.

Delivery includes the admission to the hospital, which includes the admitting history and examination, management of an uncomplicated labor, and delivery that is either vaginal or cesarean section (including any episiotomy and forceps). If the labor or delivery is complicated, you would report those services separately.

Included in *postpartum care* is the hospital visits and/or office visits after a delivery. If the postpartum care is complicated or if services were provided to the patient during the postpartum period, but the services are not generally part of the postpartum care, you would report those services separately.

The category of Vaginal Delivery, Antepartum and Postpartum Care contains codes for those times when the physician provides only part of the care. Sometimes, for example, the physician provides only the antepartum and postpartum care or only the delivery service. You must read the code descriptions carefully, as they specify what parts of the service are included in the code to guard against unbundling.

Of special note are the category codes for the patients who previously had a cesarean delivery and now for the current delivery are presenting for vaginal delivery. The category *Delivery After Previous Cesarean Delivery* is divided based on the circumstances of the current delivery—previous cesarean presenting for vaginal delivery, previous cesarean and successful vaginal delivery, and previous cesarean and current delivery ended in cesarean.

EXERCISE UU *Maternity Care and Delivery*

Code the following:

1. Laparoscopic salpingectomy of tubal ectopic pregnancy

   Code(s): ____________________

2. Version of breech presentation, successfully converted to cephalic presentation, with normal spontaneous delivery

   Code(s): ____________________

3. Thirty-year-old woman, 20 weeks' gestation, with cervical cerclage by vaginal approach

   Code(s): ____________________

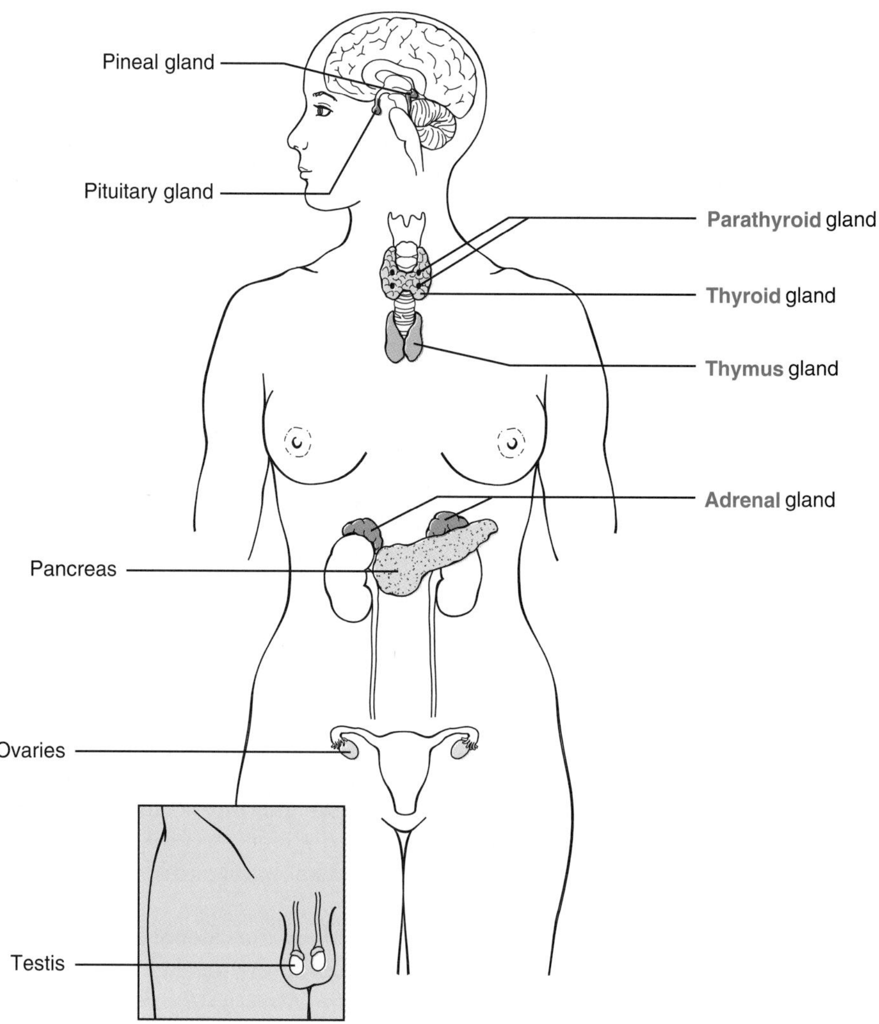

Figure 3–55
Endocrine system.

ENDOCRINE SYSTEM

Format

The endocrine system has the important job of producing and releasing hormones into the bloodstream. The endocrine glands are located throughout the body (Fig. 3–55) and regulate a wide range of body functions. (Your anatomy and physiology background is very important to you as you code.) The following exercise will serve as a guide to some of the specific terminology you will find in the Endocrine System subsection of the CPT manual.

Terminology

EXERCISE VV ***Endocrine System***

Match the following terms to the correct definitions:

1. isthmus _______
2. isthmus, thyroid _______

a. glands, located on the top of the kidneys, that produce steroid hormones

3. isthmus-ectomy _______
4. contralateral _______
5. thyroid-ectomy _______
6. thyroglossal duct _______
7. thymectomy _______
8. adrenal _______
9. thyroid _______
10. thymus _______
11. parathyroid _______

b. produces a hormone to mobilize calcium from the bones to the blood
c. connection of two regions or structures
d. surgical removal of the thyroid
e. produces hormones important to the immune response
f. surgical removal of the isthmus
g. surgical removal of the thymus
h. part of the endocrine system that produces hormones that regulate metabolism
i. tissue connection between right and left thyroid lobes
j. connection of the thyroid and the pharynx and continuation with the endoctrinal floor of the mouth
k. affecting the opposite side

Endocrine Coding Highlights

There are nine glands in the endocrine system, but only four are included in this section of the CPT manual—thyroid, parathyroid, adrenal, and thymus. The pituitary and pineal gland procedures are in the Nervous System subsection of the CPT manual, the pancreas is in the Digestive System subsection, and the ovaries and testes are in the respective Female or Male Genital System subsections.

There are only two categories in this subsection. The first category is Thyroid Gland and the second is Parathyroid, Thymus, Adrenal Glands, and Carotid Body. The *Carotid Body* refers to an area adjacent to the carotid artery that can be a site of tumors that are excised (60600).

The CPT manual lists only one incision code and one unlisted procedure code; the remaining codes are for excisions or laparoscopy. There is also an aspiration/injection code and a biopsy code, which is under the excision category. Partial/total or subtotal/total appear in many of the descriptions; *both* subtotal *and* partial *mean something less than the total.*

EXERCISE WW Endocrine System

Code the following:

1. Excision of an adenoma from posterior aspect of the thyroid gland

   Code(s): ____________________

2. Surgical removal of the thyroglossal duct cyst

   Code(s): ____________________

3. Total removal of the thymus using the transthoracic approach, radical

   Code(s): ____________________

4. Removal of tumor affixed to the carotid artery

   Code(s): ____________________

5. Partial excision of both lobes of thyroid with removal of adjacent isthmus

   Code(s): ____________________

NERVOUS SYSTEM

Format

The Nervous System subsection contains codes describing procedures done on the brain, spinal cord, nerves, and all associated parts. The subheadings are divided by anatomic site—whether it be a part of the brain or spinal column or a type of nerve. The subheadings are further divided by type of procedure. The codes deal with both the central nervous system and the peripheral nervous system.

Two Special Considerations

Punctures, Twists, or Burr Holes

The first two categories of codes (Injection, Drainage, or Aspiration and Twist Drill, Burr Hole(s), or Trephine) deal with conditions that may require holes or openings made into the brain to relieve pressure, to insert monitoring devices, to place tubing, or to inject contrast material. Twist or burr holes are made through the skull to accomplish many of the above procedures. Using twist or burr holes means that the skull stays intact except for the small openings (holes) made. Hemorrhages may also be drained with the use of these holes.

Craniectomy/Craniotomy

Codes in the category Craniectomy or Craniotomy describe craniotomy or craniectomy procedures. These procedures deal with the actual incision of the skull with possible removal of a portion of the skull to open the operative site to the surgeon for correction of the condition. Use of these codes is determined by site and condition (ie, evacuation of hematoma, supratentorial, subdural). Carefully review the descriptions for these codes before coding.

As in other subsections, there are many procedures bundled into one code, and only by careful attention to code description can you keep from unbundling surgical procedures.

When craniectomies are performed, it is not uncommon that additional grafting must take place to repair the surgical defect caused by opening the skull. These grafting procedures would be coded separately in addition to the major surgical procedure.

Terminology

EXERCISE XX Nervous System Terminology

Match the following terms to the correct definitions:

1. cranium _______
2. skull _______
3. stereotaxis _______
4. laminectomy _______
5. somatic nerve _______
6. sympathetic nerve _______
7. peripheral nerves _______
8. shunt _______
9. central nervous system _______

a. method of identifying a specific area or point in the brain
b. part of the peripheral nervous system that controls automatic body function and sympathetic nerves activated under stress
c. that part of the skeleton that encloses the brain
d. divert or make an artificial passage
e. 12 pairs of cranial nerves, 31 pairs of spinal nerves, and autonomic nervous system; connects peripheral receptors to the brain and spinal cord
f. sensory or motor nerve
g. entire skeletal framework of the head
h. surgical excision of the lamina
i. brain and spinal cord

Nervous System Coding Highlights

Surgery at Skull Base

The **skull base** is the area at the base of the cranium where the lobes of the brain rest. When lesions are found within the skull base, it often takes the skill of several surgeons working together to perform surgery dealing with these conditions. The operations found under the category Surgery of Skull Base are very involved, taking many hours to complete. The procedures are divided by the approach procedure, definitive procedure, and reconstruction/repair procedure.

The *approach procedure* is the method used to obtain exposure of the lesion (eg, anterior cranial fossa, middle cranial fossa, posterior cranial fossa). The *definitive procedure* is what was done to the lesion (eg, biopsy, repair, excision). If one physician did both the approach and the definitive procedures, both would be coded. For example, a neoplasm is excised at the base of the anterior cranial fossa, extradural, using an infratemporal preauricular approach to the midline skull base. This would be coded 61600 for the procedure (definitive procedure) and 61590 for the approach (approach procedure). Because two procedures were done—61600 and 61590—the lesser procedure, the approach, would have modifier -51.

Reconstruction or repair procedures are the various repairs that will be done to the skull on closure to rebuild the area used for entry. This last step of reconstruction or repair is reported separately only if it is extensive.

At any given point one or more physicians may be performing a separate portion of the procedure. When one surgeon performs the approach procedure, another surgeon performs the definitive procedure, and another surgeon performs the reconstruction/repair procedure, each surgeon reports the code for the specific procedure he or she individually performed. Again, if one surgeon performs more than one procedure (eg, approach procedure and definitive procedure), both codes are reported, adding modifier -51 to the secondary, additional procedure.

Aneurysms may develop in the brain, requiring surgical repair. Also present in the brain may be arteriovenous malformations, which means the arteries and veins are not in the correct anatomic position. Codes to indicate the definitive procedure or repair of these conditions are found in the category Surgery for Aneurysm, Arteriovenous Malformation, or Vascular Disease divided by the approach and method of procedures.

Cerebrospinal Fluid Shunts

A **shunt** can be considered a draining device that enables fluids to be drained from one area into another when the body is not able to perform this function on its own. In the case of cerebrospinal fluid shunts, the cerebrospinal fluid that is produced in the ventricles of the brain may not drain properly and continues to accumulate in the brain, building pressure and causing brain damage. Drains or shunts are placed from the area of collection to a drainage area to keep the fluid level within normal ranges. For instance, code 62223 describes the creation of a shunt from the ventricle to the peritoneal space (ventriculoperitoneal). This means that the shunt starts in the ventricle of the brain and ends in the peritoneum. Codes in the CSF Shunt category describe all the various types of shunting procedures, including placement of shunting devices and their repair, replacement, and removal.

Shunt systems may also be placed to drain obstructed cerebrospinal fluid from the spine. As in the previously described shunt procedures, codes from the category Shunt, Spinal CSF identify creation, replacement, removal, or insertion of a shunt system.

Spine and Spinal Cord

The subheading Spine and Spinal Cord includes codes for injections, laminectomies, excisions, repairs, and shunting. You should be familiar with terminology of parts of the spinal column, including the lamina, foramina, vertebral bodies, disks, facets, and nerve roots. The basic distinction between codes in these ranges deals with the condition (herniated intervertebral disks versus a neoplastic lesion of the spinal cord) as well as the approach (eg, anterior, posterior, costovertebral).

The complexity of the procedure is determined by the condition and approach. For example, a patient with a herniated disk at L5–S1 would require less time in surgery for the removal of the disk and decompression of the nerve root than would a patient with a neoplastic growth intertwined in the same area, because removal of a piece of disk would not be as involved as separating a lesion from multiple components of the spinal column. The approaches differ in the expertise and time required. Codes vary based on approach. A posterior approach means a surgical opening was formed from the back. An anterior approach means a surgical opening was formed from the front.

When coding spinal procedures, you should look for condition, approach, unilateral or bilateral, and multiple procedures performed.

Often when a laminectomy (removal of a vertebra) is performed, an arthrodesis (surgical fusion of joints) is also performed. In some cases spinal instrumentation (the use of rods, wires, and screws to do fusions) will also be performed. Review the operative reports and confirm all procedures performed when coding multiple procedures.

Notes throughout the Spine and Spinal Cord subsection refer you to other code ranges for commonly done additional procedures (eg, arthrodesis codes are in the Musculoskeletal subsection). Remember to use the modifier -51 for multiple procedures if more than one procedure is performed.

Nerves

Nerves are our sensing devices that carry stimuli to and from all parts of the body. Some common procedures done on nerves include injection, destruction, decompression, or suture/repair.

Nerves can be injected with anesthetic agents to cause a temporary loss of feeling. The code is chosen based on the type of nerve being injected. Nerves may also be injected to cause destruction of the nerve and permanent loss of feeling to a specific area of the body. Persons with debilitating pain may have this type of procedure done.

Neuroplasty is the decompression freeing intact nerves from scar tissue. If nerves receive excessive pressure from a source, such as scar tissue or displacement of intervertebral disk material, severe pain may occur. Movement or freeing of nerves is reported with codes from the Neuroplasty Exploration, Neurolysis, or Nerve Decompression category. Perhaps the most commonly known neuroplasty procedure is a carpal tunnel release, coded to 64721, in which the median nerve and flexor tendons of the wrist are surgically released (Fig. 3–56).

Nerves can also be removed or they can be repaired (sutured). Remember, the notes found before the repair codes in the Integumentary subsection state that if repair of nerves is necessary, codes from the Nervous System are used. The codes in the Neurorraphy and Neurorraphy with Nerve Graft categories reflect nerve repairs by the specific nerve being repaired. This category also includes codes that describe grafting by size of graft.

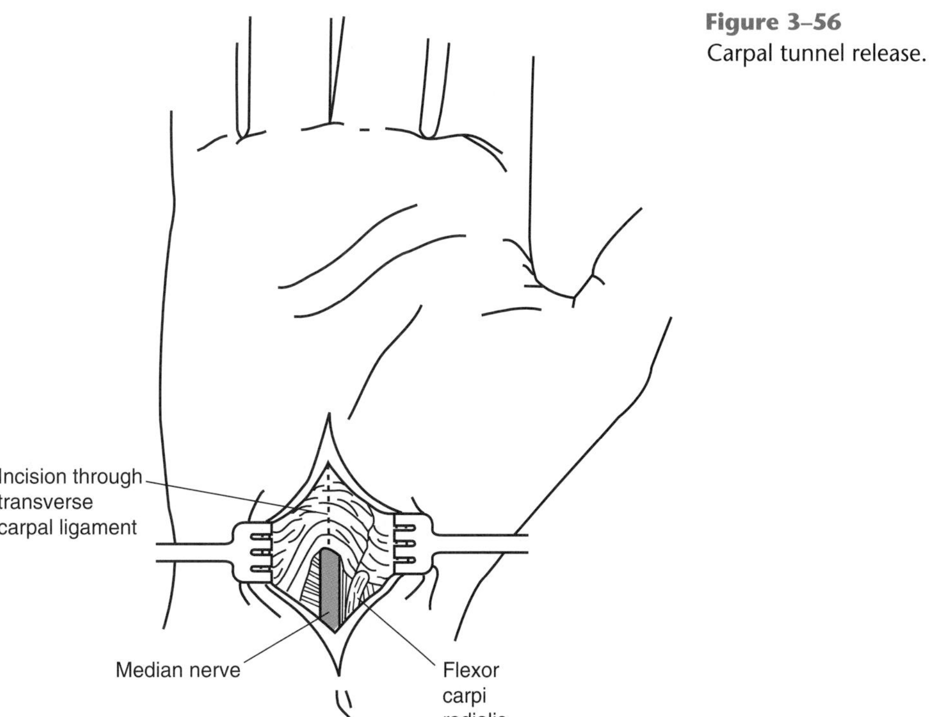

Figure 3–56
Carpal tunnel release.

EXERCISE YY *Nervous System*

Code the following:

1. Drainage of subdural hematoma using burr holes

   Code(s): ________________

2. Drainage of subdural hematoma with craniectomy

   Code(s): ________________

3. Resection of neoplasm, midline skull base, extradural, using infratemporal preauricular approach to middle cranial fossa

   Code(s): ________________

4. Removal of complete cerebrospinal fluid (CSF) shunt system, with replacement

   Code(s): ________________

5. Vertebral corpectomy T3, anterior approach, with decompression of nerve root, and diskectomy T2T3 and T3T4

   Code(s): ________________

6. Injection of anesthetic agent, facial nerve

   Code(s): ________________

7. Suture repair of sciatic nerve

   Code(s): ________________

EYE AND OCULAR ADNEXA

Format

The Eye and Ocular Adnexa subsection includes the subheadings of Eyeball, Anterior Segment, Posterior Segment, Ocular Adnexa, and Conjunctiva. There are the typical incision, excision, repair, and destruction categories, but also some that are a little different. For example, the subheading Eyeball has categories for both Removal of Eye and Removal of Foreign Bodies, although you would expect to find all removal codes in a category under one heading. Remember to use the correct modifiers when the procedure is done on two eyes.

Some code groups have different codes for patients who have been operated on before. For example, in the subsection Ocular Adnexa, the first five codes are for patients not previously operated on. Also, the subcategory Prophylaxis (preventive treatment) under the subheading Posterior Segment has notes regarding the

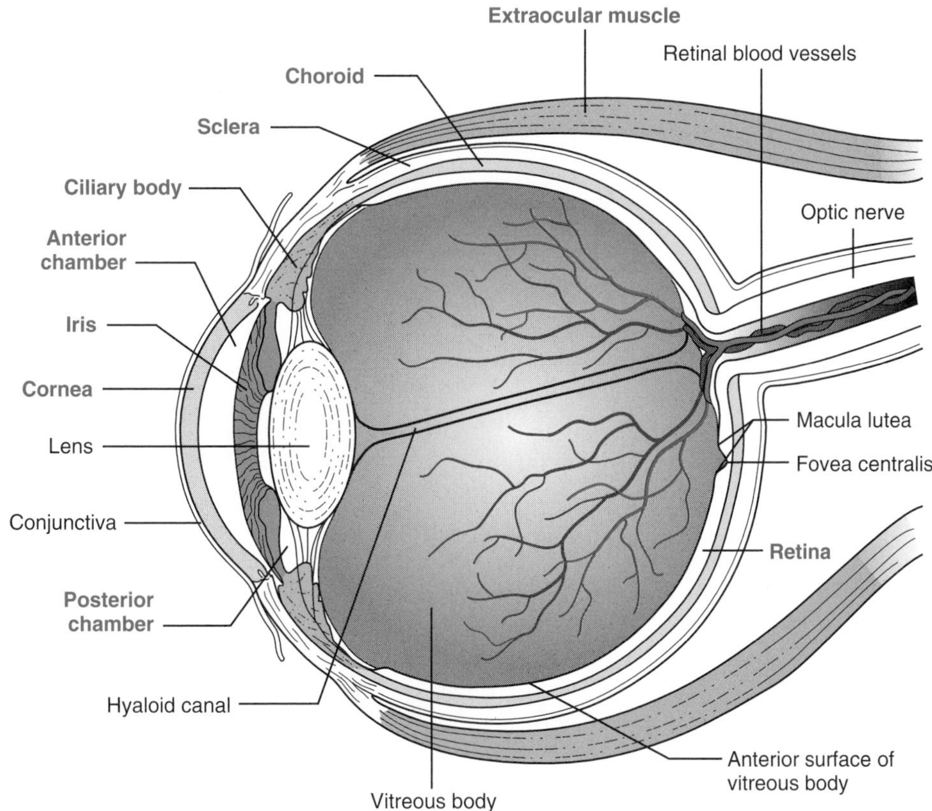

Figure 3–57
Eye and ocular adnexa.

bundling in the codes. The Prophylaxis codes include all the sessions in a treatment period. The Destruction codes in this subcategory also have "one or more sessions" included in the descriptions. Be certain to read carefully what is a part of the code.

As in all sections of the CPT manual, there are directional notes throughout that will help you think about what defines a particular code. For example, code 67850 is for the "Destruction of lesion of lid margin (up to 1 cm)." Under this description is a note in parentheses: "(For Mohs' micrographic surgery, see 17XXX–17XXX)." This helpful note gives you the category of codes to reference if the lesion destruction was done using Mohs' micrographic surgery.

Refer to Figures 3–57 to 3–60 as you prepare for the terminology exercise and coding practice.

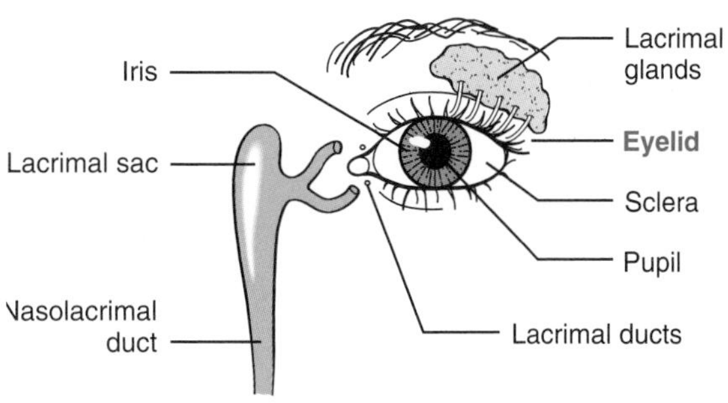

Figure 3–58
Lacrimal apparatus.

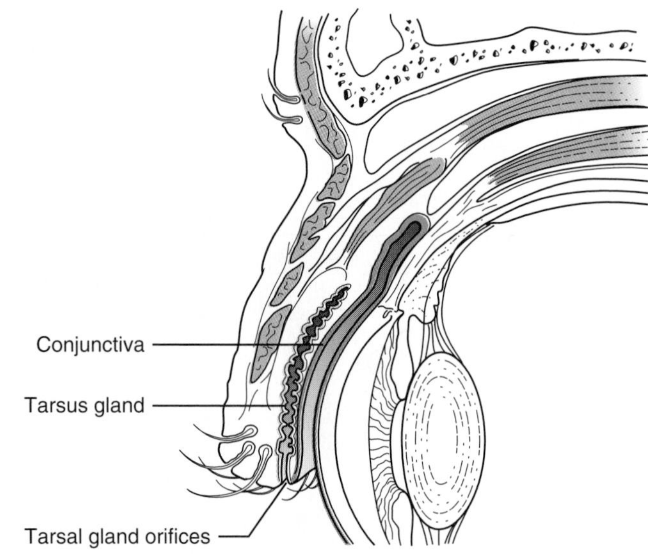

Figure 3–59
Eyelid.

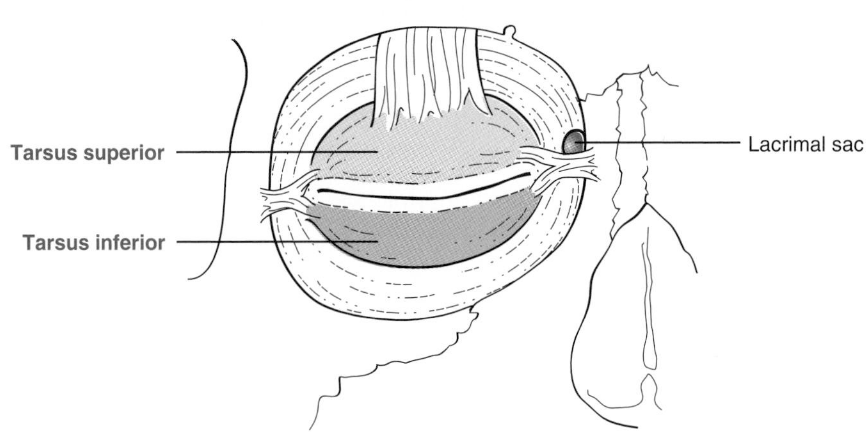

Figure 3–60
Two tarsi.

Terminology

EXERCISE ZZ *Eye and Ocular Adnexa Terminology*

Match the following terms to the correct definitions:

1. keratoplasty _______
2. evisceration _______
3. enucleation _______
4. exenteration _______
5. cataract _______
6. sclera _______
7. conjunctiva _______
8. uveal _______

a. prefix meaning eye
b. prefix meaning tear/tear duct
c. surgical repair of the cornea
d. removal of an organ(s) of a body cavity
e. opaque covering on or in the lens
f. those parts of the eye behind the lens
g. lining of the eyelids and covering of the sclera
h. removal of an organ all in one piece
i. pulling the viscera outside the body through an incision

9. tarsorrhaphy _______
10. ocular adnexa _______
11. anterior segment _______
12. posterior segment _______
13. blephar/o- _______
14. cor/o- _______
15. cycl/o- _______
16. dacry/o- _______
17. kerat/o- _______
18. ocul/o- _______
19. dacryocyst/o- _______
20. vitre/o- _______
21. astigmatism _______
22. strabismus _______

j. outer covering of the eye
k. vascular tissue of the choroid, ciliary body, and iris
l. prefix meaning cornea
m. prefix meaning pertaining to the vitreous body of the eye
n. prefix meaning ciliary body or eye muscle
o. suturing together of the eyelids
p. those parts of the eye in the front of and including the lens, orbit, extraocular muscles, and eyelid
q. orbit, extraocular muscles, and eyelid
r. prefix meaning pertaining to the lacrimal sac
s. extraocular muscle deviation resulting in unequal visual axes
t. condition in which the refractive surfaces of the eyes are unequal
u. prefix meaning eyelid
v. prefix meaning pupil

The terminology exercise and the figures are intended as a review in preparation for coding in this interesting specialty area. Having a good medical dictionary and anatomy book available will help you code better—when in doubt, check it out!

EXERCISE AAA *Eye and Ocular Adnexa*

Code the following:

1. Anterior segment of the left eye, emboli removal

   Code(s): ____________________

2. New patient strabismus surgery involving the superior oblique

   Code(s): ____________________

3. Xenon arc used in three sessions for preventive retinal detachment

   Code(s): ____________________

4. Corneal incision for revision of earlier procedure resulting in astigmatism

   Code(s): ___________________

5. Removal of left eye, muscles attached to implant

   Code(s): ___________________

AUDITORY SYSTEM

Format

The Auditory System subsection is divided into the subheadings of External Ear, Middle Ear, Inner Ear, and Temporal Bone/Middle Fossa Approach. The first three subheadings represent the anatomic divisions of the auditory system: external, middle, and internal ear (see Fig. 3–61). The categories below each subheading include introduction, incision, excision, removal of foreign body, repair,

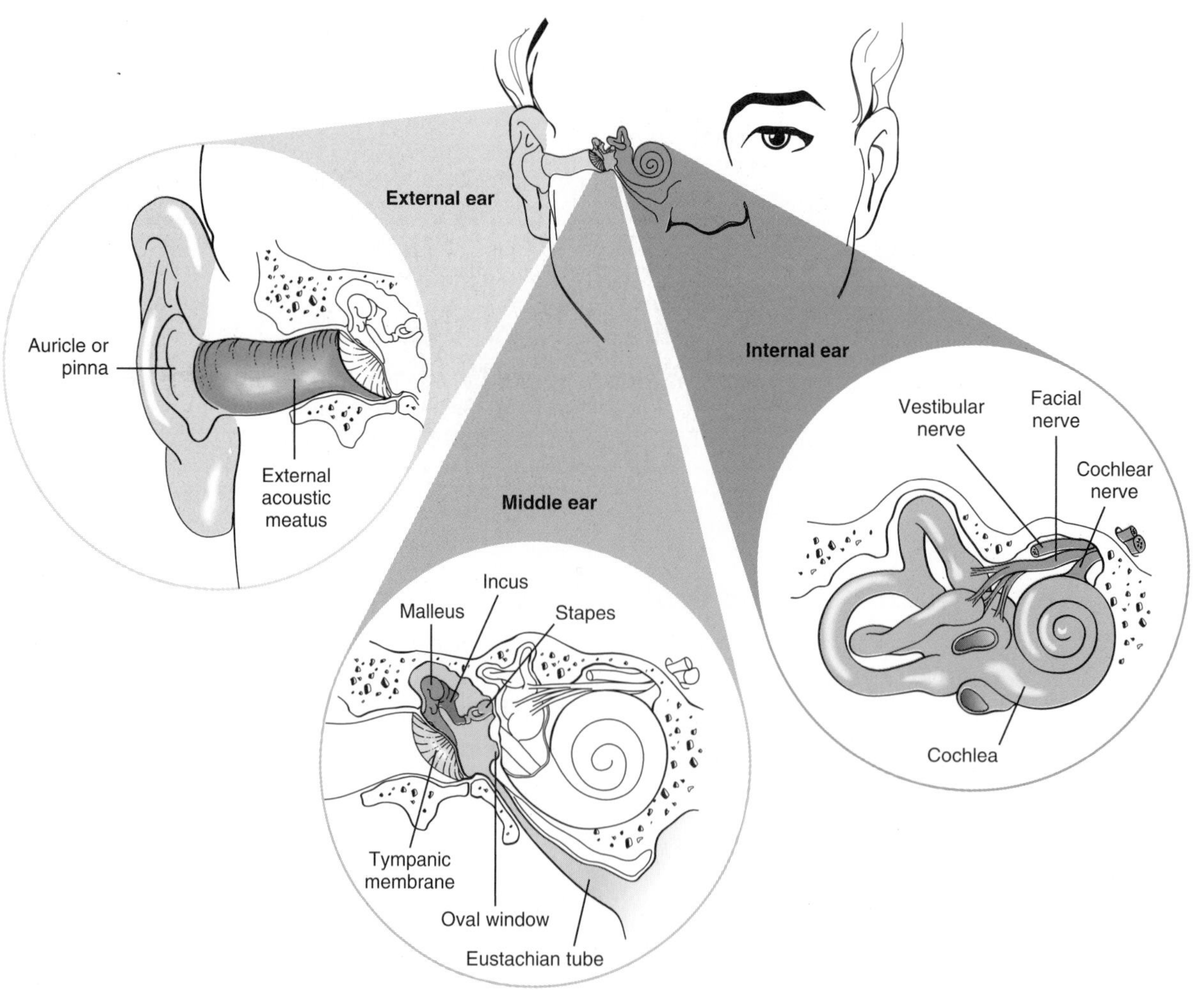

Figure 3–61
Auditory system.

and/or other procedures, depending on the particular subheading. The subheading Temporal Bone/Middle Fossa Approach contains codes that describe various surgical procedures in which the surgeon makes an incision in front of the ear. Using this incision, the surgeon performs a craniotomy and exposes the brain. The surgeon then repairs the nerve, removes a tumor, or otherwise repairs the area.

Terminology

EXERCISE BBB *Auditory System Terminology*

Match the following terms to the correct definitions:

1. aural atresia _______
2. transmastoid antrostomy _______
3. labyrinth _______
4. tympanic neurectomy _______
5. fenestration _______
6. parts of the external ear _______
7. parts of the middle ear _______
8. parts of the inner ear _______
9. mastoid- _______
10. myring- _______
11. audi- _______
12. exostosis _______
13. oto- _______
14. salping(o)- _______
15. apicectomy _______

a. prefix meaning hearing
b. auricle, pinna, external acoustic, and meatus
c. prefix meaning ear
d. prefix meaning (eustachian) tube
e. vestibule, semicircular canals, and cochlea
f. excision of the tympanic nerve
g. congenital absence of the external auditory canal
h. creation of a new opening on the inner wall of the middle ear
i. malleus, incus, and stapes
j. bony growth
k. prefix meaning posterior temporal bone
l. excision of a portion of the temporal bone
m. called a simple mastoidectomy, it creates an opening in the mastoid for drainage
n. inner connecting cavities, such as the internal ear
o. eardrum

EXERCISE CCC *Auditory System*

Code the following:

1. Labyrinthotomy with cryosurgery with multiple perfusions, transcanal

   Code(s): ____________________

2. Insertion of bilateral eustachian tubes

   Code(s): ________________

3. Transcranial approach used with a section of the vestibular nerve

   Code(s): ________________

4. Reconstruction of the right auditory canal

   Code(s): ________________

5. Establishment of an opening on the inner wall of the inner ear, semicircular canal

   Code(s): ________________

CHAPTER GLOSSARY

abortion: termination of pregnancy
abscess: localized collection of pus that will result in the disintegration of tissue over time
adrenal: glands, located on the top of the kidneys, that produce steroid hormones
allogenic: of the same species, but genetically different
allograft: tissue graft between individuals that are not of the same genotype
allotransplantation: transplantation between individuals that are not of the same genotype
amniocentesis: percutaneous aspiration of amniotic fluid
anastomosis: surgical connection of two tubular structures, such as two pieces of the intestine
aneurysm: sac of clotted blood or fluid formed in the circulatory system, ie, vein or artery
angioplasty: surgical or percutaneous procedure on a vessel to dilate the vessel opening; used in the treatment of atherosclerotic disease
anomaly: abnormality
antepartum: before childbirth
anterior segment: those parts of the eye in the front of and including the lens, orbit, extraocular muscles, and eyelid
antrotomy: cutting through the antrum wall to make an opening in the sinus
antrum: maxillary sinus
apicectomy: excision of a portion of the temporal bone
arteriovenous fistula: direct communication (passage) between an artery and vein
artery: vessel that carries oxygenated blood from the heart to body tissues
arthrodesis: surgical immobilization of a joint
arthroplasty: reshaping or reconstructing a joint
aspiration: use of a needle and a syringe to withdraw fluid
astigmatism: condition in which the refractive surfaces of the eye are unequal
atrium: chamber in the upper part of the heart
audi-: prefix meaning hearing
aural atresia: congenital absence of the external auditory canal
autogenous, autologous: from one's self
axillary nodes: lymph nodes located in the armpit
benign: not progressive or recurrent
biopsy: removal of a small piece of living tissue for diagnostic purposes
blephar/o-: prefix meaning eyelid
bronchoscopy: inspection of the bronchial tree using a bronchoscope
bulbocavernosus: muscle that constricts the vagina in a female and the urethra in a male
bulbourethral gland: rounded mass of the urethra
bypass: to go around
calculus: concretion of mineral salts, also called a stone
calycoplasty: surgical reconstruction of a recess of the renal pelvis
calyx: recess of the renal pelvis
cannulation: insertion of a tube into a duct or cavity
cardiopulmonary: refers to the heart and lungs
cardiopulmonary bypass: blood bypasses the heart through a heart-lung machine during open heart surgery

cardioverter-defibrillator: surgically placed device that directs an electrical current shock to the heart to restore rhythm
cataract: opaque covering on or in the lens
catheter: tube placed into the body to put fluid in or take fluid out
cavernosa–corpus spongiosum shunt: creation of a connection between a cavity of the penis and the urethra
cavernosa–glans penis fistulization: creation of a connection between a cavity of the penis and the glans penis, which overlaps the penis cavity
cavernosa–saphenous vein shunt: creation of a connection between the cavity of the penis and a vein
cavernosography: radiographic measurement of a cavity, ie, the main part of the penis
cavernosometry: measurement of the pressure in a cavity, ie, penis
-centesis: suffix meaning puncture of a cavity
central nervous system: brain and spinal cord
cervix uteri: rounded, cone-shaped neck of the uterus, part of which protrudes into the vagina
cesarean: surgical opening through abdominal wall for delivery
cholangiography: radiographic recording of the bile ducts
chole-: prefix meaning bile
cholecystectomy: surgical removal of the gallbladder
cholecystoenterostomy: creation of a connection between the gallbladder and intestine
chordee: condition resulting in the penis being bent downward
chorionic villus sampling (CVS): biopsy of the outermost part of the placenta
Cloquet's node: also called a gland; it is the highest of the deep groin lymph nodes
closed treatment: fracture site that is not surgically opened and visualized
colonoscopy: fiberscopic examination of the entire colon that may include part of the terminal ileum
colostomy: artificial opening between the colon and the abdominal wall
conjunctiva: lining of the eyelids and covering of the sclera
contralateral: affecting the opposite side
cor/o-: prefix meaning pupil
cordocentesis: procedure to obtain a fetal blood sample; also called a percutaneous umbilical blood sampling
corpora cavernosa: two cavities of the penis
corpus uteri: uterus
cranium: that part of the skeleton that encloses the brain
cryosurgery: destruction of lesions using extreme cold
curettage: scraping of a cavity using a spoon-shaped instrument
cycl/o-: prefix meaning ciliary body or eye muscle
cyst: closed sac containing matter or fluid
cystic hygroma: benign tumor of the lymphatic system
cystocele: herniation of the bladder into the vagina
cystolithectomy: removal of a calculus (stone) from the urinary bladder
cystolithotomy: cystolithectomy
cystometrogram (CMG): measurement of the pressures and capacity of the urinary bladder
cystoplasty: surgical reconstruction of the bladder
cystorrhaphy: suture of the bladder
cystoscopy: use of a scope to view the bladder
cystostomy: surgical creation of an opening into the bladder
cystotomy: incision into the bladder
cystourethroplasty: surgical reconstruction of the bladder and urethra
cystourethroscopy: use of a scope to view the bladder and urethra
dacry/o-: prefix meaning tear/tear duct
dacryocyst/o-: prefix meaning pertaining to the lacrimal sac
debridement: cleansing of or removing dead tissue from a wound
delivery: childbirth
dermis: second layer of skin holding blood vessels, nerve endings, sweat glands, and hair follicles
destruction: killing of tissue, possibly by electrocautery, laser, chemical, or other means
diaphragm: muscular wall that separates the thoracic and abdominal cavities
diaphragmatic hernia: hernia of the diaphragm
dilation: expansion
dislocation: placement in a location other than the original location
drainage: free flow or withdrawal of fluids from a wound or cavity
dual-chamber pacemaker: electrodes of the pacemaker are placed in both the atria and the ventricles of the heart
ear, parts of the external: auricle, pinna, external acoustic, and meatus
ear, parts of the inner: vestibule, semicircular canals, and cochlea
ear, parts of the middle: malleus, incus, and stapes
-ectomy: suffix meaning removal of part or all of an organ of the body
ectopic: pregnancy outside the uterus (ie, in the fallopian tube)
electrode: lead attached to a generator that carries the electric current from the generator to the atria or ventricles

electrodesiccation: destruction of a lesion by the use of electric current radiated through a needle
electromyography (EMG): recording of the electrical impulses of muscles
embolectomy: removal of blockage (embolism) from vessels
embolism: blockage of a blood vessel by a blood clot or other matter that has moved from another area of the body through the circulatory system
endarterectomy: incision into an artery to remove the inner lining to remove disease or blockage
endopyelotomy: procedure of the bladder and ureters with insertion of a stent
endoscopy: inspection of body organs or cavities using a lighted scope that may be placed through an existing opening or through a small incision
enterocystoplasty: surgical reconstruction of the small intestine after the removal of a cyst and usually including a bowel anastomosis
enucleation: removal of an organ(s) of a body cavity
epidermis: outer layer of skin
epididymectomy: surgical removal of the epididymis
epididymis: tube located on the top of the testes that stores sperm
epididymovasostomy: creation of a new connection between the vas deferens and epididymis
eventration: protrusion of the bowel through the viscera of the abdomen
evisceration: pulling the viscera outside the body through an incision
excision: cutting or taking away (in reference to lesion removal, it is full-thickness removal of a lesion that may include simple closure)
excisional: removal of an entire lesion for biopsy
exenteration: removal of an organ all in one piece
exostosis: bony growth
exstrophy: condition in which an organ is turned inside out
fenestration: creation of a new opening on the inner wall of the middle ear
fimbrioplasty: surgical repair of the fringe of the uterine tube
fistula: abnormal opening from one area to another area or to outside the body
fracture: break in a bone
fulguration: use of electric current to destroy tissue
fundoplasty: repair of the bottom on an organ or muscle
gastro-: prefix meaning stomach
gastrointestinal: pertaining to the stomach and intestine
gastroplasty: operation on the stomach for repair or reconfiguration
gastrostomy: artificial opening between the stomach and the abdominal wall
gloss-: prefix meaning tongue
hepat-: prefix meaning liver
hernia: organ or tissue protruding through the wall or cavity that usually contains it
hydrocele: sac of fluid
hypospadias: congenital deformity of the urethra in which the urethral opening is on the underside of the penis rather than the end
hysterectomy: surgical removal of the uterus
hysterorrhaphy: suturing of the uterus
hysteroscopy: visualization of the canal of the uterine cervix and cavity of the uterus using a scope placed through the vagina
hysterotomy: incision into the uterus
ileostomy: artificial opening between the ileum and the abdominal wall
imbrication: overlapping
incarcerated: regarding hernias, a constricted, irreducible hernia that may cause obstruction of an intestine
incision: surgically cutting into
incision and drainage: to cut and withdraw fluid
incisional: *see* incision
inguinofemoral: term that refers to the groin and thigh
injection: forcing of a fluid into a vessel or cavity
internal/external fixation: the application of pins, wires, screws, and so on to immobilize; these can be placed externally or internally
introitus: opening or entrance to the vagina
ischemia: deficient blood supply due to obstruction of the circulatory system
isthmus: connection of two regions or structures
isthmus, thyroid: tissue connection between right and left thyroid lobes
isthmusectomy: surgical removal of the isthmus
jejunostomy: artificial opening between the jejunum and the abdominal wall
jugular nodes: lymph nodes located next to the large vein in the neck
kerat/o-: prefix meaning cornea
keratoplasty: surgical repair of the cornea
Kock pouch: surgical creation of a urinary bladder from a segment of the ileum
labyrinth: inner connecting cavities, such as the internal ear
laminectomy: surgical excision of the lamina
laparoscopy: exploration of the abdomen and pelvic cavities using a scope placed through a small incision in the abdominal wall
laryngo-: prefix meaning larynx
lesion: abnormal or altered tissue, ie, wound, cyst, abscess, or boil
ligation: binding or tying off, as in constricting blood flow of a vessel or binding fallopian tubes for sterilization

litholapaxy: lithotripsy
lithotomy: incision into an organ or a duct for the purpose of removing a stone
lithotripsy: crushing of a gallbladder or urinary bladder stone followed by irrigation to wash the fragment out
lobectomy: excision of a lobe of the lung
lymph node: station along the lymphatic system
lymphadenectomy: excision of a lymph node (or nodes)
lymphadenitis: inflammation of a lymph node
lymphangiotomy: incision into a lymphatic vessel
lysis: releasing
malignant: term used to describe a cancerous tumor that grows worse over time
manipulation or reduction: words used interchangeably to mean the attempted restoration of a fracture or joint dislocation to its normal anatomic position
marsupialization: surgical procedure that creates an exterior pouch from an internal abscess
mast-: prefix meaning breast
mastoid-: prefix meaning posterior temporal bone
meatotomy: surgical enlargement of the opening of the urinary meatus
mediastinoscopy: use of an endoscope inserted through a small incision to view the mediastinum
mediastinotomy: cutting into the mediastinum
mediastinum: that area between the lungs that contains the heart, aorta, trachea, lymph nodes, thymus gland, esophagus, and bronchial tubes
myring-: prefix meaning eardrum
nephrectomy, paraperitoneal: kidney transplant
nephro-: kidney
nephrocutaneous fistula: channel from the kidney to the skin
nephrolithotomy: removal of a kidney stone through an incision made into the kidney
nephrorrhaphy: suturing of the kidney
nephrostolithotomy: creation of an artificial channel to the kidney
nephrostolithotomy, percutaneous: procedure to establish an artificial channel between the skin and the kidney
nephrostomy: creation of a channel into the renal pelvis of the kidney
nephrostomy, percutaneous: creation of a channel from the skin to the renal pelvis
nephrotomy: incision into the kidney
ocul/o-: prefix meaning eye
ocular adnexa: orbit, extraocular muscles, and eyelid
oophor-: prefix meaning ovary
oophorectomy: surgical removal of the ovary(ies)
omentum: peritoneal connection between the stomach and other internal organs
open treatment: fracture site that is surgically opened and visualized
orchiectomy: castration
orchiopexy: surgical procedure to release undescended testis
ostomy: artificial opening
oto-: prefix meaning ear
-otomy: suffix meaning incision into
oviduct: fallopian tube
pacemaker: electrical device that controls the beating of the heart by electrical impulses
paraesophageal hiatus hernia: hernia that is near the esophagus
parathyroid: produces a hormone to mobilize calcium from the bones to the blood
paring: removal of thin layers of skin by peeling or scraping
pelviolithotomy: pyeloplasty
penoscrotal: referring to the penis and scrotum
percutaneous: performed through the skin
percutaneous skeletal fixation: considered neither open nor closed; the fracture is not visualized, but fixation is placed across the fracture site under x-ray imaging
pericardium: membranous sac enclosing the heart and ends of the great vessels
perineal approach: surgical approach in the area between the thighs
perinephric cyst: cyst in the tissue around the kidney
perineum: area between the vulva and anus; also known as the pelvic floor
peripheral nerves: 12 pairs of cranial nerves, 31 pairs of spinal nerves, and autonomic nervous system; connects peripheral receptors to the brain and spinal cord
perirenal: around the kidney
peritoneoscopy: visualization of the abdominal cavity using one scope placed through a small incision in the abdominal wall and another scope placed in the vagina
perivesical: around the bladder
perivisceral: around an organ
-plasty: suffix meaning technique involving molding or surgically forming
plethysmography: determining the changes in volume of an organ part or body
pleura: covering of the lungs and thoracic cavity that is moistened with serous fluid to reduce friction during respiratory movements of the lungs
pneumo-: prefix meaning lung or air
polyp: tumor on a pedicle that bleeds easily and may become malignant
posterior segment: those parts of the eye behind the lens
postpartum: after childbirth

priapism: painful condition in which the penis is consistently erect
proctosigmoidoscopy: fiberscopic examination of the sigmoid colon and rectum
prostatotomy: incision into the prostate
punch: use of small hollow instrument to puncture a lesion
pyelo-: prefix meaning renal pelvis
pyelocutaneous: from the renal pelvis to the skin
pyelolithotomy: surgical removal of a kidney stone from the renal pelvis
pyeloplasty: surgical reconstruction of the renal pelvis
pyeloscopy: viewing of the renal pelvis using a fluoroscope after injection of contrast material
pyelostolithotomy: removal of a kidney stone and establishment of a stoma
pyelostomy: surgical creation of a temporary diversion around the ureter
pyelotomy: incision into the renal pelvis
pyloroplasty: incision and repair of the pyloric channel
reanastomosis: reconnection of a previous connection between two places, organs, or spaces
rectocele: herniation of the rectal wall through the posterior wall of the vagina
reducible: able to be corrected or put back into a normal position
renal pelvis: funnel-shaped sac in the kidney where urine is received
retroperitoneal: behind the sac holding the abdominal organs and viscera (peritoneum)
rhino-: prefix meaning nose
-rrhaphy: suffix meaning suturing
salping(o)-: prefix meaning tube
salpingectomy: surgical removal of the uterine tube
salpingostomy: creation of a fistula into the uterine tube
sclera: outer covering of the eye
seminal vesicle: gland that secretes fluid into the vas deferens
separate procedures: minor procedures that when done by themselves are coded as a procedure, but when performed with another major procedure are considered incidental and not coded separately
shaving: horizontal or transverse removal of dermal or epidermal lesions, without full-thickness excision
shunt: divert or make an artificial passage
sigmoidoscopy: fiberscopic examination of the entire rectum and sigmoid colon that may include a portion of the descending colon
single-chamber pacemaker: electrode of the pacemaker is placed only in the atrium or only in the ventricle, but not in both places
sinuses: cavities within the nasal bones
skin graft: transplantation of tissue to repair a defect
skull: entire skeletal framework of the head
soft tissue: tissues (fascia, connective tissue, muscle, etc.) surrounding a bone
somatic nerve: sensory or motor nerve
spermatocele: cyst filled with spermatozoa
splenectomy: excision of the spleen
splenoportography: radiographic procedure to allow visualization of the splenic and portal veins of the spleen
starred procedures: indicates minor procedures and services that include variable preoperative or postoperative services
stem cell: immature blood cell
stent: mold that holds a surgically placed graft in place
stereotaxis: method of identifying a specific area or point in the brain
strabismus: extraocular muscle deviation resulting in unequal visual axes
subcutaneous: tissue below dermis, primarily fat cells that insulate the body
suture: to unite parts by stitching them together
sympathetic nerve: part of the peripheral nervous system that controls automatic body function and sympathetic nerves activated under stress
symphysiotomy: cutting of the pubis cartilage to help in birthing
tarsorrhaphy: suturing together of the eyelids
thoracentesis: surgical puncture of the thoracic cavity, usually using a needle, to remove fluids
thoracic duct: collection and distribution point for lymph, and the largest lymph vessel located in the chest
thoracoscopy: use of a lighted endoscope to view the pleural spaces and thoracic cavity or perform surgical procedures
thoracostomy: cutting into the thoracic cavity to allow for enlargement of the heart or for drainage
thoracotomy: surgical incision into the thoracic cavity
thrombosis: blood clot
thymectomy: surgical removal of the thymus
thymus: produces hormones important to the immune response
thyroglossal duct: connection of the thyroid and the pharynx and continuation with the endodermal floor of the mouth
thyroid: part of the endocrine system that produces hormones that regulate metabolism
thyroidectomy: surgical removal of the thyroid
tissue transfer: piece of skin for grafting that is still partially attached to the original blood supply and is used to cover an adjacent wound area
tocolysis: repression of uterine contractions
traction: application of force to a limb

transabdominal: across the abdomen
transhepatic: across the liver
transmastoid antrostomy: called a simple mastoidectomy, it creates an opening in the mastoid for drainage
transplantation: grafting of tissue from one source to another
transthoracic: across the thorax
transureteroureterostomy: surgical connection of one ureter to the other ureter
transurethral resection, prostate: procedure performed through the urethra by means of a cystoscopy to remove part or all of the prostate
transvesical ureterolithotomy: removal of ureter stone (calculus) through the bladder
trocar needle: needle with a tube on the end, used to puncture and withdraw fluid from a cavity
tumescence: state of being swollen
tumor: swelling or enlargement; a spontaneous growth of tissue that forms an abnormal mass
tunica vaginalis: covering of the testes
tympanic neurectomy: excision of the tympanic nerve
ureterectomy: surgical removal of ureter, either totally or partially
ureterocolon: pertaining to the ureter and colon
ureterocutaneous fistula: channel from the ureter to the exterior skin
ureteroenterostomy: creation of a connection between the intestine and the ureter
ureterolithotomy: removal of a stone from the ureter
ureterolysis: freeing of the adhesions of the ureter
ureteroneocystostomy: surgical connection of the ureter to a new site on the bladder
ureteroplasty: surgical repair of the ureter
ureteropyelography: ureter and bladder radiography
ureteropyelonephrostomy: surgical connection of the ureter to a new site on the kidney
ureteropyelostomy: ureteropyelonephrostomy
ureterosigmoidostomy: surgical connection of the ureter into the sigmoid colon
ureterotomy: incision into the ureter
ureterovisceral fistula: surgical formation of a connection between the ureter and the skin
urethrocutaneous fistula: surgically created channel from the urethra to the skin surface
urethrocystography: radiography of the bladder and urethra
urethromeatoplasty: surgical repair of the urethra and meatus
urethroplasty: surgical repair of the urethra
urethrorrhaphy: suturing of the urethra
urethroscopy: use of a scope to view the urethra
uveal: vascular tissue of the choroid, ciliary body, and iris
vagina: canal from the external female genitalia to the uterus
vagotomy: surgical separation of the vagus nerve
varicocele: swelling of a scrotal vein
vas deferens: tube that carries sperm from the epididymis to the urethra
vasogram: recording of the flow in the vas deferens
vasotomy: creation of an opening in the vas deferens
vasovasorrhaphy: suturing of the vas deferens
vasovasostomy: reversal of a vasectomy
VBAC: vaginal delivery after a previous cesarean delivery
vein: vessel that carries unoxygenated blood to the heart from body tissues
vena caval thrombectomy: removal of a blood clot from the blood vessel (inferior vena cava, which is the vein trunk for the pelvic and abdominal area)
ventricle: chamber in the lower part of the heart
version: turning of the fetus from a presentation other than cephalic (head down) to cephalic for ease of birth
vesicostomy: surgical creation of a connection of the viscera of the bladder to the skin
vesicovaginal fistula: creation of a tube between the vagina and bladder
vesiculectomy: excision of the seminal vesicle
vesiculotomy: incision into the seminal vesicle
vitre/o-: prefix meaning pertaining to the vitreous body of the eye
vulva: external female genitalia including labia majora, labia minora, clitoris, and vaginal opening
wound repair, complex: involves complicated wound closure including revision, debridement, extensive undermining, and more than layered closure
wound repair, intermediate: requires closure of one or more subcutaneous tissue and superficial fascia, in addition to the skin closure
wound repair, simple: superficial wound repair, involving epidermis, dermis, and subcutaneous tissue, requiring only simple one-layer suturing

CHAPTER REVIEW Chapter 3, Part I, Theory

1. Anesthesia time is listed in ______________________________ and ______________. Units of time are determined by the third-party payer.
2. Anesthesia time begins when the anesthesiologist ________________, continues ____________________________ the procedure, and ends when____.

Match the two-digit modifiers to the correct words:

3. _____ Multiple Procedures
4. _____ Mandated Services
5. _____ Unusual Procedural Services
6. _____ Unusual Anesthesia

a. -23
b. -51
c. -32
d. -22

7. What is the one modifier that is not used with anesthesia procedures?

   ____

8. "P1" is an example of what type of modifier?

   ____

9. What word means "in a dying state"?______________________________
10. What word means "affecting the body as a whole"?

    ____

11. The letter "P" in combination with what number indicates a brain-dead patient?____
12. What type of circumstance identifies a component of anesthesia service that affects the character of the service? ____________________________
13. Anesthesia procedures are divided by what type of site?

    ____

14. What is the largest section of the six CPT manual sections?

    ____

15. How many subsections does the Surgery section have?_______________

16. The subsections in the Surgery section are according to

____

17. Measurement in the CPT manual is in what system?

____

Wound repair codes are determined by what three criteria?

18. ______________________________

19. ______________________________

20. ______________________________

What are the three classifications of wound repair?

21. ______________________________

22. ______________________________

23. ______________________________

24. What is the bilateral procedures modifier? ______________________________

____

List the three times when multiple procedures are coded:

25. ______________________________

26. ______________________________

27. ______________________________

28. Modifier -51 indicates what?

____

29. What is the name for the information that precedes section information?

____

30. What is the first subsection in the Surgery section?

____

31. If an unlisted procedure code is used, what must accompany the code?

____

32. Surgery package and surgical global fee are terms used to describe what?

____

33. What is the five-digit code number used for documentation purposes to report non-billed postoperative services provided to the patient under the umbrella of a surgery package?

____

34. The major difference in destruction of lesions is whether the lesion is

______________ or ______________.

35. The division of malignant lesion excision is based on ______________

and ______________.

Match the following terms to the correct definitions:

36. curettage _______
37. endoscopy _______
38. excision _______
39. incision _______
40. repair _______
41. -centesis _______
42. aspiration _______

a. to remedy, replace, or heal (suturing a wound)
b. cutting or taking away
c. inspection of body organs or cavities using a lighted scope that may be placed through an existing opening or through a small incision
d. scraping of a cavity using a spoon-shaped instrument
e. suffix meaning puncture of a cavity
f. surgically cutting into
g. use of a needle and a syringe to withdraw

Match the following terms to the correct definitions:

43. dermis _______
44. epidermis _______
45. debridement _______
46. paring _______
47. skin graft _______
48. tissue transfer _______
49. closed treatment _______
50. open treatment _______
51. soft tissue _______

a. tissues (fascia, connective tissue, muscle, etc.), surrounding a bone
b. second layer of skin holding blood vessels, nerve endings, sweat glands, and hair follicles
c. piece of skin for grafting that is still partially attached to the original blood supply and is used to cover an adjacent wound area
d. transplantation of tissue to repair a defect
e. cleansing or removing dead tissue from a wound
f. fracture site that is not surgically opened and visualized
g. removal of thin layers of skin by peeling or scraping
h. fracture site that is surgically opened and visualized
i. outer layer of skin

Match the following terms to the correct definitions:

52. pericardium _______
53. electrode _______
54. ventricle _______
55. atrium _______
56. artery _______
57. vein _______
58. angioplasty _______
59. anomaly _______

a. vessel that carries oxygenated blood from the heart to body tissues
b. chamber in the lower part of the heart
c. surgical or percutaneous procedure on a vessel to dilate the vessel opening; used in the treatment of atherosclerotic disease
d. chamber in the upper part of the heart
e. abnormality
f. lead attached to a generator that carries the electric current from the generator to the atria or ventricles
g. membranous sac enclosing the heart and ends of the great vessels
h. vessel that carries unoxygenated blood to the heart from body tissues

Match the following terms to the correct definitions:

60. perineum _______
61. salping(o)- _______
62. rectocele _______
63. gloss- _______
64. anastomosis _______
65. colostomy _______
66. gastrostomy _______

a. prefix meaning tube
b. prefix meaning tongue
c. area between the vulva and anus; also known as the pelvic floor
d. herniation of the rectal wall through the posterior wall of the vagina
e. surgical connection of two tubular structures, such as two pieces of the intestine
f. artificial opening between the colon and the abdominal wall
g. artificial opening between the stomach and the abdominal wall

67. What symbol in the CPT manual indicates that a procedure does not include follow-up care? ____
68. What kind of package is developed by third-party payers and may go beyond the package described in the CPT manual?

    ____
69. What two words following a procedure description alert you to the fact that you can code the procedure only if it is not done as a part of another, more major, procedure? ____

Chapter 3, Part II, Practical

What are the correct modifiers for the following as described in Appendix A of the CPT manual?

70. Multiple procedures ____________________

71. Unexpectedly terminated or reduced services ____________________

72. Extremely difficult ____________________

73. Bilateral procedure ____________________

74. Surgery component only ____________________

75. Preoperative component only ____________________

76. Postoperative component only ____________________

77. Indicates an E/M service was done on the same day as a minor procedure

    ____

78. Initial evaluation and management services with decision to do surgery,

    within the preoperative period of a major surgery ____________________

79. Assistant surgeon ____________________

Code the following cases for the surgical procedures and office visits only. Do not code the radiology services or laboratory work that may be included.

80. Dennis Smith, a 42-year-old railroad employee (established patient), has a history of severe mitral stenosis with regurgitation. He is now symptomatic and his physician recommends a mitral valve replacement to be done in 2 weeks. Dennis agrees to the surgery, and the physician does a complete examination in preparation for surgery. The physician orders a general health panel blood workup and a urinalysis (automated). Three weeks later, the physician performs the mitral valve replacement. Dennis recovers uneventfully and is discharged from the hospital 5 days later.

    Code(s): ____________________

81. Margaret Wilson, a 26-year-old mother of three (new patient), had routine screening mammography of both breasts. (You do not need to code the mammography.) A shadow was visualized in the right breast. The physician performs a biopsy (needle core). The biopsy indicates malignancy. The patient agrees to and has a mastectomy (simple, complete) 1 week later.

    Code(s): ____________________

82. Shirley Peters, age 80, a new patient, presents to the office for scissor removal of 15 skin tags.

    Code(s): ____________________

83. James Morgan, age 61, was diagnosed with a cranial neoplasm. The neurologist does a resection of the neoplasm, midline skull base, intradural, using an infratemporal preauricular approach to the middle cranial fossa.

Code(s): ____________________

84. Jennifer Prescott, age 47, has developed chest pain and difficulty breathing. Jennifer has had several episodes of coughing up thick, blood-tinged sputum. A diagnostic bronchoscopy is done with a specimen taken of the mass. The pathology report is positive for cancer, and a lobectomy is done.

Code(s): ____________________

85. Mary Carter, age 72, has an exploratory laparotomy with cholecystectomy.

Code(s): ____________________

86. Douglas O'Malley, age 31, has been having difficulty breathing and has had longstanding sinusitis. It is decided that Douglas will have a sinus endoscopy with anterior and posterior total ethmoidectomy with removal of polyps.

Code(s): ____________________

87. Sue Lind, age 29, had excision of a vaginal cyst. The pathology report comes back positive for malignancy. Her physician recommends and performs a diagnostic laparoscopy. Evidence of further malignancy of the uterus is seen and the physician does a laparoscopically assisted vaginal hysterectomy.

Code(s): ____________________

88. Martha Sellers brings her 8-year-old son Randy, a new patient, to the office for complaints of left ear pain. The physician examines Randy and identifies the problem as an abscess of the external auditory canal. The physician drains the abscess and prescribes a 10-day regimen of antibiotics.

Code(s): ____________________

89. Removal of nevus of left cheek, autograft with split-thickness skin graft of 180 sq cm.

Code(s): ____________________

90. Nipple reconstruction

Code(s): ____________________

91. Thrombectomy of arterial graft

Code(s): ____________________

92. Resection of neoplastic lesion of parasellar area; extradural

Code(s): ____________________

93. Incision and drainage of perineal abscess

    Code(s): ____________________

94. Repair of recurrent, reducible incisional hernia

    Code(s): ____________________

95. Laminotomy with decompression of nerve root and disk removal L4–L5

    Code(s): ____________________

96. Destruction of 0.4-cm malignant lesion of the neck

    Code(s): ____________________

97. Direct repair of aneurysm and graft insertion for occlusive disease of the common femoral artery

    Code(s): ____________________

98. Laparoscopic treatment of ectopic pregnancy without salpingectomy

    Code(s): ____________________

99. Suture of sciatic nerve

    Code(s): ____________________

100. Closed treatment of fractured phalanges; without manipulation

    Code(s): ____________________

101. Simple repair of a superficial wound of the genitalia; 2.4 cm

    Code(s): ____________________

102. Diagnostic laparoscopy with fulguration of oviducts

    Code(s): ____________________

103. Adjacent tissue transfer of chin defect; 9 cm^2

    Code(s): ____________________

Code the following cases:

104. *Preoperative diagnosis:* respiratory failure and ventilator dependency secondary to pneumonia and cardiac disease

    Postoperative diagnosis: same

    Procedure performed: tracheostomy

    Procedure: Before the procedure, the risks, benefits, and possible complications of the operation were explained to the patient's family, and informed consent was obtained. The patient was placed in the supine position on his bed. His neck, chest, and upper arms were prepped and draped in sterile fashion. He was given general endotracheal anesthesia. An approximate 3- to 4-cm horizontal incision was made at about the second tracheal ring. Blunt dissection was carried down to the trachea through the subcutaneous fascia and the isthmus of the thyroid. Bleeding was controlled with electrocautery. The isthmus of the thyroid was mobilized and suture ligated with 2-0 silk sutures on each side. The third cartilaginous ring was chosen for the tracheostomy site. The third tracheal ring was opened with cautery and a No. 8F Shiley tube was placed through the vertical incision. This was done after the endotracheal tube was removed under direct visualization. The balloon was inflated on the trachea. Inspiration was returned to the chest through the tracheostomy tube. Good breath sounds were noted. There was CO_2 noted on the spectrometer. Hemostasis was good. The lateral ends of the incision were approximated with interrupted sutures using 2-0 silk. The tracheostomy apparatus was tied around the patient's neck with a cloth strap. A sterile dressing was applied underneath the sides of the tracheostomy apparatus. The patient tolerated the procedure well and there were no complications. He was returned to his intensive care unit bed in stable condition.

Code(s): ____________________

105. *Preoperative diagnosis:* cholecystitis, cholelithiasis

Postoperative diagnosis: same

Procedure performed: laparoscopic cholecystectomy

Procedure: The patient was taken to the operating room, placed in the supine position, and prepped and draped in the usual sterile fashion after successful induction of general endotracheal anesthesia. An inferior periumbilical incision was made and bluntly carried down toward the anterior fascia. A Veress needle was then inserted after tenting up the abdominal wall, and the abdomen insufflated without incident. Next, a 10-mm trocar was introduced through this incision and the laparoscope passed into the peritoneum. A quick inspection revealed no obvious acute pathologic process with the exception of a few adhesions of the ascending colon and the expected adhesions to the gallbladder. Next, a 10-mm trocar was inserted through an incision in the upper abdomen, just to the left of the midline. This was passed into the peritoneum under visualization with the camera. Two 5-mm trocars were then placed in the right side and laterally on the right. Graspers were passed through these latter two trocars, and the gallbladder was retracted superiorly and anteriorly. Adhesions of the omentum were taken down bluntly and with the aid of electrocautery. Attention was then turned to the area of the porta hepatis and dissection of the structures of that region was begun. A fair amount of fibrosis and scarring was noted in this area, which hindered the progress of the dissection somewhat. Eventually, the cystic duct was identified. A clip was placed very high on the cystic duct toward the gallbladder side. Dissection was continued until the cystic artery was isolated. Three clips were placed on the cystic artery, and it was transected. Next, the cystic duct was partially transected, and through this opening a cholangiogram catheter was inserted. One intraoperative cholangiogram was obtained, which showed free flow of dye into the duodenum and into the intrahepatic biliary system, with both the right and left hepatic ducts being visualized. No filling defects were appreciated.

The cystic duct was then completely transected and two more clips placed on the proximal end. A structure that appeared to be an accessory cystic artery was dissected and clipped. Next, the gallbladder was dissected off the gallbladder bed using electrocautery. The gallbladder was entered on two occasions, and bile, which was noted to be extremely thick and dark green to black, was aspirated without difficulty. No stones were lost inside the peritoneum. Bleeding from the gallbladder bed, on occasion, was controlled with electrocautery. Irrigation was used a fair amount during this time. With the gallbladder completely dissected off the gallbladder bed, irrigation and aspiration of the gallbladder bed and the fluid that had accumulated within the abdomen during the case were done. The gallbladder was then removed through the upper 10-mm incision using a cervical dilator to spread the fascia. This required extending the incision about 0.5 cm. The gallbladder was removed and sent for pathologic examination.

Again, the gallbladder bed and porta hepatis were inspected and hemostasis achieved with electrocautery. Once hemostasis was adequate, the abdominal contents were reaspirated and all trocars were then removed under direct visualization, with no bleeding noted from inside the peritoneal cavity. The camera was removed, and the abdomen deflated. All incisions were then closed using interrupted sutures of 4-0 Vicryl in a subcuticular fashion.

The patient tolerated the procedure well with an estimated blood loss of less than 100 mL and no complications.

Code(s): ____________________

Learning About the Radiology and Pathology/ Laboratory Sections

CHAPTER TOPICS

Learning Objectives

After completing this chapter, you should be able to

1. Explain the format of the Radiology section.
2. Interpret the information contained in the Radiology Guidelines.
3. Demonstrate an understanding of Radiology terminology.
4. Code using Radiology codes.
5. Explain the format of the Pathology/Laboratory section.
6. Interpret the information contained in the Pathology/Laboratory Guidelines.
7. Demonstrate an understanding of Pathology/Laboratory terminology.
8. Code using Pathology/Laboratory codes.

AN OVERVIEW OF CODING RADIOLOGIC PROCEDURES AND THERAPIES

The Section Format

Radiology is the branch of medicine that uses radiant energy to diagnose and treat patients. The term originally was used to refer to the use of x-rays to produce radiographs but is now commonly applied to encompass all types of medical imaging. A physician who specializes in radiology is a **radiologist.** Radiologists can provide services to patients independent of or in conjunction with another physician of a different specialty. The Radiology section of the CPT manual is divided into four main subsections.

Radiology Subsections

- Diagnostic Radiology
- Diagnostic Ultrasound
- Radiation Oncology
- Nuclear Medicine

Medical Terminology Used in Radiology

The suffix *-graphy* means "making of a film" using a variety of methods. **Radiography** is a broad term used to indicate any number of methods used by radiologists to do diagnostic testing. The following exercise will familiarize you with some of the numerous radiographic procedures in the CPT manual.

EXERCISE A *Medical Terminology Used in Radiology*

The following words end in *-graphy,* meaning "making of a film." For example, in angiocardiography, *angio* means vessels and *cardio* means heart, so angiocardiography is the making of a film of the heart and vessels. What do the other *-graphy* words make a film of?

angiocardiography ______heart and vessels______

1. aortography ____________
2. arthrography ____________
3. cholangiopancreatography ____________
4. cholangiography ____________
5. cystography ____________
6. dacryocystography ____________
7. duodenography ____________
8. echocardiography ____________
9. encephalography ____________
10. epididymography ____________
11. hepatography ____________
12. hysterosalpingography ____________
13. laryngography ____________
14. lymphangiography ____________
15. myelography ____________
16. pyelography ____________
17. sialography ____________
18. sinography ____________
19. splenography ____________

20. urography ______________________________

21. venography ______________________________

22. vesiculography ______________________________

Radiographic Procedures

Here are just a few more radiographic procedures for your review:

1. **Fluoroscopy** views the inside of the body and projects it onto a television screen. Fluoroscopy provides live images and allows the study of the function of the organ (physiology) as well as the structure of the organ (anatomy).
2. **Magnetic resonance imaging (MRI)** is the use of nonionizing radiation to show the body in a cross-sectional view.
3. **Tomography** is the view of a single plane of the body by blurring out all other layers.
4. **Biometry** is the application of a statistical method to a biologic fact.

Radiographic Planes

Terminology referring to planes of the body and positioning of the body is often used in the Radiology section. A **position** is how the patient is placed during the x-ray examination, and a **projection** is the path of the x-ray beam. An example of a projection is anteroposterior, which denotes that the x-ray beam enters the patient's body on the front (anterior) side and exits the back (posterior) side. An example of a position is **prone,** which means the patient is lying on his or her anterior (front), but the entrance and exit of the x-ray beam are not specified. Familiarity with this terminology will aid you as you review the Radiology section and begin to choose the correct codes for physician services. Figure 4–1 illustrates the major planes and the surfaces of the body that can be accessed through positioning of the body.

Figure 4–2 shows proximal and distal body references. **Proximal** and **distal** are directional body references that are closest to (proximal) or farthest from (distal) the trunk of the body. These terms are relative, meaning they are used to describe the position of the part as compared with another part. Therefore, the term "proximal" describes a part as being closer to the body trunk than another part, and the term "distal" describes a part as being farther away from the body than another part. The knee would be described as being proximal to the ankle, and it would also be described as being distal to the thigh or hip.

Figure 4–3 illustrates the **anteroposterior** (AP) (front to back) position, in which the patient has his or her front (anterior) closest to the x-ray machine, and the x-ray travels through the patient from the front to the back. In Figure 4–4, the **posteroanterior** (PA) position, the patient has his or her back (posterior) located closest to the machine, and the beam travels through the patient from back to front.

Lateral positions are named for side positions. When the patient's right side is closest to the film, it is called *right lateral.* When the patient's left side is closest to the film, it is called *left lateral.* For example, Figure 4–5 shows left lateral and Figure 4–6 shows right lateral. The use of these various positions allows the

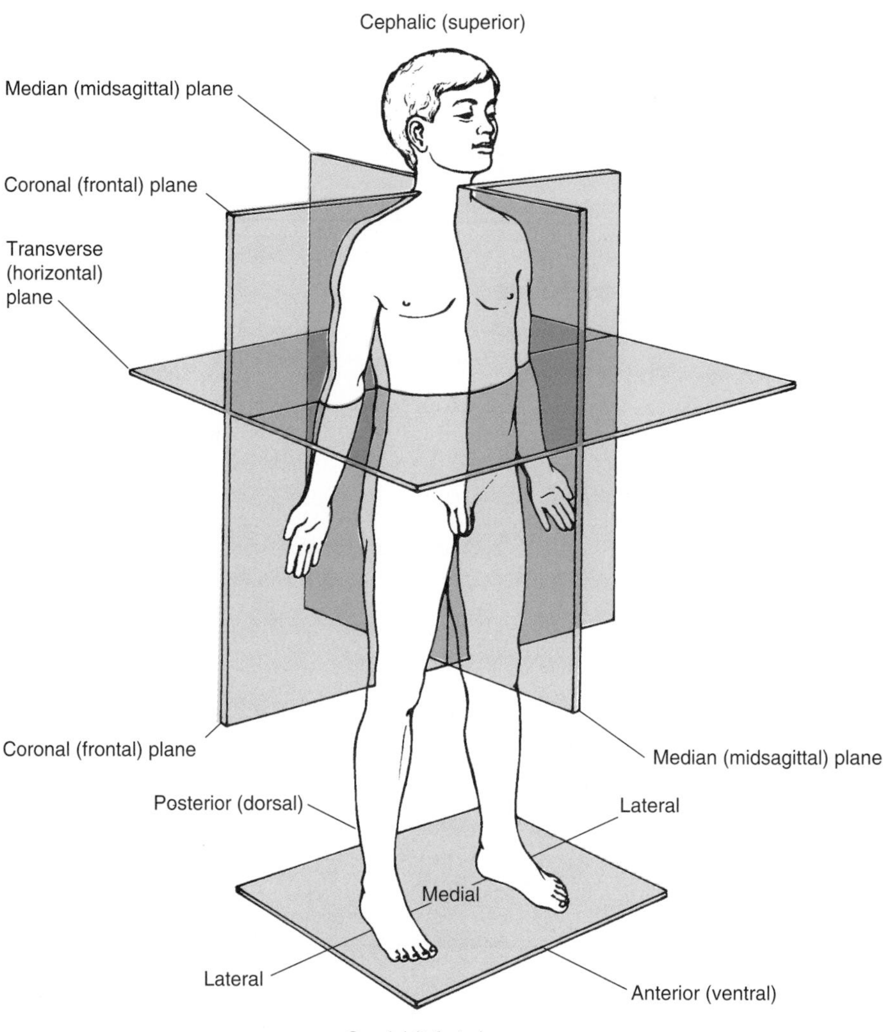

Figure 4–1
Planes of the body and terms of location and position of the body.

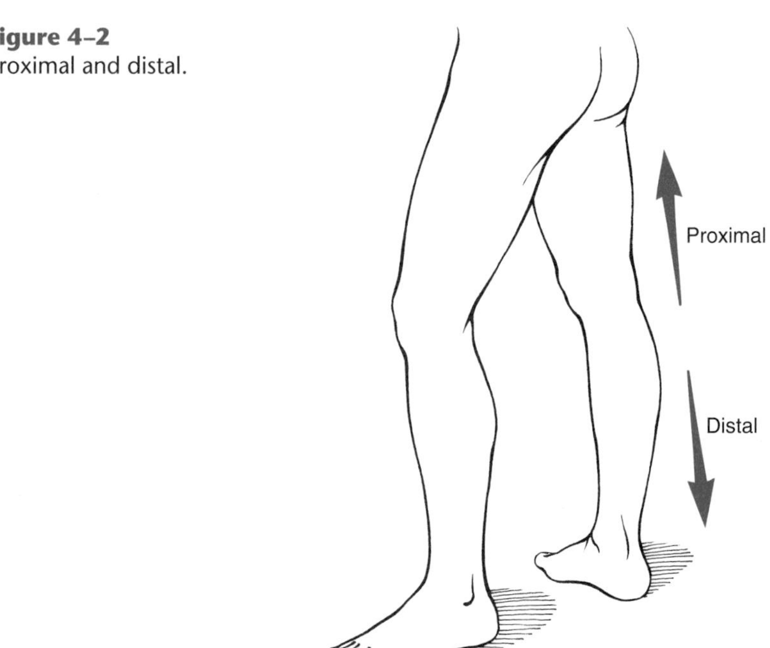

Figure 4–2
Proximal and distal.

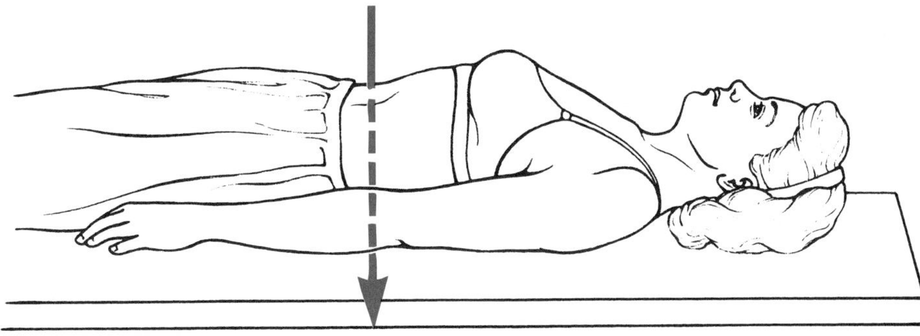

Figure 4–3
Anteroposterior (AP) projection.

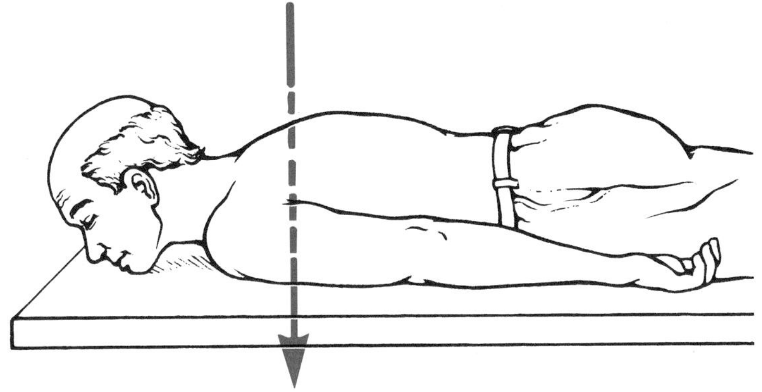

Figure 4–4
Posteroanterior (PA) projection.

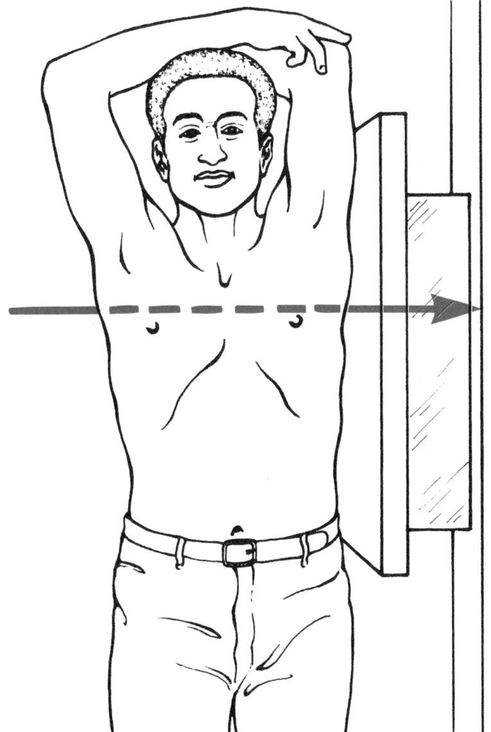

Figure 4–5
Left lateral position.

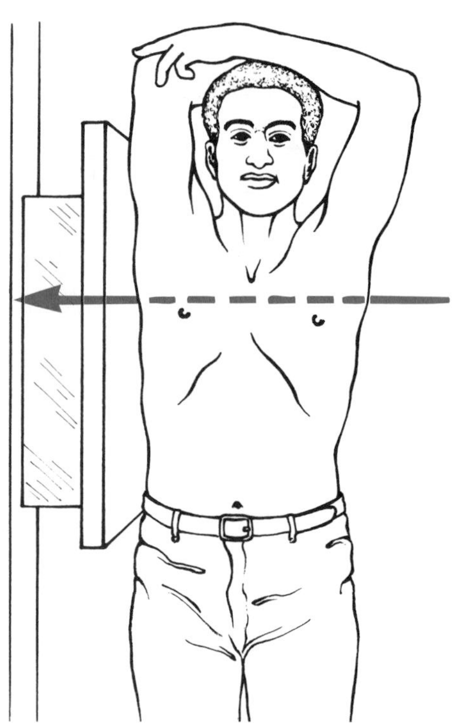

Figure 4–6
Right lateral position.

physician to view the body from different angles. Figure 4–7 shows posteroanterior and lateral positions used to view a patient's lung that contains cancer.

Dorsal, more commonly referred to as "supine," means lying on the back; **ventral,** more commonly referred to as "prone," means lying on the stomach; and *lateral* means lying on the side.

Decubitus positions are used to describe recumbent positions with the x-ray beam placed horizontally. *Ventral decubitus* (prone) is the act of lying on the stomach (Fig. 4–8*A*), and *dorsal decubitus* (supine) is the act of lying on the back (Fig. 4–8*B*). The term "decubitus," generally shortened to "decub," has special meaning in radiology. The simple act of lying on one's back would be referred to as lying supine, but if a horizontal x-ray beam is used the position becomes decubitus. The type of decubitus is determined by the body surface the patient is lying on.

Recumbent is lying down. Thus, *right lateral recumbent* is when the patient is lying down on the right side (Fig. 4–8*C*), and *left lateral recumbent* is when the patient is lying down on the left side (Fig. 4–8*D*). In the ventral decubitus position, the patient is positioned prone and the x-ray beam comes into the patient from the right side and exits on the left (Fig. 4–8*E*).

In the *left lateral decubitus* position, the patient is lying on the left side with the beam coming from the front passing through to the back (anteroposterior) (Fig. 4–8*F*).

When the patient is positioned on his or her back (dorsal decubitus) and the x-ray beam comes into the left side of the patient, the positioning is dorsal decubitus, but the view obtained is a right lateral (because the right side is closest to the film) (Fig. 4–8*G*).

The **oblique** views refer to those obtained while rotating the body so it is not in a full anteroposterior or posteroanterior position but somewhat diagonal. Oblique views are termed according to the body surface on which the patient is lying. The *left anterior oblique* (LAO) position is depicted in Figure 4–8*H* with the

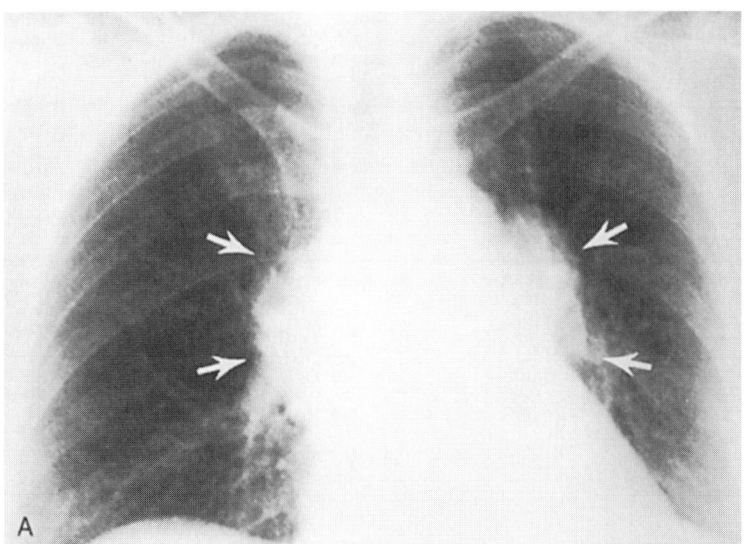

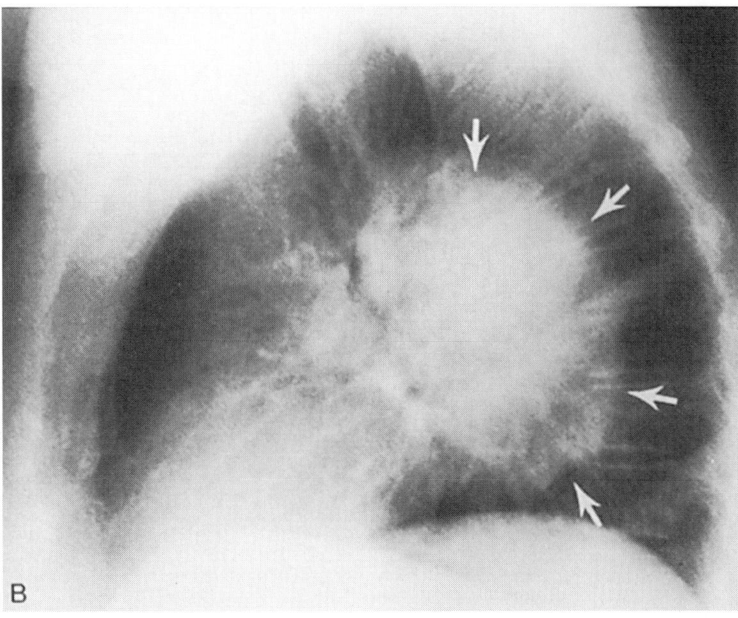

Figure 4–7
Use of posteroanterior and lateral positions to view a primary mediastinal bronchogenic carcinoma. Posteroanterior (*A*) and lateral (*B*) radiographs of this 59-year-old female smoker show a massive subcarinal mass (*arrows*) and no pulmonary mass. The subcarinal mass was surgically shown to be a large cell carcinoma of the lung. (From Woodring JH: Unusual radiographic manifestations of lung cancer. Radiol Clin North Am 28[3]:611, 1990.)

patient's left side rotated forward toward the table. The patient is lying on the left anterior aspect of his or her body. The *right anterior oblique* (RAO) position has the patient on his or her right side rotated forward toward the table as in Figure 4–8*I*.

Two more oblique views are left posterior oblique and right posterior oblique views. In the *left posterior oblique* (LPO) view, the patient is rotated so that the left posterior aspect of his or her body is against the table, as in Figure 4–8*J*. The *right posterior oblique* (RPO) view has the patient on the right side rotated back as in Figure 4–8*K*.

The last two terms that are used to describe projections are tangential and axial. **Tangential** is the patient position that allows the beam to skim the body part, which produces a profile of the structure of the body (Fig. 4–9*A*). Figure 4–9*B* illustrates the **axial** projection, which is any projection that allows the beam to pass through the body part lengthwise.

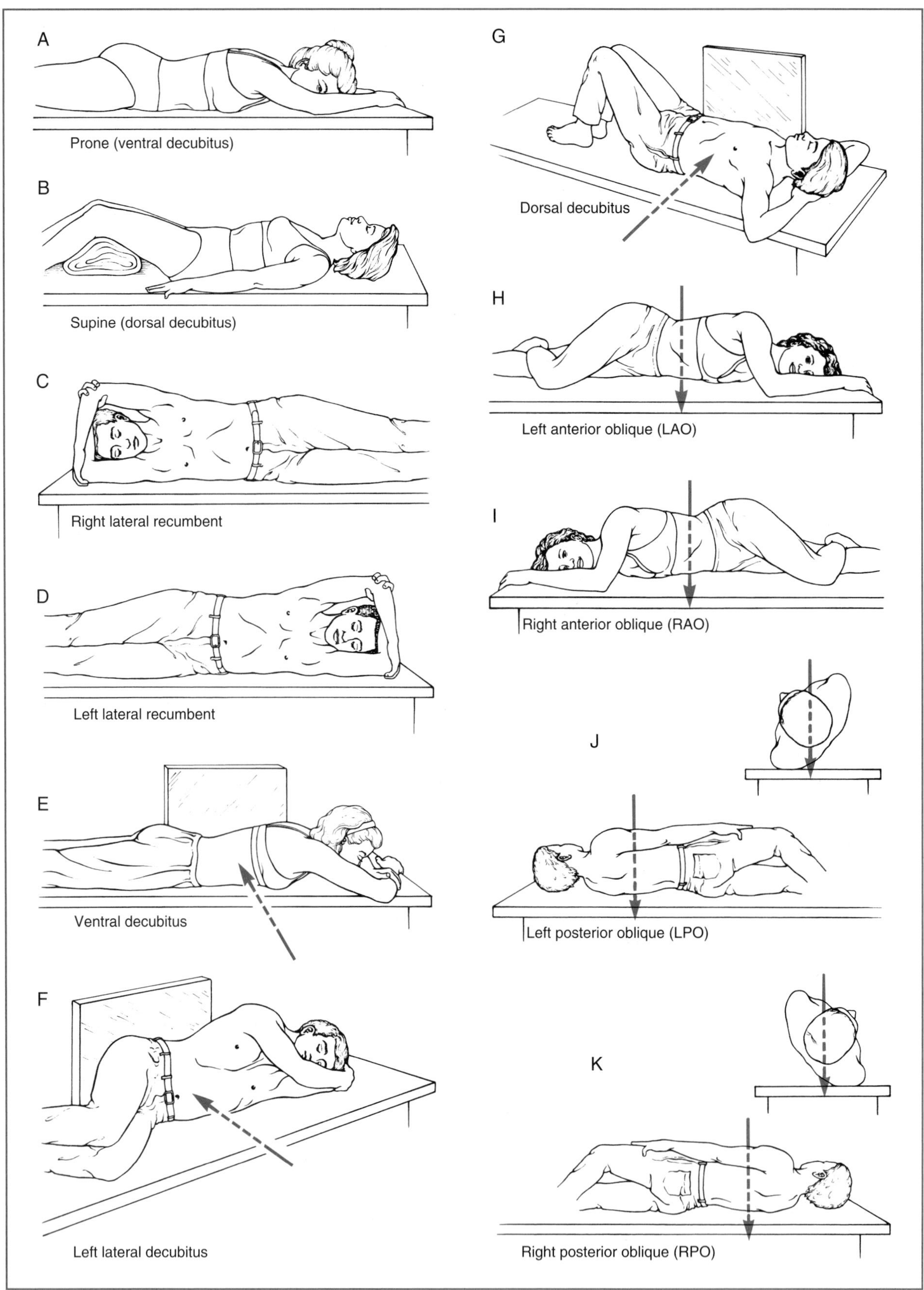

Figure 4–8
Radiographic positions. *A.* Prone (ventral decubitus). *B.* Supine (dorsal decubitus). *C.* Right lateral recumbent. *D.* Left lateral recumbent. *E.* Ventral decubitus. *F.* Left lateral decubitus. *G.* Dorsal decubitus. *H.* Left anterior oblique (LAO). *I.* Right anterior oblique (ROA). *J.* Left posterior oblique (LPO). *K.* Right posterior oblique (RPO).

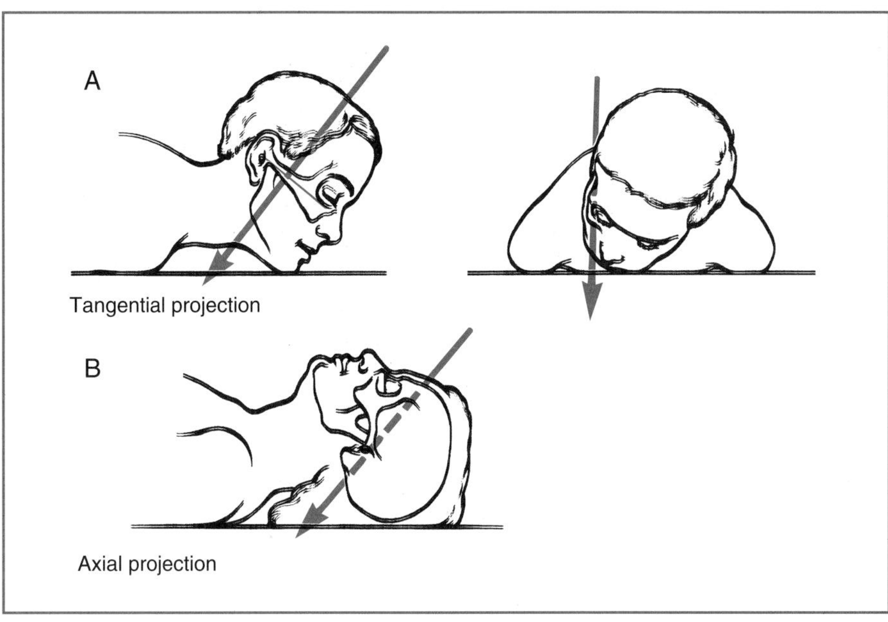

Figure 4–9
Radiographic projections.
A. Tangential projection.
B. Axial projection.

EXERCISE B *Radiographic Planes*

Fill in the blanks with the correct words:

1. What is the word that indicates how the patient is placed during the x-ray examination? ______________________

2. What is the term that indicates the path the x-ray beam travels?

____

What do the following abbreviations mean?

3. AP ______________________
4. PA ______________________
5. RAO ______________________
6. LPO ______________________
7. What term indicates a patient is lying supine or on his or her back?

____

8. What term indicates a patient is lying prone or on his or her stomach?

____

9. What term indicates a patient is lying on his or her right side?

____

10. What is the term that indicates when a patient is on his or her back and the x-ray beam comes into the right side of the patient?

____

Radiology Guidelines

As with all Guidelines, the Radiology Guidelines should be read carefully before radiologic procedures or services are coded. The Guidelines contain the unique instructions used within the section and the indications for multiple procedures, separate procedures, unlisted radiology procedure codes, and applicable modifiers.

Guidelines that are used more commonly in this section than in others are those explaining the professional, technical, and global components of a procedure. These components describe the following:

1. **Professional:** describes the services of the physician, including the supervision of the taking of the x-ray film and the interpretation with report of the x-ray films
2. **Technical:** describes the services of the technologist, as well as the use of the equipment, film, and other supplies
3. **Global:** describes the combination of the professional and technical components (1 and 2)

For example, if a patient had a radiology procedure done in a clinic that owns its own equipment, employs its own technologist(s), and also employs the radiologist who will supervise, interpret, and report on the radiologic results, the global procedure will be coded for billing. But if the radiologist is reading and interpreting films that were taken at another facility, only the professional component would be coded.

When only the professional component of the service is provided, the modifier -26 is placed behind the CPT code. Modifier -26 alerts the third-party payer to the fact that only the professional component was provided. If, for example, an independent radiology facility takes a complete chest x-ray (71030) and sends the x-rays to an independent radiologist who reads the x-rays and writes a report of the findings in the x-rays, the coding for the independent radiologist would be:

71030-26	Complete chest x-ray, four views	$XX.XX
	Professional component only	

There is no CPT modifier to indicate the technical component of radiologic services. The modifier most commonly used is the HCPCS Level II modifier -TC, which stands for technical component. HCPCS codes are for use with Medicare and Medicaid claims, which you will be learning about in Chapter 5 of this text. When submitting claims for radiologic services in which only the technical component was provided, use a CPT code followed by -TC. For example, if you were the coder for the independent radiology facility that took the complete chest x-ray (71030), you would code as follows:

71030-TC	Complete chest x-ray, four views	$XX.XX
	Technical component only	

Supervision and Interpretation

The other coding practice most commonly used in the Radiology section is called **component** or **combination coding,** which means that a code from the Radiology section as well as a code from one of the other sections must be used to fully describe the procedure. For example, interventional radiologists may inject contrast material; place stents, catheters, or guidewires; or perform any number of procedures found throughout the CPT manual. Many times before radiology procedures can be performed, a contrast material must be injected into the patient to make certain organs or vessels stand out more clearly on the radiographic image. When this contrast material is injected into the patient by the radiologist, a CPT code from the Surgery section must be used to indicate the injection procedure. Codes in the Radiology section describe only the radiology procedures, not the injections or placement of other materials necessary to do the procedure.

Suppose, for example, a voiding urethrocystography with contrast medium enhancement is performed. In this procedure, a physician injects a radioactive material into the bladder. An x-ray of the bladder (cystography) is then obtained; the x-rays show filling, voiding, and post-voiding. The injection portion of the procedure is coded with a surgery code (51600: Injection procedure for cystography or voiding urethrocystography) and the cystography is coded with a radiology code (74455: Urethrocystography, voiding, radiologic supervision and interpretation).

As a new coder, you will need to pay special attention to the information in parentheses below the codes in the Radiology section. This parenthetical material gives you information about other components of procedures. Previous editions of the CPT manual had combination codes that were used when the physician did both components of some procedures. Using the combination code replaced the use of one code from surgery and one code from radiology; but many of these combination codes have been deleted. One reason they were deleted is to allow the physicians to more specifically indicate the services provided to the patient. For example, the parenthetical phrase below code 74455 indicates that a previous combination code was deleted and directs you to code 51600 and 74455 for the complete procedure. There are many parenthetical phrases such as this throughout the Radiology section that you will want to reference when coding component procedures.

Odds and Ends

Many of the code descriptions state "radiologic supervision and interpretation" and alert you to component coding. When component coding, be certain that you read the parenthetical information that follows these component codes. Some codes are divided based on the extent of the radiologic examination, such as procedures that "specify with KUB" (kidney, ureter, and bladder). You must read the radiologist's report or the details from the medical record for the extent of the procedure. Always code to the fullest extent of the procedure.

Codes are also often divided based on if contrast materials were used. The phrase "with contrast" in the CPT manual means contrast that was administered intravascularly. If the procedure indicates that contrast was oral or rectal, the service is coded as "without contrast."

Radiographic procedures are located in the CPT manual index by the main term "X-ray" with subterms for the anatomic part (eg, hand, spine).

EXERCISE C Radiology Guidelines

Fill in the blanks using the Radiology Guidelines of your CPT manual:

1. What procedure is one that is "performed independently of, and is not immediately related to, other services"? ______________________

2. If several medical services are provided in conjunction with radiologic services to a patient on the same day, what type of procedure modifier could be used?

   ____

3. What are the four subsections of the Radiology section?

   ____

   ____

   ____

   ____

4. What is the unlisted diagnostic nuclear medicine code used for cardiovascular procedures?

   Code(s): ____________

5. What is the unlisted code used for clinical brachytherapy?

   Code(s): ____________

6. The modifier used to indicate the Professional Component only is

   ______________________.

7. What abbreviation is used to indicate a Technical Component?

   ____

The Four Radiology Subsections

Diagnostic Radiology

The most standard radiographic procedures are contained in the Diagnostic Radiology subsection of the Radiology section. This subsection describes diagnostic imaging including plain x-ray films, the use of computed axial tomography (CAT or CT) scanning, magnetic resonance imaging (MRI), magnetic resonance angiography (MRA), and angiography. CT scanning uses an x-ray beam that rotates around the patient, as illustrated in Figure 4–10. Figure 4–11 shows a right lung carcinoma of a patient and the detail that can be obtained using

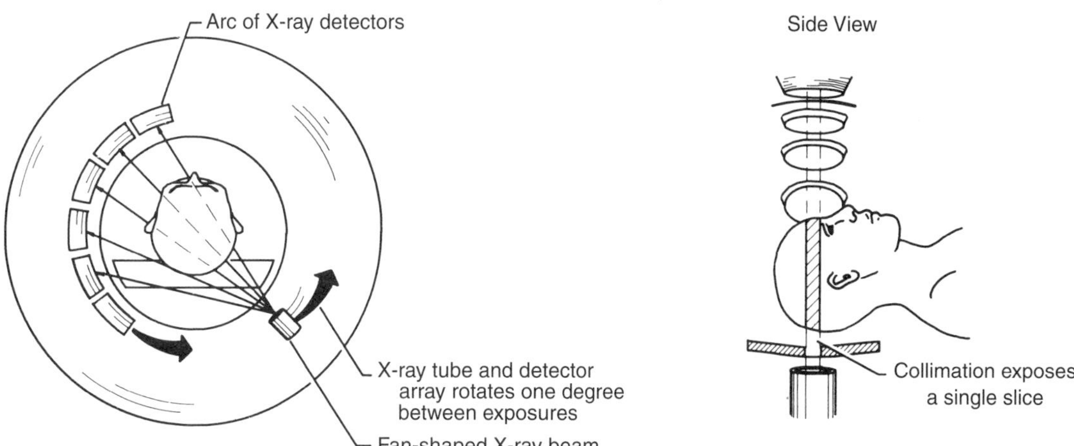

Figure 4–10
Principles of computed tomographic (CT) scanning. The x-ray tube produces a fan-shaped beam that passes through a section (slice) of the patient. This fan-shaped beam is received by a circular array of detectors at the opposite side. These detectors receive x-rays along the path through the patient's body. The detector and x-ray source rotate around the axis, producing exposures at 1-degree intervals of rotation. (From Stimac GK: Introduction to Diagnostic Imaging. Philadelphia, WB Saunders, 1992.)

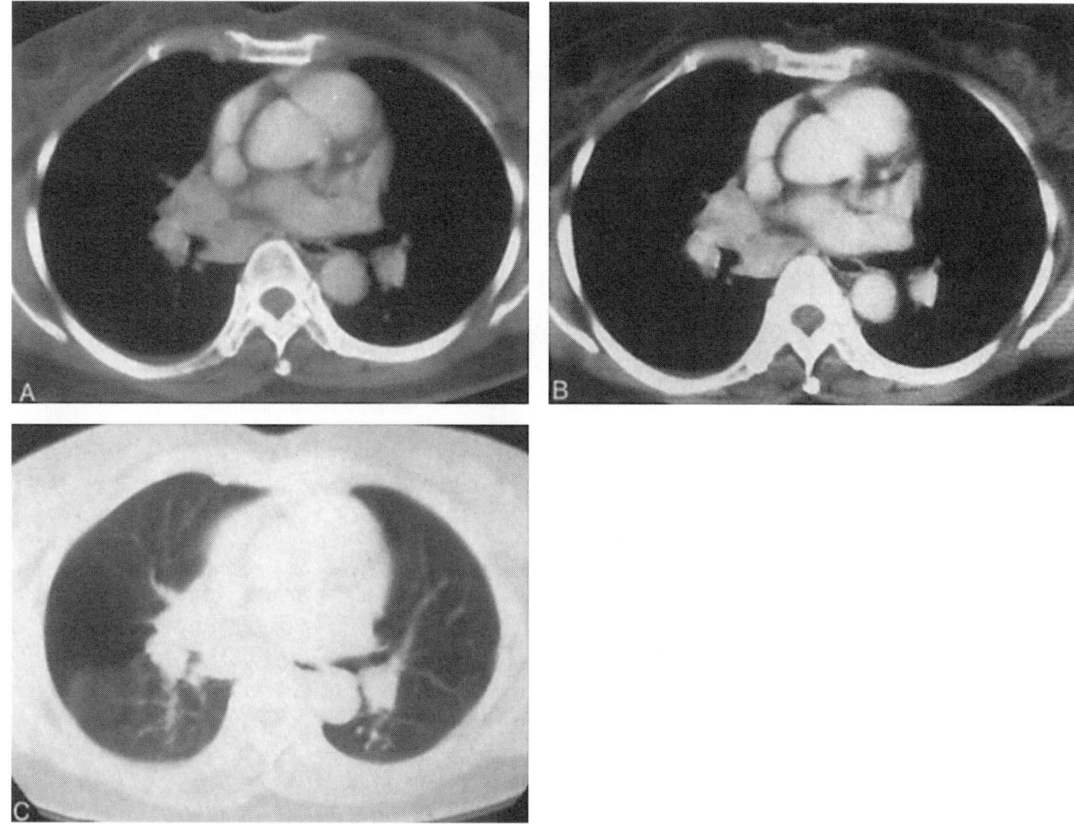

Figure 4–11
CT scans. *A.* A patient with right hilar lung carcinoma and mediastinal adenopathy showing the margins of the bones. *B.* The scan can be set to show the soft tissue. *C.* The lung organs can be shown using additional scan settings. There is greater detail than would be obtained with conventional radiographs. (Courtesy of Bruce Porter, MD.)

the CT scan. Special computer software is used with CT scanners to give three-dimensional images, which are used to study many different internal structures. Tomography, CT scanning, and MRI may include the use of injectable dyes (radiographic contrast) to aid in imaging, and the codes are divided based on whether or not contrast was used. Figure 4–12 is an example of a magnetic resonance image.

Angiography uses injectable dyes placed in the vessels to add contrast for the visualization of vessels' lumen size and condition. The lumen is the inside layer of the vessel. Angiography is used to look for abnormalities inside the vessels. Figure 4–13 shows an angiogram of the aortic arch and brachiocephalic vessels. The radiologist studies the vessels using angiography to detect conditions such as malformations, strokes, or myocarial infarctions.

Codes under the Diagnostic Radiology subsection are divided by anatomic site, from the head down. Some of the codes indicate a specific number of views, such as a minimum of three views or a single view. You should pay special attention to the description for each code and understand clearly how many views are specified in the code.

If fewer than the total number of views specified in the code are taken, modifier -52 would be used to indicate to the third-party payer that less of the procedure was performed than described by the code.

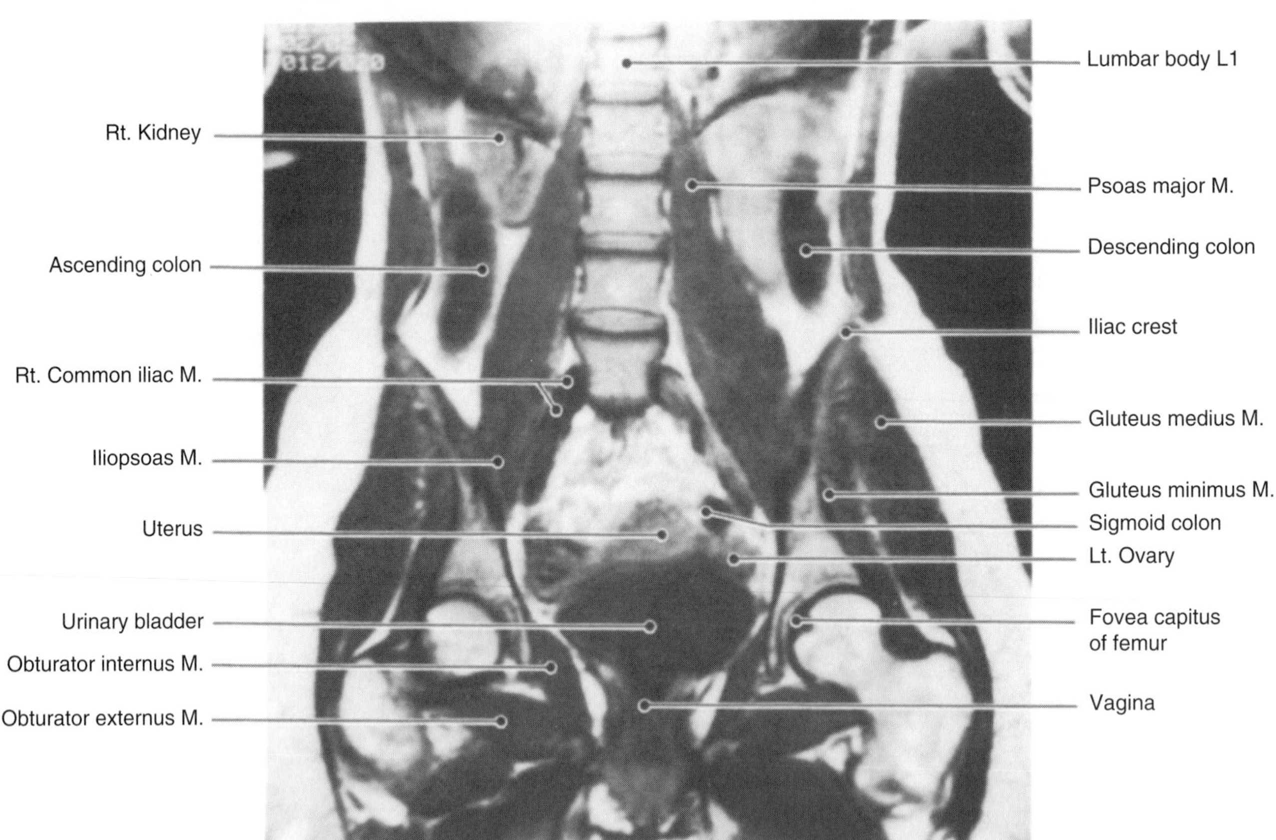

Figure 4–12
Magnetic resonance imaging produces excellent contrasts of the body. (From Christoforidis AJ: Atlas of Axial, Sagittal, and Coronal Anatomy with CT and MRI. Philadelphia, WB Saunders, 1988.)

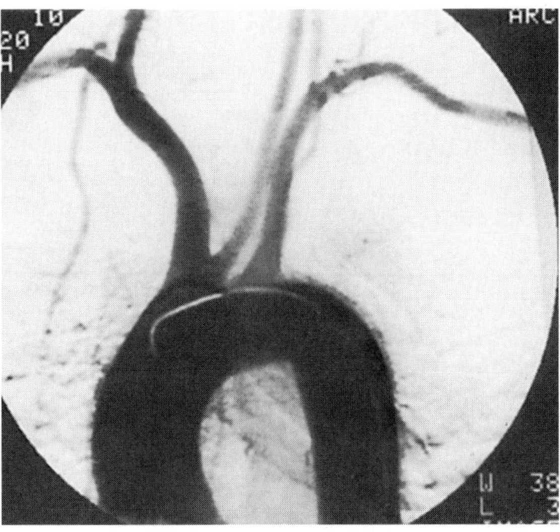

Figure 4–13
Angiography of the aortic arch and brachiocephalic vessels. (From Stimac GK: Introduction to Diagnostic Imaging. Philadelphia, WB Saunders, 1992.)

EXERCISE D *Diagnostic Radiology*

Complete the following:

1. What is the code for a mammography; bilateral?

   Code(s): ____________________

2. What is the code for an unlisted diagnostic radiologic procedure?

   Code(s): ____________________

3. Supervision and interpretation of an aortography, thoracic, by serialography

   Code(s): ____________________

   If the radiologist also injected the contrast dye for the aortography when done with a cardiac catheterization, what other code would have to be used?

   Code(s): ____________________

4. Supervision and interpretation of angiography, spinal, selective

   Code(s): ____________________

5. Radiologic examination of mastoids, two views per side

   Code(s): ____________________

6. Radiologic examination of mastoids, four views per side

   Code(s): ____________________

7. Chest x-ray four views, complete

   Code(s): ____________________

8. Chest x-ray two views, frontal and side lateral

   Code(s): ____________________

9. Scapula, complete

   Code(s): ____________________

10. Complete hip x-ray study, two views

    Code(s): ____________________

11. Urography, retrograde (moving against the flow), without KUB

    Code(s): ____________________

12. Supervision and interpretation of transluminal atherectomy, renal

    Code(s): ____________________

Diagnostic Ultrasound

The second subsection in Radiology is Diagnostic Ultrasound. **Diagnostic ultrasound** is the use of high-frequency sound waves to image anatomic structures and to detect the cause of illness and disease. It is used by the physician in the diagnosis process. Ultrasound moves at different speeds through tissue, depending on the density of the tissue. Forms and outlines of different organs can be identified with ultrasound as the sound waves move through or bounce back (echo) from the tissues.

There are many uses for ultrasound in medicine, such as showing a gallstone (Fig. 4–14) and showing triplets in the first trimester (Fig. 4–15). You may think that these ultrasound procedures do not produce a picture clear enough to be of use to the physician in the diagnosis process, but a professional trained in interpretation of ultrasound is able to clearly read these ultrasounds.

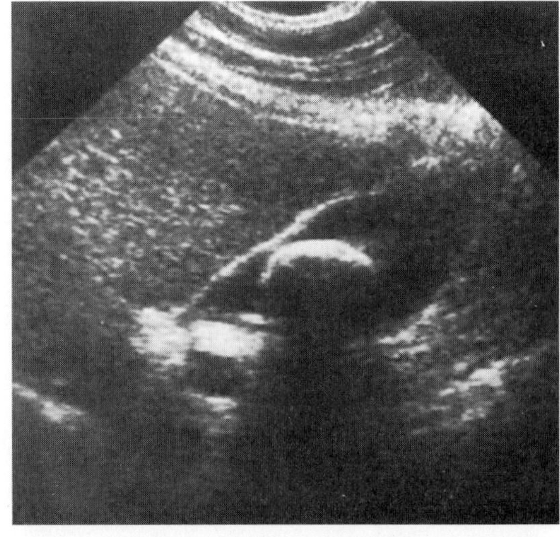

Figure 4–14
Ultrasound of the gallbladder shows shadowing of a gallstone. (From Stimac GK: Introduction to Diagnostic Imaging. Philadelphia, WB Saunders, 1992.)

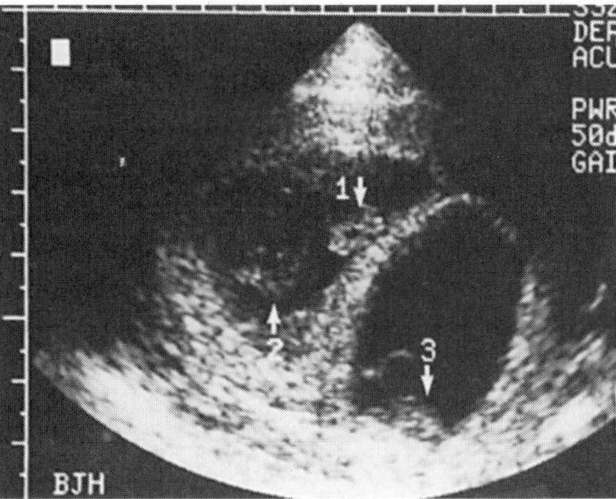

Figure 4–15
Triplets in the first trimester can be imaged on one scan. One fetus (3) is contained within its own sac with its own placenta. The other two fetuses share a placenta but are separated by a membrane. (From Benson CB, Doubilet PM: Sonography of multiple gestations. Radiol Clin North Am 28[1]:151, 1990.)

Most of the services in the Diagnostic Ultrasound subsection are located in the index of the CPT manual under the main term of Ultrasound. These terms are subdivided anatomically and by procedure, ie, guidance or drainage.

EXERCISE E Diagnostic Ultrasound

In the CPT manual, Diagnostic Ultrasound is divided into nine subheadings by body area.

Locate and list the subheadings:

1. ________________________________
2. ________________________________
3. ________________________________
4. ________________________________
5. ________________________________
6. ________________________________
7. ________________________________
8. ________________________________
9. ________________________________

Diagnostic Ultrasound Modes and Scans

There are four different types of ultrasound listed in the CPT manual: A-mode, M-mode, B-scan, and real-time scan.

A-mode: one-dimensional display reflecting the time it takes the sound wave to reach a structure and reflect back. This process maps the structure outline. "A" is for amplitude of sound return (echo).

M-mode: one-dimensional display of the movement of structures. "M" is for motion mode.

B-scan: two dimensional display of the movement of tissues and organs. "B" is for brightness mode. The sound waves bounce off tissue or organs and are projected on a black and white television screen. The strong signals display as black and the weaker signals display lighter. B-scan is also called grayscale ultrasound.

Real-time scan: two-dimensional display of both the structure and motion of tissues and organs that indicates the size, shape, and movement of the structures.

These modes and scans are used to describe the codes throughout the Diagnostic Ultrasound subsection. Codes are often divided based on what scan or mode was used. The medical record will indicate the scan or mode used.

Several codes within the subsection include the use of Doppler ultrasound. **Doppler ultrasound** is the use of sound that can be transmitted only through solids or liquids and is a specific version of ultrasonography or ultrasound. Doppler ultrasound is named for an Austrian physicist, Johann Doppler, who discovered a relationship between sound and light waves—a relationship upon which ultrasound technology was built. Doppler ultrasound is used to measure moving objects and so is ideal for measuring blood flow. Codes often state "with or without Doppler." Doppler ultrasound can be the standard black and white or color. The color Doppler translates the standard black and white to color images. Just imagine how much easier it is to see a leak in a vessel when the vessel is yellow and the blood is red. The code descriptions will specifically state "color flow Doppler."

There is some component coding, but mostly under the subheading of Ultrasonic Guidance Procedures. The parenthetical information will refer you back to the surgical procedure code. For example, code 76946 is for the radiologic supervision and interpretation of ultrasonic guidance for amniocentesis. The physician guides the insertion of a needle to withdraw fluid from the uterus. If the physician did both the radiologic portion of the procedure and the surgical procedure, you would code 59000 from the Surgery section and 76946 from the Radiology section.

The subheading Vascular Studies contains only parenthetical information that directs you to the Medicine section, Non-invasive Vascular Diagnostic Studies subsection. You will learn more about using the vascular codes in Chapter 5 of this text.

EXERCISE F *Diagnostic Ultrasound Modes and Scans*

Fill in the missing word(s), phrases, or codes for the following:

1. An echography of the spinal canal

   Code(s): ____________________

2. An echography of the chest using B-scan

   Code(s): ____________________

3. A complete abdominal echography in real-time with image documentation

   Code(s): ____________________

4. A repeat uterine echography in real-time with image documentation of a 32-week pregnant female

   Code(s): ____________________

5. A fetal profile, biophysical

   Code(s): ____________________

Radiation Oncology

The Radiation Oncology subsection of the Radiology section deals with both professional and technical treatments utilizing radiation to destroy tumors. The subsection is divided by treatment. In this subsection, special attention must be given to reporting professional and technical components. Read all of the definitions carefully to make certain you know what the code includes. Many third-party payers have developed strict guidelines determining the number of times certain procedures will be allowed within each treatment course. You should work closely with third-party payers to understand their preferred billing system.

The service codes within this subheading include codes for the initial consultation through management of the patient throughout the course of treatment. When the initial consultation occurs, the code for the service would come from the E/M section. For example, the patient might be an inpatient when the therapeutic radiologist first sees the patient for evaluation of treatment options and before a decision for treatment is made. You would code this consultation service with an Initial Inpatient Consultation code from the E/M section.

Normal follow-up care is included for three months following the completion of treatment that was reported using radiation oncology codes. You would not bill for the normal follow-up care that occurs within this three-month period.

Clinical Treatment Planning

Clinical Treatment Planning reflects professional services by the physician. It includes interpretation of special testing, tumor localization, treatment volume determination, treatment time/dosage determination, choice of treatment modality (method), determination of number and size of treatment ports, selection of appropriate treatment devices, and any other procedures necessary to adequately develop a course of treatment. A treatment plan is set up for all patients requiring radiation therapy.

There are three types of clinical treatment plans: simple, intermediate, and complex.

EXERCISE G *Clinical Treatment Planning*

Locate "Clinical Treatment Planning (External and Internal Sources)" in the CPT manual and write the definitions on the lines that follow for each type:

1. Simple: ____

   ____

   ____

2. Intermediate: ______________________________

____

____

3. Complex: ______________________________

____

____

The codes in the Clinical Treatment Planning subheading include both professional and technical components. For the professional component, the physician determines not only the treatment but also the equipment (eg, diagnostic x-ray machine) necessary to provide the treatment. For the technical component, the technologist completes the procedure (administers the treatment). Therefore, when billing for *only* the physician's services, you must use modifier -26 to indicate the *professional component–only* nature of the service.

The codes in Clinical Treatment Planning are located in the index of the CPT manual under the main term "Radiology" and the subterm "Therapeutic." Codes can also be located under the main term of the specific service, such as "Port Film."

EXERCISE H More Clinical Treatment Planning

Using the CPT manual, code the following:

1. Complex therapeutic radiology simulation–aided field setting

   Code(s): ______________

2. Therapeutic radiology treatment planning; simple

   Code(s): ______________

Medical Radiation, Physics, Dosimetry, Treatment Devices, and Special Services

Medical Radiation Physics, Dosimetry, Treatment Devices, and Special Services deals with the decision-making of the physicians as to the type of treatment (modality), dose calculation, and development of treatment devices. It is common to have several dosimetry or device changes during a treatment course. Dosimetry is the calculation of the radiation dose and placement.

Codes in this subheading are divided mostly by the level of treatment (simple, intermediate, complex). The codes are located in the index of the CPT manual under the main term "Radiation Therapy" and the subterm of the specific service, such as dose plan or treatment.

EXERCISE I Medical Radiation, Physics, Dosimetry, Treatment Devices, and Special Services

Using the CPT manual, code the following:

1. Design and construction of a bite block

   Code(s): ___________________

2. Calculation of an isodose for brachytherapy, single plane, two sources

   Code(s): ___________________

3. Teletherapy, isodose plan, simple

   Code(s): ___________________

Radiation Treatment Delivery

Radiation Treatment Delivery reflects the technical components only. These codes are used to bill for actual delivery of the radiation. Radiation treatment is delivered in units of megavoltage. A megavolt (MeV) is a unit of energy measure. While the radiation energy *delivered* by the machine is measured in megavolts, the energy that is *deposited* in the patient's tissue is measured in Rads (**r**adiation **ab**sorption **d**ose). The therapy dose in a cancer treatment would typically be in the thousands of Rads.

EXERCISE J Radiation Treatment Delivery

Using the CPT manual, code the following:

The patient receives radiation treatment delivery:

1. To a single area at 4 MeV

   Code(s): ___________________

2. With superficial voltage only

   Code(s): ___________________

3. To four separate areas with a rotational beam at 4 MeV

   Code(s): ___________________

4. For two separate areas, using three or more ports with multiple blocks up to 5 MeV

   Code(s): ___________________

5. For three or more separate areas using custom blocks, wedges, rotation beams, up to 5 MeV

   Code(s): ________________

Clinical Treatment Management

Clinical Treatment Management codes reflect professional component billing. The codes are used to bill weekly management of radiation therapy. The notes under the heading of Clinical Treatment Management state, "Weekly clinical management is based on five fractions comprising one week regardless of the time interval separating the delivery of treatment." This means these codes may be used if the patient receives a treatment at least five times within a 7-day week. It also means that if the patient receives five treatments at any time during this week (ie, skipping a day or two between treatments), these codes may still be used. You must be familiar with the definitions of the types of management—*simple, intermediate, complex,* and *conformal*—to appropriately bill physician services. The definitions are located in the notes beneath the subheading Clinical Treatment Management in the CPT manual and detail the treatments, types, and ports.

Two categories under the subheading Clinical Treatment Management are Hyperthermia and Clinical Intracavity Hyperthermia. Treatments from these categories are coded in addition to any radiation therapy or chemotherapy administered. Treatments are externally, interstitially, or intracavitarilly generated and are categorized according to the depth or probe application.

EXERCISE K Clinical Treatment Management

Using the CPT manual, code the following:

1. Five radiation management treatments, conformal

   Code(s): ________________

2. Unlisted procedure code for therapeutic radiation clinical treatment management (submission of this unlisted procedure code would necessitate a special report)

   Code(s): ________________

Clinical Brachytherapy

Clinical **brachytherapy** is the placement of radioactive material directly into or surrounding the site of the tumor. Placement may be **intercavitary** (within a body cavity) or **interstitial** (within the tissues), and material may be placed permanently or temporarily. Again, you must be familiar with the definitions of simple, intermediate, and complex applications as defined in the notes under the category Clinical Brachytherapy in the CPT manual.

The Clinical Brachytherapy codes include the physician's work related to the patient's admission to the hospital as well as the daily hospital visits.

EXERCISE L *Clinical Brachytherapy*

Using the CPT manual, code the following:

1. A simple application of a radioactive source, intracavitary

   Code(s): ________________

2. A simple application of a radioactive source, interstitial

   Code(s): ________________

3. Surface application of radioelement

   Code(s): ________________

Nuclear Medicine

Nuclear medicine deals with the placement of radionuclides within the body and the monitoring of emissions from the radioactive elements. Nuclear medicine is used not only for diagnostic studies but also for therapeutic treatment, such as treatment of thyroid conditions.

Stress tests are an example of nuclear medicine techniques. Radioactive material may be used during stress tests to monitor coronary artery blood flow. Radioactive material adheres to red blood cells. The radioactive materials on the red blood cells image the heart and indicate areas where the blood flows. The radioactive materials are injected 1 minute before the end of a stress test and then again 24 hours later for a comparison study. If the blood flow is decreased or absent, the image will show a blank area. If the coronary arteries are clear and allow blood to flow to the heart muscle, the image will show blood dispersement to all areas. If the arteries are partially blocked, the flow may be decreased but adequate during rest. During exercise, however, the necessary amount of oxygenated blood may not be adequate to keep the heart going, and that is when the chest pain may occur. During a stress test, if radionuclide dispersement is absent during exercise (showing inadequate blood supply to the area during peak demand) but is present during resting periods (showing adequate flow at rest), this is called **reversible ischemia,** meaning that heart muscle death has not occurred. With intervention, arteries may be opened or bypassed to increase the supply of blood to the muscle before heart muscle death does occur. If the radionuclide is absent during rest and exercise, the ischemia is considered **irreversible,** meaning that heart muscle death has already occurred. A stress test is one of the many uses of nuclear medicine for diagnostic purposes. As you code, you will become familiar with these various diagnostic tests and how they are reported and billed.

There are two subheadings within the Nuclear Medicine subsection—Diagnostic and Therapeutic. The subheading Diagnostic is further divided into category codes based on system, eg, endocrine system, cardiovascular system. None of the codes in the subsection includes the radiopharmaceutical(s) used for the diagnosis or therapy services. When the radiopharmaceutical(s) are supplied for diagnostic purposes, you use code 78990; and when they are supplied for therapeutic purposes, you use code 79900.

EXERCISE M Nuclear Medicine

Under which subheading in the Nuclear Medicine subsection would you look to locate codes for the following?

1. Liver ______________________
2. Thyroid ______________________
3. Spleen ______________________
4. Bone ______________________
5. Brain ______________________

AN OVERVIEW OF CODING PATHOLOGY/LABORATORY

The Guidelines for Pathology/Laboratory indicate subsections that contain notes. Most Pathology/Laboratory subsections contain notes. Whenever notes are available, be sure to read them before assigning codes from the subsection. Specific information pertinent to subsection codes are contained in the notes.

The Section Format

The Pathology/Laboratory section of the CPT manual is formatted by type of tests performed—automated multichannel, panels, assays, and so forth. The subsections are as follows.

Subsections of Pathology/Laboratory Section

- Organ- or Disease-Oriented Panels
- Drug Testing
- Therapeutic Drug Assays
- Evocative/Suppression Testing
- Consultations (Clinical Pathology)
- Urinalysis
- Chemistry
- Hematology and Coagulation
- Immunology
- Transfusion Medicine
- Microbiology
- Anatomic Pathology
- Cytopathology
- Cytogenic Studies
- Surgical Pathology
- Other Procedures

Laboratories have built-in indicators that allow additional tests to be performed without the written order of the physician. These standards are set by the medical facility and imply that when a certain test is found to be positive it is assumed that the physician would want further information on the condition. For example, if a routine urinalysis is performed, a culture is performed if a **quantitative** (positive) bacteria result is found. If a culture is performed to identify the organism, a sensitivity test is performed if the bacteria count is of a certain type or amount as predetermined by the medical facility to warrant the additional laboratory studies. You will bill only after the tests are done. This ensures that all laboratory work will be coded. Remember that what the physician orders may not be all the laboratory work done, depending on the facility policy for further tests.

The Pathology/Laboratory Subsections

Organ- or Disease-Oriented Panels

The codes in the Organ- or Disease-Oriented Panels subsection are grouped according to the usual laboratory work ordered by a physician for diagnosis or screening of various diseases or conditions. Groups of tests may be performed together depending on the situation or disease. For example, during the first obstetric visit a mother is commonly asked to have baseline laboratory tests done to ensure that appropriate antepartum care can be given. CPT code 80055 describes an obstetric panel that would typically be used for the first obstetric visit. To code for a panel from the CPT manual, each test listed in the panel description must be performed. The additional tests are coded and billed separately. The development of panels saves the facility from having to bill each test separately, and it is often more economical for the patient.

List each laboratory test separately unless the tests are part of a panel. If you list a panel, each test must be done to qualify for use of the code. You cannot use modifier -52 (reduced service) with a panel. For example, if all of the tests in the obstetric panel were done except the syphilis test, you could not code 80055 (Obstetrical Panel) with modifier -52. You would instead list separately each of the tests with the corresponding CPT code.

Be careful when coding multiple panels on the same day for the same patient. Some panels have some of the same tests included in them. For example, the obstetric panel and the hepatitis panel both have a Hepatitis B surface antigen test included in the panel. It would be inappropriate to code one test done on one patient on the same day twice.

The laboratory/pathology reports in the patient record will contain the method by which the test was done. There are many different methods for doing the various tests that you will find in this subsection. For example, a urinalysis can be automated or nonautomated and with microscopy or without microscopy. These details are necessary for you to choose the correct urinalysis code. If the details you need are not in the medical record, ask the laboratory staff or physician for further information.

EXERCISE N ***Organ- or Disease-Oriented Panels***

Complete the following:

1. Hepatic function panel code

   Code(s): ___________________

2. How many laboratory tests must be included in a hepatic function panel?

____

3. Does an obstetric panel include a rubella antibody test? ______________

4. Is blood typing ABO included in an arthritis panel? ______________

Drug Testing

Laboratory drug testing is done to identify the presence or absence of a drug. Testing that determines the presence or absence of a drug is **qualitative** (the drug is either present or not present in the specimen).

When the presence of a drug is detected in the qualitative test, there is usually a confirmation test done using a second testing method. Code 80102 is used to describe this confirmation test. The method used to conduct the confirmation is listed. Codes from the Therapeutic Drug Assay and Chemistry subsections are used to further identify the exact amount of the drug that is present. For example, a patient who has been on a medication for a long time might need to undergo testing to determine whether the drug level is therapeutic.

Refer to notes below the subsection Drug Testing for the proper coding of confirmation drug testing.

The CPT manual lists the drugs most commonly tested for. Modifier -51 is not used with pathology or laboratory codes; instead, each test is listed separately. For example, if a confirmation test was conducted for both alcohol and cocaine, code 80102 twice.

Therapeutic Drug Assays

Drug assays test for a specific drug and the amount of that drug. If qualitative information is not enough, quantitative information is needed. **Quantitative** information will determine not only the presence of a drug but also the exact amount present (or quantity present). Many types of drugs are listed under this subsection. If the drug is not listed, it is possible that quantitative analysis may be under the methodology (eg, immunoassay, radioassay).

One location for Drug Testing codes in the index of the CPT manual is under the main term "Drug," subtermed by the reason for the tests—analysis or confirmation. Therapeutic Drug Assay subsection codes can be found under the main term "Drug Assay" and subterms of the material examined, eg, amikacin, digoxin.

EXERCISE O *Therapeutic Drug Testing and Drug Assays*

Choose the correct CPT code for the following drug tests:

1. Confirmation of cocaine (qualitative)

   Code(s): ______________

2. Identify the amount of digoxin in the blood (quantitative)

   Code(s): ______________

Evocation/Suppression Testing

Evocation/Suppression testing is done to determine measurements of evocative or suppressive agents on chemical constituents. For example, code 80400 is reported when a patient undergoes testing to determine whether adrenocorticotropic hormone is being stimulated for production in the body. The physician may suspect that the patient suffers from adrenal gland insufficiency.

Consultations (Clinical Pathology)

A clinical pathologist, upon request from a primary care physician, will perform a consultation to render additional medical interpretation regarding test results. For example, a primary care physician reviews lab test results and requests a clinical pathologist to review, interpret, and prepare a written report on the findings.

There are two codes under the subsection Consultations that are reserved for clinical pathology consultations. These consultations are based on whether the consultation was limited or comprehensive. A **limited consultation** is one that is done without the pathologist's reviewing the medical record of the patient, and a **comprehensive consultation** is one in which the medical record is reviewed as a part of the consultative services. When either of these consultation codes is submitted to a third-party payer, it is accompanied by a written report.

Urinalysis and Chemistry

Many types of tests are located under the Urinalysis or Chemistry subsections. Urinalysis codes are for tests done with urine. Chemistry codes are for tests done with material from any source (eg, urine, blood, breath, feces, sputum). The main things to remember when coding from these two subsections are:

1. The identification of specific tests
2. Whether the test is automated (done by machine) or nonautomated (done by hand)
3. The number of tests done
4. Identification of combination codes for similar types of tests
5. Specifying qualitative or quantitative results
6. Methodology of testing

EXERCISE P *Urinalysis and Chemistry*

Code the following:

1. An automated urinalysis without microscopy

   Code(s): ____________________

2. Urinalysis with microscope only

   Code(s): ____________________

3. Albumin, serum

   Code(s): ____________________

4. Total and direct bilirubin

   Code(s): ____________________

5. Gases, blood pH only

   Code(s): ____________________

6. Sodium, urine

   Code(s): ____________________

7. Uric acid, blood

   Code(s): ____________________

Hematology and Coagulation

The Hematology and Coagulation subsection contains codes based on the various blood-drawing methods and tests. The method used to do the test is often what determines the code assignment. Blood counts can be manual or automated, with many variations of the tests.

There are codes within the Hematology and Coagulation subsection for bone marrow biopsy, not to be confused with bone biopsy codes from the Musculoskeletal System subsection. Bone marrow biopsy codes 85095 and 85102 differ in that 85095 is used when describing a bone marrow aspiration and 85102 is used when describing a bone marrow biopsy. Both the aspiration and biopsy can use a needle, but the biopsy takes a core of marrow while the aspiration pulls marrow from the bone. The patient record will indicate which procedure was used by the physician.

Most of the tests in the Hematology and Coagulation subsection can be located in the index of the CPT manual under the name of the test, such as prothrombin time, coagulation time, or hemogram.

EXERCISE Q *Hematology and Coagulation*

Code the following:

1. Blood count by an automated hemogram

   Code(s): ____________________

2. Blood count by an automated hemogram and platelet count with complete white blood cell count

   Code(s): ____________________

3. Blood count by a manual hemogram with a complete blood cell count

   Code(s): ____________________

4. Trocar bone marrow biopsy

   Code(s): ____________________

As you can see, there are many variations of just one test! So, read the patient record and code descriptions carefully before assigning the codes.

Immunology

Immunology codes deal with identifying conditions of the immune system caused by the action of antibodies (eg, hypersensitivity, allergic reactions, immunity, and alterations of body tissue).

EXERCISE R *Immunology*

Code the following:

1. ANA (antinuclear antibody) titer

   Code(s): ____________________

2. ASO (antistreptolysin O) screen

   Code(s): ____________________

3. Cold agglutinin screen

   Code(s): ____________________

Transfusion Medicine

The Transfusion Medicine subsection deals with testing performed on blood or blood products. Tests include the screening for antibodies, Coombs testing, autologous blood collection and processing, blood typing, compatibility testing, and preparation of and treatments performed on blood and blood products.

EXERCISE S *Transfusion Medicine*

Code the following:

1. ABO and Rh blood typing

   Code(s): ____________________

2. Irradiation of blood product, 3 units

   Code(s): ____________________

Microbiology

Microbiology deals with the study of microorganisms. Cultures for identification of organisms, as well as identification of sensitivities of the organism to antibiotics (called culture and sensitivity) are found in this subsection. Culture codes must be read carefully because some codes are used to indicate screening only to detect the presence of an organism; some codes indicate identification of specific organisms; and others indicate additional sensitivity testing to determine which antibiotic would be best for treatment of the specified bacteria. You should code all tests performed depending on whether they are quantitative or qualitative and/or a sensitivity study.

EXERCISE T *Microbiology*

Code the following:

1. If code 87081 was used to identify the presence of an organism, what does code 87163 identify? ______________________

2. If code 87116 indicates that a TB organism is present, what is code 87118 used for? ______________________

Anatomic Pathology

Anatomic Pathology deals with examination of the body fluids or tissues. Two subsections within this section are Postmortem Examination and Cytopathology.

Postmortem Examination

Postmortem Examination involves the completion of gross microscopic and limited autopsies. Codes are divided based on the extent of the examination performed. This subsection also contains codes for forensic examination and coroner's cases.

Cytopathology and Cytogenic Studies

The Cytopathology subsection deals with the laboratory work done to determine if any cellular changes are present. For example, a very common cytopathology procedure is the Papanicolaou smear (Pap smear). Cytopathology may also be performed on fluids that have been aspirated from a site, to identify cellular changes. Cytogenetic studies include tests performed for genetic and chromosomal studies.

Surgical Pathology

Surgical Pathology codes describe evaluation of specimens to determine the pathology of disease processes. When choosing the correct code for pathology, you must identify the source of the specimen and the reason for the surgical procedure. The Surgical Pathology subsection contains codes that are divided into six levels (Levels I through VI) based on the specimen examined and the level of work required by the pathologist. Pathology testing is done on all tissue removed from the body. The surgical pathology classification level is determined by the complexity of the pathologic examination.

Level I pathology code 88300 identifies specimens that normally do not need to be viewed under a microscope for pathologic diagnosis (eg, a tooth)—those for which the probability of disease or malignancy is minimal.

Level II pathology code 88302 deals with those tissues that are usually considered normal tissue and have been removed not for the probability of disease or malignancy, but for some other reason (eg, a fallopian tube for sterilization, foreskin of a newborn).

Level III pathology code 88304 is assigned for specimens with a low probability of disease or malignancy. For example, a gallbladder may be neoplastic (benign or malignant), but when the gallbladder is removed for cholecystitis (inflammation of the gallbladder), it is usually inflamed from chronic disease and not because of cancerous changes.

Level IV pathology code 88305 carries a higher probability of malignancy or decision-making for disease pathology. For example, a uterus is removed because of a diagnosis of prolapse. There is a possibility that the uterus is malignant, or there are other causes of disease pathology.

Level V pathology code 88307 classifies more complex pathology evaluations (eg, examination of a uterus that was removed for reasons other than prolapse or neoplasm).

Level VI pathology code 88309 includes examination of neoplastic tissue or very involved specimens, such as a total resection of a colon.

The remaining codes found at the end of the subsection classify specialized procedures, utilization of stains, consultations performed, preparations used, and/or instrumentation needed to complete testing.

The surgical pathology codes are located in the index under the main term "Pathology" and subterms "Surgical" and Gross and Micro Exam."

EXERCISE U Surgical Pathology

Code the following using one of the six surgical pathology codes in the CPT manual:

1. The specimen is a uterus, tubes, and ovaries. The procedure was an abdominal hysterectomy for ovarian cancer.

   Code(s): ____________________

2. The specimen is a portion of the lung. The procedure was a left lower lobe wedge resection.

   Code(s): ____________________

3. The specimen is the prostate. The procedure was a transurethral resection of the prostate.

   Code(s): ____________________

Other Procedures

Other Procedures include miscellaneous testing on body fluids, the use of special instrumentation, and testing performed on oocyte and sperm.

CHAPTER GLOSSARY

A-mode: one-dimensional ultrasonic display reflecting the time it takes the sound wave to reach a structure and reflect back; maps the structure outline

angiography: taking of x-ray films of vessels after injection of contrast material

anteroposterior: from front to back

anterior (ventral): in front of

aortography: radiographic recording of the aorta

arthrography: radiographic recording of a joint

B-scan: two-dimensional display of tissues and organs

barium enema: radiographic contrast medium–enhanced examination of the colon

bilateral: occurring on two sides

biometry: application of a statistical measure to a biologic fact

brachytherapy: therapy using radioactive sources that are placed inside the body

bronchography: radiographic recording of the lungs

caudal: same as inferior; also known as caudad; away from the head, or the lower part of the body

cavernosography: radiographic recording of the pulmonary cavity

cervical: pertaining to the neck or cervix of the uterus

cholangiography: radiographic recording of the bile ducts

cholangiopancreatography (ERCP): radiographic recording of the biliary system or pancreas

cholecystography: radiographic recording of the gallbladder

computed axial tomography (CAT or CT): procedure by which selected planes of tissue are pinpointed through computer enhancement, and images may be reconstructed by analysis of variance in absorption of the tissue

cystography: radiographic recording of the urinary bladder

cytopathology: the study of diseases of cells

dacryocystography: radiographic recording of the lacrimal sac or tear duct sac

diskography: radiographic recording of an intervertebral joint

distal: farther from the point of attachment or origin

dosimetry: scientific calculation of radiation emitted from various radioactive sources

duodenography: radiographic recording of the duodenum or first part of the small intestine

echocardiography: radiographic recording of the heart or heart walls or surrounding tissues

echoencephalography: ultrasound of the brain

echography: ultrasound procedure in which sound waves are bounced off an internal organ and the resulting image is recorded

encephalography: radiographic recording of the subarachnoid space and ventricles of the brain

epididymography: radiographic recording of the epididymis

fluoroscopy: procedure for viewing the interior of the body using x-rays and projecting the image onto a television screen

hepatography: radiographic recording of the liver

hypogastric: lowest middle abdominal area

hysterosalpingography: radiographic recording of the uterine cavity and fallopian tubes

inferior: away from the head or the lower part of the body; also known as caudad or caudal

intravenous pyelography (IVP): radiographic recording of the urinary system

laryngography: radiographic recording of the larynx

lateral: away from the midline of the body (to the side)

lymphangiography: radiographic recording of the lymphatic vessels and nodes

M-mode: one-dimensional display of movement of structures

magnetic resonance imaging (MRI): procedure that uses nonionizing radiation to view the body in a cross-sectional view

mammography: radiographic recording of the breasts

medial: toward the midline of the body

MeV: megaelectron volt

myelography: radiographic recording of the subarachnoid space of the spine

physics: scientific study of energy

posterior (dorsal): in back of

posteroanterior: from back to front

pyelography: radiographic recording of the kidneys, renal pelvis, ureters, and bladder

qualitative: measuring the presence or absence of

quantitative: measuring the presence or absence of and the amount of

Rad: radiation absorption dose, the energy deposited in patients' tissues

radiation oncology: branch of medicine concerned with the application of radiation to a tumor site for treatment (destruction) of cancerous tumors

radiograph: film on which an image is produced through exposure to x-radiation

radiologist: physician who specializes in the use of radioactive materials in the diagnosis and treatment of disease and illnesses

radiology: branch of medicine concerned with the use of radioactive substances for diagnosis and therapy

real time: two-dimensional display of both the structures and the motion of tissues and organs with the length of time also recorded as part of the study
scan: mapping of emissions of radioactive substances after they have been introduced into the body; the density can determine normal or abnormal conditions
sialography: radiographic recording of the salivary duct and branches
sinography: radiographic recording of the sinus or sinus tract
splenography: radiographic recording of the spleen
superior: toward the head or the upper part of the body; also known as cephalad or cephalic
supine: lying on the back
tomography: procedure that allows viewing of a single plane of the body by blurring out all but that particular level
transverse: horizontal
ultrasound: technique using sound waves to determine the density of the outline of tissue
unilateral: occurring on one side
uptake: absorption of a radioactive substance by body tissues; recorded for diagnostic purposes in conditions such as thyroid disease
urography: same as pyelography; radiographic recording of the kidneys, renal pelvis, ureters, and bladder
venography: radiographic recording of the veins and tributaries
vesiculography: radiographic recording of the seminal vesicles
xeroradiography: photoelectric process of radiographs

CHAPTER REVIEW Chapter 4, Part I, Theory

Without the use of the CPT manual, complete the following:

1. What is a branch of medicine that uses radiant energy to diagnose and treat patients? ____________________
2. The CPT manual divides the Radiology section into subsections of Diagnostic Radiology, ______________, ______________, and Nuclear Medicine.
3. What type of procedure is "performed independently of, and is not immediately related to, other services"? ____________________
4. If several services are provided to a patient on the same day, what type of procedure modifier could be used? ____________________
5. The modifier used to indicate the Professional Component is __________.
6. The two words that mean supervising the taking of the x-rays and reading/reporting the results of the films are __________ and ______________.
7. The name for the use of high-frequency sound waves in an imaging process that is used to diagnose patient illness is ____________________.
8. The Radiation Oncology section of the CPT manual is divided into subsections based on the ______________ of service provided to the patient.

9. The scientific study of energy is ______________________.

10. The scientific calculation of the radiation emitted from various radioactive sources is ______________________.

11. Radiation treatment delivery codes are based on the treatment area involved and further divided based on levels of what? ______________________

12. MeV stands for ______________________.

13. In the Clinical Treatment Management section codes are established based on how many fractions delivered in one week? ______________________

14. Nuclear Medicine uses these to image organs for diagnosis and treatment: ______________________

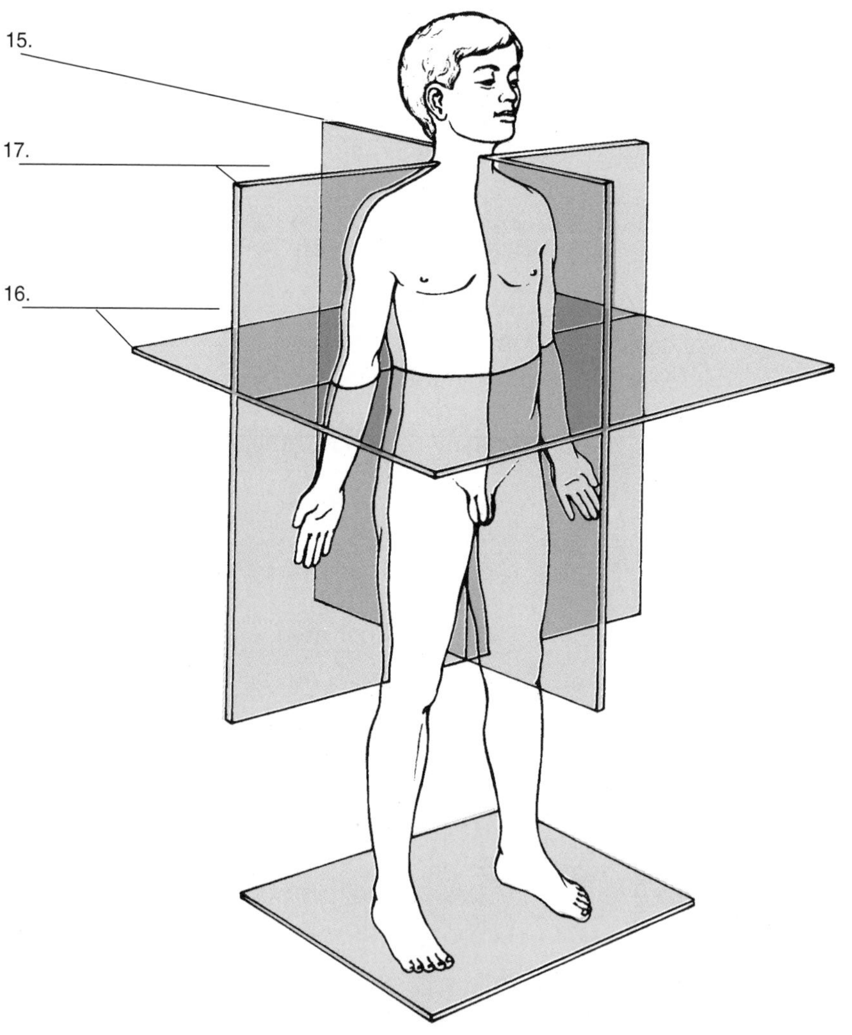

Identify the planes of the body:

15. ______________________________

16. ______________________________

17. ______________________________

Match the following terms to the correct definitions:

18. anterior (ventral) _______
19. posterior (dorsal) _______
20. superior _______
21. inferior _______
22. medial _______
23. lateral _______

a. toward the midline of the body
b. toward the head or the upper part of the body; also known as cephalad or cephalic
c. in front of
d. away from the midline of the body (to the side)
e. in back of
f. away from the head or the lower part of the body; also known as caudad or caudal

Match the following radiographic procedures to the correct structures imaged:

24. fluoroscopy _______
25. magnetic resonance imaging (MRI) _______
26. tomography _______
27. xeroradiography _______
28. barium enema _______
29. biometry _______

a. radiographic contrast medium-enhanced examination of the colon
b. procedure for viewing the interior of the body using x-rays and projecting the image onto a television screen
c. photoelectric process of radiographs
d. application of a statistical method to a biologic fact
e. procedure that uses nonionizing radiation to view the body in a cross-sectional view
f. procedure that allows viewing of a single plane of the body by blurring out all but that particular level

Match the following radiographic procedures to the correct structures imaged:

30. arthrography _______
31. cholangiography _______
32. cystography _______
33. diskography _______
34. epididymography _______
35. hysterosalpingography _______

a. uterine cavity and fallopian tubes
b. intervertebral joint
c. kidneys, renal pelvis, ureters, and bladder
d. bile ducts
e. joint
f. veins and tributaries
g. subarachnoid space of the spine
h. epididymis

36. lymph-angiography _______
37. myelography _______
38. urography _______
39. venography _______

i. urinary bladder

j. lymphatic vessels and nodes

Chapter 4, Part II, Practical

The coding exercise that follows uses codes from a variety of CPT sections.

Using the CPT manual, code the following:

40. An established patient is seen in the physician's office with the chief complaint of a persistent cough. Otherwise, the patient claims to be in good health. The physician collects a history including the chief complaint and the history of the present illness. The physical examination performed focuses on the respiratory tract. The decision-making is straightforward because the physician wants to evaluate the patient for a possible case of bronchitis.

    Code(s): ___________________

    The patient is sent to the clinic's radiology department for a two-view chest x-ray study.

    Code(s): ___________________

    The radiologist sends the x-ray results to the physician, who reviews them and decides to order a consultation from a pulmonologist from another clinic. The patient sees the other clinic's radiologist, who performs a comprehensive history and comprehensive examination with moderate complexity.

    Code(s): ___________________

    A fluoroscopic examination is done for transbronchial biopsy.

    Code(s): ___________________

    Then there is radiologic supervision and interpretation of a unilateral bronchography.

    Code(s): ___________________

41. A new patient is seen in the office for bilateral ear pain. In the history and the physical examination, the physician focuses his attention on the head, ears, nose, and throat. The physician's provisional diagnoses include otalgia and possible ear infections. The decision-making is straightforward for the physician.

    Code(s): ___________________

    The patient is sent to the clinic's radiologist for an x-ray of the ear.

    Code(s): ___________________

The patient is then sent to the clinic's ear specialist, who inserts a ventilation tube (tympanostomy) using local anesthesia.

Code(s): ____________________

42. A new patient is seen in the office for a variety of complaints, but in particular a swelling and heaviness of his right leg. The physician documents the patient's complaints, collects a comprehensive history of the present illness, performs a comprehensive review of systems, and inquires about the patient's past, family, and social history. A complete multisystem physical examination is performed. The physician's working diagnosis is edema of the lower extremity, cause to be determined. Given the nature of the problem, the physician considers the decision-making process to be highly complex.

    Code(s): ____________________

    The patient is sent to radiology for a unilateral lymphangiography of one extremity.

    Code(s): ____________________

    Another physician performs the injection procedure for the lymphangiography.

    Code(s): ____________________

43. A new patient is seen in the office with complaints of dyspnea, cough, sputum, dysphagia, and congestion in the head and neck. In order to explain this myriad of symptoms, the physician collects a detailed history including an extended history of present illness, problem-pertinent systems review, and a pertinent past, family, and social history. The physician's physical examination is detailed as well as it examines various organ systems related to the patient's complaints. During the examination, the physician notes unequal pulses on the right and left sides. The physician contemplates the possibility of an abdominal aortic aneurysm but considers the decision-making to be of low complexity.

    Code(s): ____________________

    The patient is sent to radiology for a complete abdominal echography using B-scan.

    Code(s): ____________________

44. A new patient is admitted to the hospital on an observation status after a fall at home. A comprehensive history is collected and a general, multisystem comprehensive physical examination is performed. After talking to the patient and relatives and performing the examination, the physician finds that the patient has a number of symptoms that are usually due to an increase in intracranial pressure. The physician considers this patient's problems to be of moderately severe complexity. A CT scan of the brain is done. Brain lesions are discovered, and the physician advises radiation therapy. The patient is sent to the clinic's radiology department, where an A-scan ophthalmic biometry by ultrasound echography is done. The patient has therapeutic radiology treatment planning that is simple. Later the patient has radiation

treatment delivery to a single area up to 5 MeV. The patient continues with weekly conformal radiology therapy management.

Code(s): ___________________

45. The patient is admitted to the hospital by his physician for treatment of his newly diagnosed lung cancer. The initial hospital care consists of a comprehensive history and physical examination, but the medical decision-making is of low complexity as the diagnosis has been established, and now treatment is to begin. The patient is sent to the Radiology Department for brachytherapy where a radioelement application is done.

    Code(s): ___________________

46. A patient was admitted to the hospital for removal of a pericardial clot. The physician orders chest echography (B-scan). Chest magnetic resonance (proton) imaging is also ordered. A pericardiotomy is performed for removal of clot.

    Code(s): ___________________

47. The Hematology and Coagulation subsections contain codes based on the various blood-drawing methods and tests. The method used to do the test is often a code determiner. Blood cell counts can be manual or automated, with many variations of the tests. What would the code be for an automated hemogram? What would the code be for an automated hemogram and platelet count with complete white blood cell count? A manual hemogram with a complete blood cell count?

    Code(s): ___________________

Code the following three cases with the correct pathology code from the CPT manual:

48. The specimen is tonsils and adenoids. The procedure is a tonsillectomy with adenoidectomy.

    Code(s): ___________________

49. The specimen is the appendix. The procedure is an incidental appendectomy.

    Code(s): ___________________

50. The specimen is a tooth. The procedure is an odontectomy.

    Code(s): ___________________

5 Coding in the Medicine Section and the Level II National Codes

CHAPTER TOPICS

Learning Objectives

After completing this chapter, you should be able to

1. Apply Medicine Guidelines when assigning codes.
2. Analyze the format of the Medicine section.
3. Apply the Medicine section codes.
4. List the major features of Level II, National Codes.
5. Assign Level II, National Codes and modifiers.
6. Define terminology listed in the chapter glossary.

CODING NONINVASIVE DIAGNOSTIC AND THERAPEUTIC SERVICES

The Medicine section is for coding diagnostic and therapeutic services that are generally *not invasive* (not entering a body cavity). The section begins with Guidelines applicable to all the Medicine section codes (ie, multiple procedures, separate procedures, subsection information, unlisted service/procedure codes, special reports, modifiers, and materials supplied by the physician).

The various subsections of Medicine contain many specific notes to be used with certain group(s) of codes, so be sure to read all notes that pertain to the group codes with which you are working.

The Section Format

Medicine Subsections

- Immune Globulins
- Immunization Administration for Vaccines/Toxoids
- Vaccines, Toxoids
- Therapeutic, Prophylactic, or Diagnostic Infusions
- Therapeutic or Diagnostic Injections
- Psychiatry
- Biofeedback
- Dialysis
- Gastroenterology
- Ophthalmology
- Special Otorhinolaryngologic Services
- Cardiovascular
- Noninvasive Vascular Diagnostic Services
- Pulmonary
- Allergy and Clinical Immunology
- Neurology and Neuromuscular Procedures
- Central Nervous System Assessments/Tests
- Chemotherapy Administration
- Photodynamic Therapy
- Special Dermatological Procedures
- Physical Medicine and Rehabilitation
- Osteopathic Manipulative Treatment (OMT)
- Chiropractic Manipulative Treatment
- Special Services, Procedures, and Reports
- Qualifying Circumstances for Anesthesia
- Sedation with or Without Analgesia
- Other Services and Procedures

Many specialized types of testing can be found in the Medicine section (eg, biofeedback, audiologic function tests, electrocardiograms). Codes in this section do not include the supplies used in the testing, therapy, or diagnostic treatments unless specifically stated in the code description. For example, there are codes for the prescription and fitting of an artificial eye—one code includes the supply of the artificial eye and one code does not include the supply of the artificial eye. Reading the entire code description is critical to ensure you do not unbundle the services by billing for services already included in the code. You should code

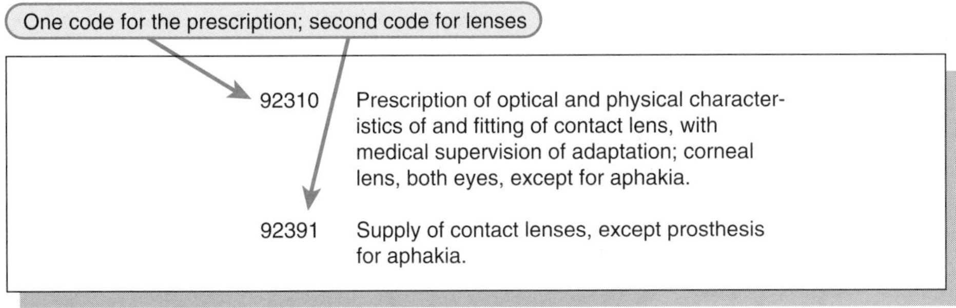

Figure 5–1
Some codes are only for the supply.

supplies, including drugs, separately unless otherwise instructed in the code information. CPT code 99070 is the supplies and materials code used to identify the supplying of drugs, trays, supplies, or materials needed to provide the service. For example, Figure 5–1 shows the code for the service of a prescription for contact lenses (92310) and the code for the supply of the contact lenses (92391). When the lenses and the prescription services are provided, both the lenses (92391) and prescription service (92310) are billed.

You will now briefly review each of the subsections in the Medicine section and assign codes to services.

Numerous Medicine Subsections

Immunization Subsections

There are two types of immunization—active or passive. **Active immunization** is the type given when it is anticipated that the person will be in contact with the disease. The active immunization agents can be a toxoid or vaccine. Toxoids are bacteria that have been made nontoxic; when injected, they produce an immune response that builds the protection that the patient has to the disease. Vaccines are viruses given in small doses that cause an immune response. **Passive immunization** doesn't cause an immune response; rather, the injected material contains a high level of antibody against a disease (eg, rabies, hepatitis B, tetanus) called immune globulins.

The first three subsections in the Medicine section are

- Immune Globulin
- Immunization Administration for Vaccines and Toxoids
- Vaccines and Toxoids

Immune Globulins

The Immune Globulins subsection is a relatively new subsection in the CPT manual. Many of the codes within the subsection were located throughout the Medicine section, but with the creation of the Immune Globulins subsection, the codes are now grouped together. The codes in this subsection identify only the immune globulin *product* and must be reported in addition to the appropriate administration code from the Therapeutic or Diagnostic Injections subsection (ie, 90782, which is a therapeutic or diagnostic injection given subcutaneously or intramuscularly).

Codes in the Immune Globulins subsection are categorized based on the type of immune globulin (rabies, hepatitis B, etc.), the method of injection (IM, IV, SQ, etc.), and the type of dose (full dose, minidose, etc.).

Immunization Administration for Vaccines/Toxoids

The Immunization Administration subsection codes are reported in conjunction with the Vaccines/Toxoids subsection codes. The codes in the Immunization Administration subsection are reported for the injection procedure. There are a variety of administration methods used to deliver the vaccine/toxoid: percutaneous, intradermal, subcutaneous, intramuscular, jet injections, intranasal, and oral administration.

Vaccines and Toxoids

The Vaccines/Toxoids subsection lists vaccine products given in immunizations. The subsection contains many codes for a single disease (eg, 90703 for tetanus toxoid) as well as codes for a combination of diseases (eg, 90701 for diphtheria, tetanus, and DPT). You must carefully review the description of the vaccine product code to determine which disease(s) is specified. When one code is available to describe multiple products given, the combination code must be used. If each vaccine were to be listed separately when a combination code is available, it would be considered unbundling.

There are codes that describe schedules for a vaccine, such as a 3-dose or 4-dose schedule. A schedule is the number of doses provided and the timing of the administration. However, the doses and timing must be exactly as specified in the code; otherwise, you should use multiple codes to identify the vaccine.

If a patient is given a vaccine in the course of an E/M service, the vaccination codes are assigned in addition to the E/M code. If the immunization is the only service that the patient receives, two codes are used to report the service: the immunization administration code is first and then the vaccine/toxoid code. Two codes are used to report the administration of immune globulins: the infusion code first and then the immune globulin code.

EXERCISE A ***Immunization Injections***

Using the CPT manual, code the following:

1. A parent brings a child in for the first time to the physician's office for an oral poliomyelitis vaccine. The physician's assistant evaluates the child and administers the vaccine orally to the child.

   Code(s): ________________

2. The following series of vaccines is indicated as having been administered to a variety of patients, and a brief history and examination were performed to assess vaccine needs and general health status. How would you code these vaccinations?

   a. New patient and the only service for the visit was a DTP (diphtheria, tetanus toxoid, pertussis) and oral poliovirus.

      Code(s): ________________

   b. An established patient, a one-year-old, was brought in for a well-baby checkup with the physician, and the following was given: DTP with injectable poliomyelitis.

      Code(s): ________________

c. A 64-year-old established patient comes in for an IM influenza virus vaccine administered by the nurse. The vaccine is the only service provided at that visit.

Code(s): ____________________

d. A new patient comes for an office visit at which the physician does an expanded problem-focused history and physical examination and also administers a DTP and *Haemophilus influenzae* B (HIB) vaccine.

Code(s): ____________________

3. A parent brings an 18-month-old infant (established patient) for a well-baby examination at which the physician administers a vaccine for diphtheria and tetanus toxoid (DT).

Code(s): ____________________

Therapeutic or Diagnostic Infusions

Therapeutic infusions are done for the purpose of healing. An **infusion** is the introducing of a liquid into the body over a long period of time, for example, fluids introduced into the vein of a patient who is dehydrated or the intravenous introduction of antibiotics into a patient with a severe infection. The physician must administer or supervise the administration of the infusion. There are only two codes in the infusion subsection, both based on the time it takes for the infusion to be completed.

Therapeutic or Diagnostic Injections

Injections are the introduction of substances into the body by the use of a needle. Codes in the Therapeutic or Diagnostic Injections subsection are determined by how the injection is introduced into the body—subcutaneous (SQ), intramuscular (IM), intravenous (IV), or intra-arterial (Fig. 5–2). Code 90782 can be used to identify any therapeutic or diagnostic injection excluding antibiotic injections since there is a code specifically for injection of antibiotics. When using either of the codes, you must specify the materials injected.

One way to locate injections in the index of the CPT manual is under the main term "Injection" and the subterm of the method (ie, intravenous, intramuscular, subcutaneous).

EXERCISE B *Injections*

Code the following injections:

1. An established patient is seen in the office for pernicious anemia. The nurse gives the patient an injection of vitamin B_{12}.

Code(s): ____________________

2. IV infusion for therapy for 1 hour

Code(s): ____________________

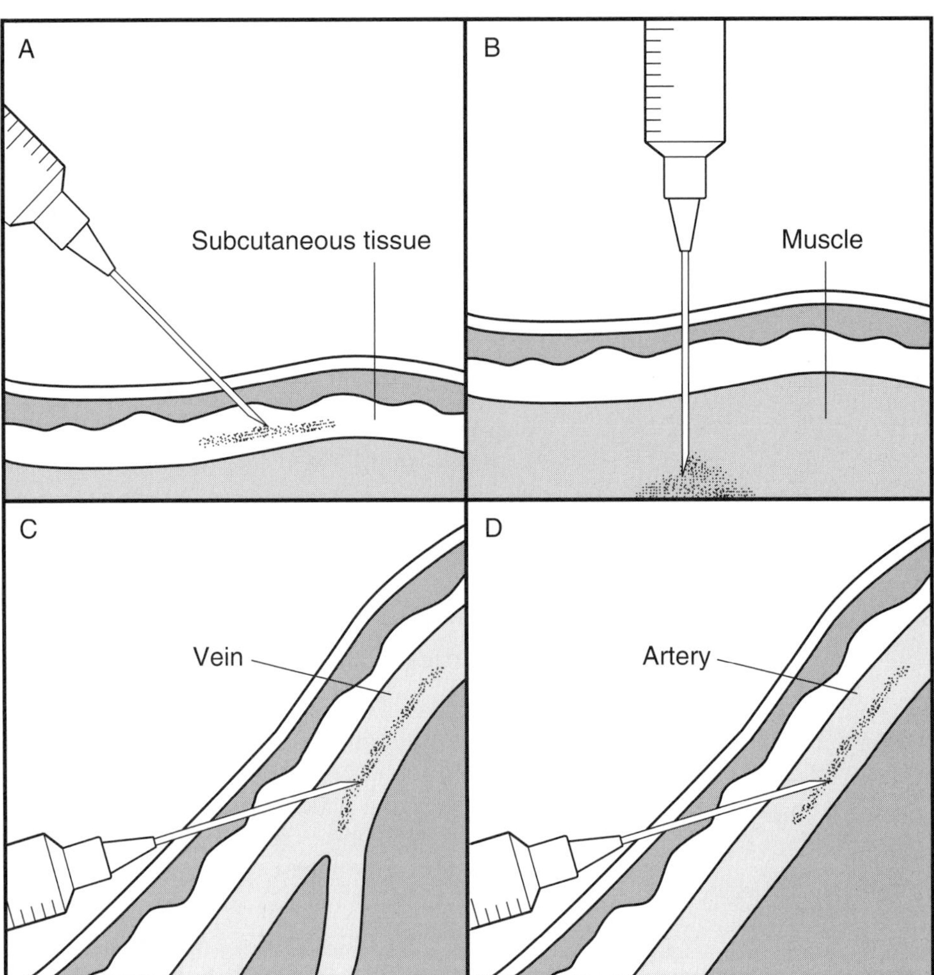

Figure 5–2
Injection methods. *A.* Subcutaneous (SQ). *B.* Intramuscular (IM). *C.* Intravenous (IV). *D.* Intra-arterial.

Psychiatry

The Psychiatry subsection has a lengthy note under the heading detailing use of psychiatric codes in conjunction with hospital and clinic E/M services. If psychiatric treatments are rendered at the same time as E/M services, both should be coded. For example, a patient is admitted to the hospital with a drug overdose secondary to depression. The physician spends 25 minutes in supportive psychotherapy with the patient several hours after he was admitted to the hospital. Services to be coded would be 99223 (Initial Hospital Care) for the E/M service provided and 90816 (Individual Medical Psychotherapy) for the psychiatric treatment. The hospital care codes include the development of orders, review and interpretation of laboratory work or other diagnostic studies, and review of therapy reports and other information from the medical record. When the services include not only a visit to the patient but also direction of a treatment team, an additional service code may be listed. You will work closely with third-party payers to determine any specific regional instructions for coding psychiatry services.

Specific descriptions dealing with services included in each of the codes appear in the Psychiatry subsection. Some codes will reflect evaluation or diagnostic services, as in CPT code 90801; some therapeutic procedures, as in 90804; and still others, which are located in the Central Nervous System Assessments/Tests, as in the psychological testing code 96100.

Time is the major billing factor for the Psychiatry subsection. Diagnostic and therapeutic time must be clearly documented in the patient record for accurate billing.

Psychiatric Diagnosis and Psychiatric Treatment are two CPT manual index locations for the psychiatric service codes.

EXERCISE C Psychiatry

Code the following:

1. Individual medical psychotherapy in office for 30 minutes

   Code(s): ______________

2. Psychological testing, 2 hours

   Code(s): ______________

3. Psychiatric evaluation of tests, medical records, or hospital data to make appropriate diagnosis and treatment plan

   Code(s): ______________

4. Initial psychiatric interview examination

   Code(s): ______________

Biofeedback

Biofeedback is the process of giving a person self-information. The information can be used by patients to gain some control over their physiologic processes such as blood pressure, heart rate, or pain. Patients are trained how to use biofeedback by a professional and then continue the use of the therapy on their own. Biofeedback training is often incorporated in individual psychophysiologic therapy. When biofeedback is part of the individual psychophysiologic therapy, a code is listed for both the biofeedback training and the individual psychophysiologic therapy (90875).

Biofeedback codes are located in the CPT manual index under the main term "Biofeedback."

EXERCISE D Biofeedback

Code the following:

1. A 40-year-old woman has been seen by the physician for several individual psychiatric sessions as the patient attempts to give up a 2-pack-a-day cigarette addiction of 15 years' duration. The patient is experiencing increased anxiety and insomnia. As a part of the last 30-minute psychiatric session, the physician taught the patient to use biofeedback in an attempt to help the patient alleviate the anxiety and insomnia. The patient was instructed to use the biofeedback techniques three times a day until the next session.

   Code(s): ______________

2. A 52-year-old man was referred to the physician by his primary care physician for psychophysiologic therapy for regulation of his blood pressure. The physician conducted a 60-minute session with the patient in which the patient was trained in the use of biofeedback.

   Code(s): ________________

Dialysis

Dialysis is the cleansing of the blood of waste products when it is not possible for the body to adequately perform the cleansing function on its own. Dialysis may be temporary, as in the case of a patient who had acute renal failure from which he or she recovers, or permanent, as in the case of patients with end-stage renal disease (ESRD) who will not recover without a kidney transplant.

The Dialysis subsection of the Medicine section is divided into types of dialysis patient training in self-dialysis. The first group of codes (End Stage Renal Disease Services) deals with dialysis of a permanent nature. The first four codes in the category reflect all services included in treating the patient with ESRD and are listed by patient age (eg, younger than 2 years of age, 2–11 years of age). Dialysis services are usually billed as a monthly fee. For those cases in which a patient may be visiting the area and will not require a full month of dialysis, daily fees may be billed using the last four codes in the ESRD category. Some third-party payers will allow E/M codes to be billed in addition to dialysis service codes, and other payers consider the dialysis codes bundled to include all the treatment necessary for the renal disease patient including the E/M services.

Hemodialysis is the routing of blood including waste products outside of the body through filters (see Fig. 3–41). After the blood is cleansed, it is returned to the body. Hemodialysis codes are billed for each day the service is provided. The codes in the hemodialysis category are based on the number of times the physician evaluates the patient during the procedure.

Peritoneal dialysis involves using the peritoneal cavity as a filter. Dialysis fluid is introduced into the cavity and left there several hours for cleansing to take place (Fig. 5–3). The dialysis fluid is then drained from the peritoneal cavity.

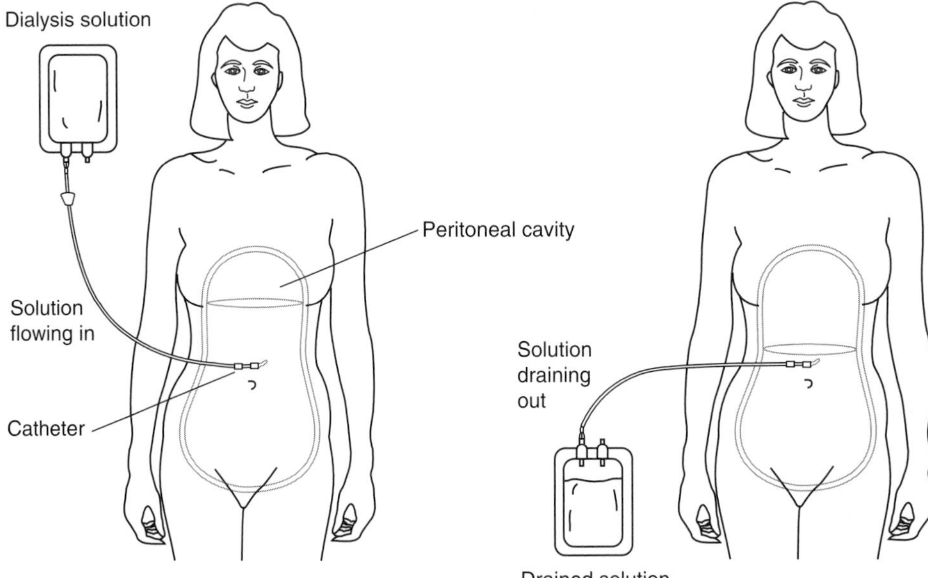

Figure 5–3
Peritoneal dialysis can be done by the patient. The dialysis solution enters the peritoneal cavity by a catheter. After the solution has been in the patient for several hours, it is drained out through the catheter.

Peritoneal dialysis is billed for each day that the service is provided. Some patients learn how to do dialysis for themselves. Dialysis teaching codes are located under Miscellaneous Dialysis Procedures.

Dialysis is the main term to be referenced in the CPT manual index.

EXERCISE E Dialysis

Using the CPT manual, code the following dialysis services:

1. Ten-year-old patient with end-stage renal disease for a full month of services

   Code(s): ___________________

2. Hemodialysis with a single physician evaluation

   Code(s): ___________________

3. Peritoneal dialysis with repeated physician evaluations

   Code(s): ___________________

Define the following words or abbreviations that are located in the subsection:

4. peritoneal ____

5. hemofiltration _______________________________________

6. ESRD ____

Gastroenterology

The Gastroenterology subsection contains many types of tests or treatments performed on the esophagus, stomach, and intestine. Several intubation codes are listed in the Gastroenterology subsection. You must carefully review the code descriptions to determine which services are bundled into the code. For example, CPT code 91055 includes intubation, collection, and preparation of specimens. Since these three services are bundled into one code, it would be incorrect to code each service individually.

EXERCISE F Gastroenterology

Using the CPT manual, code the following:

1. An acid reflux test of the esophagus with intraluminal pH electrode for detection of reflux

   Code(s): ___________________

2. Insertion, positioning, and monitoring of an intestinal bleeding tube

   Code(s): ___________________

3. Gastric intubation with washings and slide preparation for cytology

   Code(s): ____________________

Define the following words located in the subsection:

4. motility study ____

5. manometric studies ____

Ophthalmology

The notes found at the beginning of the Ophthalmology subsection describe the services included in the various types of ophthalmologic services. Ophthalmology is a very specialized field, and often the services provided and documented do not adequately fall into an E/M definition. Therefore, the AMA developed specialized codes that deal specifically with ophthalmology services. There are extensive notes preceding the codes that are required reading before you code in the subsection. The notes explain the levels of service and present excellent examples to clarify use of the codes. The general ophthalmologic services (eg, routine yearly eye examinations) are located in the subheading General Ophthalmological Services. The codes in this subsection are based on whether the patient is a new or established patient and on the complexity of service provided. Of special note are the definitions of new and established patients. Be certain to read these definitions.

The subheading Special Ophthalmological Services contains *bilateral codes.* Each service in this subheading is done on both eyes, and the codes do not require a modifier to indicate that two eyes were examined or tested. In fact, should you need to report only one eye from these codes, you would need to use modifier -52 to indicate a reduced service. It is a good idea to make a note next to the codes that are bilateral codes in the CPT manual and also make a note of modifier -52, which you would use to reduce the service for one eye.

Special Ophthalmological Service codes are those services that are not normally performed with the general eye examination. Services in this group are done for medically indicated reasons. The definitions with the codes are very comprehensive in detailing the services involved with each code.

Other codes that are found in the Ophthalmology subsection under the subheading Spectacle Services, category Supply of Materials, deal with the provision of materials to the patient (eg, contact lenses or ocular prosthesis). The refraction that is done to determine the lens prescription may be billed separately, depending on the policies set by third-party payers.

EXERCISE G *Ophthalmology*

Using the CPT manual, code the following:

1. Established patient has a comprehensive ophthalmologic service

   Code(s): ____________________

2. Fitting of contact lens for treatment of a cataract, including the lens

   Code(s): ____________________

3. Tonography (procedure to check the intraocular pressure of the eye) with a medical diagnostic evaluation with recording of findings

   Code(s): ________________

4. New patient has a comprehensive ophthalmologic service

   Code(s): ________________

5. Patient is fitted for an artificial eye; physician provided the prescription, fitting, and prosthesis

   Code(s): ________________

6. Patient is fitted for bifocal spectacles

   Code(s): ________________

7. Extended color vision examination with anomaloscope

   Code(s): ________________

Define the following words that are located in the subsection:

8. orthoptic ________________________________
9. angioscopy ________________________________
10. electroretinography ________________________________
11. anomaloscope ________________________________
12. aphakia ________________________________
13. corneosclera ________________________________

Special Otorhinolaryngologic Services

What a big word otorhinolaryngologic is! But when you take it apart it isn't so tough. "Oto" is ear, "rhino" is nose, "laryngo" is larynx, and "logy/logic" is all the knowledge about a subject—ear, nose, larynx—and all the knowledge about them—otorhinolaryngology. The services in this subsection deal with special testing or studies for the ears, nose, and larynx. Audiology (hearing) testing is found in the Special Otorhinolaryngologic Services subsection, too. An audiology test may be performed by a physician or audiologist trained in this area.

EXERCISE H *Special Otorhinolaryngologic Services*

Using the CPT manual, code the following:

1. Hearing aid check in one ear (monaural: "mon" is one and "aural" is ear)

   Code(s): ________________

2. Screening test, pure tone, air only

   Code(s): ________________

3. A nasopharyngoscopy with endoscope

   Code(s): ________________

4. Nasal function study

   Code(s): ________________

5. Positional nystagmus

   Code(s): ________________

6. Optokinetic bidirectional

   Code(s): ________________

Define the following words or abbreviations that are located in the subsection:

7. oscillating ________________________________

8. audiometry ________________________________

9. tympanometry ________________________________

10. electrocochleography ________________________________

Cardiovascular

The Cardiovascular subsection includes many invasive (entering the body) and noninvasive (not entering the body) diagnostic and therapeutic services and procedures. Cardiopulmonary resuscitation (CPR), cardioversion, percutaneous coronary angioplasties, atherectomies, and valvuloplasties are found here. A key word in this subsection is *percutaneous,* which means through the skin. If an actual surgical opening is made to open the operative site to the physician's view, treatment codes would be found in the Cardiovascular subsection of the Surgery section and not in the Cardiovascular subsection of the Medicine section.

The subsection for Cardiovascular contains the following categories:

- Therapeutic Services
- Cardiography
- Echocardiography
- Cardiac Catheterization
- Intracardiac Electrophysiological Procedures
- Other Vascular Studies
- Other Procedures

Therapeutic Services

The Therapeutic Services codes are for *invasive procedures* such as heart pacing, electrical conversion, infusions, placement of catheters, and balloon angioplasty. Divisions are often based on method (balloon or blade), location (aortic or mitral valve), or number (single or multiple vessels).

Cardiography

The Cardiography subheading is for diagnostic electrocardiographic procedures such as stress tests. Stress tests are performed to test the adequacy of oxygen getting to the heart muscle (at rest and during exercise) to indicate the presence of heart disease. The top number on a blood pressure reading is systole (heart muscle is contracting); the bottom number is diastole (heart muscle is relaxing). The heart muscle is fed by three coronary arteries and their branches. If these arteries are clear, the amount of blood going to the muscle is adequate during rest and exercise. The heart muscle is fed only during diastole. Normal blood pressure is about 120/80 mm Hg, and the normal heart rate is about 60 beats per minute. During low blood pressure, little blood and oxygen get to the heart.

As the heart beats faster, such as during exercise, the heart rate increases and diastolic pressure time decreases, meaning that there is less time to supply blood to the heart muscle. As the heart beats faster, more oxygen is also required. With narrowing of coronary arteries and branches, too little blood may circulate to the heart muscle, supplying even less oxygen than during rest, and chest pain may result as an indication of heart muscle tissue dying. Indications of heart disease during a stress test are chest pain and lengthening ST waves on the ECG, as illustrated in Figure 5–4.

The Holter monitor is similar to an **electrocardiogram (ECG),** with two leads attached to the patient. It is portable and records the patient's ECG readings for 24 hours. Leads are attached to the chest and to a cassette machine. The monitor converts the ECG readings to sound, and the sound is converted back to an ECG reading when completed. The reading is then sped up hundreds of times faster than normal by computers. Any reading that varies from a normal reading will be identified. The Q, R, and S waves are related to the contraction of the ventricles of the heart. The QRS waves and heartbeats can be monitored with Holter monitors. Cardiac arrhythmias can be identified using the Holter monitor process.

Echocardiography

Echocardiography is a noninvasive diagnostic method that uses ultrasonographic images to detect the presence of heart disease or valvular disease. A sliced image is used to detail the different walls of the heart as a transducer is placed on the

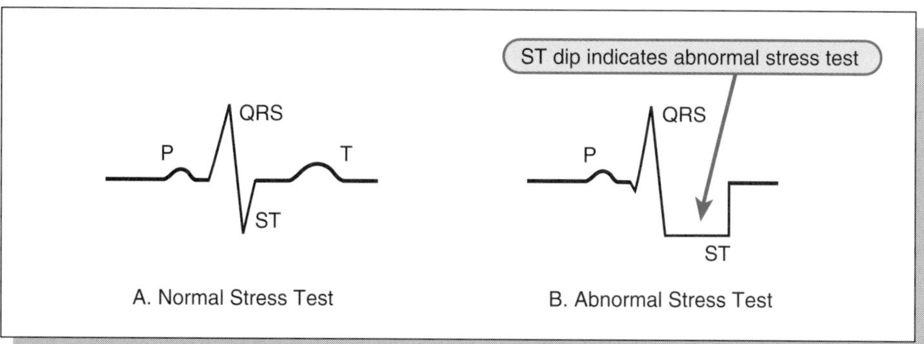

Figure 5–4
Normal and abnormal ECG test results. *A.* Normal ECG reading. *B.* Abnormal ECG reading. The ST segment dips. QRS complex and T waves are related to the contraction of the ventricles. Indications of heart disease during a stress test are chest pain and lengthened ST segments.

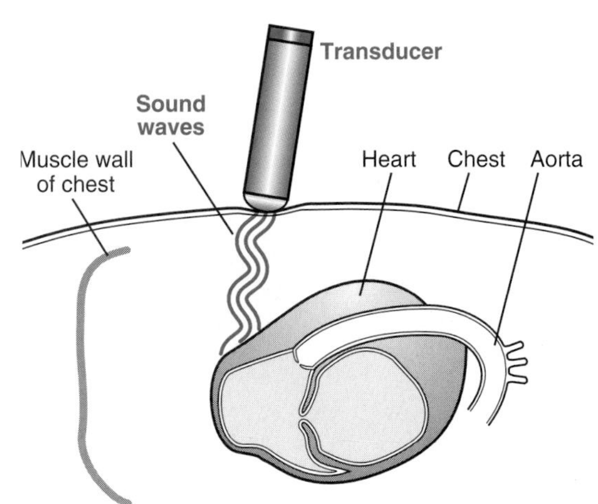

Figure 5–5
Echocardiography. A transducer is placed on the outside of the chest wall and sends sound waves through the chest. When the heart is in systole, the heart is contracting and the dots on the echocardiogram appear farther apart. When the heart is in diastole, it is relaxing and the dots on the echocardiogram appear closer together.

outside of the chest wall, sending sound waves through the chest (Fig. 5–5). As the sound reflects back from each organ wall, dots will be recorded, indicating the point of reflection. When the heart is in systole, it is contracting, and the dots on the recording appear farther apart. When the heart is in diastole, it is relaxing, and the dots on the recording appear closer together.

Cardiac Catheterization

Cardiac catheterization is an invasive diagnostic medical procedure that includes introduction, positioning, and repositioning of catheters. Cardiac catheterization is used in recording the intracardiac and intravascular pressure or obtaining blood samples for measurement of blood gases and cardiac output. When injection of contrast material is used to improve visualization, additional injection procedure codes (such as 93540 or 93544) must be used to specify the site of the injection.

EXAMPLE

During a cardiac catheterization procedure, contrast medium was injected into a bypass graft and the coronary arteries. CPT codes would be used to identify each of the three areas of injection as follows:

93540 injection into the bypass graft

93544 injection into selective coronary arteries

Each of these two codes would be reported in addition to the code reflecting the type of cardiac catheterization (eg, left and right heart catheterization, 93526). But you wouldn't be finished coding this one yet. If the cardiologist also supervises, interprets, and reports on the x-ray imaging of the angiography, codes 93555 and 93556 would be used to report the imaging services. This is a good example of component coding, which was presented first in the surgical section and then in the radiology section. Component coding requires you to examine services that were provided to the patient, identify each component or part of that service, identify who performed each component, and code each service provided.

Intracardiac Electrophysiological Procedures

As the title of these category codes implies, Intracardiac Electrophysiological Procedures contains codes to identify evaluations and procedures conducted inside the heart. The codes cover various ventricular recordings, pacing, induction of arrhythmia, stimulation after drug infusions, or ablation (removal) of catheters, and various other intracardiac evaluations or procedures. Arrhythmias (irregular heartbeats) are induced to observe how the heart will react. This is a very involved procedure and you should have a clear understanding of the specific procedures being performed before coding. Communication with the physician and the technicians is essential to ensure the accuracy of this complex coding.

Other Vascular Studies

If a patient has a pacemaker or defibrillator placed, periodic monitoring must occur. Codes to reflect these services are found in Other Vascular Studies. Codes are chosen depending on the type of pacemaker (single or dual chamber) and whether reprogramming of an existing pacemaker or defibrillator was done.

Other Procedures

The Other Procedure codes are for physician services for cardiac rehabilitation provided to outpatients, either with or without electrocardiographic monitoring. There is also an unlisted cardiovascular code following the two outpatient codes.

EXERCISE 1 ***Cardiovascular***

Code the following:

1. Routine electrocardiogram (ECG) with 12 leads, with interpretation and report

   Code(s): ____________________

2. Cardiac catheterization of the right side of the heart

   Code(s): ____________________

3. Noninvasive physiologic study of arteries of the arm, single level, bilateral

   Code(s): ____________________

4. Ambulatory blood pressure monitoring of 24 hours, using magnetic tape, including the recording, analysis, interpretation, and report

   Code(s): ____________________

5. Electronic analysis of a dual chamber pacemaker with reprogramming

   Code(s): ____________________

6. Percutaneous insertion of an intra-aorta balloon catheter

   Code(s): ____________________

Define the following words or abbreviations that are located in the subsection:

7. cardioversion ______________________________
8. phonocardiogram ______________________________
9. vectorcardiogram (VCG) ______________________________
10. apexcardiography ______________________________
11. transesophageal echocardiogram (TEE) ______________________________
12. endomyocardial ______________________________
13. plethysmography ______________________________
14. thermogram ______________________________

Keep up the hard work; you will soon be finished with the entire CPT manual.

Noninvasive Vascular Diagnostic Studies

The vascular codes in this subsection are to identify procedures conducted for veins and arteries other than the heart and great vessels. These studies use the same devices as the section on heart and great vessels echocardiography discussed previously, except that the divisions are based on the location of the vein or artery being studied.

EXERCISE J *Noninvasive Vascular Diagnostic Studies*

Code the following:

1. A patient is referred for a venous occlusion plethysmography of the left leg.

   Code(s): ____________________

2. A 34-year-old patient presents with a history of inability to sustain an erection. The physician uses a duplex scan to conduct a complete study of the arterial and venous flow.

   Code(s): ____________________

Pulmonary

Codes found in the Pulmonary subsection include therapies, such as nebulizer treatments, and diagnostic tests, such as pulmonary function tests. A nebulizer is a device that throws a spray that is inhaled and is used in treatments such as those for patients with asthma. Pulmonary function tests are used to monitor the function of the pulmonary system, such as those used to monitor the lung capacity of a patient with emphysema. In most cases, several pulmonary function tests are performed together. The data are then compiled, and a diagnosis can be made. Several indicators must be present from a variety of tests, and those tests must be performed many times with the same result each time for the results to be considered conclusive. In most cases, each type of test may be reported separately, unless specifically stated within the code description.

EXERCISE K Pulmonary

Code the following:

1. Pulmonary stress test, simple

   Code(s): ________________

2. Vital capacity, total

   Code(s): ________________

3. Bronchospasm evaluation with spirometry before and after bronchodilator treatment

   Code(s): ________________

Allergy and Clinical Immunology

You are strongly encouraged to read the notes that appear at the beginning of the Allergy and Clinical Immunology subsection. The subsection is divided into several parts. The first is Allergy Testing, which describes allergy testing by various methods (percutaneous, intracutaneous, inhalation) and the type of tests (allergenic extracts, venoms, biologicals, food). The number of tests must always be specified for billing purposes because most of these codes are paid per test.

The second subheading is Allergen Immunotherapy. Allergen Immunotherapy codes specify three types of services:

1. Injection only
2. Prescription and injection
3. Provision of antigen only

All the codes in Allergen Immunotherapy have specific notes that you must read to know if the code is for injection, prescription/injection, or antigen only. For example, code 95115 is for the injection of antigen only and does not include the antigen or the prescription, but code 95120 is for the injection, antigen, and prescription. So, careful reading of the descriptions is a necessity.

The professional service necessary to provide the immunotherapy is bundled into the code, so an office visit code would not usually be reported. If the physician provided another identifiable service at the time of the immunotherapy, an office visit could be reported. But for the patient who has only the injection, prescription, antigen, or any combination of these three, the codes already contain the professional service.

EXERCISE L Allergy and Clinical Immunology

Using the CPT manual, code the following:

1. Direct nasal mucous membrane allergy test

   Code(s): ___________________

2. Percutaneous test using allergen extracts, immediate type reaction, 10 tests

   Code(s): ___________________

3. Single injection of allergen using extract provided by the patient

   Code(s): ___________________

4. Single injection of allergen and providing extract

   Code(s): ___________________

5. Intracutaneous tests with allergy extracts, immediate type reaction, 54 tests

   Code(s): ___________________

Neurology and Neuromuscular Procedures

There are codes in the Neurology and Neuromuscular Procedures subsection for sleep testing, muscle testing (electromyography), range of motion measurements, cerebral seizure monitoring, and a variety of neurologic function tests. The codes in this subsection are usually used by physicians who specialize in neurology, called neurologists. The neurologist usually is a consultant to a physician who needs the advice and input from another physician for patients with suspected neurologic problems.

One of the specialized tests conducted in the neurology specialty area is sleep studies. **Sleep studies** are the monitoring of a patient's sleep for 6 or more hours. The studies include the tracing (technical component) and the physician's review, interpretation, and report (professional component) of the studies. If the physician did only the professional component, modifier -26 is used along with the CPT code.

Sleep studies are used to diagnose various sleep disorders and to measure the patient's response to therapy. An electroencephalogram (EEG) is a procedure that is used to record the changes in brain waves. Polysomnography is the measurement of the brain waves during sleep but with the added feature of recording during the various stages of sleep (ie, excited, relaxed, drowsy, asleep, or deep sleep). During each of these stages, the rate and amplitude (height) of the brain waves are measured and compared with normal limits. Certain neurologic conditions can be identified by the variations in the brain waves from what is within the normal limits.

Parameters are what is being measured while the sleep testing is being conducted. For example, parameters include the measurement of snoring. Another parameter is blood pressure. The parameters are listed under the subheading of Sleep Testing. Be certain to read these parameters before coding in this area. The patient's record will contain the parameters or measurements conducted during the test. Several of the category codes are based on the number of parameters being measured.

To accurately code sleep tests, you must know the parameters and stages of testing. Additionally, many codes include a time component.

The electromyographic (EMG) studies use needles and electric current to stimulate nerves and record the results. Assessments of dysphasia, developmental testing, neurobehavior status, and neuropsychological test codes are also found in this subsection.

EXERCISE M Neurology and Neuromuscular Procedures

Using the notes under the Sleep Testing subheading and the code descriptions following the notes, identify the following abbreviations:

1. NCPAP ______________________
2. EEG ______________________
3. EMG ______________________
4. EOG ______________________
5. MSLT ______________________

Code the following:

6. Awake and drowsy EEG and photic stimulation in clinic

   Code(s): ____________

7. Needle electromyography, three extremities and related paraspinal areas

   Code(s): ____________

8. Range of motion measurement and report on both legs

   Code(s): ____________

Central Nervous System Assessments/Tests

The Central Nervous System Assessments/Tests codes identify psychological testing, speech/language (aphasia) assessment, developmental progress assessments, and thinking/reasoning status examination (neurobehavioral). Except for the basic developmental testing, the codes are based on a per hour basis. The results of all the tests are to be developed into a report that is included in the patient record.

EXERCISE N Central Nervous System Assessments/Tests

Code the following (all cases were 60 minutes in length):

1. A mother presents to the office with a 10-year-old who has been referred by the child's pediatrician for his nonconformal behavior. The mother expresses

great concern for the child's inability to behave as she and the child's father believe appropriate. The physician conducts several psychological tests with this new patient, as well as a history and examination. The physician then discusses the results of the examination and test with the mother.

Code(s): ________________

2. A young executive was referred for a Minnesota Multiphasic Personality Inventory (MMPI) test by his employer. The employer requests the testing for all newly hired executives who will be working with highly sensitive government documents.

   Code(s): ________________

3. A 14-year-old is seen in the office for an assessment of the child's attention span. The child is experiencing episodes of daydreaming of increasing severity. The physician conducts a clinical assessment of the child's cognitive function.

   Code(s): ________________

Chemotherapy Administration

Chemotherapy may be provided by several modalities. For instance, some third-party payers will pay for both an IV push and infusion on the same day while others will not. The IV push quickly puts the chemotherapy into the vein, whereas the infusion is the slower introduction of the chemotherapy into the vein. Read the patient record carefully before coding to ensure that the correct modality is identified. You must also be familiar with coding requirements for chemotherapy of third-party payers in the area.

Chemotherapy codes are divided by method of treatment and length of time taken to complete the treatment. Pay special attention to the wording for each code in the subsection. Some codes will include several hours of treatment time, while others will specify each hour of treatment time; and unit billing or multiple coding may be necessary to accurately reflect the services provided. When reporting chemotherapy, be sure to add a code for the provision of the agent.

EXERCISE O *Chemotherapy Administration*

Using the CPT manual, code the following chemotherapy:

1. Chemotherapy injected into the pleural cavity with thoracentesis

   Code(s): ________________

2. Refilling and maintenance on a patient's portable pump

   Code(s): ________________

3. Chemotherapy administered subcutaneously with local anesthesia

   Code(s): ________________

4. Chemotherapy administered intravenously using the infusion technique for 1 hour

   Code(s): ____________________

5. Chemotherapy injected into the central nervous system using a lumbar puncture

   Code(s): ____________________

Special Dermatological Procedures

The dermatology codes are usually used by a dermatologist who sees a patient in an office on a consultation basis. The dermatology codes for special procedures would typically be used in addition to the E/M consultation codes. For example, a patient is referred by his family physician to a dermatologist for treatment of acne. The dermatologist conducts a history and examination and treats the patient with ultraviolet light (actinotherapy). The codes would be an Office or Other Outpatient Consultation code, depending on the level of service provided, *and* 96900 for the actinotherapy.

EXERCISE P ***Special Dermatological Procedures***

Using the CPT manual, code the following:

1. A 16-year-old patient sees a dermatologist in consultation, at which time the physician does a problem focused history and physical examination regarding the patient's acne. The physician prescribes a treatment of ultraviolet light therapy.

   Code(s): ____________________

2. Actinotherapy for a 34-year-old consultative patient with severe dermatosis. The patient receives 8 hours of treatment. The physician provided a comprehensive history and physical examination with moderately complex medical decision-making.

   Code(s): ____________________

Physical Medicine and Rehabilitation

The codes in the Physical Medicine and Rehabilitation subsection can be used by a physician or therapist. The subsection includes codes dealing with different modalities of treatments (eg, traction, whirlpool, electrical stimulation) as well as various types of patient training (eg, functional activities, gait training, massage). The codes are reported by time or treatment area, as stated in the description for the code. Unit coding is necessary if time exceeds the initial time listed. The subsection also includes other rehabilitation procedures such as shopping trips that may be arranged for residents of a Veterans' Administration Medical Center.

EXAMPLE

Coding for patient's prosthetic training of 60 minutes would be:

97520 × 4 Prosthetic training, 60 minutes

Test and measurement codes are listed by the type of testing and the time the testing takes. The type of test would be for items such as orthotics, prosthetics, and musculoskeletal or functional capacity. Note the use of type and time in the following CPT code.

EXAMPLE

97750 Physical performance test or measurement (eg, musculoskeletal, functional capacity, with written report, each 15 minutes)

Time must be noted in the documentation in the patient's medical record.

The codes in Physical Medicine and Rehabilitation are used for physical medicine/therapy as well as other rehabilitation, for example, work/community reintegration (97537).

EXERCISE Q Physical Medicine and Rehabilitation

Using the CPT manual, code the following Physical Medicine cases:

1. Application of cold packs to one area (modality)

   Code(s): ________________

2. Initial prosthetic training, 30 minutes

   Code(s): ________________

3. Physical medicine treatment procedure, gait training, 30 minutes

   Code(s): ________________

Osteopathic Manipulative Treatment (OMT)

Osteopathic manipulative treatment is a form of manual treatment applied by a physician to eliminate somatic (body) dysfunction and related disorders. Osteopathic manipulation is musculoskeletal manipulation. The codes are listed by body regions. Considered body regions are: head, cervical, thoracic, lumbar, sacral, pelvic, lower extremities, upper extremities, rib cage, and abdomen and viscera. Codes are separated by the number of body regions treated. These codes are usually used by osteopathic physicians (doctors of osteopathy, D.O.).

Chiropractic Manipulative Treatment (CMT)

The Chiropractic Manipulative Treatment subsection is divided by the number of regions manipulated. For this subsection, the *spine* is divided into five regions (cervical, thoracic, lumbar, sacral, and pelvic) and the *extraspinal* regions are divided into five regions (head, lower extremities, upper extremities, rib cage, and abdomen). Chiropractic manipulation is the manipulation of the spinal column and other structures, whereas osteopathic manipulation is the manipulation of musculoskeletal structures. Each of the codes in the Chiropractic Manipulative Treatment subsection has a professional assessment bundled into the code. An office visit code is used only if the patient had a significant separately identifiable service provided; otherwise, the service of the office visit is bundled into the code.

EXERCISE R *Manipulative Treatment*

Code the following:

1. Sally, a 43-year-old woman, presents with the complaint of a seizing pain in the area of her lower left hip. The physician conducts a patient assessment and provides an alignment to two spinal regions.

   Code(s): ____________________

2. Lumbar manipulation

   Code(s): ____________________

Special Services and Reports

Special Services and Reports is a miscellaneous subsection that includes codes that do not fit into other sections. Codes that reflect services rendered at unusual hours of the day or on holidays, for example, are considered adjunct codes and are to be used in addition to the codes for the major service. For example, if a physician goes back to the office on Sunday to meet an established patient to provide urgent, but not emergency, service, the correct E/M service code for the office visit would be used in addition to 99054 to indicate the unusual time the service was provided.

The subsection also contains codes for medical testimony, the completion of complicated reports, education services, unusual travel, and supplies. Although this subsection is small, it contains codes that are used often. Take a few minutes to become familiar with the kinds of codes listed within Special Services and Reports and then mark the subsection for future use.

The codes for Special Services are located in the CPT manual index under the main term "Special Services."

EXERCISE S *Special Services and Reports*

Using the CPT manual, code the following:

1. The physician is called to the emergency department on Sunday (this code is in addition to the basic service code for the services provided to the patient)

   Code(s): ____________________

2. Conveyance of a specimen from the physician's office to a laboratory

   Code(s): ________________

3. Supplies provided for an office visit exceeding those usually used

   Code(s): ________________

You did it! You made it all the way through the CPT! If there could be noise with a text, you would hear loud applause and horns blowing to celebrate all your hard work. Good job!

HISTORY OF NATIONAL LEVEL CODING

CPT coding is only one of a three-part coding system called HCPCS (pronounced hick-picks). The Health Care Financing Administration developed the HCFA Common Procedure Coding System in 1983. The HCPCS is a collection of codes that represent procedures, supplies, products, and services that may be provided to Medicare beneficiaries and to individuals enrolled in private health insurance programs.

Three Levels of Codes

HCPCS is divided into three levels or groups.

Level I (CPT) codes are CPT codes in the CPT manual, which was developed, maintained, and copyrighted by the AMA. The CPT is the primary coding system used in the outpatient setting to code professional services provided to the patients.

Level II codes (National Codes) are approved and maintained jointly by the Alpha-Numeric Workgroup consisting of the HCFA, the Health Insurance Association of America, and the Blue Cross and Blue Shield Association. Level II codes are five-position alphanumeric codes representing physician and nonphysician services that are not represented in the Level I codes.

Level III codes (Local Codes) were developed by Medicare carriers for use at the local (carrier) level. These are five-position alphanumeric codes representing physician and nonphysician services that are not represented in the Level I or Level II codes.

Level II National Codes

CPT codes do not cover all services that are provided to patients. Allied health care professionals—such as dentists, orthodontists, and various technical support services, such as ambulance services—are not covered under the CPT coding system. There are also no codes in the CPT system for many of the supplies that are used in patient care (eg, drugs, durable medical equipment, or orthoses). Use of national codes is mandatory on all Medicare and Medicaid claims submitted for payment for services of the previously listed professionals. Although the national codes were developed for use when billing for services rendered to Medicare patients, many third-party payers now require that providers use the national codes

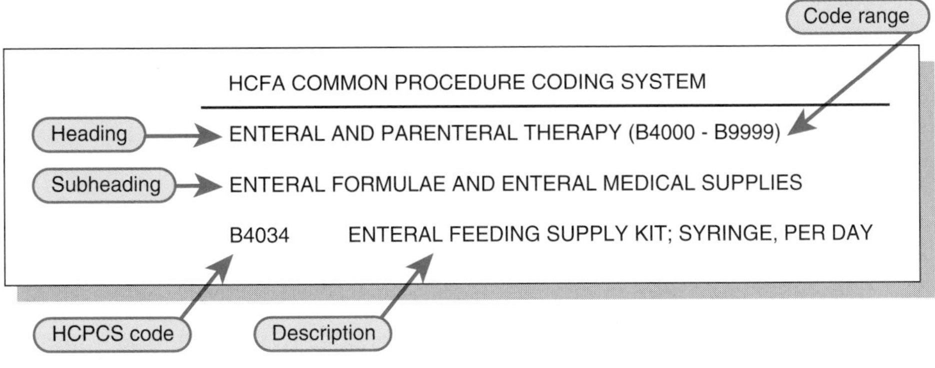

Figure 5–6
HCFA Common Procedure Coding System, National Codes. (Courtesy of U.S. Department of Health and Human Services, Health Care Financing Administration.)

when submitting bills for non-Medicare patients because the system allows continuity and specificity when billing. This uniformity also adds to the efforts to collect uniform health service data.

The first digit in a national code is a letter—A, B, D, E, G, H, J, K, L, M, P, Q, R, or V—which is followed by four numbers. Codes beginning with the letters K, G, and Q are for temporary assignment until a definitive decision can be made about appropriate code assignment. The K codes are temporary codes for durable medical equipment, G codes are temporary codes for procedures/professional services, and Q codes are temporary codes for procedures, services, and supplies. All codes and descriptions are updated annually by the HCFA. The alphanumeric listing contains headings of groups of codes as illustrated in Figure 5–6. Note that following the heading is listed the range of codes available for assignment in the category. There are also subheadings preceding the codes and the description of the codes to identify the type of codes that follow.

National codes are not used by health care facilities to code for the services provided to inpatients. Inpatient health care facilities use the diagnosis (from ICD-9-CM) as the basis for payment of their services and assign codes from ICD-9-CM, Volume 3, for inpatient procedures. The three levels of national codes are used in outpatient settings (including doctors' offices) where the basis of payment is the service rendered, not the diagnosis.

General Guidelines

The HCPCS manual includes the general guidelines for use of the national codes, a list of modifiers, the codes, a Table of Drugs, and an index. Again, we begin our study of the HCPCS manual at the index. You have to be able to locate items in the index to be able to identify the correct code. The main index terms include tests, services, supplies, orthotics, prostheses, medical equipment, drugs, therapies, and some medical and surgical procedures. The subterms of the index are listed under the main term to which they apply along with the code.

EXAMPLE

Apnea monitor is found under the entry:

Monitor
 apnea E0608

You then locate the code in the main part of the manual and read any notes that are listed with the code.

General rules for coding using the national codes are as follows:

1. Never code directly from the index. Always use both the alphanumeric listing and the index.
2. Analyze the statement or description provided that designates the item that needs a code.
3. Identify the main term in the index.
4. Check for relevant subterms under the main term. Verify the meaning of any unfamiliar abbreviations.
5. Note the code or codes found immediately after the selected main term or subterm.
6. After locating the term and the code in the index, verify the code and its full description in the alphanumeric listing to ensure the specificity of the code.
7. In most cases, for each entry a specific code is provided. In some cases, the coder is referred to a range of codes to locate the exact code desired. You must review the entire range in the numeric listing for the correct entry.

   If the code is a single number, locate that code number in the alphanumeric listing. Verify the code number and the description to be sure that you have selected the correct code that describes the item you are coding. You must review the alphanumeric listing to select the appropriate code number in this case.
8. In all cases, when locating an entry in the index, it is necessary to look at all descriptors under the main term and subterms to correctly choose the correct entry.

Code Groupings Are as Follows

- A Codes — Transportation Services, Including Ambulance; Medical and Surgical Supplies; Administrative, Miscellaneous and Investigational
- B Codes — Enteral and Parenteral Therapy
- D Codes — Dental Procedures
- E Codes — Durable Medical Equipment
- G Codes — Temporary (Procedures/Professional Services)
- J Codes — Drugs Administered Other Than Oral Method
- K Codes — Temporary (Durable Medical Equipment)
- L Codes — Orthotic Procedures
- M Codes — Medical Services
- P Codes — Pathology and Laboratory Services
- Q Codes — Temporary (Procedures, Services, and Supplies)
- R Codes — Diagnostic Radiology Services
- V Codes — Vision Services; Hearing Services

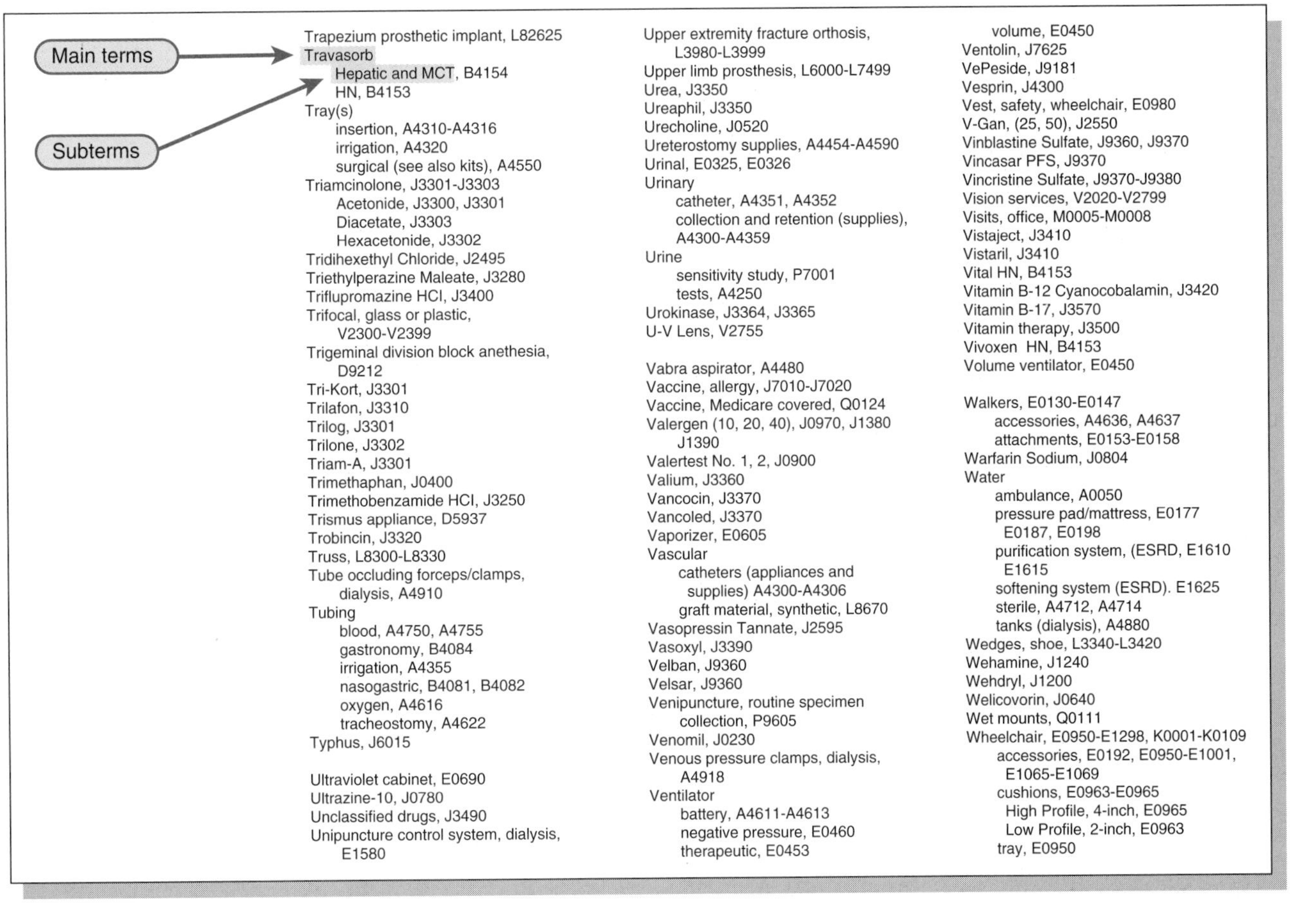

Main terms
Subterms

Trapezium prosthetic implant, L82625
Travasorb
  Hepatic and MCT, B4154
  HN, B4153
Tray(s)
  insertion, A4310-A4316
  irrigation, A4320
  surgical (see also kits), A4550
Triamcinolone, J3301-J3303
  Acetonide, J3300, J3301
  Diacetate, J3303
  Hexacetonide, J3302
Tridihexethyl Chloride, J2495
Triethylperazine Maleate, J3280
Triflupromazine HCl, J3400
Trifocal, glass or plastic, V2300-V2399
Trigeminal division block anethesia, D9212
Tri-Kort, J3301
Trilafon, J3310
Trilog, J3301
Trilone, J3302
Triam-A, J3301
Trimethaphan, J0400
Trimethobenzamide HCl, J3250
Trismus appliance, D5937
Trobincin, J3320
Truss, L8300-L8330
Tube occluding forceps/clamps, dialysis, A4910
Tubing
  blood, A4750, A4755
  gastronomy, B4084
  irrigation, A4355
  nasogastric, B4081, B4082
  oxygen, A4616
  tracheostomy, A4622
Typhus, J6015

Ultraviolet cabinet, E0690
Ultrazine-10, J0780
Unclassified drugs, J3490
Unipuncture control system, dialysis, E1580
Upper extremity fracture orthosis, L3980-L3999
Upper limb prosthesis, L6000-L7499
Urea, J3350
Ureaphil, J3350
Urecholine, J0520
Ureterostomy supplies, A4454-A4590
Urinal, E0325, E0326
Urinary
  catheter, A4351, A4352
  collection and retention (supplies), A4300-A4359
Urine
  sensitivity study, P7001
  tests, A4250
Urokinase, J3364, J3365
U-V Lens, V2755

Vabra aspirator, A4480
Vaccine, allergy, J7010-J7020
Vaccine, Medicare covered, Q0124
Valergen (10, 20, 40), J0970, J1380 J1390
Valertest No. 1, 2, J0900
Valium, J3360
Vancocin, J3370
Vancoled, J3370
Vaporizer, E0605
Vascular
  catheters (appliances and supplies) A4300-A4306
  graft material, synthetic, L8670
Vasopressin Tannate, J2595
Vasoxyl, J3390
Velban, J9360
Velsar, J9360
Venipuncture, routine specimen collection, P9605
Venomil, J0230
Venous pressure clamps, dialysis, A4918
Ventilator
  battery, A4611-A4613
  negative pressure, E0460
  therapeutic, E0453
  volume, E0450
Ventolin, J7625
VePeside, J9181
Vesprin, J4300
Vest, safety, wheelchair, E0980
V-Gan, (25, 50), J2550
Vinblastine Sulfate, J9360, J9370
Vincasar PFS, J9370
Vincristine Sulfate, J9370-J9380
Vision services, V2020-V2799
Visits, office, M0005-M0008
Vistaject, J3410
Vistaril, J3410
Vital HN, B4153
Vitamin B-12 Cyanocobalamin, J3420
Vitamin B-17, J3570
Vitamin therapy, J3500
Vivoxen HN, B4153
Volume ventilator, E0450

Walkers, E0130-E0147
  accessories, A4636, A4637
  attachments, E0153-E0158
Warfarin Sodium, J0804
Water
  ambulance, A0050
  pressure pad/mattress, E0177 E0187, E0198
  purification system, (ESRD, E1610 E1615
  softening system (ESRD). E1625
  sterile, A4712, A4714
  tanks (dialysis), A4880
Wedges, shoe, L3340-L3420
Wehamine, J1240
Wehdryl, J1200
Welicovorin, J0640
Wet mounts, Q0111
Wheelchair, E0950-E1298, K0001-K0109
  accessories, E0192, E0950-E1001, E1065-E1069
  cushions, E0963-E0965
    High Profile, 4-inch, E0965
    Low Profile, 2-inch, E0963
  tray, E0950

Figure 5–7
HCFA index, National Codes. (Courtesy of U.S. Department of Health and Human Services, Health Care Financing Administration.)

Index

The index is in alphabetical order with main terms and subterms (Fig. 5–7). The entries in the index of the national codes may be listed under more than one main term. For example, dialysis kits can be found under the two entries "Kits" or "Dialysis," as illustrated in Figure 5–8.

From the index, you turn to the code in the alphanumeric listing. The entries in the alphanumeric listing further explain what is included in the code. The dialysis kit code numbers are shown as they appear in the alphanumeric listing in Figure 5–9. Note that A4918 specifies "each," and A4910 lists examples of what can be considered supplies for dialysis. There are over 50 alphabetical modifiers

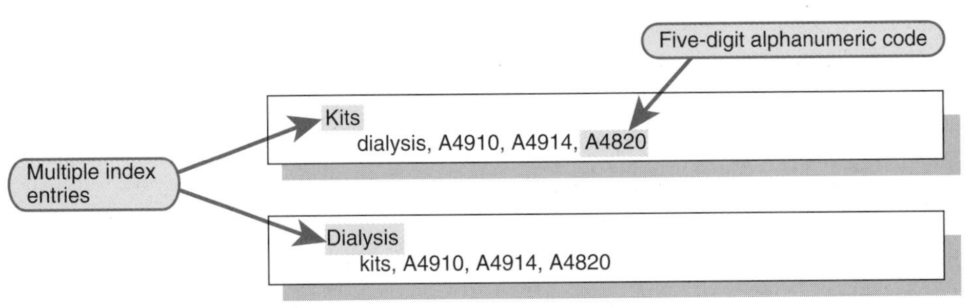

Figure 5–8
Index entries. (Courtesy of U.S. Department of Health and Human Services, Health Care Financing Administration.)

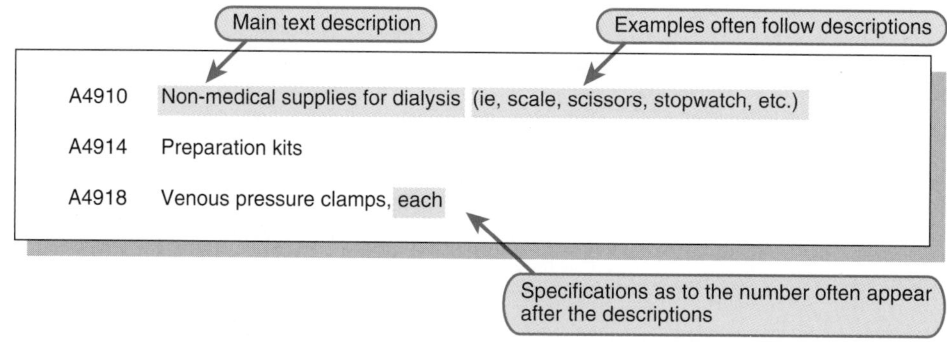

Figure 5–9
Main text display. (Courtesy of U.S. Department of Health and Human Services, Health Care Financing Administration.)

available for assignment to add further specificity to the five-digit national code. For example, modifiers can be used to specify the service provider, specify the anatomic site, or add specificity (Fig. 5–10). Appendix A of the CPT contains some of the Level II, HCPCS/National modifiers.

Table of Drugs

J codes are used to identify the drugs administered and the amounts or dosages given. The national codes contain a Table of Drugs (Fig. 5–11) to direct the user to the appropriate drug titles and the corresponding codes. J codes refer to drugs only by generic name. However, if a drug is known only by a brand or trade name, you will be directed to the generic name of the drug and then to the associated J code by a cross-reference system within the table. A *Physicians' Desk Reference* (PDR) is a valuable resource for the coder when using the Table of Drugs.

The "Route of Administration" column (see Fig. 5–11) lists the most common methods of delivering the referenced generic drug. The official definitions for Level II J codes generally describe the administration other than by oral method. Orally given drugs are not usually provided in a physician's office but are bought at a pharmacy after the visit. Therefore, with a few exceptions, orally delivered drugs are omitted from the Route of Administration column. The

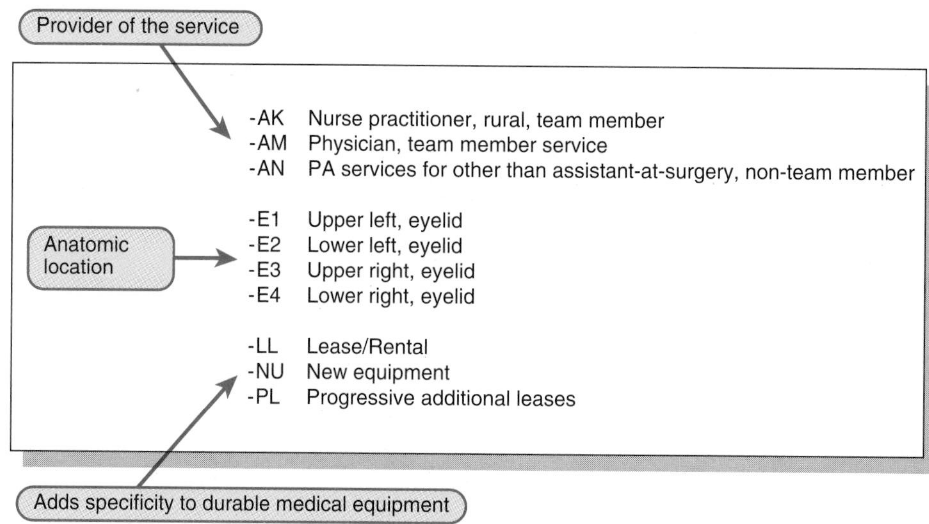

Figure 5–10
HCPCS modifiers. (Courtesy of U.S. Department of Health and Human Services, Health Care Financing Administration.)

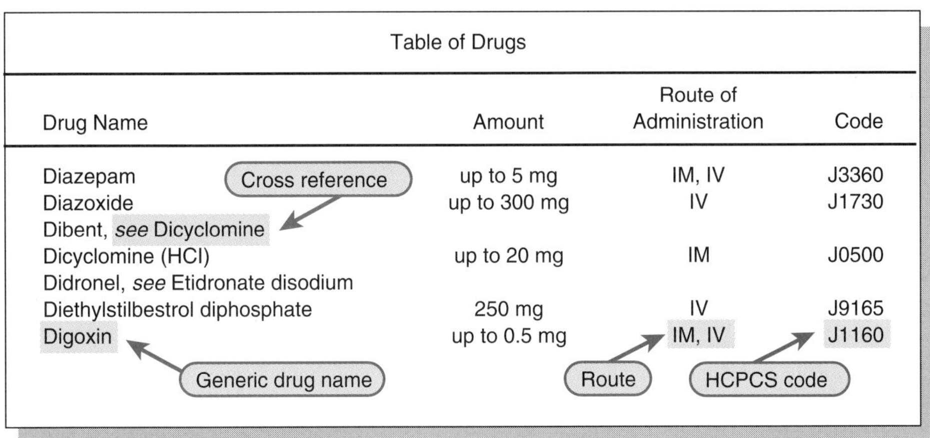

Table of Drugs

Drug Name	Amount	Route of Administration	Code
Diazepam	up to 5 mg	IM, IV	J3360
Diazoxide	up to 300 mg	IV	J1730
Dibent, *see* Dicyclomine			
Dicyclomine (HCl)	up to 20 mg	IM	J0500
Didronel, *see* Etidronate disodium			
Diethylstilbestrol diphosphate	250 mg	IV	J9165
Digoxin	up to 0.5 mg	IM, IV	J1160

Figure 5–11 Example from Table of Drugs. (Courtesy of U.S. Department of Health and Human Services, Health Care Financing Administration.)

following abbreviations and listings are used in the Route of Administration column:

IT	Intrathecal	INH	Inhalant solution
IV	Intravenous	VAR	Various routes
IM	Intramuscular	OTH	Other routes
SC	Subcutaneous		

EXERCISE T *Table of Drugs*

Define the following routes of administration for drugs:

1. Intrathecal ______________________________

____

2. Intravenous ______________________________

____

3. Intramuscular ______________________________

____

4. Subcutaneous ______________________________

____

5. Inhalant solution ______________________________

____

HCFA Common Procedure Coding System

J1120	INJECTION, ACETAZOLAMIDE SODIUM, UP TO 500 MG
J1160	INJECTION, DIGOXIN, UP TO 0.5 MG
J1165	INJECTION, PHENYTOIN SODIUM, PER 50 MG
J1170	INJECTION, HYDROMORPHONE, UP TO 4 MG
J1180	INJECTION, DYPHYLLINE, UP TO 500 MG
J1190	INJECTION, DEXRAZOXANE HYDROCHLORIDE, PER 250 MG
J1200	INJECTION, DIPHENHYDRAMINE HCL, UP TO 50 MG
J1205	INJECTION, CHLOROTHIAZIDE SODIUM, PER 500 MG

Figure 5–12
J codes. (Courtesy of U.S. Department of Health and Human Services, Health Care Financing Administration.)

Routes of Administration of Drugs

Intravenous administration includes all methods, such as gravity infusion, injections, and timed pushes. When several routes of administration are listed, the first listing is the most common method. A "VAR" posting denotes various routes of administration and is used for drugs that are commonly administered into joints, cavities, or tissues, as well as topical applications. Listings posted with "OTH" alert the coder to other administration methods, such as suppositories or catheter injections. A dash (—) in a column signifies that no information is available for that particular listing. Figure 5–12 illustrates J code information as listed in the alphanumeric listing to which you refer after locating the drug in the Table of Drugs.

Durable Medical Equipment

Durable medical equipment (DME) is equipment used by a patient with chronic disabling conditions. Claims for DME and related supplies can be paid only if the items meet the Medicare definition of covered DME and are medically necessary. The determination of medical necessity is made using documentation written by the physician. The documentation can include medical records, plans of care, discharge plans, and prescriptions or forms explicitly designed to document medical necessity. Usually these forms are referred to as Certificates of Medical Necessity (CMN) (Fig. 5–13).

Claims for other items require the use of the CMN, for example, power-operated vehicles, air fluidized beds, decubitus care pads, seat lift mechanisms, and paraffin baths.

Physician completion of the required medical documentation ensures that the DME items furnished to a Medicare beneficiary are those specifically needed for the unique medical condition of the patient. The HCFA also requires the use of form HCFA-484 for the Attending Physician's Certification of Medical Necessity for Home Oxygen Therapy (Fig. 5–14).

Effective 10/XX | DURABLE MEDICAL EQUIPMENT REGIONAL CARRIER | DMERC 02.01

CERTIFICATE OF MEDICAL NECESSITY: MANUAL/MOTORIZED WHEELCHAIRS

SECTION A CERTIFICATION: ☐ INITIAL ☐ REVISED

PATIENT NAME, ADDRESS, TELEPHONE AND HIC NO. (___) ___ - ____ HICN________	SUPPLIER NAME, ADDRESS, TELEPHONE, AND NSC NUMBER (___) ___ - ____ NSC ________
PLACE OF SERVICE ____ REPLACEMENT ITEM ____	HCPCS CODE(S) WARRANTY LENGTH TYPE
NAME AND ADDRESS OF FACILITY IF APPLICABLE (SEE BACK OF FORM):	____ ____ ____ ____

SECTION B INFORMATION BELOW TO BE COMPLETED ONLY BY THE PHYSICIAN OR PHYSICIAN'S EMPLOYEE

DIAGNOSIS (ICD9): ____ ____ ____ ____	PT. HT. ____ (IN.) PT. WT. ____ (LBS) DOB ___/___/___
I LAST EXAMINED THIS PATIENT FOR THIS CONDITION ON: ___/___/___ PT. SEX ____ (M OR F)	DATE NEEDED INITIAL ___/___/___ REVISED ___/___/___ EST. LENGTH OF NEED: # OF MONTHS: ___ 1-99 (99 = LIFETIME)

ANSWER QUESTIONS 1-4 FOR MOTORIZED WHEELCHAIR BASE, 4, 18-22 FOR MANUAL WHEELCHAIR BASE, 4-18 FOR WHEELCHAIR OPTIONS.
Use Y - Yes, N - No, or D for Does Not Apply unless otherwise noted.

[ ] 1. Does the patient have severe weakness of the upper extremities due to a neurologic or muscular disease/condition?

[ ] 2. Is the patient unable to operate a wheelchair manually?

[ ] 3. Is the patient capable of <u>safely</u> operating the controls of a power wheelchair?

[ ] 4. Would the patient be bed or chair confined without the use of a wheelchair?

[ ] 5. Does patient have quadriplegia?

[ ] 6. Does patient have a fixed hip angle?

[ ] 7. Does patient have a trunk cast or brace that requires a reclining back feature for positioning?

[ ] 8. Does the patient have a cast or brace which prevents 90 degree flexion of the knee?

[ ] 9. Does patient have a musculoskeletal condition that prevents 90 degree flexion at the knee?

[ ] 10. Does patient have excessive extensor tone of the trunk muscles?

[ ] 11. Does patient have weak neck muscles requiring support?

[ ] 12. Does patient have weak upper body muscles, upper body instability or muscle spasticity?

[ ] 13. Does patient have use of only one hand/arm and the condition is expected to last for 6 months or more?

[ ] 14. Is there hemiplegia or uncontrolled arm movements?

[ ] 15. Does patient have a need for arm height different than that available using non-adjustable arms?

[ ] 16. Does the patient need to rest in a recumbent position two or more times during the day?

[ ] 17. Is transfer between bed and wheelchair very difficult?

___ 18. How many hours per day does the patient usually spend in the wheelchair? (round up to next hour, e.g., for 3 1/2 hours, use 4) use 1-24.

[ ] 19. Is the patient able to place his/her feet on the ground for propulsion in a standard wheelchair?

[ ] 20. Is the patient able to self-propel in a standard wheelchair?

[ ] 21. Reserved for future use.

[ ] 22. Can/does patient self-propel in a lightweight wheelchair?

I certify the medical necessity of these items for this patient. Section B of this form and any statement on my letterhead attached hereto has been completed by me, or by my employee and reviewed by me. The foregoing information is true, accurate, and complete, and I understand that any falsification, omission, or concealment of material fact may subject me to civil or criminal liability.

PHYSICIAN NAME, ADDRESS	________ __/__/__ PHYSICIAN'S SIGNATURE: DATE (A STAMPED SIGNATURE IS NOT ACCEPTABLE) ☐ Attending ☐ Consulting ☐ Other ordering UPIN:________ TELEPHONE #: (___) ___ - ____

Figure 5–13
HCFA Certificate of Medical Necessity. (Courtesy of U.S. Department of Health and Human Services, Health Care Financing Administration.)

Department of Health and Human Services
Health Care Financing Administration

Form Approved
OMB No. 0938-0534

ATTENDING PHYSICIAN'S CERTIFICATION OF MEDICAL NECESSITY FOR HOME OXYGEN THERAPY *(Legible handwritten entries acceptable)*

Public reporting burden for this collection of information is estimated to average 15 minutes per response, including the time for reviewing instructions, searching existing data sources, gathering and maintaining the data needed, and completing and reviewing the collection of information. Send comments regarding this burden estimate or any other aspect of this collection of information, including suggestions for reducing this burden, to HCFA, P.O. Box 26684, Baltimore, MD 21207; and to the Office of Information and Regulatory Affairs, Office of Management and Budget, Washington, DC 20503.

Patient's Name, Address, and HIC No.	Supplier's Name, Address, and Identification No.

Certification: ☐ Initial ☐ Revised ☐ Renewed

INFORMATION BELOW TO BE ENTERED ONLY BY PHYSICIAN OR PHYSICIAN'S EMPLOYEE

1. Pertinent Diagnoses, ICD-9-CM Codes, and Findings - CHECK ALL THAT APPLY:

☐ Emphysema (492.8)
☐ COPD (496)
☐ Cor Pulmonale (416.9)
☐ Interstitial Disease (515)
☐ Other ______________
Specify Code

☐ Chronic Obstructive Bronchitis (491.2)
☐ Chronic Obstructive Asthma (493.20)
☐ Congestive Heart Failure (428.0)
☐ Secondary Polycythemia (289.0)
☐ Hematocrit 57% or more Yes☐ No☐

2.A. I last examined this patient for this condition on:
______/______/______
Month Day Year

2.B. Home oxygen prescribed:
______/______/______
Month Day Year

2.C. Estimated length of need:
☐ 1-3 months ☐ 4-12 months ☐ Lifetime

3.A. Results of Most Recent Arterial Blood Gas and/or Oxygen Saturation Tests (Patient Breathing Room Air)

	PO2	02 Saturation	Date
(1) At Rest..........			
(2) Walking..........			
(2) Sleeping.........			
(3) Exercising........			
(4) Other :			

3.C. Physician/Provider Performing Test(s) *(Printed/Typed Name and Address)*:

3.B. If performed under conditions other than room air, explain:

NOTE: If PO2 Level exceeds 59 mm Hg or the arterial blood saturation exceeds 89% at rest on room air, the claim will be disallowed without compelling medical evidence. Check block ☐ if you have attached a separate statement on your letterhead of additional documentation.

4. Oxygen Flow Rate : _____ Liters per minute ☐ Continuous (24 hrs/day)

☐ Noncontinuous (Enter hrs/day): _____ Walking _____ Sleeping _____ Exercise Program _____ Other (specify) ____________

5. Oxygen Equipment Prescribed If you have prescribed a particular form of delivery, check applicable block(s). Otherwise leave blank.

A. Supply System

(1) Stationary Source ☐ Concentrator ☐ Compressed Gas ☐ Liquid Oxygen ☐ Other

(2) Portable or Ambulatory Source ☐ Liquid Oxygen ☐ Compressed Gas ☐ Other ____________

B. Delivery System

☐ (1) Nasal Cannula
☐ (2) 02 Conserving Device
☐ Pulse 02 System
☐ Reservoir System
☐ Other ____________
☐ (3) Transtracheal Catheter
☐ (4) Other ____________

6. If you have prescribed a portable or ambulatory system, describe activities/exercise that patient regularly pursues which require this system in the home and which cannot be met by a stationary system (e.g., amount and frequency of ambulation).

CERTIFICATION

THE PATIENT HAS APPROPRIATELY TRIED OTHER TREATMENT MEASURES WITHOUT SUCCESS. OXYGEN THERAPY AND OXYGEN EQUIPMENT AS PRESCRIBED IS MEDICALLY INDICATED AND IS REASONABLE AND NECESSARY FOR THE TREATMENT OF THIS PATIENT. THIS FORM AND ANY STATEMENT ON MY LETTERHEAD ATTACHED HERETO HAS BEEN COMPLETED BY ME, OR BY MY EMPLOYEE AND REVIEWED BY ME. THE FOREGOING INFORMATION IS TRUE, ACCURATE, AND COMPLETE, AND I UNDERSTAND THAT ANY FALSIFICATION, OMISSION, OR CONCEALMENT OF MATERIAL FACT MAY SUBJECT ME TO CIVIL OR CRIMINAL LIABILITY.

Attending Physician's Signature: *(A STAMPED SIGNATURE IS NOT ACCEPTABLE)*	Date:

Physician's Name, Address, Telephone No., and Identification No.:

Form HCFA-484 (5-90)
DMERC Region D Supplier Manual *VIII - 22*

Figure 5–14
HCFA Attending Physician's Certificate of Medical Necessity for Home Oxygen Therapy. (Courtesy of U.S. Department of Health and Human Services, Health Care Financing Administration.)

EXERCISE U National Codes

With information provided in this chapter, complete the following:

1. HCPCS is divided into three levels. List the names of the levels, in order, and the level number:

   a. ______________________

   Level ______________________

   b. ______________________

   Level ______________________

   c. ______________________

   Level ______________________

2. There are three groups of codes that are used by the HCFA for temporary assignment until a definitive decision can be made about the correct code assignment. What are the alphabetical letters of these three groups of codes?

   ______________, ______________, and ______________.

3. There are over 50 modifiers in the HCPCS. Are they alphabetical or numeric modifiers? ______________________

4. What alphabetical group of codes is used to reference drugs in the HCPCS?

   ____

5. "Route of Administration" generally describes the administration of drugs by methods other than ______________________

6. What group of codes is used to reference durable medical equipment in the national codes? ______________________

Use Figure 5–7 to Figure 5–12 to answer the following questions:

7. What is the range of codes in Figure 5–7 available for coding of an allergy vaccine? ______________________

8. What is the modifier for the following (Fig. 5–10)?

   a. New equipment ______________________

   b. Lower left eyelid ______________________

   c. The services of a physician who was a member of a team that provided service ______________________

9. What is the route of administration for dicyclomine (Fig. 5–11)?

____

10. What is the amount of diazepam for code J3360 (Fig. 5–11)?

____

11. What is the J code for an injection of diazoxide (Fig. 5–11)?

____

12. What is the code range available for a high-profile cushion for a wheelchair (Fig. 5–7)? _______________

CHAPTER GLOSSARY

actinotherapy: treatment of acne using ultraviolet rays
angiography: taking of x-ray films of vessels after injection of contrast material
anomaloscope: instrument used to test color vision
anoscopy: procedure that uses a scope to examine the anus
apexcardiography: recording of the movement of the chest wall
aphakia: absence of the lens of the eye
audiometry: hearing testing
bifocal: two focuses in eyeglasses, one usually for close work and the other for improvement of distance vision
biofeedback: process of giving a person self-information
cardioversion: electrical shock to the heart to restore normal rhythm
colonoscopy: fibroscopic examination of the entire colon that may include part of the terminal ileum
corneosclera: cornea and sclera of the eye
Doppler: ultrasonic measure of blood movement
ECG: *see* electrocardiogram
echography: ultrasound procedure in which sound waves are bounced off an internal organ and the resulting image is recorded
EEG: *see* electroencephalogram
electrocardiogram (ECG): written record of the electrical action of the heart
electrocochleography: test to measure the eighth cranial nerve (hearing test)
electroencephalogram (EEG): written record of the electrical action of the brain
electromyogram (EMG): written record of the electrical activity of the skeletal muscles
electro-oculogram (EOG): written record of the electrical activity of the eye
endomyocardial: pertaining to the inner and middle layers of the heart
ESRD: end-stage renal disease
gonioscopy: use of a scope to examine the angles of the eye
hemodialysis: cleansing of the blood outside the body
hyposensitization: decreased sensitivity
hypothermia: decreased body temperature
immunotherapy: therapy to increase immunity
intramuscular: into a muscle
intravenous: into a vein
iontophoresis: introduction of ions into the body
ischemia: deficient blood supply due to obstruction of the circulatory system
modality: treatment method
monofocal: eyeglasses with one vision correction
MSLT: multiple sleep latency testing
myasthenia gravis: syndrome characterized by muscle weakness
nasopharyngoscopy: use of a scope to visualize the nose and pharynx
NCPAP: nasal continuous positive airway pressure
nystagmus: rapid involuntary eye movements
opacification: area that has become opaque (milky)
ophthalmodynamometry: test of the blood pressure of the eye
ophthalmology: body of knowledge regarding the eyes
optokinetic: movement of the eyes to objects moving in the visual field

orthoptic: corrective; in the correct place
percutaneous: through the skin
peritoneal: within the lining of the abdominal cavity
phlebotomy: cutting into a vein
phonocardiogram: recording of heart sounds
photochemotherapy: treatment by means of drugs that react to ultraviolet radiation or sunlight
plethysmography: determining the changes in volume of an organ part or body
pneumoplethysmography: determining the changes in the volume of the lung
proctosigmoidoscopy: fibroscopic examination of the sigmoid colon and rectum
retrograde: moving backward or against the usual direction of flow
spirometry: measurement of breathing capacity
subcutaneous: tissue below dermis, primarily fat cells that insulate the body
thermogram: written record of temperature variation
tonography: recording of changes in intraocular pressure in response to sustained pressure on the eyeball
tonometry: measurement of pressure or tension
transcutaneous: entering by way of the skin
transesophageal echocardiogram (TEE): echocardiogram performed by placing a probe down the esophagus and sending out sound waves to obtain images of the heart and its movement
transseptal: through the septum
tympanometry: test of the inner ear using air pressure
vectorcardiogram (VCG): continuous recording of electrical direction and magnitude of the heart

CHAPTER REVIEW Chapter 5, Part I, Theory

Without the use of the CPT manual, answer the following questions:

1. There are two types of services in the Medicine section. One is diagnostic and the other is __________.
2. What do the following abbreviations mean?
   a. IV __________
   b. IM __________
   c. SQ __________
3. The routing of blood including the waste products outside the body for cleansing is __________.
4. The dialysis that involves using the peritoneal cavity as a filter is known as what kind of dialysis? __________
5. What is the name of the test that checks the intraocular pressure of the eye?
   ____
6. What is the name of the scope that is used to examine color vision?
   ____
7. What is the word that means the body of knowledge about the ear, nose, and larynx? __________

8. In what subsection of the Medicine section would you find CPR, coronary atherectomies, and heart valvuloplasties? ______________________________

____

9. What kind of scanning uses ultrasonic technology with a display of both structure and motion with time? ______________________________

____

10. What is the name of the ultrasonic documentation that does velocity mapping and imaging? ______________________________

11. In what Medicine subsection would you find therapies such as nebulizer treatments? ______________________________

12. Percutaneous, intracutaneous, and inhalation are examples of what from the Allergy subsection? ______________________________

13. Allergenic extracts, venoms, biologicals, and food are examples of what from the Allergy subsection? ______________________________

14. If you were looking for the code number to indicate the circumstance in which a physician sees a patient between the hours of 10 PM and 8 AM, in what subsection of the Medicine section would you find that code?

____

Match the following terms to the correct definitions:

15. aphakia _______
16. echography _______
17. gonioscopy _______
18. hemodialysis _______
19. modality _______
20. nystagmus _______
21. optokinetic _______
22. percutaneous _______
23. phlebotomy _______
24. retrograde _______

a. entering by way of the skin
b. moving backward or against the usual direction of flow
c. through the skin
d. cleansing of the blood outside the body
e. test of the inner ear using air pressure
f. rapid involuntary eye movements
g. cutting into a vein
h. use of a scope to examine the angles of the eye
i. movement of the eyes to objects moving in the visual field
j. ultrasound procedure in which sound waves are bounced off an internal organ and the resulting image is recorded

25. subcutaneous _______
26. tonometry _______
27. transcutaneous _______
28. tympanometry _______

k. measurement of pressure or tension
l. tissue below dermis, primarily fat cells that insulate the body
m. absence of the lens of the eye
n. treatment method

29. What are the three levels (level number and name) of HCPCS?

a. ______________________________

b. ______________________________

c. ______________________________

30. What are the K, G, and Q codes used for in the national codes?

____

31. Can you code directly from the national code manual index?

Yes ______________ No ______________

32. Is there only one entry in the index of the national code manual for each item?

Yes ______________ No ______________

33. In what section of the national code manual would you locate the generic name of drugs? ______________________________

34. What are J codes? ______________________________

35. What administration is not listed in the Route of Administration for drugs?

____

36. Under what route of administration would suppositories or catheter injections be classified? ______________________________

37. What does the abbreviation DME stand for? ______________________________

____

Match the following administration methods for drugs:

38. OTH _______
39. IT _______
40. IV _______
41. IM _______

a. subcutaneous
b. inhalant solution
c. various routes
d. intrathecal

42. SC ______
43. INH ______
44. VAR ______

e. intramuscular
f. intravenous
g. other routes

Chapter 5, Part II, Practical

Using the CPT manual, code the following:

45. An 18-month-old established patient receives a diphtheria toxoid administered by the nurse.

    Code(s): ________________

46. An established patient received a tetanus toxoid that was administered by the physician's assistant.

    Code(s): ________________

47. DTP and an oral of poliomyelitis vaccine (live) for a new patient. A problem focused history and examination were done, and the medical decision-making was straightforward.

    Code(s): ________________

48. The physician administers an IV infusion for therapeutic purposes that takes 1 hour.

    Code(s): ________________

49. A patient brings his allergy medication into the office and has a single injection service provided by the nurse.

    Code(s): ________________

50. A patient receives the initial 30-minute training for her prosthetic arm.

    Code(s): ________________

51. A patient has a bronchospasm evaluation before and after a spirometry that was administered to monitor his lung capacity.

    Code(s): ________________

52. Nasopharyngoscopy with endoscope

    Code(s): ________________

53. A 30-year-old with end-stage renal disease received a full month of dialysis.

    Code(s): ________________

54. An esophagus acid reflux test with intraluminal pH electrode for detection of gastroesophageal reflux

    Code(s): ____________________

55. Peritoneal dialysis with a single physician evaluation

    Code(s): ____________________

56. Psychiatric evaluation of hospital records

    Code(s): ____________________

57. Esophageal intubation and collection of cytology specimens

    Code(s): ____________________

58. Supply of contact lenses to a patient

    Code(s): ____________________

59. Psychiatric diagnostic interview examination

    Code(s): ____________________

60. Hemodialysis procedure with a physician evaluation

    Code(s): ____________________

61. Hearing aid check on one ear

    Code(s): ____________________

62. Right-sided heart catheterization

    Code(s): ____________________

63. Electronic analysis of a dual chamber pacemaker system with reprogramming

    Code(s): ____________________

64. A single pulmonary stress test

    Code(s): ____________________

65. Physical medicine treatment of 30 minutes for left leg gait training

    Code(s): ____________________

66. Therapeutic phlebotomy

    Code(s): ____________________

67. Allergy prescribing, allergenic extract, and single injection

    Code(s): ____________________

68. Gastric intubation, washing, and preparation of cytology slides

    Code(s): ____________________

69. Individual, supportive, medical psychotherapy by physician in the office lasting 80 minutes

    Code(s): ____________________

Each of the following questions has a Level II code(s) in the answer. If you do not have a coding text for Level II codes, identify the item(s) that would be coded with a Level II code(s):

70. An 80-year-old man is leaving the hospital after a total right knee replacement. The physical therapist recommended that the patient use a pick-up folding walker to ambulate short distances in his home. The physician agrees and orders the walker.

    Code(s): ____________________

    HCPCS item/Code(s): ____________________

71. During a visit to the physician's office, a 50-year-old female established patient has an excision of a 1.2-cm, benign skin lesion on her back. A surgical tray is used during the procedure.

    Code(s): ____________________

    HCPCS item/Code(s): ____________________

72. The physician visits an established patient, an 83-year-old woman, at the local nursing facility for a follow-up visit. The resident has chronic massive lymphedema of her left lower leg as a result of a previous radical groin dissection surgery. The physician performs an expanded problem focused interval history and physical examination with decision-making of moderate complexity. In order to treat the lymphedema, the physician contacts a medical supply company to order a pneumatic compressor, home segmental mode with a calibrated gradient pressure monitor. The patient will also need a half leg segmental gradient pressure pneumatic appliance.

    Code(s): ____________________

    HCPCS item/Code(s): ____________________

73. A 40-year-old man is brought to the emergency department by ambulance after a two-car motor vehicle accident on a local expressway. The man is complaining of severe pain on his left side around his rib cage. He thinks the jolt of the accident caused him to hit against the driver's side door. He had no other complaints and no other signs of external injury. The emergency department physician performs an expanded problem focused history and physical examination with a moderate complexity of medical decision-

making. X-ray of the bilateral ribs, including three views, is ordered. The radiologist reports that the radiologic examination is negative for rib fractures. To support the patient's rib cage and alleviate pain, the physician orders and applies a rib belt, and the patient is discharged to his family with instructions for follow-up care within 48 hours with his family practitioner.

Code(s): ____________________

HCPCS item/Code(s): ____________________

74. An established patient with coronary artery disease is seen in his cardiologist's office for a follow-up examination. He has had repeated episodes of angina, even at rest. After collecting a comprehensive history and performing a complete cardiovascular physical examination, the physician orders an electrocardiogram with 12 leads. The physician also provides the interpretation and report for the ECG. The physician sends the patient over to the hospital radiology center for a PET myocardial perfusion imaging study. This PET will be a single study at rest.

Code(s): ____________________

HCPCS item/Code(s): ____________________

UNIT 2

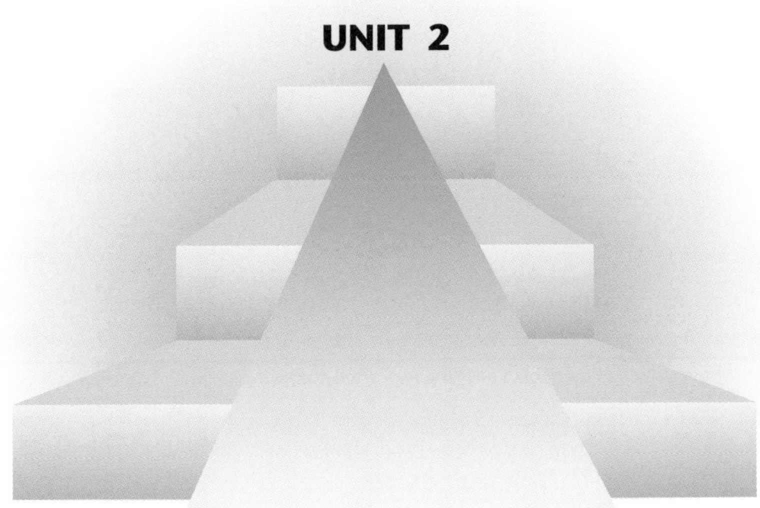

International Classification of Diseases, 9th Revision, Clinical Modification (ICD-9-CM)

6 An Overview of the ICD-9-CM

CHAPTER TOPICS

Learning Objectives

After completing this chapter, you should be able to

1. List the purposes of the ICD-9-CM.
2. Apply coding conventions when assigning codes.
3. Identify characteristics of Volumes 1, 2, and 3 formats.
4. Demonstrate use of ICD-9-CM.
5. Define chapter terminology.

WHAT IS THE ICD-9-CM?

The International Classification of Diseases, 9th Revision, Clinical Modification (ICD-9-CM) is designed for the classification of patient morbidity (sickness) and mortality (death) information for statistical purposes and for the indexing of hospital records by disease and operation for data storage and retrieval.

The ICD-9-CM is based on the ICD-9—the 9th revision of the official version of the International Classification of Diseases compiled by the World Health Organization (WHO). In February 1977, a committee was convened by the National Center for Health Statistics to provide advice and counsel to the development of a clinical modification of the ICD-9. The ICD-9-CM is the resulting **c**linical **m**odification. The term "clinical" was used to emphasize the intent of the modification to serve as a tool in the area of classification of morbidity data for indexing of medical records, medical care review, ambulatory care, other medical care programs, and basic health statistics.

Through the years, the use of the ICD-9-CM (often called the "ICD-9") has grown. The Medicare Catastrophic Coverage Act of 1988 (P.L. 100-330) required the submission of the appropriate ICD-9-CM diagnosis codes with charges billed to Medicare Part B (outpatient services). The law was later repealed, but the coding requirement still stands.

Although coding was originally accomplished to provide access to medical records through retrieval for medical research, education, and administration, codes today are used to

- facilitate payment of health services
- evaluate patients' use of health care facilities (utilization patterns)
- study health care costs
- research the quality of health care
- predict health care trends
- plan for future health care needs

The Standards of Ethical Coding was approved by the American Health Information Management Association (AHIMA) Board of Directors in April of 1991. These standards were developed by the Council on Coding and Classification to give medical records coders ethical guidelines for performing their task. The Standards are intended to impart the responsibility and importance coders have as members of the healthcare team and to support them as dignified professionals.

Standards of Ethical Coding

In this era of payment based on diagnostic and procedural coding, the professional ethics of medical records coders continues to be challenged. The following standards for ethical coding developed by the AHIMA Council on Coding and Classification are offered to guide the coder in this process.[1]

1. Diagnoses that are present on admission or diagnoses and procedures that occur during the current encounter are to be abstracted after a thorough review of the entire medical record. Those diagnoses not applicable to the current encounter should not be abstracted. Also, diagnoses that would not be abstracted if they did not influence payment should not be included.

2. Selection of the principal diagnosis and principal procedure, along with other diagnoses and procedures, must meet the definitions of the Uniform Hospital Discharge Data Set (UHDDS).

3. Assessment must be made of the documentation in the chart to assure that it is adequate and appropriate to support the diagnoses and procedures selected to be abstracted.

4. Medical record coders should use their skills, their knowledge of ICD-9-CM and CPT, and any available resources to select diagnostic and procedural codes.

5. Medical record coders should not change codes or narratives of codes so that the meanings are misrepresented. Nor should diagnoses or procedures be included or excluded because the payment will be affected. Statistical clinical data is an important result of coding, and maintaining a quality database should be a conscientious goal.

6. Physicians should be consulted for clarification when they enter conflicting or ambiguous documentation in the chart.

7. The medical record coder is a member of the healthcare team, and as such, should assist physicians who are unfamiliar with ICD-9-CM, CPT, or DRG methodology by suggesting resequencing or inclusion of diagnoses or procedures when needed to more accurately reflect the occurrence of events during the encounter.

8. The medical record coder is expected to strive for the optimal payment to which the facility is legally entitled, but it is unethical and illegal to maximize payment by means that contradict regulatory guidelines.

[1]The Official Coding Guidelines, published by the Cooperating Parties (American Hospital Association, American Health Information Management Association, Health Care Financing Administration and National Center for Health Statistics), should be followed in all facilities regardless of payment source.

Figure 6–1
Standards of Ethical Coding. (From American Health Information Management Association, 1991.)

The use and results of coding are widespread and evident in our everyday lives. Many people hear the results of coding on a regular basis and don't even know it. Anytime you listen to the news and hear the newscaster refer to a specific number of AIDS cases in the United States or read about an epidemic of measles in your local newspaper, you are seeing the results of ICD-9-CM coding. The ICD-9-CM is totally compatible with its parent system, ICD-9, thus meeting the need for comparability of morbidity and mortality statistics at the international level. The ICD-9-CM is a classification system to track morbidity and mortality. A classification system means that each condition or disease can be coded to only one code as much as possible to ensure the validity and reliability of data.

Coding must be performed correctly and consistently to produce meaningful statistics. (Refer to Fig. 6–1 for the Standards of Ethical Coding.) To code accurately, it is necessary to have a working knowledge of medical terminology and to understand the guidelines, terminology, and conventions of the ICD-9-CM. Transforming verbal descriptions of diseases, injuries, conditions, and procedures into numerical designations is a complex activity and should not be undertaken without proper training. Learning to use the ICD-9-CM codes will be a valuable tool to you in any health care career.

EXERCISE A What Is the ICD-9-CM?

Using the information presented in this text, complete the following:

1. The ICD-9-CM is designed for the classification of patient

   ______________________________ or

   ______________________________.

2. The ICD-9-CM manual is based on what text developed by the World Health Organization? ______________________________

3. The CM in ICD-9-CM stands for

   ______________________________.

4. Name four of the six reasons why the ICD-9-CM codes are used today.

   ____

   ____

   ____

   ____

5. The ICD-9-CM is used to translate what descriptive information into numeric codes? ______________________________ and

   ____

FORMAT AND CONVENTIONS USED IN THE ICD-9-CM

Several publishing companies produce editions of the ICD-9-CM manual. All editions are based on the official government version of the ICD-9-CM. This text is based on the official government version. The ICD-9-CM manual is published in a three-volume set:

Volume 1 Diseases: Tabular List

Volume 2 Diseases: Alphabetic Index

Volume 3 Procedures: Tabular List and Alphabetic Index

Volume 1 contains the disease and condition codes with the code descriptions (nomenclature) as well as the Supplementary Classification of Factors Influencing Health Status and Contact with Health Services (V codes) and External Causes of Injury and Poisoning (E codes). Volume 2 is the Alphabetic Index for Volume 1. Volumes 1 and 2 are used in inpatient and outpatient settings to substantiate medical services (medical necessity) by assigning diagnosis codes. Volume 3, used for coding procedures, contains codes for surgical, therapeutic, and diagnostic procedures and is used primarily by hospitals. ICD-9-CM codes are reported on the HCFA-1500 insurance claim form used in physicians' offices and the UB-92 form used in hospitals (Fig. 6–2). Private insurance carriers also require ICD-9-CM codes when submitting for payment for services.

There are four groups whose function it is to deal with in-depth coding principles and practices: Health Care Financing Administration (HCFA), National Center for Health Statistics, American Health Information Management Association (AHIMA), and American Hospital Association (AHA).

To begin the study of ICD-9-CM codes, you will first review the format of each volume. The objective of the review is to introduce you to the format and content of the volumes. When the review has been completed, you will begin to practice locating codes for various diseases and illnesses using the ICD-9-CM manual, since the only way to learn to code is to practice. For now, just relax, and let's take a look at the format and content of each volume of the ICD-9-CM.

You would think that you would begin your study of ICD-9-CM with Volume 1, but you will begin with Volume 2 because this volume is the index. Volume 2 is located at the beginning of the ICD-9-CM manual, followed by Volume 1. You began the practice of the CPT manual with learning how to locate items in the index and moved on to the main text. We will use that same approach with the ICD-9-CM. But first, you need to know about the conventions that are used in all volumes.

Conventions

The ICD-9-CM manual contains symbols, abbreviations, punctuation, and notations called conventions. Some conventions are used in all three volumes of the ICD-9-CM manual, and others are used in only one or two volumes. The ICD-9-CM manual contains a list of the conventions and definitions to be used when assigning codes. It is important that you be familiar with the conventions as you prepare to use the ICD-9-CM codes.

NEC

NEC *(not elsewhere classifiable)* is to be used only when the information at hand specifies a condition but there is no more specific separate code for that condition in the coding manual.

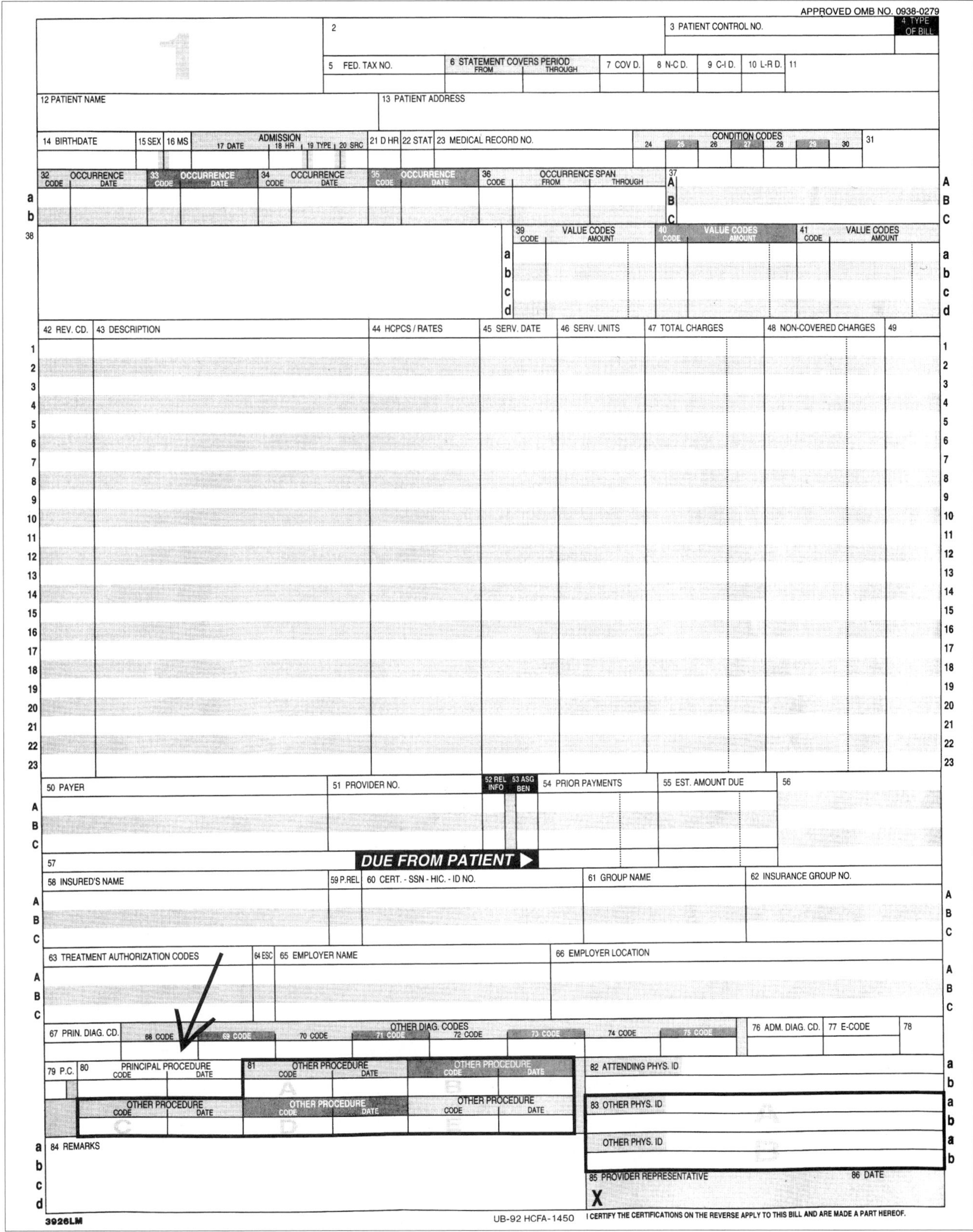

APPROVED OMB NO. 0938-0279

1 | 2 | 3 PATIENT CONTROL NO. | 4 TYPE OF BILL

5 FED. TAX NO. | 6 STATEMENT COVERS PERIOD FROM THROUGH | 7 COV D. | 8 N-C D. | 9 C-I D. | 10 L-R D. | 11

12 PATIENT NAME | 13 PATIENT ADDRESS

14 BIRTHDATE | 15 SEX | 16 MS | ADMISSION 17 DATE 18 HR 19 TYPE 20 SRC | 21 D HR | 22 STAT | 23 MEDICAL RECORD NO. | CONDITION CODES 24 25 26 27 28 29 30 | 31

32 OCCURRENCE CODE DATE | 33 OCCURRENCE CODE DATE | 34 OCCURRENCE CODE DATE | 35 OCCURRENCE CODE DATE | 36 OCCURRENCE SPAN CODE FROM THROUGH | 37 A B C

a b

38

39 VALUE CODES CODE AMOUNT | 40 VALUE CODES CODE AMOUNT | 41 VALUE CODES CODE AMOUNT

a b c d

42 REV. CD. | 43 DESCRIPTION | 44 HCPCS / RATES | 45 SERV. DATE | 46 SERV. UNITS | 47 TOTAL CHARGES | 48 NON-COVERED CHARGES | 49

1 2 3 4 5 6 7 8 9 10 11 12 13 14 15 16 17 18 19 20 21 22 23

50 PAYER | 51 PROVIDER NO. | 52 REL INFO | 53 ASG BEN | 54 PRIOR PAYMENTS | 55 EST. AMOUNT DUE | 56

A B C

57 DUE FROM PATIENT ▶

58 INSURED'S NAME | 59 P.REL | 60 CERT. - SSN - HIC. - ID NO. | 61 GROUP NAME | 62 INSURANCE GROUP NO.

A B C

63 TREATMENT AUTHORIZATION CODES | 64 ESC | 65 EMPLOYER NAME | 66 EMPLOYER LOCATION

A B C

67 PRIN. DIAG. CD. | OTHER DIAG. CODES 68 CODE 69 CODE 70 CODE 71 CODE 72 CODE 73 CODE 74 CODE 75 CODE | 76 ADM. DIAG. CD. | 77 E-CODE | 78

79 P.C. | 80 PRINCIPAL PROCEDURE CODE DATE | 81 OTHER PROCEDURE CODE DATE A | OTHER PROCEDURE CODE DATE B | 82 ATTENDING PHYS. ID a b

OTHER PROCEDURE CODE DATE C | OTHER PROCEDURE CODE DATE D | OTHER PROCEDURE CODE DATE E | 83 OTHER PHYS. ID A a b | OTHER PHYS. ID B a b

84 REMARKS a b c d | 85 PROVIDER REPRESENTATIVE X | 86 DATE

3926LM UB-92 HCFA-1450 I CERTIFY THE CERTIFICATIONS ON THE REVERSE APPLY TO THIS BILL AND ARE MADE A PART HEREOF.

Figure 6–2
UB-92 HCFA-1450 is used by inpatient facilities for claims submissions. (Courtesy of U.S. Department of Health and Human Services, Health Care Financing Administration.)

EXAMPLE

244.8 Other specified acquired hypothyroidism
Secondary hypothyroidism NEC

NOS

NOS *(not otherwise specified)* is the equivalent of "unspecified." It is used when the information at hand does not permit a more specific code assignment. The coder should ask the physician for more specific information so that the proper code assignment can be made.

EXAMPLE

159 Malignant neoplasm of other and ill-defined sites within the digestive organs and peritoneum

159.0 Intestinal tract, part unspecified
Intestine NOS

[ ]

Brackets are used to enclose synonyms, alternative wording, or explanatory phrases, and are found in the Tabular List.

EXAMPLE

426.89 Other
Dissociation:
atrioventricular [AV]
interference
isorhythmic
Nonparoxysmal AV nodal tachycardia

( )

Parentheses are used to enclose supplementary words that may be present or absent in the statement of a disease or procedure without affecting the code number to which it is assigned. Parentheses are found in both the Alphabetic Index and the Tabular List.

EXAMPLE

158 Malignant neoplasm of retroperitoneum and peritoneum

158.8 Specified parts of peritoneum
Cul-de-sac (of Douglas)
Mesentery

:

Colons are used in the Tabular List after an incomplete term that needs one or more of the modifiers that follow in order to make it assignable to a given category.

EXAMPLE

628 Infertility, Female

628.4 Of cervical or vaginal origin
Infertility associated with:
anomaly of cervical mucus
congenital structural anomaly
dysmucorrhea

}

Braces are used to enclose a series of terms, each of which is modified by the statement appearing at the right of the brace.

EXAMPLE

473 Chronic sinusitis

Includes: abscess, empyema, infection, suppuration } (chronic) of sinus (accessory) (nasal)

□

The lozenge symbol printed in the left margin preceding the disease code denotes a four-digit number unique to the ICD-9-CM manual. The content of these codes in the ICD-9-CM is not the same as those in ICD-9. The lozenge symbol is used only in Volume 1, Diseases: Tabular List. Coders seldom concern themselves with the differences between ICD-9-CM and ICD-9. These differences would be important to researchers.

EXAMPLE

□ **296.12 Manic disorder, recurrent episode, moderate**

§

The section mark indicates that a footnote is located at the bottom of the page.

EXAMPLE

§ **E807 Railway accident of unspecified nature**

The footnote on the page states:

§ Requires fourth digit.

Bold Type

Bold type is used for all codes and titles in the Tabular List in Volume 1.

EXAMPLE

244.8 Other specified acquired hypothyroidism
Secondary hypothyroidism NEC

Italicized Type

Italicized type is used for all exclusion notes and to identify those codes that are not usually sequenced as the principal diagnosis. Italicized type codes cannot be assigned as a principal diagnosis because they always follow another code. Italicized codes are to be sequenced in the order specified in the Alphabetic Index.

EXAMPLE

420.0 Acute pericarditis in diseases classified elsewhere

Code first underlying disease, as:
actinomycosis (039.8)
amebiasis (006.8)
nocardiosis (039.8)
tuberculosis (017.9)
uremia (585)

[ ]

Slanted brackets used in Volume 2, Alphabetic Index, are used to enclose the *manifestation* of the underlying condition. When a code is listed inside the slanted brackets, you must sequence that code after the underlying condition code.

EXAMPLE

Diabetic retinal hemorrhage

Hemorrhage, hemorrhagic (nontraumatic) 459.0
retina, retinal (deep) (superficial) (vessels) 362.81
diabetic 250.5 *[362.01]*

You would sequence the code 250.5 and then 362.01 to indicate that the retinal hemorrhage was due to diabetes.

Includes

"Includes" notes further define or provide examples and can apply to the chapter, section, or category. The notes at the beginning of a chapter apply to the entire chapter, the notes at the beginning of the section apply to that entire section, and the notes at the beginning of the category apply to the entire category. You need to refer back to the beginning of the chapter or section for any Includes notes that refer to an entire chapter or section because the Includes notes are not repeated within the chapter or section. Includes notes can also be found before or after category codes.

"Includes" at the beginning of a chapter:

EXAMPLE

1. INFECTIOUS AND PARASITIC DISEASES (001-139)

Note: Categories for "late effects" of infectious and parasitic diseases are to be found at 137-139.

INCLUDES diseases generally recognized as communicable or transmissible as well as a few diseases of unknown but possibly infectious origin

EXCLUDES *acute respiratory infections* (460-466)
carrier or suspected carrier of infectious organism (V02.0-V02.9)
certain localized infections
influenza (487.0-487.8)

"Includes" at the beginning of section:

EXAMPLE

TUBERCULOSIS (010-018)

INCLUDES infection by Mycobacterium tuberculosis (human) (bovine)

EXCLUDES *congenital tuberculosis* (771.2)
late effects of tuberculosis (137.0-137.4)

"Includes" at the beginning of a category: (applies to the entire category):

EXAMPLE

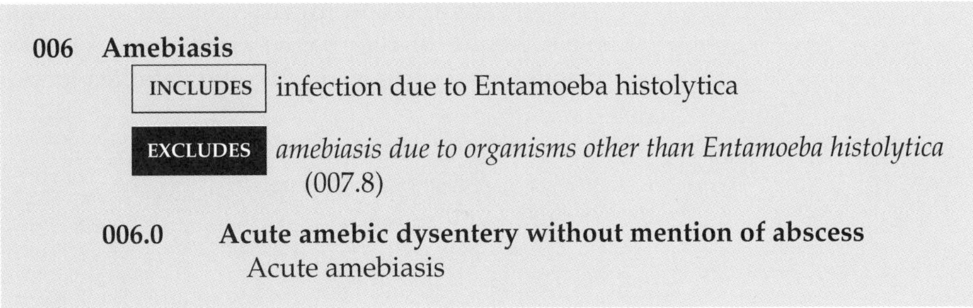

006 Amebiasis

INCLUDES infection due to Entamoeba histolytica

EXCLUDES *amebiasis due to organisms other than Entamoeba histolytica* (007.8)

006.0 Acute amebic dysentery without mention of abscess
Acute amebiasis

Excludes

"Excludes" indicates terms that are to be coded elsewhere. *Excludes* notes can be located at the beginning of a chapter or section or below a category or subcategory. *Excludes* notes can be used for three reasons:

1. The condition may have to be coded elsewhere.

EXAMPLE

861 Injury to heart and lung

EXCLUDES *injury to blood vessels of thorax* (901.0-901.9)

This *Excludes* note indicates that injuries to the blood vessels of the thorax are assigned within the codes 901.1-901.9 and are not assigned within the codes in 861.

2. The code cannot be assigned if the associated condition is present.

EXAMPLE

§463 Acute tonsillitis

EXCLUDES *streptococcal tonsillitis* (034.0)

If the tonsillitis is due to streptococcal organism, it would be coded as 034.0, not 463.

3. Additional code(s) may be required to fully explain the condition.

EXAMPLE

4. DISEASES OF BLOOD AND BLOOD-FORMING ORGANS (280-289)

EXCLUDES *Anemia complicating pregnancy or the puerperium* (648.2)

This *Excludes* tells you that you should code 648.2 to indicate the complication of pregnancy followed by an additional code to specify the type of anemia.

Use Additional Code

You add information (by assigning an additional code) to provide a more complete picture of the diagnosis or procedure. The use of an additional code is mandatory if supporting documentation is found in the record.

EXAMPLE

510 Empyema
Use additional code to identify infectious organism (041.0-041.9)

Code First Underlying Disease

"Code first underlying disease" is used in those categories not intended as the principal diagnosis. In such cases, the code, title, and instructions appear in italics. The note requires that the underlying disease (etiology) be sequenced first.

EXAMPLE

366.4 Cataract associated with other disorders

366.41 Diabetic cataract
Code first diabetes (250.5)

By following this convention, diabetes 250.5 is sequenced first, followed by diabetic cataract 366.41.

And/With

Although the two words "and/with" in everyday language have similar meanings, in ICD-9-CM terminology they have special significance and meaning. The "and" means "and/or," whereas the "with" indicates there are "two conditions" included in the code.

EXAMPLE

474 Chronic disease of tonsils and adenoids

The code 474 is used to identify the disease as one of tonsils and/or adenoids.

EXAMPLE

366.4 Cataract associated with other disorders

366.41 Diabetic cataract

The code 366.4 indicates that the patient has cataracts along with another disorder, perhaps diabetes. To assign code 366.41, you have to be sure that both conditions are present.

EXERCISE B *Conventions*

Match the abbreviations, punctuation, symbols, and words to the correct descriptions:

1. [ ] _______
2. NOS _______
3. : _______
4. § _______
5. italics _______
6. *Excludes* _______
7. Includes _______
8. } _______
9. NEC _______
10. ( ) _______

a. must be modified by an additional term to complete the code description

b. used in Volume 2 to enclose the disease manifestation codes that are to be recorded as secondary diagnoses to the diagnosis for the etiology

c. typeface used for all codes and titles in Volume 1

d. indicates the use of code assignment for "other" when a more specific code does not exist

e. encloses a series of terms that modify the statement to the right

f. encloses synonyms, alternative words, or explanatory phrases

g. equals unspecified

11. *[ ]* ______

12. bold type ______

h. typeface used for all exclusion notes or diagnosis codes not to be used for principal diagnosis

i. footnote or section mark

j. appears under a three-digit code title to further define or explain category content

k. encloses supplementary words that do not affect the code assignment

l. indicates terms that are to be coded elsewhere

Answer the following True or False questions about conventions:

13. Includes and *Excludes* notes have no bearing on the code selection.

____

14. Brackets enclose synonyms, alternate wordings, or explanatory phrases.

____

VOLUME 2: ALPHABETIC INDEX

Modifiers

A main term in the index may be followed by a series of terms in parentheses. The presence or absence of these parenthetical terms in the diagnosis has no effect on the selection of the code listed for the main term. These are called **nonessential modifiers.**

EXAMPLE

Ileus (adynamic) (bowel) (colon) (inhibitory) (intestine) (neurogenic) (paralytic) 560.1

The nonessential modifiers are the words "(adynamic) (bowel) (colon)," etc. Nonessential modifiers are words that may be used to clarify the diagnosis but do not affect the code. The code for ileus is 560.1, and the code for adynamic ileus is also 560.1. The addition of the modifier "adynamic" does not affect the code assignment.

A main term may also be followed by a list of subterms that do have an effect on the selection of the appropriate code for a given diagnosis. These subterms are indented under the main term and offer additional specificity.

EXAMPLE

Incoordination
esophageal-pharyngeal (newborn) 787.2
muscular 781.3
papillary muscle 429.81

The term in parentheses "(newborn)" is nonessential and merely supplementary. The indented subterms are essential modifiers, such as muscular or papillary muscle.

General adjectives such as "acute," "chronic," "epidemic," or "hereditary" and references to anatomic site, such as "arm," "stomach," and "uterus," will appear as main terms, but they will have only a "*see*" or "*see also* condition" reference.

EXAMPLE

Hereditary—*see* condition

Uterus—*see* condition

Note: "*see* condition" means that you are to look up the actual condition being described, not the main term condition.

Cross References

Cross references provide the coder with possible modifiers for a term or its synonyms. There are three types of cross references:

1. *see*
2. *see also*
3. *see* category

The "*see*" cross reference is an explicit direction to look elsewhere. It is used for anatomic sites and many general adjective modifiers not normally used in the Alphabetic Index. The "*see*" cross reference is also used to reference the appropriate main term under which all the information concerning a specific disease will be found.

EXAMPLE

Encephalomeningitis—*see* Meningoencephalitis

Endamebiasis—*see* Amebiasis

Kidney—*see* condition

Leukosis—*see* Leukemia

Lipofibroma (M8851/0)—*see* Lipoma, by site

The "*see also*" cross reference directs you to look under another main term if all the information being searched for cannot be located under the first main term entry.

EXAMPLE

Laryngoplegia—(*see also* Paralysis, vocal cord) 478.30

The "*see* category" cross reference directs you to Volume 1, Tabular List for important information governing the use of the specific code.

EXAMPLE

Late—*see also* condition
effect(s) (of)—*see also* condition
abscess
intracranial or intraspinal (conditions classifiable to 324)—*see* category 326

Notes

Certain main terms are followed by notes that are used to define terms and give coding instructions.

EXAMPLE

Amputation
traumatic (complete) (partial)
arm 887.4
at or above elbow 887.2
complicated 887.3

Note: "Complicated" includes traumatic amputation with delayed healing, delayed treatment, foreign body, or major infection

Mandatory Fifth Digit

Notes are also used to list the fifth-digit subclassifications for subcategories—such as the entries "Tuberculosis" or "Diabetes mellitus." Only the four-digit code is given for the individual entry, and you must refer to the note following the main term to locate the appropriate fifth-digit subclassification. For example, Figure 6–3 shows the fifth digit's use when coding diabetes.

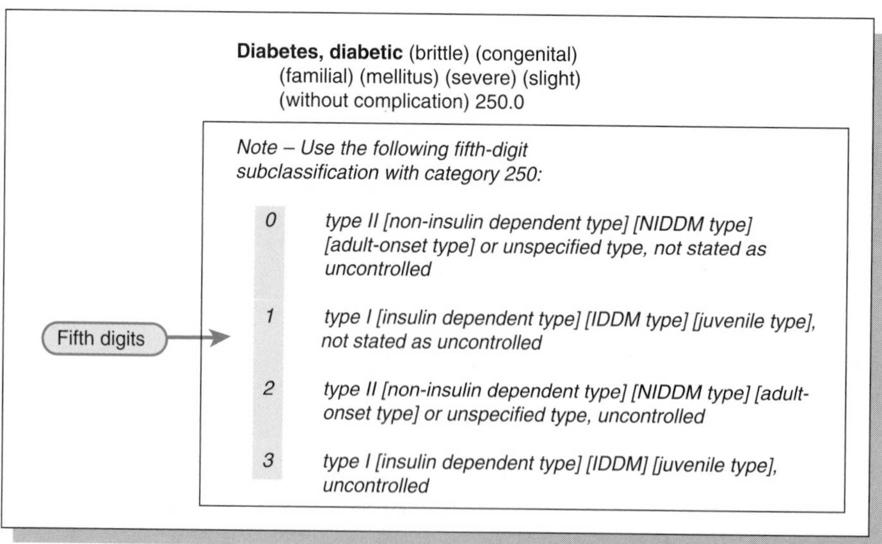

Figure 6–3
Index to Diseases, fifth digit, diabetes. (From International Classification of Diseases, 9th Revision. U.S. Department of Health and Human Services, Public Health Service, Health Care Financing Administration.)

Eponyms

Eponyms (diseases or syndromes named for persons) are listed both as main terms in their appropriate alphabetical sequence and under the main terms "Disease" or "Syndrome." A description of the disease or syndrome is usually included in parentheses following the eponym.

EXAMPLE

Crigler-Najjar disease or syndrome
(congenital hyperbilirubinemia) 277.4

Disease
Crigler-Najjar (congenital hyperbilirubinemia) 277.4

Syndrome
Crigler-Najjar (congenital hyperbilirubinemia) 277.4

The cross reference feature will be very helpful to you as you code using the ICD-9-CM.

EXERCISE C More Conventions

Match the convention to the definition:

1. *see* category _______
2. subterms _______
3. NEC _______
4. NOS _______
5. *see* _______
6. Notes _______
7. modifiers _______
8. *see also* _______
9. eponym _______

a. terms in parentheses or following main terms that may or may not be essential
b. terms indented under main terms, considered essential modifiers
c. explicit direction to look elsewhere
d. follows code descriptions to define and give instructions
e. means "unspecified"
f. directs coder to look under another term if all information isn't found under the first term
g. directs coder to use Volume 1, Tabular List, for additional information
h. disease/syndrome named for a person
i. tells the coder to use code assignment for "other" if a more specific code does not exist

Fill in the blank for the following questions:

10. Which coding convention advises you that a more specific code is not available? ____________________

11. What directs you to look under another main term?

____

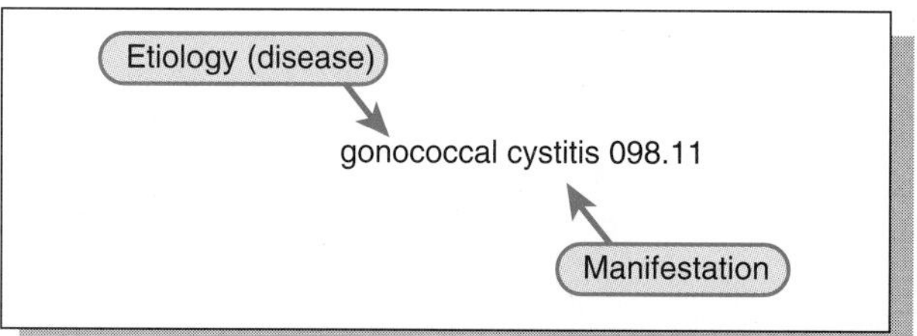

Figure 6–4
Manifestation and etiology, combination code. (From International Classification of Diseases, 9th Revision. U.S. Department of Health and Human Services, Public Health Service, Health Care Financing Administration.)

Etiology and Manifestation of Disease

For certain conditions it is important to record both the etiology (cause) and the manifestation (symptom) of the disease. In many cases recording of etiology and manifestations can be accomplished with the use of a single five-digit code. The single five-digit code is termed a **combination code.** For example, Figure 6–4 shows etiology and manifestation combined in one code. The etiology is gonococcal, and the manifestation is cystitis; both are represented by the code 098.11.

For some conditions it is not possible to provide specific fifth-digit subclassifications giving both etiology and manifestation. Multiple coding is then required. In such cases the two facets of the disease—etiology and manifestation—are coded individually as in Figure 6–5.

It is important to record the multiple codes in the same sequence they are used in the Alphabetic Index.

Chapter 7 provides more information about the use of combination and multiple codes.

Hypertension Table

The Hypertension Table is found in the Alphabetic Index under the main term "Hypertension." The table contains a complete list of all conditions due to or associated with hypertension. The table classifies the hypertension conditions according to malignant, benign, or unspecified. Hypertension codes will be discussed in more detail under the hypertension guidelines in Chapter 7.

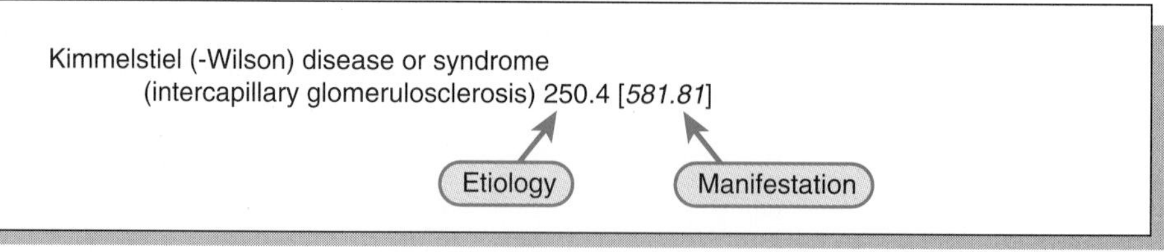

Figure 6–5
Manifestation and etiology, multiple coding. (From International Classification of Diseases, 9th Revision. U.S. Department of Health and Human Services, Public Health Service, Health Care Financing Administration.)

Neoplasms

Neoplasms are tumors. It takes two steps to locate the neoplasm code in the Alphabetic Index. The first step is to locate the neoplasm by its name or its morphology. For example, glioma, lymphoma, and adenoma are considered histologic types and are found in the Alphabetic Index. This is where you will locate the M codes to classify the morphology of the tumor. You follow the instructions in the Index to reach the proper code in the Tabular List. If you wanted to locate the correct neoplasm code for adenocarcinoma, you would find the following entry in the Index.

EXAMPLE

Adenocarcinoma (M8140/3)—*see also*
Neoplasm, by site, malignant

This *"see also"* instruction means you are to refer to the Neoplasm Table to locate the appropriate code.

The second step is to locate the Neoplasm Table in the Alphabetic Index under "N" for neoplasm. The Neoplasm Table is established based on anatomic site. A comprehensive list of anatomic sites with subterms for more specificity is found in this table under the main term "Neoplasm." The table contains six columns, as indicated in Figure 6–6. For each site there are six possible code numbers according to whether the neoplasm in question is malignant, and then further specifying the malignancy as primary, secondary, or in situ (confined to the original site); benign;

Neoplasm **INDEX TO DISEASES**

	Malignant					
	Primary	Secondary	Ca in situ	Benign	Uncertain Behavior	Unspecified
Neoplasm, neoplastic—*continued*						
breast (connective tissue) (female) (glandular tissue) (soft parts)	174.9	198.81	233.0	217	238.3	239.3
areola	174.0	198.81	233.0	217	238.3	239.3
male	175.0	198.81	233.0	217	238.3	239.3
axillary tail	174.6	198.81	233.0	217	238.3	239.3
central portion	174.1	198.81	233.0	217	238.3	239.3
contiguous sites	174.8	—	—	—	—	—
ectopic sites	174.8	198.81	233.0	217	238.3	239.3
inner	174.8	198.81	233.0	217	238.3	239.3
lower	174.8	198.81	233.0	217	238.3	239.3
lower-inner quadrant	174.3	198.81	233.0	217	238.3	239.3
lower-outer quadrant	174.5	198.81	233.0	217	238.3	239.3
male	175.9	198.81	233.0	217	238.3	239.3
areola	175.0	198.81	233.0	217	238.3	239.3
ectopic tissue	175.9	198.81	233.0	217	238.3	239.3
nipple	175.0	198.81	233.0	217	238.3	239.3
mastectomy site (skin)	173.5	198.2	—	—	—	—
specified as breast tissue	174.8	198.81	—	—	—	—
midline	174.8	198.81	233.0	217	238.3	239.3
nipple	174.0	198.81	233.0	217	238.3	239.3

Figure 6–6
M Codes, Section 1, Index to Disease, breast. (From International Classification of Diseases, 9th Revision. U.S. Department of Health and Human Services, Public Health Service, Health Care Financing Administration.)

of uncertain behavior; or of unspecified nature. A malignant tumor is one that becomes progressively worse, and a benign tumor is one that is not malignant.

EXERCISE D Neoplasms

Referring to Figure 6–6, fill in the codes for the following:

1. Secondary malignant tumor of a male, breast, nipple

   Code(s): ________________

2. Benign neoplasm, breast, female

   Code(s): ________________

Morphology codes are used to supplement the appropriate ICD-9-CM neoplasm code. A complete listing of morphology codes is found in Appendix A of Volume 1, Morphology of Neoplasms, and is presented later in this chapter. M codes are optional; whether you assign the codes may depend on facility policy.

Sections

Volume 2: Alphabetic Index serves as an index to Volume 1, Tabular List. Everything in the index is by condition—meaning diagnosis, signs, symptoms, or conditions (such as pregnancy, admission, encounter, or complication). Volume 2: Alphabetic Index contains three sections, as illustrated in Figure 6–7.

Section 1 contains terms referring to diseases and injuries in alphabetical order.

Section 2 is the Table of Drugs and Chemicals and includes codes for poisonings and external causes of injury from drugs or chemicals.

Section 3 is the Index to External Causes (E Codes) and is an alphabetical index to the cause of an accident or injury.

Figure 6–7
Volume 2, Table of Contents. (From International Classification of Diseases, 9th Revision. U.S. Department of Health and Human Services, Public Health Service, Health Care Financing Administration.)

TABLE OF CONTENTS

Volume 2

Section 1: Index to Diseases and Injuries

Section 1 is the largest portion of the Alphabetic Index. To locate a code in the Tabular List, you must first locate the possible code(s) in the Alphabetic Index. The Index has main terms (conditions) in bold print, and indented subterms (modifying words for additional specificity) are in regular print.

Main Terms and Subterms

Main terms in the Alphabetic Index are in bold with subterms indented two spaces to the right.

EXAMPLE

Fracture
styloid process
metacarpal (closed) 815.02
open 815.12

Each term is followed by the code(s) applying to the term (Fig. 6–8). The Alphabetic Index includes the most diagnostic terms currently in use. Some types of codes may be a little difficult to find, such as those dealing with complications, late effects, and V codes.

Section 2: Table of Drugs and Chemicals

Section 2, Table of Drugs and Chemicals, contains a classification of drugs and other chemical substances associated with poisoning and external causes of adverse effects.

In Figure 6–9 the Table of Drugs and Chemicals shows that column 1 (Substance) contains the name of the drug or chemical. Column 2 (Poisoning) contains the list of poisoning codes. The remaining five columns are the E codes that are assigned to indicate how the poisoning or adverse effect occurred. Remember, E codes are never the principal diagnosis. The table headings pertaining to external causes are defined as follows:

Accident (E850-E869): accidental overdose of drug, wrong substance given or taken, drug taken inadvertently, accidents in the use of drugs and biological agents in medical and surgical procedures, and external causes of poisonings classifiable to 980-989.

Therapeutic Use (E930-E949): a correct substance properly administered in therapeutic or prophylactic dosage as the external cause of adverse effects.

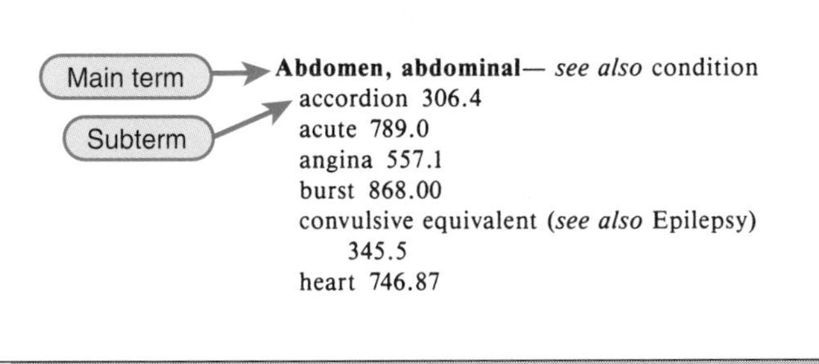

Figure 6–8
Volume 2, Format. (From International Classification of Diseases, 9th Revision. U.S. Department of Health and Human Services, Public Health Service, Health Care Financing Administration.)

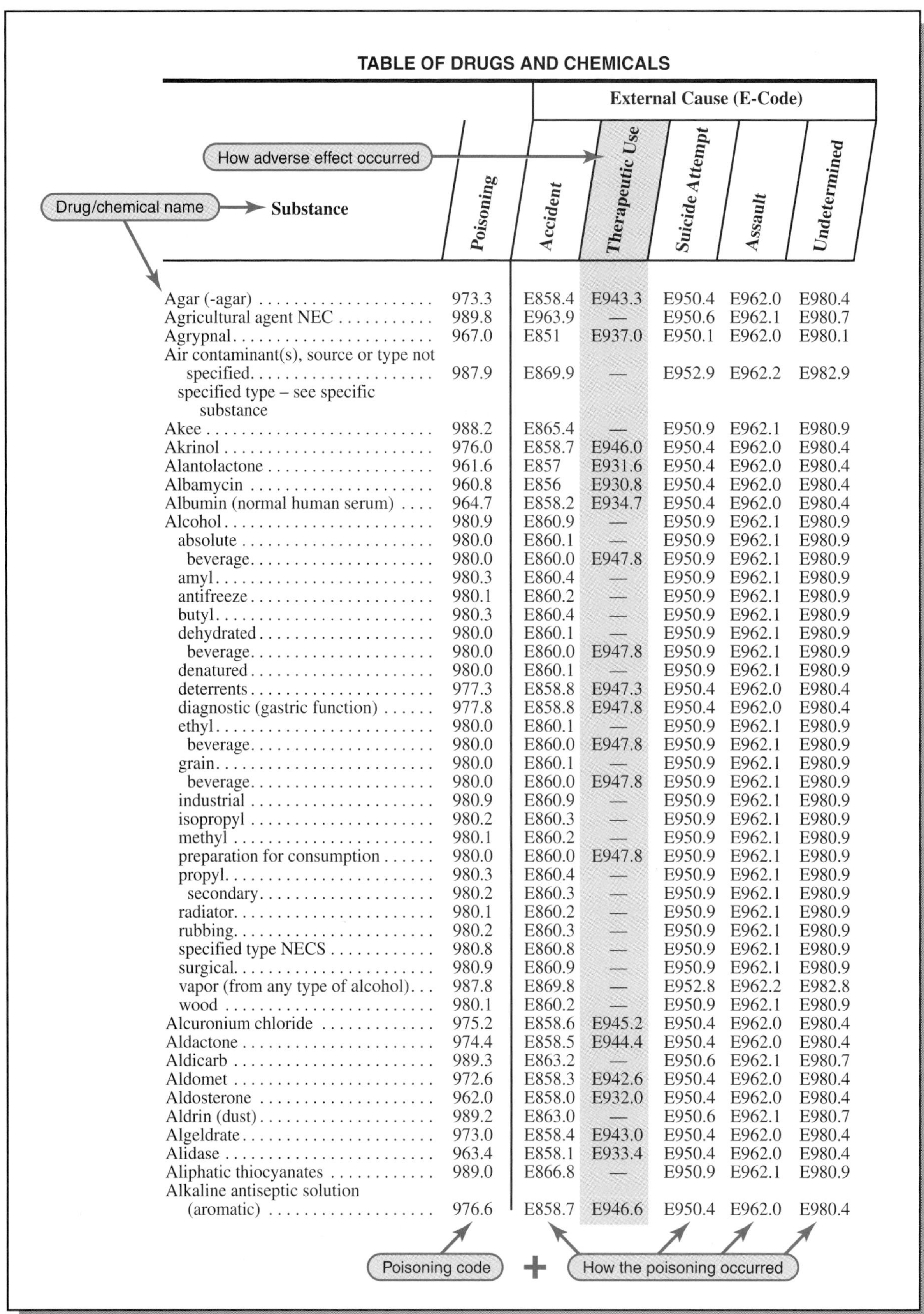

TABLE OF DRUGS AND CHEMICALS

		External Cause (E-Code)				
Substance	Poisoning	Accident	Therapeutic Use	Suicide Attempt	Assault	Undetermined
Agar (-agar)	973.3	E858.4	E943.3	E950.4	E962.0	E980.4
Agricultural agent NEC	989.8	E963.9	—	E950.6	E962.1	E980.7
Agrypnal	967.0	E851	E937.0	E950.1	E962.0	E980.1
Air contaminant(s), source or type not specified	987.9	E869.9	—	E952.9	E962.2	E982.9
specified type – see specific substance						
Akee	988.2	E865.4	—	E950.9	E962.1	E980.9
Akrinol	976.0	E858.7	E946.0	E950.4	E962.0	E980.4
Alantolactone	961.6	E857	E931.6	E950.4	E962.0	E980.4
Albamycin	960.8	E856	E930.8	E950.4	E962.0	E980.4
Albumin (normal human serum)	964.7	E858.2	E934.7	E950.4	E962.0	E980.4
Alcohol	980.9	E860.9	—	E950.9	E962.1	E980.9
absolute	980.0	E860.1	—	E950.9	E962.1	E980.9
beverage	980.0	E860.0	E947.8	E950.9	E962.1	E980.9
amyl	980.3	E860.4	—	E950.9	E962.1	E980.9
antifreeze	980.1	E860.2	—	E950.9	E962.1	E980.9
butyl	980.3	E860.4	—	E950.9	E962.1	E980.9
dehydrated	980.0	E860.1	—	E950.9	E962.1	E980.9
beverage	980.0	E860.0	E947.8	E950.9	E962.1	E980.9
denatured	980.0	E860.1	—	E950.9	E962.1	E980.9
deterrents	977.3	E858.8	E947.3	E950.4	E962.0	E980.4
diagnostic (gastric function)	977.8	E858.8	E947.8	E950.4	E962.0	E980.4
ethyl	980.0	E860.1	—	E950.9	E962.1	E980.9
beverage	980.0	E860.0	E947.8	E950.9	E962.1	E980.9
grain	980.0	E860.1	—	E950.9	E962.1	E980.9
beverage	980.0	E860.0	E947.8	E950.9	E962.1	E980.9
industrial	980.9	E860.9	—	E950.9	E962.1	E980.9
isopropyl	980.2	E860.3	—	E950.9	E962.1	E980.9
methyl	980.1	E860.2	—	E950.9	E962.1	E980.9
preparation for consumption	980.0	E860.0	E947.8	E950.9	E962.1	E980.9
propyl	980.3	E860.4	—	E950.9	E962.1	E980.9
secondary	980.2	E860.3	—	E950.9	E962.1	E980.9
radiator	980.1	E860.2	—	E950.9	E962.1	E980.9
rubbing	980.2	E860.3	—	E950.9	E962.1	E980.9
specified type NECS	980.8	E860.8	—	E950.9	E962.1	E980.9
surgical	980.9	E860.9	—	E950.9	E962.1	E980.9
vapor (from any type of alcohol)	987.8	E869.8	—	E952.8	E962.2	E982.8
wood	980.1	E860.2	—	E950.9	E962.1	E980.9
Alcuronium chloride	975.2	E858.6	E945.2	E950.4	E962.0	E980.4
Aldactone	974.4	E858.5	E944.4	E950.4	E962.0	E980.4
Aldicarb	989.3	E863.2	—	E950.6	E962.1	E980.7
Aldomet	972.6	E858.3	E942.6	E950.4	E962.0	E980.4
Aldosterone	962.0	E858.0	E932.0	E950.4	E962.0	E980.4
Aldrin (dust)	989.2	E863.0	—	E950.6	E962.1	E980.7
Algeldrate	973.0	E858.4	E943.0	E950.4	E962.0	E980.4
Alidase	963.4	E858.1	E933.4	E950.4	E962.0	E980.4
Aliphatic thiocyanates	989.0	E866.8	—	E950.9	E962.1	E980.9
Alkaline antiseptic solution (aromatic)	976.6	E858.7	E946.6	E950.4	E962.0	E980.4

Figure 6–9
Section 2, Table of Drugs and Chemicals. (From International Classification of Diseases, 9th Revision. U.S. Department of Health and Human Services, Public Health Service, Health Care Financing Administration.)

Suicide Attempt (E950-E952): instances in which self-inflicted injuries or poisonings are involved.
Assault (E961-E962): injury or poisoning inflicted by another person with the intent to injure or kill.
Undetermined (E980-E982): to be used when the intent of the poisoning or injury cannot be determined whether it was intentional or accidental.

The table also contains the American Hospital Formulary Service (AHFS) List numbers, which can be used to classify new drugs not listed in the table by name. The AHFS List numbers are found in the Table of Drugs and Chemicals under the main term "Drug." The AHFS List numbers and their ICD-9-CM equivalents are also found in Appendix C of Volume 1, Tabular List.

Although certain substances are indexed with one or more subentries, the majority are listed according to one use or state. It is recognized that many substances may be used in various ways, in medicine and in industry, and may cause adverse effects or poisoning whatever the state of the agent (ie, solid, liquid, or gas). In cases in which the reported data indicate a use or state not in the table, or which is clearly different from the one listed, an attempt should be made to classify the substances in the form that most nearly expresses the reported facts.

EXERCISE E Table of Drugs and Chemicals

Code the following:

1. Poisoning by the ingestion of the beverage of grain alcohol

   Code(s): ________________

2. Undetermined poisoning by antifreeze

   Code(s): ________________

3. (E code) Accidental overdose due to therapeutically used akrinol

   Code(s): ________________

Manifestations (symptoms or signs) of poisonings or adverse effects of drugs and chemicals are found in Section 1, under the specific symptom or disease. For example, Figure 6–10 illustrates the location of the symptom "Rash" in Volume 2, the Alphabetic Index. If the symptom of the drug poisoning or adverse effect was a rash, the subterm "drug (internal use)" directs you to 693.0.

Turn to code 693.0 in Volume 1, Tabular List.

4. What does the description of the code state?

   ____

Note the statement below the code: "Use additional E code to identify drug." In this case the condition is rash. So, when you see this statement, you know you have to identify the drug that *caused* the rash.

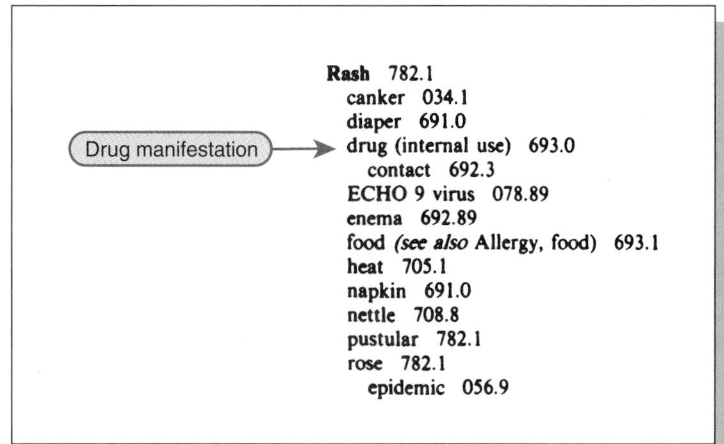

Figure 6–10
Index to Diseases, Rash. (From International Classification of Diseases, 9th Revision. U.S. Department of Health and Human Services, Public Health Service, Health Care Financing Administration.)

Section 3: Alphabetic Index to External Causes of Injuries and Poisonings (E Code)

Section 3: Alphabetic Index to External Causes of Injuries and Poisonings is the index for the E codes. The index classifies environmental events (tornados, floods), circumstances, and other conditions as the cause of injury and other adverse effects alphabetically. *E codes are never used as a principal diagnosis.* Rather, E codes are used to clarify the cause of an injury or adverse effect.

E code terms describe the circumstances under which an accident, injury, or act of violence occurred. The main terms in this section usually represent the type of accident or violence (eg, assault, collision), with the specific agent or other circumstance listed below the main term. "Collision" in Figure 6–11 is the *type* of accident, and listed below collision are the *circumstances* of the accident.

You must be sure to read all the information under a term before choosing the code. Be sure to check for fourth-digit specificity for railway accidents, motor vehicle traffic and nontraffic accidents, other road vehicle accidents, water transport accidents, and air and space transport accidents shown in the Index to External Causes section.

VOLUME 1: TABULAR LIST

Divisions

Volume 1: Tabular List is the listing of all the code numbers and their descriptions available for assignment. When the exact word is not found in the Tabular List but is found in the Alphabetic Index, you must trust the code provided in the Alphabetic Index as being correct because the Index contains words the Tabular doesn't. This saves space in the Tabular List. Anything that can happen, in the way of injury or disease, to a human body has a code number within Volume 1. Although there are certainly many things that can happen to us, the people who developed the ICD-9-CM not only included them all but organized them in a systematic way. Volume 1 is divided into two major divisions:

1. Classification of Diseases and Injuries
2. Supplementary Classification

INDEX TO EXTERNAL CAUSES **Collision**

Type

Circumstance

Collision (accidental) — *continued*
- motor vehicle (on public highway) (traffic accident) — *continued*
  - and — *continued*
    - fallen — *continued*
      - tree E815
    - guard post or guard rail E815
    - inter-highway divider E815
    - landslide, fallen or not moving E815
      - moving E909
    - machinery (road) E815
    - nonmotor road vehicle NEC E813
    - object (any object, person, or vehicle off the public highway resulting from a noncollision motor vehicle nontraffic accident) E815
      - off, normally not on, public highway resulting from a noncollision motor vehicle traffic accident E816
    - pedal cycle E813
    - pedestrian (conveyance) E814
    - person (using pedestrian conveyance) E814
    - post or pole (lamp) (light) (signal) (telephone) (utility) E815
    - railway rolling stock, train, vehicle E810
    - safety island E815
    - street car E813
    - traffic signal, sign, or marker (temporary) E815
    - tree E815
    - tricycle E813
    - wall of cut made for road E815
  - due to cataclysm — *see* categories E908, E909
  - not on public highway, nontraffic accident E822
    - and
      - animal (carrying person, property) (herded) (unattended) E822
      - animal-drawn vehicle E822
      - another motor vehicle (moving), except off-road motor vehicle E822
        - stationary E823
      - avalanche, fallen, not moving E823
        - moving E909
      - landslide, fallen, not moving E823
        - moving E909
      - nonmotor vehicle (moving) E822
        - stationary E823
      - object (fallen) (normally) (fixed) (movable but not in motion) (stationary) E823
        - moving, except when falling from, set in motion by, aircraft or cataclysm E822

Collision (accidental) — *continued*
- motor vehicle (on public highway) (traffic accident) — *continued*
  - not on public highway, nontraffic accident — *continued*
    - and — *continued*
      - pedal cycle (moving) E822
        - stationary E823
      - pedestrian (conveyance) E822
      - person (using pedestrian conveyance) E822
      - railway rolling stock, train, vehicle (moving) E822
        - stationary E823
      - road vehicle (any) (moving) E822
        - stationary E823
      - tricycle (moving) E822
        - stationary E823
- off-road type motor vehicle (not on public highway) E821
  - and
    - animal (being ridden) (-drawn vehicle) E821
    - another off-road motor vehicle, except snow vehicle E821
    - other motor vehicle, not on public highway E821
    - other object or vehicle NEC, fixed or movable, not set in motion by aircraft, motor vehicle on highway, or snow vehicle, motor-driven E821
    - pedal cycle E821
    - pedestrian (conveyance) E821
    - railway train E821
  - on public highway — *see* Collision, motor vehicle
- pedal cycle E826
  - and
    - animal (carrying person, property) (herded) (unherded) E826
    - animal-drawn vehicle E826
    - another pedal cycle E826
    - nonmotor road vehicle E826
    - object (fallen) (fixed) (movable) (moving) not falling from or set in motion by aircraft, motor vehicle, or railway train NEC E826
    - pedestrian (conveyance) E826
    - person (using pedestrian conveyance) E826
    - street car E826
- pedestrian(s) (conveyance) E917.9
  - with fall E886.9
    - in sports E886.0
  - and
    - crowd, human stampede (with fall) E917.1
    - machinery — *see* Accident, machine

Figure 6–11
Section 3, Index to External Causes. (From International Classification of Diseases, 9th Revision. U.S. Department of Health and Human Services, Public Health Service, Health Care Financing Administration.)

TABLE OF CONTENTS

Figure 6–12
Volume 1, Diseases: Table of Contents. (From International Classification of Diseases, 9th Revision. U.S. Department of Health and Human Services, Public Health Service, Health Care Financing Administration.)

Classification of Diseases and Injuries

The Classifications of Diseases and Injuries is the main part of the ICD-9-CM Volume 1 and consists of 17 chapters with codes from 001-999. Figure 6–12 illustrates that most chapters are based on body system (eg, nervous system [Chapter 6], respiratory system [Chapter 8], and digestive system [Chapter 9]). Some chapters are based on the cause or type of the disease (eg, infections and parasitic diseases [Chapter 1] and neoplasms [Chapter 2]). Figure 6–13 indicates the format of each chapter as

Chapter
A chapter is the main division in the ICD-9-CM manual.

Section
A section is a group of three-digit categories that represent a group of conditions or related conditions.

Category
A three-digit category is a code that represents a single condition or disease.

Subcategory
A four-digit subcategory code provides more information or specificity as compared to the three-digit code in terms of the cause, site, or manifestation of the condition. You must assign the fourth digit if available.

Subclassification
A five-digit subclassification code adds even more information and specificity to the condition description. You must assign the fifth digit if available.

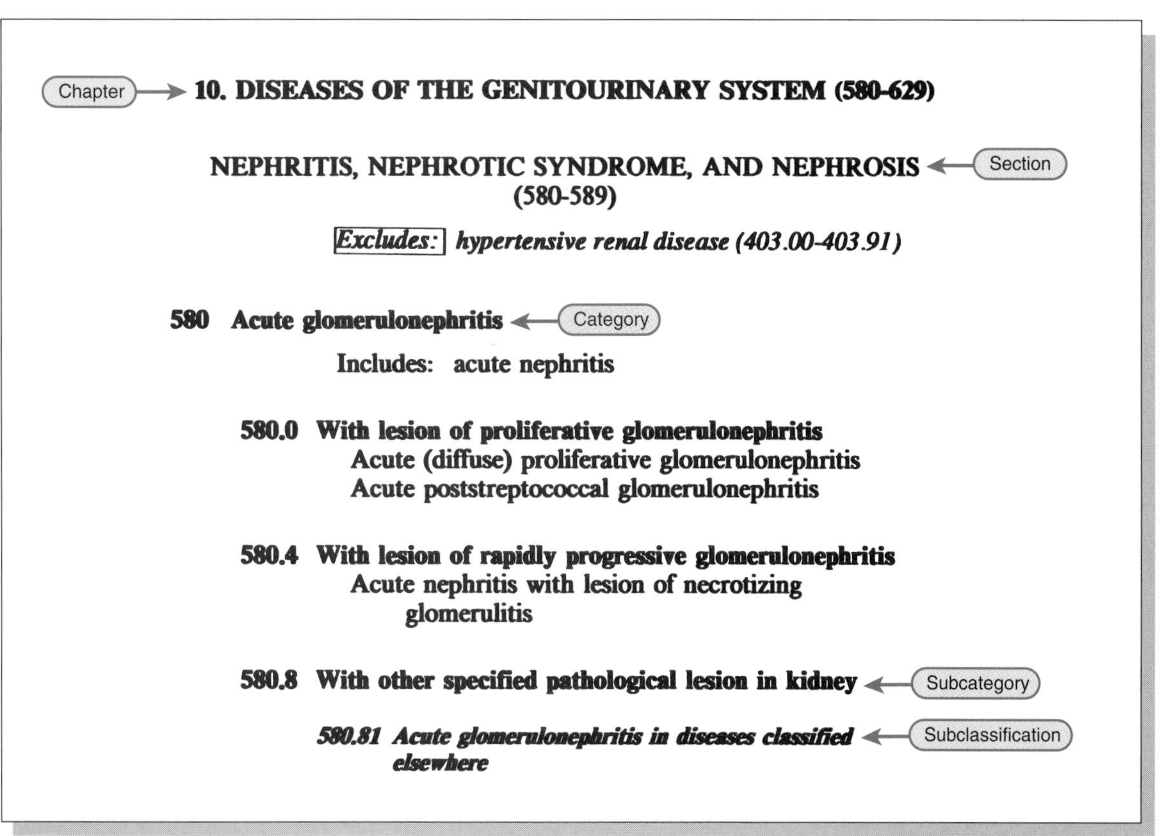

Figure 6–13
Volume 1, Diseases: format. (From International Classification of Diseases, 9th Revision. U.S. Department of Health and Human Services, Public Health Service, Health Care Financing Administration.)

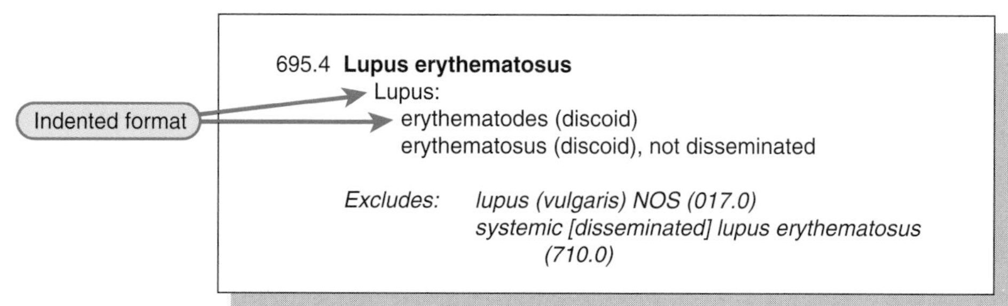

Figure 6–14
Indented format. (From International Classification of Diseases, 9th Revision. U.S. Department of Health and Human Services, Public Health Service, Health Care Financing Administration.)

EXERCISE F ICD-9-CM Chapter Format

Using ICD-9-CM Volume 1: Tabular List, locate the first page of Chapter 3 and answer the following questions about the chapter:

1. The name of the chapter: ______________________________
2. The name of the first section: ______________________________
3. The description of the first category: ______________________________
4. The description of the first subcategory: ______________________________

The information in this activity was important to your learning because it will enable you to communicate effectively about information in the ICD-9-CM manual using common terminology.

Figure 6–14 illustrates the indented format used in Volume 1 for ease of reference.

The basic ICD-9-CM code is a three-digit code, as shown in Figure 6–15. Each code is a *rubric* (something under which something else is classed). Both the code number and entry are in bold type. Diagnosis codes always contain at least three digits before the decimal point. If the diagnosis code is "1," it is written 001. Procedure codes from Volume 3 always consist of at least two digits before the decimal point. You can always tell a procedure code from a diagnosis code by the number of digits before the decimal point.

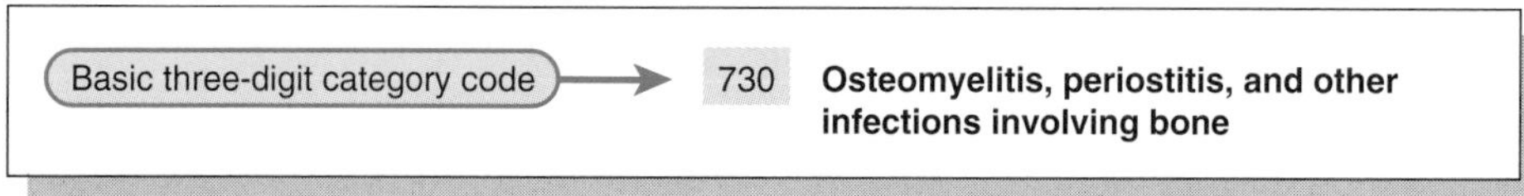

Figure 6–15
ICD-9-CM three-digit category code. (From International Classification of Diseases, 9th Revision. U.S. Department of Health and Human Services, Public Health Service, Health Care Financing Administration.)

EXAMPLE

496	Diagnosis
27.54	Procedure
461.9	Diagnosis
21.1	Procedure

The addition of the fourth and fifth digits to the basic three-digit code provides greater specificity to the numeric designation of the patient's condition and reduces third-party returns. When four digits (one digit after the decimal point) are used, they are called *subcategory* codes. If five digits are used (two digits after the decimal point), they are called *subclassification* codes. Figure 6–16 shows the first three digits of the code used to identify the disease "Osteomyelitis, periostitis, and other infections involving bone"; the fourth digit provides further specificity by distinguishing between "acute" and "chronic" osteomyelitis.

Not all codes have fourth or fifth digits, but when a fourth or fifth digit is available, it must be used. It is a good idea to highlight the codes with which a fifth digit is listed. This will serve as a reminder to you to always use that fifth digit. For an example of the fifth digit, code 730 appears with a list of fifth digits that are used to identify the location of acute osteomyelitis as:

0	site unspecified
1	shoulder region
2	upper arm
3	forearm
4	hand
5	pelvic region and thigh
6	lower leg
7	ankle and foot
8	other specified sites
9	multiple sites

You indicate that acute osteomyelitis was located in the patient's shoulder with the use of the fifth digit "1" added to the 730.0 code (Fig. 6–17).

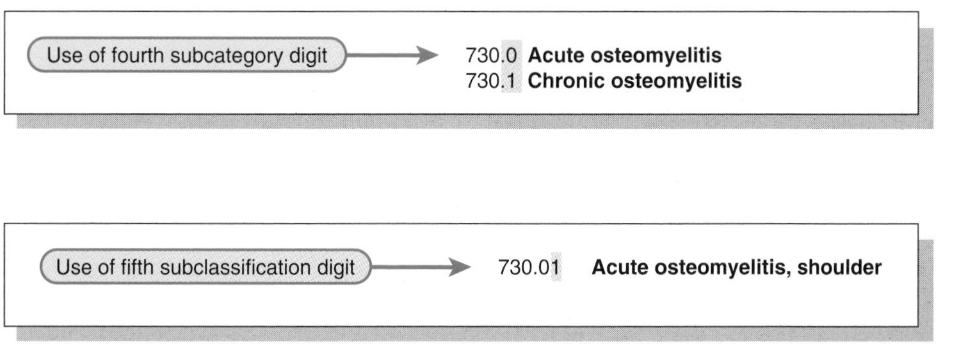

Figure 6–16
ICD-9-CM four-digit subcategory code.

Figure 6–17
ICD-9-CM five-digit subclassification code.

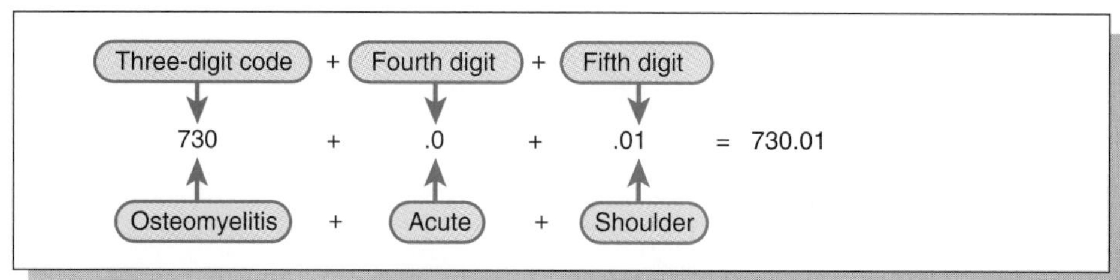

Figure 6–18 Specificity in ICD-9-CM codes.

Remember that the goal is to be as accurate, as complete, and as specific as possible. Figure 6–18 illustrates how adding the fourth and fifth digits adds specificity to the information you knew about the patient's condition.

EXERCISE G *Five-Digit Specificity*

Locate the first page of Chapter 13, Diseases of the Musculoskeletal System and Connective Tissues, in the ICD-9-CM manual. Notes immediately following the chapter title indicate the fifth-digit subclassifications and the specific categories with which these fifth digits are used. Read the notes for Chapter 13.

The following is a part of the fifth-digit subclassifications used with categories 711-712, 715-716, 718-719, and 730:

0 **site unspecified**
1 **shoulder region**
Acromioclavicular
Glenohumeral
Sternoclavicular } Joint(s)
Clavicle
Scapula
2 **upper arm**
Elbow joint
Humerus

The various joints of the shoulder region or the elbow joint and humerus of the upper arm are the specific anatomic terms to which the main term refers. The use of the "2" indicates the elbow joint or the humerus, etc. These anatomic terms serve to provide further specificity to the code selection.

Locate code 711 in the ICD-9-CM, then answer the following:

The patient record states: Pyogenic arthritis in lower leg.

1. What would the correct five-digit code be?

 Code(s): ____________________

2. Is the use of the fifth digit optional? ____________________

3. How is specificity added to ICD-9-CM codes?

 ____

 ____

Supplementary Classification

The Supplementary Classification in Volume 1 contains the following:

1. Supplementary Classification of Factors Influencing Health Status and Contact with Health Services (V codes)
2. Supplementary Classification of External Causes of Injury and Poisoning (E codes)

Supplementary Classification of Factors Influencing Health Status and Contact with Health Services (V Codes)

V codes from the Supplementary Classification of Factors Influencing Health Status and Contact with Health Services are found under such main term references as admission, examination, history, observation, and problem. V codes are used under the following circumstances:

- When a person who is not currently sick encounters the health services for some specific purpose, such as to act as a donor or receive a vaccination
- When a person with a known disease or injury presents for specific treatment of that condition—such as dialysis, chemotherapy, or cast change
- When a circumstance may influence a patient's health status
- To indicate the birth status and outcome of delivery of a newborn

The Supplementary Classification is located near the back of Volume 1 and contains three- or four-digit code numbers preceded by the letter V. The codes in this section are called V codes. The V codes deal with occasions when persons who are not currently sick use health care services. This can arise mainly in two ways:

1. When a person who is currently not sick encounters the health services for some specific purpose, such as to act as donor of an organ or tissue, to receive a preventive vaccination, or to discuss a problem that is in itself not a disease or injury. Occurrences such as these will be fairly rare among hospital inpatients but will be relatively more common among outpatient health clinics.

EXAMPLE

Code V59.4 indicates a donor of a kidney who is not sick but encounters health care:

V59 **Donors**

V59.4 **Kidney**

V59 is the category and V59.4 is the subcategory. You would first locate "Donor, kidney" in the Index (Volume 2), and then verify code V59 in the V codes in the Tabular List.

EXAMPLE

A well child receives a polio vaccination:

V04 **Need for prophylactic vaccination and inoculation against certain viral diseases**

V04.0 **Poliomyelitis**

Code V04.0 indicates a patient who is not ill but encounters health care for a polio vaccination. V04 is the category and V04.0 is the subcategory.

The Index (Volume 2) entry is "vaccination, poliomyelitis." If you want to indicate that a child had been in contact with poliomyelitis, assign code V01.3, which has an Index location of "Contact, poliomyelitis."

EXAMPLE

A student seeks health care to discuss a problem with school:

V62 Other psychosocial circumstances

V62.3 Educational circumstances
Dissatisfaction with school environment

V62 is the category code and V62.3 is the subcategory code.

Code V62.3 indicates a patient who is not ill but encounters health care for a psychosocial circumstance. Index location is "Dissatisfaction with, education."

2. When some circumstance or problem is present that influences the person's health status but is not in itself a current illness or injury. For example, a family history of malignant neoplasms is significant to the patient's health care.

EXAMPLE

V16 Family history of malignant neoplasm

V16.0 Gastrointestinal tract

V16 is the category and V16.0 is the subcategory. The Index location is "History, family, malignant neoplasm, gastrointestinal tract." If, however, the diagnosis was a personal history of malignant neoplasm, the Index location would be "History, malignant, neoplasm, gastrointestinal tract" and the code would be V10.00.

EXAMPLE

V45 Other postsurgical states

V45.01 Cardiac pacemaker

V45 is the category, V45.0 is the subcategory, and V45.01 is the subclassification code. The Index location would be "Cardiac, device, pacemaker, in situ."

EXERCISE H More V Codes

Locate the V codes in the ICD-9-CM manual in Volume 2, Index, and then in Volume 1, Tabular.

Code the following:

1. A person who has been in contact with smallpox

   Index location: ____________________

   Code(s): ____________________

2. Prophylactic vaccination against smallpox

   Index location: ____________________

   Code(s): ____________________

3. Personal history of malignant neoplasm of the tongue

   Index location: ____________________

   Code(s): ____________________

Supplementary Classification of External Causes of Injury and Poisoning (E Codes)

The E codes are located in the "Supplementary Classification of External Causes of Injury and Poisoning (E800-E999)" behind the V codes in the ICD-9-CM manual. The E codes are numerical designations for causes of injuries and poisonings.

The E code section permits the classification of environmental events, circumstances, and conditions as the cause of injury, poisoning, and other adverse effects. With E codes, anything that can injure or have an adverse effect on a human body can be coded. The E codes can supply a code if you were injured while pearl diving (E910.3), injured when a window on a railroad car falls on you (E806.9), or pecked by a bird (E906.8). They are all in the E codes! These are rather far-fetched examples, granted, but they show how extensive and specific the codes are.

When a code from the E section is used, it is used in addition to a code from the Tabular List of the ICD-9-CM. The E code classification is used as an additional code for more detail. Most groups of E codes have Includes or *Excludes* notes for further detail on using the codes in the group. Be sure to read these notes as you begin to code.

E codes have their own index. You can locate the E code index term in Volume 2 and then turn to the code(s) directed to in the E code Supplementary Classification of Volume 1.

The following information presents E code(s) available in each group and an example of the type of code located in each range. The use of the fourth digit adds specificity as to who was injured in the accident. For example, if the injured person was the driver of the car involved in a motor vehicle accident, the fifth digit would be "0." If the injured person was a passenger in the vehicle the fifth digit would be "1." E code terms are located first in the E code index in Volume 2 and then in the E code Supplementary Classification of Volume 1.

Some states have made the assignment of E codes mandatory and the general use of E codes has increased significantly. At the beginning of Chapter 17, Injury and Poisoning (800-999) the note tells you to "Use E code(s) to identify the cause and intent of the injury or poisoning (E800-E999)."

EXERCISE I E Codes

Using an ICD-9-CM manual, locate the correct code number for each of the following in Volume 2 and then in Volume 1:

1. Railway (E800-E807)
   Railway accident involving derailment without antecedent collision, injuring a porter

   E code index term(s): ___________________

   Code(s): ___________________

2. Motor Vehicle Traffic (E810-819)
   Motor vehicle traffic accident involving collision with other vehicle, driver injured

   E code index term(s): ___________________

   Code(s): ___________________

3. Motor Vehicle Nontraffic (E820-E825)
   Nontraffic accident of other off-road and motor vehicle, pedal cyclist injured

   E code index term(s): ___________________

   Code(s): ___________________

4. Other Road Vehicle (E826-E829)
   Horse being ridden, rider injured, and nonmotor vehicle collision

   E code index term(s): ___________________

   Code(s): ___________________

5. Water Transport (E830-E838)
   Accident to watercraft causing other injury, occupant of small powered boat injured due to collision

   E code index term(s): ___________________

   Code(s): ___________________

You are ready to move on to the appendices. There is much interesting information waiting for you in the appendices.

THE FIVE APPENDICES IN VOLUME 1

Volume 1 contains five appendices:

Appendix A	Morphology of Neoplasms
Appendix B	Glossary of Mental Disorders
Appendix C	Classification of Drugs by American Hospital Formulary Service List Number and Their ICD-9-CM Equivalents
Appendix D	Classification of Industrial Accidents According to Agency
Appendix E	List of Three-Digit Categories

(*Note:* In some commercially published ICD-9-CM texts, Appendix E or F is a listing of complications and comorbidities for the Diagnosis Related Groups—to be discussed in Chapter 8.)

Appendices are included as a reference to the coder to:

- provide further information about the patient's clinical picture
- further define a diagnostic statement
- aid in classifying new drugs
- reference three-digit categories

The appendices are termed Appendix A, B, C, D, and E to indicate their position in the back of Volume 1 of the ICD-9-CM manual.

Appendix A, Morphology of Neoplasms

The World Health Organization has published an adaptation of the International Classification of Diseases for Oncology (ICD-O). The ICD-O contains codes for the morphology of tumors. Morphology is the study of neoplasms. The morphology codes consist of five digits: the first four identify the histologic type of the neoplasm and the fifth indicates the behavior of the neoplasm.

Examples of the type of neoplasm are epithelial, papillary, basal cell, and adenomas. Refer to a medical dictionary if you are not certain of any of the types of neoplasms presented in Appendix A.

Examples of the behavior of the neoplasm are benign, malignant, and carcinoma in situ. In situ means the neoplasm has not spread from another site and is located in its normal place.

The ICD-O one-digit behavior code is as follows:

/0 Benign

/1 Uncertain whether benign or malignant

Borderline malignancy

/2 Carcinoma in situ

Intraepithelial

Noninfiltrating

Noninvasive

/3 Malignant, primary site

/6 Malignant, metastatic site

Secondary site

/9 Malignant, uncertain whether primary or metastatic site

A primary site is the originating site of the tumor, and a secondary site is the metastatic site (spread from primary to secondary).

Appendix B, Glossary of Mental Disorders

The psychiatric terms that appear in ICD-9-CM Chapter 5, Mental Disorders, are listed in alphabetical order in Appendix B. Appendix B contains terminology from a variety of psychiatric sources, describing elements required to be present to use each code. Many of the terms in Appendix B appear in Chapter 5 of the ICD-9-CM manual. The Glossary of Mental Disorders is useful when a code describes a psychiatric term that you are not sure of. For example, the following shows a diagnostic code and code description.

EXAMPLE

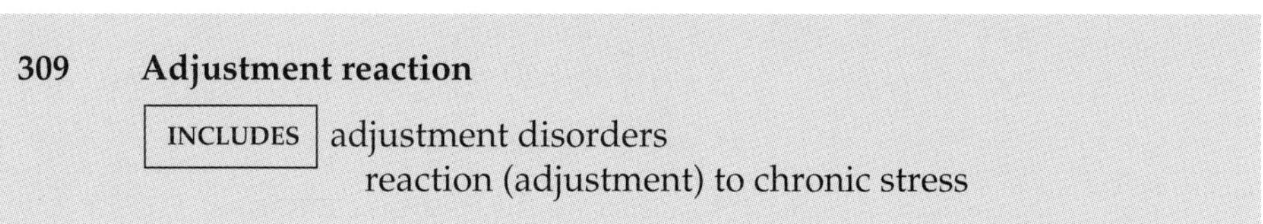

309 Adjustment reaction

INCLUDES adjustment disorders
reaction (adjustment) to chronic stress

If you did not know what was meant by "Adjustment reaction," you could locate the term "Adjustment reaction" in the Glossary of Mental Disorders. You would find a complete description of the term. A portion of the description follows:

> **Adjustment reaction or disorder:** Mild or transient disorders lasting longer than acute stress reactions which occur in individuals of any age without any apparent pre-existing mental disorder. Such disorders are often relatively circumscribed or situation-specific, are generally reversible, and usually last only a few months. They are usually closely related in time and content to stresses such as bereavement, migration, or other experiences. Reactions to major stress that last longer than a few days are also included. In children such disorders are associated with no significant distortion of development.

You will find Appendix B a helpful tool as you begin to code psychiatric conditions.

Appendix C, Drugs

This alphabetized subsection is entitled "Classification of Drugs by American Hospital Formulary Service List Number and Their ICD-9-CM Equivalents." (Have you noticed how few short titles there are in the ICD-9-CM?) A division of the American Hospital Formulary Service (AHFS) regularly publishes a coded listing of drugs. These AHFS codes are up to five digits. Each begins with a number, then a colon, and up to four additional digits to provide specificity.

EXAMPLE

AHFS		ICD-9-CM
8:12.04	Antifungal Antibiotics	960.1

Note that the ICD-9-CM code and the AHFS poisoning codes mean the same thing. For example, both AHFS 8:12.04 and ICD-9-CM 960.1 are "Antifungal Antibiotics."

Appendix D, Industrial Accidents

The subsection titled "Classification of Industrial Accidents According to Agency" contains three-digit codes to identify occupational hazards. The subsection is divided into

1. Machines
2. Means of Transport and Lifting Equipment
3. Other Equipment
4. Materials, Substances and Radiation
5. Working Environments
6. Other Agencies, Not Elsewhere Classified (NEC)
7. Agencies Not Classified for Lack of Sufficient Data

The identification of occupational hazards is especially important in coding injury/death that is job related. Statisticians analyze the data and make statements about risks of various occupations based on the data collected from the forms completed by health care workers.

Appendix E, Three-Digit Categories

Appendix E is a list of all the three-digit codes in the ICD-9-CM presented by each chapter. The categories are labeled from 1 through 17.

EXAMPLE

1. INFECTIOUS AND PARASITIC DISEASES
Intestinal infectious diseases (001-009)

001	Cholera
002	Typhoid and paratyphoid fevers
003	Other salmonella infections
004	Shigellosis
005	Other food poisoning (bacterial)
006	Amebiasis
007	Other protozoal intestinal diseases
008	Intestinal infections due to other organisms
009	Ill-defined intestinal infections

Reviewing Appendix E is a good way to get a quick overview of all of the codes in the ICD-9-CM manual.

EXERCISE J *The Five Appendices in Volume 1*

In which appendix would you find the following information?

1. Glossary of Mental Disorders ____________________
2. Classification of Industrial Accidents According to Agency ____________________
3. Morphology of Neoplasms ____________________
4. List of Three-Digit Categories ____________________
5. Classification of Drugs by American Hospital Formulary Service List

   ____

6. In what appendix of the ICD-9-CM manual would you find the code to identify an injury resulting from a job-related accident with a machine?

   ____

VOLUME 3: PROCEDURES

History

An important new development occurred with the publication of the ICD-9-CM manual—a Classification of Procedures in Medicine was added. Although some countries, notably the United States, had included classifications of surgical procedures in their adaptations of the ICD-9-CM since 1959, international agreement in classification of procedures was never reached. The classification of procedures was never included in the ICD-9-CM manual itself but has always been a separate volume.

The WHO had recognized the growing need for a classification of procedures used in medicine and in 1971 sponsored an international working party that was convened by the American Hospital Association to coordinate the recommendations for a classification of procedures, with the primary emphasis on surgery. The International Conference for the 9th Revision of the International Classification of Diseases was convened at WHO Headquarters in Geneva in 1975. From that gathering, a proposal for a classification of procedures was submitted. The recommendations of the working party were to publish the provisional procedures classification as a supplement to the ICD-9. When the ICD-9 manual was published, a series of separate sections called fascicles (supplements) were also published. Each fascicle provides a classification of a different mode (type) of therapy (eg, surgery, radiology, and laboratory procedures).

Subsequently, the ICD-9-CM was published in a three-volume set, including Volume 3, Procedures. Volume 3 was drawn primarily from WHO's Fascicle V, "Surgical Procedures." At the same time, the codes in Volume 3 were expanded from three to four digits to allow for greater detail.

Volume 3 of the ICD-9-CM manual did not maintain compatibility with the

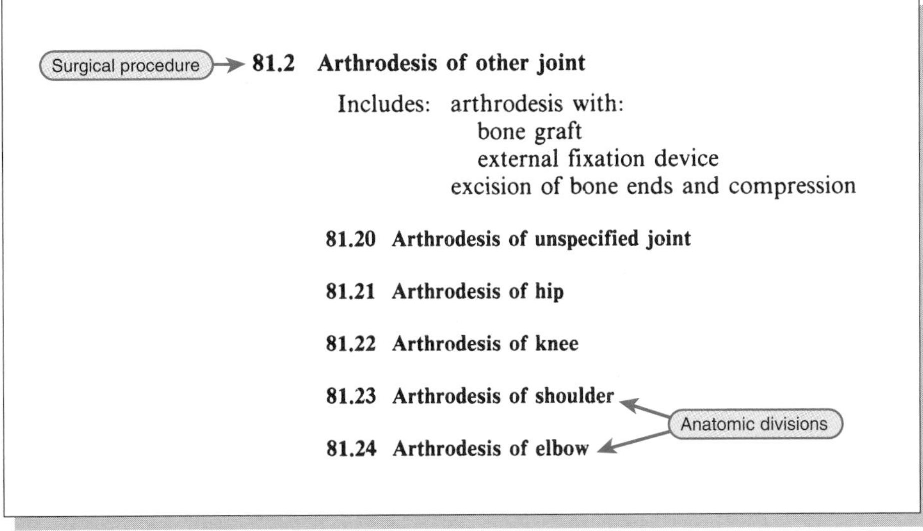

81.2 Arthrodesis of other joint

Includes: arthrodesis with:
bone graft
external fixation device
excision of bone ends and compression

81.20 Arthrodesis of unspecified joint

81.21 Arthrodesis of hip

81.22 Arthrodesis of knee

81.23 Arthrodesis of shoulder

81.24 Arthrodesis of elbow

Figure 6–19
Volume 3, Surgical procedures. (From International Classification of Diseases, 9th Revision. U.S. Department of Health and Human Services, Public Health Service, Health Care Financing Administration.)

ICD-9 as Volume 1 and 2 had done. A different approach was taken in the development of Volume 3 that was deemed more appropriate to a classification system that would deal with surgical and therapeutic procedures.

Format

Approximately 90% of the codes in Volume 3 refer to surgical procedures (Fig. 6–19). The remaining 10% of the codes are diagnostic and therapeutic procedures, as shown in Figure 6–20. For the most part, nonsurgical procedures are segregated from the surgical procedures and confined to the codes 87-99.

Therapeutic procedure → **88.4 Arteriography using contrast material**

Includes: angiography of arteries
arterial puncture for injection of
contrast material
radiography of arteries (by fluoroscopy)
retrograde arteriography

Note: The fourth-digit subclassification identifies the site to be viewed, not the site of injection.

Excludes: *arteriography using:*
radioisotopes or radionuclides (92.01-92.19)
ultrasound (88.71-88.79)
fluorescein angiography of eye (95.12)

88.40 Arteriography using contrast material, unspecified site

Figure 6–20
Volume 3, Therapeutic procedures. (From International Classification of Diseases, 9th Revision. U.S. Department of Health and Human Services, Public Health Service, Health Care Financing Administration.)

Volume 3 is not used in physicians' offices because procedures done by physicians in their offices are coded using the CPT codes. Hospitals use Volume 3 extensively to code services provided to inpatients for surgery, therapy, and diagnostic procedures. Hospitals use the ICD-9-CM codes to bill for facility fees (eg, operating room, room/board, nurses, supplies). For example, a patient is admitted for a total abdominal hysterectomy. The physician would report his or her services and bill for the service of the total abdominal hysterectomy using the CPT code 58150. The hospital would report and bill for facility services for the hysterectomy procedure using the ICD-9-CM procedure code 68.4. The physician and the hospital would report the patient's diagnosis using an ICD-9-CM diagnosis code. If the patient in this example had a diagnosis of chronic endometriosis, both the physician and the hospital would indicate the patient's diagnosis and the reason for their services due to endometriosis of the uterus using the ICD-9-CM code of 617.0.

TABLE OF CONTENTS

Figure 6–21
Volume 3, Table of Contents. (From International Classification of Diseases, 9th Revision. U.S. Department of Health and Human Services, Public Health Service, Health Care Financing Administration.)

EXERCISE K *Table of Contents*

The Table of Contents, Volume 3 (Fig. 6–21) indicates the 16 chapters in Volume 3. Note that each chapter is based on a body system, except for Chapters 13 and 16.

1. What is Chapter 13? ____________________

2. What is Chapter 16? ____________________

Tabular List

Volume 3 has abbreviations, punctuation, symbols, and words similar to those used in Volumes 1 and 2. The following are the conventions that are the same in all volumes:

1. Abbreviations of NEC and NOS
2. Punctuation symbols of brackets, parentheses, colons, and braces
3. Boldface type for all codes and titles
4. Italicized type for all exclusion notes
5. Instructional notations of Includes and *Excludes*

"Code also" has two purposes in Volume 3: to code

1. each component of a procedure
2. the use of special adjunctive (at the same time) procedures or equipment

These instructions are not mandatory but serve as a reminder to code these additional procedures if they were performed.

Using the following ICD-9-CM code as an example, let us take a closer look at the code to make sure you understand what the procedure is and how the "Code also" is used.

EXAMPLE

42.6 Antesternal anastomosis of esophagus
Code also any synchronous:
esophagectomy (42.40-42.42)
gastrostomy (43.1)

You won't find the word antesternal in most medical dictionaries. It is at this time that your skill at taking the word apart will help you out. The prefix "ante" means before, and "sternal" refers to sternum. Anastomosis is the joining together of two openings; in this case it is an opening into the esophagus. The location of the opening into the esophagus is above the sternum, which stated in medical lingo is antesternal anastomosis of esophagus. "Synchronous" means occurring at the same time; "esophagectomy" is the removal of a part of the esophagus, and "gastrostomy" is the creation of an opening into the stomach. The statement from code 42.6 is translated into "Code also any [esophagectomy or gastrostomy] occurring at the same time." You need to know what the terminology you work with means to know what you are coding. The study of terminology is a lifelong endeavor. There are always new words to be discovered. Just remember to always look up any word you are not certain of and take the time to understand the word in the context in which it is used. If you make a practice of doing this, you will soon find that you have a very dependable medical terminology vocabulary.

An example of the second use of the instruction notation "Code also," to code the use of special adjunctive (accessory) procedures or equipment, follows.

EXAMPLE

39.21 Caval-pulmonary artery anastomosis
Code also cardiopulmonary bypass (39.61)

The "Code also" note below code 39.21 directs you to code 39.61, which is the code for extracorporeal (outside the body) circulation. Extracorporeal circulation is an auxiliary procedure done with heart surgery.

EXERCISE L *Terminology*

State the definition of the following terms:

1. cava(l) ______________________
2. pulmonary ______________________
3. anastomosis ______________________
4. cardiopulmonary ______________________
5. extracorporeal ______________________
6. What is a "caval-pulmonary artery anastomosis"?

   ____

   ____
7. What does a heart-lung machine do for the patient who is having a caval-pulmonary artery anastomosis?

   ____

   ____

Alphabetic Index

The Alphabetic Index is an important complement to the Tabular List because the index contains many procedure terms that do not appear in the Tabular List. Terms in the list of included procedures under the two-digit category code of the

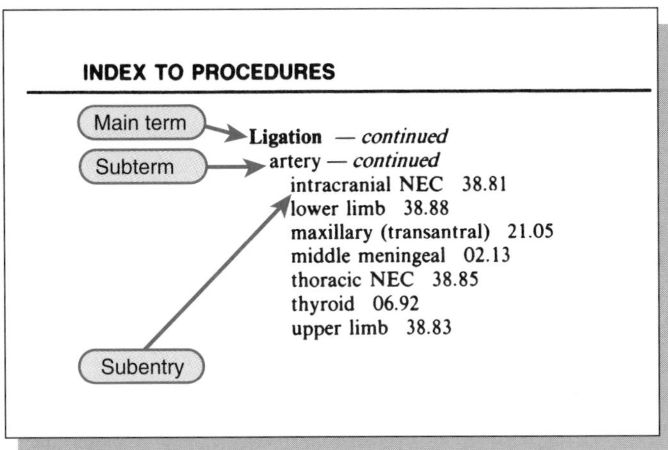

Figure 6–22
Index to procedures. (From International Classification of Diseases, 9th Revision. U.S. Department of Health and Human Services, Public Health Service, Health Care Financing Administration.)

Tabular List are not meant to be exhaustive; they serve as examples of the content of the category. The index, however, includes most procedure terms currently in use in North America. When the exact word is not found in the Tabular List but is found in the Alphabetic Index, you must trust the code given in the Alphabetic Index as being correct.

Never code directly from the Alphabetic Index. After locating a code in the index, refer to that code in the Tabular List for important instructions. Instructions in the form of notes suggesting the use of additional codes and exclusion notes that indicate the circumstances under which a procedure would be coded elsewhere are found only in the Tabular List.

The Alphabetic Index is primarily arranged by procedure (Fig. 6–22) into main terms and subterms. Procedure codes are numbers only with no alphabetical characters. The classification is based on a two-digit structure with two additional digits when necessary for additional specificity.

Figure 6–23 indicates the two-digit category codes, three-digit subcategory codes, and the four-digit subclassifications codes contained in the Tabular List. All category codes in Volume 3 are two-digit codes, whereas all the category codes in Volume 1 are three-digit codes.

The *sequence* of the Alphabetic Index is a letter-by-letter alphabetical order. Letter-by-letter alphabetizing ignores single spaces and single hyphens and produces sequences.

EXAMPLE

opening

open reduction

Upon first consideration, you would think that these two words were not in correct alphabetical order; "open" should come before "opening." The old filer's rule of "nothing comes before something" does not apply here. To alphabetize "opening" and "open reduction," you consider the beginning of the two words as "o-p-e-n"; the fifth letter in "opening" is "i" and the fifth letter in "open reduction" is "r." For alphabetizing purposes, the terms are considered as

opening

openreduction

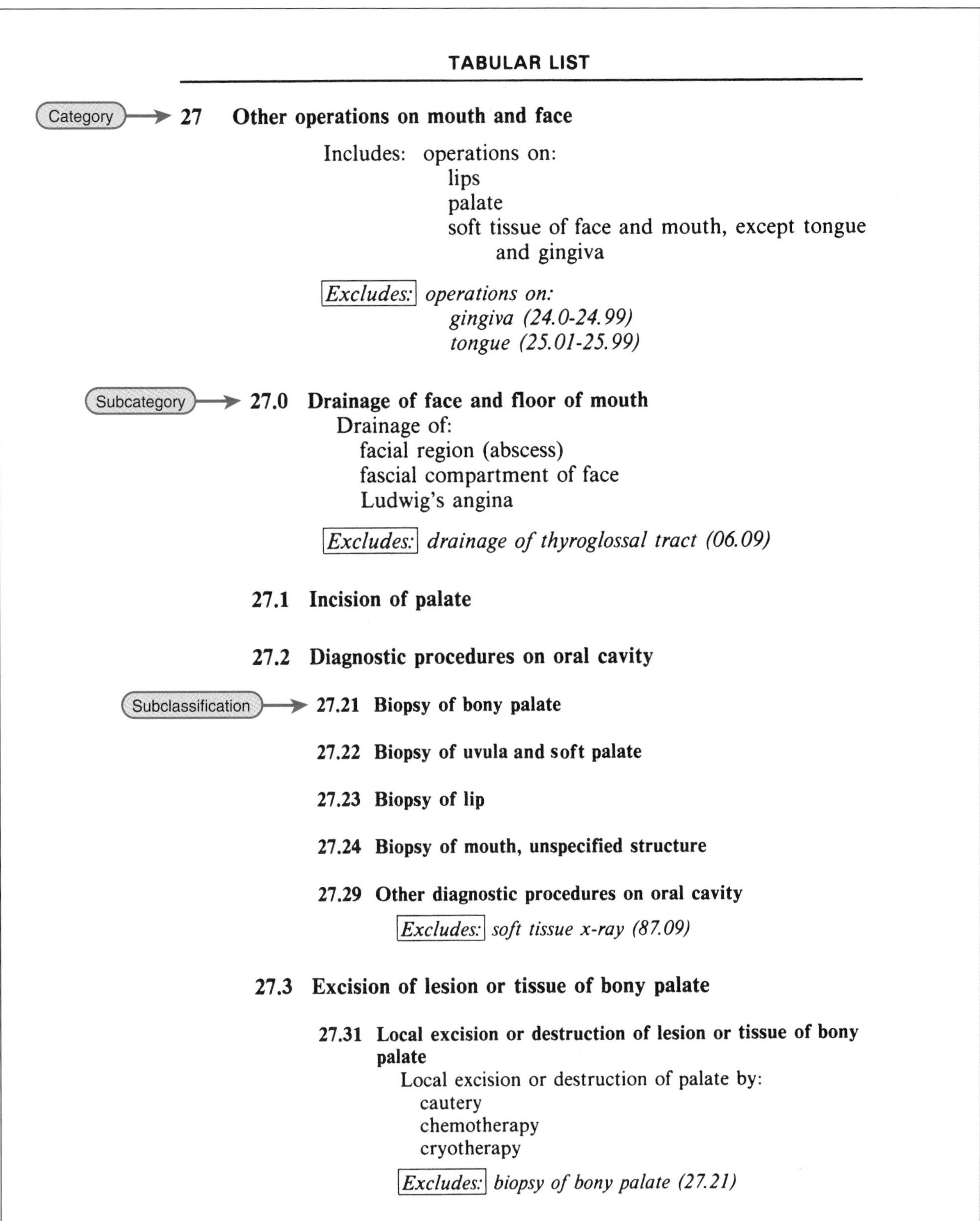

TABULAR LIST

27 Other operations on mouth and face

Includes: operations on:
lips
palate
soft tissue of face and mouth, except tongue and gingiva

Excludes: *operations on:*
gingiva (24.0-24.99)
tongue (25.01-25.99)

27.0 Drainage of face and floor of mouth

Drainage of:
facial region (abscess)
fascial compartment of face
Ludwig's angina

Excludes: *drainage of thyroglossal tract (06.09)*

27.1 Incision of palate

27.2 Diagnostic procedures on oral cavity

27.21 Biopsy of bony palate

27.22 Biopsy of uvula and soft palate

27.23 Biopsy of lip

27.24 Biopsy of mouth, unspecified structure

27.29 Other diagnostic procedures on oral cavity

Excludes: *soft tissue x-ray (87.09)*

27.3 Excision of lesion or tissue of bony palate

27.31 Local excision or destruction of lesion or tissue of bony palate

Local excision or destruction of palate by:
cautery
chemotherapy
cryotherapy

Excludes: *biopsy of bony palate (27.21)*

Figure 6–23
Volume 3, format. (From International Classification of Diseases, 9th Revision. U.S. Department of Health and Human Services, Public Health Service, Health Care Financing Administration.)

Operation
Beck I (epicardial poudrage) 36.39
Beck II (aorto-coronary sinus shunt) 36.39
Beck-Jianu (permanent gastrostomy) 43.19

Figure 6–24
Numbers.

Numbers, whether Arabic (1, 2, 3), Roman (I, II, III), or ordinal (first, second, third), are all placed in numeric sequence *before* alphabetical characters. Simply stated, numbers come before letters (Fig. 6–24).

The *prepositions* "as," "by," and "with" immediately follow the main term to which they refer. When multiple prepositional references are present, they are listed in alphabetical sequence.

The Alphabetic Index is organized by main terms that are printed in bold typeface. Main terms usually identify the type of procedure performed, rather than the anatomic site involved.

A main term may be followed by a series of terms in parentheses. The presence or absence of these parenthetical terms in the procedure description has no effect on the selection of the code listed for the main term. These parenthetical terms are called nonessential modifiers. For example, all of the following words in parentheses are nonessential modifiers.

EXAMPLE

Clipping
aneurysm (basilar) (carotid) (cerebellar)
(cerebellopontine) (communicating artery) (vertebral) 39.51

A main term may also be followed by a list of subterms (modifiers) that do have an effect on the selection of the appropriate code for a given procedure. These subterms form individual line entries and describe essential differences in site or surgical technique (eg, see Fig. 6–25).

Terms that identify incisions are listed as main terms in the Alphabetic Index. If the incision was made only for the purpose of performing further surgery, the instruction "*omit* code" is given. The incision for the surgical procedure is bundled into the surgical code and would therefore not be coded separately.

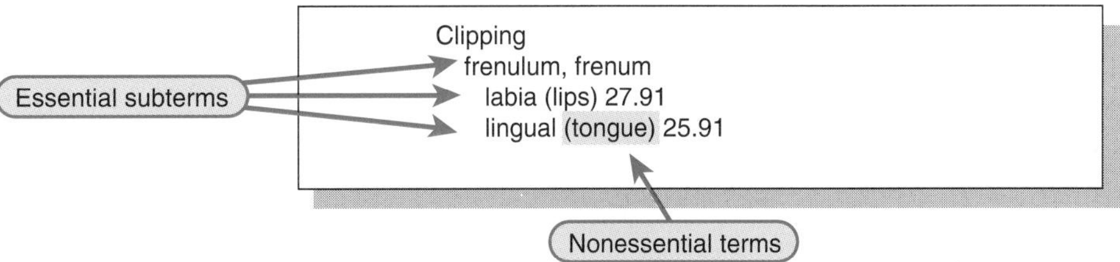

Figure 6–25
Essential and nonessential subterms. (From International Classification of Diseases, 9th Revision. U.S. Department of Health and Human Services, Public Health Service, Health Care Financing Administration.)

EXAMPLE

Arthrotomy 80.10
as operative approach—*omit* code with
arthrography—*see* Arthrogram
arthroscopy—*see* Arthroscopy
injection of drug 81.92
removal of prothesis (*see also* Removal, prosthesis, joint structures) 80.00
ankle 80.17
elbow 80.12

For some operative procedures it is necessary to record the individual components of the procedure. In these instances the Alphabetic Index will list both codes.

EXAMPLE

Code 57.87 describes the reconstruction of the urinary bladder, and 45.51 indicates the intestinal resection (cutting out of a portion of the intestine) necessary to create the ileal bladder.

Ileal bladder
closed 57.87 *[45.51]*

It is important to record these codes in the same sequence used in the Alphabetic Index.

Cross references provide the coder with possible modifiers for a term or its synonyms. There are three types of cross references:

1. "*see*" is an explicit direction to look elsewhere. It is used with terms that do not define the type of procedure performed.

EXAMPLE

Bacterial smear—*see* Examination, microscopic

2. "*see also*" directs the coder to look under another main term because all of the information being searched for cannot be located under the first main term entry.

EXAMPLE

Immunization—*see also* Vaccination

3. "*see* category" directs the coder to the Tabular List for further information or specific site references.

EXAMPLE

Osteolysis—*see* category 78.4

Notes are used in the index to list fourth-digit subclassifications for those categories that use the same fourth digit. In these cases, only the three-digit code is given for the individual entry; you must refer to the note following the main term to obtain the appropriate fourth digit. For an example of a note, see Figure 6–26.

The fourth-digit subclassification codes also appear in the Tabular List with the category codes 90 and 91.

EXAMPLE

Operations named for persons (eponyms) are listed both as main terms in their appropriate alphabetical sequence and under the main term "Operation." A description of the procedure or anatomic site affected usually follows the eponym.

Under the "O":

Operation
  Thompson
    cleft lip repair 27.54
    correction of lymphedema 40.9
    quadricepsplasty 83.86
    thumb opposition with bone graft 82.69

Under the "T":

Thompson operation
  cleft lip repair 27.54
  correction of lymphedema 40.9
  quadricepsplasty 83.86
  thumb opposition with bone graft 82.69

90 Microscopic examination - I

The following fourth-digit subclassification is for use with categories in section 90 to identify type of examination:

1 bacterial smear
2 culture
3 culture and sensitivity
4 parasitology
5 toxicology
6 cell block and Papanicolaou smear
9 other microscopic examination

Fourth digit also appears in the tabular list under the categories

Figure 6–26
Volume 3, Notes, Alphabetic Index. (From International Classification of Diseases, 9th Revision. U.S. Department of Health and Human Services, Public Health Service, Health Care Financing Administration.)

EXERCISE M Procedures

Code the following using Volume 3:

1. Flexible sigmoidoscopy

   Code(s): ___________________

2. Vasectomy

   Code(s): ___________________

3. Closed reduction of maxillary fracture

   Code(s): ___________________

4. Transfusion of 2 units packed cells

   Code(s): ___________________

5. Control of epistaxis by cauterization

   Code(s): ___________________

6. Closed (endoscopic) biopsy of the esophagus

   Code(s): ___________________

7. Thoracentesis

   Code(s): ___________________

8. Closed reduction dislocation finger

   Code(s): ___________________

9. Incision of cornea to remove foreign body

   Code(s): ___________________

10. Laparoscopic appendectomy

    Code(s): ___________________

11. Endocervical biopsy

    Code(s): ___________________

12. Needle biopsy of the left breast

    Code(s): ___________________

13. Chemotherapy for cancer

    Code(s): ___________________

14. Excision lesion elbow joint

    Code(s): ____________________

15. Incision and drainage pilonidal sinus

    Code(s): ____________________

Congratulations! You have now completed the study of the arrangement of the information in the ICD-9-CM manual. The knowledge that you have gained will be used as the foundational information that will be built on in Chapter 7. In Chapter 7 you will begin further work with the correct assignment and sequencing of ICD-9-CM codes.

CHAPTER GLOSSARY

acute: of sudden onset and short duration
benign: not progressive or recurrent
chronic: of long duration
combination code: single five-digit code used to identify etiology and manifestations of a disease
communicable disease: disease that can be transmitted from one person to another or from one species to another.
etiology: study of causes of diseases
histology: study of minute structures, composition, and function of tissues
infectious disease carrier: person who has a communicable disease
infectious disease contact: encounter with a person who has a disease that can be communicated or transmitted
manifestation: sign of a disease
malignant: used to describe a cancerous tumor that grows worse over time
morbidity: condition of being diseased or morbid
morphology: study of neoplasms
mortality: death
multiple coding: use of more than one code to identify both etiology and manifestation of a disease, as contrasted with combination coding
neoplasm: new tumor growth that can be benign or malignant
rubric: heading used as a direction or explanation as to what follows and the way in which the information is to be used. In ICD-9-CM coding, the rubric is the three-digit code that precedes the four- and five-digit codes.
secondary site: place to which a malignant tumor has spread; metastatic site
V codes: numerical designations preceded by the letter "V" used to classify persons who are not currently sick when they encounter health services
World Health Organization (WHO): group that deals with health care issues on a global basis

CHAPTER REVIEW

Match the appendix to the information contained in the appendix:

1. Appendix A _______
2. Appendix B _______
3. Appendix C _______
4. Appendix D _______
5. Appendix E _______

a. Industrial Accidents
b. Classification of Drugs
c. Morphology of Neoplasms
d. Three-Digit Categories
e. Mental Disorders

Circle the correct answer for each of the following:

6. The ICD-9-CM is designed to classify what two things?
   a. sickness and disease
   b. symptoms and illness
   c. causes of morbidity and mortality
   d. diagnosis and disease

7. Which of the following is *not* a stated use for the ICD-9-CM?
   a. facilitate payment of health services
   b. study health care costs
   c. plan for future health care needs
   d. evaluate appropriateness of treatment

Match the ICD-9-CM volume number to the correct name of the volume:

8. Volume 1 _______
9. Volume 2 _______
10. Volume 3 _______

a. Tabular List and Alphabetic Index for Procedures
b. Diseases: Alphabetic Index
c. Diseases: Tabular List

Identify the format of the chapters in the ICD-9-CM Volume 1, Tabular List, in the proper sequence from first to last:

11. _______
12. _______
13. _______
14. _______
15. _______

a. subcategory
b. chapter
c. subclassification
d. section
e. category

Are the following statements about V codes True or False?

16. primarily deals with persons who are not ill but use health care ___________

17. do not use fourth digits ___________

18. can indicate place of birth as before admission or after admission ___________

Circle the correct answer for the following:

19. The primary purpose of E codes is to
   a. identify environmental events
   b. designate causes of injuries and poisonings
   c. both a and b
   d. neither a nor b

20. Morphology is the science of
   a. human anatomy
   b. physiologic function
   c. neoplasms
   d. tissue

21. Epithelial, papillary, basal cell, and adenomas are examples of
    a. secondary sites
    b. carcinomas
    c. borderline malignancies
    d. histologic types

22. Benign, malignant, and carcinoma in situ are examples of types of
    a. secondary sites
    b. neoplasm behavior
    c. borderline malignancy
    d. primary sites

Match the abbreviations, punctuation, symbols, words, or typeface to the correct descriptions:

23. [ ] _______
24. NOS _______
25. : _______
26. § _______
27. italics _______
28. *Excludes* _______
29. Includes _______
30. } _______
31. NEC _______
32. ( ) _______
33. *[ ]* _______
34. bold type _______

a. incomplete term that needs one of the modifiers to make a code assignable
b. used in Volume 2 to enclose the disease and procedure codes that are to also be recorded with the code they are listed with
c. typeface used for all codes and titles in Volume 1
d. information is not available to code to a more specific category
e. encloses a series of terms that are modified by the statement to the right
f. encloses synonyms, alternative words, or explanatory phrases
g. equals unspecified
h. typeface used for all exclusion notes
i. footnote or section note
j. appears under a three-digit code title to further define or explain category content
k. encloses supplementary words and doesn't affect the code
l. indicates terms that are to be coded elsewhere

Match the convention to the definition:

35. *see* category _______
36. modifiers _______
37. NEC _______
38. NOS _______
39. *see* _______

a. indented under main term and essential to code selection
b. terms in parentheses that are nonessential
c. explicit direction to look elsewhere
d. follow terms to define and give instructions
e. means unspecified

40. Notes _______

41. subterms _______

42. *see also* _______

43. eponym _______

f. directs coder to look under another term since all information isn't under the first term

g. directs coder to Volume 1

h. disease/syndrome named for a person

i. means "other"

Circle the correct answer for each of the following:

44. Volume 3 is used primarily by which of the following?
    a. clinics
    b. ambulatory centers
    c. hospitals
    d. nursing homes

45. Volume 3 is used to code what type of procedures?
    a. surgical
    b. therapeutic
    c. diagnostic
    d. all of the above

Identify if the following statements are True or False:

46. The location of the Includes and *Excludes* notes has no bearing on the code selection.

    ____

47. Use of fourth and fifth digits, if available, is mandatory.

    ____

48. If the same condition is listed as both acute and chronic, the chronic condition is sequenced first.

    ____

49. Four-digit codes are referred to as subcategory codes in Volume 1.

    ____

50. In Volume 2, Alphabetic Index, when the main term is modified by terms listed in parentheses following the main term, these modifiers are considered essential for code selection.

    ____

Underline the main term in the following:

51. Grief reaction

52. Fractured radius and ulna

53. Bowel obstruction

54. Erb's palsy

55. Supervision of high-risk pregnancy

56. Aortic stenosis

57. Rapid respirations

58. Actinomycosis meningitis

Identify as category, subcategory, and subclassification:

59. 066.1 ____________________

60. 070.43 ____________________

61. 220 ____________________

62. 274.11 ____________________

63. 284.9 ____________________

64. 337.21 ____________________

Are the following codes procedure codes or diagnosis codes?

65. 214.0 ____________________

66. 251.0 ____________________

67. 31.41 ____________________

68. 37.96 ____________________

69. 663.61 ____________________

Chapter 6, Part II, Practical

Using an ICD-9-CM manual, answer the following questions:

70. What does the *Excludes* note state under category code 175? ____________________

____

71. What does the Includes note state under category 444? ____________________

____

72. Under category 805, which codes use the subclassification 0-8? ____________________

____

73. Would code 362.72 be sequenced as the principal diagnosis? ____________________

____

7 Using the ICD-9-CM

CHAPTER TOPICS

Learning Objectives

After completing this chapter, you should be able to

1. Understand the official coding principles.
2. Define principal and primary diagnosis.
3. Explain reporting other (additional) diagnoses.
4. Assign ICD-9-CM codes to the highest level of specificity.
5. Properly sequence ICD-9-CM codes.
6. Apply ICD-9-CM guidelines and coding conventions.
7. Apply basic coding guidelines to classifying outpatient services.
8. Recognize the major parts of ICD-10-PCS.

SOME GENERAL GUIDELINES

As was discussed in Chapter 6, Official Coding and Reporting Guidelines have been developed and approved for coding and reporting by the Cooperating Parties for ICD-9-CM: American Hospital Association (AHA), American Health Information Management Association (AHIMA), Health Care Financing Administration (HCFA), and the National Center for Health Statistics. The Central Office on ICD-9-CM of the American Hospital Association staffs guideline development activities, and the Cooperating Parties oversee the guidelines.

General Guidelines

The number that appears to the left of the coding guideline in this text is the number of the guideline as listed in the Official Coding and Reporting Guidelines published by the HCFA. For the purposes of this text, the guidelines will sometimes appear out of order. For example, the two guidelines regarding burns are 8.3 and 2.11 and are presented together as you learn about sequencing burns. Appendix A of this text presents the guidelines in their entirety in numeric order.

In the examples in this text, main terms and subterms are often noted for you after the term enclosed in parentheses to help you locate the terms in the Alphabetic Index. Remember, the extensive cross reference system within the ICD-9-CM allows the coder many options for locating codes in the Alphabetic Index. The examples and subsequent identification of main terms and subterms represent only one way the term can be located.

You will be practicing coding using the ICD-9-CM throughout this chapter. You need to practice using the steps that are always necessary to assign an ICD-9-CM code. If you begin your ICD-9-CM coding using these steps, you will develop good coding habits that will last throughout your career.

1. Identify the main term(s) in the diagnostic statement.
2. Locate the main term(s) in the Alphabetic Index (Volume 2) (referred to in this text as the Index).
3. Review any subterms under the main term in the Index.
4. Follow any cross reference instructions, such as *see also.*
5. Verify the code(s) selected from the Index in the Tabular List (Volume 1) (referred to in this text as the Tabular).
6. Refer to any instructional notations in the Tabular.
7. Assign codes to the highest level of specificity. For example, if a fourth digit is available, you cannot assign only a three-digit code, and if a fifth digit is available, you cannot assign only a four-digit code.
8. Code the diagnosis until all elements are completely identified.

The guideline will be presented, followed by examples or exercises to illustrate the rule(s).

1.1 USE OF BOTH THE ALPHABETIC INDEX AND THE TABULAR LIST

A. Use both the Alphabetic Index and the Tabular List when locating and assigning a code. Reliance on only the Alphabetic Index or the Tabular List leads to errors in code assignment and less specificity in code selection.

B. Locate each item in the Alphabetic Index and verify the code selected in the Tabular List. Read and be guided by instructional notations that appear in both the Alphabetic Index and the Tabular List.

EXAMPLES

Use of Both the Alphabetic Index and the Tabular List

Diagnosis: Hodgkin's Disease

Index: **Hodgkin's** (main term)

disease (subterm) 201.9

Tabular: **201 Hodgkin's disease** [category code]

201.9 Hodgkin's disease, Unspecified [subcategory code]

Code: 201.9X Hodgkin's Disease [subclassification code]

Verify 201.9 in the Tabular and note that the code requires a fifth-digit assignment of 0 to 8 to indicate the disease location. You would have missed the required fifth-digit subclassification if you had used only the Index and not verified the code in the Tabular.

Diagnosis: Stroke, due to vertebral artery occlusion

Index: **Stroke** (main term) 436

Tabular: **436 Acute, but ill-defined, cerebrovascular disease**

EXCLUDES *any condition classifiable to categories 430-435*

Reading the *Excludes* note under stroke, 436, in the Tabular, you can identify that 436 can be used only if the stroke description is not classifiable to 430-435. You then must reference the occlusion portion of the diagnosis.

Index: **Occlusion**

artery, vertebral

Tabular: **433 Occlusion and stenosis of precerebral arteries**

0 without mention of cerebral infarction

1 with cerebral infarction

433.2 Vertebral artery

Code: 433.20 Stroke, due to vertebral artery occlusion

The diagnosis statement "fits" or is classifiable to 433.20. You would have incorrectly coded the diagnosis to 436 if you had not verified the code in the Tabular. There are no shortcuts in this process: Always check the Tabular.

Official Coding and Reporting Guidelines

1.2 LEVEL OF SPECIFICITY IN CODING

Diagnostic and procedure codes must be used at their highest level of specificity.

A. Assign three-digit codes only if there are no four-digit codes within that code category.
B. Assign four-digit codes only if there is no fifth-digit subclassification for that category.
C. Assign the five-digit subclassification code for those categories where it exists.

EXAMPLES

Level of Specificity

Three-Digit Category

Diagnosis: Subarachnoid hemorrhage

Index: **Hemorrhage,** subarachnoid, nontraumatic 430

Tabular: **430 Subarachnoid hemorrhage** [category code]

Code: 430 Subarachnoid hemorrhage

Diagnosis: AIDS

Index: **AIDS** 042

Tabular: **042 Human immunodeficiency virus (HIV) disease** [category code]

Code: 042 AIDS

Both of the preceding diagnostic statements are correctly assigned to three-digit category codes because there are no four-digit subcategory codes available within either code.

Four-Digit Subcategory

Diagnosis: Crohn's disease of large intestine

Index: **Crohn's disease** (see also Enteritis, regional) 555.9

Tabular: **555 Regional enteritis (Includes: Crohn's disease)** [category code]

555.1 Large intestine [subcategory code]

Code: 555.1 Crohn's disease of large intestine

Diagnosis: Cellulitis of the upper right leg

Index: **Cellulitis,** leg

Tabular: **682 Other cellulitis and abscess** [category code]

682.6 leg, except foot [subcategory code]

Code: 682.6 Cellulitis of the upper right leg

Both of the preceding diagnostic statements are correctly assigned to four-digit subcategory codes because no five-digit subclassification codes are available.

Five-Digit Subclassification

Diagnosis: RUQ abdominal pain

Index: **Pain,** abdominal

Tabular: **789.0 Abdominal pain** [subcategory code]

789.01 Right upper quadrant [subclassification code]

Code: 789.01 RUQ abdominal pain

Diagnosis: Bilateral, congenital bowing of right femur

Index: **Bowing**

femur 736.89

congenital 754.42

Tabular: **754 Certain congenital musculoskeletal deformities** [category code]

754.4 Congenital genu recurvatum and bowing of long bones of leg [subcategory code]

754.42 Congenital bowing of femur [subclassification code]

Code: 754.42 Bilateral, congenital bowing of right femur

Both of the preceding diagnostic statements are correctly assigned to five-digit subclassification codes, having been carried out to the highest level of specificity available.

EXERCISE A *Level of Specificity in Coding*

Identify and fill in the category, subcategory, and subclassifications of the following:

1. Diagnosis: Recurrent right inguinal hernia, with obstruction

   Index: **Hernia**

   inguinal 550.9

   Tabular: **550 Inguinal hernia** ____________________

   550.1 Inguinal hernia, with obstruction, without mention of gangrene ____________________

   550.11 Inguinal hernia, with obstruction, without mention of gangrene, unilateral __________

2. Diagnosis: Transient hypertension, 30 weeks' gestation, undelivered

   Index: **Hypertension**

   transient

   of pregnancy (soubrette) 642.3

   Tabular: **642 Hypertension complicating pregnancy, childbirth, and the puerperium** ____________________

   642.3 Transient hypertension of pregnancy __________

   642.33 Antepartum condition or complication _____

Official Coding and Reporting Guidelines

1.3 OTHER (NEC) AND UNSPECIFIED (NOS) CODE TITLES

Codes labeled "other specified" (NEC—not elsewhere classified) or "unspecified" (NOS—not otherwise specified) are used only when neither the diagnostic statement nor a thorough review of the medical record provides adequate information to permit assignment of a more specific code.

A. Use the code assignment for "other" or NEC when the information at hand specifies a condition but no separate code for the condition is provided.
B. Use "unspecified" (NOS) when the information at hand does not permit either a more specific or "other" code assignment.

When the Alphabetic Index assigns a code to a category labeled "other (NEC)" or to a category labeled "unspecified (NOS)" refer to the Tabular List and review the titles and inclusion terms in the subdivisions under that particular three-digit category (or subdivision under the four-digit code) to determine if the information at hand can be appropriately assigned to a more specific code.

EXAMPLES

NEC

Diagnosis: Pneumonia due to gram-negative bacteria

Index: **Pneumonia**

gram-negative bacteria NEC 482.83

Tabular: **482.8 Pneumonia due to other specified bacteria**

482.83 Other gram-negative bacteria

Code: 482.83 Pneumonia due to gram-negative bacteria

Code 482.83 identifies gram-negative bacteria pneumonia that cannot be classified more specifically into the other subclassifications. The other subclassifications within 482.8 are for anaerobes, *Escherichia coli [E. coli]*, "other than gram-negative" bacteria, Legionnaire's disease, and other specified bacteria. None of these other subclassifications can be assigned to the diagnostic statement.

NEC can be used in two ways:

1. NEC directs the coder to look under other classifications if appropriate. Other subterms or *Excludes* notes may provide hints as to what the other classifications may be.
2. NEC is used when the ICD-9-CM does not have any codes that provide greater specificity.

NOS

Diagnosis: Bronchitis

Index: **Bronchitis** 490

Tabular: **490 Bronchitis, not specified as acute or chronic**

Bronchitis NOS

Code: 490 Bronchitis

The diagnosis was not specified by the practitioner as acute or chronic; therefore, the "not otherwise specified" code 490 must be assigned. In this situation, it would be appropriate for the coder to request specificity from the practitioner.

1.4 AND 2.3 ACUTE AND CHRONIC CONDITIONS

If the same condition is described as both acute (subacute) and chronic and separate subentries exist in the Alphabetic Index at the same indentation level, code both and sequence the acute (subacute) code first.

See Figure 7–1 for the format of acute pancreatitis and chronic pancreatitis. Both acute and chronic forms of pancreatitis are subcategorized under code 577.

EXAMPLES

Acute and Chronic Conditions

Diagnosis: Acute and chronic thyroiditis

Index: **Thyroiditis**

acute 245.0

chronic 245.8

Tabular: **245 Thyroiditis**

245.0 Acute thyroiditis

245.8 Other and unspecified chronic thyroiditis

Sequence: 245.0, 245.8 Acute and chronic thyroiditis

Note that the acute form of thyroiditis is sequenced before the chronic as directed by Guideline 2.3.

Diagnosis: Acute and chronic pericarditis

Index: **Pericarditis**

acute 420.90

chronic 423.8

Tabular: **420 Acute pericarditis**

420.9 Other and unspecified acute pericarditis

420.90 Acute pericarditis, unspecified

Tabular: **423 Other diseases of pericardium**

423.8 Other specified diseases of the pericardium

Sequence: 429.90, 423.8 Acute and chronic pericarditis

577.0 Acute pancreatitis

Abscess of pancreas	Pancreatitis:
Necrosis of pancreas:	NOS
acute	acute (recurrent)
infective	apoplectic
	hemorrhagic
	subacute
	suppurative

Excludes: *mumps pancreatitis (072.3)*

577.1 Chronic pancreatitis

Chronic pancreatitis:	Pancreatitis:
NOS	painless
infectious	recurrent
interstitial	relapsing

Figure 7–1
Indent level of acute and chronic. (From International Classification of Diseases, 9th Revision. U.S. Department of Health and Human Services, Public Health Service, Health Care Financing Administration.)

Note that while the Index directs you to code 423.8 for chronic pericarditis, when the Tabular is verified, there is no mention of "chronic pericarditis." This is an example of a common coding situation in which you must "trust the Index." When the condition is both acute and chronic, and both acute and chronic are listed in the Alphabetic Index as separate entries at the same indentation level, the acute *code is sequenced first.*

1.5 COMBINATION CODE

A single code used to classify two diagnoses or a diagnosis with an associated secondary process (manifestation) or an associated complication is called a combination code. Combination codes are identified by referring to subterm entries in the Alphabetic Index and by reading the inclusion and exclusion notes in the Tabular List.

A. Assign only the combination code when that code fully identifies the diagnostic conditions involved or when the Alphabetic Index so directs. Multiple coding should not be used when the classification provides a combination code that clearly identifies all of the elements documented in the diagnosis. When the combination code lacks necessary specificity in describing the manifestation or complication, an additional code may be used as a secondary code.

The following is an example of a combination code that classifies a diagnosis (hypertension) with a secondary manifestation (congestive heart failure).

EXAMPLES

Combination Codes

Diagnosis: Congestive heart failure due to hypertension

(*Note:* Beginning with this Index example, the main term will be listed first and subsequent subterm(s) will follow on the same line, separated by a comma. Index main terms and subterms will be listed on separate lines only if separate lines add to the clarity of the example.)

Index: **Failure,** heart, congestive, hypertensive 402.91

Tabular: **402 Hypertensive heart disease**

402.9 Unspecified

402.91 with congestive heart failure

Code: 402.91 Congestive heart failure due to hypertension

The diagnosis of congestive heart failure due to hypertension is fully described by the single code 402.91.

Another example of a diagnosis (streptococcal) and manifestation (pharyngitis—sore throat) assigned to a combination code is as follows:

Diagnosis: Streptococcal pharyngitis

Index: **Pharyngitis,** streptococcal 034.0

Tabular: **034 Streptococcal sore throat and scarlet fever**

034.0 Streptococcal sore throat

Septic:	Streptococcal:
angina	angina
sore throat	laryngitis
	pharyngitis
	tonsillitis

The single code 034.0 fully describes the diagnosis of streptococcal pharyngitis.

Code(s): 034.0 Streptococcal pharyngitis

EXERCISE B ***Combination Codes***

Fill in the codes for the following using combination coding:

1. Pneumonia due to *Haemophilus influenzae*

   Code(s): ____________________

2. Candidiasis of the mouth (thrush)

   Code(s): ____________________

3. Enteritis due to *Clostridium difficile*

   Code(s): ____________________

4. Hypertensive cerebrovascular disease

   Code(s): ____________________

5. Closed fracture of the tibia and fibula

   Code(s): ____________________

Official Coding and Reporting Guidelines

1.6 MULTIPLE CODING OF DIAGNOSES

Multiple coding is required for certain conditions not subject to the rules for combination codes.

Instructions for conditions that require multiple coding appear in the Alphabetic Index and the Tabular List:

A. Alphabetic Index: Codes for both etiology and manifestation of a disease appear following the subentry term, with the second code italicized and in slanted brackets. Assign both codes in the same sequence in which they appear in the Alphabetic Index.
B. Tabular List: Instructional terms, such as "Code first . . . ," "Use additional code for any . . . ," and "Note . . . ," indicate when to use more than one code.
   1. "Code also underlying disease"—Assign the codes for both the manifestation and the underlying cause. The codes for manifestations cannot be used (designated) as principal diagnosis.
   2. "Use additional code, if desired, to identify manifestation, as . . ."—Assign also the code that identifies the manifestation, such as, but not limited to, the examples listed. The codes for manifestations cannot be used (designated) as principal diagnosis.
C. Apply multiple coding instructions throughout the classification where appropriate, whether or not multiple coding directions appear in the Alphabetic Index or the Tabular List. Avoid indiscriminate multiple coding of irrelevant information, such as symptoms or signs characteristic of the diagnosis.

EXAMPLES

Multiple Coding

Diagnosis: Diabetic retinopathy with type I diabetes

(*Note:* Retinopathy is the manifestation and diabetes is the etiology or cause of the retinopathy.)

Index: **Retinopathy,** diabetic 250.5 [362.01]

The Index subterm "diabetic" identifies the code for the etiology as 250.5 and directs you to the code for the manifestation of *[362.01]* retinopathy. The italicized code is never sequenced first as the principal diagnosis but is used to identify a manifestation.

Tabular: **250 Diabetes mellitus**

250.5 Diabetes with ophthalmic manifestations

Use additional code to identify manifestation

250.51 Type I, not stated as uncontrolled

Code 250.51 is the correct code to describe the diabetes (etiology). The statement "Use additional code to identify manifestation" directs you to assign a code that identifies the manifestation (retinopathy).

Tabular: **362 Other retinal disorders**

362.0 Diabetic retinopathy

Code first diabetes 250.5

362.01 Background diabetic retinopathy

Note that the *"Code first diabetes"* directs you to the etiology code.

Code: 250.51, 362.01 Diabetic retinopathy with type I diabetes

The multiple codes fully describe the diagnostic statement. The guideline directs you to place the etiology code first, followed by the manifestation code. Let's review another example of multiple coding.

Diagnosis: Staphylococcal cellulitis of the face

(Staphylococcal infection is the etiology and cellulitis is the manifestation.)

Index: **Cellulitis,** face (any part, except eye) 682.0

Tabular: **682 Other cellulitis and abscess**

682.0 Face

Code(s): 682.0 Cellulitis of the face

You now must identify the etiology code.

Index: **Infection,** staphylococcal NEC 041.10

Tabular: **041 Bacterial infection in conditions classified elsewhere and of unspecified site**

Note: This category is to be used as an additional code to identify the bacterial agent in diseases classifed elsewhere. This category is also used to classify bacterial infections of unspecified nature or site.

041.1 Staphylococcus

041.10 Staphylococcus, unspecified

Code: 682.0, 041.10 Staphylococcal cellulitis of the face

Note that it is acceptable to sequence the manifestation code first in this example because code 682.0 is not italicized in the Tabular, and the instructional notation listed under category 682 in the Tabular specifically states "Use additional code to identify organism, . . ."

EXERCISE C Multiple Coding

Using multiple codes, fill in the codes for the following diagnoses:

1. Chronic prostatitis due to streptococcus

   Code(s): ____________________

2. Acute bronchitis due to *Pseudomonas*

   Code(s): ____________________

3. Gangrene due to diabetes mellitus, type I

   Code(s): ____________________

4. Urinary tract infection due to *Escherichia coli*

   Code(s): ____________________

5. Amyloid cardiomyopathy

   Code(s): ____________________

1.8 UNCERTAIN DIAGNOSIS

If the diagnosis documented at the time of discharge is qualified as "probable," "suspected," "likely," "questionable," "possible," or "rule out," code the condition as if it existed or was established. The bases for these guidelines are the diagnostic workup, arrangements for further workup or observation, and initial therapeutic approach that correspond most closely with the established diagnosis.

The basis for this guideline is that the diagnostic workup, arrangements for further workup, observation, or therapies are the same whether treating the confirmed condition or ruling it out.

Because hospitals are paid a lump sum (DRG amount) for each hospitalization, the facility resources used are averaged. In an outpatient setting, only confirmed diagnoses may be coded. Rule out, possible, or probable diagnoses are coded to the chief complaint or sign or symptom that occasioned the visit. In an outpatient setting, each visit in the process of confirming a diagnosis is coded/billed.

EXAMPLES

Uncertain Diagnosis

Hospital Inpatient

Diagnosis: <u>Probable</u> bronchitis (code as bronchitis)

Index: **Bronchitis** 490

Tabular: **490 Bronchitis**

Hospital Inpatient

Diagnosis: Rule out Graves' disease (code as Graves' disease)

Index: **Graves' Disease** 242.0

Tabular: **242.00 Toxic diffuse goiter** (Graves' disease)

Clinic Outpatient

Diagnosis: Chest pain, rule out myocardial infarction (code as chest pain)

Index: **Pain(s),** chest 786.50

Tabular: **786.50 Chest pain, unspecified**

Clinic Outpatient

Diagnosis: Cough and fever, probably pneumonia (code as cough and fever)

Index: **Cough** 786.2

Index: **Fever** 780.6

Tabular: **786.2 Cough**
780.6 Pyrexia of unknown origin (fever)

Official Coding and Reporting Guidelines

1.9 IMPENDING OR THREATENED CONDITION

Code any condition described at the time of discharge as "impending" or "threatened" as follows:

A. If it did occur, code as confirmed diagnosis.
B. If it did not occur, reference the Alphabetic Index to determine if the condition has a subentry term for "impending" or "threatened" and also reference main term entries for Impending and for Threatened.
   1. If the subterms are listed, assign the given code.
   2. If the subterms are not listed, code the existing forerunner condition(s) and not the condition described as impending or threatened.

EXAMPLES

Impending or Threatened Condition

Diagnosis: Threatened abortion

Index: **Threatened,** abortion 640.0

Tabular: **640 Hemorrhage in early pregnancy**

640.0 Threatened abortion

Code: 640.03 Threatened abortion

Diagnosis: Impending myocardial infarction

Index: **Impending,** myocardial infarction 411.1

Tabular: **411 Other acute and subacute forms of ischemic heart disease**

411.1 Intermediate coronary syndrome

Impending infarction Preinfarction syndrome

Preinfarction angina Unstable angina

Code: 411.1 Impending myocardial infarction

If the infarction had occurred, you would have coded it as a confirmed diagnosis by coding myocardial infarction (with the appropriate fifth digit to denote the episode of care).

EXERCISE D Impending or Threatened Conditions

Fill in the codes for the following:

1. Evolving stroke

   Code(s): ____________________

2. Impending delirium tremens

   Code(s): ____________________

3. Threatened miscarriage

   Code(s): ____________________

4. Threatened labor

   Code(s): ____________________

5. Impending coronary syndrome

   Code(s): ____________________

Selection of Principal Diagnosis

Official Coding and Reporting Guidelines

The circumstances of inpatient admission always govern the selection of principal diagnosis. The principal diagnosis is defined in the Uniform Hospital Discharge Data Set (UHDDS) as "that condition established after study to be chiefly responsible for occasioning the admission of the patient to the hospital for care."

The principal diagnosis is sequenced first. In an outpatient setting, it is important to indicate as the first diagnosis the main reason for the visit, as well as subsequent diagnoses to substantiate adjunct services (such as laboratory and radiology). In other settings, this first diagnosis is sometimes called the primary diagnosis. The terminology "principal diagnosis" only refers to the acute care setting and is used in conjunction with the DRG payment scheme.

Official Coding and Reporting Guidelines

In determining the principal diagnosis, the coding directives in the ICD-9-CM manuals, Volumes I, II, and III, take precedence over all other guidelines. The importance of consistent, complete documentation in the medical record cannot be overemphasized. Without such documentation the application of all coding guidelines is a difficult, if not an impossible, task.

2.1 CODES FOR SYMPTOMS, SIGNS, AND ILL-DEFINED CONDITIONS

Codes for symptoms, signs, and ill-defined conditions from Chapter 16 (Symptoms, Signs, and Ill-Defined Conditions) are not to be used as principal diagnosis when a related definitive diagnosis has been established.

EXERCISE E *Symptoms, Signs, and Ill-Defined Conditions*

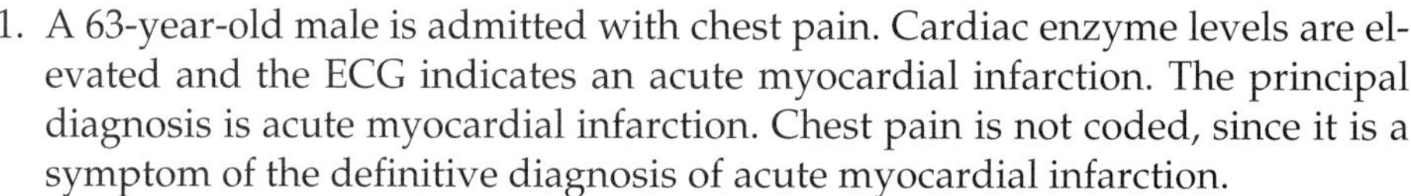

1. A 63-year-old male is admitted with chest pain. Cardiac enzyme levels are elevated and the ECG indicates an acute myocardial infarction. The principal diagnosis is acute myocardial infarction. Chest pain is not coded, since it is a symptom of the definitive diagnosis of acute myocardial infarction.

   Let's code this case together.

   a. For an acute myocardial infarction, infarction is the manifestation. "Acute" indicates the episode of care and "myocardial" indicates the general site of the infarction.

   b. Locate "infarction" in the Index.

   c. Under the term "Infarct, infarction" you should next locate the subterm "myocardial." Note after "myocardium, myocardial" you find "acute. . . ." and are directed to code 410.9.

   d. Now turn to 410.9 in the Tabular, Volume 1.

   e. Under **"410.9 Unspecified site"** you are presented with a notation that a fifth digit is required.

   f. Go back to the three-digit category code 410 where the fifth digits are listed. The "0" fifth digit is for an unspecified episode of care, the "1" fifth digit is for initial episode of care, and the "2" fifth digit is for a subsequent episode of care. The myocardial infarction was diagnosed during this visit, so that would fit the initial episode of care definition in the ICD-9-CM. The correct fifth digit is "1."

g. The complete, correct code is 410.91.

Now you try one.

2. A patient is admitted to the hospital with severe flank pain and hematuria. A urinalysis is done and it is positive for *Escherichia coli.* The discharge summary states acute pyelonephritis.

   a. What is the principal diagnosis? ______________________

   b. Locate the principal diagnosis in the Index. What code does the Index direct you to locate?

      Code(s): ______________

   c. Locate the code in the Tabular. What is the three-digit category code and the title of the category you were directed to?

      Code(s) and title: ______________________________

   d. Was there mention of a lesion in the case above? ______________

   e. What is the correct five-digit code for this case? ______________

   f. Why do you think "severe flank pain and hematuria" are noted on this patient case? ______________________________

Wait, you're not finished with this case yet. Go back to the three-digit category code 590 and look at the entry immediately under the "Infections of Kidney." A note states, "Use additional code to identify organism, such as **Escherichia coli [E. coli]** *(041.4)." You also code 041.4 to indicate the type of infection present. You have to be very careful to read all notes in the category before coding. If, in the end, you arrived at codes 590.10 and 041.4, you did a fine job.*

2.2 CODES IN BRACKETS

Codes in brackets in the Alphabetic Index can never be sequenced as principal diagnosis. Coding directives require that the codes in brackets be sequenced in the order specified in the Alphabetic Index.

EXERCISE F Codes in Brackets

1. A patient was admitted with the diagnosis of malarial hepatitis.

    a. You might not be sure if the principal diagnosis is hepatitis or malaria.

    b. Locate "malaria" in the Index. Under the subterm "any type, with" you will find "hepatitis 084.9 *[573.2]*." The slanted brackets alert you that *[573.2]* cannot be sequenced as the principal diagnosis.

    c. Locate "hepatitis" and then the subterm "malarial." You again find 084.9 *[573.2]*.

    d. Both Index entries directed you to the principal diagnosis of malaria. Hepatitis can be a manifestation of malaria. The slanted brackets in 084.9 *[573.2]* indicate that this hepatitis is a manifestation of the condition malaria. "Hepatitis" is the condition and "malarial" describes the hepatitis.

    e. Under the four-digit code of 084.9 locate "Malarial" and then "Hepatitis." 084.9 Malaria is the principal diagnosis and *[573.2]* hepatitis is the complication, and you would record both, 084.9, 573.2.

You do the next one.

2. The patient's record states: systemic lupus erythematosus with lung involvement.

    a. When you locate the term "erythematosus" in the Index, what do you find? ____________________

    b. Locate the main term "Lupus," the subterm "erythematosus," and the second subterm "systemic," and the last subterm "with lung involvement." What codes are you directed to?

    Code(s): ____________

    c. What is the title of the three-digit category code located in the Tabular for the codes from b above?

    ____

    d. What does the three-digit category code include? ____________

    ____

    e. Under the three-digit category code you are also directed to "Use additional code to identify manifestation." Such as:

    ____

That last entry tells you that you are to use *[517.8]* (lung involvement) if the principal diagnosis is in the three-digit category code 710 and further specified as "with lung involvement." This patient has lung involvement, so be alert to the use of the code in the brackets.

f. What four-digit code designates the principal diagnosis of "systemic lupus erythematosus"?

Code(s): ________________

g. What are the two complete codes for this case?

Code(s): ________________

2.4 TWO OR MORE INTERRELATED CONDITIONS, EACH POTENTIALLY MEETING THE DEFINITION FOR PRINCIPAL DIAGNOSIS

When there are two or more interrelated conditions (such as disease in the same ICD-9-CM chapter or manifestation characteristically associated with a certain disease) potentially meeting the definition of principal diagnosis, either condition may be sequenced first, unless the circumstances of the admission, the therapy provided, the Tabular List, or the Alphabetic Index indicate otherwise.

EXERCISE G *Two or More Interrelated Conditions*

1. A patient is admitted with chest pain, shortness of breath, and a heart murmur. The patient undergoes a diagnostic cardiac catheterization, which shows two-vessel coronary artery disease and severe mitral (valve) stenosis. It is recommended that bypass surgery with mitral valve replacement be performed as soon as possible.

   The patient has two conditions, each of which has the potential to be the principal diagnosis: mitral valve stenosis and coronary artery disease.

   a. Locate stenosis in the Index: both "mitral" and "valve" tell the type and site of stenosis the patient has—the condition is stenosis. Under the main term "Stenosis," locate the subterm "mitral." The words in parentheses indicate the kinds of mitral stenosis, such as valve, chronic, or inactive. You are looking for valve, so the correct four-digit category code for the mitral valve stenosis is likely to be 394.0.

   b. Locate coronary artery disease by locating the main term "Disease" and the subterms "artery" and "coronary." The entry you find refers you to "*see* Arteriosclerosis, coronary." Under the main term "Arteriosclerosis" and the subterm "coronary (artery)" you will be directed to code 414.00. If the Tabular validates codes 394.0 and 414.00, either code could be sequenced first because none of the information indicates one condition is more the principal diagnosis than the other.

   Now you do one.

2. A patient is involved in a car accident and is admitted with an open fracture of the right humerus and an open fracture of the distal femur. Both fractures

will require open reduction, which means that the fracture will be repaired using an open incision into the fracture site.

a. What are the two diagnoses?

____

Either of these diagnoses may be listed first, because both are addressed and plans are made to treat both surgically. They were equally the reason for admission to the hospital.

b. Under what main term in the Index would you look to locate both diagnoses?

____

c. After the main term "Fracture," what would be the first subterm for the fracture of the right humerus?

____

d. What is the word that appears in parentheses after this first subterm you just identified in c above?

____

Because your patient's case states "open," you know that 812.20 is not the correct code because 812.20 specifies "closed." Go farther down the list of subterms to "Fracture, humerus, open." What is the code for open?

Code(s): ______________

e. In the Tabular, does the code you chose in the Index fit the description?

____

You still have to locate the code for the open fracture of distal femur.

f. After looking in the Index using the main term fracture, what is the subterm you would locate?

____

g. What is the word in parentheses after the first subterm?

____

h. What is the next subterm? ______________________________

i. What does this subterm direct you to do?

____

j. When you take the subterm direction, what is the next subterm that you must use to get to the code?

____

k. What is the code that you are directed to look up under "Fracture, femur, open, lower end, open"?

Code(s): ________________

l. After checking the code in the Tabular, is the code correct?

____

Official Coding and Reporting Guidelines

2.5 TWO OR MORE DIAGNOSES THAT EQUALLY MEET THE DEFINITION FOR PRINCIPAL DIAGNOSIS

In the usual instance when two or more diagnoses equally meet the criteria for principal diagnosis as determined by the circumstances of admission, diagnostic workup and/or therapy provided, and the Alphabetic Index, Tabular List, or another coding guideline does not provide sequencing direction, any one of the diagnoses may be sequenced first.

EXERCISE H *Two or More Diagnoses*

1. A patient is admitted with weakness, diarrhea of 2 days' duration, diaphoresis, and abdominal pain. The attending physician lists the diagnoses as viral gastroenteritis and dehydration. Intravenous fluids with electrolyte supplements are ordered.

   a. Locate "Gastroenteritis" as the main term in the Index and then the subterm "viral." When you do this you will be directed to code 008.8 (unspecified) because the record does not specify the organism type.

   b. After you have located code 008.8 in the Tabular and made sure it is the correct code, look for any notes under the three-digit category code to see if there are any fifth digits that need to be assigned.

   c. The correct code was 008.8 and there were no fifth digits to be assigned. Now you need to code the other diagnosis of dehydration. It seems almost too good to be true: There is only one word in the diagnosis. "Dehydration" is the main term. Dehydration appears in the Index, and it points to only one code. Check out the code 276.5 in the Tabular.

   d. The Tabular confirms that 276.5 is for dehydration or volume depletion and there is no note regarding any *Excludes* that concerns this case. There is no fifth digit with the category. The correct code is 276.5.

   e. Remember when two equally important diagnoses are indicated, it does not matter which code is sequenced first. So, the two codes for this case can be stated 008.8 and 276.5 or 276.5 and 008.8. The order of the codes may not seem too earth-shattering right now, but the order of the codes is significant. Later in this text, you will learn about how the hospital payment is made to the hospital by third-party payers based on the diagnosis codes. One of these diagnoses may reimburse higher than the other; therefore, selection of the principal diagnosis is critically important.

Now you have the opportunity to do the next case.

2. A patient is admitted with heavy menstrual bleeding of 2 days' duration, severe abdominal pain, and anemia due to acute blood loss. The patient is given medication intravenously to control the pain and bleeding. She also receives two units of packed cells for the anemia.

   a. What is the medical term for heavy menstrual/uterine bleeding?

      ____

   b. The medical term from the question above is the first diagnosis that you will need to locate. What code does the Index indicate and the Tabular of the text confirm as a code for the first diagnosis?

      Code(s): ______________

   c. The second diagnosis is what? ______________________

   d. Locate the second diagnosis code and confirm your finding in the Tabular. (Hint: The subterms for the second code are "blood loss" and "acute.") What is the code?

      Code(s): ______________

Official Coding and Reporting Guidelines

2.6 TWO OR MORE COMPARATIVE OR CONTRASTING CONDITIONS

In those rare instances when two or more contrasting or comparative diagnoses are documented as "either/or" (or similar terminology), they are coded as if the diagnoses were confirmed and the diagnoses are sequenced according to the circumstances of the admission. If no further determination can be made as to which diagnosis should be principal, either diagnosis may be sequenced first.

EXERCISE I *Two or More Comparative or Contrasting Conditions*

1. A patient is admitted to the hospital with chest pain, nausea, and dyspnea. The patient has a history of a prior myocardial infarction 2 years ago. The pain is atypical. An ECG and cardiac enzyme study (creatine phosphokinase) are ordered, as well as an upper gastrointestinal series to rule out esophageal reflux. Diagnosis by the attending physician is myocardial infarction or esophageal reflux.

   a. Infarction is located by the main term "Infarct, infarction" and subterm "myocardium." In the Tabular, there is a notation of five-digit subclassifications that are used with category 410 codes. You might think that the patient was having a subsequent episode of care until you read the definitions attached to the fifth digits for initial and subsequent. "Subsequent" refers to a patient who has received care for the condition within

8 weeks. This patient was diagnosed and treated 2 years ago, so this episode is considered an initial episode of care and has the "1" fifth digit. The correct code is 410.91.

b. The second diagnosis is reflux, esophageal, located in the Index under the main term "Reflux" and subterm "esophageal." You are directed to code 530.81. After checking this in the Tabular to be sure this is the correct code with no exclusions or additions, you have the second of the two contrasting conditions, 530.81. Only further evaluation by the physician will finally determine what the principal diagnosis is; but for now, the case has been coded to the most specificity possible with the information available in the patient record. Either diagnosis may be selected as the principal diagnosis. You may want to consider which code would result in the higher reimbursement.

Here's a case for you to code.

2. A 75-year-old man is admitted with severe low back pain. He is known to have prostate cancer as well as severe spondylosis. Spine x-ray films and a bone scan are ordered. Differential diagnoses are compression fracture versus bone metastases from prostate cancer. (*Note:* The physician would have to be consulted to determine whether prostate cancer is "current" or "history of.")

   a. What is the main term for compression fracture?

   ____

   b. Using "compression" as the subterm, what are you directed to do?

   ____

   Before you continue to look up other possible subterms, you need to consider why the patient has severe low back pain. You know that it is from a disease process taking place in the patient's body, but you do not know the cause at this time. This is known as pathologic. "Pathologic" is a subterm. Under "Fracture" locate "pathologic" and then the subterm "vertebrae." You are then forwarded to 733.13. Is that the correct code according to the Tabular?

   ____

   c. The second diagnosis in the differential diagnoses is metastases from prostate cancer. Locating cancer in the Index you find: "*see* also Neoplasm, by site, malignant." The potential neoplasm is of the bone. "Neoplasm" is the main term and "bone" is a subterm. Secondary is the type of malignancy because the record states that this patient has had a history of prostate cancer (primary) and now has the potential to have bone (secondary) cancer. Under the "Secondary" column, what is the correct code for "Neoplasm, bone" for this patient?

   Code(s): ______________

   An additional code would be assigned for the prostate cancer.

The difference between Guidelines 2.6 and 2.7 is the way the physician states the final diagnosis. In the Guideline 2.6 examples, there are symptoms documented but the physician states "X versus Y" instead of listing the symptoms. In Guideline 2.7, the physician states the diagnosis as "symptoms due to X versus Y."

2.7 A SYMPTOM(S) FOLLOWED BY CONTRASTING/ COMPARATIVE DIAGNOSES

When a symptom(s) is followed by contrasting/comparative diagnoses, the symptom code is sequenced first. All the contrasting/comparative diagnoses should be coded as suspected conditions.

EXERCISE J A Symptom(s) Followed by Contrasting/Comparative Diagnoses

1. The patient presents with knee pain of 3 months' duration, with no known trauma, either bucket-handle tear of medial meniscus or loose body in the knee joint. The final diagnosis is knee pain due to bucket-handle tear of medial meniscus versus loose body in the knee joint.

   There will be three codes for this case: one for the pain in the knee joint, one for the tear in the meniscus, and one for the loose body in the knee joint.

   a. Using "Pain, joint, knee" for the first condition, what is the correct code?

      Code(s): ____________________

   b. Using "Tear, meniscus, bucket handle, old," what is the correct second code?

      Code(s): ____________________

   c. Using "Loose, body, joint, knee," what is the correct third code?

      Code(s): ____________________

Official Coding and Reporting Guidelines

2.8 CODES FROM THE V71.0-V71.9 SERIES, OBSERVATION AND EVALUATION FOR SUSPECTED CONDITIONS

Codes from the V71.0-V71.9 series are assigned as principal diagnoses for encounters or admissions to evaluate the patient's condition when there is some evidence to suggest the existence of an abnormal condition or following an accident or other incident that ordinarily results in a health problem, and where no supporting evidence for the suspected condition is found and no treatment is currently required. The fact that the patient may be scheduled for continuing observation in the office/clinic setting following discharge does not limit the use of this category.

EXERCISE K Observation and Evaluation for Suspected Conditions

1. The patient fell off his motorcycle when turning too sharply and hit his head on the sidewalk. The patient was wearing a helmet. The examination revealed no outwardly apparent head injury. The only injury noted on examination was abrasion of the elbow. The patient was admitted overnight to the hospital for observation to rule out head injury.

   There will be two codes on this case: one for the observation of the injury (a V code) and one for the abrasion.

   a. Hospital observation is located in the Index under the main term "Observation." Listed under the main term are the reasons for observation, which you know by the word "for" in parentheses after the main term. The subterm is "accident NEC." Check the code in the Tabular. What is the V code?

      Code(s): ____________________

   b. The second code is for the abrasion to the elbow. When you locate "abrasion" in the Index, you are referred to "*see also* Injury, superficial, by site." What is the code for the abrasion?

      Code(s): ____________________

      (See cross reference in the Tabular, and discover if a fourth digit is needed for specificity.)

2. A patient is admitted for observation and further evaluation following an alleged rape.

   a. There is only one code for this case. What is that V code?

      Code(s): ____________________

2.9 ORIGINAL TREATMENT PLAN NOT CARRIED OUT

Sequence as the principal diagnosis the condition which after study occasioned the admission to the hospital, even though treatment may not have been carried out due to unforeseen circumstances.

EXERCISE L Original Treatment Plan Not Carried Out

1. A patient is admitted to the hospital for an elective cholecystectomy. The patient has chronic cholecystitis, and gallstones were visualized on x-ray films. After admission, it is noticed that the patient has a fever, is coughing, and shows some patchy infiltrates on the chest x-ray film. Surgery is canceled because the patient may have pneumonia.

   This case will have three codes: the cholecystitis, pneumonia, and surgery not done.

a. The cholecystitis is chronic (subterm) with calculus (subterm), without mention of obstruction. What is the code?

Code(s): ________________

b. The pneumonia code?

Code(s): ________________

c. The surgery not done is located in the Index under "Surgery, not done because of." Why was the surgery not done?

____

d. What is the code for the surgery not done?

Code(s): ________________

There is no procedure code submitted because no procedure was done.

2. A patient is admitted for elective sterilization by tubal ligation. The patient and her husband decide not to go through with the surgery, and the surgery is canceled.

a. How many codes will there be for this case and what are the main terms for each?

____

b. What is the V code for the sterilization?

Code(s): ________________

c. What is the code for the surgery not done?

Code(s): ________________

TWO SPECIAL TYPES OF CODES YOU NEED TO KNOW ABOUT

There are 17 chapters in Volume 1, Tabular List, of the ICD-9-CM. Each of the chapters represents a different organ system or topic. You will review each of the chapters, but first, there are some special codes that you need to know about—V codes and late effects.

V Codes

Let's begin with the V codes. In the Tabular the V codes follow code 999.9. If you have an ICD-9-CM available, locate the V codes now. Notice that V codes are only two digits before the decimal point with a V preceding the number. V codes can be located in the Index like any other code. Often, the most difficult thing about the V code is locating it in the Index. To help you become familiar with how to locate the V code in the Index, review the following most common Index terms for locating V codes:

Admission	Examination	Replacement
Aftercare	Fitting of	Screening
Attention to	Follow up	Status
Boarder	Health, Healthy	Supervision (of)
Care (of)	History	Test
Carrier	Maintenance	Transplant
Checking	Maladjustment	Unavailability of medical facilities
Contraception	Observation	Vaccination
Counseling	Problem	
Dialysis	Procedure (surgical)	
Donor	Prophylactic	

V codes are most often used in outpatient settings, that is, ambulatory care centers, physician offices, and outpatient departments of hospitals. There are three circumstances in which V codes are used:

1. A patient is not currently sick but receives health care services.

EXAMPLE

An elderly patient comes to the clinic for an influenza vaccination. The patient is not currently sick but receives health care services of a vaccination.

Index: **Vaccination,** prophylactic, influenza V04.8

Tabular: **V04 Need for prophylactic vaccination and inoculation against certain viral diseases**

V04.8 Influenza

Code: V04.8 Influenza vaccination

2. A patient with a known disease or injury receives health services for specific treatment of the disease or injury.

EXAMPLE

A patient with breast cancer reports to the outpatient department of the hospital for a chemotherapy session. The patient is not currently sick but receives health care services for specific treatment of cancer.

Index: **Chemotherapy,** encounter (for) V58.1

Tabular: **V58 Other and unspecified aftercare**

V58.1 Chemotherapy

Code: V58.1 Chemotherapy treatment

The breast cancer (174.9) would also be coded, but you will learn about the details of that later in the chapter; for now, concentrate on the use of the V codes. V codes should not be mistaken for prodecure codes. There is an ICD-9-CM procedure code to identify chemotherapy (99.25). Facility policy and the setting will determine the assignment of the procedure code.

3. A circumstance or problem is present that influences a patient's health status but is not in itself a current illness or injury.

EXAMPLE

A patient who is allergic to penicillin was admitted to the hospital for treatment of pneumonia using intravenous antibiotic. The patient received health services for the pneumonia, but the patient's allergy to penicillin was a special consideration of the treatment received.

Index: **History** (personal) of, allergy to, antibiotic agent NEC V14.1, penicillin V14.0

Tabular: **V14 Personal history of allergy to medicinal agents**

V14.0 Penicillin

Code: V14.0 History of allergy to penicillin

Additionally, the pneumonia (486) would be coded, but you are focusing only on the use of V codes right now.

EXERCISE M *V Codes*

Fill in the V code(s) for the following:

1. Admission for cardiac pacemaker adjustment

   Code(s): ________________

2. Insertion of subdermal implantable contraceptive

   Code(s): ________________

3. Personal history of cancer of the prostate

   Code(s): ________________

4. Baby in for MMR (measles, mumps, rubella) vaccination

   Code(s): ________________

5. Screening mammogram

   Code(s): ________________

6. Clinic visit for pre-employment physical examination

   Code(s): ________________

7. Family history of diabetes mellitus

   Code(s): ________________

8. Encounter for dressing change

   Code(s): ____________________

9. Admission for breast implant

   Code(s): ____________________

10. Examination following treatment for a fracture

    Code(s): ____________________

11. History of allergy to penicillin

    Code(s): ____________________

12. Observation for alleged rape

    Code(s): ____________________

13. Problem with career choice

    Code(s): ____________________

14. Status, postoperative, transplant of heart valve

    Code(s): ____________________

15. Vaccination for smallpox

    Code(s): ____________________

Often, the patient record will state "history of" a disease: for example, "history of diabetes mellitus." This does not mean that the patient no longer has diabetes mellitus, but that the patient's medical history includes diabetes mellitus. You would not assign a V code to indicate a previous history of diabetes mellitus, but instead would assign the code for the current disease of diabetes mellitus (250.0X). If there is any question regarding the current status of the disease, check with the physician. You may also want to offer some physician education regarding documentation of past history of diseases.

Late Effects

Late effect codes are not assigned to a separate chapter in the Tabular. Instead, you must first identify a case as a late effect and then code it as such. You use late effect codes when the acute phase of the illness or injury has passed. Sometimes an acute illness or injury will leave the patient with a residual health problem that remains after the illness or injury has resolved. The residual is coded first and then the late effect code is assigned to indicate the cause of the residual. Note that the late effect code is accessed in the Index under the main term "Late." An example would be scars that remain after a severe burn.

In most instances, two codes will be assigned—one code for the residual that is being treated and one code that will indicate the cause (late effect) of the residual. There is no time limit for the development of a residual. It may be evident at the time of the acute illness or it may occur months after an injury. It is also possible that a patient may develop more than one residual. For example, a patient who has had a stroke may develop right-sided hemiparesis and aphasia.

2.10 RESIDUAL CONDITION OR NATURE OF THE LATE EFFECT

The residual condition or nature of the late effect is sequenced first, followed by the late effect code for the cause of the residual condition, except in a few instances where the Alphabetic Index or Tabular List directs otherwise.

For example, a person cannot have a current hip fracture (820.8) and late effect of hip fracture (905.3). The code is either a current injury or a condition caused by the prior injury. It cannot be both at the same time.

Official Coding and Reporting Guidelines

1.7 LATE EFFECT

A late effect is the residual effect (condition produced) after the acute phase of an illness or injury has terminated. There is no time limit on when a late effect code can be used. The residual may be apparent early, such as in cerebrovascular accident cases, or it may occur months or years later, such as that due to a previous injury.

Coding of late effects requires two codes:

A. The residual condition or nature of the late effect.
B. The cause of the late effect.

The residual condition or nature of the late effect is sequenced first, followed by the cause of the late effect, except in those few instances where the code for late effect is followed by a manifestation code identified in the Tabular List and title or the late effect code has been expanded (at the fourth- and fifth-digit levels) to include the manifestation(s).

The code for the acute phase of an illness or injury that led to the late effect is never used with a code for the cause of the late effect.

Official Coding and Reporting Guidelines

A. LATE EFFECT OF CEREBROVASCULAR DISEASE

Category 438 is used to indicate conditions classifiable to categories 430-437 as the causes of late effects (neurologic deficits), themselves classified elsewhere. These "late effects" include neurologic deficits that persist after initial onset of conditions classifiable to 430-437. The neurologic deficits caused by cerebrovascular disease may be present from the onset or may arise at any time after the onset of the condition classifiable to 430-437.

Codes from category 438 may be assigned on a health care record with codes from 430-437 if the patient has a current CVA and deficits from an old CVA.

Assign code V12.59 (and not a code from category 438) as an additional code for history of cerebrovascular disease when no neurologic deficits are present.

EXAMPLE

Diagnosis: Dysphagia due to a previous cerebrovascular accident

Residual: Dysphagia

The dysphagia is a problem that remains following the acute illness of the cerebrovascular accident.

Cause: Cerebrovascular accident

(This patient had a previous cerebrovascular accident.)

Terms to code: Dysphagia [residual]

Cerebrovascular accident [cause]

EXERCISE N *Residual and Cause Terms*

Write the term(s) that represent the residual and the cause on the lines provided for the following:

1. Scars of the face from third-degree burns suffered 1 year ago

   Residual ____________________

   Cause ____________________

2. Constrictive pericarditis due to old tuberculosis infection

   Residual ____________________

   Cause ____________________

3. Residual foreign body in femur due to gunshot injury years ago

   Residual ____________________

   Cause ____________________

4. Mental retardation due to previous poliomyelitis

   Residual ____________________

   Cause ____________________

5. Leg pain from old fracture of femur

   Residual ____________________

   Cause ____________________

As Guideline 1.7 indicates, you usually sequence the code for the residual condition first, followed by the late effect code. To locate the late effects codes in the ICD-9-CM, use the entry "Late Effects" in the Index. There are numerous subterms that describe the various late effects. Review and become familiar with the late effects subterms.

EXAMPLE

The following are the steps that you would take to correctly code the example of dysphagia due to a previous cerebrovascular accident as used in the preceding example.

Diagnosis: Dysphagia due to a previous cerebrovascular accident

Index: **Late, cerebrovascular disease with dysphagia** 438.82

EXERCISE O Residual and Cause Codes

Now you identify the residual and cause terms and then code the following diagnoses:

1. Traumatic arthritis following fracture of the left ankle 3 years ago

   Residual ______________________

   Code(s): __________

   Cause ______________________

   Code(s): __________

2. Aphasia due to cerebrovascular accident 6 months ago (Requires one combination code.)

   Residual ______________________

   Cause ______________________

   Code: __________

3. Sensorineural deafness due to previous meningitis

   Residual ______________________

   Code(s): __________

   Cause ______________________

   Code(s): __________

4. Severe mental retardation due to previous viral encephalitis

   Residual ______________________________

   Code(s): ______________

   Cause ______________________________

   Code(s): ______________

5. Nonunion of left tibia fracture (closed)

   Residual ______________________________

   Code(s): ______________

   Cause ______________________________

   Code(s): ______________

6. Osteoporosis due to previous poliomyelitis

   Residual ______________________________

   Code(s): ______________

   Cause ______________________________

   Code(s): ______________

7. Flaccid hemiplegia affecting dominant side due to cerebrovascular accident 4 months ago

   Residual and Cause ______________________________

   Code: ______________

CHAPTER-SPECIFIC GUIDELINES

Infectious and Parasitic Diseases

Chapter 1 in the Tabular is Infectious and Parasitic Diseases, which classifies diseases according to the etiology or cause of the disease. Because infectious or parasitic conditions can affect different parts of our body, the chapter contains a wide variety of codes.

In this chapter there are many instances of combination coding and multiple coding. Remember: *Combination coding* applies when one code fully describes the condition. *Multiple coding* is acceptable when it takes more than one code to fully describe the condition.

EXAMPLE

Combination Coding

Diagnosis: Candidiasis infection of the mouth

Index: **Candidiasis,** candidal 112.9, mouth 112.0

Tabular: **112.0 Candidiasis of mouth**

Code: 112.0 Candidiasis infection of the mouth

The code 112.0 fully describes the diagnosis.

Multiple Coding

Diagnosis: Urinary tract infection due to *Escherichia coli (E. coli)*

Index: **Infection,** infected, infective, urinary (tract) NEC 599.0

Tabular: **599.0 Urinary tract infection, site not specified**

Use additional code to identify organism, such as *Escherichia coli [E. coli]* (041.4)

Code 599.0 does not fully describe the condition. The instructions in the Tabular for code 599.0 state that you are to also code the organism causing the urinary tract infection. To locate a causative organism, you locate the main term "infection" in the Index and then the subterm of the specific organism.

EXAMPLE

Index: **Infection,** infected, infective, *Escherichia coli* NEC 041.4

Tabular: **041 Bacterial infection in conditions classified elsewhere and of unspecified site**

041.4 *Escherichia coli [E. coli]*

Codes: 599.0, 041.4 Urinary tract infection due to *Escherichia coli (E. coli)*

Multiple coding was necessary to fully describe the infection of the urinary tract and the causative organism of *E. coli.*

Human Immunodeficiency

Another important category in Chapter 1 is 042 Human Immunodeficiency Virus (HIV) Disease. Review the guidelines for HIV codes.

HUMAN IMMUNODEFICIENCY VIRUS (HIV) INFECTIONS

10.1 CODE ONLY CONFIRMED CASES OF HIV INFECTION/ILLNESS.

This is an exception to Guideline 1.8, which states, "If the diagnosis documented at the time of discharge is qualified as 'probable,' 'suspect,' 'likely,' 'questionable,' 'possible,' or 'still to be ruled out,' code the condition as if it existed or was established." In this context, confirmation does not require documentation of positive serology or culture for HIV; the physician's diagnostic statement that the patient is HIV positive, or has an HIV-related illness, is sufficient.

10.2 SELECTION OF HIV CODE

042 Human Immunodeficiency Virus (HIV) Disease
Patients with an HIV-related illness should be coded to 042, Human Immunodeficiency Virus [HIV] Disease.

V08 Asymptomatic Human Immunodeficiency Virus (HIV) Infection
Patients with physician-documented asymptomatic HIV infections who have never had an HIV-related illness should be coded to V08, Asymptomatic Human Immunodeficiency Virus [HIV] Infection.

795.71 Nonspecific Serologic Evidence of Human Immunodeficiency Virus [HIV]
Code 795.71, Nonspecific serologic evidence of human immunodeficiency virus [HIV] should be used for patients (including infants) with inconclusive HIV test results.

10.3 PREVIOUSLY DIAGNOSED HIV-RELATED ILLNESS

Patients with any known prior diagnosis of an HIV-related illness should be coded to 042. Once a patient has developed an HIV-related illness, the patient should always be assigned code 042 on every subsequent admission. Patients previously diagnosed with any HIV illness (042) should never be assigned with 795.71 or V08.

10.4 SEQUENCING

The sequencing of diagnoses for patients with HIV-related illnesses follows Guideline 2 for selection of principal diagnosis. That is, the circumstances of admission govern the selection of principal diagnosis, that condition established after study to be chiefly responsible for occasioning the admission of the patient to the hospital for care.

Patients who are admitted for an HIV-related illness should be assigned a minimum of two codes: first assign code 042 to identify the HIV disease and then sequence additional codes to identify the other diagnoses.

If a patient is admitted for an HIV-related condition, the principal diagnosis should be 042, followed by additional diagnosis codes for all reported HIV-related conditions.

If a patient with HIV disease is admitted for an unrelated condition (such as a traumatic injury), the code for the unrelated condition (e.g., the nature of injury code) should be the principal diagnosis. Other diagnoses would be 042 followed by additional diagnosis codes for all reported HIV-related conditions.

Whether the patient is newly diagnosed or has had previous admissions for HIV conditions (or has expired) is irrelevant to the sequencing decision.

10.5 HIV INFECTIONS IN PREGNANCY, CHILDBIRTH, AND PUERPERIUM

During pregnancy, childbirth, or the puerperium, a patient admitted because of an HIV-related illness should receive a principal diagnosis of 647.8X, other specified infectious and parasitic diseases in the mother classifiable elsewhere, but complicating the pregnancy, childbirth, or the puerperium, followed by 042 and the code(s) for the HIV-related illness(es). This is an exception to the sequencing rule found in 10.4 above.

Patients with asymptomatic HIV infection status admitted during pregnancy, childbirth, or the puerperium should receive codes of 647.8X and V08.

10.6 ASYMPTOMATIC HIV INFECTION

V08 Asymptomatic human immunodeficiency virus (HIV) infection, is to be applied when the patient without any documentation of symptoms is listed as being HIV positive, known HIV, HIV test positive, or similar terminology. Do not use this code if the term AIDS is used or if the patient is treated for any HIV-related illness or is described as having any condition(s) resulting from his/her HIV positive status; use code 042 in these cases.

10.7 INCONCLUSIVE LABORATORY TEST FOR HIV

Patients with inconclusive HIV serology, but no definitive diagnosis or manifestations of the illness may be assigned code 795.71, inconclusive serologic test for Human Immunodeficiency Virus [HIV].

10.8 TESTING FOR HIV

If the patient is asymptomatic but wishes to know his/her HIV status, use code V73.89, Screening for other specified viral disease. Use code V69.8, Other problems related to lifestyle, as a secondary code if an asymptomatic patient is in a known high-risk group for HIV. Should a patient with signs or symptoms or illness, or a confirmed HIV-related diagnosis be tested for HIV, code the signs and symptoms or the diagnosis. An additional counseling code V65.44 may be used if counseling is provided during the encounter for the test.

When the patient returns to be informed of his/her HIV test results, use code V65.44, HIV counseling, if the results of the test are negative. If the results are positive but the patient is asymptomatic, use code V08, Asymptomatic HIV infection. If the results are positive and the patient is symptomatic, use code 042, HIV infection, with codes for the HIV-related symptoms or diagnosis. The HIV counseling code may also be used if counseling is provided for patients with positive test results.

As stated in Guideline 10.1, you do not assign 042 to a patient's record or insurance claim unless the diagnosis of HIV is a confirmed diagnosis. The assignment of the code prior to a confirmation may cause the patient many unwarranted problems if the patient does not have HIV. Use extreme caution when assigning the 042.

Official Coding and Reporting Guidelines

7 SEPTICEMIA AND SEPTIC SHOCK

When the diagnosis of septicemia with shock or the diagnosis of general sepsis with septic shock is documented, code and list the septicemia first and report the septic shock code as a secondary condition. The septicemia code assignment should identify the type of bacteria if it is known.

Sepsis and septic shock associated with abortion, ectopic pregnancy, and molar pregnancy are classified to category codes in Chapter 11 (630-639).

Negative or inconclusive blood cultures do not preclude a diagnosis of septicemia in patients with clinical evidence of the condition.

EXERCISE P *Infectious and Parasitic Diseases*

Code the following infectious diseases:

1. Viral gastroenteritis

   Code(s): ____________________

2. Septicemia due to *Pseudomonas* with septic shock

   Code(s): ____________________

3. Acute poliomyelitis

   Code(s): ____________________

4. Candidal vaginal infection

   Code(s): ____________________

5. Viral hepatitis A

   Code(s): ____________________

6. Tinea pedis

   Code(s): ____________________

7. Herpes zoster

   Code(s): ____________________

8. Acute prostatitis due to *streptococcus*

   Code(s): ____________________

9. Viral syndrome

   Code(s): ____________________

10. Exposure to HIV

    Code(s): ____________________

11. Asymptomatic HIV

    Code(s): ____________________

12. Positive HIV blood test (asymptomatic)

    Code(s): ____________________

13. Kaposi's sarcoma due to AIDS

    Code(s): ____________________

14. AIDS with *Pneumocystis carinii* pneumonia

    Code(s): ____________________

Neoplasms

Chapter 2 in the Tabular is similar to Chapter 1, Infectious and Parasitic Diseases, in that it classifies diseases according to the etiology or cause of the disease. Neoplastic conditions can affect all parts of the body. Before you learn more about what is in Chapter 2, we will quickly review some of the specific terminology.

EXERCISE Q *Neoplasms Terminology*

Match the following terms to the correct definitions:

1. neoplasm _______
2. malignant _______
3. primary _______
4. secondary _______
5. benign _______
6. in situ _______
7. uncertain behavior _______
8. unspecified nature _______
9. morphology _______

a. not progressive or recurrent
b. malignancy that is located within the original site of development
c. used to describe a cancerous tumor that grows worse over time
d. study of neoplasms
e. refers to the behavior of a neoplasm as neither malignant nor benign but having characteristics of both malignant and benign
f. when the behavior or histology of a neoplasm is not known or not specified
g. site to which a malignant tumor has spread
h. site of origin or where the tumor originated
i. new tumor growth that can be benign or malignant

Locating a code for a neoplasm is a two-step process:

1. First, locate the morphology or histologic type of the neoplasm in the Index, for example, carcinoma, adenocarcinoma, sarcoma, melanoma, lymphoma, lipoma, adenoma.
2. Once you have located the morphology, review all modifiers and subterms, and then follow the instructions or verify the code listed. Most often you will be instructed to turn to the Neoplasm Table in the Index to find the code.

When you locate the morphology of the neoplasm, you can identify the "M" or morphology code. The M codes are in parentheses following the morphology. M codes are optional, so facility policy would determine their usage.

M codes are an alphanumeric code and are listed in Appendix A of the ICD-9-CM code book. The alphanumeric structure of the morphology codes starts with the letter M, followed by four digits that indicate the histologic type of neoplasm, and a slash, followed by a fifth digit that indicates the behavior.

Behavior

/0 =	Benign
/1 =	Uncertain whether benign or malignant
	Borderline malignancy
/2 =	Carcinoma in situ
	Intraepithelial
	Noninfiltrating
	Noninvasive
/3 =	Malignant, primary site
/6 =	Malignant, metastatic site
	Secondary site
/9 =	Malignant, uncertain whether primary or metastatic site

EXAMPLE

ICD-9-CM Codes and Morphology Codes

Diagnosis:	Adenocarcinoma of the upper-outer quadrant right breast with metastasis to the axillary lymph nodes.
Index:	**Adenocarcinoma** (M8140/3)—*see also* Neoplasm, by site, malignant
Neoplasm Table:	Breast, upper-outer quadrant 174.4 (primary column)
	Lymph, lymphatic, gland (secondary column), axilla, axillary 196.3
Tabular:	**174 Malignant neoplasm of female breast**
	174.4 Upper-outer quadrant

196 Secondary and unspecified malignant neoplasm of lymph nodes

196.3 Lymph nodes of axilla and upper limb

Codes: 174.4, 196.3 Adenocarcinoma of the upper outer quadrant right breast with metastasis to the axillary lymph nodes.

But, wait, you're not done yet. You have two M codes to assign to this diagnosis before you are finished—one for the primary adenocarcinoma and one for a secondary adenocarcinoma. Both M codes will have the same histologic type of adenocarcinoma, but the fifth digit will be different to indicate the primary and secondary behaviors.

Index: **Adenocarcinoma** (M8140/3)—*see also* Neoplasm, by site, malignant

M code: **primary** adenocarcinoma of the breast, M8140/**3**

M code: **secondary** adenocarcinoma of the axillary lymph nodes, M8140/**6**

ICD-9-CM and M Codes: 174.4, M8140/3, 196.3, M8140/6 Adenocarcinoma of the upper-outer quadrant right breast with metastasis to the axillary lymph nodes.

Note that the M codes are sequenced after the ICD-9-CM diagnosis code to which they refer.

Official Coding and Reporting Guidelines

2.13 NEOPLASMS

A. If the treatment is directed at the malignancy, designate the malignancy as the principal diagnosis, except when the purpose of the encounter or hospital admission is for radiotherapy session(s), V58.0, or for chemotherapy session(s), V58.1, in which instance the malignancy is coded and sequenced second.
B. When a patient is admitted for the purpose of radiotherapy or chemotherapy and develops complications, such as uncontrolled nausea and vomiting or dehydration, the principal diagnosis is Encounter for radiotherapy, V58.0, or Encounter for chemotherapy, V58.1.
C. When an episode of inpatient care involves surgical removal of a primary site or secondary site malignancy followed by adjunct chemotherapy or radiotherapy, code the malignancy as the principal diagnosis, using codes in the 140-198 series or, where appropriate, in the 200-203 series.
D. When the reason for admission is to determine the extent of the malignancy, or for a procedure such as paracentesis or thoracentesis, the primary malignancy or appropriate metastatic site is designated as the principal diagnosis, even though chemotherapy or radiotherapy is administered.
E. When the primary malignancy has been previously excised or eradicated from its site and there is no adjunct treatment directed to that site and no evidence of

any remaining malignancy at the primary site, use the appropriate code from the V10 series to indicate the former site of primary malignancy. Any mention of extension, invasion, or metastasis to a nearby structure or organ or to a distant site is coded as a secondary malignant neoplasm to the site and may be the principal diagnosis in the absence of the primary site.

F. When a patient is admitted because of a primary neoplasm with metastasis and treatment is directed toward the secondary site only, the secondary neoplasm is designated as the principal diagnosis even though the primary malignancy is still present.

G. Symptoms, signs, and ill-defined conditions listed in Chapter 16 characteristic of, or associated with, an existing primary or secondary site malignancy cannot be used to replace the malignancy as principal diagnosis, regardless of the number of admissions or encounters for treatment and care of the neoplasm.

H. Coding and sequencing of complications associated with the malignancy neoplasm or with the therapy thereof are subject to the following guidelines:

1. When admission is for management of an anemia associated with the malignancy, and the treatment is only for anemia, the anemia is designated as the principal diagnosis and is followed by the appropriate code(s) for the malignancy.
2. When admission is for management of an anemia associated with chemotherapy or radiotherapy and the only treatment is for the anemia, the anemia is designated as the principal diagnosis followed by the appropriate code(s) for the malignancy.
3. When the admission is for management of dehydration due to the malignancy or the therapy, or a combination of both, and only the dehydration is being treated (intravenous rehydration), the dehydration is designated as the principal diagnosis, followed by the code(s) for the malignancy.
4. When the admission is for treatment of a complication resulting from a surgical procedure performed for the treatment of an intestinal malignancy, designate the complication as the principal diagnosis if treatment is directed at resolving the complication.

V codes are also frequently used when coding neoplasms. There are V codes present in the ICD-9-CM to indicate the personal history of a malignant neoplasm (V10.00-V10.9). These history codes are used to indicate a primary malignant neoplasm that is no longer present. Remember in the V code section you were presented with information about documenting a "history of" a disease. Be careful in determining whether the physician is indicating a past and current history of a condition or a true past "history of." With neoplasms there is often a true "history of" whereby the condition previously existed but is no longer present.

There are also encounter codes for chemotherapy (V58.1) and radiotherapy (V58.0). When coding an encounter for chemotherapy or radiotherapy, code the V code first, followed by the active code for the malignant neoplasm even if that neoplasm has already been removed. As long as the neoplasm is being treated as adjunctive therapy following a surgical removal of the cancer, you can code that neoplasm as if it still exists. You would not assign a "history of" V code because the neoplasm is the reason for the treatment. Instead, the neoplasm is coded as a current or active disease.

EXERCISE R Neoplasms

1. A patient is admitted for chemotherapy for ovarian cancer.

   There are two codes needed for this case: one for the encounter for chemotherapy and the other for the malignant, primary, ovarian neoplasm.

   Locate in the Index and verify in the Tabular the two codes necessary to code this case.

   Code(s): ____________________

2. A patient is admitted for radiation therapy for metastatic bone cancer. The patient had a mastectomy for breast cancer 3 years earlier.

   There is a code for the admission for radiation management, which will be a V code; a code for the secondary, malignant, bone neoplasm; and a V code for the history of malignant neoplasm of the breast. What are these three codes?

   Code(s): ____________________

3. A patient is admitted with chest pain, shortness of breath, and a history of bloody sputum. Diagnostic x-ray film shows a mass in the bronchial tube. A diagnostic bronchoscopy is performed and is positive for cancer. The pathology report states "metastatic carcinoma of bronchus, primary unknown." The patient chooses to have chemotherapy performed.

   a. What is the description of the principal diagnosis? ____________________

   b. What is the subsequent diagnosis description? ____________________

   c. Is metastatic carcinoma of the bronchus considered a primary or secondary malignant neoplasm? ____________________

   d. What are the diagnosis codes for this case?

      Code(s): ____________________

4. A patient is admitted with uncontrolled nausea and vomiting after chemotherapy treatment for lung cancer.

   a. How many codes would be needed to accurately reflect this case? _____

   b. What is the principal diagnosis? ____________________

   c. What is the secondary diagnosis? ____________________

   d. What is the code for the principal diagnosis?

      Code(s): ____________________

   e. What is the code for the secondary diagnosis?

      Code(s): ____________________

Unknown Site or Unspecified

There is an entry, "unknown site or unspecified," on the Neoplasm Table. This code, 199.1, is used to indicate either an unknown or an unspecified primary or secondary malignancy. If there is a known secondary site, there must be a code assigned to the primary site or history of a primary site. It is possible for a primary site to be unknown.

EXAMPLE

Diagnosis: Metastatic bone cancer.

This statement indicates that the bone cancer is a secondary neoplasm, but there is no indication of the location of the primary site.

Index:	**Cancer** (M8000/3)—*see also* Neoplasm, by site, malignant
Neoplasm Table:	Bone 198.5 (secondary)
	Unknown site or unspecified 199.1 (primary)
Tabular:	**198 Secondary malignant neoplasm of other specified site**
	198.5 Bone and bone marrow
Tabular:	**199 Malignant neoplasm without specification of site**
	199.1 Other
Codes:	198.5, 199.1 Metastatic bone cancer (if the treatment is for the secondary site)
	199.1, 198.5 Metastatic bone cancer (if the treatment is for the primary site)

The sequencing of the primary and secondary neoplasms is dependent on the treatment circumstances documented in the health record. If treatment was directed toward the secondary malignancy, that code would be sequenced first. If treatment is focused on determining the site of the unknown primary, that code would be sequenced first.

EXERCISE S *More Neoplasms*

Practice assigning ICD-9-CM codes as well as the appropriate M codes for the following neoplasms:

1. Multiple myeloma

   Code(s): ________________

2. Carcinoma in situ cervix

   Code(s): ________________

3. Cancer of the sigmoid colon with spread to the peritoneum

   Code(s): ____________________

4. Adenocarcinoma of the prostate with metastasis to the bone

   Code(s): ____________________

5. Metastatic cancer to the brain; primary unknown

   Code(s): ____________________

6. Metastatic carcinoma of the breast to the lungs; the breast carcinoma has been removed by mastectomy

   Code(s): ____________________

7. Admission for radiotherapy for lymphoma nodes of the neck

   Code(s): ____________________

8. Tumor abdomen

   Code(s): ____________________

9. Lipoma subcutaneous tissue of the face

   Code(s): ____________________

10. Hepatocellular adenoma

    Code(s): ____________________

Endocrine, Nutritional, and Metabolic Diseases and Immunity Disorders

Chapter 3 in the Tabular describes diseases or conditions affecting the endocrine system. The endocrine system involves glands that are located throughout the body and are responsible for secreting hormones into the bloodstream. Also included in Chapter 3 are diseases or conditions that affect nutritional and metabolic status as well as disorders of the immune system.

One of the frequently used category codes in Chapter 3 is 250 Diabetes Mellitus. When you locate diabetes in the Index, you will note that many of the subterms have two codes listed. The 250.X code will be followed by an italicized code in brackets. This is because multiple coding is common with the diabetes code inasmuch as both the manifestation (symptom) and the etiology (cause—diabetes) are coded.

EXAMPLE

Index: **Diabetes,** retinopathy, background, 250.5 *[362.01]*

There are four five-digit subclassifications for use with category 250. It is essential that you read these before assigning codes for diagnosis of diabetes (DM). The fifth digits identify the type of diabetes: 2 is type II [non-insulin dependent type] [NIDDM type] [adult onset type] or unspecified type, uncontrolled; and 3 is type I [insulin dependent type] [IDDM] [juvenile type], uncontrolled. NIDDM refers to non-insulin dependent diabetes mellitus and IDDM refers to insulin dependent diabetes mellitus. It is possible for a type II diabetic to receive insulin, so it is best if the health care providers document the type. You should not assume that because a patient is receiving insulin that he or she is insulin dependent. In order to appropriately assign the fifth digits 2 or 3, uncontrolled diabetes, the physician must document that the patient's DM is uncontrolled or out-of-control. If a complication is specified (250.1-250.8), assign the appropriate fourth and fifth digits; do not use the .9 (unspecified).

EXAMPLE

Diagnosis: Diabetic iritis

Index: **Diabetes, diabetic,** iritis 250.5 *[364.42]*

The first code (250.5) indicates the etiology (diabetes) and the second code *[364.42]* indicates the manifestation (iritis). You need two codes to describe diagnosis. You will always code first the etiology and then the manifestation.

Tabular: **250.5 Diabetes with ophthalmic manifestations**

Use additional code, if desired, to identify manifestation, as:

364.4 Vascular disorders of iris and ciliary body

The Tabular also indicates that a fifth digit should be added for greater specificity.

Tabular: **364.4 Vascular disorders of iris and ciliary body**

364.42 Rubeosis iridis

Even though the 364.42 entry above does not specifically indicate iritis, you trust the code that is listed in the Index. You could also look up the main term "Iritis" in the Index and be directed to the same codes.

Index: **Iritis** 364.3, diabetic 250.5 *[364.42]*

You are directed to the same codes.

Code(s): 250.50, 364.42 Diabetic iritis

The codes must be sequenced in this order and indicate that iritis is a manifestation of the diabetes.

To code a disease or condition as a manifestation of diabetes mellitus it must be stated that the disease or condition is diabetic or due to the diabetes. A cause-and-effect relationship must be evident. If you are unsure of the relationship, you must clarify this with the physician.

If a cause-and-effect relationship is not evident, the following codes would be assigned.

EXAMPLE

Diagnosis: Diabetes mellitus and iritis

Index: **Diabetes, diabetic** 250.0

Note—Use the following fifth-digit subclassification with category 250:

The "Note" in the Index directs you to use a fifth digit for greater specificity.

Tabular: **250.0 Diabetes mellitus without mention of complication**

Index: **Iritis** 364.3

Tabular: **364.3 Unspecified iridocyclitis**

Code(s): 250.00 Diabetes and 364.3 Iritis

Note that codes (250.00 and 364.3) are different because a cause-and-effect relationship was not established—the iritis is not a manifestation of the diabetes in this case.

EXERCISE T *Endocrine Diseases*

Fill in the codes for the following:

1. Addison's disease

   Code(s): ___________________

2. Dehydration

   Code(s): ___________________

3. Diabetes mellitus with hypoglycemic coma

   Code(s): ___________________

4. Graves' disease with thyrotoxic crisis

   Code(s): ___________________

5. Vitamin K deficiency

   Code(s): ___________________

6. Gangrene, left great toe, due to diabetes mellitus, insulin dependent

   Code(s): ___________________

7. Diabetic nephropathy, type II, uncontrolled

   Code(s): ___________________

8. Hypercholesterolemia

   Code(s): ___________________

9. Stein-Leventhal syndrome

   Code(s): ________________

10. Hypothyroidism

   Code(s): ________________

Diseases of the Blood and Blood-Forming Organs

Chapter 4, Diseases of the Blood and Blood-Forming Organs, is a short chapter with only 10 categories. The *anemia category* is often used from this chapter because anemia is the most common blood disease. Anemia is the main term under which you will find the many subterms that relate to anemia. In addition to the numerous subterms for anemia, many of the subterms have lengthy additional subterms listed under them.

There are two anemias that are easy to confuse—anemia of chronic disease and chronic anemia. These two diagnostic statements do not have the same meaning. In "anemia of chronic disease," the word "chronic" describes the nature of the disease that is the cause of the anemia, for example, "Anemia due to chronic renal failure." The chronic renal failure is the chronic disease causing anemia. Code anemia (285.9) and chronic renal failure (585) separately. In the diagnostic statement "chronic anemia," the word "chronic" describes a type of anemia. Let's see what difference these diagnostic statements make in code assignment.

EXAMPLE

Diagnosis: Anemia of chronic disease

In this diagnosis statement, you do not know what the chronic disease is.

Index: **Anemia** 285.9

The Index has no subterm that further directs you to a chronic disease.

Tabular: **285.9 Anemia,** unspecified

Code: 285.9 Anemia of chronic disease

Diagnosis: Chronic anemia

Index: **Anemia** 285.9, chronic simple 281.9

In this example, the Index does indicate a subterm that further directs you to chronic simple 281.9.

Tabular: **281.9 Unspecified deficiency anemia**

Code: 281.9 Chronic anemia

If there is any question about how to classify an anemia, check with the physician.

EXERCISE U Diseases of the Blood and Blood-Forming Organs

Fill in the codes for the following:

1. Pernicious anemia

   Code(s): ________________

2. Disseminated intravascular coagulation (DIC)

   Code(s): ________________

3. Hemophilia

   Code(s): ________________

4. Acute blood loss anemia

   Code(s): ________________

5. Familial polycythemia

   Code(s): ________________

6. Screening for iron deficiency anemia

   Code(s): ________________

7. Folate deficiency anemia due to dietary causes

   Code(s): ________________

8. Von Willebrand's disease

   Code(s): ________________

9. Idiopathic eosinophilia

   Code(s): ________________

10. Sickle-cell thalassemia

    Code(s): ________________

Mental Disorders

Chapter 5 in the Tabular is Mental Disorders. The chapter includes four sections: organic psychotic conditions; other psychoses; neurotic, personality, and other nonpsychotic mental disorders; and mental retardation.

Appendix B in the ICD-9-CM is the Glossary of Mental Disorders. Your understanding of the definitions of these mental disorders is necessary to enable you to code these diagnoses accurately. When assigning codes from Chapter 5, you need to take extra care to select the appropriate code(s) and code only diagnoses that are documented in the medical record. Mental disorders can also be difficult to code because physicians are not always as specific in their diagnostic statements as the coder might need as required by the coding in this chapter. When in doubt, always check with the physician. Just one term in the medical record can make a big difference in the code(s) you use.

You should be aware that there is a V code for history of alcoholism (V11.3). Instead of using that code you use the alcoholism code (303.9x) with a fifth digit of "3," which specifies "in remission." It is rare to assign code V11.3 because the disease of alcoholism cannot be cured.

Five-Digit Subclassification

A five-digit subclassification is provided for categories 303-305 to indicate the patient's pattern of use of alcohol or drugs:

-0:	unspecified	
-1:	continuous:	Alcohol: refers to daily intake of large amounts of alcohol or regular heavy drinking on weekends or days off from work Drugs: daily or almost daily use of drugs
-2:	episodic:	Alcohol: refers to alcoholic binges lasting weeks or months, followed by long periods of sobriety Drugs: indicates short periods between drug use or use on weekends.
-3:	remission:	Refers either to a complete cessation of alcohol or drug intake or to the period during which a decrease toward cessation is taking place

Another often encountered instance is when you are instructed to "Use additional code to identify the associated neurological condition" or "Use additional code to identify cerebral atherosclerosis (437.0)," etc. Pay close attention to the instructions given in the Tabular when you see these instructions.

EXAMPLE

Diagnosis: Arteriosclerotic dementia with delirium

Index: **Dementia** 294.8, arteriosclerotic (simple type) (uncomplicated) 290.40, with, delirium 290.41

Tabular: **290 Senile and presenile organic psychotic conditions**

290.4 Arteriosclerotic dementia

Use additional code to identify cerebral atherosclerosis (437.0)

290.41 Arteriosclerotic dementia with delirium

Tabular: **437 Other and ill-defined cerebrovascular disease**

437.0 Cerebral atherosclerosis

Codes: 290.41, 437.0 Arteriosclerotic dementia with delirium

EXERCISE V Mental Disorders

Now you have a chance to show your skill by coding the following:

1. Alzheimer's dementia

   Code(s): ____________________

2. Depression with anxiety

   Code(s): ____________________

3. Profound mental retardation

   Code(s): ____________________

4. Anorexia nervosa

   Code(s): ____________________

5. Delirium tremens due to chronic alcoholism, continuous

   Code(s): ____________________

6. Chronic schizophrenia, paranoid-type

   Code(s): ____________________

7. Drug withdrawal syndrome due to dependence on heroin

   Code(s): ____________________

8. Tobacco abuse

   Code(s): ____________________

9. Antisocial personality disorder

   Code(s): ____________________

10. Panic attack

    Code(s): ____________________

Diseases of the Nervous System and Sense Organs

Chapter 6, Diseases of the Nervous System and Sense Organs, in the Tabular describes diseases or conditions affecting the central nervous system and the peripheral nervous system. It also includes disorders and diseases of the eyes and ears.

The chapter uses some combination codes in which one code identifies both the manifestation and the etiology.

EXAMPLE

Diagnosis: Pneumococcal meningitis

This diagnostic statement means the meningitis is due to the pneumococcal bacteria.

Index: **Meningitis**, pneumococcal 320.1

Tabular: **320 Bacterial meningitis**

320.1 Pneumococcal meningitis

Code: 320.1 Pneumococcal meningitis

Code 320.1 includes the manifestation of meningitis and also the etiology of pneumococcal organism.

In Chapter 6, you will also find conditions that are manifestations of other diseases. These categories are typed in italics in the Tabular and provide instructions to code the underlying disease process first.

EXAMPLE

Diagnosis: Chronic iridocyclitis due to sarcoidosis

Index: **Iridocyclitis** NEC 364.3, chronic, in, sarcoidosis 135 *[364.11]*

Entries such as 135 *[364.11]* instruct you to code the sarcoidosis (135) first, followed by the chronic iridocyclitis (364.11). Both codes need to be verified in the Tabular.

Tabular: **135 Sarcoidosis**

Tabular: **364 Disorders of iris and ciliary body**

364.11 Chronic *iridocyclitis in diseases classified elsewhere*

Code first underlying disease, as:

sarcoidosis (135)

tuberculosis (017.3)

Codes: 135, 364.11 Chronic iridocyclitis due to sarcoidosis

Category 345 Epilepsy is also in Chapter 6, but the physician must specifically indicate "epilepsy" before the code can be assigned. If the episode was for a seizure disorder or convulsions other than epilepsy, the code would be 780.39. You should clarify any questions about the diagnosis with the physician.

EXERCISE W *Diseases of the Nervous System and Sense Organs*

Fill in the codes for the following:

1. Meningitis due to *Proteus morganii*

   Code(s): ________________

2. Multiple sclerosis

   Code(s): ____________________

3. Acute otitis media

   Code(s): ____________________

4. Primary open angle glaucoma

   Code(s): ____________________

5. Bell's palsy

   Code(s): ____________________

6. Infected meibomian gland

   Code(s): ____________________

7. Peripheral retinal edema

   Code(s): ____________________

8. Meniere's disease in remission

   Code(s): ____________________

9. Encephalitis due to infectious mononucleosis

   Code(s): ____________________

10. Petit mal epilepsy

    Code(s): ____________________

Diseases of the Circulatory System

Chapter 7, Diseases of the Circulatory System, in the Tabular contains diseases of heart and blood vessels.

Hypertension is probably one of the most common conditions coded in this chapter. The Hypertension Table is located in the Index, as shown in Figure 7–2. This table provides a complete listing of all conditions due to or associated with hypertension. The first column identifies the hypertensive condition, such as accelerated, antepartum, cardiovascular disease, cardiorenal, and cerebrovascular disease. The remaining three columns, entitled malignant, benign, and unspecified, constitute the subcategories of hypertensive disease.

Malignant hypertension is an accelerated, severe form of hypertension, manifested by headaches, blurred vision, dyspnea, and uremia. This type of hypertension usually causes permanent organ damage. **Benign hypertension** is a continuous, mild blood pressure elevation. **Unspecified hypertension** has not been specified as either benign or malignant.

INDEX TO DISEASES **Hypertension**

	Malignant	Benign	Unspecified
Hypertension, hypertensive (arterial) (arteriolar) (crisis) (degeneration) (disease) (essential) (fluctuating) (idiopathic) (intermittent) (labile) (low renin) (orthostatic) (paroxysmal) (primary) (systemic) (uncontrolled) (vascular)	401.0	(#1) 401.1	(#3) 401.9
with			
heart involvement (conditions classifiable to 425.8, 428, 429.0-429.3, 429.8, 429.9 due to hypertension) *(see also* Hypertension, heart)	402.00	402.10	402.90
with kidney involvement — *see* Hypertension, cardiorenal			
renal involvement (only conditions classifiable to 585, 586, 587) (excludes conditions classifiable to 584) *(see also* Hypertension, kidney)	403.00	403.10	403.90
with heart involvement — *see* Hypertension, cardiorenal			
failure (and sclerosis) (*see also* Hypertension, kidney)	403.01	403.11	(#4) 403.91
sclerosis without failure (*see also* Hypertension, kidney)	403.00	403.10	403.90
accelerated (*see also* Hypertension, by type, malignant)	401.0	—	—
antepartum — *see* Hypertension, complicating pregnancy, childbirth, or the puerperium			
cardiorenal (disease)	404.00	404.10	404.90
with			
heart failure (congestive)	404.01	404.11	404.91
and renal failure	404.03	404.13	404.93
renal failure	404.02	404.12	404.92
and heart failure (congestive)	404.03	404.13	404.93
cardiovascular disease (arteriosclerotic) (sclerotic)	(#2) 402.00	402.10	402.90
with			
heart failure (congestive)	402.01	402.11	402.91
renal involvement (conditions classifiable to 403) (*see also* Hypertension, cardiorenal)	404.00	404.10	404.90
cardiovascular renal (disease) (sclerosis) (*see also* Hypertension, cardiorenal)	404.00	404.10	404.90

Condition

Figure 7–2
Hypertension Table, Index to Diseases. (From International Classification of Diseases, 9th Revision. U.S. Department of Health and Human Services, Public Health Service, Health Care Financing Administration.)

There is no defined threshold of blood pressure above which an individual is considered hypertensive. Commonly, a sustained diastolic pressure of above 90 mm Hg and a sustained systolic pressure of above 140 mm Hg constitutes hypertension.

Benign hypertension remains fairly stable over the years and is compatible with a long life; but if untreated, it is an important risk factor in coronary heart disease and cerebrovascular disease.

Malignant hypertension is frequently associated with abrupt onset and runs a course measured in months. It causes irreversible organ damage and often ends with renal failure or cerebral hemorrhage. Usually a person with malignant hypertension will complain of headaches and vision difficulties. Blood pressure of 200/140 mm Hg is common.

Hypertensive heart disease refers to the secondary effects on the heart of prolonged sustained systemic hypertension. The heart has to work against greatly increased resistance in the form of high blood pressure. The primary effect is thickening of the left ventricle, which finally results in heart failure.

There are two sections in this chapter that have instructions to "Use additional code, if desired, to identify presence of hypertension (401.0-405.9)." The sections are Ischemic Heart Disease (410-414) and Cerebrovascular Disease (430-438). There are also a number of guidelines that pertain to hypertension or other hypertensive disease processes.

4.1 HYPERTENSION, ESSENTIAL, OR NOS

Assign hypertension (arterial) (essential) (primary) (systemic) (NOS) to category code 401 with the appropriate fourth digit to indicate malignant (.0), benign (.1), or unspecified (.9). Do not use either .0 malignant or .1 benign unless medical record documentation supports such a designation.

4.2 HYPERTENSION WITH HEART DISEASE

Certain heart conditions (425.8, 428, 429.0-429.3, 429.8, 429.9) are assigned to a code from category 402 when a causal relationship is stated (due to hypertension) or implied (hypertensive). Use only the code from category 402. The same heart conditions (425.8, 428, 429.0-429.3, 429.8, 429.9) with hypertension, but without a stated causal relationship, are coded separately. Sequence according to the circumstances of the admission.

4.3 HYPERTENSIVE RENAL DISEASE WITH CHRONIC RENAL FAILURE

Assign codes from category 403, Hypertensive renal disease, when conditions classified to categories 585-587 are present. Unlike hypertension with heart disease, ICD-9-CM presumes a cause-and-effect relationship and classifies chronic renal failure with hypertension as hypertensive renal disease. (Acute renal failure is not included in this cause-and-effect relationship.)

4.4 HYPERTENSIVE HEART AND RENAL DISEASE

Assign codes from combination category 404, Hypertensive heart and renal disease, when both hypertensive renal disease and hypertensive heart disease are stated in the diagnosis. Assume a relationship between the hypertension and the renal disease, whether or not the condition is so designated.

4.5 HYPERTENSIVE CEREBROVASCULAR DISEASE

First assign codes from 430-438, Cerebrovascular disease, then the appropriate hypertension code from categories 401-405.

4.6 HYPERTENSIVE RETINOPATHY

Two codes are necessary to identify the condition. First assign code 362.11, Hypertensive retinopathy, then the appropriate code from categories 401-405 to indicate the type of hypertension.

4.7 HYPERTENSION, SECONDARY

Two codes are required; one to identify the underlying condition and one from category 405 to identify the hypertension. Sequencing of codes is determined by the reason for admission to the hospital.

4.8 HYPERTENSION, TRANSIENT

Assign code 796.2, Elevated blood pressure reading without diagnosis of hypertension, unless patient has an established diagnosis of hypertension. Assign code 642.3X for transient hypertension of pregnancy.

4.9 HYPERTENSION, CONTROLLED

Assign appropriate code from categories 401-405. This diagnostic statement usually refers to an existing state of hypertension under control by therapy.

4.10 HYPERTENSION, UNCONTROLLED

Uncontrolled hypertension may refer to untreated hypertension or hypertension not responding to current therapeutic regimen. In either case, assign the appropriate code from categories 401-405 to designate the state and type of hypertension. Code to the type of hypertension.

Guideline 4.3 instructs you to assume that there is a cause-and-effect relationship between hypertension and renal diseases that are categorized in the range of codes 585-587. The physician might not indicate that they are related, but the coder must assume this relationship.

EXAMPLE

Diagnosis: Chronic renal failure and hypertension

There is nothing in the above diagnostic statement to indicate that the two diseases are related. Let's see how this would be coded. The guidelines instruct you to code as if there were a cause-and-effect relationship between the chronic renal failure and hypertension. Therefore, the diagnosis would be coded as hypertensive chronic renal failure.

Index: **Failure, failed,** renal 586, chronic 585, hypertensive or with hypertension (*see also* hypertension, kidney), 403.91

Tabular: **403 Hypertensive renal disease**

403.9 Unspecified

Code 403.9 is not complete until you assign the appropriate fifth digit. You have a choice of "0" without mention of renal failure, or "1" with renal failure. Chronic renal failure is present in the diagnosis statement, so a fifth digit of 1 is assigned.

Code: 403.91 Chronic renal failure, hypertension

The code for chronic renal failure is 585; however, when you locate code 585 in the Tabular there is an *"Excludes"* note that states: "*. . . with any condition classifiable to 401 (403.0-403.9 with a fifth digit 1).*" Thus, chronic renal failure due to hypertension cannot be classified to code 585.

Code *410* Acute myocardial infarction requires a fifth-digit assignment and includes specific instructions that must be carefully read.

A fifth digit of "1" indicates an initial episode and can be assigned to the same patient for a different admission providing treatment for the initial episode of care for the MI. A patient could be diagnosed with acute myocardial infarction and be transferred to a larger facility for further investigation and care. The diagnoses at both facilities would sequence the acute myocardial infarction first, and the five-digit assignment would be "1" at both facilities.

A fifth digit of "2" indicates subsequent care and is used when a patient is readmitted for testing or further care within 8 weeks of the initial episode. For example, a patient had an acute myocardial infarction and was discharged from the hospital. Four weeks later, that same patient was admitted for a cardiovascular procedure. The myocardial infarction would be coded 410.92, to indicate a subsequent episode. Note that code 412 is assigned for a healed myocardial infarction that is not showing any symptoms (asymptomatic). You would not assign a V code history of MI in this situation.

As you review the following examples, refer to Figure 7–2 for the codes highlighted for each example.

EXAMPLES

Hypertension

Diagnosis: Congestive heart failure with benign hypertension

Tabular: **428.0 Congestive heart failure**

401.1 Hypertension, benign (indicated as 1 on Fig. 7–2)

The key word in the above diagnosis statement is "with," which indicates two conditions. Both the congestive heart failure and the benign hypertension are coded because each is a separate condition.

Diagnosis: Dilated cardiomyopathy due to malignant hypertension

Tabular: **402.00 Cardiomyopathy** (indicated as 2 on Fig. 7–2) due to:

hypertension—See Hypertension with heart involvement malignant

In this example, the hypertension caused the cardiomyopathy. The key words here are "due to," which indicates that one condition caused the other condition.

Diagnosis: Acute renal failure with hypertension

Tabular: **584.9 Renal failure,** acute

Tabular: **401.9 Hypertension** (indicated as 3 on Fig. 7–2)

At first, you identify that you would code the hypertension separately because the word "with" is included in the diagnostic statement. Under hypertension, renal involvement, on Figure 7–2, you will see an *"Excludes"* note. The note indicates that conditions classifiable to 584 (acute renal failure) are excluded from the codes for renal involvement. The condition in this example is acute renal failure, 584; therefore, you cannot assign the renal involvement hypertension codes. Codes 585-587 imply that acute renal failure is not assumed to have a cause-and-effect relationship with hypertension. Be sure to read all notes before you assign any code. Thus, the code for the hypertension in this example is 401.9, Hypertension, unspecified. When you next note the diagnosis, "renal failure," you may think that only one code is to be assigned. The key term included in this diagnosis was "acute" renal failure.

Diagnosis: Hypertension with chronic renal failure

Index: **403.91 Hypertension, with renal involvement, failure** (indicated as 4 on Fig. 7–2)

Figure 7–3 shows the portion of the Hypertension Table that includes the "secondary" hypertension codes. *Secondary hypertension* means that the hypertension is caused by another condition.

EXAMPLE

Diagnosis: Secondary, benign hypertension, due to renal artery occlusion

Tabular: **405.11 Hypertension,** secondary, due to renal (artery), occlusion, benign (indicated as 5 on Fig. 7–3)

In the previous example, the renal artery occlusion caused the hypertension and so is correctly coded to category 405. You would also assign a code to the renal artery occlusion (593.81) because the renal artery occlusion is causing the secondary hypertension. Sequence the occlusion first.

EXAMPLE

Code: 593.81, 405.11 Secondary, benign hypertension, due to renal artery occlusion

The renal artery occlusion is causing the hypertension and when treated may result in the "disappearance" of the hypertension.

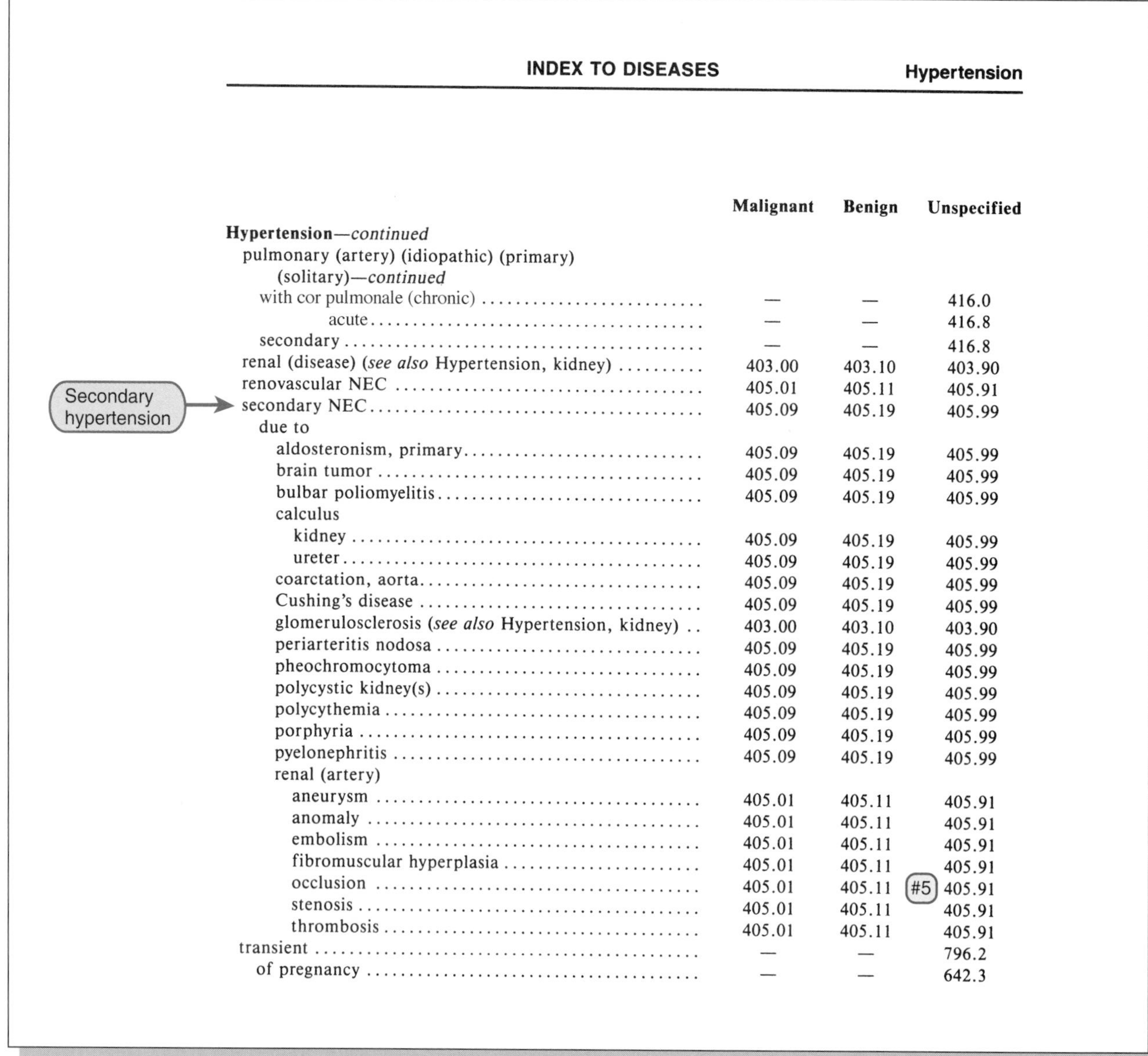

INDEX TO DISEASES — Hypertension

	Malignant	Benign	Unspecified
Hypertension—*continued*			
pulmonary (artery) (idiopathic) (primary) (solitary)—*continued*			
with cor pulmonale (chronic)	—	—	416.0
acute	—	—	416.8
secondary	—	—	416.8
renal (disease) (*see also* Hypertension, kidney)	403.00	403.10	403.90
renovascular NEC	405.01	405.11	405.91
secondary NEC	405.09	405.19	405.99
due to			
aldosteronism, primary	405.09	405.19	405.99
brain tumor	405.09	405.19	405.99
bulbar poliomyelitis	405.09	405.19	405.99
calculus			
kidney	405.09	405.19	405.99
ureter	405.09	405.19	405.99
coarctation, aorta	405.09	405.19	405.99
Cushing's disease	405.09	405.19	405.99
glomerulosclerosis (*see also* Hypertension, kidney)	403.00	403.10	403.90
periarteritis nodosa	405.09	405.19	405.99
pheochromocytoma	405.09	405.19	405.99
polycystic kidney(s)	405.09	405.19	405.99
polycythemia	405.09	405.19	405.99
porphyria	405.09	405.19	405.99
pyelonephritis	405.09	405.19	405.99
renal (artery)			
aneurysm	405.01	405.11	405.91
anomaly	405.01	405.11	405.91
embolism	405.01	405.11	405.91
fibromuscular hyperplasia	405.01	405.11	405.91
occlusion	405.01	405.11	405.91
stenosis	405.01	405.11	405.91
thrombosis	405.01	405.11	405.91
transient	—	—	796.2
of pregnancy	—	—	642.3

Figure 7–3
Secondary hypertension. (From International Classification of Diseases, 9th Revision. U.S. Department of Health and Human Services, Public Health Service, Health Care Financing Administration.)

Official Coding and Reporting Guidelines

4.11 ELEVATED BLOOD PRESSURE

For a statement of elevated blood pressure without further specificity, assign code 796.2, Elevated blood pressure reading without diagnosis of hypertension, rather than a code from category 401.

EXERCISE X Diseases of the Circulatory System

Fill in the codes for the following:

1. Congestive heart failure

   Code(s): ____________________

2. Acute subendocardial infarction, initial episode

   Code(s): ____________________

3. Secondary hypertension due to periarteritis nodosa

   Code(s): ____________________

4. Cerebral infarction due to thrombosis, brain

   Code(s): ____________________

5. Subarachnoid hemorrhage

   Code(s): ____________________

6. Hypertension, uncontrolled

   Code(s): ____________________

7. Atrial fibrillation

   Code(s): ____________________

8. Mitral valve insufficiency

   Code(s): ____________________

9. Arteriosclerotic cardiovascular disease

   Code(s): ____________________

10. Septic myocarditis due to staphylococcus

    Code(s): ____________________

11. Abdominal aortic aneurysm

    Code(s): ____________________

12. Elevated blood pressure

    Code(s): ____________________

13. Congestive heart failure due to hypertension

    Code(s): ________________

14. Retinopathy due to hypertension, controlled

    Code(s): ________________

Diseases of the Respiratory System

Chapter 8, Diseases of the Respiratory System, in the Tabular includes diseases and disorders of the respiratory tract, which starts with the nasal passages and follows a path to the lungs. Note that at the beginning of Chapter 8 there is an instructional note that covers the entire chapter. The note states that you are to "Use additional code to identify infectious organism." You should be aware that in this chapter the organism is already identified in some codes, and you would not assign an additional code to identify the specific infectious organism.

EXAMPLES

Diagnosis: Pneumonia due to *Klebsiella pneumoniae*

Index: **Pneumonia,** *Klebsiella pneumoniae,* 482.0

Tabular: **482 Other bacterial pneumonia**

482.0 Pneumonia due to *Klebsiella pneumoniae*

Code: 482.0 Pneumonia due to *Klebsiella pneumoniae*

The code 482.0 is a combination code that includes the disease process (pneumonia) with the causative organism (*Klebsiella pneumoniae*). In this instance, you would not need to assign an additional code because the organism is identified in the code 482.0.

Diagnosis: Acute maxillary sinusitis due to *Haemophilus influenzae*

Index: **Sinusitis** (accessory) (nasal) (hyperplastic) (nonpurulent) (purulent) (chronic) 473.9

acute 461.9

maxillary 461.0

Tabular: **461 Acute sinusitis**

461.0 Maxillary

Index: **Infection, infected, infective** (opportunistic), *Haemophilus influenzae* NEC 041.5

Tabular: **041 Bacterial infection in conditions classified elsewhere and of unspecified site**

041.5 *Haemophilus influenzae [H. influenzae]*

Codes: 461.0, 041.5 Acute maxillary sinusitis due to *Haemophilus influenzae*

The respiratory condition of chronic obstructive pulmonary disease (COPD) falls within the category 496 Chronic airway obstruction NEC. The note under code 496 indicates that this code cannot be assigned with any code from categories 491-493. The *"Excludes"* note under code 496 indicates that COPD specified "(as) (with) asthma (493.2)" cannot be assigned to code 496. The *Excludes* note sends you elsewhere in the ICD-9-CM.

EXAMPLE

Diagnosis: COPD with asthma

Index: **Asthma, asthmatic** (bronchial) (catarrh) (spasmodic) 493.9,
with, chronic obstructive pulmonary disease (COPD) 493.2

Tabular: **493 Asthma**

493.2 Chronic obstructive asthma

This code is not complete yet because it needs a fifth digit. You have two fifth digit choices; either

0 without mention of status asthmaticus, or

1 with status asthmaticus

To code the asthma with status asthmaticus, the physician provides specific documentation of the condition. If the clinical condition is severe enough that you suspect that the patient has status asthmaticus, clarification with the physician should be sought.

Code: 493.20 COPD with asthma

EXERCISE Y Diseases of the Respiratory System

Fill in the codes for the following:

1. Croup

   Code(s): ____________________

2. Respiratory failure due to congestive heart failure

   Code(s): ____________________

3. COPD with chronic bronchitis

   Code(s): ____________________

4. Influenza with acute bronchitis

   Code(s): ____________________

5. Pneumonia due to *Haemophilus influenzae*

   Code(s): ____________________

6. Postoperative pneumothorax

   Code(s): ________________

7. Chronic ethmoidal sinusitis

   Code(s): ________________

8. Upper respiratory infection

   Code(s): ________________

9. Status asthmaticus

   Code(s): ________________

10. Nasal polyp

    Code(s): ________________

Diseases of the Digestive System

Chapter 9, Diseases of the Digestive System, in the Tabular describes diseases or conditions affecting the digestive system. Digestion starts when food is taken into the mouth and follows the gastrointestinal tract until it leaves the body through the anus. The categories are sequenced in a manner that follows that path, starting with disorders of the teeth.

Throughout the chapter, as in other chapters, you must pay close attention to fifth-digit assignment and carefully read the *Excludes* notes and any other instructions. Also important in the chapter is the presence of *hemorrhage* associated with the diseases. The physician may not always indicate the presence of hemorrhage, and the coder must review the record and then clarify with the physician the appropriate code assignment.

EXAMPLES

Diagnosis: Diverticulitis of the colon with hemorrhage

Index: **Diverticulitis** (acute), colon (perforated) 562.11, with hemorrhage 562.13

Note that the presence of hemorrhage makes a difference in the code assignment.

Tabular: **562 Diverticula of intestine**

562.13 Diverticulitis of colon with hemorrhage

Code: 562.13 Diverticulitis of the colon with hemorrhage

Category **578 Gastrointestinal hemorrhage** has an *Excludes* note that is very important:

EXCLUDES *that with mention of:*

angiodysplasia of stomach and duodenum (537.83)

angiodysplasia of intestine (569.85)

diverticulitis, intestine:
large (562.13)
small (562.03)
diverticulosis, intestine:
large (562.12)
small (562.02)
gastritis and duodenitis (535.0-535.6)
ulcer:
duodenum (532.0-532.9)
gastric (531.0-531.9)
gastrojejunal (534.0-534.9)
peptic (533.0-533.9)

If you are coding a diagnosis of GI (gastrointestinal) hemorrhage with any of the listed *Excludes* diagnoses, you are instructed to code GI hemorrhages elsewhere and not use the codes from category 578.

Diagnosis: Gastrointestinal hemorrhage due to acute antral ulcer

Index: **Ulcer, ulcerated, ulcerating, ulceration, ulcerative** 707.9, antral—*see* ulcer, stomach, stomach (eroded) (peptic) (round) 531.9, acute 531.3, with hemorrhage 531.0

Tabular: **531 Gastric ulcer**

531.0 Acute with hemorrhage

Code 531.0 is not a complete code. You must assign a fifth digit. There is no mention of obstruction in the diagnosis, so the fifth digit assigned would be 0, without mention of obstruction.

Index: **Hemorrhage, hemorrhagic** (nontraumatic) 459.0

Gastrointestinal (tract) 579.9

Tabular: **578 Gastrointestinal hemorrhage**

Excludes: that with mention of:

Ulcer:

gastric (531.0-532.9)

Code: 531.00 Gastrointestinal hemorrhage due to acute antral ulcer

At this point, you discover the importance of the *Excludes* notes for 578 Gastrointestinal hemorrhage, which states that the hemorrhage is included in the ulcer code. That is one reason why it is so important to verify code assignment in the Tabular. It is only when you check the Tabular that you will know for certain any of the Includes or *Excludes* that are not listed anywhere else. So be certain to always, always check the Tabular before assigning a code.

EXERCISE Z *Diseases of the Digestive System*

Fill in the codes for the following:

1. Appendicitis with peritonitis

   Code(s): ________________

2. Gastrointestinal bleeding due to acute duodenal ulcer

   Code(s): ________________

3. Acute and chronic cholecystitis with cholelithiasis

   Code(s): ________________

4. Gastroenteritis

   Code(s): ________________

5. Gastroesophageal reflux

   Code(s): ________________

6. Obstructed left inguinal hernia, recurrent

   Code(s): ________________

7. Alcoholic gastritis with hemorrhage; chronic alcoholism

   Code(s): ________________

8. Peptic ulcer disease

   Code(s): ________________

9. Acute and chronic gingivitis

   Code(s): ________________

10. Adynamic ileus

    Code(s): ________________

Diseases of the Genitourinary System

Chapter 10, Diseases of the Genitourinary System, in the Tabular includes conditions and diseases of the male and female genital organs and urinary tract. Disorders of the breast (categories 610-611) are also included in the chapter.

Once again, when you are dealing with infections of the urinary tract or the genital organs, you are instructed to use an additional code to identify the organism.

EXAMPLE

Diagnosis: Acute prostatitis due to *Streptococcus*

Index: **Prostatitis** (congestive) (suppurative) 601.9

acute 601.0

Tabular: **601 Inflammatory diseases of prostate**

601.1 Acute prostatitis

Index: **Infection, infected, infective** (opportunistic)

streptococcal NEC 041.00

Tabular: **041 Bacterial infection in conditions classified elsewhere and of unspecified site**

041.0 *Streptococcus*

041.00 *Streptococcus,* unspecified

Codes: 601.1, 041.00 Acute prostatitis due to *Streptococcus*

EXERCISE AA Diseases of the Genitourinary System

Fill in the codes for the following diagnostic statements:

1. Pelvic inflammatory disease (PID)

   Code(s): ____________________

2. Hematuria

   Code(s): ____________________

3. Acute and chronic pyelonephritis

   Code(s): ____________________

4. Benign prostatic hypertrophy (BPH)

   Code(s): ____________________

5. Fibrocystic breast disease

   Code(s): ____________________

6. Calculus (stone) of the kidney

   Code(s): ____________________

7. Acute cystitis due to *Escherichia coli*

   Code(s): ____________________

8. Phimosis

   Code(s): ________________

9. Rectocele with cystocele with complete uterine prolapse

   Code(s): ________________

10. Amenorrhea

   Code(s): ________________

Complications of Pregnancy, Childbirth, and the Puerperium

Chapter 11, Complications of Pregnancy, Childbirth, and the Puerperium, of the Tabular is probably the most difficult chapter from which to code. One reason is because pregnancy and childbirth are natural functions and physicians often overlook documentation of diagnoses that should be coded. Another reason is that there is extensive use of multiple coding in the chapter. Also, fifth-digit assignment for pregnancy is often difficult to determine. There are instructions noted throughout this chapter that must be read thoroughly. Obstetric coding can also be difficult because you may not use this chapter as frequently as some of the other chapters, so you won't be as familiar with the special notes and coding instructions.

An ectopic or molar pregnancy is one in which the fertilized ovum implants outside the uterus, usually in the fallopian tube. Ectopic and Molar Pregnancy (630-633) contains instructions to use an additional code from category 639 to identify any complication(s).

Category 639, Complications following abortion and ectopic and molar pregnancies, provides instructional guidelines for the use of this code. You cannot use 639, complications, with any code from categories 634-638 because the complications are classified according to the fourth-digit subcategory codes. As stated previously, you use 639, complications, to identify any complications for code 630-633. You also use 639, complications, when the complication is the reason for the medical care and the abortion, ectopic, or molar pregnancy was taken care of during a previous episode.

Complications mainly related to pregnancy (640-648) designate fifth-digit subclassifications that are of special note:

0 unspecified as to episode of care or not applicable
1 delivered, with or without mention of antepartum condition
2 delivered, with mention of postpartum complication
3 antepartum condition or complication
4 postpartum condition or complication

The fifth digit "0" is used when an abortion is due to or associated with a complication from the chapter. To use the fifth digits "1" and "2," a delivery must occur during that stay. The "1" is assigned to those conditions that are with or without an antepartum condition. The fifth digits "3" and "4" are used when no delivery has occurred during that stay or visit. The "3" is used for antepartum conditions, and the "4" for postpartum conditions. When you review the categories and subcategories throughout the chapter, you will note that many subcategories may indicate that you can use only certain fifth digits with a particular code. For example, with code 641.1, Hemorrhage from placenta previa, the only fifth digits that can be used are "0," "1," and "3." Neither "2" nor "4" can be used because placenta previa occurs before the baby is delivered.

When coding multiple diagnoses from one inpatient stay, certain combinations of fifth digits are used to classify that stay or visit. These fifth-digit combinations are

1 only, or with 2; NOT with 0, 3, or 4
2 only, or with 1; NOT with 0, 3, or 4
3 only, NOT with 0, 1, 2, or 4
4 only, NOT with 0, 1, 2, or 4

Category 650, Normal delivery, cannot be used with any other code that falls within the range 630-676 because these codes refer to other than normal delivery. Code 650 is used only when the following is documented:

- A full-term, single liveborn infant is delivered.
- There are no antepartum or postpartum conditions classifiable to 630-676.
- The presentation is cephalic, requiring minimal assistance without fetal manipulation or the use of instrumentation.
- An episiotomy can be performed.

Most deliveries do not fit the above criteria for a 650 Normal Delivery code assignment.

Category V27 Outcome of delivery can be assigned as an additional code to the mother's record. This is indexed under the term "Outcome."

2.16 COMPLICATION OF PREGNANCY

When a patient is admitted because of a condition that is either a complication of pregnancy or that is complicating the pregnancy, the code for the obstetric complication is the principal diagnosis. An additional code may be assigned as needed to provide specificity.

EXAMPLE

Diagnosis: Iron deficiency anemia complicating pregnancy, antepartum

Index: **Pregnancy** (single) (uterine) (without sickness) V22.2

complicated (by) 646.9

anemia (conditions classifiable to 280-285) 648.2

Tabular: **648.2 Anemia**

This code is not complete because it lacks fifth-digit assignment and there are instructions to "Use additional code(s) to identify the condition," which means to identify the type of anemia. The code book states that you can assign fifth digits 0-4. No delivery has occurred and the condition is stated as being antepartum; therefore the fifth digit "3" is assigned. The next step is to locate the additional code to identify the type of anemia.

EXAMPLE

Index: **Anemia** 285.9, deficiency 281.9, iron (Fe) 280.9

Tabular: **280.9 Iron deficiency anemia, unspecified**

Codes: 648.23, 280.9 Iron deficiency anemia complicating pregnancy, antepartum

The first code, 648.23, indicates that the anemia is a complication of the pregnancy, and the second code, 280.9, provides greater specificity as to the type of anemia.

Chapter 4 can be somewhat confusing at the beginning because there is an *Excludes* note that states: *"anemia complicating pregnancy or the puerperium (648.2)."* In Chapter 11 you are directed to "Also code the condition." This means that anemias are assumed to be complications of pregnancy and you should follow the instructions given for code 648.2. The code from the obstetric chapter would be sequenced first followed by the anemia code.

OBSTETRICS

Introduction

These guidelines have been developed and approved by the Cooperating Parties in conjunction with the Editorial Advisory Board of Coding Clinic and the American College of Obstetricians and Gynecologists, to assist the coder in coding and reporting obstetric cases. Where feasible, previously published advice has been incorporated. Some advice in these new guidelines may supersede previous advice. The guidelines are provided for reporting purposes. Health care facilities may record additional diagnoses as needed for internal data needs.

5.1 GENERAL RULES

A. Obstetric cases require codes from Chapter 11, codes in the range 630-677, Complications of Pregnancy, Childbirth, and the Puerperium. Should the physician document that the pregnancy is incidental to the encounter, then code V22.2 should be used in place of any of any Chapter 11 codes. It is the physician's responsibility to state that the condition being treated is not affecting the pregnancy.
B. Chapter 11 codes have sequencing priority over codes from other chapters. Additional codes from other chapters may be used in conjunction with Chapter 11 codes to further specify conditions.
C. Chapter 11 codes are to be used only on the maternal record, never on the record of the newborn.
D. An outcome of delivery code, V27.0-V27.9, should be included on every maternal record when a delivery has occurred. These codes are not to be used on subsequent records or on the newborn record.

5.2 SELECTION OF PRINCIPAL DIAGNOSIS

A. The circumstances of the encounter govern the selection of the principal diagnosis.
B. In episodes when no delivery occurs the principal diagnosis should correspond to the principal complication of the pregnancy which necessitated the encounter. Should more than one complication exist, all of which are treated or monitored, any of the complications codes may be sequenced first.
C. When a delivery occurs, the principal diagnosis should correspond to the main circumstances or complication of the delivery. In cases of cesarean deliveries, the principal diagnosis should correspond to the reason the cesarean was performed, unless the reason for admission was unrelated to the condition resulting in the cesarean delivery.
D. For routine prenatal visits when no complications are present, codes V22.0, Supervision of normal first pregnancy, and V22.1, Supervision of other normal pregnancy, should be used as principal diagnoses. These codes should not be used in conjunction with Chapter 11 codes.
E. For prenatal outpatient visits for patients with high-risk pregnancies, a code from category V23, Supervision of high-risk pregnancy, should be used as the principal diagnosis. Secondary Chapter 11 codes may be used in conjunction with these codes if appropriate. A thorough review of any pertinent *Excludes* note is necessary to be certain that these V codes are being used properly.

5.3 CHAPTER 11 FIFTH DIGITS

A. Categories 640-648, 651-676 have required fifth digits that indicate whether the encounter is antepartum, postpartum, and whether a delivery has also occurred.
B. The fifth digits which are appropriate for each code number are listed in brackets under each code. The fifth digits on each code should all be consistent with each other. That is, should a delivery occur all of the fifth digits should indicate the delivery.

5.4 FETAL CONDITIONS AFFECTING THE MANAGEMENT OF THE MOTHER

Codes from category 655, Known or suspected fetal abnormality affecting management of the mother, and category 656, Other fetal and placental problems affecting the management of the mother, are assigned only when the fetal condition is actually responsible for modifying the management of the mother, i.e., by requiring diagnostic studies, additional observation, special care, or termination of pregnancy. The fact that the fetal condition exists does not justify assigning a code from this series to the mother's record.

5.5 NORMAL DELIVERY, 650

A. Code 650 is for use in cases when a woman is admitted for a full-term normal delivery and delivers a single, healthy infant without any complications antepartum, during the delivery, or postpartum during the delivery episode.
B. 650 may be used if the patient had complications at some point during her pregnancy but the complication is not present at the time of the admission for delivery.
C. Code 650 is always a principal diagnosis. It is not to be used if any other code

from Chapter 11 is needed to describe a current complication of the antenatal, delivery, or perinatal period. Additional codes from other chapters may be used with code 650 if they are not related to or are in any way complicating the pregnancy.

D. V27.0, Single liveborn, is the only outcome of delivery code appropriate for use with 650.

5.6 PROCEDURE CODES

A. In cases of cesarean delivery, the selection of the principal diagnosis should correspond to the reason the cesarean delivery was performed unless the reason for admission was unrelated to the condition resulting in the cesarean delivery.

B. A delivery procedure code should not be used for a woman who has delivered prior to admission to the hospital. Any postpartum repairs should be coded.

5.7 THE POSTPARTUM PERIOD

A. The postpartum period begins immediately after delivery and continues for 6 weeks following delivery.

B. A postpartum complication is any complication occurring within the 6 week period.

C. Chapter 11 codes may also be used to describe pregnancy related complications after the 6 week period should the physician document that a condition is pregnancy related.

D. Postpartum complications that occur during the same admission as the delivery are identified with a fifth digit of "2." Subsequent admissions for postpartum complications should be identified with a fifth digit of "4."

E. When the mother delivers outside the hospital prior to admission and is admitted for routine postpartum care and no complications are noted, code V24.0, Postpartum care and examination immediately after delivery, should be assigned as the principal diagnosis.

5.8 ABORTIONS

A. Fifth digits are required for abortion categories 634-637. Fifth digit 1, incomplete, indicates that all of the products of conception have not been expelled from the uterus. Fifth digit 2, complete, indicates that all products of conception have been expelled from the uterus prior to the episode of care.

B. A code from categories 640-648 and 651-657 may be used as additional codes with an abortion code to indicate the complication leading to the abortion. Fifth digit 3 is assigned with codes from these categories when used with an abortion code because the other fifth digits will not apply. Codes from the 660-669 series are not to be used for complications of abortion.

C. Code 639 is to be used for all complications following abortion. Code 639 cannot be assigned with codes from categories 634-638.

D. Abortion with Liveborn Fetus. When an attempted termination of pregnancy results in a liveborn fetus, assign code 644.21, Early onset of delivery, with an appropriate code from category V27, Outcome of Delivery. The procedure code for the attempted termination of pregnancy should also be assigned.

E. Retained Products of Conception Following an Abortion. Subsequent admissions for retained products of conception following a spontaneous or legally induced abortion are assigned the appropriate code from category 634, Spontaneous abortion, or legally induced abortion, with a fifth digit of "1" (incomplete). This advice is appropriate even when the patient was discharged previously with a discharge diagnosis of complete abortion.

5.9 CODE 677, LATE EFFECT OF COMPLICATION OF PREGNANCY, CHILDBIRTH, AND THE PUERPERIUM

A. Code 677, Late effect of complication of pregnancy, childbirth, and the puerperium is for use in those cases when an initial complication of a pregnancy develops a sequelae requiring care or treatment at a future date.
B. This code may be used at any time after the initial postpartum period.
C. This code, like all late effect codes, is to be sequenced following the code describing the sequelae of the complication.

EXERCISE BB Complications of Pregnancy, Childbirth, and the Puerperium

Fill in the codes for the following:

1. Blighted ovum

   Code(s): ____________________

2. Incomplete spontaneous abortion; dilation and curettage (D&C) performed

   Code(s): ____________________

3. False labor of 38-week pregnancy, undelivered

   Code(s): ____________________

4. Vaginal delivery of liveborn single infant with fourth-degree perineal laceration. Obstetrical laceration repaired (include appropriate V code for outcome of delivery).

   Code(s): ____________________

5. Obstructed labor due to cephalopelvic disproportion. Liveborn single infant delivered by lower segment cesarean section.

   Code(s): ____________________

6. A 35-year-old female at 32 weeks' gestation is seen with complaints of pain and burning with urination and is diagnosed with a urinary tract infection.

   Code(s): ____________________

7. A 29-year-old female at 28 weeks' gestation has uncontrolled type I diabetes.

   Code(s): ____________________

Diseases of the Skin and Subcutaneous Tissue

Chapter 12, Diseases of the Skin and Subcutaneous Tissue, in the Tabular describes diseases or conditions of the integumentary system. This chapter is one of the shorter chapters in the ICD-9-CM manual. When reviewing the first categories listed, such as 681, 682, and 683, you will note that multiple coding may be necessary with some conditions.

EXAMPLE

Diagnosis: Cellulitis right small finger due to *Staphylococcus aureus*

Index: **Cellulitis** (diffuse) (with lymphangitis) (*see also* abscess) 682.9, finger (intrathecal) (periosteal) (subcutaneous) (subcuticular) 681.00

Tabular: **681 Cellulitis and abscess of finger and toe**

681.0 Finger

681.00 Cellulitis and abscess, unspecified

There is an instructional note that tells you to identify the organism when assigning code 681.00. To locate the code for the causative organism you look up the main term "infection" in the Index.

Index: **Infection, infected, infective** (opportunistic) 136.9, staphylococcal, NEC 041.10, aureus 041.11

Tabular: **041 Bacterial infection in conditions classified elsewhere and of unspecified site**

041.1 ***Staphylococcus***

041.11 ***Staphylococcus aureus***

The Tabular states, "Use additional code, if desired, to identify organism, such as *Staphylococcus* (041.1)." Code 041.1 must have a fifth-digit assignment before it can be assigned, and you would know this only if you verified the code in the Tabular.

Code(s): 681.00, 041.11 Cellulitis right small finger due to *Staphylococcus aureus*

The code for the organism is used as an additional code and is sequenced after the disease or condition.

EXERCISE CC *Diseases of the Skin and Subcutaneous Tissue*

Fill in the codes for the following:

1. Pruritus

   Code(s): ________________

2. Heat rash

   Code(s): ________________

3. Psoriasis

   Code(s): ____________________

4. Decubitis ulcer coccyx

   Code(s): ____________________

5. Dermatitis due to poison ivy

   Code(s): ____________________

6. Cellulitis left foot and ankle due to *Staphylococcus*

   Code(s): ____________________

7. Scleroderma

   Code(s): ____________________

8. Acne

   Code(s): ____________________

9. Paronychia finger

   Code(s): ____________________

10. Pilonidal cyst

    Code(s): ____________________

Diseases of the Musculoskeletal System and Connective Tissue

Chapter 13, Diseases of the Musculoskeletal System and Connective Tissue, in the Tabular describes diseases or conditions of the bone, joints, and muscles. It is important to refer to the note at the beginning of the chapter because this is where you will find the information on the fifth-digit subclassifications that are used for categories 711-712, 715-716, 718-719, and 730. If you turn to category 711, you will see the fifth-digit subclassifications again, but not in the same detail as at the beginning of the chapter.

EXAMPLE

Diagnosis:	Pyogenic arthritis of the wrist
Index:	Arthritis, arthritic (acute) (chronic) (subacute) 716.9 pyogenic or pyemic 711.0
Tabular:	**711 Arthropathy associated with infections**
	711.0 Pyogenic arthritis

Code 711.0 is not a valid code because you still need to assign a fifth digit to indicate the site. When reviewing the subclassifications, you must identify whether the wrist is part of the forearm or part of the hand. You need to refer to that note at the beginning of the chapter, where you will note that fifth digit " '3' forearm includes the radius, ulna and wrist joint."

Code: 711.03 Pyogenic arthritis of the wrist

Pathologic or spontaneous fractures are also coded in Chapter 13. A pathologic or *spontaneous fracture* is a break in the bone that occurs because of a bone disease or a change surrounding the bone tissue that makes the bone weak. For a pathologic fracture, you code the fracture and the disease process responsible for the fracture, such as osteoporosis or metastatic cancer of the bone. It is possible to have a small trauma associated with a pathologic fracture. Suppose, for example, an elderly woman with severe osteoporosis bumps her hip against the doorway and sustains a fractured hip. This would be classifiable as a pathologic fracture because a person with healthy bones would not fracture the hip as the result of a small trauma such as bumping the hip on a doorway. If there is any question about whether a fracture is pathologic or due to the trauma, ask the physician what caused the fracture.

A pathologic fracture is serious because healing may be delayed by the underlying bone disease. Also, if a pathologic fracture is documented and no other disease process is indicated, review the record or clarify with the physician the underlying cause of the fracture.

EXAMPLE

Diagnosis: Pathologic fracture of the hip due to severe osteoporosis

Index: **Fracture** (abduction) (adduction) (avulsion) (compression) (crush) (dislocation) (oblique) (separation) (closed) 829.0 pathologic (cause unknown) 733.10 hip 733.14

Tabular: **733.1 Pathologic fracture**

733.14 Pathologic fracture of neck of femur

Index: **Osteoporosis** (generalized) 733.00

Tabular: **733.0 Osteoporosis**

733.00 Osteoporosis, unspecified

Codes: 733.14, 733.00 Pathologic fracture of the hip due to severe osteoporosis

Instructions with category 730 Osteomyelitis, periostitis, and other infections involving bone direct you to identify any organism as an additional code. It is easy to miss the instructions when they are stuck between an *"Excludes"* note and the list of fifth-digit subclassifications. Highlight these instructions in your ICD-9-CM until you become familiar with their use when coding in this area.

EXERCISE DD Diseases of the Musculoskeletal System and Connective Tissue

Fill in the codes for the following:

1. Rheumatoid arthritis

   Code(s): ____________________

2. Pain in the neck

   Code(s): ____________________

3. Recurrent dislocation right shoulder

   Code(s): ____________________

4. Systemic lupus erythematosus with lung involvement

   Code(s): ____________________

5. Spontaneous fracture left humerus due to metastatic bone cancer; history of cancer of the breast previously excised

   Code(s): ____________________

6. Arthritis due to ulcerative colitis

   Code(s): ____________________

7. Osteoarthritis of the cervical spine

   Code(s): ____________________

8. Calcaneal spur

   Code(s): ____________________

9. Bunion right big toe

   Code(s): ____________________

10. Acute osteomyelitis left patella due to *Staphylococcus*

    Code(s): ____________________

Congenital Anomalies and Certain Conditions Originating in the Perinatal Period

Chapters 14 and 15, Congenital Anomalies and Certain Conditions Originating in the Perinatal Period, in the Tabular describe congenital anomalies and conditions that originate in the perinatal period. An *anomaly* is an abnormality of a structure or organ. *Congenital* means that it is an abnormality that one was born with. Some anomalies are noticeable and discovered at birth. Sometimes, it may be a number of months or even years before an anomaly is discovered. If there is any question about whether a condition is acquired or congenital, you can review the record or clarify with the physician.

The *perinatal period* extends through 28 days following birth. Codes from this chapter can still be used beyond that time frame, but as the chapter title indicates, the condition must have originated during the perinatal period.

6 NEWBORN GUIDELINES

Definition

The newborn period is defined as beginning at birth and lasting through the 28th day following birth.

The following guidelines are provided for reporting purposes. Hospitals may record other diagnoses as needed for internal data use.

General Rule

All clinically significant conditions noted on routine newborn examination should be coded. A condition is clinically significant if it requires:

- clinical evaluation
- therapeutic treatment
- diagnostic procedures
- extended length of hospital stay
- increased nursing care and/or monitoring
- has implications for future health care needs

Note: The newborn guidelines listed previously are the same as the general coding guidelines for other diagnoses, except for the final item regarding implications for future health care needs. Whether a condition is clinically significant can be determined only by the physician.

6.1 USE OF CODES V30-V39

When coding the birth of an infant, assign a code from categories V30-V39, according to the type of birth. A code from this series is assigned as a principal diagnosis, and assigned only once to a newborn at the time of birth.

6.2 NEWBORN TRANSFERS

If the newborn is transferred to another institution, the V30 series is not used.

6.3 USE OF CATEGORY V29

A. Assign a code from V29, Observation and evaluation of newborns and infants for suspected conditions not found, to identify those instances when a healthy newborn is evaluated for a suspected condition that is determined after study not to be present. Do not use a code from category V29 when the patient has identified signs or symptoms of a suspected problem; in such case, code the sign or symptom.

B. A V29 code is to be used as a secondary code after the V30, Outcome of delivery, code. It may also be assigned as a principal code for readmissions or encounters when the V30 code no longer applies. It is for use only for healthy newborns and infants for which no condition after study is found to be present.

6.4 MATERNAL CAUSES OF PERINATAL MORBIDITY

Codes from categories 760-763, Maternal causes of perinatal morbidity and mortality, are assigned only when the maternal condition has actually affected the fetus or newborn. The fact that the mother has an associated medical condition or experiences some complication of pregnancy, labor, or delivery does not justify the routine assignment of codes from these categories to the newborn record.

6.5 CONGENITAL ANOMALIES

Assign an appropriate code from categories 740-759, Congenital Anomalies, when a specific abnormality is diagnosed for an infant. Such abnormalities may occur as a set of symptoms or multiple malformations. A code should be assigned for each presenting manifestation of the syndrome if the syndrome is not specifically indexed in ICD-9-CM.

6.6 CODING OF OTHER (ADDITIONAL) DIAGNOSES

A. Assign codes for conditions that require treatment or further investigation, prolong the length of stay, or require resource utilization.
B. Assign codes for conditions that have been specified by the physician as having implications for future health care needs. Note: This guideline should not be used for adult patients.
C. Assign a code for Newborn conditions originating in the perinatal period (categories 760-779), as well as complications arising during the current episode of care classified in other chapters, only if the diagnoses have been documented by the responsible physician at the time of transfer or discharge as having affected the fetus or newborn.
D. Insignificant conditions or signs or symptoms that resolve without treatment are not coded.

6.7 PREMATURITY AND FETAL GROWTH RETARDATION

Codes from categories 764 and 765 should not be assigned based solely on recorded birthweight or estimated gestational age, but upon the attending physician's clinical assessment of maturity of infant.

Note: Since physicians may utilize different criteria in determining prematurity, do not code the diagnosis of prematurity unless the physician documents this condition.

As Guideline 6.1 states, code the birth from categories V30-V39. This code is only used *once* on the birth record because it indicates the type of birth. If the baby is transferred to another facility, a code from categories V30-V39 would not be assigned.

On the baby's birth record the appropriate V code is sequenced first. If there are any other conditions or congenital anomalies documented, those are coded as secondary diagnoses.

EXAMPLE

Diagnosis: Newborn male delivered by cesarean section in the hospital with Down's syndrome

Index: **Newborn** (infant) (liveborn), single, born in hospital (without mention of cesarean delivery or section) V30.00 with cesarean delivery or section V30.01

Tabular: **V30 Single liveborn**

You are instructed to check the fourth and fifth digits. The code is not complete until you have coded it to the fifth-digit subclassification. In this case, the code would be V30.01, as indicated in the Index.

Index: **Syndrome**—*see also* disease, Down's (mongolism) 758.0

Tabular: **758 Chromosomal anomalies**

758.0 Down's syndrome

Codes: V30.01, 758.0 Newborn male delivered by cesarean section in the hospital; Down's syndrome

In the preceding example, if that baby was transferred to a second facility for treatment of the Down's syndrome there would be no V code to identify the delivery. The V code can only be used once as the principal diagnosis at the birthing facility. The principal diagnosis code would be Down's syndrome (758.0) at the second facility.

You have to be careful about assigning codes from 760-763 categories, Maternal Causes of Perinatal Morbidity and Mortality. Many times the mother will have a condition, but that condition has no untoward (negative) effect on the baby or fetus. Codes from these categories are to be used only when the maternal condition has affected the health of the newborn.

EXERCISE EE Congenital Anomalies and Certain Conditions Originating in the Perinatal Period

Fill in the codes for the following:

1. Congenital absence of the earlobe

   Code(s): ________________

2. Newborn male delivered in the hospital via vaginal delivery. Undescended left testicle (will re-evaluate in 6 weeks)

   Code(s): ________________

3. Three-year-old diagnosed with fragile X syndrome

   Code(s): ________________

4. Newborn was transferred to our facility with a congenital dislocation of right hip

   Code(s): ________________

5. Newborn female delivered in the hospital by cesarean delivery with evidence of cleft palate and cleft lip

   Code(s): ____________________

6. Fetal alcohol syndrome

   Code(s): ____________________

Symptoms, Signs, and Ill-Defined Conditions

Chapter 16, Symptoms, Signs, and Ill-Defined Conditions, in the Tabular includes symptoms, signs, abnormal results of investigations and other ill-defined conditions.

You use the codes from Chapter 16 when

- no more specific diagnosis can be made after investigation
- signs and symptoms existing at the time of the initial encounter proved to be transient or a cause could not be determined
- a patient fails to return and all you have is a provisional diagnosis
- a case is referred elsewhere before a definitive diagnosis could be made
- a more precise diagnosis was not available for any other reason
- certain symptoms that represent important problems in medical care exist and that it might be desired to classify in addition to a known cause

You do not code from Chapter 16 when a definitive diagnosis is available. Consider, for example, the diagnostic statement: "Right lower quadrant abdominal pain due to acute appendicitis." The code for right lower quadrant abdominal pain is 789.03, which is located in Chapter 16. But because the reason for the pain is the acute appendicitis, you would not include the code for the symptom of abdominal pain. The only code you would assign would be 540.9 for the acute appendicitis.

You do not code from Chapter 16 when the symptom is considered to be an integral part of the disease process. Consider, for example, the diagnostic statement: "Cough and fever with pneumonia." Both cough and fever are symptoms of the pneumonia; therefore, you would not assign codes for either symptom. The only code you would assign is 486 for the pneumonia.

A disease reference book comes in handy until you become more familiar with disease symptoms. If you do not know which symptoms are associated with a given disease, look this up in a reference or ask a colleague.

Finding the codes for *abnormal investigations* in the Index is a little tricky. The codes are found under the main term "Findings, abnormal, without diagnosis (examination) (laboratory test)." Some entries may also be found under the main term "Elevation."

EXAMPLE

Diagnosis:	Abnormal liver scan
Index:	**Findings, abnormal, without diagnosis** (examination) (laboratory test) 796.4, scan NEC 794.9, liver 794.8
Tabular:	**794 Nonspecific abnormal results of function studies**
	794.8 Liver
Code:	794.8 Abnormal liver scan

EXERCISE FF *Symptoms, Signs, and Ill-Defined Conditions*

Fill in the codes for the following:

1. Presyncope

   Code(s): ____________________

2. Pleuritic-type chest pain

   Code(s): ____________________

3. Abnormal mammogram

   Code(s): ____________________

4. Seizure disorder

   Code(s): ____________________

5. Elevated blood pressure reading

   Code(s): ____________________

6. Hepatomegaly

   Code(s): ____________________

7. Epistaxis

   Code(s): ____________________

8. Proteinuria

   Code(s): ____________________

9. Nausea and vomiting

   Code(s): ____________________

10. Polydipsia

    Code(s): ____________________

Injury and Poisoning

Official Coding and Reporting Guidelines

11 GUIDELINES FOR CODING EXTERNAL CAUSES OF INJURIES, POISONINGS AND ADVERSE EFFECTS OF DRUGS (E CODES)

Introduction: These guidelines are provided for those who are currently collecting E codes in order that there will be standardization in the process. If your institution plans to begin collecting E codes, these guidelines are to be applied. The use of E codes is supplemental to the application of basic ICD-9-CM codes. E codes are never to be recorded as principal diagnosis (first listed in the outpatient setting) and are not required for reporting to the Health Care Financing Administration.

Injuries are a major cause of mortality, morbidity, and disability. In the United States, the care of patients who suffer intentional and unintentional injuries and poisonings contributes significantly to the increase in medical care costs. External causes of injury and poisoning codes (E codes) are intended to provide data for injury research and evaluation of injury prevention strategies. E codes capture how the injury or poisoning happened (cause), the intent (unintentional or accidental; or intentional, such as suicide or assault), and the place where the event occurred. Some major categories of E codes include:

- transport accidents
- poisoning and adverse effects of drugs, medicinal substances and biologicals
- accidental falls
- accidents caused by fire and flames
- accidents due to natural and environmental factors
- late effects of accidents, assaults or self-injury
- assaults or purposely inflicted injury
- suicide or self-inflicted injury

These guidelines apply for the coding and collection of E codes from records in hospitals, outpatient clinics, emergency departments, other ambulatory care settings and physician offices except when other specific guidelines apply. (See Reporting Diagnostic Guidelines for Hospital-based Outpatient Services/Reporting Requirements for Physician Billing.)

11.1 GENERAL E CODE CODING GUIDELINES

A. An E code may be used with any code in the range of 001-V82.9 which indicates an injury, poisoning, or adverse effect due to an external cause.
B. Assign the appropriate E code for all initial treatments of an injury, poisoning, or adverse effect of drugs.
C. Use a late effect E code for subsequent visits when a late effect of the initial injury or poisoning is being treated. There is no late effect E code for adverse effects of drugs.
D. Use the full range of E codes to completely describe the cause, the intent, and the place of the occurrence, if applicable, for all injuries, poisonings, and adverse effects of drugs.
E. Assign as many E codes as necessary to fully explain each cause. If only one E code can be recorded, assign the E code most related to the principal diagnosis.
F. The selection of the appropriate E code is guided by the Index to External Causes which is located after the alphabetical index to diseases and by Inclusion and Exclusion notes in the Tabular List.
G. An E code can never be a principal (first listed) diagnosis.

11.2 PLACE OF OCCURRENCE GUIDELINE

Use an additional code from category E849 to indicate the Place of Occurrence for injuries and poisonings. The Place of Occurrence describes the place where the event occurred and not the patient's activity at the time of the event.

Do not use E849.9 if the place of occurrence is not stated.

11.3 POISONINGS AND ADVERSE EFFECTS OF DRUGS, MEDICINAL AND BIOLOGICAL SUBSTANCE GUIDELINES

A. Do not code directly from the Table of Drugs and Chemicals. Always refer back to the Tabular List.
B. Use as many codes as necessary to describe completely all drugs, medicinal or biological substances.
C. If the same E code would describe the causative agent for more than one adverse reaction, assign the code only once.
D. If two or more drugs, medicinal or biological substances are reported, code each individually unless the combination code is listed in the Table of Drugs and Chemicals. In that case, assign the E code for the combination.
E. When a reaction results from the interaction of a drug(s) and alcohol, use poisoning codes and E codes for both.
F. If the reporting format limits the number of E codes that can be used in reporting clinical data, code the one most related to the principal diagnosis. Include at least one from each category (cause, intent, place) if possible.

If there are different fourth-digit codes in the same three-digit category, use the code for "Other specified" of that category. If there is no "Other specified" code in that category, use the appropriate "Unspecified" code in that category.

If the codes are in different three-digit categories, assign the appropriate E code for other multiple drugs and medicinal substances.

11.4 MULTIPLE CAUSE E CODE CODING GUIDELINES

If two or more events cause separate injuries, an E code should be assigned for each cause. The first listed E code will be selected in the following order:

1. E codes for child and adult abuse take priority over all other E codes—see Child and Adult Abuse Guidelines
2. E codes for cataclysmic events take priority over all other E codes except child and adult abuse
3. E codes for transport accidents take priority over all other E codes except cataclysmic events and child and adult abuse

The first listed E code should correspond to the cause of the most serious diagnosis due to an assault, accident, or self-harm, following the order of hierarchy in the preceding list.

11.5 CHILD AND ADULT ABUSE GUIDELINES

A. When the cause of an injury or neglect is intentional child or adult abuse, the first listed E code should be assigned from categories E960-E968, Homicide and injury purposely inflicted by other persons (except category E967). An E code from category E967, Child and adult battering and other maltreatment, should be added as an additional code to identify the perpetrator, if known.

B. In cases of neglect when the intent is determined to be accidental, E code E904.0, Abandonment or neglect of infant and helpless person, should be the first listed E code.

11.6 UNKNOWN OR SUSPECTED INTENT GUIDELINES

A. If the intent (accident, self-harm, assault) of the cause of an injury or poisoning is unknown or unspecified, code the intent as undetermined E980-E989.
B. If the intent (accident, self-harm, assault) of the cause of an injury or poisoning is questionable, probable or suspected, code the intent as undetermined E980-E989.

11.7 UNDETERMINED CAUSE

When the intent of an injury or poisoning is known, but the cause is unknown, use codes: E928.9, Unspecified accident, E958.9, Suicide and self-inflicted injury by unspecified means, and E968.9, Assault by unspecified means.

These E codes should rarely be used as the documentation in the medical record, in both the inpatient and outpatient settings, should normally provide sufficient detail to determine the cause of the injury.

11.8 LATE EFFECTS OF EXTERNAL CAUSE GUIDELINES

A. Late effect E codes exist for injuries and poisonings but not for adverse effects of drugs, misadventures, and surgical complications.
B. A late effect E code (E929, E959, E969, E977, E989, or E999) should be used with any report of a late effect or sequela resulting from a previous injury or poisoning (905-909).
C. A late effect E code should never be used with a related current nature of injury code.

11.9 MISADVENTURES AND COMPLICATIONS OF CARE GUIDELINES

A. Assign a code in the range of E870-E876 if misadventures are stated by the physician.
B. Assign a code in the range of E878-E879 if the physician attributes an abnormal reaction or later complication to a surgical or medical procedure, but does not mention misadventure at the time of the procedure as the cause of the reaction.

Chapter 17, Injury and Poisoning, in the Tabular is a very long chapter that includes the codes that range from 800 to 999. At the beginning of this chapter there are notes that provide you with specific instructions for the entire chapter. A recent addition to this chapter is the statement that coders should "Use E code(s) to identify the cause and intent of the injury or poisoning (E800-E999)." You learned how to assign E codes in Chapter 6.

There are numerous guidelines that pertain to injuries and poisonings. See the following illustrations.

Official Coding and Reporting Guidelines

2.12 MULTIPLE INJURIES

When multiple injuries exist, the code for the most severe injury as determined by the attending physician is sequenced first.

2.11 MULTIPLE BURNS

Sequence first the code that reflects the highest degree of burn when more than one burn is present. (See also Burns Guideline 8.3.)

8.3 CURRENT BURNS AND ENCOUNTERS FOR LATE EFFECTS OF BURNS

Current burns (940-948) are classified by depth, extent and, if desired, by agent (E code). By depth burns are classified as first degree (erythema), second degree (blistering), and third degree (full-thickness involvement).

A. All burns are coded with the highest degree of burn sequenced first.
B. Classify burns of the same local site (three-digit category level, 940-947) but of different degrees to the subcategory identifying the highest degree recorded in the diagnosis.
C. Non-healing burns are coded as acute burns. Necrosis of burned skin should be coded as a non-healed burn.
D. Assign code 958.3, Posttraumatic wound infection, not elsewhere classified, as an additional code for any documented infected burn site.
E. When coding multiple burns, assign separate codes for each burn site. Category 946, Burns of multiple specified sites, should only be used if the location of the burns is not documented. Category 949, Burn, unspecified, is extremely vague and should rarely be used.
F. Assign codes from category 948, Burns, classified according to extent of body surface involved, when the site of the burn is not specified or when there is a need for additional data. It is advisable to use category 948 as additional coding when needed to provide data for evaluating burn mortality, such as that needed by burn units. It is also advisable to use category 948 as an additional code for reporting purposes when there is mention of third-degree burn involving 20 percent or more of the body surface.

   In assigning a code from category 948:

   1. Fourth-digit codes are used to identify the percentage of total body surface involved in a burn (all degrees).
   2. Fifth-digits are assigned to identify the percentage of body surface involved in a third-degree burn.
   3. Fifth-digit zero (0) is assigned when less than 10 percent or when no body surface is involved in a third-degree burn.

   Category 948 is based on the classic rule of nines in estimating body surface involved: head and neck are assigned nine percent, each arm nine percent, each leg 18 percent, the anterior trunk 18 percent, posterior trunk 18 percent, and genitalia one percent. Physicians may change these percentage assignments when necessary to accommodate infants and children who have proportionately larger heads than adults and patients who have large buttocks, thighs, or abdomen that involve burns.

G. Encounters for the treatment of the late effects of burns (i.e., scars or joint contractures) should be coded to the residual condition (sequelae) followed by the appropriate late effect code (906.5-906.9). A late effect E code may also be used, if desired.

H. When appropriate, both a sequela with a late effect code, and a current burn code may be assigned on the same record.

8.4 DEBRIDEMENT OF WOUNDS, INFECTION, OR BURN

A. For coding purposes, excisional debridement, 86.22, is assigned only when the procedure is performed by a physician.
B. For coding purposes, nonexcisional debridement performed by the physician or nonphysician health care professional is assigned to 86.28. Any excisional type procedure performed by nonphysician is assigned to 86.28.

8.1 CODING FOR MULTIPLE INJURIES

When coding multiple injuries such as fracture of tibia and fibula, assign separate codes for each injury unless a combination code is provided, in which case the combination code is assigned. Multiple injury codes are provided in ICD-9-CM, but should not be assigned unless information for a more specific code is not available.

A. The code for the most serious injury, as determined by the physician, is sequenced first.
B. Superficial injuries such as abrasions or contusions are not coded when associated with more severe injuries of the same site.
C. When a primary injury results in minor damage to peripheral nerves or blood vessels, the primary injury is sequenced first with additional code(s) from categories 950-957, Injury to nerves and spinal cord, and/or 900-904, Injury to blood vessels. When the primary injury is to the blood vessels or nerves, that injury should be sequenced first.

8.2 MULTIPLE FRACTURES

The principle of multiple coding of injuries should be followed in coding multiple fractures. Multiple fractures of specified sites are coded individually by site in accordance with both the provisions within categories 800-829 and the level of detail furnished by medical record content. Combination categories for multiple fractures are provided for use when there is insufficient detail in the medical record (such as trauma cases transferred to another hospital); when the reporting form limits the number of codes that can be used in reporting pertinent clinical data; or when there is insufficient specificity at the fourth-digit or fifth-digit level. More specific guidelines are as follows:

A. Multiple fractures of same limb classifiable to the same three-digit or four-digit category are coded to that category.
B. Multiple unilateral or bilateral fractures of same bone(s) but classified to different fourth-digit subdivisions (bone part) within the same three-digit category are coded individually by site.
C. Multiple fracture categories 819 and 828 classify bilateral fractures of both upper limbs (819) and both lower limbs (828), but without any detail at the fourth-digit level other than open and closed type of fracture.
D. Multiple fractures are sequenced in accordance with the severity of the fracture and the physician should be asked to list the fracture diagnoses in the order of severity.

Fracture is the first section in the chapter and contains the codes assigned for fractures caused by trauma. A fracture not indicated as closed or open should be classified as closed. If you have doubt, check with the physician as to the nature of the fracture. A dislocation and fracture of the same bone would be coded to the fracture site. The cross reference "see" is a mandatory instruction telling you to go to "fracture" and not to code the dislocation separately. When you locate the main term "dislocation" in the Index, you are directed to "*see* Fracture, by site." You locate "fracture" in the Index by the anatomic location of the fracture.

EXAMPLES

Diagnosis: Fracture, right patella with abrasions of the site

Index: **Fracture,** patella (closed) 822.0

Tabular: **822 Fracture of patella**

822.0 Closed

Code(s): 822.0 Fracture, right patella with abrasions of the site

When a fracture is not specified as open or closed, assign a code as a closed fracture. You would not assign a code for the abrasions when there is a more severe injury (the fracture) at the same site.

Diagnosis: Fractured hip with dislocation

Index: **Dislocation,** with fracture—*see* Fracture by site

The "*see* Fracture by site" means the dislocation is included with the fracture code.

Index: **Fracture,** hip (closed) 820.8

Tabular: **820 Fracture of neck of femur**

820.8 Unspecified part of neck of femur, closed

Code(s): 820.8 Fractured hip with dislocation

The guidelines for *burns* direct you to sequence the highest degree of burn first. If you are coding a third-degree burn of the hand and a second-degree burn of the chest wall, you would sequence the code for the third-degree burn of the hand first, followed by the second-degree burn of the chest.

If different degrees of burns are documented at the same site, assign a code to the highest degree only. If, for example, the patient has first- and second-degree burns to the hand, you would code only the second-degree burn or the second-degree burn to the hand.

Facilities may choose to capture data regarding the extent of body area burned. In this case, the Rule of Nines is applied. The ICD-9-CM index entry is "Burn, extent."

Burns are located in the Index by referring to the main term "Burn," subterms according to the site (abdomen or thigh), and finally the degree of burn (second or third).

EXAMPLES

Diagnosis: First- and second-degree burn to the back

Index: **Burn,** back, second degree 942.24

Tabular: **942 Burn of trunk**

942.2 Blisters, epidermal [second degree]

A fifth digit is used to indicate the specific location of the burn to the trunk. In this case, the fifth digit "4" is used to indicate the location of "back."

Code(s): 942.24 First- and second-degree burn to the back

Note that the diagnosis includes first- and second-degree burns and the code assigned indicates second-degree burns: You code only the highest degree when the burns are of the same site.

Diagnosis: Second-degree burn, chin, and third-degree burn, scapular region

Index: **Burn,** chin, second 941.24

Tabular: **941 Burn of face, head, and neck**

941.2 Blisters, epidermal loss [second degree]

A fifth digit is used to indicate the specific location of the burn to the face, head, or neck. In this case, the fifth digit "4" is used to indicate the location of "chin."

Index: **Burn,** scapular region, third degree 943.36

Tabular: **943 Burn of upper limb, except wrist and hand**

943.3 Deep necrosis of underlying tissues [deep third degree] without mention of loss of body part

A fifth digit is used to indicate the specific location of the burn. In this case, the fifth digit "6" is used to indicate the location of "scapular region."

Code(s): 943.36, 941.24 Third-degree burn, scapular region, and second-degree burn, chin

EXERCISE GG *Burns*

Code the burn, extent of the body surface involved, and percentage of body surface burned using the Rule of Nines.

1. A 3-year-old pulls a pan of hot grease off the stove and receives third-degree burns of the abdomen and second-degree burns of the thigh.

   Code(s): ____________________

2. Infected third-degree burn, left thigh

   Code(s): ____________________

3. First- and second-degree burn, right foot, due to bonfire

   Code(s): ________________

4. Non-healing burn, right hand. Excisional debridement performed by physician

   Code(s): ________________

5. Second-degree burn, right forearm; first-degree burn, right little finger; and third-degree burns, right chest wall

   Code(s): ________________

Wounds (lacerations) are found under the main term "Wound." There are three subcategories for some of the wound codes. These injuries can be classified as

1. without mention of complication
2. complicated
3. with tendon involvement

A *complicated wound* is one that includes documentation of delayed healing, delayed treatment, foreign body, or major infection.

EXAMPLE

Diagnosis:	Infected wound of the right knee.
Index:	**Wound,** knee 891.0, complicated 891.1
Tabular:	**891 Open wound of knee, leg [except thigh], and ankle**
	891.1 Complicated
Codes:	891.1 Infected wound of the right knee

The coding of adverse effects and poisonings is probably the most difficult part of this chapter. It takes some practice to distinguish between an adverse effect and a poisoning. Because the physician is probably not going to use those specific terms in the diagnostic statement, you must question the physician if you are uncertain whether the diagnosis is an adverse effect or poisoning.

Official Coding and Reporting Guidelines

9 ADVERSE EFFECTS AND POISONING

The properties of certain drugs, medicinal and biological substances, or combinations of such substances, may cause toxic reactions. The occurrence of drug toxicity is classified in ICD-9-CM as follows.

9.1 ADVERSE EFFECT

When the drug was correctly prescribed and properly administered, code the reaction plus the appropriate code from the E930-E949 series. Adverse effects of therapeutic substances correctly prescribed and properly administered (toxicity, synergistic reaction, side effect, and idiosyncratic reaction) may be due to (1) differences among patients, such as age, sex, disease, and genetic factors, and (2) drug-related factors, such as type of drug, route of administration, duration of therapy, dosage, and bioavailability. Codes from the E930-E949 series must be used to identify the causative substance for an adverse effect of drug, medicinal and biological substance, correctly prescribed and properly administered. The effect, such as tachycardia, delirium, gastrointestinal hemorrhaging, vomiting, hypokalemia, hepatitis, renal failure, or respiratory failure, is coded and followed by the appropriate code from the E930-E949 series.

An *adverse effect* occurs when a drug was correctly prescribed and properly administered and the patient develops a reaction. Everything was done correctly by the physician and the patient, but there is a reaction or adverse effect to the drug.

When coding adverse effect, you code the effect first, followed by the E code from the therapeutic column on the Table of Drugs and Chemicals.

EXAMPLE

Diagnosis:	Urticaria due to penicillin (properly taken and prescribed)
Index:	**Urticaria** 708.9, due to, drugs 708.0
Tabular:	**708 Urticaria**
	708.0 Allergic urticaria
Drug Table:	Penicillin (any type) E930.0
Tabular:	**E930 Antibiotics**
	E930.0 Penicillins
Codes:	708.0, E930.0 Urticaria due to penicillin

The E codes from this section (E930-E949) are considered required E codes. Thus, therapeutic E codes for adverse effects must be assigned. E codes are never assigned as a principal diagnosis but are always considered an additional code.

There is a code available for an *unknown adverse effect.* If the physician documented reaction due to penicillin and you cannot determine from the record what the exact adverse effect was, you would code unknown adverse effect. Adverse effects can be found in the Index under the main term "Effect, adverse" and the subterm "drugs and medicinals correct substance properly taken 995." The correct codes for adverse effect due to penicillin are 995.2 and E930.0.

A *poisoning* occurs when drugs or other chemical substances are taken not according to a physician's instruction. Poisonings occur in a variety of ways:

- the wrong dosage is given in error, either during medical treatment or by nonmedical personnel such as a mother or taken by self
- the medication is given to the wrong person

- the medication is taken by the wrong person
- medication overdose
- medications (prescription or over-the-counter) in combination with alcohol/other recreational drugs
- over-the-counter medications taken in combination with prescription medications without physician approval

Official Coding and Reporting Guidelines

2.14 POISONING

When coding a poisoning or reaction to the improper use of a medication (e.g., wrong dose, wrong substance, wrong route of administration) the poisoning code is sequenced first, followed by a code for the manifestation. If there is also a diagnosis of drug abuse or dependence to the substance, the abuse or dependence is coded as an additional code.

9.2 POISONING (960-979)

For poisoning when an error was made in drug prescription or in the administration of the drug by a physician, nurse, patient, or other person, use the appropriate code from the 960-979 series. If an overdose of a drug was intentionally taken or administered and resulted in drug toxicity, it would be coded as a poisoning (960-979 series). If a nonprescription drug or medicinal agent was taken in combination with a correctly prescribed and properly administered drug, any drug toxicity or other reaction resulting from the interaction of the two drugs would be classified as a poisoning.

Poisoning codes are found in the Table of Drugs and Chemicals. You must always sequence the poisoning code first, then code any manifestation of the poisoning such as coma. You also assign the corresponding E code from the Table. If there is no documentation to indicate otherwise, you use the E code from the accidental column.

You CANNOT use an E code from the therapeutic column (E930-E940) with a poisoning code.

EXAMPLE

Diagnosis: Coma due to accidental overdose of Valium

When you look up the main term "Overdose" in the Index, you are referred to the Table of Drugs and Chemicals.

Table of Drugs: Valium 969.4 (poisoning)

E853.2 (accidental)

Tabular: **969 Poisoning by psychotropic agents**

969.4 Benzodiazepine-based tranquilizers

Tabular:	**E853 Accidental poisoning by tranquilizers**
	E853.2 Benzodiazepine-based tranquilizers
Index:	**Coma 780.01**
Tabular:	**780 General symptoms**
	780.01 Coma
Codes:	969.4, 780.01, E853.2 Coma due to accidental overdose of Valium

Note that the poisoning code is sequenced first, followed by the manifestation and then the E code.

If there is no manifestation (coma in the above case) of the poisoning, you would assign only the poisoning code with the appropriate E code. When a patient has a poisoning that involves more than one drug or chemical, there could be a different poisoning code and E code for each drug or chemical. There are many codes to review when coding poisonings!

Official Coding and Reporting Guidelines

2.15 COMPLICATIONS OF SURGERY AND OTHER MEDICAL CARE

When the admission is for treatment of a complication resulting from surgery or other medical care, the complication code is sequenced as the principal diagnosis. If the complication is classified to the 996-999 series (complications), an additional code for the specific complication may be assigned.

When coding complications of surgical or medical care, you must be careful to make sure that there are actual complications present. A surgical complication is one that takes place as a result of the procedure. Just because a complication occurs following a procedure does not mean the complication is a surgical complication. Do not assume a cause-and-effect relationship. Clarify any doubt or questions with the physician.

EXERCISE HH *Injury/Poisoning and Complications*

In the Index, you will find complications of medical and surgical procedures under the main term "Complications." Locate "Complications" in the Index.

What code does the Index direct you to for the following complications?

1. Breast implants, infection

   Code(s): ____________________

2. Bone marrow graft, rejection

   Code(s): ____________________

3. Surgical procedures, stitch abscess

   Code(s): ____________________

4. Cardiac pacemaker, (device) mechanical complication

   Code(s): ____________________

Now fill in the code for the following diagnostic statements:

5. Palpitations due to overdose of monoamine oxidase

   Code(s): ____________________

6. Fracture, right clavicle

   Code(s): ____________________

7. Sprain, left ankle

   Code(s): ____________________

8. Abrasion, right elbow

   Code(s): ____________________

9. First- and second-degree burn, forehead

   Code(s): ____________________

10. Concussion

    Code(s): ____________________

11. Foreign body (penny) in stomach

    Code(s): ____________________

12. Contusion, left hip

    Code(s): ____________________

13. Traumatic amputation, right foot, without complications

    Code(s): ____________________

14. Open wound, right hand

    Code(s): ____________________

15. A 5-year-old presents with a rash following ingestion of erythromycin (properly prescribed) for an ear infection.

    (Hint: There are two codes for this case: one for the rash and an E code from the Table of Drugs and Chemicals for the adverse reaction to the therapeutic use of erythromycin.) What are the two codes?

Code(s): ___________________

16. A patient develops gastrointestinal bleeding while taking Motrin as prescribed for abdominal cramping. (Hint: Two conditions need to be coded. You will need to consult the Physician's Desk Reference to find out what Motrin is called in its generic form.)

    Code(s): ___________________

17. A patient is admitted with nausea, weakness, sweating, and tachycardia following a gastrectomy. A diagnosis of dumping syndrome is made.

    a. The condition here is dumping syndrome. What is the code for this condition?

       Code(s): ___________________

    b. Why is the code 997.4, gastrointestinal complications, not correct to use?

       ____

18. A patient develops acute renal failure following a cardiac catheterization and is admitted for dialysis.

    a. There are two conditions in the case. What are they?

       ______________________________ and ______________________________

    b. What are the two codes for these conditions?

       Code(s): ___________________

19. A patient died from an overdose of heroin. (Hint: Use the Table of Drugs and Chemicals and assign an E code.) What are the codes?

    Code(s): ___________________

20. A patient is lethargic with severe abdominal cramping and vomiting following ingestion of five Tylenol with codeine and a bottle of vodka. There are six codes for this case. (*Note:* Unless intent is specified, the incident is considered accidental when assigning E codes.)

    a. Codeine, poisoning

       Code(s): ___________________

    b. Acetaminophen, poisoning

       Code(s): ___________________

    c. Alcohol, beverage

       Code(s): ___________________

d. Lethargy

Code(s): ________________

e. Vomiting

Code(s): ________________

f. Cramp, abdominal, unspecified site

Code(s): ________________

MORE GENERAL GUIDELINES

You have now reviewed all of the chapter-specific guidelines. However, there are a few more guidelines to review.

Other diagnoses are defined as "all conditions that coexist at the time of admission, that develop subsequently, or that affect the treatment received and/or the length of stay. Diagnoses that relate to an earlier episode which have no bearing on the current hospital stay are to be excluded."

Reporting Other (Additional) Diagnoses

The general rule is that for reporting purposes, the definition for "other diagnoses" is interpreted as additional conditions that affect patient care in terms of requiring the following:

- clinical evaluation, or
- therapeutic treatment, or
- diagnostic procedures, or
- extended length of hospital stay, or
- increased nursing care and/or monitoring

The listing of the diagnoses on the attestation statement is the responsibility of the attending physician.

3.1 PREVIOUS CONDITIONS

If the physician has included a diagnosis in the final diagnostic statement, such as the discharge summary or the face sheet, it should ordinarily be coded. Some physicians include in the diagnostic statement resolved conditions or diagnoses and status post procedures from previous admission that have no bearing on the current stay. Such conditions are not to be reported and are coded only if required by hospital policy.

However, history codes (V10-V19) may be used as secondary codes if the historical condition or family history has an impact on current care or influences treatment.

EXERCISE 11 *Previous Conditions*

Circle the conditions in the following diagnostic lists that would not be coded:

1. herpes zoster
   history of hysterectomy
   diabetes
2. influenza
   hypertension (currently controlled on medication)
   history of peptic ulcer disease

Official Coding and Reporting Guidelines

3.2 DIAGNOSES NOT LISTED IN THE FINAL DIAGNOSTIC STATEMENT

When the physician has documented what appears to be a current diagnosis in the body of the record, but has not included the diagnosis in the final diagnostic statement, the physician should be asked whether the diagnosis should be added.

3.3 CONDITIONS THAT ARE AN INTEGRAL PART OF A DISEASE PROCESS

Conditions that are integral to the disease process should not be assigned as additional codes.

3.4 CONDITIONS THAT ARE NOT AN INTEGRAL PART OF A DISEASE PROCESS

Additional conditions that may not be associated routinely with a disease process should be coded when present.

3.5 ABNORMAL FINDINGS

Abnormal findings (laboratory, x-ray, pathologic, and other diagnostic results) are not coded and reported unless the physician indicates their clinical significance. If the findings are outside the normal range and the physician has ordered other tests to evaluate the condition or prescribed treatment, it is appropriate to ask the physician whether the diagnosis should be added.

EXERCISE JJ Other Diagnoses

Circle those diagnoses that should not be coded:

1. acute myocardial infarction
   chest pain
   shortness of breath
   congestive heart failure
2. fractured hip
   hip pain
   contusion of hip

In the following cases, would anemia be coded?

3. A patient is admitted with a fractured femur and undergoes an open reduction. Laboratory values following surgery show a hemoglobin level of 8 mg/dL. No additional workup is done or treatment is provided.

   ____

4. A patient is also admitted for reduction of a hip fracture but receives two units of blood following two reports of hemoglobin volumes of 7 and 8 mg/dL.

   ____

In the following case, would the potassium level be coded?

5. A patient with gastroenteritis has a blood sample drawn that shows low levels of potassium. The physician initials the test result but does not order potassium supplements or additional laboratory studies.

   ____

All Guidelines are located in Appendix B of this text.

BASIC CODING GUIDELINES FOR OUTPATIENT SERVICES

Official Coding and Reporting Guidelines

DIAGNOSTIC CODING AND REPORTING GUIDELINES FOR OUTPATIENT SERVICES (HOSPITAL-BASED AND PHYSICIAN OFFICE)

Introduction

These revised coding guidelines for outpatient diagnoses have been approved for use by hospitals/physicians in coding and reporting hospital-based outpatient services and physician office visits.

Information about the use of certain abbreviations, punctuation, symbols, and other conventions used in the ICD-9-CM Tabular List (code numbers and titles) can be found in the section at the beginning of the ICD-9-CM on "Conventions Used in the Tabular List." Information about the correct sequence to use in finding a code is described in the Introduction to the Alphabetic Index of ICD-9-CM.

The terms encounter and visit are often used interchangeably in describing outpatient service contacts and, therefore, appear together in these guidelines without distinguishing one from the other.

Coding guidelines for outpatient and physician reporting of diagnoses will vary in a number of instances from those for inpatient diagnoses, recognizing that:

- The Uniform Hospital Discharge Data Set (UHDDS) definition of principal diagnosis applies only to inpatients in acute, short-term, general hospitals.
- Coding guidelines for inconclusive diagnoses (probable, suspected, rule out, etc.) were developed for inpatient reporting and do not apply to outpatients.
- Diagnoses often are not established at the time of the initial encounter/visit. It may take two or more visits before the diagnosis is confirmed.

The most critical rule involves beginning the search for the correct code assignment through the Alphabetic Index. Never begin searching initially in the Tabular List as this will lead to coding errors.

BASIC CODING GUIDELINES FOR OUTPATIENT SERVICES

A. The appropriate code or codes from 001.0 through V82.9 must be used to identify diagnoses, symptoms, conditions, problems, complaints, or other reason(s) for the encounter/visit.

B. For accurate reporting of ICD-9-CM diagnosis codes, the documentation should describe the patient's condition, using terminology which includes specific diagnoses as well as symptoms, problems, or reasons for the encounter. There are ICD-9-CM codes to describe all of these.

C. The selection of codes 001.0 through 999.9 will frequently be used to describe the reason for the encounter. These codes are from the section of ICD-9-CM for the classification of diseases and injuries (eg, infectious and parasitic diseases; neoplasms; symptoms, signs, and ill-defined conditions, etc.).

D. Codes that describe symptoms and signs, as opposed to diagnoses, are acceptable for reporting purposes when an established diagnosis has not been diagnosed (confirmed) by the physician. Chapter 16 of ICD-9-CM, Symptoms, Signs, and Ill-Defined Conditions (codes 780.0-799.9), contains many, but not all codes for symptoms.

E. ICD-9-CM provides codes to deal with encounters for circumstances other than a disease or injury. The Supplementary Classification of Factors Influencing Health Status and Contact with Health Services (V01.0-V82.9) is provided to deal with occasions when circumstances other than a disease or injury are recorded as diagnosis or problems.

F. ICD-9-CM is composed of codes with either 3, 4, or 5 digits. Codes with 3 digits are included in ICD-9-CM as the heading of a category of codes that may be further subdivided by the use of fourth and/or fifth digits which provide greater specificity.

   A three-digit code is to be used only if it is not further subdivided. Where fourth-digit subcategories and/or fifth-digit subclassifications are provided, they must be assigned. A code is invalid if it has not been coded to the full number of digits for that code.

G. List first the ICD-9-CM code for the diagnosis, condition, problem, or other reason for encounter/visit shown in the medical record to be chiefly responsible for the services provided. List additional codes that describe any coexisting conditions.

H. Do not code diagnoses documented as "probable," "suspected," "questionable," "rule out," or "working diagnosis." Rather, code the condition(s) to the highest degree of certainty for that encounter/visit, such as symptoms, signs, abnormal test results, or other reason for the visit.

Please note: This is contrary to the coding practices used by hospitals and medical record departments for coding the diagnosis of hospital inpatients.

I. Chronic diseases treated on an ongoing basis may be coded and reported as many times as the patient receives treatment and care for the condition(s).

J. Code all documented conditions that coexist at the time of the encounter/visit, and require or affect patient care treatment or management. Do not code conditions that were previously treated and no longer exist. However, history codes (V10-V19) may be used as secondary codes if the historical condition or family history has an impact on current care or influences treatment.

K. For patients receiving diagnostic services only during an encounter/visit, sequence first the diagnosis, condition, problem, or other reason for encounter/visit shown in the medical record to be chiefly responsible for the outpatient services provided during the encounter/visit. Codes for other diagnoses (e.g., chronic conditions) may be sequenced as additional diagnoses.

L. For patients receiving therapeutic services only during an encounter/visit, sequence first the diagnosis, condition, problem, or other reason for encounter/visit shown in the medical record to be chiefly responsible for the outpatient services provided during the encounter/visit. Codes for other diagnoses (e.g., chronic conditions) may be sequenced as additional diagnoses.

M. The only exception to this rule is that for patients receiving chemotherapy, radiation therapy, or rehabilitation, the appropriate V code for the service is listed first, and the diagnosis or problem for which the service is being performed is listed second.

N. For patients receiving preoperative evaluations only, sequence a code from category V72.8, Other specified examinations, to describe the pre-op consultations. Assign a code for the condition to describe the reason for the surgery as an additional diagnosis. Code also any findings related to the pre-op evaluation.

O. For ambulatory surgery, code the diagnosis for which the surgery was performed. If the postoperative diagnosis is known to be different from the preoperative diagnosis at the time the diagnosis is confirmed, select the postoperative diagnosis for coding, since it is the most definitive.

OVERVIEW OF ICD-10-CM AND ICD-10-PCS

Development of the ICD-10

The tenth edition of the *International Classification of Diseases* was issued in 1993 by the World Health Organization (WHO), and WHO is responsible for maintaining the ICD. ICD-10 does not include a procedure classification (Volume 3). World governments are responsible for adapting the ICD-10 to suit their country's needs. For example, Australia uses the ICD-10-AM, ie, the ICD-10-**A**ustralian **M**odification. The governments are responsible for ensuring that their country's modification conforms with the WHO convention for the ICD-10. In the United States, the Health Care Financing Administration (HCFA) is responsible for developing the procedure classification entitled the ICD-10-PCS (PCS stands for **P**rocedure **C**oding **S**ystem). The National Center for Health Statistics (NCHS) is responsible for the disease classification system (Volumes 1 and 2) entitled ICD-10-CM (CM stands for **C**linical **M**odification). The ICD-10-CM and ICD-10-PCS are scheduled for introduction sometime after the year 2004.

The ICD-10 is already widely used in Europe, but conversion to the new edition in the United States has taken a great deal of implementation time. One reason for the additional time needed for conversion is that the ICD-9-CM is the basis for the hospital billing system in the United States. In addition, Diagnosis Related Groups (DRG) is the prospective payment system in place for reimbursement of Medicare hospital inpatient stays and the DRG system is based on the ICD-9-CM.

At the time of publication of this textbook, the final versions of the ICD-10-CM and ICD-10-PCS had not been released. Therefore, all information presented here is from the draft version of the ICD-10-CM information.

Development of the ICD-10-CM to Replace ICD-9-CM, Volumes 1 and 2

The ICD-10-CM will replace ICD-9-CM, Volumes 1 and 2. Prior to the implementation of the new edition, extensive consultation and review with physican groups, clinical coders, and others must take place. The NCHS has established a twenty-member Technical Advisory Panel made up of representatives of the health care and coding communities to provide input during the development of the tenth edition.

Improvements in the ICD-10-CM

Notable improvements in the content and format of the ICD-10-CM include the:

- addition of information relevant to ambulatory and managed care encounters
- expanded injury codes

  Extensive expansion of the injury codes allows for greater specificity. For example, S50.351 is the new code for "Superficial foreign body of right elbow."
- creation of combination diagnosis/symptom codes to reduce the number of codes needed to fully describe a condition

  For example, I25.12 is the new code for "Atherosclerotic heart disease with unstable angina." Under the ICD-9-CM, two codes are required to classify both diagnoses.
- addition of a sixth character

  For example, S06.336 is the new code for "Contusion and laceration of brainstem with prolonged [> than 24 hrs.] loss of consciousness. . . ."
- incorporation of common fourth- and fifth-digit subclassifications

  For example, F10.04 is the new code for "Alcohol abuse with alcohol-induced mood disorder."
- updating and added specificity of diabetes mellitus

  For example, E11.21 is the new code for "Type 2 diabetes mellitus with nephropathy."
- greater specificity in code assignment

Structure of the System

ICD-10-CM contains 21 chapters and excludes the supplementary classifications found in ICD-9-CM. The E and V codes from ICD-9-CM have been incorporated throughout ICD-10-CM. Chapter titles in ICD-10-CM remain the same except for two new chapters: Chapter VII, Diseases of the Eye and Adnexa; and Chapter VIII, Diseases of the Ear and Mastoid Process.

Crosswalk

As a part of the conversion, a *crosswalk* has been developed. This crosswalk converts ICD-9-CM codes to ICD-10-CM codes. Figure 7–4 illustrates a section of the crosswalk. Sometimes, more than one ICD-10-CM code will crosswalk from the ICD-9-CM code. For these instances, the possible matches are noted in a "Best Match" column. For example, in Figure 7–4 the ICD-9-CM code 281.1, Vitamin B12 deficiency anemia NEC, has five possible matches with ICD-10-CM codes. In the Best Match column the symbol "#a" indicates that the best match for 281.1 would be ICD-10-CM code D51.9. Every ICD-9-CM code is crosswalked in this manner to ICD-10-CM code(s).

Index

The Index for the ICD-10-CM is alphabetical, as illustrated in Figure 7–5. As in the ICD-9-CM, the Index is arranged with main terms in bold typeface and subterms are indented under the main term. Following the index entry is a code. Sometimes, only the first four digits of the code are given. To ensure that you have chosen the correct code and/or to obtain the remaining digits, you must reference the Tabular.

Tabular

The 21 chapters of the Tabular are arranged in numeric order after the first letter assigned to the chapter. For example, the letter R is assigned to the chapter regarding symptoms. Figure 7–6 illustrates a portion of the chapter on symptoms.

Figure 7–4
ICD-9-CM to ICD-10-CM Conversion (crosswalk). (Courtesy of U.S. Department of Health and Human Services, Health Care Financing Administration.)

ICD-9-CM to ICD-10-CM Conversion
Diseases of theBlood and Blood-forming Organs
(pound sign (#) following ICD-10-CM code indicates the best match of one to many matches)

ICD-9-CM Code	ICD-9-CM Abbreviated Title	ICD-10-CM Code	Best Match	ICD-10-CM Abbreviated Title
280	IRON DEFICIENCY ANEMIAS			
280.0	IRON DEF ANEM DT BL LOSS	D50.0		CHRONIC BLOOD LOSS ANEMIA
280.1	IRON DEF ANEM DT DIET	D50.8		FE DEFICIENCY ANEMIA NEC
280.8	IRON DEFICIT ANEMIAS NEC	D50.1		SIDEROPENIC DYSPHAGIA
280.8	IRON DEFICIT ANEMIAS NEC	D50.8	#b	FE DEFICIENCY ANEMIA NEC
280.9	IRON DEFICIT ANEMIA NOS	D50.9		FE DEFICIENCY ANEMIA NOS
281	OTHER DEFICIENCY ANEMIAS			
281.0	PERNICIOUS ANEMIA	D51.0		PERNICIOUS ANEMIA
281.1	VIT B12 DEFIC ANEMIA NEC	D51.1		HEREDIT MEGALOBLAST ANEM
281.1	VIT B12 DEFIC ANEMIA NEC	D51.2		TRANSCOBALAMIN DEF ANEM
281.1	VIT B12 DEFIC ANEMIA NEC	D51.3		DIETARY B12 DEF ANEM NEC
281.1	VIT B12 DEFIC ANEMIA NEC	D51.8		B12 DEFICIENC ANEM NEC
281.1	VIT B12 DEFIC ANEMIA NEC	D51.9	#a	B12 DEFICIENC ANEM NOS

ICD-10-CM Best Match for 281.1

Best Match Designation

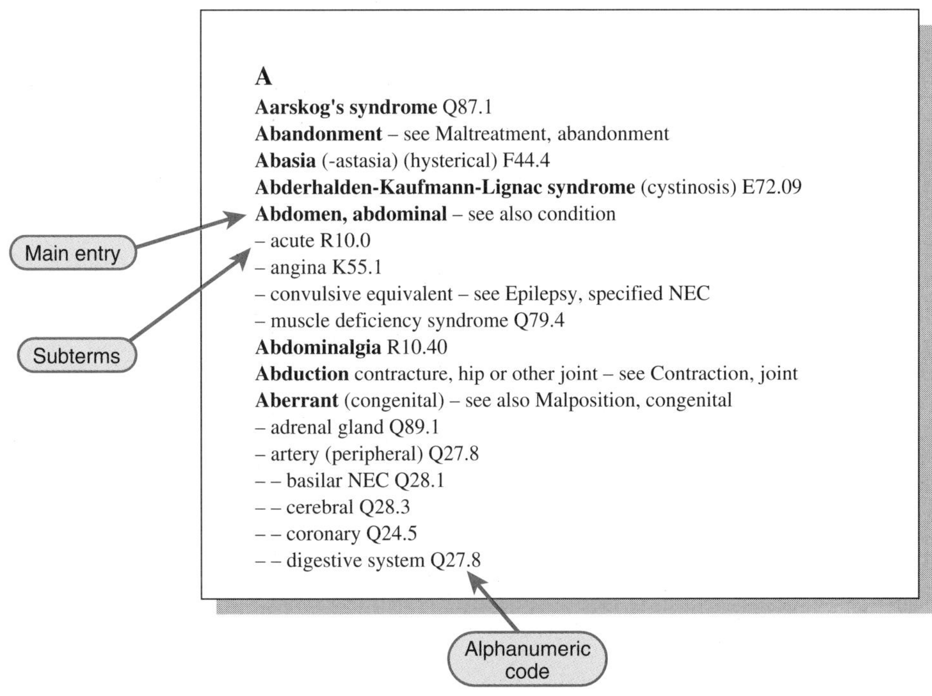

A
Aarskog's syndrome Q87.1
Abandonment – see Maltreatment, abandonment
Abasia (-astasia) (hysterical) F44.4
Abderhalden-Kaufmann-Lignac syndrome (cystinosis) E72.09
Abdomen, abdominal – see also condition
– acute R10.0
– angina K55.1
– convulsive equivalent – see Epilepsy, specified NEC
– muscle deficiency syndrome Q79.4
Abdominalgia R10.40
Abduction contracture, hip or other joint – see Contraction, joint
Aberrant (congenital) – see also Malposition, congenital
– adrenal gland Q89.1
– artery (peripheral) Q27.8
– – basilar NEC Q28.1
– – cerebral Q28.3
– – coronary Q24.5
– – digestive system Q27.8

Figure 7–5
ICD-10-CM Index. (Courtesy of U.S. Department of Health and Human Services, Health Care Financing Administration.)

Note that in the index (Figure 7–5) the main entry is "Abdomen, abdominal" and the first subterm is "acute," directing the coder to the Tabular location of "R10.0." Now, note in the Tabular (Figure 7–6) the location of "R10.0" as "Acute abdomen."

Developing the ICD-10-PCS to Replace ICD-9-CM, Volume 3

The new structure will allow more expansion than was possible with the ICD-9-CM. Because the ICD-9-CM lacks specificity (exactness) and does not provide for sufficient expansion to support government payment systems and data needs, HCFA contracted with 3M Health Information Systems to develop the ICD-10-PCS to replace ICD-9-CM procedure codes for reporting inpatient procedures.

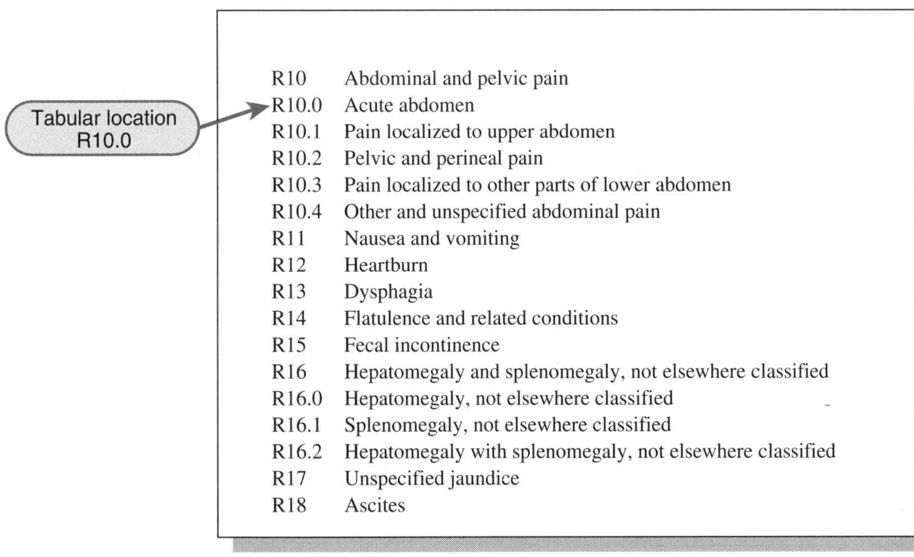

R10	Abdominal and pelvic pain
R10.0	Acute abdomen
R10.1	Pain localized to upper abdomen
R10.2	Pelvic and perineal pain
R10.3	Pain localized to other parts of lower abdomen
R10.4	Other and unspecified abdominal pain
R11	Nausea and vomiting
R12	Heartburn
R13	Dysphagia
R14	Flatulence and related conditions
R15	Fecal incontinence
R16	Hepatomegaly and splenomegaly, not elsewhere classified
R16.0	Hepatomegaly, not elsewhere classified
R16.1	Splenomegaly, not elsewhere classified
R16.2	Hepatomegaly with splenomegaly, not elsewhere classified
R17	Unspecified jaundice
R18	Ascites

Figure 7–6
ICD-10-CM Tabular. (Courtesy of U.S. Department of Health and Human Services, Health Care Financing Administration.)

Four major objectives guided the development of ICD-10-PCS:

1. **Completeness** There should be a unique code for all substantially different procedures. Currently, procedures on different body parts, with different approaches or of different types, are sometimes assigned to the same code.
2. **Expandability** As new procedures are developed, the structure of ICD-10-PCS should allow for their incorporation as unique codes.
3. **Multiaxial** ICD-10-PCS should have a structure such that each code character has, as much as possible, the same meaning, both within the specific procedure section and across procedure sections.
4. **Standardized Terminology** While the meaning of specific words can vary in common usage, ICD-10-PCS should not include multiple meanings for the same term; each term should be assigned a specific meaning, and ICD-10-PCS should include definitions of the terminology.

A complete, expandable, multiaxial ICD-10-PCS with standardized terminology will allow coding specialists to determine accurate codes with minimal effort.

Seven Characters of ICD-10-PCS

ICD-10-PCS has a seven-character alphanumeric code structure. Each character has up to 34 different values: 10 digits (0–9) and 24 letters (A–H, J–N, and P–Z) may be assigned to each character. The letters O and I are not used in order to avoid confusion with the digits 0 and 1. In the ICD-10-PCS the term "procedure" is used to refer to the complete designation of the seven characters. Procedures are divided into sections according to the type of procedure.

Character 1 Identifies the Section

The first character of the procedure code identifies the section. To assign an ICD-10-PCS code, the section where the procedure is coded must be identified. For example, a chest x-ray is in the Imaging section, a breast biopsy is in the Medical and Surgical section, and crisis intervention is in the Mental Health section. Each section is identified by a specific character—number or letter. Section titles and numbers/letters are shown in Figure 7–7.

Figure 7–7
Sections of ICD-10-PCS. (Courtesy of U.S. Department of Health and Human Services, Health Care Financing Administration.)

	Sections
0	Medical and Surgical
1	Obstetrics
2	Placement
3	Administration
4	Measurement and Monitoring
5	Imaging
6	Nuclear Medicine
7	Radiation Oncology
8	Osteopathic
9	Rehabilitation and Diagnostic Audiology
B	Extracorporeal Assistance and Performance
C	Extracorporeal Therapies
D	Laboratory
F	Mental Health
G	Chiropractic
H	Miscellaneous

EXERCISE KK ICD-10-PCS First Character

Using Figure 7–7, identify the first character that would be assigned to the following procedures:

1. _____ Gait training (Rehabilitation)
2. _____ Cesarean section (Obstetrics)
3. _____ Computerized tomography, spine (Imaging)
4. _____ Cholecystectomy (Medical/Surgical)
5. _____ Insertion of radium into cervix (brachytherapy) (Nuclear Medicine)
6. _____ Cranioplasty (Medical/Surgical)

Changing Characters

Characters 2 through 7 have a standard meaning within each section, but may have different meanings across sections. The meanings for each character are described in each section. For example, Figure 7–8 shows the meanings of the seven characters for the Medical and Surgical sections while Figure 7–9 shows the meanings for the Imaging section. Notice that several characters have different meanings across these sections. For instance, the third character in medical and surgical procedures (Figure 7–8) is used to define the root *operation* (extraction, insertion, removal, etc.), whereas the third character in imaging procedures (Figure 7–9) is used to define the root *type* (fluoroscopy, MRI, CT, ultrasonography, etc.).

Each code MUST include seven characters. If a character is not applicable for a specific procedure, the letter Z is used.

Character 2 Is the Body System

The second character identifies the body system in all sections except Rehabilitation and Mental Health. In these two sections, the second character identifies the type of procedure performed.

Character 3 Is the Root Operation

The third character identifies the root operation in all sections except Radiation Oncology, Rehabilitation, and Mental Health. In many sections, only a few root operations are performed, and these operations are defined for use in that section. The Medical and Surgical section uses an extensive list of root operations.

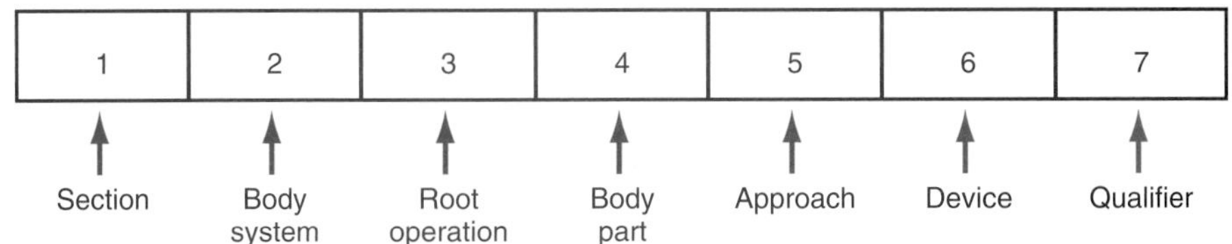

Figure 7–8
Medical and surgical procedures. (Courtesy of U.S. Department of Health and Human Services, Health Care Financing Administration.)

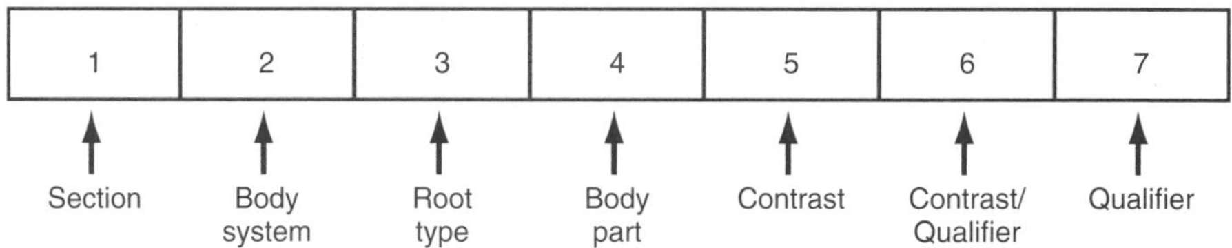

Figure 7–9
Imaging procedures. (Courtesy of U.S. Department of Health and Human Services, Health Care Financing Administration.)

The Obstetrics and Placement sections use some of these same root operations as well as section-specific root operations. See Table 7–1 for a list of the Medical and Surgical root operations definitions, explanations, and examples.

TABLE 7–1 Medical and Surgical Root Operations

0	**Alteration**	**Definition:** Modifying the natural anatomic structure of a body part without affecting the function of the body part **Explanation:** Principle purpose is to improve appearance. **Examples:** Face lift Breast augmentation
1	**Bypass**	**Definition:** Altering the route of passage of the contents of a tubular body part **Explanation:** Rerouting contents around an area of a body part to another distal (downstream) area in the normal route; to another different but similar route and body part; or to an abnormal route and another dissimilar body part. **Encompasses:** Diversion, reroute, shunt **Examples:** Gastrojejunal bypass Coronary artery bypass
2	**Change**	**Definition:** Taking out or off a device from a body part and putting back an identical or similar device in or on the same body part without cutting or puncturing the skin or a mucous membrane **Explanation:** Requires no invasive intervention **Example:** Change a drainage tube
3	**Control**	**Definition:** Stopping, or attempting to stop, postprocedural bleeding **Explanation:** Confined to postprocedural bleeding and limited to the Anatomic Regions, Upper Extremities, and Lower Extremities Body Systems **Examples:** Control of postprostatectomy bleeding Control of postpneumonectomy bleeding
4	**Creation**	**Definition:** Making a new structure that does not physically take the place of a body part **Explanation:** Confined to sex change operations where genitalia are made **Encompasses:** Formation **Examples:** Create an artificial vagina in a male Create an artificial penis in a female
5	**Destruction**	**Definition:** Eradicating all or a portion of a body part **Explanation:** The actual physical destruction of all or a portion of a body part by the direct use of energy, force, or a destructive agent. There is no tissue taken out. **Encompasses:** Ablation, cauterization, coagulation, crush, electrocoagulation, fulguration, mash, obliteration **Examples:** Fulgurate a rectal polyp Crush a fallopian tube

TABLE 7–1 Medical and Surgical Root Operations *Continued*

6	**Detachment**	**Definition:** Cutting off all or a portion of an extremity **Explanation:** Pertains only to extremities. The body part determines the level of the detachment. All of the body parts distal to the detachment level are detached. **Encompasses:** Amputation **Examples:** Shoulder disarticulation Below-knee amputation
7	**Dilation**	**Definition:** Expanding the orifice or the lumen of a tubular body part **Explanation:** Stretching by pressure using intraluminal instrumentation **Examples:** Dilate the trachea Dilate the anal sphincter
8	**Division**	**Definition:** Separating, without taking out, all or a portion of a body part **Explanation:** Separating into two or more portions by sharp or blunt dissection **Encompasses:** Bisection **Examples:** Bisect an ovary Spinal cordotomy Divide a patent ductus
9	**Drainage**	**Definition:** Taking or letting out fluids and/or gases from a body part **Explanation:** The fluids or gases may be normal or abnormal. **Encompasses:** Aspiration, evacuation, marsupialization, needle, puncture, rupture, stab, suction, tap, unbridle, undercut, window **Examples:** I & D of an abscess Thoracentesis
B	**Excision**	**Definition:** Cutting out or off, without replacement, a portion of a body part **Explanation:** Involves the act of cutting using a sharp instrument or other method such as a hot knife or laser **Encompasses:** Biopsy, core needle biopsy, debridement, debulk, fine needle aspiration, punch, shuck, trim, wedge **Examples:** Partial nephrectomy Wedge ostectomy Pulmonary segmentectomy
C	**Extirpation**	**Definition:** Taking or cutting out solid matter from a body part **Explanation:** Taking out solid matter (which may or may not have been broken up) by cutting with either a sharp instrument or other method such as a hot knife or laser, by blunt dissection, by pulling, by stripping, or by suctioning, with the intent not to take out any appreciable amount of the body part. The solid matter may be imbedded in the tissue of the body part or in the lumen of a tubular body part. **Examples:** Sequestrectomy Cholelithotomy
D	**Extraction**	**Definition:** Taking out or off all or a portion of a body part **Explanation:** The body part is not completely dissected free but is pulled or stripped by the use of force (eg, manual, suction, etc.) from its location. **Encompasses:** Abrasion, avulsion, strip **Examples:** Tooth extraction Vein stripping Dermabrasion
F	**Fragmentation**	**Definition:** Breaking down solid matter in a body part **Explanation:** Physically breaking up solid matter not normally present in a body part such as stones and foreign bodies. The breakup may be accomplished by direct physical force or shock waves applied directly or indirectly through intervening layers. The resulting debris is not taken out but is passed from the body or absorbed by the body. The solid matter may be in the lumen of a tubular body part or in a body cavity. **Encompasses:** Pulverization **Examples:** Lithotripsy, urinary stones Lithotripsy, gallstones

Table continued on following page

TABLE 7–1 Medical and Surgical Root Operations *Continued*

G	**Fusion**	**Definition:** Joining together portions of an articular body part, rendering the articular body part immobile **Explanation:** Confined to joints **Examples:** Spinal fusion Ankle arthrodesis
H	**Insertion**	**Definition:** Putting in a nonbiologic appliance that monitors, assists, performs, or prevents a physiologic function, but does not physically take the place of a body part **Encompasses:** Cutdown, implantation, passage **Examples:** Implant a radioactive element Insert a diaphragmatic pacemaker
J	**Inspection**	**Definition:** Visually and/or manually exploring a body part **Explanation:** Looking at a body part directly or with an optical instrument or feeling the body part directly or through intervening body layers **Encompasses:** Check, enter, examination, exploration, expose, open, probe **Examples:** Diagnostic arthroscopy Exploratory laparotomy
K	**Map**	**Definition:** Locating the route of passage of electrical impulses and/or locating functional areas in a body part **Explanation:** Confined to the cardiac conduction mechanism and the central nervous system **Encompasses:** Localization **Examples:** Map cardiac conduction pathways Locate cortical areas
L	**Occlusion**	**Definition:** Completely closing the orifice or lumen of a tubular body part **Explanation:** Can be accomplished intraluminally or extraluminally **Encompasses:** Clamp, clip, embolization, interruption, ligation, stoppage, suture, ligation **Examples:** Ligate the vas deferens Fallopian tube ligation
M	**Reattachment**	**Definition:** Putting back in or on all or a portion of a body part **Explanation:** Pertains only to body parts or appendages that have been severed. May or may not involve the re-establishment of vascular and nervous supplies. **Encompasses:** Replantation **Examples:** Reattach penis Reattach a hand Replant parathyroids
N	**Release**	**Definition:** Freeing a body part **Explanation:** Eliminating abnormal compression or restraint by force or sharp or blunt dissection. Some of the restraining tissue may be taken out, but none of the body part itself is taken out. **Encompasses:** Decompression, free, lysis, mobilization, relaxation, relief, section, take down **Examples:** Lyse peritoneal adhesions Free median nerve
P	**Removal**	**Definition:** Taking out or off a device from a body part **Explanation:** May or may not involve invasive penetration **Examples:** Remove a drainage tube Remove a cardiac pacemaker
Q	**Repair**	**Definition:** Restoring, to the extent possible, a body part to its natural anatomic structure **Explanation:** An operation of exclusion. Most of the other operations are some type of repair, but if the objective of the procedure is one of the other operations, then that operation is coded. If none of the other operations is performed to accomplish the repair, then the operation "repair" is coded.

TABLE 7–1 Medical and Surgical Root Operations *Continued*

		Encompasses: Closure, correction, fix, reconstruction, reduction, reformation, reinforcement, restoration, stitch, suture **Examples:** Tracheoplasty Suture laceration Herniorrhaphy
R	**Replacement**	**Definition:** Putting in or on biologic or synthetic material that physically takes the place of all or a portion of a body part **Explanation:** The biologic material may be living similar or dissimilar tissue from the same individual or nonliving similar or dissimilar tissue from the same individual, another individual, or animal. The body part replaced may have been previously taken out, previously replaced, or may be taken out concurrently with the replacement. **Examples:** Replace external ear with synthetic prosthesis Total hip replacement Replacement of part of the aorta Free skin graft Pedicle skin graft
S	**Reposition**	**Definition:** Moving to its normal location or other suitable location all or a portion of a body part **Explanation:** The body part repositioned is aberrant, compromised, or may have been detached. If attached, it may or may not be detached to accomplish the repositioning. **Examples:** Reposition undescended testicle Reposition an aberrant kidney
T	**Resection**	**Definition:** Cutting out or off, without replacement, all of a body part **Explanation:** Involves the act of cutting with either a sharp instrument or other method such as a hot knife or laser **Examples:** Total gastrectomy Pneumonectomy Total nephrectomy
V	**Restriction**	**Definition:** Partially closing the orifice or lumen of a tubular body part **Explanation:** Can be accomplished intraluminally or extraluminally **Encompasses:** Band, cerclage, collapse, compression, pack, tamponade **Examples:** Fundoplication Cervical cerclage
W	**Revision**	**Definition:** Correcting a portion of a previously performed procedure **Explanation:** Redoing a portion of a previously performed procedure that has failed to function as intended. Revisions exclude the complete redo of the procedure and procedures to correct complications that do not require the redoing of a portion of the original procedure, such as the control of bleeding. **Examples:** Revise hip replacement Revise gastroenterostomy
X	**Transfer**	**Definition:** Moving, without taking out, all or a portion of a body part to another location to take over the function of all or a portion of a body part **Explanation:** The body part transferred is not detached from the body. Its vascular and nerve supply remain intact. The body part whose function is taken over may or may not be similar. **Encompasses:** Transposition **Examples:** Nerve transfer Tendon transfer
Y	**Transplantation**	**Definition:** Putting in or on all or a portion of a living body part taken from another individual or animal to physically take the place and/or function of all or a portion of a similar body part **Explanation:** The native body part may or may not be taken out. The transplanted body part may either physically take the place of the native body part or simply take over all or a portion of its function. **Examples:** Lung transplant Kidney transplant

EXERCISE LL Root Operation

Place the character for the root operation term before its definition:

1. ______ Taking or letting out fluids and/or gases from a body part
2. ______ Freeing a body part
3. ______ Taking out or off a device from a body part
4. ______ Visually and/or manually exploring a body part
5. ______ Restoring to the extent possible a body part to its natural anatomic structure
6. ______ Altering the route of passage of the contents of a tubular body part
7. ______ Cutting out or off, without replacement, all of a body part
8. ______ Eradicating all or a portion of a body part
9. ______ Correcting a portion of a previously performed procedure
10. ______ Cutting out or off, without replacement, a portion of a body part

1 Bypass
4 Destruction
7 Drainage
8 Excision
L Release
M Removal
N Repair
R Resection
G Inspection
T Revision

A Closer Look at Root Operations

The root operation is described by one of the main terms as outlined in Table 7–1 (eg, alteration, destruction, transfer). These root operations can be grouped into types of operations, such as operations that always involve devices: insertion, replacement, removal, change. Table 7–2 shows the root operations grouped by types.

TABLE 7–2 Root Operations by Type

Operation	Action	Object	Modification	Example
		Operations that take out or eliminate all or a portion of a body part		
Excision	Cutting out or off	Portion of a body part	Without replacement of the body part	Sigmoid polypectomy
Resection	Cutting out or off	All of a body part	Without replacement of the body part	Total nephrectomy
Extraction	Taking out or off	All or a portion of a body part	Without replacement of the body part	Tooth extraction
Destruction	Eradicating	All or a portion of a body part	Without taking out any of the body part Without replacement of the body part	Fulgurate rectal polyp
Detachment	Cutting off	All or a portion of an extremity	Without replacement of the extremity	Below-knee amputation

TABLE 7–2 Root Operations by Type *Continued*

Operation	Action	Object	Modification	Example
		Operations that involve putting in or on, putting back, or moving living body parts		
Transplantation	Putting in or on	All or a portion of a living body part	Taken from other individual or animal; physically takes the place and/or function of all or a portion of a body part	Heart transplant
Reattachment	Putting back in or on	All or a portion of a body part	Body part was detached	Reattach finger
Reposition	Move	All or a portion of a body part	Put in its normal or other suitable location. Body part may or may not be detached	Reposition of undescended testicle
Transfer	Move	All or a portion of a body part	Without taking out the body part; takes over function of similar body part	Tendon transfer
		Operations that take out or eliminate solid matter, fluids, or gases from a body part		
Drainage	Taking or letting out	Fluid and/or gases from a body part	Without taking out any of the body part	I & D of an abscess
Extirpation	Taking or cutting out	Solid matter in a body part	Without taking out any of the body part	Sequestrectomy
Fragmentation	Breaking down	Solid matter in a body part	Without taking out any of the body part or any of the solid matter	Lithotripsy, gallstones
		Operations that only involve examination of body parts and regions		
Inspection	Visual and/or manual exploration	A body part		Diagnostic arthroscopy
Map	Locating	Route of passage of electrical impulses Functional areas in a body part		Cardiac conduction pathways Locate cortical areas
		Operations that can be performed only on tubular body parts		
Bypass	Altering the route of passage	Contents of tubular body part	May include use of living tissue, nonliving biologic material or synthetic material which does not take the place of the body part	Gastrojejunal bypass
Dilation	Expanding	Orifice or lumen of a tubular body part	By application of pressure	Dilate anal sphincter
Occlusion	Completely closing	Orifice or lumen of a tubular body part		Fallopian tube ligation
Restriction	Partially closing	Orifice or lumen of a tubular body part		Cervical cerclage
		Operations that always involve devices		
Insertion	Putting in	Nonbiologic appliance	Does not physically take the place of body part	Pacemaker insertion
Replacement	Putting in or on	Biologic or synthetic material; living tissue taken from same individual	Physically takes the place of all or a portion of a body part	Total hip replacement
Removal	Taking out or off	Device		Remove cardiac pacemaker
Change	Taking out or off and putting back	Identical or similar device	Without cutting or puncturing the skin or mucous membrane	Change a drainage tube
		Miscellaneous operations		
Alteration	Modifying	Natural anatomic structures of a body part	Without affecting function of a body part	Face lift
Creation	Making	New structure	Does not physically take the place of a body part	Artificial vagina

Table continued on following page

TABLE 7–2 Root Operations by Type *Continued*

Operation	Action	Object	Modification	Example
Control	Stopping or attempting to stop	Postprocedural bleeding		Postprostatectomy bleeding
Division	Separating	A body part	Without taking out any of the body part	Bisect ovary
Fusion	Joining together	An articular body part	Rendering body part immobile	Spinal fusion
Release	Freeing	A body part	By eliminating compression or restriction; without taking out any of the body part	Lyse peritoneal adhesions
Repair	Restoring	To the extent possible, a body part to its natural anatomic structure	May include use of living tissue, nonliving biologic material, or synthetic material which does not take the place or take over the function of the body part	Hernia repair
Revision	Correcting	Portion of a previously performed procedure	Procedure failed to function as intended	Revise hip replacement

EXERCISE MM ***Root Operation Terms***

Using Table 7–2, identify the root operation term for each example:

1. ___________ Tendon transfer
2. ___________ Appendectomy
3. ___________ Diagnostic bronchoscopy
4. ___________ Kidney transplant
5. ___________ Cardioverter-defibrillator implantation
6. ___________ Removal of pulse generator for pacemaker
7. ___________ Lithotripsy, bladder stone
8. ___________ Fallopian tube ligation
9. ___________ Elbow replacement revision
10. ___________ Lysis peritoneal adhesions

The Index

ICD-10-PCS codes are described both in the Index and in the Tabular Listing. The Index, which allows codes to be located by an alphabetic lookup, is divided into two parts. The first part of the Index includes the following sections:

- Medical and Surgical
- Obstetrics
- Placement

- Measurement and Monitoring
- Administration
- Extracorporeal Assistance and Performance
- Extracorporeal Therapies
- Miscellaneous Sections

The first part of the Index is arranged by root operation terms with subentries by:

- Body System
- Body Part
- Operation (for Revision)
- Device (for Change)

The Index may also be consulted for a specific operation term such as "Hysterectomy," where a cross-reference directs you to see "Resection, Female Reproductive System, OVT." Although you need to become very familiar with the root operations, you may be able to locate a code for a specific operation such as an appendectomy more rapidly by looking under the term "Appendectomy" than by consulting the root operation term "Resection," subterms "*by* Body Part," and "Appendix." See Figure 7–10 for an example of the Index of ICD-10-PCS.

Fasciectomy – see Resection, Bursa, Ligaments, Fascia 0MB....
Fasciectomy – see Excision, Bursa, Ligaments, Fascia 0MT....
Fascioplasty – see Repair, Bursa, Ligaments, Fascia 0MG....
Fine Needle Aspiration – see Excision
Fix – see Repair
Flushing – see Irrigation
Formation – see Creation
Fragmentation
  by Body System
    Anatomical Regions 0XF....
    Central Nervous System 00F...
    Eye 08F...
    Female Reproduction System 0VF....
    Gastrointestinal System 0DF...
    Heart & Great Vessels 02F....
    Hepatobiliary System & Pancreas 0FF....
    Mouth & Throat 0CF....
    Respiratory System 0BF....
    Urinary System 0TF....
  by Body Part
    Ampulla of Vater 0FFB....
    Anus 0DFQ....
    Appendix 0DFJ....
    Bladder 0TF8....
    Bladder Neck 0TF9....
    Bronchus
      Lingula 0BF9....
      Lower Lobe 0BF....
      Main 0BF....
      Middle Lobe, Right 0BF5....
      Segmental, Lingula 0BF9....
      Upper Lobe 0BF....

Figure 7–10
ICD-10-PCS Index. (Courtesy of U.S. Department of Health and Human Services, Health Care Financing Administration.)

The second part of the Index covers the remaining sections. This part is also arranged by root operations. For example:

- Imaging—Fluoroscopy by Body System, by Body Part
- Nuclear Medicine—Nonimaging Assay by Body System, by Body Part
- Osteopathic—Treatment by Region

Codes may also be located in the second part of the Index by specific procedures such as a "Chest x-ray—see Plain Radiography, Anatomical Regions." The Index refers you to a specific entry in the Tabular List by providing the first three or four digits of the procedure code. It is always necessary to refer to the Tabular List to obtain the complete code since the Index contains only the first few numbers and letters.

The Tabular List Completes the Code

The Tabular List provides the remaining characters needed to complete the code given in the Index. The Tabular List is arranged by sections and most sections are subdivided by body systems. For each body system, the Tabular List begins with a listing of the operatons performed, ie, the root operations. When a procedure involves distinct parts, multiple codes are provided. For example, a section of the listing of the operations performed for the central nervous system is as follows.

- Bypass
- Change
- Destruction
- Division
- Drainage
- Excision

The Tabular List for each body system also includes a listing of the body parts, approaches, devices, and qualifiers for that system. These listings are followed by separate tables for each root operation in the body system. At the top of each of the tables is the name of the section, body system, and root operation, as well as the definition of the root operation. The list is formatted as a grid, with rows and columns. The four columns in the grid represent the last four characters of the code (which are labeled Body Part, Approach, Device, and Qualifier for the Obstetrics and Medical and Surgical sections). Each row in the grid specifies the allowable combinations of the last four characters. For example, looking at the grid in Figure 7–11, you can see that the code for delivery of retained products of conception is 10Y1BZZ:

1 Obstetrics
0 Pregnancy
Y Delivery
1 Products of Conception, Retained
B Transorifice Intraluminal
Z None
Z None

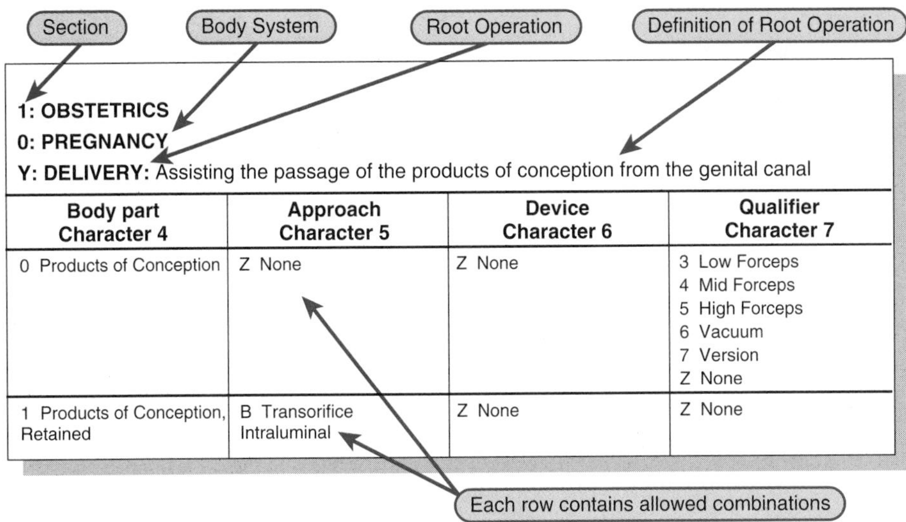

1: OBSTETRICS
0: PREGNANCY
Y: DELIVERY: Assisting the passage of the products of conception from the genital canal

Body part Character 4	Approach Character 5	Device Character 6	Qualifier Character 7
0 Products of Conception	Z None	Z None	3 Low Forceps 4 Mid Forceps 5 High Forceps 6 Vacuum 7 Version Z None
1 Products of Conception, Retained	B Transorifice Intraluminal	Z None	Z None

Figure 7–11
ICD-10-PCS Tabular. (Courtesy of U.S. Department of Health and Human Services, Health Care Financing Administration.)

Code 10Y1BZZ would be the only allowable code for "Products of Conception, Retained" since you may not complete a code by choosing entries from different rows (a row may consist of multiple entries in a box). Thus the code 10Y1BZ6 is not permitted, since the qualifier 6 can be used only with the body part 0; it cannot be used with body part 1. If you begin the code with "0, Products of Conception," you must continue to choose from the available numbers or letters in that same line. So, with the qualifier 6, the code would have to be 10Y0ZZ6.

EXERCISE NN ICD-10-PCS Format

Complete the following:

Achievement of the four major objectives guiding the development of ICD-10-PCS will result in a classification system that is:

1. ____________________
2. ____________________
3. ____________________
4. ____________________

Provide the requested information about the ICD-10-PCS code structure:

5. The ICD-10-PCS has a __________ character code structure.
6. The characters in ICD-10-PCS are __________.
7. Each character has up to __________ different values.
8. The letters __________ are not used as character values.
9. The complete specification of seven characters describes a(n) __________ in ICD-10-PCS.

CHAPTER GLOSSARY

AHA: American Hospital Association

AHIMA: American Health Information Management Association

anomaly: abnormality

asymptomatic: not showing any of the typical symptoms of a disease or condition

benign: not progressive or recurrent

benign hypertension: hypertensive condition with a continuous, mild blood pressure elevation

combination code: single five-digit code used to identify etiology and manifestations of a disease

comparative conditions: patient conditions that are documented as "either/or" in the patient record

congenital: existing from birth

Crohn's disease: regional enteritis

debridement: cleansing of or removing dead tissue from a wound

HCFA: Health Care Financing Administration

Hodgkin's disease: malignant lymphoma

hypertension, uncontrolled: untreated hypertension or hypertension that is not responding to the therapeutic regimen

hypertensive heart disease: the secondary effects on the heart of prolonged, sustained systemic hypertension; the heart has to work against greatly increased resistance, causing increased blood pressure

in situ: malignancy that is within the original site of development

italicized code: ICD-9-CM code that can never be sequenced as the principal diagnosis

late effect: residual effect (condition produced) after the acute phase of an illness or injury has terminated

lesion: abnormal or altered tissue, ie, wound, cyst, abscess, or boil

malignancy: used in reference to a cancerous tumor

malignant: used to describe a cancerous tumor that grows worse over time

malignant hypertension: accelerated, severe form of hypertension, manifested by headaches, blurred vision, dyspnea, and uremia; usually causes permanent organ damage

morphology: study of neoplasms

myocardial infarction (MI): necrosis of the myocardium resulting from interrupted blood supply

NEC: not elsewhere classified

neoplasm: new tumor growth that can be benign or malignant

NOS: not otherwise specified

Official Coding and Reporting Guidelines: rules of coding diagnosis codes (ICD-9-CM) published by the Editorial Advisory Board of Coding Clinic

pericarditis: swelling of the sac surrounding the great vessels and the heart

principal diagnosis: defined in the Uniform Hospital Discharge Data Set (UHDDS) as "that condition established after study to be chiefly responsible for occasioning the admission of the patient to the hospital for care: the principal diagnosis is sequenced first

prophylactic: substance or agent that offers some protection from disease

residual: that which is left behind or remains

Rule of Nines: rule used to estimate burned body surface in burn patients

RUQ: right upper quadrant

secondary site: place to which a malignant tumor has spread, metastatic site

sequela: a condition that follows an illness

slanted brackets: indicate that the ICD-9-CM code can never be sequenced as the principal diagnosis

thyroiditis: a thyroid gland inflammation

UHDDS: Uniform Hospital Discharge Data Set

uncertain behavior: refers to the behavior of a neoplasm as neither malignant nor benign but having characteristics of both malignant and benign

uncertain diagnosis: diagnosis documented at the time of discharge as "probable," "suspected," "likely," "questionable," "possible," or "rule out"

unspecified hypertension: hypertensive condition that has not been specified as either benign or malignant hypertension

unspecified nature: when the behavior or histology of a neoplasm is not known or is not specified

CHAPTER REVIEW Chapter 7, Part I, Theory

List, define, or describe the following, as directed:

1. The UHDDS definition of a Principal Diagnosis is: ______________________

    ____

    ____

    ____

2. List two of the four cooperating parties that agree on coding principles:

    ____

    ____

Chapter 7, Part II, Practical

Using the ICD-9-CM and coding guidelines, fill in the codes for the following:

1. Combined spinal cord degeneration with pernicious anemia

    Code(s): ____________________

2. Carcinoma, in situ, of skin of lip, vermilion border

    Code(s): ____________________

3. Bilateral occlusion of carotid arteries

    Code(s): ____________________

4. Subacute bacterial endocarditis

    Code(s): ____________________

5. Nephrogenic diabetes insipidus

    Code(s): ____________________

6. Ovarian cyst

    Code(s): ____________________

7. Uterine fibroids complicating pregnancy, 23 weeks' gestation

    Code(s): ____________________

8. Acute and chronic bronchitis

   Code(s): ___________________

9. Group B streptococcal pneumonia

   Code(s): ___________________

10. Obstructed labor caused by cephalopelvic disproportion, delivered liveborn male

    Code(s): ___________________

11. Term birth, delivered by cesarean section, with intrauterine growth retardation

    Code(s): ___________________

12. Alzheimer's disease

    Code(s): ___________________

13. Hypertension with end-stage renal disease

    Code(s): ___________________

14. Anal fistula

    Code(s): ___________________

15. Positive occult blood in stools

    Code(s): ___________________

16. Peptic ulcer, bleeding

    Code(s): ___________________

17. Acute anterior wall myocardial infarction

    Code(s): ___________________

18. Aneurysm of right coronary artery

    Code(s): ___________________

19. Sarcoidosis with cardiomyopathy

    Code(s): ___________________

20. Type I diabetes mellitus, uncontrolled, with diabetic nephropathy

    Code(s): ___________________

21. Mobitz II atrioventricular block

    Code(s): ____________________

22. Atherosclerosis of lower extremity with claudication

    Code(s): ____________________

23. Welder's keratitis

    Code(s): ____________________

24. Endocarditis secondary to typhoid fever

    Code(s): ____________________

25. Transient visual loss

    Code(s): ____________________

Fill in the ICD-9-CM codes for the following cases:

26. Mr. Jones presents to the emergency department with acute abdominal pain. After a thorough examination and diagnostic x-ray film, Mr. Jones is diagnosed with acute small bowel obstruction and taken immediately to surgery.

    Code(s): ____________________

27. Mrs. Smith is at 32 weeks' gestation and is admitted with severe bleeding with abdominal cramping. An emergency ultrasound is done and fetal monitors are applied. She is diagnosed with total placenta previa with indications of fetal distress. An emergency cesarean section is done, with delivery of a viable male infant.

    Code(s): ____________________

28. Mr. Jensen is status post colon resection 3 months ago for sigmoid colon cancer and is now admitted for adjunct chemotherapy.

    Code(s): ____________________

29. Miss Halliday is an 80-year-old woman who presents to the emergency department with a history of abdominal pain, fever, and burning with urination. Urine culture is obtained, and Miss Halliday is admitted for workup to rule out urosepsis.

    Code(s): ____________________

30. Mr. Johnson is admitted to the hospital with chest and epigastric pain. He is evaluated by the emergency department physician with a diagnosis of "rule out myocardial infarction." Mr. Johnson is then transferred to a larger facility for further workup.

    Code(s): ____________________

In the following cases, identify the principal diagnosis and all other diagnoses. Assign the appropriate ICD-9-CM codes.

CASE STUDY ONE

History of Present Illness

The patient is a 68-year-old female, status post motor vehicle accident 3 months ago. The patient had an open fracture that was treated initially with traction for 6 to 8 weeks. After initial treatment with traction, the patient was placed in a cast brace. She presents with a complaint of pain in the left femur and inability to bear weight on her leg. The patient was referred from an orthopedic surgeon. The past medical history was significant for no history of myocardial infarction or renal disease and no asthma. The patient had undergone no previous procedures with the exception of debridement of the open fracture. Otherwise the patient's history was unremarkable. The patient was taking no medications and had no known allergies. She underwent a preoperative workup including gallium scan.

Physical Examination

The heart, lungs, and abdomen were benign. The left knee had 30-degree extension lag. There was motion with the knee approximately 30 degrees from horizontal axis to 90 degrees of flexion. The patella was difficult to palpate, and it was very difficult to tell at the time of examination whether motion was occurring at the fracture or whether it was occurring at the knee joint. The vascular examination was unremarkable.

Laboratory Data and Course in Hospital

The x-ray film showed nonunion of the left femur. The gallium scan obtained preoperatively was unremarkable, and there was no evidence of infection.

Treatment

On May 14, the patient underwent open reduction and internal fixation of the left femur fracture with a 90-degree dynamic condylar screw and side plate. The patient tolerated the procedure well. She received two units of her own autologous blood at the time of surgery. Postoperatively she was quite anemic with hemoglobin of 6 to 7 mg/dL. The patient was asymptomatic clinically, and her vascular examination was intact. On postoperative day 2, she had motion in the left knee from 0 to 30 degrees of flexion. She was placed in continuous passive motion and was up with physical therapy but non-weight-bearing on the left leg. Physical therapy was tolerated well. The hospital course was benign. The wound was clean and dry, and the neurovascular examination was unchanged. The x-ray films obtained before discharge showed maintenance of alignment of the left femur. The patient's staples were removed on postoperative day 7. She was placed in a cast brace and was discharged home after being independent in physical therapy.

Final Diagnosis

Nonunion of the left femur

Procedure

Open reduction and internal fixation of the left femur with 90-degree screw and site plate.

31. Code(s): ____________________

CASE STUDY TWO

History of Present Illness

This 50-year-old disabled male is a resident of a nursing home who was admitted because of marked congestion and respiratory distress. He is known to have mental retardation with frequent urinary tract and pulmonary infections. He has a recurrent epileptic disorder that is well controlled on Dilantin.

Physical Examination

On admission vital signs were a temperature of 101°F, respiratory rate of 32 breaths per minute, heart rate of 82 beats per minute, and blood pressure of 120/70 mm Hg. Examination of the chest revealed bilateral crepitations. There was moderate redness and edema of the scrotal skin.

Laboratory Data and Course in Hospital

His white blood cell count was 8.5; hemoglobin, 12.9 g/dL; polymorphonuclear leukocytes, 64; bands, 19; lymphocytes, 10; monocytes, 6; and eosinophils, 1. Urinalysis showed moderate bacterial and 1 + white blood cell count. Urine culture showed mixed flora. The repeat urine culture showed *Providencia stuartii* sensitive to Fortaz. Sputum culture revealed the presence of methicillin-resistant *Staphylococcus aureus,* sensitive to vancomycin. Chest x-ray film showed bilateral pulmonary infiltrates. Arterial blood gases on room air showed a Po_2 of 48, Pco_2 of 30, and pH of 7.50. When repeated with the patient on oxygen, Po_2 was 66, Pco_2 was 36, and pH was 7.45. The patient was treated with intravenous vancomycin and intravenous Fortaz. His pulmonary infiltrate decreased. His oral intake has been somewhat poor, and he has been given intravenous fluids off and on. The nursing staff at the nursing home relates his intake in terms of eating and taking fluids is much better. His medications at the nursing home will include Dilantin, 200 mg twice a day; Tegretol, 400 mg 8 AM, 4 PM, and 200 mg at 8 PM; and Cipro, 500 mg twice a day; and his other maintenance medication will be continued. This patient is being discharged today.

Final Diagnosis

Acute respiratory insufficiency

Bilateral pneumonia

Mental retardation

Epilepsy

32. Code(s): ____________________

CASE STUDY THREE

History of Present Illness

The patient is an 80-year-old female with a known history of advanced metastatic carcinoma of the breast. The patient has been admitted because of increased shortness of breath and severe pain. The pain was worse in her left chest, and this was associated with increased shortness of breath. At the time of admission, the patient was in so much pain that she was unable to remember her history. The patient initially presented for congestive heart failure over a year ago. This was subsequently found to be secondary to metastatic breast cancer, after left mastectomy, 3 years ago. The patient had previously been on chemotherapy.

Course in Hospital

The patient was treated initially with intravenous pain medication to control her pain, and subsequently her condition became stable on oral medication. By the time of discharge, the patient was stable on oral Vicodin. She was able to eat. Admission blood urea nitrogen (BUN) was 38 mg/dL with creatinine of 1.3 mg/dL secondary to dehydration. By the time of discharge, these levels had improved. Admission glucose of 225 mg/dL was down to 110 mg/dL at discharge.

Discharge Diagnoses

Uncontrolled pain, secondary to widely metastatic breast carcinoma

Dehydration

Type II diabetes mellitus, uncontrolled

33. What is the principal diagnosis and the code for the principal diagnosis for this patient?

    Diagnosis and code(s): ______________________________

34. What are the other diagnoses for this patient and what are the codes for these other diagnoses?

    Diagnosis and code(s): ______________________________

    ____

    ____

UNIT 3

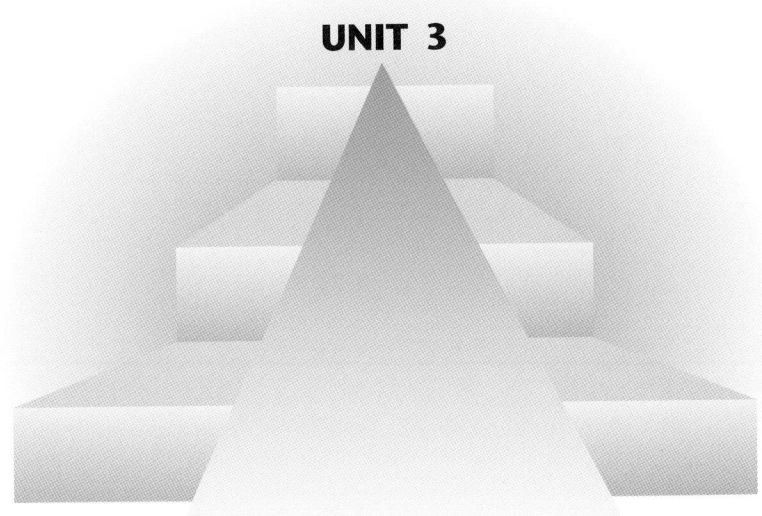

An Overview of Reimbursement

8 Third-Party Reimbursement Issues

CHAPTER TOPICS

Learning Objectives

After completing this chapter, you should be able to

1. Distinguish between Medicare Part A and Part B.
2. Define a "participating provider."
3. Locate information in the *Federal Register*.
4. Identify major elements of the DRG system.
5. Choose the correct DRG.
6. Explain the purpose of PROs.
7. Explain the RBRVS system.
8. State the structure of the APG and APC systems.
9. Understand the framework of Medicare Fraud and Abuse.
10. Identify the major components of Managed Health Care.

INTRODUCTION

You now have an understanding of the coding systems used in the outpatient and inpatient health care settings. Each of the coding systems plays a key role in the reimbursement to the providers of patient health care services. In your role as a medical coder, it is your responsibility to ensure that you code accurately and completely to optimize reimbursement for services provided.

Today, the elderly are the fastest growing segment of our population. Medical advances have people living longer and healthier than ever before. Consider that in 1949 there were four persons age 19 and under for every one person age 65 and older; in 2030 there will be one person age 19 and under for every one person older than age 65.[1]

Persons enrolled for Medicare coverage increased from 19.5 million in 1967 to 38.1 million in 1996, a 95% increase.[2] Medicare is big business, with Medicare spending at $159.9 billion in 1997.[3]

National Trends[1,2]

Ratio of Children 18 and Younger to Persons 65+

- 4:1 1949
- 2:1 1988
- 1:1 2030

Increasing numbers of elderly, technologic advances, and improved access to health care have all increased consumer use of health care services. As more people use health care services, coding will become even more important for appropriate reimbursement and cost control.

You must understand that your responsibility is to ensure that the data are as accurate as possible, not only for classification and study purposes but also to obtain appropriate reimbursement. Ethical issues surface and must be dealt with by coding personnel. Guidelines must always be followed for assignment. Instruction from internal and external sources (eg, administration, peer review organizations, third-party payers) that may increase reimbursement but conflict with coding guidelines must be discussed and resolved. The principal diagnosis must match the documentation. The sequencing for diagnosis-related group (DRG) payment must always be substantiated by the medical records. Upcoding (maximizing), assignment of comorbidity/complications based only on a laboratory value, and using nonphysician impressions/assessments without physician agreement are all clearly fraudulent, prompting ethical concerns when coding for reimbursement.

Reimbursement usually comes from third-party payers. By far, the largest third-party payer is the government through the Medicare program. Since the Medicare program has such an important role in reimbursement, the rules and regulations that govern Medicare reimbursement will be your first topic of study.

THE BASIC STRUCTURE OF THE MEDICARE PROGRAM[4,5]

The Medicare program was established in 1965 with the passage of the Social Security Act. The Medicare Program dramatically increased the involvement of the government in health care. The program consisted of Part A (Hospital Insurance) and Part B (Supplemental Medical Insurance). Part A pays for the cost of hospital/facility care, and Part B pays for physician services and durable medical equipment that are not paid for under Part A. Medicare was originally designed for people 65 and over, but later, people who were eligible for disability benefits from Social Security were also covered under the Medicare program along with those with permanent kidney failure. Individuals covered under Medicare are called **beneficiaries.**

The Secretary of the Department of Health and Human Services (DHHS) is responsible for the administration of the federal Medicare program. Within the Department, the operation of Medicare is delegated to the Health Care Financing Administration (HCFA). The funds to run Medicare are generated from payroll taxes paid by employers and employees. The Social Security Administration is responsible for collecting and handling the funds. HCFA's function is to promote the general welfare of the public. Its stated goals are

1. protect and improve beneficiary health and satisfaction
2. promote the fiscal integrity of HCFA programs
3. purchase the best value health care for beneficiaries
4. promote beneficiary and public understanding of HCFA and its programs
5. foster excellence in the design and administration of HCFA's programs
6. provide leadership in the broader public interest to improve health

HCFA handles the daily operation of the Medicare program through the use of fiscal intermediaries (FI). The **fiscal intermediary** does the "paperwork" for Medicare. A fiscal intermediary is usually an insurance company that bids for a contract with HCFA to handle the Medicare program in a specific area. The monies for Medicare flow from the Social Security Administration through HCFA to the fiscal intermediary and, finally, are paid to beneficiaries and providers.

Physicians, hospitals, and other suppliers that furnish care or supplies to Medicare patients are called **providers.** Providers must be licensed by local and state health agencies to be eligible to provide Medicare patients services or supplies. Providers must also meet various additional Medicare requirements before payment can be made for their services.

Medicare pays for 80% of covered charges, and the beneficiary pays the remaining 20%. The beneficiary pays deductibles, premiums, and coinsurance payments. (The 1999 deductible for Part A was $768[6] and $100 for Part B.[7]) The **coinsurance** is the 20% that Medicare does not pay. Often, beneficiaries will have additional insurance to cover out-of-pocket expenses. The maximum out-of-pocket amounts are set each year according to formulas established by Congress and published in the *Federal Register*. New amounts usually begin each January 1.

What Is a Participating Provider?[5]

Fiscal intermediaries process the claims sent in by providers of the services according to Medicare guidelines. Providers can sign a **participating provider agreement** with the FI to accept assignment on all claims submitted to Medicare. *Accepting assignment* means that the provider will accept what Medicare pays and not bill the patient for the difference between what the service costs and what Medicare pays. For example, a participating provider renders a service that costs $100 and bills Medicare for the service, Medicare pays $58, and the provider accepts the Medicare payment as payment in full. Now, you are probably asking yourself why anyone would agree to this. The patient does not pay the $42 difference, nor does Medicare. The amount is written off by the provider as if the service really cost only $58 to provide. This is a good deal for Medicare and the patient, but what about the provider? Why would he or she agree to decreased payments?

There are incentives to be a participating provider. Congress has mandated the following:

For **participating providers (PAR):**

- direct payment on all claims
- 5% higher fee schedule than nonparticipating providers
- faster processing on assigned claims
- name listed in the PAR directory made available to each Medicare patient with identification as a PAR provider who accepts assignment on all claims
- hospital referrals for outpatient care must provide the patient with the name and address of at least one participating provider

For **nonparticipating providers:**

- payment goes to the patient on all claims
- 5% less on the fee schedule than participating providers
- slower processing on nonassigned claims
- statement on the Explanation of Benefits (EOB) sent to the patient reminding the patient that the use of a participating physician will lower his or her out-of-pocket expenses

For **fiscal intermediaries:**

- bonus for each recruited and enrolled participating provider
- name listed in the PAR directory made available to each Medicare patient with identification as non-PAR provider who accepts assignment on all claims

There are incentives for providers to participate in the Medicare program! Incentives backed by Congress. Currently, half of all physicians in the nation are participating providers.

Services Paid Under Part A: Hospital Insurance[5]

Hospitals submit bills for Part A services by using ICD-9-CM codes and the DRG assignment. DRGs are discussed later in this chapter. Beneficiaries are automatically eligible for Part A, hospital insurance, when they are eligible for Medicare benefits.

During a hospital inpatient stay, Part A pays for a semiprivate room (two to four beds), meals and special diet, plus all other medically necessary services except personal convenience items and private-duty nurses. Part A can also help pay for inpatient care in a Medicare-certified skilled nursing facility if the patient's condition requires daily skilled nursing or rehabilitation services that can be provided only in a skilled nursing facility. Skilled nursing care means care that can be performed only by or under the supervision of licensed nursing personnel. Skilled rehabilitation services may include such services as physical therapy performed by or under the supervision of a professional therapist. The skilled nursing care and skilled rehabilitation services received must be based on physician's orders. Part A pays for a semiprivate room in the skilled nursing facility, plus meals, nursing services, and drugs. Personal convenience items, private-duty nurses, and custodial nursing home services are provided to covered beneficiaries with chronic long-term illnesses or disabilities.[5]

Part A can pay for covered home health care visits from a participating home health agency. The visits can include part-time skilled nursing care and physical therapy or speech therapy when the services are approved by a physician.

Hospice provides relief care (palliative) and support care to terminally ill patients. Part A also pays for hospice care to terminally ill patients when a physician has certified that the patient is terminally ill, the patient has elected to receive care from a hospice rather than the standard Medicare benefits, and the hospice is Medicare certified. Items covered include nursing services, physician services, and certain other medically necessary covered services.[5]

Part B: Supplementary Insurance Must Be Purchased

Part B is not automatically provided to beneficiaries when they become eligible for Medicare. Instead, beneficiaries must purchase the benefits with a monthly premium ($45.50 in 1999).[7] Part B helps pay for medically necessary physicians' services, outpatient hospital services, home health care, and a number of other medical services and supplies that are not covered by Part A. These Part B services are billed using the ICD-9-CM codes for the diagnosis, CPT codes for the procedure (service), and HCPCS codes (national codes) for the additional supplies and services.

EXERCISE A *Medicare*

Using the information presented in this chapter, complete the following:

1. The major third-party reimburser in the United States is

   ____

2. The Medicare program was established in what year? ________________

3. Hospital Insurance is Medicare, Part ______________________________.

4. Supplemental Medical Insurance is Medicare, Part ________________.

5. What two groups of persons were added to those eligible for Medicare benefits after the initial establishment of the Medicare program?

   ____

   ____

6. To what government organization did the Secretary of the Department of Health and Human Services delegate the responsibility for administering the Medicare program?

   ____

7. What government organization handles the funds for the Medicare program?

   ____

8. There are three items that the Medicare beneficiaries are responsible to pay before Medicare will begin to pay for services. What are these three items?

____

____

____

CHECK THIS OUT!

The HCFA website is located at http://www.hcfa.gov and contains information on the Medicare program. Through this website you can link to the Public Use Files (PUFs), which house useful provider information on the Medicare program.

THE IMPORTANCE OF THE *FEDERAL REGISTER*

The *Federal Register* is the official publication of all "Presidential Documents," "Rules and Regulations," "Proposed Rules," and "Notices." When the government institutes national changes, the changes are published in the *Federal Register*. You must be aware of the changes that are listed in the *Federal Register* that relate to reimbursement of Medicare to correctly submit Medicare charges. Most of the information in this chapter is about rules that the government has developed and introduced through the *Federal Register*. You might wonder why so much time is to be spent on learning how to follow the guidelines set by the government for reimbursement when it is only one third-party payer. The answer is simple: Because the government is the largest third-party payer in the nation, even a slight change in the rules governing reimbursement to providers can have a major consequence. For example, there has been a 45% decrease in the number of inpatient hospital beds from 1975 to 1996.[2] Much of this decrease is directly related to the government-implemented inpatient reimbursement system that you will learn about in this chapter—diagnosis-related groups. Often more than 33% of the patients in a hospital are Medicare patients. Because the government is such an important payer in health care, you must know how to interpret the government's directives published in the *Federal Register*. In addition, many commercial insurers are adopting Medicare payment philosophies for their own reimbursement policies. The government has changed health care reimbursement through the Medicare program, and even more changes are promised.

If you have the *Federal Register* available to you through a library, locating and reviewing some of the issues would be an excellent educational activity for you.

CHECK THIS OUT!

You can access the *Federal Register* on the website for the National Archives and Records Administration at http://www.access.gpo.gov/nara. This site houses issues of the *Federal Register* from 1994 forward.

The October editions of the *Federal Register* are of special interest to *hospital facilities* because the hospital updates are released in that edition. *Outpatient facili-*

ties are especially interested in the November or December editions of the *Federal Register* because Medicare reimbursements for outpatient services are published in that edition. Each year, when changes to the various payment systems are proposed, the proposed changes are published early in the year and a period of several months is offered for interested parties to comment and make suggestions on the proposed changes. The final rules are published in the fall editions. The changes presented in fall editions of the *Federal Register* are for implementation in the following calendar year.

Figure 8–1 shows a copy of a portion of a *Federal Register* and is marked to indicate the location of the following[8]:

1. The issuing office of the regulation
2. Subject of the notice
3. Agency
4. Action
5. Summary
6. Dates
7. Addresses
8. For further information contact
9. Supplementary information

Items 1–9 always come before the "Final Rule," which is the official statement of the entire rule.

EXERCISE B *Federal Register*

Answer the following questions:

1. What edition of the *Federal Register* is of special interest to hospital facilities?

 ____

2. What edition of the *Federal Register* is of special interest to outpatient facilities? ______________________________

Using Figure 8–1, answer the following questions:

3. What is the issuing office? ______________________________
4. What is the last date for comment to be received on this proposal?

 ____

5. The "Summary" section in Figure 8–1 indicates that the 1999 Medicare physician fee schedule conversion factor was what dollar amount? ____________
6. According to the "For Further Information Contact:" section in Figure 8–1, who could give you further information related to the issue of physician assistants? ______________________________

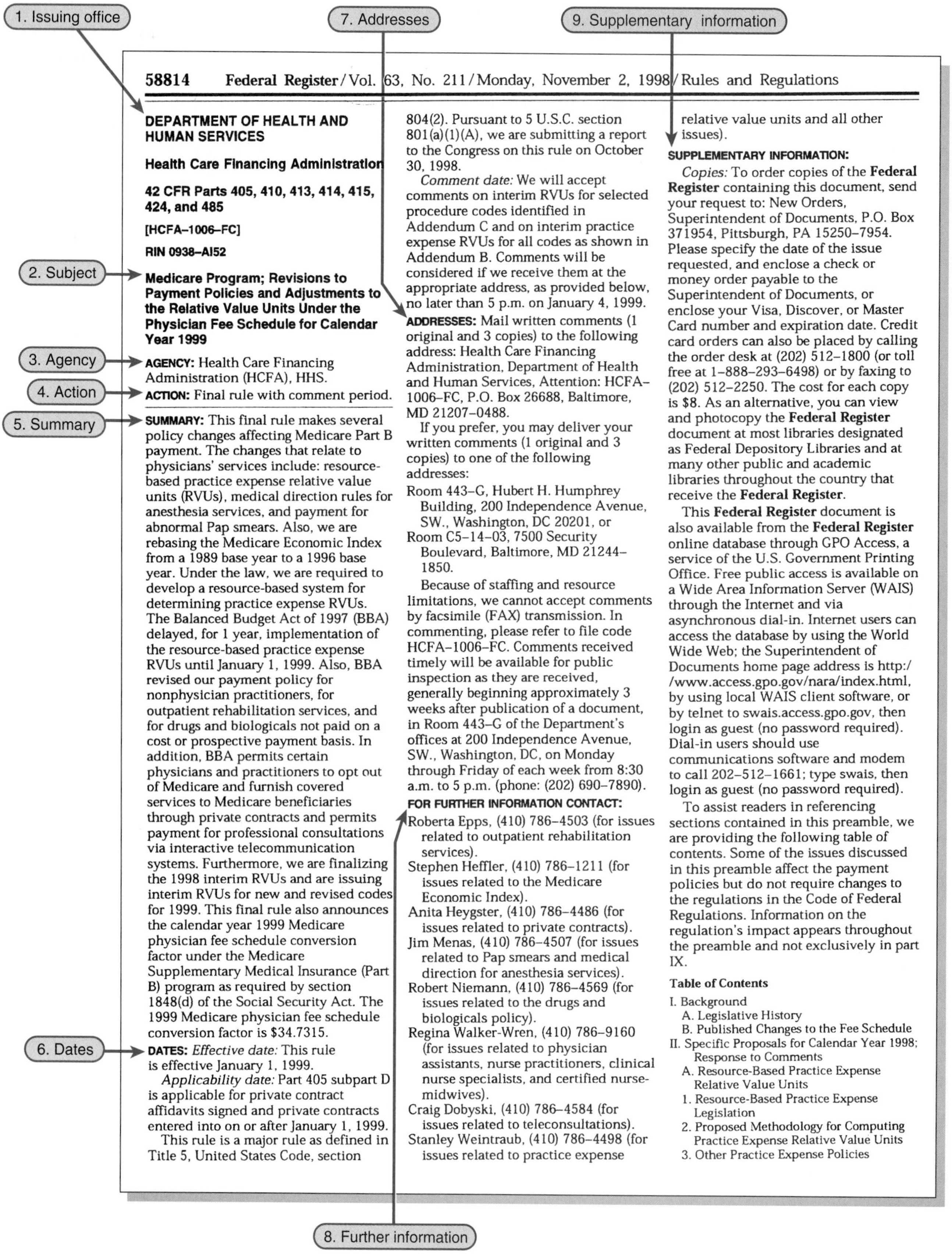

58814 Federal Register / Vol. 63, No. 211 / Monday, November 2, 1998 / Rules and Regulations

DEPARTMENT OF HEALTH AND HUMAN SERVICES

Health Care Financing Administration

42 CFR Parts 405, 410, 413, 414, 415, 424, and 485

[HCFA–1006–FC]

RIN 0938–AI52

Medicare Program; Revisions to Payment Policies and Adjustments to the Relative Value Units Under the Physician Fee Schedule for Calendar Year 1999

AGENCY: Health Care Financing Administration (HCFA), HHS.

ACTION: Final rule with comment period.

SUMMARY: This final rule makes several policy changes affecting Medicare Part B payment. The changes that relate to physicians' services include: resource-based practice expense relative value units (RVUs), medical direction rules for anesthesia services, and payment for abnormal Pap smears. Also, we are rebasing the Medicare Economic Index from a 1989 base year to a 1996 base year. Under the law, we are required to develop a resource-based system for determining practice expense RVUs. The Balanced Budget Act of 1997 (BBA) delayed, for 1 year, implementation of the resource-based practice expense RVUs until January 1, 1999. Also, BBA revised our payment policy for nonphysician practitioners, for outpatient rehabilitation services, and for drugs and biologicals not paid on a cost or prospective payment basis. In addition, BBA permits certain physicians and practitioners to opt out of Medicare and furnish covered services to Medicare beneficiaries through private contracts and permits payment for professional consultations via interactive telecommunication systems. Furthermore, we are finalizing the 1998 interim RVUs and are issuing interim RVUs for new and revised codes for 1999. This final rule also announces the calendar year 1999 Medicare physician fee schedule conversion factor under the Medicare Supplementary Medical Insurance (Part B) program as required by section 1848(d) of the Social Security Act. The 1999 Medicare physician fee schedule conversion factor is $34.7315.

DATES: *Effective date:* This rule is effective January 1, 1999.

Applicability date: Part 405 subpart D is applicable for private contract affidavits signed and private contracts entered into on or after January 1, 1999.

This rule is a major rule as defined in Title 5, United States Code, section 804(2). Pursuant to 5 U.S.C. section 801(a)(1)(A), we are submitting a report to the Congress on this rule on October 30, 1998.

Comment date: We will accept comments on interim RVUs for selected procedure codes identified in Addendum C and on interim practice expense RVUs for all codes as shown in Addendum B. Comments will be considered if we receive them at the appropriate address, as provided below, no later than 5 p.m. on January 4, 1999.

ADDRESSES: Mail written comments (1 original and 3 copies) to the following address: Health Care Financing Administration, Department of Health and Human Services, Attention: HCFA–1006–FC, P.O. Box 26688, Baltimore, MD 21207–0488.

If you prefer, you may deliver your written comments (1 original and 3 copies) to one of the following addresses:

Room 443–G, Hubert H. Humphrey Building, 200 Independence Avenue, SW., Washington, DC 20201, or

Room C5–14–03, 7500 Security Boulevard, Baltimore, MD 21244–1850.

Because of staffing and resource limitations, we cannot accept comments by facsimile (FAX) transmission. In commenting, please refer to file code HCFA–1006–FC. Comments received timely will be available for public inspection as they are received, generally beginning approximately 3 weeks after publication of a document, in Room 443–G of the Department's offices at 200 Independence Avenue, SW., Washington, DC, on Monday through Friday of each week from 8:30 a.m. to 5 p.m. (phone: (202) 690–7890).

FOR FURTHER INFORMATION CONTACT:

Roberta Epps, (410) 786–4503 (for issues related to outpatient rehabilitation services).

Stephen Heffler, (410) 786–1211 (for issues related to the Medicare Economic Index).

Anita Heygster, (410) 786–4486 (for issues related to private contracts).

Jim Menas, (410) 786–4507 (for issues related to Pap smears and medical direction for anesthesia services).

Robert Niemann, (410) 786–4569 (for issues related to the drugs and biologicals policy).

Regina Walker-Wren, (410) 786–9160 (for issues related to physician assistants, nurse practitioners, clinical nurse specialists, and certified nurse-midwives).

Craig Dobyski, (410) 786–4584 (for issues related to teleconsultations).

Stanley Weintraub, (410) 786–4498 (for issues related to practice expense relative value units and all other issues).

SUPPLEMENTARY INFORMATION:

Copies: To order copies of the **Federal Register** containing this document, send your request to: New Orders, Superintendent of Documents, P.O. Box 371954, Pittsburgh, PA 15250–7954. Please specify the date of the issue requested, and enclose a check or money order payable to the Superintendent of Documents, or enclose your Visa, Discover, or Master Card number and expiration date. Credit card orders can also be placed by calling the order desk at (202) 512–1800 (or toll free at 1–888–293–6498) or by faxing to (202) 512–2250. The cost for each copy is $8. As an alternative, you can view and photocopy the **Federal Register** document at most libraries designated as Federal Depository Libraries and at many other public and academic libraries throughout the country that receive the **Federal Register**.

This **Federal Register** document is also available from the **Federal Register** online database through GPO Access, a service of the U.S. Government Printing Office. Free public access is available on a Wide Area Information Server (WAIS) through the Internet and via asynchronous dial-in. Internet users can access the database by using the World Wide Web; the Superintendent of Documents home page address is http://www.access.gpo.gov/nara/index.html, by using local WAIS client software, or by telnet to swais.access.gpo.gov, then login as guest (no password required). Dial-in users should use communications software and modem to call 202–512–1661; type swais, then login as guest (no password required).

To assist readers in referencing sections contained in this preamble, we are providing the following table of contents. Some of the issues discussed in this preamble affect the payment policies but do not require changes to the regulations in the Code of Federal Regulations. Information on the regulation's impact appears throughout the preamble and not exclusively in part IX.

Table of Contents

Figure 8–1
Example of page from the *Federal Register*. (From *Federal Register*, November 2, 1998, Vol. 63 (211):58814.)

UNDERSTANDING INPATIENT DIAGNOSIS-RELATED GROUPS (DRGs)[9]

This patient classification system provides a means of relating the type of patients a hospital treats (case mix) to the costs incurred by the hospital. The design and development of the DRGs began in the late 1960s at Yale University. The initial motivation for developing the DRGs was to create a framework for monitoring the quality of care and the utilization of services in a hospital setting. The first large-scale application of the DRGs was in the late 1970s in New Jersey. The New Jersey State Department of Health used DRGs as the basis of a prospective payment system in which hospitals were reimbursed a fixed DRG-specific amount for each patient treated. In 1982, the Tax Equity and Fiscal Responsibility Act (TEFRA) modified the Medicare hospital reimbursement limits to include a system based on DRGs. In 1983, Congress amended the Social Security Act to include a national DRG-based hospital prospective payment system for all Medicare patients.

Prospective payment rates based on DRGs have been established as the basis of the Medicare's hospital reimbursement system. The evolution of the DRGs and their use as the basic unit of payment in Medicare's hospital reimbursement system represents a recognition of the basic role that a hospital's case mix plays in determining its costs. (Case mix will be more fully explained later, but, for now, case mix is the types of patients a hospital usually serves.) Currently, hospitals are paid according to the DRG and a hospital payment rate. The hospital payment rate for Medicare patients is based on the type of hospital, geographic area, the designation of urban or rural, and other factors that affect the cost of providing care. In the past, hospital characteristics such as teaching status and bed size were used to explain the cost differences among hospitals. However, such characteristics failed to account for the cost impact of a hospital's case mix. Individual hospitals have often attempted to justify higher cost by stating that they treated a more complex mix of patients or that the patients they treated were simply "sicker." Everyone agreed that more complex cases cost a hospital more to treat, but exactly how to define and measure a hospital's case mix was a very complex matter.

The categories (type of illness and volume) of patients treated by a hospital represent the complexity of the hospital's case load and are referred to as the hospital's **case mix**. The concept of case mix complexity has been used to refer to a set of patient attributes that include

- severity of illness
- prognosis
- treatment difficulty
- need for intervention
- resource intensity

Each of these attributes has an exact meaning that describes a particular aspect of a hospital case mix:

Severity of illness refers to the levels of loss of function and mortality that may be experienced by patients with a particular disease.

Prognosis refers to the probable outcome of an illness, including the likelihood of improvement or deterioration in the severity of the illness, the likelihood of recurrence, and the probable life span.

Treatment difficulty refers to the patient management problems that a particular illness presents to the health care provider. Such management problems are associated with illnesses without a clear pattern of symptoms, illnesses requiring sophisticated and technically difficult procedures, and illnesses requiring close monitoring and supervision.

Need for intervention relates to the consequences in terms of severity of illness that the lack of immediate or continuing care would produce.

Resource intensity refers to the volume and type of diagnostic, therapeutic, and bed services used in the management of a particular illness.

There are two ways to use the term "case mix complexity." Clinicians use it to mean that the patient has a greater severity of illness, presents greater treatment difficulty, has a poor prognosis, or has a greater need for intervention. *Administrators and regulators*, however, usually use "case mix complexity" to indicate the patient's need for more resources with respect to the cost of providing care. Often the two interpretations of case mix complexity are closely related, but they can be very different for certain kinds of patients. For example, terminal cancer patients are very severely ill and have a poor prognosis, but in the end states they frequently require few hospital resources beyond basic nursing care.

Because the purpose of the DRGs is to relate a hospital's case mix to the resource demands and associated costs experienced by the hospital, a hospital having a more complex case mix from a DRG perspective means that the hospital treats patients who require more hospital resources—not necessarily that the hospital treats patients having a greater severity of illness, a greater treatment difficulty, a poorer prognosis, or a greater need for intervention.

Major Diagnostic Categories (MDCs)

The process of forming the DRGs was begun by dividing all possible principal diagnoses into 23 principal diagnosis areas referred to as major diagnostic categories (MDCs). Two new MDCs were created in the eighth version of the DRGs, for a total of 25 MDCs. The MDCs are displayed in Figure 8–2. Physician panels developed the diagnoses in each MDC to correspond to a single organ system (respiratory system, circulatory system, digestive system) and generally to be associated with a particular medical specialty. This was done because most clinical care is organized around medical specialties. Not all diseases and disorders can be assigned to an organ system (eg, systemic infections), and so a number of non–organ system categories exist: Systemic Infectious Diseases, Myeloproliferative Diseases, and Poorly Differentiated Neoplasms. Each of the DRGs is defined by a particular set of patient attributes:

- principal diagnosis
- secondary diagnosis
- procedures
- age
- sex
- discharge status

A tree diagram (flow chart) depicts the DRG structure for each MDC. Tree diagrams use several symbols to describe the different types of decisions made when determining DRG assignment. Figure 8–3 indicates the symbols and the definitions of each.

Major Diagnostic Categories

1 - Diseases and Disorders of the Nervous System
2 - Diseases and Disorders of the Eye
3 - Diseases and Disorders of the Ear, Nose, Mouth and Throat
4 - Diseases and Disorders of the Respiratory System
5 - Diseases and Disorders of the Circulatory System
6 - Diseases and Disorders of the Digestive System
7 - Diseases and Disorders of the Hepatobiliary System and Pancreas
8 - Diseases and Disorders of the Musculoskeletal System and Connective Tissue
9 - Diseases and Disorders of the Skin, Subcutaneous Tissue and Breast
10 - Endocrine, Nutritional and Metabolic Diseases and Disorders
11 - Diseases and Disorders of the Kidney and Urinary Tract
12 - Diseases and Disorders of the Male Reproductive System
13 - Diseases and Disorders of the Female Reproductive System
14 - Pregnancy, Childbirth and the Puerperium
15 - Newborns and Other Neonates with Conditions Originating in the Perinatal Period
16 - Diseases and Disorders of the Blood and Blood Forming Organs and Immunological Disorders
17 - Myeloproliferative Diseases and Disorders, and Poorly Differentiated Neoplasms
18 - Infectious and Parasitic Diseases (Systemic or Unspecified Sites)
19 - Mental Diseases and Disorders
20 - Alcohol/Drug Use and Alcohol/Drug Induced Organic Mental Disorders
21 - Injuries, Poisonings and Toxic Effects of Drugs
22 - Burns
23 - Factors Influencing Health Status and Other Contacts with Health Services
24 - Multiple Significant Trauma
25 - Human Immunodeficiency Virus Infections

Figure 8–2
Major Diagnostic Categories of the Diagnosis-Related Groups. (From Diagnosis Related Groups, Version 14.0, Definitions Manual, 3M Health Information Systems.)

A diamond indicates that a decision is being made on a single variable as opposed to a search of several variables. This symbol is used when the decision variable in the DRG structure is principal diagnosis, discharge status, or age.

A circle indicates a decision is being made by searching several variables. For example, a circle is used when all listed secondary diagnoses are searched to determine if a complication or comorbidity is present. A circle is also used when the decision in the DRG structure involves the presence of an operating room procedure or the presence of a particular diagnosis as either the principal diagnosis or as a secondary diagnosis.

A square indicates that DRG assignment has been completed.

A pointer indicates that the tree diagram structure is continued on another page.

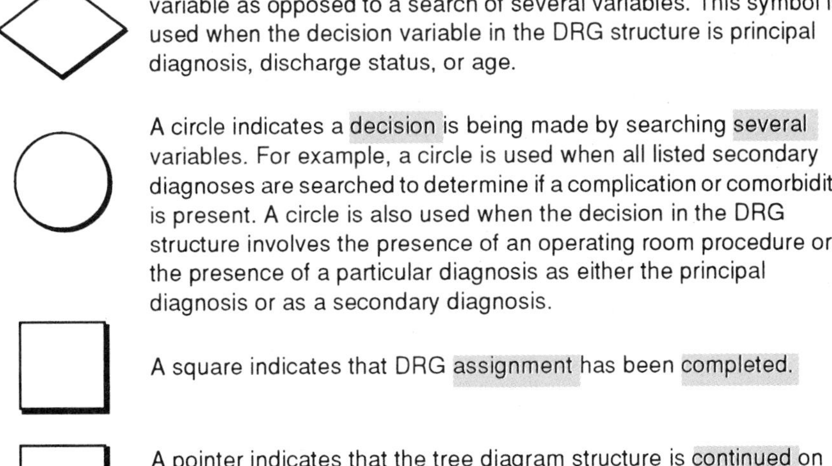

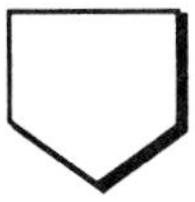

Figure 8–3
DRG symbols used in tree diagrams for each Major Diagnostic Category. (From Diagnosis Related Groups, Version 14.0, Definitions Manual, 3M Health Information Systems.)

All patient classification begins with the diagnosis and the pre-MDC flow chart or tree diagram as shown in Figure 8–4. For example, if the patient is admitted to the hospital for a tracheostomy, DRG 483 is assigned; for a liver transplant, the patient is assigned to DRG 480. If the patient was not admitted for a tracheostomy or a liver transplant, the next question in the tree diagram asks if the patient was admitted for a bone marrow transplant (481), and so on down the tree diagram. If the patient was not admitted for one of the principal diagnoses noted on the flow chart of pre-MDCs, the patient classification moves on to one of the remaining 23 MDCs. When surgical procedures are classified, additional hospital resources are used with the surgical procedure MDCs (eg, operating room, recovery room, anesthesia). For this reason most MDCs were initially divided into medical and surgical groups. Figure 8–5 shows the typical division depending on whether a surgical procedure was performed.

Patients are considered surgical if they have a procedure performed that requires the use of the operating room. If a patient has multiple surgical procedures, the DRG assignment is based on a surgical ranking of most to least resource-intensive (surgical hierarchy). For example, if a patient had both a dilation and curettage and a hysterectomy, the hysterectomy would use more resources and would be the basis of the DRG selection. The definition of principal diagnosis is one that is performed for definitive treatment rather than one performed for diagnostic or exploratory purposes or one that was necessary to take care of a complication.

DRG selection is based on the principal diagnosis selection if no surgery is performed. DRG selection is also based on complications, comorbidities, and the patient's age. Physician panels classified each diagnosis code based on whether the diagnosis, when presented with a secondary condition, would be considered a substantial complication or comorbidity. A substantial *complication or comorbidity* was considered a condition that increased the length of stay in the hospital by at least 1 day in at least 75% of the patients. For example, pneumonia is considered a substantial complication or comorbidity whereas benign hypertension is not. The same basic list of complications and comorbidities is used in most DRGs.

The patient's age is sometimes used in the definition of the DRGs. Pediatric patients are often assigned to separate DRGs. Age is used because extremely young or extremely old patients often require more resources. Also, patient discharge status is a consideration in assignment of a DRG. For example, separate DRGs were formed for burn patients and newborns if the patients were transferred to another acute care facility. Separate DRGs were also formed for patients with alcoholism or drug abuse who left the facility against medical advice, for patients with acute myocardial infarction, and for newborns who died.

There are also five DRGs that contain patients whose records contain inconsistent or invalid information. DRGs 468, 476, and 477 are for records that indicate that the patient had a surgical procedure unrelated to the diagnosis. Typically, these patients would be admitted for a diagnosis requiring no surgery but develop a complication unrelated to the principal diagnosis and have an operating room procedure performed for the complication or have a diagnostic procedure performed for another concurrent principal diagnosis. For example, a patient who has a principal diagnosis of congestive heart failure and develops acute cholecystitis and whose only procedure is a cholecystectomy will be assigned to DRG 468 since the cholecystectomy is considered an extensive procedure and is unrelated to the reason for admission.

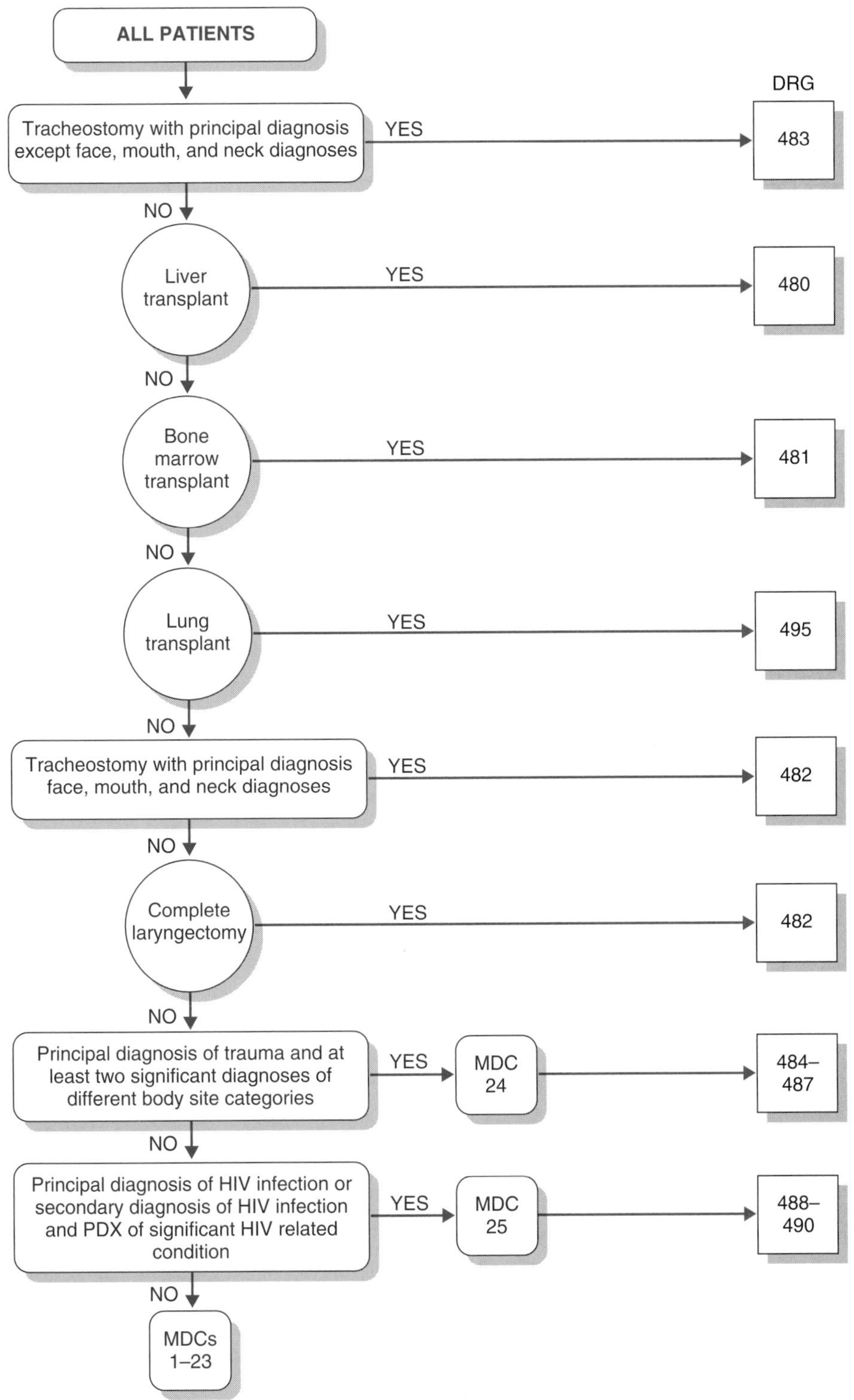

Figure 8–4
Pre-MDC flow chart, HCFA Grouper Version 12.0. (From Diagnosis Related Groups, Version 14.0, Definitions Manual, 3M Health Information Systems.)

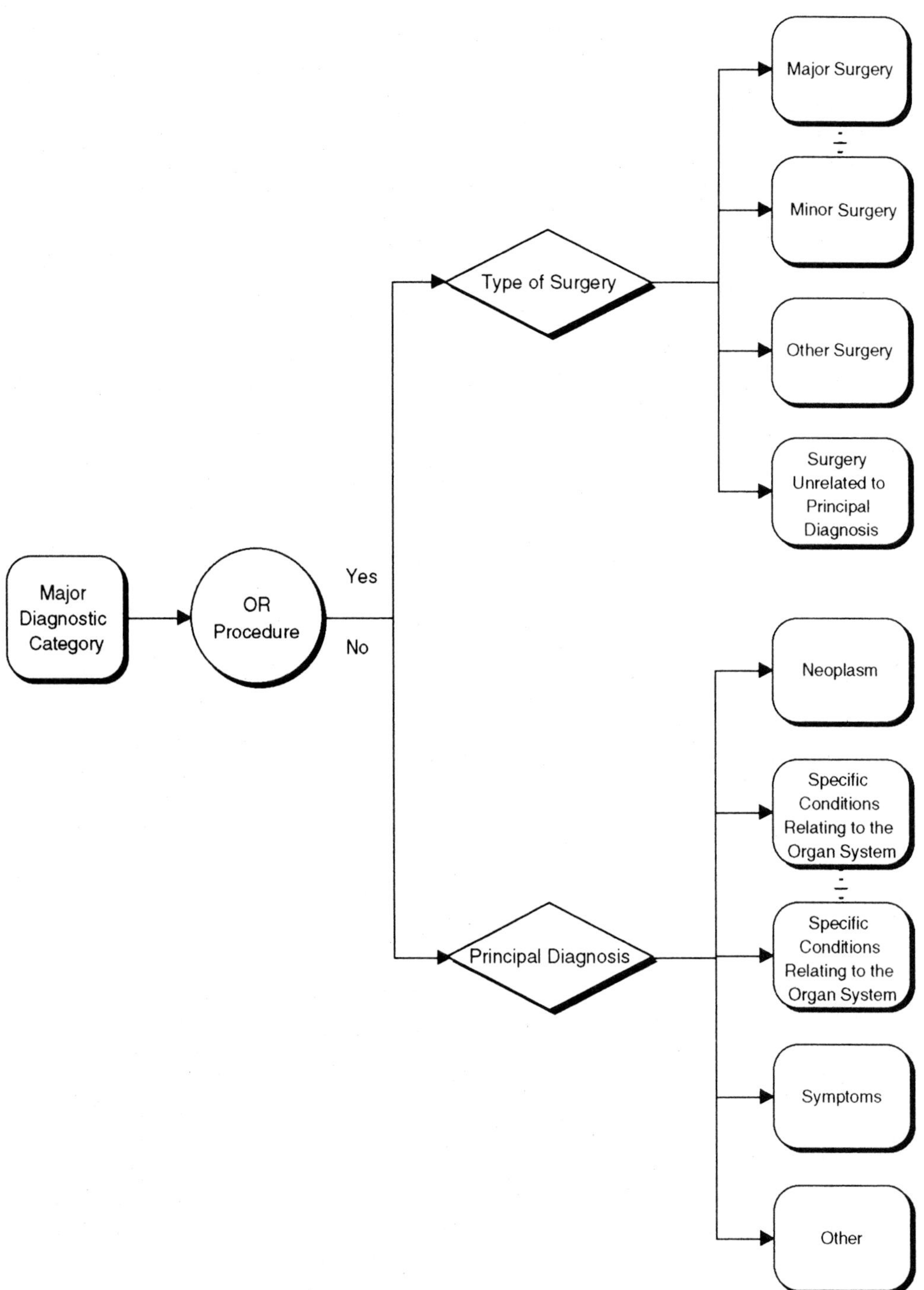

Figure 8–5
Typical DRG structure for a Major Diagnostic Category. The Medical and Surgical Classes are further divided based on the age of the patient or the presence of complications or comorbidities. (From Diagnosis Related Groups, Version 14.0, Definitions Manual, 3M Health Information Systems.)

Patients are assigned to DRG 469 when a selected principal diagnosis, although a valid ICD-9-CM code, is not precise enough to allow the patient to be assigned to a DRG. For example, ICD-9-CM code 646.90 is an unspecified complication of pregnancy with the episode of care unspecified. The diagnosis code does not indicate the type of complication nor whether the episode of care was antepartum, postpartum, or for delivery. Because DRG definitions assign patients to different sets of DRGs depending on whether the episode of care was antepartum, postpartum, or for delivery, a patient with a principal diagnosis that did not indicate the specificity would be assigned to 469 for principal diagnosis. DRG 470 is for certain types of record errors that may affect the DRG assignment. For example, a patient who is age 154 would be assigned to 470 if the correct choice of DRG depended on the age of the patient because the age is an obvious error.

With the principal diagnosis of the patient, you can locate the correct DRG. A computer program, called a grouper, is used to input the principal diagnosis and other critical information about a patient (secondary diagnosis, procedures, age, sex, discharge status). The grouper then provides the correct DRG assignment for the case based on the information the coder provides. For now, you are going to use the best computer of all to calculate a DRG—your brain. Did you know that it would take a computer that was as tall as a 33-story building to hold all of the capability your brain has! You have tremendous potential! The computer is only as "smart" as the operator. You will be the operator of the grouper, and the quality of the information you input will determine the quality of the information output. Understanding how the grouper works will help you to identify the correct information to input into the computer.

Tree Diagrams Guide You

Each MDC has a flow chart, called a "tree." Each flow chart has the codes available for selection located within symbols that have particular meaning. The tree diagram uses decision symbols to guide you through the diagram. The symbols are like road signs to make sure you stay on the right path.

EXERCISE C ***Terminal DRG***

Using Figure 8–6, the flow chart for Diseases and Disorders of the Respiratory System, let's locate a DRG together.

A 72-year-old patient was admitted to the hospital for pneumonia.

You begin on the left side of Figure 8–6 at the circle labeled "OR Procedure." This patient did not have surgery, so move on down the "No" path until you arrive at the question that asks if "Ventilator Support" was used. There is no indication in the patient information of ventilator support, so you continue down the "No" path to the off-page connector "1" symbol, which tells you that there is another page. Figure 8–7 shows that next page. From the pointer "1," you arrive at the decision symbol labeled "Principal Diagnosis." You have five principal diagnosis categories from which to choose on this medical page: "Pulmonary Embolism," "Infections and Inflammations," "Neoplasm," "Major Chest Trauma," and "Pleural Effusion." This patient has an infection of the lungs, so you follow the line down from the principal diagnosis category of "Infections and Inflammations." The decision operation "Age > 17" asks the age of the patient as older than 17, yes or no. This patient was 72, so you follow the line down the "Yes" path.

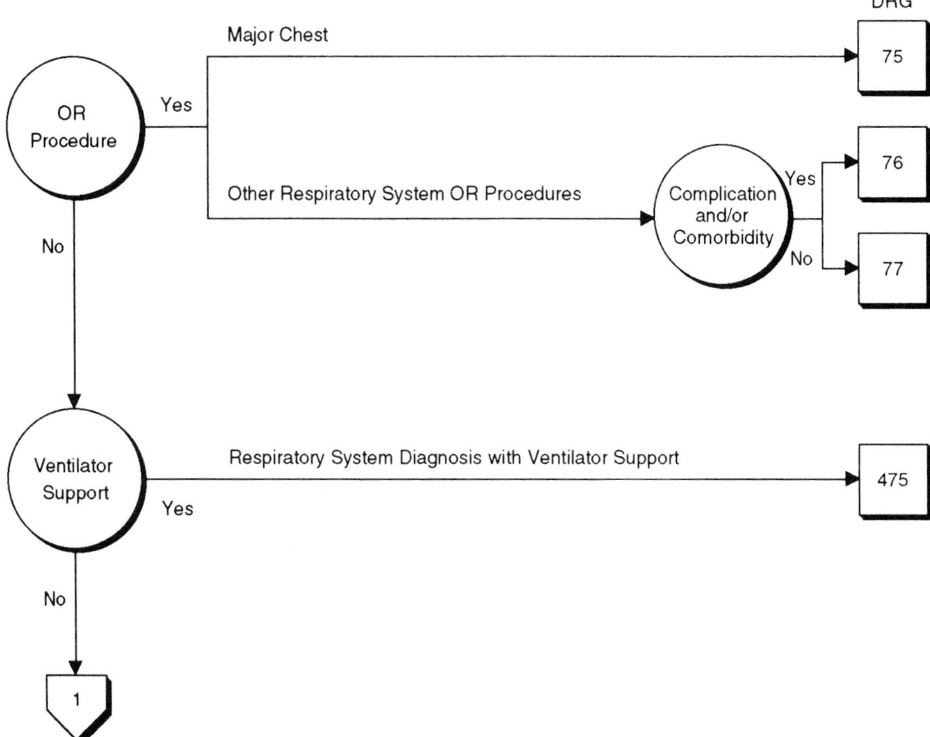

Figure 8–6
Major Diagnostic Category 4, Diseases and Disorders of the Respiratory System, Surgical Partitioning. (From Diagnosis Related Groups, Version 14.0, Definitions Manual, 3M Health Information Systems.)

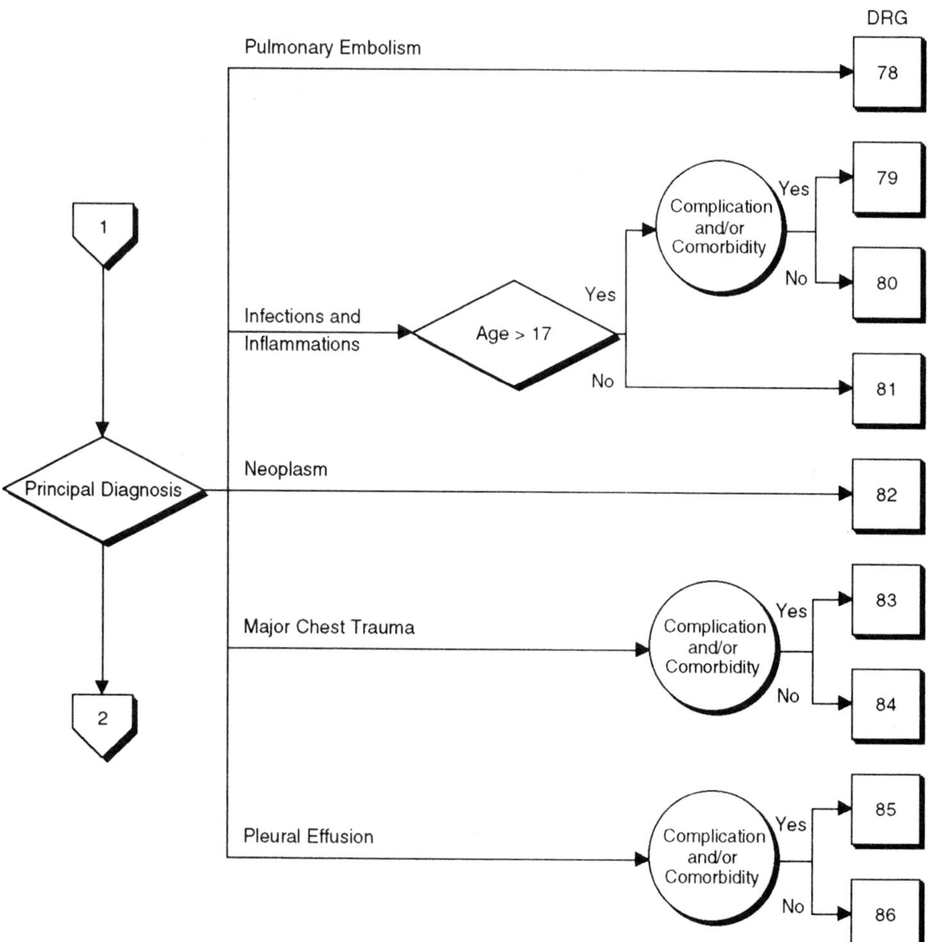

Figure 8–7
Major Diagnostic Category 4, Diseases and Disorders of the Respiratory System, Medical Partitioning. (From Diagnosis Related Groups, Version 14.0, Definitions Manual, 3M Health Information Systems.)

Next, you are presented with the question of whether the patient had any "Complication and/or Comorbidity." There was no indication of any comorbidity or complication. You proceed along the "No" path and arrive at the correct DRG for this case, 80.

Now you do one. Using Figure 8–7, locate the correct DRG for the following:

1. The patient is an 82-year-old admitted with the principal diagnosis of iatrogenic pulmonary embolism and infarction (iatrogenic means "physician-induced") (ICD-9-CM 415.11).

   DRG: ________________

2. A 42-year-old patient is admitted with the principal diagnosis of major chest trauma (without complications)—three fractured ribs, larynx, and trachea (ICD-9-CM code 807.03).

   DRG: ________________

Connecting the ICD-9-CM and the DRG

In the DRG manual, each of the DRG numbers has assigned to it a group of ICD-9-CM codes along with the principal diagnosis statement. For example, Question 1 in Exercise C has a principal diagnosis of iatrogenic pulmonary embolism and infarction, which is identified by ICD-9-CM code 415.11. Figure 8–8 shows this diagnosis code as it appears in the ICD-9-CM. The DRG manual also lists 415.11 under DRG 78, Pulmonary Embolism (Fig. 8–9). (Note that in the DRG manual, the decimal point used in the ICD-9-CM code is deleted because the computer does not need the decimal point.) Therefore, in Question 1, the patient's diagnosis of iatrogenic pulmonary embolism and infarction, 415.11, automatically is classified to DRG 78 by the grouper. Any of the principal diagnoses listed under DRG 78 (Fig. 8–9) is automatically assigned to DRG 78 based on the ICD-9-CM code you input into the computer.

Also, Question 2 in Exercise C has an ICD-9-CM code of 807.03 (three fractured ribs, larynx, and trachea). Figure 8–10 shows the diagnosis code as it appears in the ICD-9-CM. The ICD-9-CM code 807.03 is listed in the group of codes for DRG 84 in the description of DRGs (Fig. 8–11).

As you can see from the previous exercise, your coding ability and the completeness of the medical record are critical for the correct DRG assignment. The computer follows the flow charts just as you did when you assigned the DRGs for Questions 1 and 2 above. The advantage is that the computer can quickly accomplish the task of DRG assignment for you. However, the assignment will only be as accurate as the information you input. What a difference the correct DRG assignment can make in the reimbursement received by the hospital for the patient care!

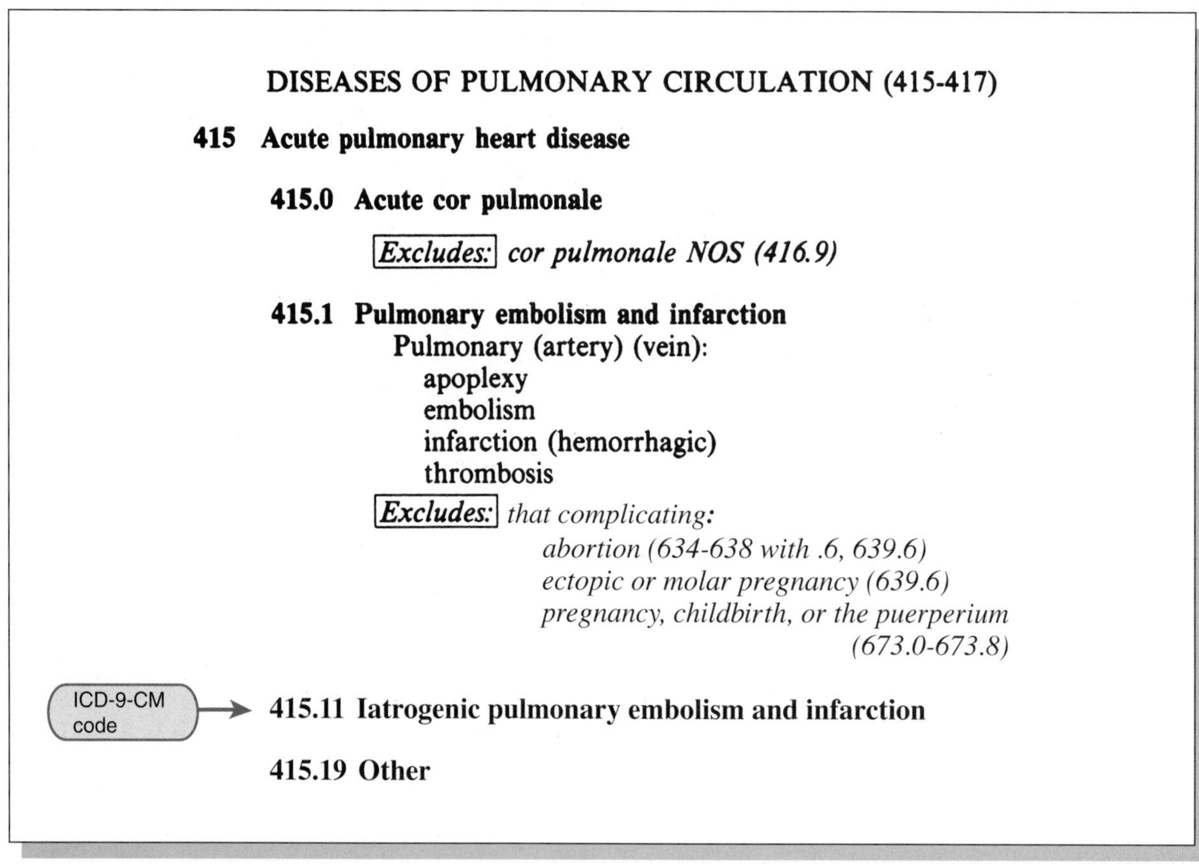

DISEASES OF PULMONARY CIRCULATION (415-417)

415 Acute pulmonary heart disease

415.0 Acute cor pulmonale

Excludes: *cor pulmonale NOS (416.9)*

415.1 Pulmonary embolism and infarction
Pulmonary (artery) (vein):
apoplexy
embolism
infarction (hemorrhagic)
thrombosis

Excludes: *that complicating:*
abortion (634-638 with .6, 639.6)
ectopic or molar pregnancy (639.6)
pregnancy, childbirth, or the puerperium (673.0-673.8)

415.11 Iatrogenic pulmonary embolism and infarction

415.19 Other

Figure 8–8
ICD-9-CM diagnosis code for iatrogenic pulmonary embolism and infarction. (From International Classification of Diseases, 9th Revision. U.S. Department of Health and Human Services, Public Health Service, Health Care Financing Administration.)

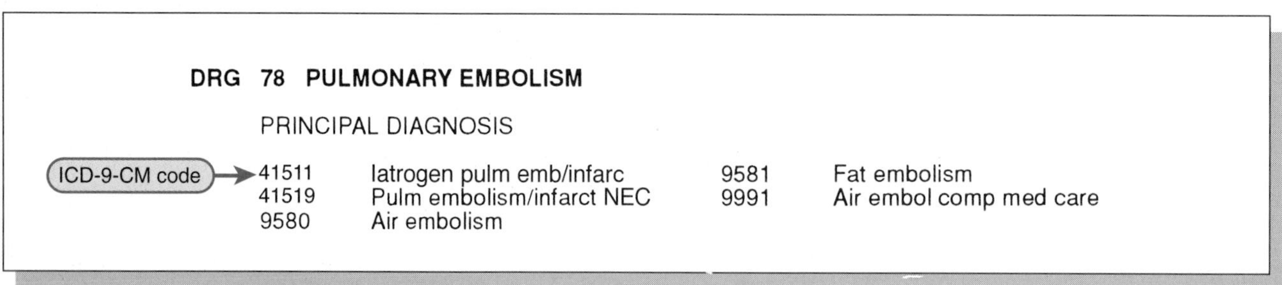

DRG 78 PULMONARY EMBOLISM

PRINCIPAL DIAGNOSIS

41511	Iatrogen pulm emb/infarc	9581	Fat embolism
41519	Pulm embolism/infarct NEC	9991	Air embol comp med care
9580	Air embolism		

Figure 8–9
Section on MDC 4, Definition of DRGs showing ICD-9-CM code for iatrogenic pulmonary embolism and infarction. (From Diagnosis Related Groups, Version 14.0, Definitions Manual, 3M Health Information Systems.)

ICD-9-CM code → **807 Fracture of rib(s), sternum, larynx, and trachea**

The following fifth-digit subclassification is for use with codes 807.0-807.1:

- **0 rib(s), unspecified**
- **1 one rib**
- **2 two ribs**
- **3 three ribs**
- **4 four ribs**
- **5 five ribs**
- **6 six ribs**
- **7 seven ribs**
- **8 eight or more ribs**
- **9 multiple ribs, unspecified**

807.0 Rib(s), closed

807.1 Rib(s), open

807.2 Sternum, closed

807.3 Sternum, open

807.4 Flail chest

807.5 Larynx and trachea, closed
Hyoid bone
Thyroid cartilage
Trachea

807.6 Larynx and trachea, open

Figure 8–10
ICD-9-CM diagnosis code for three fractured ribs—closed. (From International Classification of Diseases, 9th Revision. U.S. Department of Health and Human Services, Public Health Service, Health Care Financing Administration.)

DRG 84 MAJOR CHEST TRAUMA W/O CC

PRINCIPAL DIAGNOSIS

ICD-9-CM code →

Code	Description	Code	Description
80703	Fracture three ribs-clos	80718	Fx eight/more ribs-open
80704	Fracture four ribs-close	80719	Fx mult ribs NOS-open
80705	Fracture five ribs-close	8072	Fracture of sternum-clos
80706	Fracture six ribs-closed	8073	Fracture of sternum-open
80707	Fracture seven ribs-clos	8074	Flail chest
80708	Fx eight/more rib-closed	83961	Dislocat sternum-closed
80709	Fx mult ribs NOS-closed	83971	Dislocation sternum-open
80710	Fracture rib NOS-open	8483	Sprain of ribs
80711	Fracture one rib-open	84840	Sprain of sternum NOS
80712	Fracture two ribs-open	84841	Sprain sternoclavicular
80713	Fracture three ribs-open	84842	Sprain chondrosternal
80714	Fracture four ribs-open	84849	Sprain of sternum NEC
80715	Fracture five ribs-open	8600	Traum pneumothorax-close
80716	Fracture six ribs-open	8601	Traum pneumothorax-open
80717	Fracture seven ribs-open	8602	Traum hemothorax-closed

Figure 8–11
Section on MDC 4, Definition of DRGs showing ICD-9-CM code for three fractured ribs—closed. (From Diagnosis Related Groups, Version 14.0, Definitions Manual, 3M Health Information Systems.)

As an example of how sequencing of complications and comorbidity can affect the reimbursement amount, consider the following actual case:

CASE STUDY ONE

The principal diagnosis was congestive heart failure (428.0). Additional diagnoses were morbid obesity (278.01), diabetes (250.00), coronary atherosclerosis (414.0), psoriasis (696.1), depressive disorder (311), unspecified personality disorder (301.9), hypercholesterolemia (272.0), cardiomegaly (429.3), and initial episode, subendocardial infarction (410.71). The result of code 410.71 being listed as the tenth diagnosis was a reimbursement of $4,702. If 410.71 is within the top nine diagnoses, the reimbursement is $7,055. This is a $2,353 loss to the hospital because of the incorrect sequencing of a complication.

CASE STUDY TWO

A patient had a diskectomy and had postoperative cardiac arrhythmias documented. The arrhythmias being identified as a complication would upgrade the DRG 215 (back and neck procedures without complication) code to DRG 214 (back and neck procedures with complication) (Fig. 8–12). This change will amount to $2,334 in additional reimbursement to the hospital.

CASE STUDY THREE

A patient had a transurethral resection without complication (DRG 311). Postoperatively, cardiac complications (DRG 477) developed. Assignment of DRG 477 would move the case from $1,546 to $4,301—an increase in reimbursement of $2,755 (Fig. 8–13).

Correct DRG assignment makes good "cents."

All ICD-9-CM codes considered as complications or comorbidities (C/C) for a DRG are a part of the DRG system and are listed in the DRG manual in Appendix C. Figure 8–14 shows a page of Appendix C, Diagnoses Defined as Complications or Comorbidities, in the Diagnosis-Related Groups, Definition Manual. The

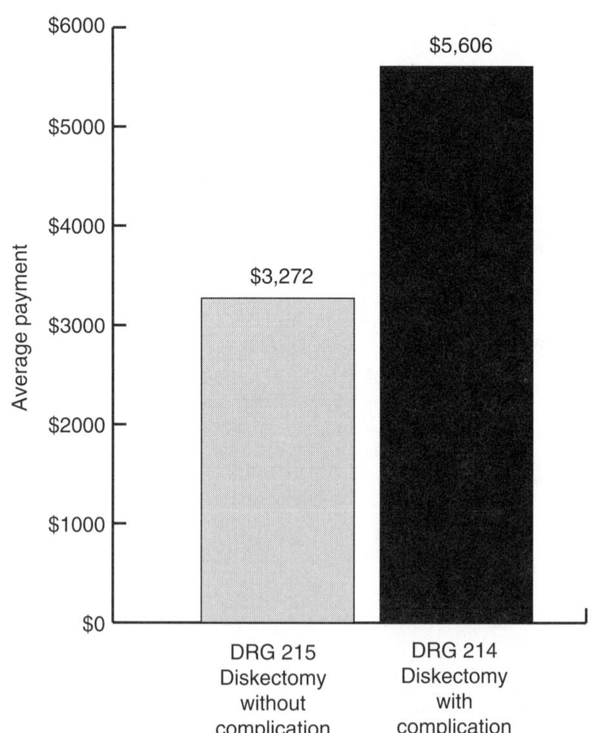

Figure 8–12
DRG assignment for diskectomy with or without complications. (Reproduced from *A Minute for the Medical Staff: Complications of medical and surgical care.* 1993 Opus Communications, Inc., P.O. Box 1168, Marblehead, MA 01945, 781-639-1872.)

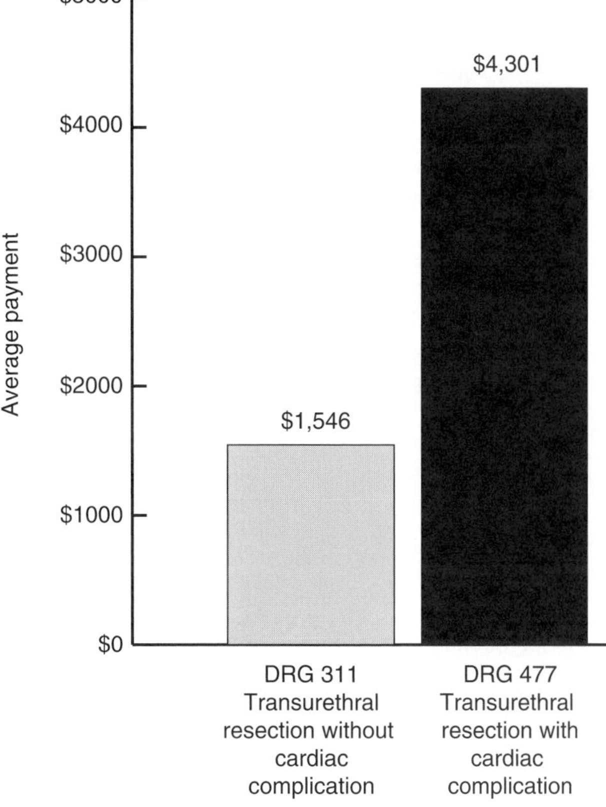

Figure 8–13
DRG assignment for transurethral resection with or without cardiac complications. (Reproduced from *A Minute for the Medical Staff: Complications of medical and surgical care.* 1993 Opus Communications, Inc., P.O. Box 1168, Marblehead, MA 01945, 781-639-1872.)

complication/comorbidity ICD-9-CM code is displayed in bold typeface with an abbreviated diagnosis statement following the code. For example, in Figure 8–14, listed as a complication/comorbidity is ICD-9-CM code 83914, dislocation of the fourth cervical vertebra—open (top of the second column, "83914 Disloc 4th cerv vert-opn"). The codes listed under 83914 are the principal diagnoses for which a dislocation of the fourth cervical vertebra (open) is not considered a complication.

For example, the first range of principal diagnosis codes listed under 83914 is 80500 to 80518. Code 805 identifies "Fractures of the vertebral column" with the fourth digit identifying cervical, thoracic, lumbar, or other location; and the fifth digit specifying which cervical vertebra was fractured—first, second, third, etc. Code 805.14 represents the diagnosis of "fracture of the fourth cervical vertebral (open)." A "fracture of the fourth cervical vertebra" (80514) cannot be a complication/comorbidity (C/C) for "dislocation of the fourth cervical vertebra" (83914).

As another example, codes 80600 to 80619 are listed as principal diagnoses that also cannot use 83914 as a C/C. Codes in the 80600 to 80619 range are for vertebra fractures with spinal cord injury with the fourth digit identifying cervical, thoracic, lumbar, or sacrum/coccyx location; and the fifth digit specifying the extent and level of the spinal injury. Again, the complication of a dislocation of the fourth cervical vertebra would not be considered a complication to the fracture of the same vertebra because the C/C is closely related to the principal diagnosis. So, even though complications increase the reimbursement for a diagnosis, the DRG system specifies which complications cannot be considered with a given principal diagnosis, and all complications must be adequately documented in the medical record.

APPENDIX C - DIAGNOSES DEFINED AS COMPLICATIONS OR COMORBIDITIES

83901 Disloc 1st cerv vert-cl
80500-80518,80600-80619,
8068-8069,83900-83918,8470,
8488-8489,8798-8799,9290-9299,
95200-95209,9588,9598-9599

83902 Disloc 2nd cerv vert-cl
80500-80518,80600-80619,
8068-8069,83900-83918,8470,
8488-8489,8798-8799,9290-9299,
95200-95209,9588,9598-9599

83903 Disloc 3rd cerv vert-cl
80500-80518,80600-80619,
8068-8069,83900-83918,8470,
8488-8489,8798-8799,9290-9299,
95200-95209,9588,9598-9599

83904 Disloc 4th cerv vert-cl
80500-80518,80600-80619,
8068-8069,83900-83918,8470,
8488-8489,8798-8799,9290-9299,
95200-95209,9588,9598-9599

83905 Disloc 5th cerv vert-cl
80500-80518,80600-80619,
8068-8069,83900-83918,8470,
8488-8489,8798-8799,9290-9299,
95200-95209,9588,9598-9599

83906 Disloc 6th cerv vert-cl
80500-80518,80600-80619,
8068-8069,83900-83918,8470,
8488-8489,8798-8799,9290-9299,
95200-95209,9588,9598-9599

83907 Disloc 7th cerv vert-cl
80500-80518,80600-80619,
8068-8069,83900-83918,8470,
8488-8489,8798-8799,9290-9299,
95200-95209,9588,9598-9599

83908 Disloc mult cerv vert-cl
80500-80518,80600-80619,
8068-8069,83900-83918,8470,
8488-8489,8798-8799,9290-9299,
95200-95209,9588,9598-9599

83910 Disloc cerv vert NOS-opn
80500-80518,80600-80619,
8068-8069,83900-83918,8470,
8488-8489,8798-8799,9290-9299,
95200-95209,9588,9598-9599

83911 Disloc lst cerv vert-opn
80500-80518,80600-80619,
8068-8069,83900-83918,8470,
8488-8489,8798-8799,9290-9299,
95200-95209,9588,9598-9599

83912 Disloc 2nd cerv vert-opn
80500-80518,80600-80619,
8068-8069,83900-83918,8470,
8488-8489,8798-8799,9290-9299,
95200-95209,9588,9598-9599

83913 Disloc 3rd cerv vert-opn
80500-80518,80600-80619,
8068-8069,83900-83918,8470,
8488-8489,8798-8799,9290-9299,
95200-95209,9588,9598-9599

83914 Disloc 4th cerv vert-opn
80500-80518,80600-80619,
8068-8069,83900-83918,8470,
8488-8489,8798-8799,9290-9299,
95200-95209,9588,9598-9599

83915 Disloc 5th cerv vert-opn
80500-80518,80600-80619,
8068-8069,83900-83918,8470,
8488-8489,8798-8799,9290-9299,
95200-95209,9588,9598-9599

83916 Disloc 6th cerv vert-opn
80500-80518,80600-80619,
8068-8069,83900-83918,8470,
8488-8489,8798-8799,9290-9299,
95200-95209,9588,9598-9599

83917 Disloc 7th cerv vert-opn
80500-80518,80600-80619,
8068-8069,83900-83918,8470,
8488-8489,8798-8799,9290-9299,
95200-95209,9588,9598-9599

83918 Disloc mlt cerv vert-opn
80500-80518,80600-80619,
8068-8069,83900-83918,8470,
8488-8489,8798-8799,9290-9299,
95200-95209,9588,9598-9599

8500 Concussion w/o coma
80000-80199,80300-80499,
8500-85219,85221-85419,
8738-8739,8798-8799,9050,
9251-9252,9290-9299,9588-9590,
9598-9599

8501 Concussion-brief coma
80000-80199,80300-80499,
8500-85219,85221-85419,
8738-8739,8798-8799,9050,
9251-9252,9290-9299,9588-9590,
9598-9599

8502 Concussion-moderate coma
80000-80199,80300-80499,
8500-85219,85221-85419,
8738-8739,8798-8799,9050,
9251-9252,9290-9299,9588-9590,
9598-9599

8503 Concussion-prolong coma
80000-80199,80300-80499,
8500-85219,85221-85419,
8738-8739,8798-8799,9050,
9251-9252,9290-9299,9588-9590,
9598-9599

8504 Concussion-deep coma
80000-80199,80300-80499,
8500-85219,85221-85419,
8738-8739,8798-8799,9050,
9251-9252,9290-9299,9588-9590,
9598-9599

8505 Concussion w coma NOS
80000-80199,80300-80499,
8500-85219,85221-85419,
8738-8739,8798-8799,9050,
9251-9252,9290-9299,9588-9590,
9598-9599

Figure 8–14
Appendix C, Diagnoses Defined as Complications or Comorbidities. (From Diagnosis Related Groups, Version 14.0, Definitions Manual, 3M Health Information Systems.)

EXERCISE D DRG Information

After locating the principal diagnosis in your ICD-9-CM, use Figure 8–14 to answer the following:

1. Can C/C of a concussion with a brief coma be used with a principal diagnosis of a cerebral laceration with open intracranial wound?

___

2. Can C/C of a dislocation of the third cervical vertebra (closed) be used as a C/C with the principal diagnosis of whiplash?

___

3. Can the C/C of dislocation of the sixth cervical vertebra (open) be used as a C/C with the principal diagnosis of injury to the external carotid artery?

___

Fill in the blanks with the correct word(s):

4. The design and development of the DRGs began in the late 1960s at which university?

___

5. The first large-scale application of the DRGs was in the late 1970s in what state?

___

6. The types of illness and volume of patients treated by a hospital represent the complexity of the hospital's

___

7. The concept of case mix complexity has been used to refer to a set of patient attributes that include these five things:

___

___

___

___

___

8. Each of the DRGs is defined by a set of six patient attributes, which include

___

___

____

____

____

9. How many MDCs are there? ______________________________

10. What two things are defined as a condition that increased the patient's length of stay in the hospital by at least 1 day in at least 75% of the patients?

    ______________________ and ______________________

11. What age is sometimes used in definition of the patients?

    ____

12. What are three DRGs that are used to indicate the patient had a surgery unrelated to the principal diagnosis?

    ______________, ______________, ______________

13. What are MDC flow charts also called?

    ____

THE PURPOSE OF PEER REVIEW ORGANIZATIONS (PROs)[5]

An attempt to monitor payment and ensure quality care for hospital services came about when Congress amended the Social Security Act of 1972 and established the Professional Standards Review Organization (PSRO). The PSRO was a voluntary group of physicians who monitored the necessity of hospital admissions and reviewed the treatment costs and medical records of hospitals. But the cost of operating the PSRO was more than what the program saved each year. Congress wanted a program that had stricter controls over Medicare reimbursement for inpatient costs. Congress was concerned that within the Prospective Payment System of DRGs there was an incentive for hospitals to increase admission, increase readmissions, and code hospital stays into higher-priced diagnostic categories to receive higher payments. So, Congress created control peer review organizations (PROs). The creation of the PROs (also known as Quality Improvement Organizations) was made possible under the provision of TEFRA, which gave the HCFA the right to contract with private organizations for peer review purposes.

The review services of the PROs were intended to determine

1. Whether the services provided or proposed were reasonable and medically necessary for (a) the diagnosis and treatment of an illness or injury; (b) improving the function of the patient; (c) prevention of illness; or (d) management of a terminal illness.
2. Whether the services that were proposed to be provided on an inpatient basis could actually be provided on an outpatient basis.
3. The medical necessity, reasonableness, and appropriateness of the care.

4. Whether a hospital had misrepresented admission or discharge information or had taken action that results in (a) unnecessary admission; (b) unnecessary multiple admissions; (c) any other inappropriate medical practices with respect to the beneficiary; or (d) the potential of premature discharge.
5. The validity of all information supplied by the provider.
6. The completeness and adequacy of hospital care provided.
7. The quality of services meets professionally recognized standards of health care.

The review obligations of the PROs are outlined in HCFA's Scope of Work document, which defines the type and number of health records that must be reviewed. The focus of the Scope of Work includes

- increased educational and focused review
- patterns of care and outcome
- differences that occur regularly versus isolated cases
- identification of patterns and variations
- cooperation with the community (education and reports)

Here are six types of reviews that are performed by the PROs:

1. Admission
2. Discharge
3. Quality
4. DRG validation
5. Coverage
6. Procedure

The review begins with a nonphysician reviewer, usually a nurse, who screens the records based on guidelines established by HCFA. For example, an elective surgical admission is reviewed based on six criteria: (1) adequacy of assessment of physiologic functional impairment, (2) preoperative evaluation, (3) operative protocol, (4) postoperative management, (5) recovery, and (6) discharge. Each includes items that are to be reviewed (eg, operative protocol requires a review of the patient's preparation for surgery, anesthesia, and surgical procedure). See Figure 8–15 for an excerpt of the HCFA guidelines for the PRO quality criteria. The PRO quality criteria were originally published in the *Federal Register* on January 18, 1989.

The nonphysician reviewer forwards cases that do not meet the criteria to a physician. The physician then reviews the records to identify if any unnecessary services were provided or if the services were provided on an inpatient basis when they could have been provided in an outpatient setting. If the physician reviewer believes that the care was inappropriate, a letter outlining the problem with the record is sent to the attending physician and to the hospital. Both the attending physician and the hospital must respond to the problems identified in the letter within 20 days. The PRO can either dismiss the case and approve the admission or deny reimbursement for the admission and declare medical mismanagement.

Medical mismanagement problems are classified by three levels of severity:

1. Without the potential for significant adverse effects on the patient
2. With the potential for significant adverse effects on the patient
3. With significant adverse effects on the patient

HCFA's guidelines for PRO quality criteria

Admissions for acute medical conditions

1. Initial assessment—adequacy of initial assessment of:
   a. respiratory function
   b. cardiac function
   c. neurologic function
   d. biochemical/metabolic status
   e. gastrointestinal status
2. Stabilization—restoration of:
   a. respiratory function
   b. cardiac function
   c. fluid volume and chemical balance
3. Definitive diagnosis—identification of:
   a. the immediate cause of hospitalization:
      i. failure of organ system
      ii. infectious process
   b. significant comorbidities
   c. other major reversible problems
   d. adequate diagnostic workup
   e. documentation
   f. comments
   g. complications
4. Definitive therapy—
   a. physiologic support
   b. pharmacologic intervention:
      i. selection of agents
      ii. determination of proper doses
      iii. consideration of toxicity drug interactions
      iv. consideration of interactions with comorbidities
   c. surgical evaluation—specialty consultation
   d. provision of device:
      i. selection and fitting
      ii. training
   e. referral/transfer
5. Recovery—
   a. titration of therapeutic agents and supports
   b. mgmt. of intercurrent infections
   c. mgmt. of complications related to comorbidities
6. Discharge—
   a. physiologic stability sufficient for ambulatory care
   b. plan for followup and aftercare/sociologic setting
   c. rehabilitation

Chronic medical conditions

1. Adequacy of assessment of deterioration of function—
   a. measures of deficit and residual function/reserve
      i. vital organs
      ii. biochem/metabolic status
      iii. motor capability
      iv. sensory limitation pain
      v. psychologic
      vi. social situation
   b. comorbidities
2. Management—
   a. pharmacologic
      i. agent selection
      ii. dosage titration
      iii. drug interactions
      iv. interactions with comorbidities
   b. device
      i. selection and fitting
      ii. training
   c. surgical evaluation/referral
3. Discharge—
   a. assessment of restoration of function/physiologic stability
   b. plan for followup and aftercare/sociologic setting

Elective surgical admissions

1. Adequacy of assessment of physiologic/functional impairment—
   a. underlying disorder and stage of progression
   b. comorbidities
   c. evaluation of medical/interventional radiologic mgmt. alternatives
   d. need for procedures
   e. documentation
2. Preoperative evaluation—
   a. cardiac
   b. pulmonary
   c. neurologic
   d. renal
   e. endocrine metabolic
   f. hydration and electrolytes (anesthetic staging)
   g. radiologic assessment
3. Operative protocol—
   a. preparation
      i. gastrointestinal
      ii. antibiotic prophylaxis
      iii. sedation
   b. anesthesia
      i. agent route
      ii. ventilation
      iii. hemodynamic monitor
      iv. intravenous fluids (volume electrolytes)
   c. surgical procedure
      i. appropriateness and adequacy
      ii. support staff
      iii. operative complications
4. Post-operative mgmt.—
   a. vital signs
   b. stabilization
      i. ventilation
      ii. hemodynamics
   c. neurologic status/sensorium
5. Recovery—
   a. physiologic support
   b. wound management

Figure 8–15
HCFA guidelines for peer review organization quality criteria. (From *Federal Register,* Jan. 18, 1989, pp. 1965–1966.)

Adverse effects are defined by HCFA as (1) unnecessarily prolonged treatment, complications, or readmissions; and (2) patient management that results in anatomic or physiologic impairment or disability.

Each of the levels of severity is assigned a score and a record is kept of the providers, physicians, and hospitals that indicates the numbers and severity of occurrences. At preset levels, the PRO intervenes. Interventions can include education, intensified review, denial of payments, other corrective interventions, notification of licensing and accreditation bodies, and sanctions. Ultimately, sanctions may be levied in two situations: (1) when substantial violations occurred in a substantial number of cases; (2) when a gross or flagrant violation took place, causing danger to health, safety, or well-being of a patient.

c. mgmt. of current infections
d. mgmt. of comorbidities
e. other postop complications
6. Discharge—
a. physiologic stability
b. wound stability
c. management of temporary functional deficit
d. plan for followup and aftercare/sociological setting

Acute surgical admissions

1. Initial assessment—adequacy of initial assessment of:
a. cardiac output/blood volume
b. ventilation
c. biochemical/metabolic balance
d. neurologic status/sensorium
2. Stabilization—
a. respiration
b. cardiac output/blood volume
c. biochemical/metabolic balance
3. Identification of affected organ/lesion—
a. history/physical
b. radiology (imaging)
c. laboratory
d. other diagnostic procedures
e. documentation
4. Preoperative evaluation management—
a. cardiac
b. pulmonary
c. neurologic
d. electrolytes/hematology
e. renal function
f. assessment of medical or interventional radiologic alternatives
5. Operative protocol—
a. preparation
i. gastrointestinal
ii. antibiotic prophylaxis
iii. sedation
b. anesthesia
i. agent route
ii. ventilation
iii. hemodynamic cardiovascular
iv. intravenous fluids (volume, electrolytes)
c. surgical procedure
i. appropriateness, adequacy
ii. support staff
iii. operative complications
6. Post-operative mgmt.—
a. vital signs
b. stabilization
i. ventilation
ii. hemodynamics
c. neurologic status/sensorium
7. Recovery—
a. physiologic support
b. wound management
c. mgmt. of intercurrent infections
d. mgmt. of comorbidities
e. other postoperative complications
8. Discharge—
a. physiologic ability
b. wound stability
c. mgmt. of temporary functional deficit
d. plan for followup and aftercare sociologic setting

Admissions for trauma

1. Initial assessment—adequacy of initial assessment of:
a. anatomic damage
b. respiratory function
c. cardiac function, blood volume
d. neurologic status
e. biochemical/metabolic
2. Stabilization—
a. correction of stabilization of anatomic injury
b. respiratory function
c. cardiac function/blood volume
3. Evaluation/diagnosis—
a. collateral injuries
i. radiology
ii. invasive procedures
b. comorbidities
4. Corrective treatment—
a. surgical (see acute surgical admissions)
b. physiologic support
c. physical therapy/rehab.
5. Discharge—
a. stability of injury
b. physiologic stability
c. functional capacity
d. followup and aftercare
e. rehabilitation
f. sociologic evaluation support

Acute psychiatric admissions

1. Assessment—adequacy of initial assessment of:
a. degree of functional impairment
b. underlying physiologic disorder
c. comorbidities
d. history
e. medical status
f. documentation
g. mental status
h. assessment for potential harm to self or others
2. Management—
a. underlying physiologic disorder
b. pharmacologic
i. agent
ii. titration of dosage
iii. drug interactions
iv. interactions with comorbidities
c. surgical
d. other therapy: electric shock therapy, analysis, psychotherapy, rehab, etc.
3. Disposition—
a. functional capacity
b. followup monitoring
c. aftercare/sociologic support

Federal Register, Jan. 18, 1989. pp. 1965–1966

Figure 8–15
Continued

EXERCISE E *Peer Review Organizations*

Fill in the blanks with the correct word(s):

1. The creation of Peer Review Organizations was made possible under the provision of what act?

____

2. What is the name of the document that is produced by HCFA that defines the type and number of health records that must be reviewed?

____

3. What are the six types of review that are performed by the PROs?

____

____

____

____

____

____

4. What are the three levels of medical mismanagement?

____

____

____

WHAT IS THE OUTPATIENT RESOURCE-BASED RELATIVE VALUE SCALE (RBRVS)?[5,9]

Physician payment reform was implemented to

1. decrease Medicare expenditures
2. redistribute physician payment more equitably
3. ensure quality health care at a reasonable rate

Before January 1, 1992, payment under Medicare Part B for physicians' services was based on a reasonable charge that, under the Social Security Act, could not exceed the lowest of the (1) physician's actual charge for the service, (2) physician's customary charge for the service, or (3) prevailing charges of physicians for similar services in the locality.

The act also required that the local prevailing charge for a physician's service not exceed the level in effect for that service in the locality for the fiscal year ending on June 30, 1973. There was some provision made for changes in the level based on economic changes. When there were economic changes in the country, the Medicare Economic Index (MEI) reflected these changes. Until 1992, the MEI tied increases in the Medicare prevailing charges to increases in physicians' practice costs and general wage rates throughout the economy as compared with the index base year. The MEI was first published in the *Federal Register* on June 16, 1975, and has been recalculated annually since then.

Congress mandated the MEI as part of the 1972 Amendments to the Social Security Act. The 1972 Amendment to the Act did not specify the particular type of index to be used; however, the present form of the MEI follows the recommendations outlined by the Senate Finance Committee in its report accompanying the legislation. The MEI attempts to present an equitable measure for changes in the costs of physicians' time and operating expenses of physicians.

A major change took place in Medicare in 1989 with the enactment of the Omnibus Budget Reconciliation Act of 1989 (OBRA), Public Law 101-239. Section 6102 of PL 101-239 amended Title XVIII of the Social Security Act by adding Section 1848, "Payment for Physician Services." The new section contained three major elements:

1. Establishment of standard rates of increase of physician services' expenditures
2. Replacement of the reasonable charge payment mechanism with a fee schedule for physicians' services
3. Replacement of the maximum actual allowable charge (MAAC), which limits the total amount nonparticipating physicians can charge

Revisions were made and a new Omnibus Budget Reconciliation Act of 1990 was passed. OBRA 1990 contained several modifications and clarifications to the PL 101-239 provisions establishing the physician fee schedule. This final rule required that before January 1 of each year, beginning with 1992, the Secretary shall establish, by regulation, fee schedules that establish payment amounts for all physician's services furnished in all fee schedule areas for the year.

The physician fee schedule is updated each April 15 and is composed of three basic elements:

1. The relative value units for each service
2. A geographic adjustment factor to adjust for regional variations in the cost of operating a health care facility
3. A national conversion factor

Medicare volume performance standards have been developed to be used as a tool to monitor annual increases in Part B expenditures for physician services and, when appropriate, to adjust payment levels to reflect the success or failure in meeting the performance standards. Various financial protections have been designed and instituted on behalf of the Medicare beneficiary. Uniformity of administration and standardization of procedures, policies, and coding have been implemented so that all Medicare carriers communicate on the same level using the same language.

National Fee Schedule[5]

Beginning January 1, 1992, the Medicare Fee Schedule (MFS) replaced the reasonable charge payment system. All physicians' services are paid using the amounts indicated on the new MFS. Reimbursement is made at 80% of the fee schedule amount, subject to the annual Part B Medicare deductible. The fee schedule applies to Medicare payment for physicians' services and supplies furnished "incidental to" physicians' services, outpatient physical and occupational therapy services, diagnostic tests, and radiology services. The fee schedule applies when payment is made to either physicians or suppliers.

Relative Value Unit[5]

Nationally, unit values have been assigned for each service (CPT code) determined on the resources necessary for the physician to perform the service. By analyzing a service, a Harvard team was able to identify its separate parts and assign each part a relative value unit (RVU). These parts or components were

1. Work. The work component was identified as the amount of time, the intensity of effort, and the technical expertise required for the physician to provide the service.
2. Overhead. The overhead component was identified as the allocation of costs associated with the physician's practice (eg, rent, staffing, supplies) required to provide a service.
3. Malpractice. The malpractice component was identified as the cost of medical malpractice insurance coverage associated with providing service.

The sum of the units established for each component of the service equals the total RVUs for a service.

A relative value of 1 has been established for the mid-level established patient office visit (99213). All other services are valued at, above, or below this service relative to the work, overhead, and malpractice expenses associated with the service.

Geographic Practice Cost Index[5]

The Urban Institute developed scales that measure cost differences between areas. The Geographic Practice Cost Indices (GPCIs) have been established for each of the prevailing charge localities. Entire states are often considered a locality for purposes of physician payment reform. The GPCIs reflect the relative costs of practice in a given locality compared with a national average. The national average is 1. A separate GPCI has been established and is applied to each component of a service. For example, the GPCIs for Minnesota are .999 for work, .971 for overhead, and .748 for malpractice insurance.

Conversion Factor[5]

The conversion factor (CF) is a national dollar amount that is applied to all services paid on the Medicare Fee Schedule basis. Congress provided a CF to be used to convert RVUs to dollars. The CF is updated annually based on the data sources, which indicate

- percent changes to the Medicare Economic Index (MEI)
- percent changes in physician expenditures
- the relationship of expenditures to the volume performance standards
- change in access and quality

Conversion factors differ according to the type of service provided (eg, medical, surgical, nonsurgical).

The Transition[5]

To prevent extreme fluctuation in Medicare reimbursement amounts, some of the fee schedule amounts are subject to a 5-year transitional phase-in. A historical payment base (HPCB) charge was established for all services to use in a comparison with the fee schedule allowance. Simply put, this means that Medicare allowed 5 years to bring the prices for services to the fee schedule amounts. Those prices that were higher than the fee schedule slowly dropped during this period, and those that were lower were slowly raised. By 1996, all prices for services reflected the fee schedule amount.

Medicare Volume Performance Standards[5]

The Medicare Volume Performance Standards (MVPS) are best thought of as an object. "It" represents the government's estimate of how much growth is appropriate for nationwide physician expenditures paid by the Part B Medicare program. The purpose of MVPS is to guide Congress in its consideration of the appropriate annual payment update.

The Secretary of Health and Human Services must make MVPS recommendations to Congress by April 15 for the upcoming fiscal year, and by May 15, the Physician Payment Review Commission (PPRC) must make its recommendations for the fiscal year. Congress has until October 15 to establish the MVPS by either accepting or modifying the two proposed MVPS recommendations.

If Congress does not react by October 15, the MVPS rate is established using a default mechanism. If the default mechanism is used, the Secretary would then be required to publish a notice in the *Federal Register*, containing the formula to derive MVPS.

Variations in health care usage by Medicare patients occur every year. Because Medicare strives for balanced billing, if HCFA agrees to pay for additional services not previously paid for or increases the weights of CPT codes, thus increasing reimbursement, then discounts are taken across the board so that more money than authorized is not spent and the budget is balanced.

Beneficiary Protection[5]

There are several provisions in Physician Payment Reform that were designed to protect Medicare beneficiaries:

1. As of September 1, 1990, all providers must file claims for their Medicare patients (free of charge). In addition, claims must be submitted within 1 year of the date of service or they will be subject to a 10% reduction in payment.
2. The Omnibus Budget Reconciliation Act of 1989 requires the physician to accept the amount paid for eligible Medicaid services (mandatory assignment).
3. Effective January 1, 1991, the Maximum Actual Allowable Charge (MAAC) limitations that applied to unassigned physician charges were replaced by new billing limits called "limiting charges." The provisions of the new limitations state that nonparticipating physicians and suppliers cannot charge more than the stated limiting charge on unassigned claims.

Limiting Charge[5]

In 1991 and 1992, the limiting charge was specific to each physician. Beginning in 1993, the limiting charge for a service has been the same for all physicians within a locality regardless of specialty. The limiting charge for each service also appears on the beneficiary's Explanation of Medicare Benefits.[5]

The limiting charge applies to every service listed in the Medicare Physicians' Fee Schedule that is performed by a nonparticipating physician. This includes global, professional, and technical services performed by a physician. When a nonphysician provider (eg, portable x-ray supplier, laboratory technician) provides the technical component of a service that is on the fee schedule, the limiting charge does not apply. CPT codes are assigned many different prices. The amount determined by multiplying the RVU weight by the geographic index and the conversion factor is called the "fee schedule" amount. If a physician is participating, he or she receives the fee schedule amount. If the physician is nonparticipating, the fee schedule amount or the allowable payment is slightly less than the participating physician's payment. The limiting amount is a percentage over the allowable (eg, 115% times the allowable amount). The limiting charge is important because that is the maximum amount a Medicare patient can be billed for a service. For covered services, Medicare usually pays 80% of the allowable amount. The beneficiary is then "balance billed," which means that the patient is billed the difference between what Medicare pays and the limiting charge.

EXAMPLE

Limiting charge is	$115	(Maximum charge)
Allowable is	$100	
Medicare pays	$80	(Medicare pays 80%)
Patient is billed	$35	($20, 20% of $100, and $15, the remainder of the limiting charge maximum)

Physicians may round the limiting charge to the nearest dollar if they do this consistently for all services.

Uniformity Provision[5]

Equitable use of the Medicare fee schedule requires a payment system with uniform policy and procedures. Because the relative value for the work component for a service is the same nationwide (except for a geographic practice cost adjustment), it is important that when physicians across the country are paid for a service they are paid for the same amount or "package" of work. For example, the preoperative and postoperative periods included in the payment must be the same. To prevent variation in interpretation, standard definitions of services are required.

A comprehensive survey of carrier policies resulted in HCFA's issuing a standardization policy for the following items:

- Evaluation and management services
- Visits and procedures on the same day
- Global surgery packages
- Starred procedures
- Endoscopies
- Multiple/bilateral/incidental surgeries
- Assistant/team surgeon
- Outpatient limits
- Inpatient visits—concurrent care
- Site of service differentials
- Travel/mileage charges
- Specimen handling

- Injections and other "incident to" services
- Modifiers used for payment differential purposes
- Place and type of service

Adjustments[5]

Whenever an adjustment to the full fee schedule amount is made on a service, the limiting charge for that service must be adjusted. Medicare has provided adjusted limiting charges to providers for services in which the site of service limitation applies, the assistant-at-surgery limitation applies, multiple surgery limitations applies, and when only a portion of the global surgical package is being provided. These adjustments are identified on the physician disclosure, which is provided to all physicians during the participating enrollment period each year.

Adjustments to the limiting charge must be manually calculated before submitting unassigned claims for all services in which a fee schedule limitation applies.

Payments to nonparticipating physicians will not exceed 95% of the physician fee schedule for a service.

Site of Service Limitations[5]

Services that are primarily performed in office settings will be subject to a payment discount if they are performed in outpatient hospital departments. There is a national list of procedures that are performed 50% of the time in the office setting. These procedures are subject to site of service limitations. "Site of service limitation" means that a discount is taken on any service that is performed in a setting other than a clinic setting. For instance, an arthrocentesis is normally performed in the office. If a physician provides this service in a hospital outpatient setting, the limiting charge will be less than that for the office setting. This is because the hospital will also be billing Medicare for the use of the room and supplies. Medicare has a built-in practice expense or overhead for the clinic setting (the RVU weight for practice expense), and Medicare doesn't want to pay twice for the overhead. So, part of the overhead is reduced from the physician's payment to make up for the hospital payment. For these procedures, the practice expense RVU is reduced by 50%. Payment is the lower of the actual charge or the reduced fee schedule amount. Physicians who bill an emergency department visit will not be subject to the outpatient limit for these services.

Surgical Modifier Circumstances[5]

Multiple Surgery

General

If a surgeon performs more than one procedure on the same patient on the same day, discounts will be made on all subsequent procedures. Medicare will pay 100% of the fee for the highest value procedure, 50% for the second most expensive procedure, and 25% for the third, fourth, and fifth procedures. Discounting is why the service (CPT code) that you place the modifier on is so important! Each procedure after the fifth procedure will require documentation and special carrier review to determine the payment amount. These discount amounts are subject to review every year by HCFA.

Commercial insurers often follow different discount limits than Medicare, as established by their own individual reimbursement policies.

Endoscopic Procedures[5]

In the case of multiple endoscope procedures, Medicare will allow the full value of the highest valued endoscopy, plus the difference between the next highest endoscopy and the base endoscopy. As in all other reimbursement issues, some non-Medicare carriers follow this pricing method, others follow their own established multiple procedure discounting policies.

Dermatologic Surgery

For certain dermatology services, there are CPT codes that indicate that multiple surgical procedures have been performed. When the CPT code description states "additional," the general multiple procedure rules will not apply.

Providers Furnishing Part of the Global Fee Package

Under the fee schedule, Medicare will pay the same amount for surgical services if they are furnished by several physicians as if only one physician furnished all of the services in the global package.

Medicare will pay each physician directly for his or her part of the global surgery services. The policy is written with the assumption that the surgeon always furnishes the usual and necessary preoperative and intraoperative services and also, with a few exceptions, in-hospital postoperative services. In most cases, the surgeon also furnishes the postoperative office services necessary to ensure normal recovery from the surgery. Recognizing that there are cases in which the surgeon turns over the out-of-hospital recovery care to another physician, Medicare has determined percentages for families of procedures for paying usual out-of-hospital postoperative care if furnished by someone other than the surgeon. These are weighted percentages based on the percentage of total global surgical work.

Again, become familiar with individual third-party payer policies, because some may not split their global payments in this manner.

Physicians Who Assist at Surgery

Physicians assisting the primary physician in a procedure will receive a set percentage of the total fee for the service. Medicare will set the payment level for assistants-at-surgery at 16% of the fee schedule amount for the global surgical service. Non-Medicare payers may set this percentage at 20% or more.

Two Surgeons and Surgical Team

When two surgeons of different specialties perform a procedure, each is paid an equal percentage of the global fee. For co-surgeons, Medicare pays 125% of the global fee, dividing the payment equally between the two surgeons (or each will receive 62.5% of the global fee). No payment will be made for an assistant-at-surgery in these cases.

For team surgery, a medical director will determine the payment amounts on an individual basis.

Purchased Diagnostic Services

For physicians who bill for a diagnostic test performed by an outside supplier, the fee schedule amount is limited to the lower of the billing physician's fee schedule amount or the price he or she paid for the service.

Reoperations

The amount paid by Medicare for a return trip to the operating room for treatment of a complication is limited to the intraoperative portion of the code that best describes the treatment of the complications.

When an unlisted procedure is billed because no other code exists to describe the treatment, payment is based on a maximum of 50% of the value of the intraoperative services originally performed.

Commercial insurance companies again have their own guidelines. Many do not take discounts for these subsequent surgical procedures.

EXERCISE F ***RBRVS***

Fill in the blanks with the correct words:

1. What does RBRVS stand for? ______________________________

   ____

2. The Medicare Economic Index is published in what publication? __________

   ____

3. In 1989, a major change took place in Medicare with the enactment of

   ____

   ____

4. Medicare publishes the Medicare Fee Schedule and usually pays what percentage of the amounts indicated for services? ______________

5. The three components of work, overhead, and malpractice are part of an RVU. What do the initials RVU stand for? ______________

6. According to the Physician Payment Reform, providers must file claims for their Medicare patients within what time period? ______________

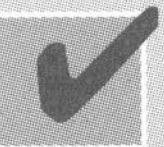

CHECK THIS OUT!

HCFA publishes the RVUs on their website (www.hcfa.gov) under the Public Use Files (PUFs). Click on "Students" and then on "Public Use Files." In the medical office, you may be responsible for downloading the new RVUs when they are posted, usually in October each year.

THE PROSPECTIVE PAYMENT SYSTEM FOR THE SKILLED NURSING FACILITY

Effective July 1, 1998, a per diem prospective payment system (PPS) for skilled nursing facilities (SNFs) was implemented to cover all costs (routine, ancillary, and capital) related to services provided to Medicare Part A beneficiaries. Federal rates were established using FY 1995 cost reports, and per diem payments are case-mix adjusted according to a classification system entitled Resource Utilization Groups III (RUGS III). (*Note:* FY stands for fiscal year.)

Information collected by completing the Minimum Data Set 2.0 (MDS 2.0) resident assessment instrument (RAI) determines the amount of per diem payments for each SNF admission. Payments are case-mix adjusted based on data from the MDS 2.0 and relative weights determined by SNF staff time. The per diem rate is adjusted for geographic variation in wages, using the hospital wage index, and rates are expected to increase each federal fiscal year using a "SNF market basket index (minus one percentage point in FY 2000 through FY 2002)." A blending of the facility-specific payment rate with the federal case-mix–adjusted rate will apply during the three-year phase-in period.

TWO MEDICARE REIMBURSEMENT SYSTEMS—APG & APC

Medicare payments for hospital services, both inpatient and outpatient, were historically based on the customary and reasonable cost of a service. In 1983, the law that governs Medicare was revised to move from this cost-based payment to a prospective payment system (PPS) for hospital inpatients. Outpatient hospital services continued to operate on the cost-based system. Advances in medical technology and changes in practices (such as more outpatient surgery) brought a shift in the site of medical care from the inpatient to the outpatient setting. In the years that followed, Congress enacted many laws to try to curb this shift to outpatient-based services, to no avail. OBRA 1986 (Omnibus Budget Reconciliation Act of 1986) contained a requirement to replace the existing outpatient hospital cost-based system with a PPS. Also, as a part of OBRA 1986 came the ability to require hospitals to report claims for services under the HCFA Common Procedure Coding System (HCPCS). This coding requirement provided data to HCFA on the specific services being provided on an outpatient basis. These data were used to develop the outpatient PPS.

HCFA conducted research into ways to classify outpatient services for the purposes of developing the outpatient PPS. The resulting report cited the Ambulatory Patient Groups (APGs), developed by 3M Health Information Systems under a cooperative grant with HCFA, as the most promising classification system for grouping outpatient services, and recommended that APG-like groups be used in the hospital PPS. The APG-like groups were named Ambulatory Patient Classifications (APCs) and were scheduled for implementation January 1, 1999. However, that date was delayed owing to concerns with Year 2000 (Y2K) computer issues. Implementation is scheduled for soon after January 1, 2000.

Both the APGs and APCs will be used in health care facilities for reimbursement of patient services.

An Introduction to Ambulatory Patient Groups (APGs)[10,11]

The HCFA in cooperation with 3M Company has developed a prospective payment system for hospital outpatient facility fees called Ambulatory Patient Groups (APGs). The General Accounting Office was ordered by Congress to convert to the APG system starting with radiology and other diagnostic services. The OBRA 1986 required HCFA to develop a prospective payment system for outpatient facilities. This outpatient system mirrors the inpatient DRG system. The inpatient system was very cost-effective, and the government is seeking to continue the cost savings on the outpatient side of health care. The APG system is a facility payment system for outpatient care, just as the DRG is a facility payment system for inpatient care. The APGs were scheduled to be fully implemented nationally on January 1, 1996; however, the federal funding was not appropriated to make the transition. Some facilities have already implemented APGs because a number of state agencies and private payers are using the system for reimbursement. Mandatory implementation for Medicare services is anticipated after January 1, 2000. Medicare will notify the facilities 90 days prior to implementation.

APGs are a patient classification system designed to explain the amount and type of resources used in an ambulatory visit. APGs differ from DRGs because they are a patient classification system designed to explain the amount and type of resources used in an ambulatory visit. DRGs are a patient classification system that provided a means of relating the type of patients a hospital treats to the costs incurred by the hospital for the care of inpatients. The APG services are classified into either medical visits or procedure visits, as shown in Figure 8–16. The assignment of the APG is based on the information routinely collected on the Medicare claim form and consists of the diagnosis code (ICD-9-CM), the procedures code (CPT), and the age and sex of the patient. Significant procedure APGs are divided based on the twelve body systems. Each procedure was assigned to a body system and then subdivided based on the method of the procedure (eg, endoscopy, catheterization, needle). The complexity of the procedure was also an aspect of the division of the procedure into APGs.

Medical APGs were divided based on the coded diagnosis that was the reason for the visit. The etiology of the diagnosis was then used to subdivide the APGs. Considered as etiologies: well care, malignancy, trauma, poisoning, pregnancy, neonate, or other. Further division was based on body system. There are 83 medical APGs. Figure 8–17 shows the initial medical APG logic flow chart. Note that in Figure 8–17 the diamond shape labeled "Etiology" has further divisions from it, such as the subdivision "Malignancy." From this subdivision comes further subdivision, as shown in Figure 8–18. Malignancy is divided based on the site, "Hematological," "Prostatic," "Lung," "Breast," "GI," "Skin," or "Other." Each site is assigned a three-digit APG. If the site of the malignancy was the lung, the APG code would be 433. The APGs Definitions Manual includes Appendix C (Fig. 8–19), which lists all APGs available for assignment. There are 290 APGs within the classification system (Fig. 8–20).

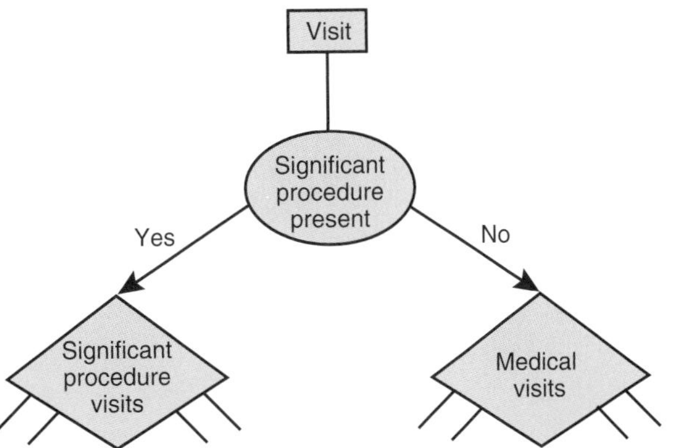

Figure 8–16
APG partition based on the presence of significant procedure.

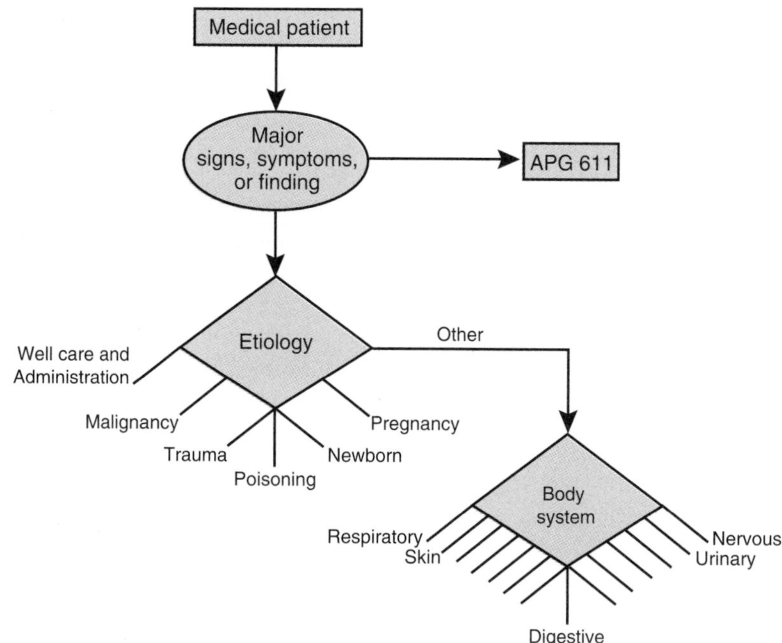

Figure 8–17
Initial APG medical flow chart.

Ambulatory care data are highly influenced by RVU (Relative Value Unit) scales. The RVU scales provide a measure of resource use, physician time, and knowledge necessary to treat a patient.[10] Thus, ambulatory charges for a procedure do not necessarily reflect the actual needs of an individual patient but are based on the established RVU for the procedure. Data about the extent of services are often simply a reflection of the established RVU scales. For example, there are different CPT codes for excisions of benign and malignant skin lesions. RVU and charge data implied that excisions of malignant skin lesions of the same site and size used significantly more resources than those of benign skin lesions. However, whether the lesion is malignant or benign is usually not known at the time

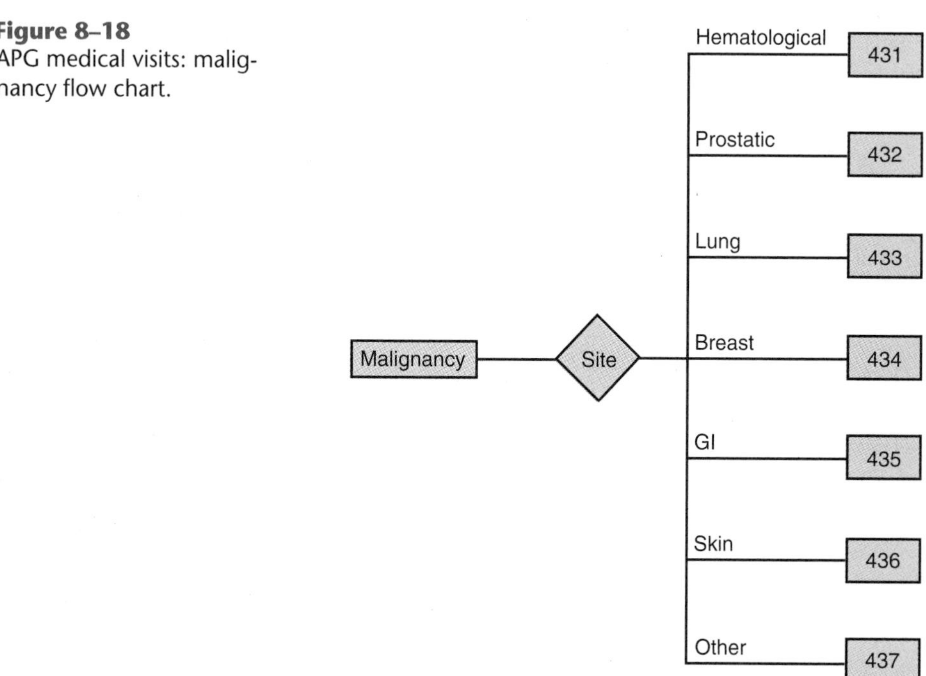

Figure 8–18
APG medical visits: malignancy flow chart.

APPENDIX C - LIST OF APGS

MEDICAL APGS

APC 24 MALIGNANCY

431 HEMATOLOGICAL MALIGNANCY
432 PROSTATIC MALIGNANCY
433 LUNG MALIGNANCY
434 BREAST MALIGNANCIES
435 GI MALIGNANCIES
436 SKIN MALIGNANCY
437 OTHER MALIGNANCIES

APC 25 POISONING

451 POISONING

APC 26 TRAUMA

461 HEAD AND SPINE INJURY
462 MINOR SKIN AND SOFT TISSUE INJURIES EXCEPT BURNS
463 SKIN AND SOFT TISSUE INJURIES EXCEPT BURNS
464 FRACTURE, DISLOCATION AND SPRAIN
465 BURNS
466 OTHER INJURIES

Figure 8–19
Appendix C from *Ambulatory Patient Groups Definitions Manual* listing APGs. (From Ambulatory Patient Group Definitions Manual, Version 2.0, 3M Health Information Systems. Available from 3M Health Information Systems, 100 Barnes Road, Wallingford, CT 06492.)

Type of APG	Count
Significant Procedure and Therapy	139
Medical	83
Laboratory	20
Radiology	11
Pathology	3
Anesthesia	1
Ancillary Tests and Procedures	16
Ancillary Mental Illness and Substance Abuse Svcs	2
Incidental Procedures	2
Chemotherapy Drugs	5
Errors	8
Total	290

Figure 8–20
Types of APGs.

of the procedure but is established when a pathology report is returned. Furthermore, the excision of a malignant and benign skin lesion of the same site and size is basically the same procedure except that a wider margin is excised for lesions that are suspected to be malignant. The procedure APGs do not differentiate between malignant and benign skin excisions.[10]

In the outpatient setting, the diversity of sites of service (eg, same-day-surgery units, emergency departments, and outpatient clinics), the wide variation in the reasons patients require outpatient care (eg, well care to critical trauma care), and the high percentage of cost associated with ancillary services (ie, the cost of ancillary services or those additional services necessary can often exceed the cost of the base visit) necessitate a patient classification scheme that can precisely reflect the services rendered to the patient. The APGs address the diversity within the outpatient setting by assigning patients to multiple APGs. For example, if a patient had two procedures performed plus a chest x-ray film and a blood test, there would be four APGs assigned to the patient (ie, one APG for each of the two procedures, one APG for the chest x-ray film, and one for the blood test). In a prospective payment system, each APG would have a standard payment rate.

Packaging refers to the inclusion of certain ancillary services into the payment for the visit, similar to the surgery package. The significant procedure or medical visit combined with the packaged ancillary services would be considered as a single unit. In the case of ambulatory surgery, for example, a packaged visit would combine the significant procedure with the related ancillary services into a single payment amount.

A uniform packaging of ancillaries was selected for use in the APG payment model. The APGs included in the uniform packaging were primarily simple laboratory tests (eg, basic chemistry), simple pathology, anesthesia, simple radiology (eg, plain films), other minor tests (eg, electrocardiograms), and minor procedures and therapies (eg, spirometry). In general, the ancillaries in the uniform packaging included ancillaries that are performed for a wide range of different types of visits and were relatively low cost compared with the average cost of the procedure and medical APGs. A few ancillaries were also included that were a routine part of one particular type of visit (eg, obstetric ultrasound). Only relatively low cost ancillaries were included in the uniform packaging. The cost of medical surgical supplies, drugs, and all other facility-related costs are included in the payment for a significant procedure or medical visit. The only exception is the cost of chemotherapeutic agents.

In addition to significant procedure consolidation and ancillary packaging, the visit payment computation could also include discounting. Discounting refers to a reduction in the standard payment rate for an APG. The need for discounting occurs when multiple procedures or ancillaries are performed. For example, discounting could compensate for the reduced cost per procedure of doing multiple significant procedures at the same time. When multiple significant procedures are performed, in general, the patient preparation, use of the operating room, and recovery time are shared between the two procedures. Thus, the cost of doing two procedures at the same time is less than the cost of doing the two procedures at two different times. Discounting can also be used to provide a financial incentive not to repeat the same ancillary service multiple times. Because the performance of multiple ancillaries in the same APG may be clinically necessary and appropriate, there is no consolidation of ancillaries within the same APG. Thus, each nonpackaged ancillary in the same APG will result in an additional payment. However, to provide some financial incentive not to repeat ancillary tests, multiple ancillaries in the same APG could be discounted. The level of any discounting is a policy decision and would be determined during system implementation. The final APG payment system is depicted in Figure 8–21.

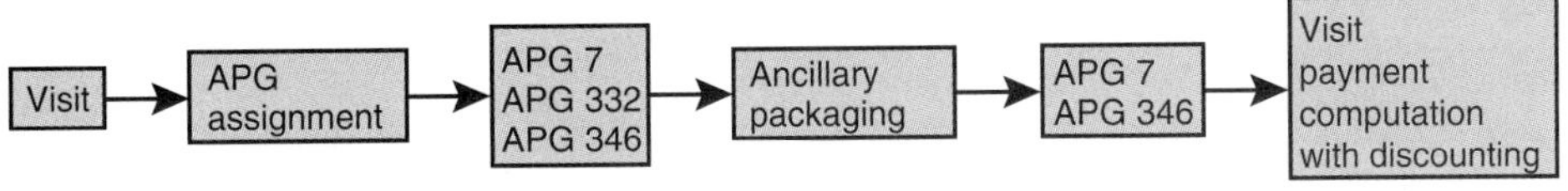

Figure 8–21
Significant procedure consolidation and ancillary packaging for APGs.

A visit-based APG prospective payment system with significant procedure consolidation, uniform ancillary packaging, and multiple APG discounting combined to form the basis for a prospective payment system for outpatients under Medicare.

Introduction to Ambulatory Patient Classifications (APCs)

When 3M Health Information Systems developed the APGs under the grant from HCFA, they also developed a second system. The second system was revised by HCFA and subsequently titled Ambulatory Patient Classifications (APCs). APCs are a system to reimburse facilities for Medicare outpatient health care. Once past the computer concerns of January 1, 2000, HCFA will finalize the APC reimbursement system and mandate implementation with a 90-day notice to the health care facilities.

APCs will be mandatory for all hospital outpatient services. They will include inpatient services covered under Part B for beneficiaries who are entitled to Part A benefits but who have exhausted their Part A benefits or otherwise are not in a covered Part A hospital stay. Patients who receive partial hospitalization services furnished by community mental health centers will also qualify to have their services paid under the prospective payments system of APCs. In general, the definition for a hospital outpatient is an individual who is not an inpatient of the hospital but who is registered as an outpatient.

The way beneficiary coinsurance is determined for the services included under the PPS has also changed. A coinsurance amount will initially be calculated for each APC based on 20% of the national median charge for services in the APC. The coinsurance amount for an APC will not change until such time as the amount becomes 20% of the total APC payment.

Figure 8–22 shows the broad range of categories of services provided under the Medicare program and which categories are paid under the APC rate. The APC system consists of 346 groups of services that are covered under this hospital outpatient prospective payment system. ICD-9-CM codes are assigned into a major diagnostic categories (MDCs). Figure 8–23 illustrates the listing of ICD-9-CM codes assigned to MDCs. Each procedure is then assigned into a group of APCs and the payment rate and beneficiary coinsurance portion are identified (Fig. 8–24). The services are identified by HCPCS codes and descriptions, as illustrated in Figure 8–25. The APCs identify the packaged services that are included in each APC. Packaged services are those that are recognized as contributing to the cost of the services in the APC, but that Medicare does not pay for separately. Under the APC system, packaged services include the operating room, recovery room, anesthesia, medical/surgical supplies, pharmaceuticals, observation, blood, intraocular lenses, casts and splints, donor tissue, and various incidental services such as venipuncture. Also bundled into the APC will be any medical visit that takes place on the same date of service as a scheduled outpatient surgery. Registration of the patient, taking of vital signs, insertion of an IV, preparation for surgery, etc, are packaged into and paid for as a part of the APC group to which the surgical procedure or service is classified.

STATUS INDICATORS[11] (How Medicare pays for various services when they are billed for hospital outpatients)	
Service	**Status**
Pulmonary Rehabilitation; Clinical trial	Non-paid.
Inpatient Procedures	Bill as inpatient.
Durable Medical Equipment, Prosthetics and Orthotics	DMEPOS Fee Schedule.
Non-covered Items and Services	Non-paid.
Physical, Occupational and Speech Therapy	Rehab Fee Schedule.
Ambulance	Ambulance Fee Schedule.
EPO for ESRD patients	National Rate.
Clinical Diagnostic Laboratory Services	Lab Fee Schedule.
Physician Services for ESRD patients	Bill to carrier.
Screening Mammography	Lower of Charge or National Rate.
Incidental Services, packaged into APC rate	Packaged; no additional payment allowed.
Partial Hospitalization Services	Paid per diem.
Significant Procedure, not reduced when multiple	Paid under hospital outpatient PPS (APC rate).
Significant Procedure, multiple procedure reduction applies	Paid under hospital outpatient PPS (APC rate).
Visit to Clinic or Emergency Department	Paid under hospital outpatient PPS (APC rate).
Ancillary Service	Paid under hospital outpatient PPS (APC rate).

Figure 8–22
A listing of groups of services and the payment status for each group. (From *Federal Register,* Vol. 63, No. 173, Tuesday, September 8, 1998, p 47561.)

ADDENDUM F.– ICD-9 CODES WITH MAJOR DIAGNOSTIC CATEGORIES (MDCs) FOR PAYMENT OF MEDICAL VISITS UNDER THE HOSPITAL OUTPATIENT PPS–Continued

ICD-9-CM	ICD-9 Description	MDC
57451	CHOLEDOCHLITH NOS W OBST	41
5750	ACUTE CHOLECYSTITIS	41
5752	OBSTRUCTION GALLBLADDER	41
5753	HYDROPS OF GALLBLADDER	41
5754	PERFORATION GALLBLADDER	41
5755	FISTULA OF GALLBLADDER	41
5756	GB CHOLESTEROLOSIS	41
5758	DIS OF GALLBLADDER NEC	41
5759	DIS OF GALLBLADDER NOS	41
5760	POSTCHOLECYSTECTOMY SYND	41
5761	CHOLANGITIS	41
5762	OBSTRUCTION OF BILE DUCT	41
5763	PERFORATION OF BILE DUCT	41
5763	FISTULA OF BILE DUCT	41

ICD-9-CM Diagnosis Code

Diagnosis Code Description

Major Diagnostic Category (MDC) for each ICD-9-CM Code

Figure 8–23
ICD-9-CM codes assigned to Major Diagnostic Categories (MDCs). (From *Federal Register,* Vol. 63, No. 173, Tuesday, September 8, 1998, p 47901.)

ADDENDUM A.– LIST OF PROPOSED HOSPITAL OUTPATIENT AMBULATORY PAYMENT CLASSES WITH STATUS INDICATORS, RELATIVE WEIGHTS, PAYMENT WEIGHTS, PAYMENT RATES, AND COINSURANCE RATES–Continued

APC[11]	Group title	Status indicator	Relative weight	Payment rate	National unadjusted coinsurance	Minimum unadjusted coinsurance
063	Level III Chemotherapeutic agents	X	2.89	$146.43	$110.97	$29.29
064	Level IV Chemotherapeutic agents	X	4.17	$211.29	$140.12	$42.26
089	Neuropsychological Testing	X	2.54	$128.70	$37.29	$25.74
090	Monitoring psychiatric drugs	X	0.85	$43.07	$12.43	$8.61
091	Brief Individual Psychotherapy	S	1.09	$55.23	$14.01	$11.05
092	Extended Individual Psychotherapy	S	1.57	$79.55	$21.92	$15.91
093	Family Psychotherapy	S	1.54	$78.03	$20.11	$15.61
094	Group Psychotherapy	S	1.24	$62.83	$20.11	$12.57
121	Level I needle biopsy/aspiration	T	0.67	$33.95	$20.91	$6.79
122	Level II needle biopsy/aspiration	T	4.87	$246.76	$115.03	$49.35
131	Level I incision & drainage	T	1.94	$98.30	$36.61	$19.66
132	Level II incision & drainage	T	6.04	$306.04	$134.13	$61.21
137	Nail procedures	T	0.46	$23.31	$4.66	$4.66
141	Level I Destruction of lesion	T	0.59	$29.90	$9.49	$5.98
142	Level II Destruction of lesion	T	3.77	$191.02	$73.00	$38.20
151	Level I debridement /destruction	T	1.74	$88.16	$35.71	$17.63
152	Level II debridement /destruction	T	10.43	$528.48	$261.71	$105.70
161	Level I excision/biopsy	T	3.50	$177.34	$75.48	$35.47
162	Level II excision/biopsy	T	5.67	$287.30	$125.43	$57.46
163	Level III excision/biopsy	T	10.69	$541.66	$264.65	$108.33
181	Level I skin repair	T	2.19	$110.97	$43.84	$22.19
182	Level II skin repair	T	4.00	$202.68	$84.98	$40.54
183	Level III skin repair	T	11.17	$565.98	$286.46	$113.20
184	Level IV skin repair	T	15.17	$768.66	$396.40	$153.73
197	Incision/excision breast	T	12.13	$614.62	$310.75	$122.92
198	Breast reconstruction/mastectomy	T	19.17	$971.33	$530.20	$194.27
200	Arthrocentesis & Ligament/Tendon Injection	T	1.89	$95.77	$39.10	$19.15

APC number

Service Description

Payment Rate

Payment Coinsurance Rate

Figure 8–24
APCs with group titles and payment rates. (From *Federal Register,* Vol. 63, No. 173, Tuesday, September 8, 1998, p 47616.)

ADDENDUM B.–PROPOSED HOSPITAL OUTPATIENT DEPARTMENT (HOPD) PAYMENT STATUS BY HCPCS CODE AND RELATED INFORMATION—Continued

CPT[1]/ HCPCS[2]	HOPD status indicator	Description	Proposed APC	Relative weight	Proposed payment rate	National unadjusted coinsurance	Minimum unadjusted coinsurance
J9340	X	Thiotepa injection	063	2.89	$152.79	$110.97	$30.56
J9350	X	Topotecan	061	1.04	$54.85	$36.61	$10.97
J9360	X	Vinblastine sulfate inj	061	1.04	$54.85	$36.61	$17.83
J9370	X	Vincristine sulfate 1 MG inj	062	1.69	$89.13	$36.61	$8.61
J9375	X	Vincristine sulfate 2 MG inj	063	2.89	$152.79	$110.97	$30.56
J9380	X	Vincristine sulfate 5 MG inj	063	2.89	$152.79	$110.97	$30.56
J9390	X	Vinorelbine tartrate/10 mg	061	1.04	$54.85	$36.61	$10.97
J9600	X	Portimer sodium	061	1.04	$54.85	$36.61	$10.97
J9999	X	Chemotherapy drug	061	1.04	$54.85	$36.61	$10.97

HCPCS or CPT Code for Service

Description

Payment Rate

Patient Coinsurance Rate

Figure 8–25
Individual HCPCS or CPT codes assigned to payment rate. (From *Federal Register,* Vol. 63, No. 173, Tuesday, September 8, 1998, p 47744.)

EXERCISE G *APGs and APCs*

Fill in the blanks:

1. What two groups cooperated to develop the APGs? ______________________

____

2. The DRG is to inpatients as the APG is to ______________________

3. What is the term that is used in the APG system to refer to the inclusion of certain ancillary services into the payment for the visit? ______________________

____

4. How many days' notice will HCFA give before implementation of APCs?

____

5. The APC system consists of how many groups of services? ______________

6. The APC coinsurance amount for beneficiaries is based on what percent of the national median charge? ______________________

Use Figure 8–18 to answer the following:

7. What is the APG for prostatic malignancy? ______________________

8. What is the APG for gastrointestinal malignancy? ______________________

MEDICARE FRAUD AND ABUSE[12]

What Are Fraud and Abuse?

The Medicare program is subject to fraud and abuse, as is any third-party payer program. But because Medicare is the largest third-party payer, it has the most comprehensive anti–fraud and abuse program. You will need to understand the specifics of the Medicare fraud and abuse program because you will be filing Medicare claims. The HCFA is responsible for establishing the regulations that monitor the Medicare program for fraud and abuse.

Medicare defines fraud as "the intentional deception or misrepresentation that an individual knows to be false or does not believe to be true and makes it knowing that the deception could result in some unauthorized benefit to himself/herself or some other person."[12] So fraud involves both deliberate intention to deceive and an expectation of an unauthorized benefit. By this definition, it is fraud when a claim is filed for a service rendered to a Medicare patient when that service was not actually provided. How could this type of fraud happen? The fact is that most Medicare patients sign a standing approval, which is kept in the patient's file in the medical office. Having a standing approval is convenient for the patient and for the coding staff: After the patient has received a service, the Medicare claim is filed automatically, without patient's having to sign the form again. But a standing approval also makes it easy for unscrupulous persons to submit charges for services never provided. The possibility also exists for extra services to be submitted in addition to services that were provided (upcoding). Suppose, for example, a patient came in for an office visit and a claim was submitted for an in office surgical procedure. That's also fraud.

The most frequent kind of fraud arises from a false statement or misrepresentation made, or caused to be made, that results in additional payment under the Medicare program.

Who Are the Violators?

The violator may be a physician or other practitioner, a hospital or other institutional provider, a clinical laboratory or other supplier, an employee of any provider, a billing service, a beneficiary, a Medicare carrier employee, or any person in a position to file a claim for Medicare benefits. Since you will be the person filing Medicare claims, you need to be careful about the claims that you submit—it's important to validate that the service was provided by consulting the medical record or the physician.

Fraud schemes range from those committed by individuals acting alone to broad-based activities perpetrated by institutions or groups of individuals, sometimes employing sophisticated telemarketing and other promotional techniques to lure consumers into serving as the unwitting tools in the schemes. Seldom do such perpetrators target just one insurer; nor do they focus exclusively on either the public or private sector. Rather, most are found to be defrauding several private- and public-sector victims, such as Medicare, simultaneously.

What Forms Does Fraud Take?

The most common forms of Medicare fraud are

- billing for services not furnished
- misrepresenting the diagnosis to justify a payment
- soliciting, offering, or receiving a kickback
- unbundling or "exploding" charges
- falsifying certificates of medical necessity, plans of treatment, and medical records to justify payment
- billing for additional services not furnished as billed—ie, upcoding
- routine waiver of co-payment

Who Says What Is Fraudulent?

HCFA administers the Medicare program. HCFA's responsibilities include managing contractor claims payment, fiscal audit and/or overpayment prevention and recovery, and the development and monitoring of payment safeguards necessary to detect and respond to payment errors or abusive patterns of service delivery. Within HCFA's Bureau of Program Operations is the Office of Benefits Integrity (OBI), which oversees Medicare's payment safeguard program, including carrier and intermediary operations related to fraud, audit, medical review, the collection of overpayments, and the imposition of civil monetary penalties (CMPs) for certain violations of Medicare law.

The Office of the Inspector General (OIG), Department of Health and Human Services, is responsible for developing an annual work plan that outlines the ways in which the Medicare program is monitored to identify fraud or abuse. The plan is a published public document that gives the evaluation methods and approaches that will be taken the following year to monitor the Medicare program. For example, in the 1999 Work Plan the following is listed as the review for E/M services:

ACCURACY AND CARRIER MONITORING OF PHYSICIAN VISIT CODING[13]

We will assess whether physicians are correctly coding evaluation and management services in locations other than teaching hospitals and whether carriers are adequately monitoring physician coding. In 1992, Medicare began using new visit codes that were developed by the American Medical Association for reimbursing physicians for evaluation and management services. Generally, the codes represent the type and complexity of services provided and patient status, such as new or established. Previous work by the OIG has found that physicians do no accurately or uniformly use visit codes. Our analysis will build upon this previous work and add more definitive data on the accuracy of physician visit coding.

This excerpt from OIG Work Plan identifies E/M service as a specific area to be monitored in the following year. The OIG charges the *fiscal intermediaries* (carriers) with doing the actual monitoring. (Recall that insurance companies bid for the opportunity to be the fiscal intermediary for Medicare and handle the payments to providers for Medicare services. The OIG Work Plan sets the broad boundaries for monitoring the Medicare program for fraud and abuse.

The Specific Regulations Are in the MCM

HCFA establishes the specific regulations in the *Medicare Carriers Manual* (MCM) for the carriers to follow. You will deal with MCM regulations as you code Medicare claims in order to know what is allowable. The MCM regulations that deal with Medicare fraud and abuse are numbered 14000 to 14032. The following are selected excerpts from these regulations *addressed to the carriers:*

14000. FRAUD AND ABUSE—BACKGROUND[12]

The effort to prevent and detect fraud, abuse, and waste is a cooperative one that involves beneficiaries, Medicare contractors, providers, Peer Review Organizations (PROs), State Medicaid Fraud Control Units (MFCUs), and Federal agencies such as HCFA, Office of Inspector General (OIG), DHHS, the Federal Bureau of Investigation (FBI), and the Department of Justice (DOJ).

You are responsible for assisting Medicare in protecting the program's Trust Fund from those persons and entities that would seek payment for items and services under false or fraudulent circumstances. This includes effectively developing cases of suspected fraud to the fullest potential possible before you refer them to the OIG, Office of Investigations (OI) Field Office. OI is responsible for determining if federal and/or civil statutes have been violated. Ensure that you make only appropriate payments and that you take appropriate steps to recover any mistaken payments. This can be accomplished through actions such as suspension of payments, denial of payments, and recovery of overpayments. These options are discussed in more detail in 14004, 14008, 14017, and 14018.

This chapter explains the actions you are to take to protect the Medicare Trust Funds and applies to all Medicare carriers, including Durable Medical Equipment

Regional Carriers (DMERCs). It provides general guidelines and suggestions for preventing and detecting fraud and abuse, and for developing incidents of suspected fraud and abuse.

Each investigation is unique and should be tailored to the specific circumstances involved. The guidelines provided here should not be interpreted as requiring a specific course of action or establishing any specific requirements on the part of the government or its agents with respect to any investigation. Similarly, these guidelines should not be interpreted as creating any rights in favor of any person, including the subject of an investigation.

MCMs Referring to Part B Fraud

14001. PART B MEDICARE FRAUD[12]

Fraud is the intentional deception or misrepresentation that an individual knows to be false or does not believe to be true and makes it, knowing that the deception could result in some unauthorized benefit to himself/herself or some other person. The most frequent kind of fraud arises from a false statement or misrepresentation made, or caused to be made, that is material to entitlement or payment under the Medicare program. The violator may be a physician or other practitioner, a supplier of durable medical equipment, an employee of a physician or supplier, a carrier employee, a billing service, a beneficiary, or any other person or business entity in a position to bill the Medicare program or to otherwise benefit from such billing.

Attempts to defraud the Medicare program may take a variety of forms. The following are some examples of how fraud may be perpetrated in the Medicare medical insurance program:

- Billing for services or supplies that were not provided. This includes billings for "no shows," ie, billing Medicare for services that were not actually furnished because patients failed to keep their appointments;
- Misrepresenting the diagnosis for the patient to justify the services or equipment furnished;
- Altering claim forms to obtain a higher payment amount;
- Deliberately applying for duplicate payment, eg, billing both Medicare and the beneficiary for the same service or billing both Medicare and another insurer in an attempt to get paid twice;
- Soliciting, offering, or receiving a kickback, bribe, or rebate, eg, paying for a referral of patients in exchange for the ordering of diagnostic tests and other services or medical equipment;
- Unbundling or "exploding" charges, eg, the billing of a multichannel set of lab tests to appear as if the individual tests had been performed.
- Completing Certificates of Medical Necessity (CMNs) for patients not personally and professionally known by the provider;
- Misrepresenting the services rendered (upcoding or the use of procedure codes not appropriate for the item or service actually furnished), amounts charged for services rendered, identity of the person receiving the services, dates of services, etc;
- Billing for noncovered services, eg, routine foot care billed as a more involved form of foot care to obtain payment;
- Participating in schemes that involve collusion between a provider and a benefi-

ciary, or between a supplier and a provider, and result in higher costs or charges to the Medicare program;

- Using another person's Medicare card to obtain medical care;
- Utilizing split billing schemes (eg, billing procedures over a period of days when all treatment occurred during one visit);
- Participating in schemes that involve collusion between a provider and a carrier employee where the claim is assigned, eg, the provider deliberately overbills for services, and the carrier employee then generates adjustments with little or no awareness on the part of the beneficiary;
- Manipulating claims data on unassigned claims for one's own benefit, eg, through manipulation of beneficiary address or the claims history record, a carrier employee could generate adjustment payments against many beneficiary records and cause payments to be mailed to an address known only to him/her; and
- Billing based on "gang visits," eg, a physician visits a nursing home and bills for 20 nursing home visits without furnishing any specific service to, or on behalf of, individual patients.

Although some of the preceding practices initially may be considered abusive rather than fraudulent activities, they may evolve into fraud. *Note:* The term "provider" means physicians, practitioners, and other suppliers of health care services/supplies.

Some of the Ways Reviews Are Conducted

The reviews of Medicare claims take a wide variety of methods, the following is an excerpt from the MCM on ideas for reviews.[12]

E. Conduct Reviews.—Conduct a variety of reviews to determine the appropriateness of payments even when there is no evidence of fraud. Some or all of the following reviews are to be done, depending on your funding level. They include:

- Sampling of claims for a variety of items and services to determine propriety of payments;
- Telephone contacts with beneficiaries to verify the delivery of items and services;
- Random validation checks of physician licensure;
- Reviews of original certificates of medical necessity;

How Does Medicare Find Out About Suspected Fraud?

The MCMs identify a number of ways in which leads on fraud can come to Medicare carriers.[12]

14005. FRAUD DETECTION LEADS

A variety of sources may be used to identify potential fraud and abuse situations. They include but are not limited to:

- Referrals from MR or carrier quality assurance (QA) staff;
- Suggestions/referrals from HCFA components, other Federal agencies, State agencies, contractors, PROs, or other sources, concerning areas where they have experienced problems or identified program matters that do not seem to be properly addressed in current policy. These suggestions may be provided directly or

may be implicit in various reports and other materials produced in the course of evaluation and audit activities, eg, contractor evaluations, State assessment, HCFA-directed surveys, contractor or State audits of providers;

- Leads developed through data analysis, pattern detection, or link analysis methods, or produced by State and contractor systems or other sources that indicate aberrancies such as excessive costs, upcoding, or questionable charging practices;
- Complaints or questions from providers, beneficiaries, Medicaid recipients, or private citizens;
- Referrals from the RO, SSA, HCFA and/or from any component of OIG;
- Aberrancies detected through internal controls, postpayment and other reviews, audits, or inspections;
- OI and HCFA fraud alerts;
- Investigative leads from ongoing fraud and abuse case review activity; and
- Ideas stemming from ongoing or completed inspections.

Two Types of Medicare Alerts

Medicare distributes alerts on fraud and abuse to carriers, providers, and beneficiaries throughout the year. As part of the MCM, the following are the current alerts[12]:

14019. FRAUD AND ABUSE ALERTS.

14019.1 TYPES OF FRAUD ALERTS.—There are two types of fraud alerts, National Medicare Fraud Alerts (NMFAs) and Restricted Medicare Fraud Alerts (RFAs).

A. National Medicare Fraud Alerts.—The most commonly issued alert is the NMFA. These alerts do not identify specific providers or other entities suspected of committing fraud. They focus on a particular scheme or scam and are intended to serve as a fraud detection lead.

The following is a sample of Unrestricted Fraud Alert.

Unrestricted National Medicare Fraud Alert (UMFA 9605, Issued July 12, 1997: Billing Protective Pads as HIP Abduction Orthotics)[14]

Supplier submitted claims for hip abduction orthotic devices when it was actually supplying a protective pad unit. In addition, claims were submitted for a large number of the supplies which were refused and returned.

A survey of several nursing/residential facilities indicated the following:

1) The item provided is not a "hip orthotic," but is a set of cushioned plastic pads, designed to protect the hip from fracture, in the event of a fall, and was so marketed by the representative of the supplier;
2) Many of the units known as "Hip guards," were returned to the supplier upon receipt and examination by the beneficiaries and/or facility staff;
3) The certificates of medical necessity provided by the supplier failed to support the need for a genuine hip orthotic.

The following is a sample of Restricted Fraud Alert.

Restricted National Medicare Fraud Alert (RMFA 9612, Issued October 30, 1996: Fraudulent Billing for 24 Hour Cardiac Monitoring)[15]

Provider was billing Medicare for 24-hour attended monitoring, receipt of transmissions, and 24-hour attended monitoring, recording, for beneficiaries residing in New Jersey, New York, Puerto Rico and Florida. The Florida and Puerto Rico beneficiaries reported to the Florida carrier that they are visited by a nurse in their home; the equipment (event recorder) is hooked up for approximately 20 minutes to 30 minutes; then the equipment is removed and the nurse takes it with her when she leaves. This continues on a monthly basis.

Provider billed for patient demand single or multiple event recording with presymptom memory loop and 24-hour attended monitoring, (G0006), 24-hour attended monitoring, recording (G0005), and postsymptom telephonic transmission of EKG rhythm strip; 24-hour attended monitoring (G0015). Eighty-six percent of the beneficiaries being billed in New York resided in Florida while only 6% lived in New York. The majority of beneficiaries contacted stated they did not know this provider nor the address of the provider.

Medical Policy for 24-hour monitoring requires that the event recorder be attached to the patient in the doctor's office and the patient wears the monitor home. This permits the patient to record an EKG at the onset of symptoms (ie, dizziness, palpitations, or syncope) or in response to a doctor's order (ie, immediately following strong exertion). Most devices also permit the patient to simultaneously voice-record in order to describe symptoms and/or activity. A supplier of the service must be capable of receiving and recording transmissions. This includes receipt of the EKG signal as well as voice transmission relating any associated services. The person receiving the transmission must be a technician, nurse or physician trained in interpreting EKGs and abnormal rhythms. A physician must be available for immediate consultation to review the transmission in case of significant symptoms or EKG abnormalities. The provider of the service must maintain hard copy documentation of test results and interpretation along with copies of the ordering/referring physician's order for the study.

Who Makes Complaints of Fraud and Abuse?

The definition of a complaint of fraud or abuse is as follows[12]:

14020.1 DEFINITION OF A COMPLAINT OF FRAUD OR ABUSE.—A complaint is a statement, oral or written, alleging that a provider, supplier, or beneficiary received a Medicare benefit of monetary value, directly or indirectly, overtly or covertly, in cash or in kind, to which he or she is not entitled under current Medicare law, regulations, or policy. Included are allegations of misrepresentation and violations of Medicare requirements applicable to persons or entities that bill for covered items and services. Use this definition for workload reporting purposes on Schedule G. Examples of complaints include:

- Allegations that items or services were not received;
- Allegations that services received are inconsistent with the services billed (as indicated on the Explanation of Medicare Benefits (EOMB));

- Allegations that a provider or supplier has billed both the beneficiary and Medicare for the same item or service;
- Allegations regarding waiver of copayments or deductibles;
- Allegations that a supplier or provider has misrepresented itself as having an affiliation with an agency or department of the State, local, or Federal government, whether expressed or implied; and
- Beneficiary inquiries concerning payment for an item or service, that in his/her opinion, far exceeds reasonable payment for the item or service that the beneficiary received (eg, the supplier or physician has "upcoded" to receive higher payment).

Not all complaints made to Medicare are considered fraud or abuse; the following are not fraud or abuse complaints:

- Complaints (or inquiries) regarding Medicare coverage policy;
- Complaints (or inquiries) regarding the status of claims;
- Requests for claims appeal;
- Complaints regarding the appeals process; or
- Complaints concerning providers or suppliers (other than those complaints meeting the criteria established above) that are general in nature and are policy or program oriented.

What Is the Difference between Abuse and Fraud?

Abuse is different from fraud, although the two words have been used together throughout the MCM. The following defines abuse:

14022. DEVELOPMENT OF ABUSE CASES[12]

14022.1 GENERAL.—Correcting and preventing program abuse are functions of the MR Unit. The difference between abuse reviews and fraud reviews is essentially that the abuse situation involves a review of the propriety or medical necessity of services that are billed. Fraud reviews are geared towards determining, for example, whether or not billed services were, in fact, furnished. Abuse reviews generally occur after your claims processing activity, although they may arise as a result of information obtained during the claims processing cycle.

What's a Kickback?

Kickbacks are not allowable under the Medicare or Medicaid program. The following is the law that defines what a kickback is and the penalties for kickbacks that involve the Medicare program[12]:

B. Anti-Kickback Statute Implications.—The Medicare and Medicaid anti-kickback statue provides the following:

Whoever knowingly and willfully solicits or receives any remuneration (including any kickback, bribe, or rebate) directly or indirectly, overtly or covertly, in cash or in kind, in return for referring a patient to a person for the furnishing or arranging for the furnishing of any item or service for which payment may be made in whole or in part under Medicare, Medicaid or a State health care program, or in return for purchasing, leasing, or ordering or arranging for or recommending purchasing, leasing, or ordering any good facility, service, or item for which payment may be made in whole or in part under Medicare, Medicaid or a State health program, shall be guilty of a felony and upon conviction thereof, shall be fined not more than $25,000 or imprisoned for not more than five years, or both. 42 U.S.C. 1320a-7b(b), Section 1128B(b) of the Act.

There is a "safe harbor" clause in the statute that protects certain types of discounting of medical services. For example, an HMO might contract with a laboratory for all laboratory services and receive a discounted price for those services. Not all discounts are protected.

The following types of discounts are *not* protected[12]:

- Rebates offered to beneficiaries;
- Cash payments;
- Furnishing an item or service free of charge or at a reduced charge in exchange for any agreement to buy a different item or service;
- Reduction in price applicable to one payer but not to Medicare or a State health care program; and
- Routine reduction or waiver of any coinsurance or deductible amount owed by a program beneficiary.

Out of Compliance Is Not a Good Place to Be!

If an organization or individual if found to be not in compliance with any of the fraud and abuse regulations, the carrier can impose a number of remedies. The following remedies are addressed to the fiscal intermediaries:

14029.2 ADMINISTRATIVE REMEDIES CONSIDERED INITIALLY[12]

A. Educational Contact and/or Warning.—Inform the provider of questionable or improper practices, the correct procedure to be followed, and that continuation of the improper practice may result in administrative sanctions.

B. Revocation of Assignment Privileges.—Revocation of a provider's assignment privileges is a possible administrative action that may be taken in appropriate situations. Use revocation of assignment privileges as an administrative sanction to deny payment while criminal prosecution is being considered or is in process.

C. Withholding of Payments/Recovery of Overpayments.—In cases involving abuse, OIG may, in conjunction with HCFA, ask you to notify the provider or other supplier of your intention to suspend payment, in whole or in part, and the reasons for making the suspension (42 CFR 405.371(a)). The provider or other supplier has 15 days following the date of notification to submit additional evidence, unless an extension is granted.

D. Referral of Situations to State Licensing Boards or Medical/Professional Societies.—Refer instances of apparent unethical or improper practices or unprofessional conduct to State licensing authorities, medical boards, the PRO, or professional societies for review and possible disciplinary action. It may be appropriate to refer a provider to the PRO for action by a State licensing agency or medical society. If a case requires immediate attention, refer it directly to the State licensing agency or medical society and send a copy of the referral to the PRO. (See 14013.C.)

Review the following list of violations for which the Secretary of Health may impose financial penalties on individuals or organizations that are found guilty of fraud or abuse.

The Secretary may also impose a civil monetary penalty against a person who presents or causes to be presented a request for payment in violation of[12]:

- A Medicare assignment agreement;
- An agreement with the State Medicaid agency not to charge a person in excess of permitted limits;
- A Medicare participating physician or supplier agreement; or
- An agreement not to charge patients for services denied as a result of a determination of an abuse of PPS. A person that gives false or misleading information regarding PPS that could reasonably be expected to influence a discharge decision is also subject to the imposition of a civil monetary penalty.

Other situations where civil monetary penalties may be applied include:

- Violation of assignment requirements for certain diagnostic clinical lab tests (1833(h));
- Violation of assignment requirements for nurse-anesthetist services (1833(1));
- Any supplier who refuses to supply rented DME supplies without charge after rental payments may no longer be made (effective January 1, 1989) (1834(a));
- Nonparticipating physician or supplier violation of charge limitation provisions for radiology services (effective January 1, 1989) (1834(b));
- Violation of assignment requirement for physician assistant services (1842(b));
- Medicare nonparticipating physician's violation of limiting charge limits;
- Nonparticipating physician's violation of charge limitations (1842(j));
- Nonparticipating physician's violation of charge limitation provision for services to inherent reasonableness provisions, specified overpriced procedures, specified cataract procedures, A-mode ophthalmic ultrasound procedures, medical direction of nurse-anesthetists, and for certain purchased diagnostic procedures where mark-up is prohibited (effective July 1, 1988 for cataract procedures) (1842(j));
- Physician billing for assistants at cataract surgery without prior approval of PRO (1842(k));
- Nonparticipating physician's violation of refund requirements for medically unnecessary services (1842(l));
- Nonparticipating physician's violation of refund provision for unassigned claims for elective surgery (1842(m));
- Physician charges in violation of assignment provision for certain purchased diagnostic procedures where mark-up is prohibited or where a payment is prohibited for these procedures due to failure to disclose required information (1842(n));
- Hospital unbundling of outpatient surgery costs (1866(g)); and
- Hospital and responsible physician "dumping" of patients (1867).

How to Protect Yourself

As you can see from the preceding information about Medicare Fraud and Abuse, HCFA is very serious about identifying those that try to take advantage of the program. As the person submitting the Medicare claims, you are one of those HCFA holds responsible to submit truthful and accurate claims. If you are unsure about a charge or a request, check with the physician or other supervisory personnel to ensure that you are submitting the correct charges for each patient. In this way, you protect the Medicare program, your facility, and yourself.

THE MANAGED HEALTH CARE CONCEPT

Health care in the United States is the best in the world, and people come from all over the world to access the health care that U.S. residents take for granted. Physicians and health care have traditionally been held in high esteem by U.S. citizens. Whatever it took to provide access to high-quality health care is what these citizens demanded. Historically, the government responded to these demands by funding the research, facilities, and services necessary to keep the U.S. health system on the cutting edge of medical advances. But the research, facilities, and services are extremely expensive, and many U.S. citizens are also demanding a balanced federal budget.

Health care services in the United States are undergoing rapid change. The U.S. health care system has been financed through traditional health insurance systems, which paid providers on a fee-for-service basis and allowed beneficiaries relative freedom to select health care providers. Health insurance has become an important benefit of employment. Employers became the primary purchasers of health insurance, and the rising cost of health care is reflected in the premiums employers pay and the subsequent decrease in employer-sponsored coverage. Private purchasers of health insurance have also seen a steady increase in their health insurance premiums, until many are forced to go "bare," forgoing health insurance due to the high costs. Fewer people now have health insurance coverage as a benefit of their employment. The number of uninsured people increased from 36 million in 1990 to nearly 40 million in 1994,[16] and the number of uninsured continues to rise as employers and individuals find health care insurance out of their reach. "People who are uninsured, underinsured, chronically ill, or disabled are likely to have increasing difficulties gaining access to health care as the ability of institutions to subsidize care continues to erode."[17] One solution that is gaining widespread use to contain health care costs is managed health care.

Managed health care is a term that refers to the concept of establishing networks of health care providers that offer an array of health care services under one organization. A managed health care organization may be a group of physicians, hospitals, and health plans responsible for the health services for an enrolled individual or group. The organization coordinates the total health care services required by its enrollees. The purpose of managed health care is to provide cost-effectiveness of services and theoretically to improve the health care services provided to the enrollee by ensuring access to all required health services.

There are many models used to deliver the managed health care: Health Maintenance Organizations (HMOs), Individual Practice Associations (IPAs), Group Practice, Multiple Option Plan, Medicare Risk HMOs, Preferred Provider Organizations (PPOs), and the Staff model. Each of these models delivers managed health care using a different structure.

In 1994, about 18% of the U.S. population (47 million persons) were enrolled in HMOs and about 23% of the population (60 million) received coverage through a PPO.[17] The HMO and PPO enrollees are 41% of the U.S. population. The use of managed health care approach varies widely based on geography. Many regions have little managed care and others have enrollment that represents over 50% of the population. In 1994, 65% of employees of large and medium-sized companies were in managed care. In 1996, 70% of workers in firms with more than 200 employees were in managed care.[18] In 1997, more than 85% of the enrolled workforce was in some type of a managed care plan.[2] The rising percentage of those employees opting for a managed care health plan for their employees indicates the employers' search for cost containment in offering the benefit of health coverage for employees.

The managed care industry has evolved from the small, regional nonprofit plans to the large, national, for-profit companies. Eleven national managed care companies now account for half of all HMO enrollment.

The pressure on the government to cut expenses and balance the budget guarantees the continued increases in the market share for managed care. The government mandated the use of managed care within the Medicaid program. Over one fourth of all Medicaid beneficiaries are currently enrolled in managed care plans in 45 states.[19] The number of Medicaid beneficiaries enrolled in managed care continues to increase.

In the early stages of development, the managed care market included networks that allowed the enrollees a broad choice of providers. As the market segments for managed care expand, the choices for the enrollees decreased.

Types of HMOs

A **Managed Care Organization** (MCO) is a group that is responsible for the health care services offered to an enrolled group or person. The organization coordinates or manages the care of the enrollee. The MCO contains costs by negotiating with various health care entities—hospitals, clinics, laboratories, etc—for a discounted rate for services provided to its enrollees. Providers of the health care services must receive prior approval from the MCO before services are rendered. For example, a physician may want to conduct a certain high-cost diagnostic test on a patient, but before the test can be conducted, the MCO must give the physician approval. The MCO uses a gatekeeper, usually a primary care physician to the patient, that can authorize the patient's need to seek health care services outside the established organization. For example, a certain specialist may not be available within the MCO, and the primary care physician can recommend that the enrollee be referred to the specialist. If the enrollee were to see the specialist without the recommendation of the primary care physician and approval of the MCO, the enrollee would be responsible for all charges incurred. MCOs develop practice guidelines that evaluate the appropriateness and medical necessity of medical care provided to the enrollee by the physicians, which gives the MCO control over what care is provided to the enrollee.

A **Preferred Provider Organization** (PPO) is a group of providers who form a network and who have agreed to provide services to enrollees at a discounted rate. Enrollees are usually responsible for paying a portion of the costs (cost sharing) when using a PPO provider. Enrollees who seek health care outside of the PPO providers pay an additional out-of-pocket cost. The out-of-pocket costs are established by the PPO to discourage use of outside providers. The PPOs do not use a gatekeeper, but they do have strict guidelines for what are approved expenses and what the enrollee will pay.

The **Health Maintenance Organization** (HMO) is a delivery system that allows the enrollee access to all health care services. The HMO is the "total package" approach to health care organizations, and the out-of-pocket expenses are minimal. However, the enrollee is assigned a primary care physician who manages all the health care needs of the enrollee and acts as the gatekeeper for the enrollee. Services are prepaid by the HMO. For example, the HMO pays a laboratory to provide services at a negotiated price and the services are prepaid by the HMO. The gatekeeper has authority to allow the enrollee access to the services available or authorize services outside of those the HMO has available. The gatekeeper has strong incentives to contain costs for the HMO by controlling and managing the health care services provided to the enrollee. The HMO can directly employ the physician in the **Staff Model** HMO or contract the physician through the **Individual Practice Associations** (IPA) model in which the physician provides services for a set fee. Either way, the physician has an incentive to service the cost containment needs of the HMO.

Exclusive Provider Organizations (EPO) have many of the same features of the HMO except that the providers of the services are not prepaid. Instead, the providers are paid on a fee-for-service basis. The **Group Practice Model** (GPM) is a form of HMO in which an organization of physicians contracts with the HMO to provide services to the enrollees of the HMO. A payment is negotiated and the HMO pays the group, and then the group pays the individual physicians.

A **Medicare Risk HMO** is a Medicare-funded alternative to the standard Medicare supplemental coverage. The Risk HMO is a standard HMO; however, it is provided to Medicare beneficiaries rather than the traditional fee-for-service model historically used by Medicare. The enrollees pay out-of-pocket if they choose to go outside the network of providers. **Point-of-Service** (POS) benefits allow the enrollee in a Medicare Risk HMO to receive services outside the HMO's health care network, but at increased cost in copayments, in coinsurance, or in a deductible. The POS benefit is one that the Risk HMO may choose to offer; but it is not required, and HCFA does not provide any additional funding for this benefit. However, the HMO that offers this option is more attractive to a potential enrollee, because the lack of access to providers outside of a predefined network is the main reason people do not join a managed health care organization. The POS benefit option is also referred to as an *open-ended HMO* or a *self-referral option.* The POS benefit is attractive not only to Medicare Risk plan enrollees who wish to be treated by providers not available in their plan's network but also to those who travel and would like access to routine medical care while temporarily (for fewer than 90 days) out of their plan's service area.

Managed health care is now part of the fabric of the U.S. health care system. The "richer" plans of traditional insurance companies are often no longer an option to a great segment of the population.

Drawbacks of the HMO

There are some significant drawbacks to the HMO concept in terms of access to health care. Consider that providers (physicians in particular) have an incentive to keep treatment costs to a minimum. Traditionally, a physician's primary concern was what was in the best interest of the patient, not what was in the best interest of containment of cost. This fundamental change transformed physicians into the gatekeepers for the third-party payer and third-party payers into the developers of the guidelines that ultimately control the services patients can and do receive. The patient/physician relationship has shifted to a physician/third-party payer relationship, which leaves the patient at the mercy of the third-party payer. Many lawsuits have been brought by patients who allege lack of treatment caused patient harm or sometimes death. Cost containment issues, and hence HMOs, bring along many ethical and legal implications that will continue to involve patients, providers, and third-party payers.

CHAPTER GLOSSARY

APCs (Ambulatory Patient Categories): patient classification that provides a payment system for outpatients

assignment: Medicare's payment for the service, which participating physicians agree to accept as payment in full

CF (conversion factor): national dollar amount that is applied to all services paid on the Medicare Fee Schedule basis

DHHS: Department of Health and Human Services

DRGs (Diagnosis-Related Groups): disease classification system that relates the type of inpatients a hospital treats (case mix) to the costs incurred by the hospital

Exclusive Provider Organization (EPO): similar to a Health Maintenance Organization except that the providers of the services are not prepaid, but rather are paid on a fee-for-service basis

Federal Register: official publication of all "Presidential Documents," "Rules and Regulations," "Proposed Rules," and "Notices"; government-instituted national changes are published in the *Federal Register*

Group Practice Model: an organization of physicians who contract with an Health Maintenance Organization to provide services to the enrollees of the HMO

grouper: computer used to input the principal diagnosis and other critical information about a patient and then provide the correct DRG code

HCFA: Health Care Financing Administration

Health Maintenance Organization (HMO): a health care delivery system in which an enrollee is assigned to a primary care physician who manages all the health care needs of the enrollee

Individual Practice Association (IPA): an organization of physicians who provide services for a set fee. Health Maintenance Organizations often contract with the IPA for services to their enrollees

MAAC (Maximum Actual Allowable Charge): limitation on the total amount that can be charged by physicians who are not participants in Medicare

Managed Care Organization (MCO): a group that is responsible for the health care services offered to an enrolled group of persons

MDC (Major Diagnostic Categories): division of all principal diagnoses into 25 mutually exclusive principal diagnosis areas within the DRG system

MEI (Medicare Economic Index): government-mandated index that ties increases in the Medicare prevailing charges to economic indicators

Medicare Risk HMO: a Medicare-funded alternative to the standard Medicare supplemental coverage

MFS (Medicare Fee Schedule): schedule that listed the allowable charges for Medicare services; was replaced by the Medicare reasonable charge payment system

MVPS (Medical Volume Performance Standards): government's estimate of how much growth is appropriate for nationwide physician expenditures paid by the Part B Medicare program

OBRA (Omnibus Budget Reconciliation Act of 1989): act that established new rules for Medicare reimbursement

Part A: Medicare's Hospital Insurance; covers hospital/facility care

Part B: Medicare's Supplemental Medical Insurance; covers physician services and durable medical equipment that are not paid for under Part A

participating provider program: Medicare providers who have agreed in advance to accept assignment on all Medicare claims

Preferred Provider Organization (PPO): a group of providers who form a network and who have agreed to provide services to enrollees at a discounted rate

prognosis: probable outcome of an illness

PROs (Peer Review Organizations): groups established to review hospital admission and care

PSRO (Professional Standards Review Organization): voluntary physicians' organization designed to monitor the necessity of hospital admissions, treatment costs, and medical records of hospitals

RBRVS (Resource-Based Relative Value Scale): scale designed to decrease Medicare expenditures, redistribute physician payment, and ensure quality health care at a reasonable rate

resource intensity: refers to the relative volume and type of diagnostic, therapeutic, and bed services used in the management of a particular illness

RVU (Relative Value Unit): unit value that has been assigned for each service

severity of illness: refers to the levels of loss of function and mortality that may be experienced by patients with a particular disease

Staff Model: a Health Maintenance Organization that directly employs the physicians who provide services to enrollees

TEFRA (Tax Equity and Fiscal Responsibility Act): act that contains language to reward cost-conscious health care providers

CHAPTER REVIEW Chapter 8, Part I, Theory

1. What two insurance programs were established in 1965 by amendments to the Social Security Act?

____

____

2. The Secretary of DHHS has delegated responsibility for Medicare to which department?

____

____

3. Who administers funds for Medicare?

____

4. Who is eligible for Medicare? ______________________________

____

5. What are the six types of reviews defined in the Scope of Work that are performed by the PROs?

______________________ ______________________

______________________ ______________________

______________________ ______________________

6. List three goals of Physician Payment Reform:

____

____

____

7. List the three components of the relative value unit:

____

____

____

8. What does UHDDS stand for?

____

9. What is the fastest growing segment of our population today?

____

10. What is the name of the groups that handle the daily operations of the Medicare program?

____

11. Hospitals submit bills to Medicare using what codes? ______________

12. What edition of the *Federal Register* would the hospitals be especially interested in?

____

13. What editions would the outpatient facilities be interested in?

____

14. Where and when did the design and the development of the DRGs begin?

____

15. What was the first state to use the DRG system on a wide scale?

____

16. Some hospitals justified their higher costs of patient care by stating that they treated what type of patients?

____

17. The concept of case mix complexity has been used to refer to a set of five patient attributes. Name three of the five.

____

____

____

18. What does MDC stand for? ______________________________

19. What is the total number of MDCs? ___________________________

20 Explain what is considered a substantial complication or comorbidity.

____

____

21. What three DRGs indicate that a patient had a surgery unrelated to the diagnosis?

____

22. Under what act were the PROs made possible?

____

23. Under what act was a major change in Medicare in 1989 made possible?

____

24. What do the initials RVU stand for?

____

25. Can a physician charge a patient to complete a Medicare form?

____

References

1. Resident Population of the United States: Middle Series Projections, p 2015–2030, by Age and Sex; U.S. Bureau of the Census; March 1996.
2. 1996 HCFA Statistics. Bureau of Data Management, HCFA Pub No 03394, Sept 1996.
3. Highlights, National Health Expenditures, 1997, Health Care Financing Administration, p 1.
4. *Federal Register* 59(121), Friday, June 24, 1994, p 32753.
5. Blue Cross and Blue Shield of Minnesota's Medicare coding manual. St. Paul, MN.
6. *Federal Register* 63 (203), October 21, 1998, p 56199.
7. *Federal Register* 63 (203), October 21, 1998, p 56201.
8. *Federal Register* 63 (211), November 2, 1998, p 58814.
9. Diagnosis Related Groups, Version 14.0, Definitions Manual.
10. Ambulatory Patient Groups Definitions Manual, Version 2.0. 3M Health Information Systems, 100 Barnes Road, Wallingford, CT 06492.
11. *Federal Register* 63 (173), September 8, 1998, p 47554–47555.
12. 1999 Medicare Carriers Manual, Fraud and Abuse, Health Care Financing Administration, 14000–14032.
13. Department of Health and Human Services, Office of the Inspector General, Fiscal Year 1999 Work Plan, Health Care Financing Administration, p 12.
14. Unrestricted Medicare Fraud Alert 9605, July 12, 1996, Health Care Financing Administration.
15. Restricted Medicare Fraud Alert 9612, October 1996, Health Care Financing Administration.
16. Mechanic R, Dobson A, Yu, S: The Impact of Managed Care on Clinical Research: A Preliminary Investigation. The Commonwealth Fund, January 1996.
17. Health Care Coverage and Access Program. Picker/Commonwealth Program on Health Care Quality and Managed Care, March 1996. (There is no author as this is from a page covering a list of research this group has funded.)
18. Davis K: Health Services Research and the Changing Health Care system. Briefing, Notes, The Commonwealth Fund, March 1996.
19. Blumenthal D: Case Studies of Academic Health Centers Preparing for Managed Competition. The Commonwealth Fund, March 1995.

APPENDIX A Official ICD-9-CM Guidelines for Coding and Reporting

The Public Health Service and the Health Care Financing Administration of the U.S. Department of Health and Human Services present the following guidelines for coding and reporting using the International Classification of Diseases, 9th Revision, Clinical Modification (ICD-9-CM). These guidelines should be used as a companion document to the official versions of the ICD-9-CM.

These guidelines for coding and reporting have been developed and approved by the cooperating parties for ICD-9-CM: American Hospital Association, American Health Information Management Association, Health Care Financing Administration and the National Center for Health Statistics. These guidelines previously appeared in the Coding Clinic for ICD-9-CM, published by the American Hospital Association.

These guidelines have been developed to assist the user in coding and reporting in situations where the ICD-9-CM manual does not provide direction. Coding and sequencing instructions in the three ICD-9-CM manuals take precedence over any guidelines.

These guidelines are not exhaustive. The cooperating parties are continuing to conduct review of these guidelines and develop new guidelines as needed. Users of the ICD-9-CM should be aware that only guidelines approved by the cooperating parties are official. Revision of these guidelines and new guidelines will be published by the U.S. Department of Health and Human Services when they are approved by the cooperating parties.

OFFICIAL GUIDELINES FOR CODING AND REPORTING

Table of Contents

1. GENERAL INPATIENT CODING GUIDELINES

1.1 Use of Both Alphabetic Index and Tabular List

A. Use both the Alphabetic Index and the Tabular List when locating and assigning a code. Reliance on only the Alphabetic Index or the Tabular List leads to errors in code assignments and less specificity in code selection.

B. Locate each term in the Alphabetic Index and verify the code selected in the Tabular List. Read and be guided by instructional notations that appear in both the Alphabetic Index and the Tabular List.

1.2 Level of Specificity in Coding

Diagnostic and procedure codes are to be used at their highest level of specificity:

Assign three-digit codes only if there are no four-digit codes within that code category.

Assign four-digit codes only if there is no fifth-digit subclassification for that category.

Assign the fifth-digit subclassification code for those categories where it exists.

1.3 Other (NEC) and Unspecified (NOS) Code Titles

Codes labeled "other specified" (NEC not elsewhere classified) or "unspecified" (NOS not otherwise specified) are used only when neither the diagnostic statement nor a thorough review of the medical record provides adequate information to permit assignment of a more specific code.

Use the code assignment for "other" or NEC when the information at hand specifies a condition but no separate code for that condition is provided.

Use "unspecified" (NOS) when the information at hand does not permit either a more specific or "other" code assignment.

When the Alphabetic Index assigns a code to a category labeled "other (NEC)" or to a category labeled "unspecified (NOS)," refer to the Tabular List and review the titles and inclusion terms in the subdivisions under that particular three-digit category (or subdivision under the four-digit code) to determine if the information at hand can be appropriately assigned to a more specific code.

1.4 Acute and Chronic Conditions

If the same condition is described as both acute (subacute) and chronic and separate subentries exist in the Alphabetic Index at the same indentation level, code both and sequence the acute (subacute) code first.

1.5 Combination Code

A single code used to classify two diagnoses or a diagnosis with an associated secondary process (manifestation) or an associated complication is called a combination code. Combination codes are identified by referring to subterm entries in the Alphabetic Index and by reading the inclusion and exclusion notes in the Tabular List.

A. Assign only the combination code when that code fully identifies the diagnostic conditions involved or when the Alphabetic Index so directs. Multiple coding should not be used when the classification provides a combination code that clearly identifies all of the elements documented in the diagnosis. When the combination code lacks necessary specificity in describing the manifestation or complication, an additional code may be used as a secondary code.

1.6 Multiple Coding of Diagnoses

Multiple coding is required for certain conditions not subject to the rules for combination codes.

Instructions for conditions that require multiple coding appear in the Alphabetic Index and the Tabular List.

A. Alphabetic Index: Codes for both etiology and manifestation of a disease appear following the subentry term, with the second code in brackets. Assign both codes in the same sequence in which they appear in the Alphabetic Index.

B. Tabular List: Instructional terms, such as "Code first . . . ," "Use additional code for any . . . ," and "Note . . . ," indicate when to use more than one code.

"Code first underlying disease"—Assign the codes for both the manifestation and underlying cause. The codes for manifestations cannot be used (designated) as principal diagnosis.

"Use additional code, to identify manifestation, as . . . "—Assign also the code that identifies the manifestation, such as, but not limited to, the examples listed. The codes for manifestations cannot be used (designated) as principal diagnosis.

C. Apply multiple coding instructions throughout the classification where appropriate, whether or not multiple coding directions appear in the Alphabetic Index or the Tabular List. Avoid indiscriminate multiple coding or irrelevant information, such as symptoms or signs characteristic of the diagnosis.

1.7 Late Effect

A late effect is the residual effect (condition produced) after the acute phase of an illness or injury has terminated. There is no time limit on when a late effect code can be used. The residual may be apparent early, such as in cerebrovascular accident cases, or it may occur months or years later, such as that due to a previous injury.

Coding of late effects requires two codes:

The residual condition or nature of the late effect
The cause of the late effect

The residual condition or nature of the late effect is sequenced first, followed by the cause of the late effect, except in those few instances where the code for late effect is followed by a manifestation code identified in the Tabular List and title or the late effect code has been expanded (at the fourth- and fifth-digit levels) to include the manifestation(s).

The code for the acute phase of an illness or injury that led to the late effect is never used with a code for the cause of the late effect.

A. Late Effects of Cerebrovascular Disease

Category 438 is used to indicate conditions classifiable to categories 430-437 as the causes of late effects (neurologic deficits), themselves classified elsewhere. These "late effects" include neurologic deficits that persist after initial onset of conditions classifiable to 430-437. The neurologic deficits caused by cerebrovascular disease may be present from the onset or may arise at any time after the onset of the condition classifiable to 430-437.

Codes from category 438 may be assigned on a health care record with codes from 430-437, if the patient has a current CVA and deficits from an old CVA.

Assign code V12.59 (and not a code from category 438) as an additional code for history of cerebrovascular disease when no neurologic deficits are present.

1.8 Uncertain Diagnosis

If the diagnosis documented at the time of discharge is qualified as "probable," "suspected," "likely," "questionable," "possible," or "still to be ruled out," code the condition as if it existed or was established. The bases for these guidelines are the diagnostic workup, arrangements for further workup or observation, and initial therapeutic approach that correspond most closely with the established diagnosis.

1.9 Impending or Threatened Condition

Code any condition described at the time of discharge as "impending" or "threatened" as follows:

If it did occur, code as confirmed diagnosis.

If it did not occur, reference the Alphabetic Index to determine if the condition has a subentry term for "impending" or "threatened" and also reference main term entries for Impending and for Threatened.

If the subterms are listed, assign the given code.
If the subterms are not listed, code the existing forerunner condition(s) and not the condition described as impending or threatened.

2. SELECTION OF PRINCIPAL DIAGNOSIS

The circumstances of inpatient admission always govern the selection of principal diagnosis. The principal diagnosis is defined in the Uniform Hospital Discharge Data Set (UHDDS) as "that condition established after study to be chiefly responsible for occasioning the admission of the patient to the hospital for care."

In determining principal diagnosis the coding directives in the ICD-9-CM manuals, Volumes I, II, and III, take precedence over all other guidelines.

The importance of consistent, complete documentation in the medical record cannot be overemphasized. Without such documentation the application of all coding guidelines is a difficult, if not impossible, task.

2.1 Codes for symptoms, signs, and ill-defined conditions.
Codes for symptoms, signs, and ill-defined conditions from Chapter 16 are not to be used as principal diagnosis when a related definitive diagnosis has been established.

2.2 Codes in brackets.
Codes in brackets in the Alphabetic Index can never be sequenced as principal diagnosis. Coding directives require that the codes in brackets be sequenced in the order as they appear in the Alphabetic Index.

2.3 Acute and chronic conditions.
If the same condition is described as both acute (subacute) and chronic and separate subentries exist in the Alphabetic Index at the same indentation level, code both and sequence the acute (subacute) code first.

2.4 Two or more interrelated conditions, each potentially meeting the definition for principal diagnosis.
When there are two or more interrelated conditions (such as diseases in the same ICD-9-CM chapter or manifestations characteristically associated with a certain disease) potentially meeting the definition of principal diagnosis, either condition may be sequenced first, unless the circumstances of the admission, the therapy provided, the Tabular List, or the Alphabetic Index indicate otherwise.

2.5 Two or more diagnoses that equally meet the definition for principal diagnosis.
In the unusual instance when two or more diagnoses equally meet the criteria for principal diagnosis as determined by the circumstances of admission, diagnostic workup and/or therapy provided, and the Alphabetic Index, Tabular List, or another coding guideline does not provide sequencing direction, any one of the diagnoses may be sequenced first.

2.6 Two or more comparative or contrasting conditions.
In those rare instances when two or more contrasting or comparative diagnoses are documented as "either/or" (or similar terminology), they are coded as if the diagnoses were confirmed and the diagnoses are sequenced according to the circumstances of the admission. If no further determination can be made as to which diagnosis should be principal, either diagnosis may be sequenced first.

2.7 A symptom(s) followed by contrasting/comparative diagnoses.
When a symptom(s) is followed by contrasting/comparative diagnoses, the symptom code is sequenced first. All the contrasting/comparative diagnoses should be coded as suspected conditions.

2.8 Codes from the V71.0-V71.9 series, Observation and evaluation for suspected conditions.
Codes from the V71.0-V71.9 series are assigned as principal diagnoses for encounters or admissions to evaluate the patient's condition when

there is some evidence to suggest the existence of an abnormal condition or following an accident or other incident that ordinarily results in a health problem, and where no supporting evidence for the suspected condition is found and no treatment is currently required. The fact that the patient may be scheduled for continuing observation in the office/clinic setting following discharge does not limit the use of this category.

2.9 Original treatment plan not carried out.
Sequence as the principal diagnosis the condition which after study occasioned the admission to the hospital, even though treatment may not have been carried out due to unforeseen circumstances.

2.10 Residual condition or nature of late effect.
The residual condition or nature of the late effect is sequenced first, followed by the late effect code for the cause of the residual condition, except in a few instances where the Alphabetic Index or Tabular List directs otherwise.

2.11 Multiple burns.
Sequence first the code that reflects the highest degree of burn when more than one burn is present. (See also Burns guideline 8.3.)

2.12 Multiple injuries.
When multiple injuries exist, the code for the most severe injury as determined by the attending physician is sequenced first.

2.13 Neoplasms.

A. If the treatment is directed at the malignancy, designate the malignancy as the principal diagnosis, except when the purpose of the encounter or hospital admission is for radiotherapy session(s), V58.0, or for chemotherapy session(s), V58.1, in which instance the malignancy is coded and sequenced second.

B. When a patient is admitted for the purpose of radiotherapy or chemotherapy and develops complications such as uncontrolled nausea and vomiting or dehydration, the principal diagnosis is Encounter for radiotherapy, V58.0, or Encounter for chemotherapy, V58.1.

C. When an episode of inpatient care involves surgical removal of a primary site or secondary site malignancy followed by adjunct chemotherapy or radiotherapy, code the malignancy as the principal diagnosis, using codes in the 140-198 series or where appropriate in the 200-203 series.

D. When the reason for admission is to determine the extent of the malignancy, or for a procedure such as paracentesis or thoracentesis, the primary malignancy or appropriate metastatic site is designated as the principal diagnosis, even though chemotherapy or radiotherapy is administered.

E. When the primary malignancy has been previously excised or eradicated from its site and there is no adjunct treatment directed to that site and no evidence of any remaining malignancy at the primary site, use the appropriate code from the V10 series to indicate the former site of primary malignancy. Any mention of extension, invasion, or metastasis to a nearby structure or organ or to a distant site is coded as a secondary malignant neoplasm to that site and may be the principal diagnosis in the absence of the primary site.

F. When a patient is admitted because of a primary neoplasm with metastasis and treatment is directed toward the secondary site only, the secondary neoplasm is designated as the principal diagnosis even though the primary malignancy is still present.

G. Symptoms, signs, and ill-defined conditions listed in Chapter 16 characteristic of, or associated with, an existing primary or secondary site malignancy cannot be used to replace the malignancy as principal diagnosis, regardless of the number of admissions or encounters for treatment and care of the neoplasm.

H. Coding and sequencing of complications associated with the malignant neoplasm or with the therapy thereof are subject to the following guidelines:

When admission is for management of an anemia associated with the malignancy, and the treatment is only for anemia, the anemia is designated as the principal diagnosis and is followed by the appropriate code(s) for the malignancy.

When the admission is for management of an anemia associated with chemotherapy or radiotherapy and the only treatment is for the anemia, the anemia is designated as the principal diagnosis followed by the appropriate code(s) for the malignancy.

When the admission is for management of dehydration due to the malignancy or the therapy, or a combination of both, and only the dehydration is being treated (intravenous rehydration), the dehydration is designated as the principal diagnosis, followed by the code(s) for the malignancy.

When the admission is for treatment of a complication resulting from a surgical procedure performed for the treatment of an intestinal malignancy, designate the complication as the principal diagnosis if treatment is directed at resolving the complication.

2.14 Poisoning.
When coding a poisoning or reaction to the improper use of a medication (eg, wrong dose, wrong substance, wrong route of administration) the poisoning code is sequenced first, followed by a code for the manifestation. If there is also a diagnosis of drug abuse or dependence to the substance, the abuse or dependence is coded as an additional code.

2.15 Complications of surgery and other medical care.
When the admission is for treatment of a complication resulting from surgery or other medical care, the complication code is sequenced as the principal diagnosis. If the complication is classified to the 996-999 series, an additional code for the specific complication may be assigned.

2.16 Complication of pregnancy.
When a patient is admitted because of a condition that is either a complication of pregnancy or that is complicating the pregnancy, the code for the obstetric complication is the principal diagnosis. An additional code may be assigned as needed to provide specificity.

3. REPORTING OTHER (ADDITIONAL) DIAGNOSES

A joint effort between the attending physician and coder is essential to achieve complete and accurate documentation, code assignment, and reporting of diagnoses and procedures.

These guidelines have been developed and approved by the Cooperating Parties to assure both the physician and the coder in identifying those diagnoses that are to be reported in addition to the principal diagnosis. Hospitals may record other diagnoses as needed for internal data use.

The UHDDS definitions are used by acute care short-term hospitals to report inpatient data elements in a standardized manner. These data elements and their definitions can be found in the July 31, 1985, *Federal Register* (Vol. 50, No. 147), pp. 31038-40.

The UHDDS item #11-b defines Other Diagnoses as "all conditions that coexist at the time of admission, that develop subsequently, or that affect the treatment received and/or the length of stay. Diagnoses that relate to an earlier episode which have no bearing on the current hospital stay are to be excluded."

General Rule

For reporting purposes the definition for "other diagnoses" is interpreted as additional conditions that affect patient care in terms of requiring:

clinical evaluation; or
therapeutic treatment; or
diagnostic procedures; or
extended length of hospital stay; or
increased nursing care and/or monitoring.

The following guidelines are to be applied in designating "other diagnoses" when neither the Alphabetic Index nor the Tabular List in ICD-9-CM provide direction.

The listing of the diagnoses on the attestation statement is the responsibility of the attending physician.

3.1 Previous conditions.
If the physician has included a diagnosis in the final diagnostic statement, such as the discharge summary or the face sheet, it should ordinarily be coded. Some physicians include in the diagnostic statement resolved conditions or diagnoses and status-post procedures from previous admission that have no bearing on the current stay. Such conditions are not to be reported and are coded only if required by hospital policy.

However, history codes (V10-V19) may be used as secondary codes if the historical condition or family history has an impact on current care or influences treatment.

3.2 Diagnoses not listed in the final diagnostic statement.
When the physician has documented what appears to be a current diagnosis in the body of the record, but has not included the diagnosis in the final diagnostic statement, the physician should be asked whether the diagnosis should be added.

3.3 Conditions that are an integral part of a disease process.
Conditions that are integral to the disease process should not be assigned as additional codes.

3.4 Conditions that are not an integral part of a disease process.
Additional conditions that may not be associated routinely with a disease process should be coded when present.

3.5 Abnormal findings.
Abnormal findings (laboratory, x-ray, pathologic, and other diagnostic results) are not coded and reported unless the physician indicates their clinical significance. If the findings are outside the normal range and the physician has ordered other tests to evaluate the condition or prescribed treatment, it is appropriate to ask the physician whether the diagnosis should be added.

4. HYPERTENSION

4.1 Hypertension, Essential, or NOS
Assign hypertension (arterial) (essential) (primary) (systemic) (NOS) to category code 401 with the appropriate fourth digit to indicate malignant (.0), benign (.1), or unspecified (.9). Do not use either .0 malignant or .1 benign unless medical record documentation supports such a designation.

4.2 Hypertension with Heart Disease
Certain heart conditions (425.8, 428, 429.0-429.3, 429.8, 429.9) are assigned to a code from category 402 when a causal relationship is stated (due to hypertension) or implied (hypertensive). Use only the code from category 402.
The same heart conditions (425.8, 428, 429.0-429.3, 429.8, 429.9) with hypertension, but without a stated casual relationship, are coded separately. Sequence according to the circumstances of the admission.

4.3 Hypertensive Renal Disease with Chronic Renal Failure
Assign codes from category 403, Hypertensive renal disease, when conditions classified to categories 585-587 are present. Unlike hypertension with heart disease, ICD-9-CM presumes a cause-and-effect relationship and classifies renal failure with hypertension as hypertensive renal disease.

4.4 Hypertensive Heart and Renal Disease
Assign codes from combination category 404, Hypertensive heart and renal disease, when both hypertensive renal disease and hypertensive heart disease are stated in the diagnosis. Assume a relationship between the hypertension and the renal disease, whether or not the condition is so designated.

4.5 Hypertensive Cerebrovascular Disease.
First assign codes from 430-438, Cerebrovascular disease, then the appropriate hypertension code from categories 401-405.

4.6 Hypertensive Retinopathy
Two codes are necessary to identify the condition. First assign the code from subcategory 362.11, Hypertensive retinopathy, then the appropriate code from categories 401-405 to indicate the type of hypertension.

4.7 Hypertension, Secondary
Two codes are required: one to identify the underlying condition and one from category 405 to identify the hypertension. Sequencing of codes is determined by the reason for admission to the hospital.

4.8 Hypertension, Transient
Assign code 796.2, Elevated blood pressure reading without diagnosis of hypertension, unless patient has an established diagnosis of hypertension. Assign code 642.3x for transient hypertension of pregnancy.

4.9 Hypertension, Controlled
Assign appropriate code from categories 401-405. This diagnostic statement usually refers to an existing state of hypertension under control by therapy.

4.10 Hypertension, Uncontrolled
Uncontrolled hypertension may refer to untreated hypertension or hypertension not responding to current therapeutic regimen. In either case, assign the appropriate code from categories 401-405 to designate the stage and type of hypertension. Code to the type of hypertension.

4.11 Elevated Blood Pressure
For a statement of elevated blood pressure without further specificity, assign code 796.2, Elevated blood pressure reading without diagnosis of hypertension, rather than a code from category 401.

5. OBSTETRICS

Introduction

These guidelines have been developed and approved by the Cooperating Parties in conjunction with the Editorial Advisory Board of Coding Clinic and the American College of Obstetricians and Gynecologists, to assist the coder in coding and reporting obstetric cases. Where feasible, previously published advice has been incorporated. Some advice in these new guidelines may supersede previous advice. The guidelines are provided for reporting purposes. Health care facilities may record additional diagnoses as needed for internal data needs.

5.1 General Rules

A. Obstetric cases require codes from chapter 11, codes in the range 630-677, Complications of Pregnancy, Childbirth, and the Puerperium. Should the physician document that the pregnancy is incidental to the encounter, then code V22.2 should be used in place of any chapter 11 codes. It is the physician's responsibility to state that the condition being treated is not affecting the pregnancy.

B. Chapter 11 codes have sequencing priority over codes from other chapters. Additional codes from other chapters may be used in conjunction with chapter 11 codes to further specify conditions.

C. Chapter 11 codes are to be used only on the maternal record, never on the record of the newborn.

D. An outcome of delivery code, V27.0-V27.9, should be included on every maternal record when a delivery has occurred. These codes are not to be used on subsequent records or on the newborn record.

5.2 Selection of Principal Diagnosis

A. The circumstances of the encounter govern the selection of the principal diagnosis.

B. In episodes when no delivery occurs the principal diagnosis should correspond to the principal complication of the pregnancy which necessitated the encounter. Should more than one complication exist, all of which are treated or monitored, any of the complications codes may be sequenced first.

C. When a delivery occurs the principal diagnosis should correspond to the main circumstances or complication of the delivery. In cases of cesarean deliveries, the principal diagnosis should correspond to the reason the cesarean was performed, unless the reason for admission was unrelated to the condition resulting in the cesarean delivery.

D. For routine prenatal visits when no complications are present codes V22.0, Supervision of normal first pregnancy, and V22.1, Supervision of other normal pregnancy, should be used as principal diagnoses. These codes should not be used in conjunction with chapter 11 codes.

E. For prenatal outpatient visits for patients with high-risk pregnancies, a code from category V23, Supervision of high-risk pregnancy, should be used as the principal diagnosis. Secondary chapter 11 codes may be used in conjunction with these codes if appropriate. A thorough review of any pertinent excludes note is necessary to be certain that these V codes are being used properly.

5.3 Chapter 11 Fifth digits

A. Categories 640-648, 651-676 have required fifth digits which indicate whether the encounter is antepartum, postpartum, and whether a delivery has also occurred.

B. The fifth digits which are appropriate for each code number are listed in brackets under each code. The fifth digits on each code should all be consistent with each other. That is, should a delivery occur all of the fifth digits should indicate the delivery.

5.4 Fetal Conditions Affecting the Management of the Mother.

Codes from category 655, Known or suspected fetal abnormality affecting management of the mother, and category 656, Other fetal and placental problems affecting the management of the mother, are assigned only when the fetal condition is actually responsible for modifying the management of the mother, ie, by requiring diagnostic studies, additional observation, special care, or termination of pregnancy. The fact that the fetal condition exists does not justify assigning a code from this series to the mother's record.

5.5 Normal Delivery, 650

A. Code 650 is for use in cases when a woman is admitted for a full-term normal delivery and delivers a single, healthy infant without any complications antepartum, during the delivery, or postpartum during the delivery episode.

B. 650 may be used if the patient had a complication at some point during her pregnancy but the complication is not present at the time of the admission for delivery.

C. Code 650 is always a principal diagnosis. It is not to be used if any other code from chapter 11 is needed to describe a current complication of the antenatal, delivery, or perinatal period. Additional codes from other chapters may be used with code 650 if they are not related to or are in any way complicating the pregnancy.

D. V27.0, Single liveborn, is the only outcome of delivery code appropriate for use with 650.

5.6 Procedure Codes

A. In cases of cesarean delivery, the selection of the principal diagnosis should correspond to the reason the cesarean delivery was performed unless the reason for admission was unrelated to the condition resulting in the cesarean delivery.

B. A delivery procedure code should not be used for a woman who has delivered prior to admission to the hospital. Any postpartum repairs should be coded.

5.7 The Postpartum Period

A. The postpartum period begins immediately after delivery and continues for 6 weeks following delivery.

B. A postpartum complication is any complication occurring within the 6 week period.

C. Chapter 11 codes may also be used to describe pregnancy-related complications after the 6 week period should the physician document that a condition is pregnancy related.

D. Postpartum complications that occur during the same admission as the delivery are identified with a fifth digit of "2." Subsequent admissions for postpartum complications should identified with a fifth digit of "4."

E. When the mother delivers outside the hospital prior to admission and is admitted for routine postpartum care and no complications are noted, code V24.0, Postpartum care and examination immediately after delivery, should be assigned as the principal diagnosis.

5.8 Abortions

A. Fifth digits are required for abortion categories 634-637. Fifth digit 1, incomplete, indicates that all of the products of conception have not been expelled from the uterus. Fifth digit 2, complete, indicates that all products of conception have been expelled from the uterus prior to the episode of care.

B. A code from categories 640-648 and 651-657 may be used as additional codes with an abortion code to indicate the complication leading to the abortion.

Fifth digit 3 is assigned with codes from these categories when used with an abortion code because the other fifth digits will not apply. Codes from the 660-669 series are not to be used for complications of abortion.

C. Code 639 is to be used for all complications following abortion. Code 639 cannot be assigned with codes from categories 634-638.

D. Abortion with Liveborn Fetus. When an attempted termination of pregnancy results in a liveborn fetus assign code 644.21, Early onset of delivery, with an appropriate code from category V27, Outcome of Delivery. The procedure code for the attempted termination of pregnancy should also be assigned.

E. Retained Products of Conception following an abortion. Subsequent admissions for retained products of conception following a spontaneous or legally induced abortion are assigned the appropriate code from category 634, Spontaneous abortion, or legally induced abortion, with a fifth digit of "1" (incomplete). This advice is appropriate even when the patient was discharged previously with a discharge diagnosis of complete abortion.

5.9 Code 677, Late effect of complication of pregnancy, childbirth, and the puerperium

A. Code 677, Late effect of complication of pregnancy, childbirth, and the puerperium, is for use in those cases when an initial complication of a pregnancy develops a sequelae requiring care or treatment at a future date.

B. This code may be used at any time after the initial postpartum period.

C. This code, like all late effect codes, is to be sequenced following the code describing the sequelae of the complication.

6. NEWBORN GUIDELINES

Definition

The newborn period is defined as beginning at birth and lasting through the 28th day following birth.

The following guidelines are provided for reporting purposes. Hospitals may record other diagnoses as needed for internal data use.

General Rule

All clinically significant conditions noted on routine newborn examination should be coded. A condition is clinically significant if it requires:

- clinical evaluation; or
- therapeutic treatment; or

- diagnostic procedures; or
- extended length of hospital stay; or
- increased nursing care and/or monitoring; or
- has implications for future health care needs.

Note: The preceding list of newborn guidelines are the same as the general coding guidelines for "other diagnoses," except for the final bullet regarding implications for future health care needs. Whether or not a condition is clinically significant can only be determined by the physician.

6.1 Use of Codes V30-V39
When coding the birth of an infant, assign a code from categories V30-V39, according to the type of birth. A code from this series is assigned as a principal diagnosis, and assigned only once to a newborn at the time of birth.

6.2 Newborn Transfers
If the newborn is transferred to another institution, the V30 series is not used.

6.3 Use of Category V29

A. Assign a code from category V29, Observation and evaluation of newborns and infants for suspected conditions not found, to identify those instances when a healthy newborn is evaluated for a suspected condition that is determined after study not to be present. Do not use a code from category V29 when the patient has identified signs or symptoms of a suspected problem; in such cases, code the sign or symptom.

B. A V29 code is to be used as a secondary code after the V30, Outcome of delivery, code. It may also be assigned as a principal code for readmissions or encounters when the V30 code no longer applies. It is for use only for healthy newborns and infants for which no condition after study is found to be present.

6.4 Maternal Causes of Perinatal Morbidity
Codes from categories 760-763, Maternal causes of perinatal morbidity and mortality, are assigned only when the maternal condition has actually affected the fetus or newborn. The fact that the mother has an associated medical condition or experiences some complication of pregnancy, labor or delivery does not justify the routine assignment of codes from these categories to the newborn record.

6.5 Congenital Anomalies
Assign an appropriate code from categories 740-759, Congenital Anomalies, when a specific abnormality is diagnosed for an infant. Such abnormalities may occur as a set of symptoms or multiple malformations. A code should be assigned for each presenting manifestation of the syndrome if the syndrome is not specifically indexed in ICD-9-CM.

6.6 Coding of Other (Additional) Diagnoses

A. Assign codes for conditions that require treatment or further investigation, prolong the length of stay, or require resource utilization.

B. Assign codes for conditions that have been specified by the physician as having implications for future health care needs.

Note: This guideline should not be used for adult patients.

C. Assign a code for Newborn conditions originating in the perinatal period (categories 760-779), as well as complications arising during the current episode of care classified in other chapters, only if the diagnoses have been documented by the responsible physician at the time of transfer or discharge as having affected the fetus or newborn.

D. Insignificant conditions or signs or symptoms that resolve without treatment are not coded.

6.7 Prematurity and Fetal Growth Retardation

Codes from categories 764 and 765 should not be assigned based solely on recorded birthweight or estimated gestational age, but upon the attending physician's clinical assessment of maturity of the infant. *Note:* Since physicians may utilize different criteria in determining prematurity, do not code the diagnosis of prematurity unless the physician documents this condition.

7. SEPTICEMIA AND SEPTIC SHOCK

When the diagnosis of septicemia with shock or the diagnosis of general sepsis with septic shock is documented, code and list the septicemia first and report the septic shock code as a secondary condition. The septicemia code assignment should identify the type of bacteria if it is known.

Sepsis and septic shock associated with abortion, ectopic pregnancy, and molar pregnancy are classified to category codes in chapter 11 (630-639).

Negative or inconclusive blood cultures do not preclude a diagnosis of septicemia in patients with clinical evidence of the condition.

8. TRAUMA

8.1 Coding for Multiple Injuries

When coding multiple injuries such as fracture of tibia and fibula, assign separate codes for each injury unless a combination code is provided, in which case the combination code is assigned. Multiple injury codes are provided in ICD-9-CM, but should not be assigned unless information for a more specific code is not available.

A. The code for the most serious injury, as determined by the physician, is sequenced first.

B. Superficial injuries such as abrasions or contusions are not coded when associated with more severe injuries of the same site.

C. When a primary injury results in minor damage to peripheral nerves or blood vessels, the primary injury is sequenced first with additional code(s) from categories 950-957, Injury to nerves and spinal cord, and/or 900-904, Injury to blood vessels. When the primary injury is to the blood vessels or nerves, that injury should be sequenced first.

8.2 Coding for Multiple Fractures

The principle of multiple coding of injuries should be followed in coding multiple fractures. Multiple fractures of specified sites are coded individually by site in accordance with both the provisions within categories 800-829 and the level of detail furnished by medical record content. Combination categories for multiple fractures are provided for use when there is insufficient detail in the medical record (such as trauma cases transferred to another hospital), when the reporting form limits the number of codes that can be used in reporting pertinent clinical data, or when there is insufficient specificity at the fourth-digit or fifth-digit level. More specific guidelines are as follows:

A. Multiple fractures of same limb classifiable to the same three-digit or four-digit category are coded to that category.
B. Multiple unilateral or bilateral fractures of same bone(s) but classified to different fourth-digit subdivisions (bone part) within the same three-digit category are coded individually by site.
C. Multiple fracture categories 819 and 828 classify bilateral fractures of both upper limbs (819) and both lower limbs (828), but without any detail at the fourth-digit level other than open and closed type of fractures.
D. Multiple fractures are sequenced in accordance with the severity of the fracture and the physician should be asked to list the fracture diagnoses in the order of severity.

8.3 Current Burns and Encounters for Late Effects of Burns

Current burns (940-948) are classified by depth, extent and, if desired, by agent (E code). By depth burns are classified as first degree (erythema), second degree (blistering), and third degree (full-thickness involvement).

A. All burns are coded with the highest degree of burn sequenced first.
B. Classify burns of the same local site (three-digit category level, (940-947)) but of different degrees to the subcategory identifying the highest degree recorded in the diagnosis.
C. Non-healing burns are coded as acute burns. Necrosis of burned skin should be coded as a non-healed burn.
D. Assign code 958.3, Posttraumatic wound infection, not elsewhere classified, as an additional code for any documented infected burn site.
E. When coding multiple burns, assign separate codes for each burn site.

   Category 946, Burns of multiple specified sites, should only be used if the location of the burns are not documented.

   Category 949, Burn, unspecified, is extremely vague and should rarely be used.

F. Assign codes from category 948, Burns classified according to extent of body surface involved, when the site of the burn is not specified or when there is a need for additional data. It is advisable to use category 948 as additional coding when needed to provide data for evaluating burn mortality, such as that needed by burn units. It is also advisable to use category 948 as an additional code for reporting purposes when there is mention of a third-degree burn involving 20 percent or more of the body surface. In assigning a code from category 948:

   Fourth-digit codes are used to identify the percentage of total body surface involved in a burn (all degree).
   Fifth-digits are assigned to identify the percentage of body surface involved in third-degree burn.
   Fifth-digit zero (0) is assigned when less than 10 percent or when no body surface is involved in a third-degree burn.

   Category 948 is based on the classic "rule of nines" in estimating body surface involved: head and neck are assigned nine percent, each arm nine percent, each leg 18 percent, the anterior trunk 18 percent, posterior trunk 18 percent, and genitalia one percent. Physicians may change these percentage assignments where necessary to accommodate infants and children who have proportionately larger heads than adults and patients who have large buttocks, thighs, or abdomen that involve burns.

G. Encounters for the treatment of the late effects of burns (i.e., scars or joint contractures) should be coded to the residual condition (sequelae) followed by the appropriate late effect code (906.5-906.9). A late effect E code may also be used, if desired.

H. When appropriate, both a sequelae with a late effect code, and a current burn code may be assigned on the same record.

8.4 Debridement of Wound, Infection, or Burn

A. For coding purposes, excisional debridement, 86.22, is assigned only when the procedure is performed by a physician.

B. For coding purposes, nonexcisional debridement performed by the physician or nonphysician health care professional is assigned to 86.28. Any "excisional" type procedure performed by a nonphysician is assigned to 86.28.

9. ADVERSE EFFECTS AND POISONING

The properties of certain drugs, medicinal and biological substances or combinations of such substances, may cause toxic reactions. The occurrence of drug toxicity is classified in ICD-9-CM as follows:

9.1 Adverse Effect

When the drug was correctly prescribed and properly administered, code the reaction plus the appropriate code from the E930-E949 series.

Adverse effects of therapeutic substances correctly prescribed and properly administered (toxicity, synergistic reaction, side effect, and idiosyncratic reaction) may be due to (1) differences among patients, such as age, sex, disease, and genetic factors, and (2) drug-related factors, such as type of drug, route of administration, duration of therapy, dosage, and bioavailability.

Codes from the E930-E949 series must be used to identify the causative substance for an adverse effect of drug, medicinal and biological substances, correctly prescribed and properly administered. The effect, such as tachycardia, delirium, gastrointestinal hemorrhaging, vomiting, hypokalemia, hepatitis, renal failure, or respiratory failure, is coded and followed by the appropriate code from the E930-E949 series.

9.2 Poisoning

Poisoning when an error was made in drug prescription or in the administration of the drug by physician, nurse, patient, or other person, use the appropriate code from the 960-979 series. If an overdose of a drug was intentionally taken or administered and resulted in drug toxicity, it would be coded as a poisoning (960-979 series). If a nonprescribed drug or medicinal agent was taken in combination with a correctly prescribed and properly administered drug, any drug toxicity or other reaction resulting from the interaction of the two drugs would be classified as a poisoning.

10. HUMAN IMMUNODEFICIENCY VIRUS (HIV) INFECTIONS

10.1 Code only confirmed cases of HIV infection/illness.

This is an exception to guideline 1.8 which states "If the diagnosis documented at the time of discharge is qualified as 'probable,' 'suspected,' 'likely,' 'questionable,' 'possible,' or 'still to be ruled out,' code the condition as if it existed or was established. . . ."

In this context, "confirmation" does not require documentation of positive serology or culture for HIV; the physician's diagnostic statement that the patient is HIV positive, or has an HIV-related illness is sufficient.

10.2 Selection of HIV code

042 Human Immunodeficiency Virus [HIV] Disease
Patients with an HIV-related illness should be coded to 042, Human Immunodeficiency Virus [HIV] Disease.

V08 Asymptomatic Human Immunodeficiency Virus [HIV] Infection
Patients with physician-documented asymptomatic HIV infections who have never had an HIV-related illness should be coded to V08, Asymptomatic Human Immunodeficiency Virus [HIV] Infection.

795.71 Nonspecific Serologic Evidence of Human Immunodeficiency Virus [HIV]

Code 795.71, Nonspecific serologic evidence of human immunodeficiency virus [HIV], should be used for patients (including infants) with inconclusive HIV test results.

10.3 Previously diagnosed HIV-related illness
Patients with any known prior diagnosis of an HIV-related illness should be coded to 042. Once a patient has developed an HIV-related illness, the patient should always be assigned code 042 on every subsequent admission. Patients previously diagnosed with any HIV illness (042) should never be assigned to 795.71 or V08.

10.4 Sequencing
The sequencing of diagnoses for patients with HIV-related illnesses follows guideline 2 for selection of principal diagnosis. That is, the circumstances of admission govern the selection of principal diagnosis, "that condition established after study to be chiefly responsible for occasioning the admission of the patient to the hospital for care."

Patients who are admitted for an HIV-related illness should be assigned a minimum of two codes: first assign code 042 to identify the HIV disease and then sequence additional codes to identify the other diagnoses. If a patient is admitted for an HIV-related condition, the principal diagnosis should be 042, followed by additional diagnosis codes for all reported HIV-related conditions.

If a patient with HIV disease is admitted for an unrelated condition (such as a traumatic injury), the code for the unrelated condition (e.g., the nature of injury code) should be the principal diagnosis. Other diagnoses would be 042 followed by additional diagnosis codes for all reported HIV-related conditions.

Whether the patient is newly diagnosed or has had previous admissions for HIV conditions (or has expired) is irrelevant to the sequencing decision.

10.5 HIV Infection in Pregnancy, Childbirth, and the Puerperium
During pregnancy, childbirth or the puerperium, a patient admitted because of an HIV-related illness should receive a principal diagnosis of 647.6X, Other specified infectious and parasitic diseases in the mother classifiable elsewhere, but complicating the pregnancy, childbirth or the puerperium, followed by 042 and the code(s) for the HIV-

related illness(es). This is an exception to the sequencing rule found in 10.4 above.

Patients with asymptomatic HIV infection status admitted during pregnancy, childbirth, or the puerperium should receive codes of 647.6X and V08.

10.6 Asymptomatic HIV Infection

V08 Asymptomatic human immunodeficiency virus [HIV] infection, is to be applied when the patient without any documentation of symptoms is listed as being "HIV positive," "known HIV," "HIV test positive," or similar terminology. Do not use this code if the term "AIDS" is used or if the patient is treated for any HIV-related illness or is described as having any condition(s) resulting from his/her HIV positive status; use 042 in these cases.

10.7 Inconclusive Laboratory Test for HIV

Patients with inconclusive HIV serology, but no definitive diagnosis or manifestations of the illness may be assigned code 795.71, Inconclusive serologic test for Human Immunodeficiency Virus [HIV]

10.8 Testing for HIV

If the patient is asymptomatic but wishes to know his/her HIV status, use code V73.89, Screening for other specified viral disease. Use code V69.8, Other problems related to lifestyle, as a secondary code if an asymptomatic patient is in a known high-risk group for HIV. Should a patient with signs or symptoms or illness, or a confirmed HIV-related diagnosis be tested for HIV, code the signs and symptoms or the diagnosis. An additional counseling code V65.44 may be used if counseling is provided during the encounter for the test.

When the patient returns to be informed of his/her HIV test results use code V65.44, HIV counseling, if the results of the test are negative. If the results are positive but the patient is asymptomatic use code V08, Asymptomatic HIV infection. If the results are positive and the patient is symptomatic use code 042, HIV infection, with codes for the HIV-related symptoms or diagnosis. The HIV counseling code may also be used if counseling is provided for patients with positive test results.

11. GUIDELINES FOR CODING EXTERNAL CAUSES OF INJURIES, POISONINGS, AND ADVERSE EFFECTS OF DRUGS (E Codes)

Introduction

These guidelines are provided for those who are currently collecting E codes in order that there will be standardization in the process. If your institution plans to begin collecting E codes, these guidelines are to be applied. The use of E codes is supplemental to the application of basic ICD-9-CM codes. E codes are never to be recorded as principal diagnosis (first listed in the outpatient setting) and are not required for reporting to the Health Care Financing Administration.

Injuries are a major cause of mortality, morbidity, and disability. In the United States, the care of patients who suffer intentional and unintentional injuries and poisonings contributes significantly to the increase in medical care costs. External causes of injury and poisoning codes (E codes) are intended to provide data for injury research and evaluation of injury prevention strategies. E codes capture how the injury or poisoning happened (cause), the intent (unintentional or accidental; or intentional, such as suicide or assault), and the place where the event occurred. Some major categories of E codes include:

transport accidents
poisoning and adverse effects of drugs, medicinal substances and biologicals

accidental falls
accidents caused by fire and flames
accidents due to natural and environmental factors
late effects of accidents, assaults, or self-injury
assaults or purposely inflicted injury
suicide or self-inflicted injury

These guidelines apply for the coding and collection of E code from records in hospitals, outpatient clinics, emergency departments, other ambulatory care settings and physician offices except when other specific guidelines apply. (See Reporting Diagnostic Guidelines for Hospital-based Outpatient Services/Reporting Requirements for Physician Billing.)

11.1 General E Code Coding Guidelines

A. An E code may be used with any code in the range of 001-V82.9 which indicates an injury, poisoning, or adverse effect due to an external cause.
B. Assign the appropriate E-code for all initial treatments of an injury, poisoning, or adverse effect of drugs.
C. Use a late effect E code for subsequent visits when a late effect of the initial injury or poisoning is being treated. There is no late effect E code for adverse effects of drugs.
D. Use the full range of E codes to completely describe the cause, the intent and the place of occurrence, if applicable, for all injuries, poisonings, and adverse effects of drugs.
E. Assign as many E codes as necessary to fully explain each cause. If only one E code can be recorded, assign the E code most related to the principal diagnosis.
F. The selection of the appropriate E code is guided by the Index to External Causes which is located after the Alphabetical Index to diseases and by Inclusion and Exclusion notes in the Tabular List.
G. An E code can never be a principal (first listed) diagnosis.

11.2 Place of Occurrence Guideline

Use an additional code from category E849 to indicate the Place of Occurrence for injuries and poisonings. The Place of Occurrence describes the place where the event occurred and not the patient's activity at the time of the event.

Do not use E849.9 if the place of occurrence is not stated.

11.3 Poisonings and Adverse Effects of Drugs, Medicinal and Biological Substances Guidelines

A. Do not code directly from the Table of Drugs and Chemicals. Always refer back to the Tabular List.
B. Use as many codes as necessary to describe completely all drugs, medicinal or biological substances.
C. If the same E code would describe the causative agent for more than one adverse reaction, assign the code only once.
D. If two or more drugs, medicinal or biological substances are reported, code each individually unless the combination code is listed in the Table of Drugs and Chemicals. In that case, assign the E code for the combination.
E. When a reaction results from the interaction of a drug(s) and alcohol, use poisoning codes and E codes for both.
F. If the reporting format limits the number of E codes that can be used in reporting clinical data, code the one most related to the

principal diagnosis. Include at least one from each category (cause, intent, place) if possible.

If there are different fourth digit codes in the same three digit category, use the code for "Other specified" of that category. If there is no "Other specified" code in that category, use the appropriate "Unspecified" code in that category.

If the codes are in different three digit categories, assign the appropriate E code for other multiple drugs and medicinal substances.

11.4 Multiple Cause E Code Coding Guidelines

If two or more events cause separate injuries, an E code should be assigned for each cause. The first listed E code will be selected in the following order:

E codes for child and adult abuse take priority over all other E codes—see Child and Adult abuse guidelines
E codes for cataclysmic events take priority over all other E codes except child and adult abuse
E codes for transport accidents take priority over all other E codes except cataclysmic events and child and adult abuse

The first list E code should correspond to the cause of the most serious diagnosis due to an assault, accident, or self-harm, following the order of hierarchy in the preceding list.

11.5 Child and Adult Abuse Guideline

A. When the cause of an injury or neglect is intentional child or adult abuse, the first listed E code should be assigned from categories E960-E968, Homicide and injury purposely inflicted by other persons, (except category E967). An E code from category E967, Child and adult battering and other maltreatment, should be added as an additional code to identify the perpetrator, if known.
B. In cases of neglect when the intent is determined to be accidental E code E904.0, Abandonment or neglect of infant and helpless person, should be the first listed E code.

11.6 Unknown or Suspected Intent Guideline

A. If the intent (accident, self-harm, assault) of the cause of an injury or poisoning is unknown or unspecified, code the intent as undetermined E980-E989.
B. If the intent (accident, self-harm, assault) of the cause of an injury or poisoning is questionable, probable or suspected, code the intent as undetermined E980-E989.

11.7 Undetermined Cause

When the intent of an injury or poisoning is known, but the cause is unknown, use codes: E928.9, Unspecified accident, E958.9, Suicide and self-inflicted injury by unspecified means, and E968.9, Assault by unspecified means.

These E codes should rarely be used as the documentation in the medical record, in both the inpatient and outpatient settings, should normally provide sufficient detail to determine the cause of the injury.

11.8 Late Effects of External Cause Guidelines

A. Late effect E codes exist for injuries and poisonings but not for adverse effects of drugs, misadventures, and surgical complications.

B. A late effect E code (E929, E959, E969, E977, E989, or E999) should be used with any report of a late effect or sequela resulting from a previous injury or poisoning (905-909).

C. A late effect E code should never be used with a related current nature of injury code.

11.9 Misadventures and Complications of Care Guidelines

A. Assign a code in the range of E870-E876 if misadventures are stated by the physician.

B. Assign a code in the range of E878-E879 if the physician attributes an abnormal reaction or later complication to a surgical or medical procedure, but does not mention misadventure at the time of the procedure as the cause of the reaction.

12. DIAGNOSTIC CODING AND REPORTING GUIDELINES FOR OUTPATIENT SERVICES (HOSPITAL-BASED AND PHYSICIAN OFFICE)
Revised October 1, 1995

Introduction

These revised coding guidelines for outpatient diagnoses have been approved for use by hospitals/physicians in coding and reporting hospital-based outpatient services and physician office visits. These guidelines replace the official guidelines on the October 1, 1994 CD-ROM.

Information about the use of certain abbreviations, punctuation, symbols, and other conventions used in the ICD-9-CM Tabular List (code numbers and titles), can be found in the section at the beginning of the ICD-9-CM on "Conventions Used in the Tabular List." Information about the correct sequence to use in finding a code is described in the "Introduction" to the Alphabetic Index of ICD-9-CM.

The terms encounter and visit are often used interchangeably in describing outpatient service contacts and, therefore, appear together in these guidelines without distinguishing one from the other.

Coding guidelines for outpatient and physician reporting of diagnoses will vary in a number of instances from those for inpatient diagnoses, recognizing that:

The Uniform Hospital Discharge Data Set (UHDDS) definition of principal diagnosis applies only to inpatients in acute, short-term, general hospitals.

Coding guidelines for inconclusive diagnoses (probable, suspected, rule out, etc.) were developed for inpatient reporting and do not apply to outpatients.

Diagnoses often are not established at the time of the initial encounter/visit. It may take two or more visits before the diagnosis is confirmed.

The most critical rule involves beginning the search for the correct code assignment through the Alphabetic Index. Never begin searching initially in the Tabular List as this will lead to coding errors.

Basic Coding Guidelines for Outpatient Services

A. The appropriate code or codes from 001.0 through V82.9 must be used to identify diagnoses, symptoms, conditions, problems, complaints, or other reason(s) for the encounter/visit.

B. For accurate reporting of ICD-9-CM diagnosis codes, the documentation should describe the patient's condition, using terminology which includes specific diagnoses as well as symptoms, problems, or reasons for the encounter. There are ICD-9-CM codes to describe all of these.

C. The selection of codes 001.0 through 999.9 will frequently be used to describe the reason for the encounter. These codes are from the section of ICD-9-CM for the classification of diseases and injuries (e.g., infectious and parasitic diseases; neoplasms; symptoms, signs, and ill-defined conditions, etc.).

D. Codes that describe symptoms and signs, as opposed to diagnoses, are acceptable for reporting purposes when an established diagnosis has not been diagnosed (confirmed) by the physician. Chapter 16 of ICD-9-CM, Symptoms, Signs, and Ill-Defined Conditions (codes 780.0-799.9) contain many, but not all codes for symptoms.

E. ICD-9-CM provides codes to deal with encounters for circumstances other than a disease or injury. The Supplementary Classification of factors Influencing Health Status and Contact with Health Services (V01.0-V82.9) is provided to deal with occasions when circumstances other than a disease or injury are recorded as diagnosis or problems.

F. ICD-9-CM is composed of codes with either 3, 4, or 5 digits. Codes with 3 digits are included in ICD-9-CM as the heading of a category of codes that may be further subdivided by the use of fourth and/or fifth digits which provide greater specificity.

A three-digit code is to be used only if it is not further subdivided. Where fourth-digit subcategories and/or fifth-digit subclassifications are provided, they must be assigned. A code is invalid if it has not been coded to the full number of digits required for that code.

G. List first the ICD-9-CM code for the diagnosis, condition, problem, or other reason for encounter/visit shown in the medical record to be chiefly responsible for the services provided. List additional codes that describe any coexisting conditions.

H. Do not code diagnoses documented as "probable," "suspected," "questionable," "rule out," or "working diagnosis." Rather, code the condition(s) to the highest degree of certainty for that encounter/visit, such as symptoms, signs, abnormal test results, or other reason for the visit.

Please note: This is contrary to the coding practices used by hospitals and medical record departments for coding the diagnosis of hospital inpatients.

I. Chronic diseases treated on an ongoing basis may be coded and reported as many times as the patient receives treatment and care for the condition(s).

J. Code all documented conditions that coexist at the time of the encounter/visit, and require or affect patient care treatment or management. Do not code conditions that were previously treated and no longer exist. However, history codes (V10-V19) may be used as secondary codes if the historical condition or family history has an impact on current care or influences treatment.

K. For patients receiving diagnostic services only during an encounter/visit, sequence first the diagnosis, condition, problem, or other reason for encounter/visit shown in the medical record to be chiefly responsible for the outpatient services provided during the encounter/visit. Codes for other diagnoses (e.g., chronic conditions) may be sequenced as additional diagnoses.

L. For patients receiving therapeutic services only during an encounter/visit, sequence first the diagnosis, condition, problem, or other reason for encounter/visit shown in the medical record to be chiefly responsible for the outpatient services provided during the encounter/visit. Codes for other diagnoses (e.g., chronic conditions) may be sequenced as additional diagnoses.

M. The only exception to this rule is that patients receiving chemotherapy, radiation therapy, or rehabilitation, the appropriate V code for the service is listed first, and the diagnosis or problem for which the service is being performed listed second.

N. For patients receiving preoperative evaluations only, sequence a code from category V72.8, Other specified examinations, to describe the pre-op consultations. Assign a code for the condition to describe the reason for the surgery as an additional diagnosis. Code also any findings related to the pre-op evaluation.

O. For ambulatory surgery, code the diagnosis for which the surgery was performed. If the postoperative diagnosis is known to be different from the preoperative diagnosis at the time the diagnosis is confirmed, select the postoperative diagnosis for coding, since it is the most definitive.

APPENDIX B Documentation Guidelines for Evaluation and Management Services

TABLE OF CONTENTS

Documentation Guidelines for Evaluation and Management Services*

I. INTRODUCTION

What Is Documentation and Why Is It Important?

Medical record documentation is required to record pertinent facts, findings, and observations about an individual's health history including past and present illnesses, examinations, tests, treatments, and outcomes. The medical record chronologically documents the care of the patient and is an important element contributing to high quality care. The medical record facilitates:

- the ability of the physician and other health care professionals to evaluate and plan the patient's immediate treatment, and to monitor his/her health care over time.
- communication and continuity of care among physicians and other health care professionals involved in the patient's care;
- accurate and timely claims review and payment;
- appropriate utilization review and quality of care evaluations; and
- collection of data that may be useful for research and education.

An appropriately documented medical record can reduce many of the "hassles" associated with claims processing and may serve as a legal document to verify the care provided, if necessary.

What Do Payers Want and Why?

Because payers have a contractual obligation to enrollees, they may require reasonable documentation that services are consistent with the insurance coverage provided. They may request information to validate:

- the site of service;
- the medical necessity and appropriateness of the diagnostic and/or therapeutic services provided; and/or
- that services provided have been accurately reported.

II. GENERAL PRINCIPLES OF MEDICAL RECORD DOCUMENTATION

The principles of documentation listed below are applicable to all types of medical and surgical services in all settings. For Evaluation and Management (E/M) services, the nature and amount of physician work and documentation varies by type of service, place of service and the patient's status. The following list of gen-

*Developed jointly by the American Medical Association (AMA) and the Health Care Financing Administration (HCFA).

eral principles may be modified to account for these variable circumstances in providing E/M services.

1. The medical record should be complete and legible.
2. The documentation of each patient encounter should include:
   - reason for the encounter and relevant history, physical examination findings and prior diagnostic test results;
   - assessment, clinical impression or diagnosis;
   - plan for care; and
   - date and legible identity of the observer.
3. If not documented, the rationale for ordering diagnostic and other ancillary services should be easily inferred.
4. Past and present diagnoses should be accessible to the treating and/or consulting physician.
5. Appropriate health risk factors should be identified.
6. The patient's progress, response to and changes in treatment, and revision of diagnosis should be documented.
7. The CPT and ICD-9-CM codes reported on the health insurance claim form or billing statement should be supported by the documentation in the medical record.

III. DOCUMENTATION OF E/M SERVICES

This publication provides definitions and documentation guidelines for the three key components of E/M services and for visits which consist predominantly of counseling or coordination of care. The three *key* components—history, examination, and medical decision making—appear in the descriptors for office and other outpatient services, hospital observation services, hospital inpatient services, consultations, emergency department services, nursing facility services, domiciliary care services, and home services. While some of the text of CPT has been repeated in this publication, the reader should refer to CPT for the complete descriptors for E/M services and instructions for selecting a level of service. Documentation guidelines are identified by the symbol •*DG*.

The descriptors for the levels of E/M services recognize seven components which are used in defining the levels of E/M services. These components are:

- history;
- examination;
- medical decision making;
- counseling;
- coordination of care;
- nature of presenting problem; and
- time.

The first three of these components (ie, history, examination and medical decision making) are the key components in selecting the level of E/M services. In the case of visits which consist *predominantly* of counseling or coordination of care, time is the key or controlling factor to qualify for a particular level of E/M service.

Because the level of E/M service is dependent on two or three key components, performance and documentation of one component (eg, examination) at the highest level does not necessarily mean that the encounter in its entirety qualifies for the highest level of E/M service.

These Documentation Guidelines for E/M services reflect the needs of the typical adult population. For certain groups of patients, the recorded information may vary slightly from that described here. Specifically, the medical records of infants, children, adolescents and pregnant women may have additional or modified information recorded in each history and examination area.

As an example, newborn records may include under history of the present illness (HPI) the details of mother's pregnancy and the infant's status at birth; social history will focus on family structure; family history will focus on congenital anomalies and hereditary disorders in the family. In addition, the content of a pediatric examination will vary with the age and development of the child. Although not specifically defined in these documentation guidelines, these patient group variations on history and examination are appropriate.

A. Documentation of History

The levels of E/M services are based on four types of history (Problem Focused, Expanded Problem Focused, Detailed, and Comprehensive). Each type of history includes some or all of the following elements:

- Chief complaint (CC);
- History of present illness (HPI);
- Review of systems (ROS); and
- Past, family and/or social history (PFSH).

The extent of history of present illness, review of systems and past, family and/or social history that is obtained and documented is dependent upon clinical judgment and the nature of the presenting problem(s).

The chart below shows the progression of the elements required for each type of history. To qualify for a given type of history all three elements in the table must be met. (A chief complaint is indicated at all levels.)

History of Present Illness (HPI)	Review of Systems (ROS)	Past, Family, and/or Social History (PFSH)	Type of History
Brief	N/A	N/A	*Problem Focused*
Brief	Problem Pertinent	N/A	*Expanded Problem Focused*
Extended	Extended	Pertinent	*Detailed*
Extended	Complete	Complete	*Comprehensive*

- DG: The CC, ROS and PFSH may be listed as separate elements of history, or they may be included in the description of the history of the present illness.
- DG: A ROS and/or a PFSH obtained during an earlier encounter does not need to be re-recorded if there is evidence that the physician reviewed and updated the previous information. This may occur when a physician

updates his or her own record or in an institutional setting or group practice where many physicians use a common record. The review and update may be documented by:

- describing any new ROS and/or PFSH information or noting there has been no change in the information; and
- noting the date and location of the earlier ROS and/or PFSH.

- DG: The ROS and/or PFSH may be recorded by ancillary staff or on a form completed by the patient. To document that the physician reviewed the information, there must be a notation supplementing or confirming the information recorded by others.
- DG: If the physician is unable to obtain a history from the patient or other source, the record should describe the patient's condition or other circumstance which precludes obtaining a history.

Definitions and specific documentation guidelines for each of the elements of history are in the following list.

Chief Complaint (CC)

The CC is a concise statement describing the symptom, problem, condition, diagnosis, physician recommended return, or other factor that is the reason for the encounter, usually stated in the patient's words.

- DG: The medical record should clearly reflect the chief complaint.

History of Present Illness (HPI)

The HPI is a chronological description of the development of the patient's present illness from the first sign and/or symptom or from the previous encounter to the present. It includes the following elements:

- location,
- quality,
- severity,
- duration,
- timing,
- context,
- modifying factors, and
- associated signs and symptoms.

Brief and *extended* HPIs are distinguished by the amount of detail needed to accurately characterize the clinical problem(s).

A *brief* HPI consists of one to three elements of the HPI.

- DG: The medical record should describe one to three elements of the present illness (HPI).

An *extended* HPI consists of at least four elements of the HPI or the status of at least three chronic or inactive conditions.

- DG: The medical record should describe at least four elements of the present illness (HPI), or the status of at least three chronic or inactive conditions.

Review of Systems (ROS)

A ROS is an inventory of body systems obtained through a series of questions seeking to identify signs and/or symptoms which the patient may be experiencing or has experienced.

For purposes of ROS, the following systems are recognized:

- Constitutional symptoms (eg, fever, weight loss)
- Eyes
- Ears, Nose, Mouth, Throat
- Cardiovascular
- Respiratory
- Gastrointestinal
- Genitourinary
- Musculoskeletal
- Integumentary (skin and/or breast)
- Neurological
- Psychiatric
- Endocrine
- Hematologic/Lymphatic
- Allergic/Immunologic

A *problem pertinent* ROS inquires about the system directly related to the problem(s) identified in the HPI.

- DG: The patient's positive responses and pertinent negatives for the system related to the problem should be documented.

An *extended* ROS inquires about the system directly related to the problem(s) identified in the HPI and a limited number of additional systems.

- DG: The patient's positive responses and pertinent negatives for two to nine systems should be documented.

A *complete* ROS inquires about the system(s) directly related to the problem(s) identified in the HPI *plus* all additional body systems.

- DG: At least ten organ systems must be reviewed. Those systems with positive or pertinent negative responses must be individually documented. For the remaining systems, a notation indicating all other systems are negative is permissible. In the absence of such a notation, at least ten systems must be individually documented.

Past, Family and/or Social History (PFSH)

The PFSH consists of a review of three areas:

- past history (the patient's past experiences with illnesses, operations, injuries and treatments);
- family history (a review of medical events in the patient's family, including diseases which may be hereditary or place the patient at risk); and
- social history (an age appropriate review of past and current activities).

For certain categories of E/M services that include only an interval history, it is not necessary to record information about the PFSH. Those categories are subsequent hospital care, follow-up inpatient consultations and subsequent nursing facility care.

A *pertinent* PFSH is a review of the history area(s) directly related to the problem(s) identified in the HPI.

- DG: At least one specific item from any of the three history areas must be documented for a pertinent PFSH.

A *complete* PFSH is a review of two or all three of the PFSH history areas, depending on the category of the E/M service. A review of all three history areas is required for services that by their nature include a comprehensive assessment or reassessment of the patient. A review of two of the three history areas is sufficient for other services.

- DG: At least one specific item from two of the three history areas must be documented for a complete PFSH for the following categories of E/M services: office or other outpatient services, established patient; emergency department; domiciliary care, established patient; and home care, established patient.

- DG: At least one specific item from each of the three history areas must be documented for a complete PFSH for the following categories of E/M services: office or other outpatient services, new patient; hospital observation services; hospital inpatient services, initial care; consultations; comprehensive nursing facility assessments; domiciliary care, new patient; and home care, new patient.

B. Documentation of Examination

The levels of E/M services are based on four types of examination:

- *Problem Focused*—a limited examination of the affected body area or organ system.
- *Expanded Problem Focused*—a limited examination of the affected body area or organ system and any other symptomatic or related body area(s) or organ system(s).
- *Detailed*—an extended examination of the affected body area(s) or organ system(s) and any other symptomatic or related body area(s) or organ system(s).
- *Comprehensive*—a general multi-system examination, or complete examination of a single organ system and other symptomatic or related body area(s) or organ system(s).

These types of examinations have been defined for general multi-system and the following single organ systems:

- Cardiovascular
- Ears, Nose, Mouth and Throat
- Eyes
- Genitourinary (Female)
- Genitourinary (Male)
- Hematologic/Lymphatic/Immunologic

- Musculoskeletal
- Neurological
- Psychiatric
- Respiratory
- Skin

A general multi-system examination or a single organ system examination may be performed by any physician regardless of specialty. The type (general multi-system or single organ system) and content of examination are selected by the examining physician and are based upon clinical judgment, the patient's history, and the nature of the presenting problem(s).

The content and documentation requirements for each type and level of examination are summarized following and described in detail in tables beginning on page 571. In the tables, organ systems and body areas recognized by CPT for purposes of describing examinations are shown in the left column. The content, or individual elements, of the examination pertaining to that body area or organ system are identified by bullets (•) in the right column.

Parenthetical examples, "(eg, . . .)," have been used for clarification and to provide guidance regarding documentation. Documentation for each element must satisfy any numeric requirements (such as "Measurement of *any three of the following seven . . .*") included in the description of the element. Elements with multiple components but with no specific numeric requirement (such as "Examination of *liver* and *spleen*") require documentation of at least one component. It is possible for a given examination to be expanded beyond what is defined here. When that occurs, findings related to the additional systems and/or areas should be documented.

- DG: Specific abnormal and relevant negative findings of the examination of the affected or symptomatic body area(s) or organ system(s) should be documented. A notation of "abnormal" without elaboration is insufficient.
- DG: Abnormal or unexpected findings of the examination of any asymptomatic body area(s) or organ system(s) should be described.
- DG: A brief statement or notation indicating "negative" or "normal" is sufficient to document normal findings related to unaffected area(s) or asymptomatic organ system(s).

General Multi-System Examinations

General multi-system examinations are described in detail beginning on page 571. To qualify for a given level of multi-system examination, the following content and documentation requirements should be met:

- *Problem Focused Examination*—should include performance and documentation of one to five elements identified by a bullet (•) in one or more organ system(s) or body area(s).
- *Expanded Problem Focused Examination*—should include performance and documentation of at least six elements identified by a bullet (•) in one or more organ system(s) or body area(s).
- *Detailed Examination*—should include at least six organ systems or body areas. For each system/area selected, performance and documentation of at least two elements identified by a bullet (•) is expected. Alternatively, a de-

tailed examination may include performance and documentation of at least twelve elements identified by a bullet (•) in two or more organ systems or body areas.

- *Comprehensive Examination*—should include at least nine organ systems or body areas. For each system/area selected, all elements of the examination identified by a bullet (•) should be performed, unless specific directions limit the content of the examination. For each area/system, documentation of at least two elements identified by a bullet is expected.

Single Organ System Examinations

The single organ system examinations recognized by CPT are described in detail beginning on page 574. Variations among these examinations in the organ systems and body areas identified in the left columns and in the elements of the examinations described in the right columns reflect differing emphases among specialties. To qualify for a given level of single organ system examination, the following content and documentation requirements should be met:

- *Problem Focused Examination*—should include performance and documentation of one to five elements identified by a bullet (•), whether in a box with a shaded or unshaded border.
- *Expanded Problem Focused Examination*—should include performance and documentation of at least six elements identified by a bullet (•), whether in a box with a shaded or unshaded border.
- *Detailed Examination*—examinations other than the eye and psychiatric examinations should include performance and documentation of at least twelve elements identified by a bullet (•), whether in box with a shaded or unshaded border.

  Eye and psychiatric examinations should include the performance and documentation of at least nine elements identified by a bullet (•), whether in a box with a shaded or unshaded border.
- *Comprehensive Examination*—should include performance of all elements identified by a bullet (•), whether in a shaded or unshaded box. Documentation of every element in each box with a shaded border and at least one element in each box with an unshaded border is expected.

Content and Document Requirements

General Multi-System Examination

System/Body Area	Elements of Examination
Constitutional	• Measurement of **any three of the following seven** vital signs: 1) sitting or standing blood pressure, 2) supine blood pressure, 3) pulse rate and regularity, 4) respiration, 5) temperature, 6) height, 7) weight (may be measured and recorded by ancillary staff) • General appearance of patient (eg, development, nutrition, body habitus, deformities, attention to grooming)
Eyes	• Inspection of conjunctivae and lids • Examination of pupils and irises (eg, reaction to light and accommodation, size and symmetry) • Ophthalmoscopic examination of optic discs (eg, size, C/D ratio, appearance) and posterior segments (eg, vessel changes, exudates, hemorrhages)

Table continues on following page

General Multi-System Examination *Continued*

System/Body Area	Elements of Examination
Ears, Nose, Mouth and Throat	• External inspection of ears and nose (eg, overall appearance, scars, lesions, masses) • Otoscopic examination of external auditory canals and tympanic membranes • Assessment of hearing (eg, whispered voice, finger rub, tuning fork) • Inspection of nasal mucosa, septum and turbinates • Inspection of lips, teeth and gums • Examination of oropharynx: oral mucosa, salivary glands, hard and soft palates, tongue, tonsils and posterior pharynx
Neck	• Examination of neck (eg, masses, overall appearance, symmetry, tracheal position, crepitus) • Examination of thyroid (eg, enlargement, tenderness, mass)
Respiratory	• Assessment of respiratory effort (eg, intercostal retractions, use of accessory muscles, diaphragmatic movement) • Percussion of chest (eg, dullness, flatness, hyperresonance) • Palpation of chest (eg, tactile fremitus) • Auscultation of lungs (eg, breath sounds, adventitious sounds, rubs)
Cardiovascular	• Palpation of heart (eg, location, size, thrills) • Auscultation of heart with notation of abnormal sounds and murmurs Examination of: • carotid arteries (eg, pulse amplitude, bruits) • abdominal aorta (eg, size, bruits) • femoral arteries (eg, pulse amplitude, bruits) • pedal pulses (eg, pulse amplitude) • extremities for edema and/or varicosities
Chest (Breasts)	• Inspection of breasts (eg, symmetry, nipple discharge) • Palpation of breasts and axillae (eg, masses or lumps, tenderness)
Gastrointestinal (Abdomen)	• Examination of abdomen with notation of presence of masses or tender ness • Examination of liver and spleen • Examination for presence or absence of hernia • Examination (when indicated) of anus, perineum and rectum, including sphincter tone, presence of hemorrhoids, rectal masses • Obtain stool sample for occult blood test when indicated
Genitourinary	**MALE:** • Examination of the scrotal contents (eg, hydrocele, spermatocele, tenderness of cord, testicular mass) • Examination of the penis • Digital rectal examination of prostate gland (eg, size, symmetry, nodularity, tenderness) **FEMALE:** Pelvic examination (with or without specimen collection for smears and cultures), including • Examination of external genitalia (eg, general appearance, hair distribution, lesions) and vagina (eg, general appearance, estrogen effect, discharge, lesions, pelvic support, cystocele, rectocele) • Examination of urethra (eg, masses, tenderness, scarring) • Examination of bladder (eg, fullness, masses, tenderness) • Cervix (eg, general appearance, lesions, discharge) • Uterus (eg, size, contour, position, mobility, tenderness, consistency, descent or support) • Adnexa/parametria (eg, masses, tenderness, organomegaly, nodularity)
Lymphatic	Palpation of lymph nodes in **two or more** areas: • Neck • Axillae • Groin • Other

General Multi-System Examination *Continued*

System/Body Area	Elements of Examination
Musculoskeletal	• Examination of gait and station • Inspection and/or palpation of digits and nails (eg, clubbing, cyanosis, inflammatory conditions, petechiae, ischemia, infections, nodes) Examination of joints, bones and muscles of **one or more of the following six** areas: 1) head and neck; 2) spine, ribs and pelvis; 3) right upper extremity; 4) left upper extremity; 5) right lower extremity; and 6) left lower extremity. The examination of a given area includes: • Inspection and/or palpation with notation of presence of any misalignment, asymmetry, crepitation, defects, tenderness, masses, effusions • Assessment of range of motion with notation of any pain, crepitation or contracture • Assessment of stability with notation of any dislocation (luxation), subluxation or laxity • Assessment of muscle strength and tone (eg, flaccid, cog wheel, spastic) with notation of any atrophy or abnormal movements
Skin	• Inspection of skin and subcutaneous tissue (eg, rashes, lesions, ulcers) • Palpation of skin and subcutaneous tissue (eg, induration, subcutaneous nodules, tightening)
Neurologic	• Test cranial nerves with notation of any deficits • Examination of deep tendon reflexes with notation of pathological reflexes (eg, Babinski) • Examination of sensation (eg, by touch, pin, vibration, proprioception)
Psychiatric	• Description of patient's judgment and insight Brief assessment of mental status including: • orientation to time, place and person • recent and remote memory • mood and affect (eg, depression, anxiety, agitation)

CONTENT AND DOCUMENTATION REQUIREMENTS

Level of Exam	*Perform and Document:*
Problem Focused	**One to five** elements identified by a bullet.
Expanded Problem Focused	**At least six** elements identified by a bullet.
Detailed	**At least two** elements identified by a bullet **from each of six areas/systems** OR **at least twelve** elements identified by a bullet **in two or more areas/systems.**
Comprehensive	Perform **all elements** identified by a bullet in **at least nine** organ systems or body areas and document **at least two** elements identified by a bullet **from each of nine areas/systems.**

Cardiovascular Examination

System/Body Area	Elements of Examination
Constitutional	• Measurement of **any three of the following seven** vital signs: 1) sitting or standing blood pressure, 2) supine blood pressure, 3) pulse rate and regularity, 4) respiration, 5) temperature, 6) height, 7) weight (may be measured and recorded by ancillary staff) • General appearance of patient (eg, development, nutrition, body habitus, deformities, attention to grooming)
Head and Face	
Eyes	• Inspection of conjunctivae and lids (eg, xanthelasma)
Ears, Nose, Mouth and Throat	• Inspection of teeth, gums and palate • Inspection of oral mucosa with notation of presence of pallor or cyanosis
Neck	• Examination of jugular veins (eg, distension; a, v or cannon a waves) • Examination of thyroid (eg, enlargement, tenderness, mass)
Respiratory	• Assessment of respiratory effort (eg, intercostal retractions, use of accessory muscles, diaphragmatic movement) • Auscultation of lungs (eg, breath sounds, adventitious sounds, rubs)
Cardiovascular	• Palpation of heart (eg, location, size and forcefulness of the point of maximal impact; thrills; lifts; palpable S3 or S4) • Auscultation of heart including sounds, abnormal sounds and murmurs • Measurement of blood pressure in two or more extremities when indicated (eg, aortic dissection, coarctation) Examination of: • Carotid arteries (eg, waveform, pulse amplitude, bruits, apical-carotid delay) • Abdominal aorta (eg, size, bruits) • Femoral arteries (eg, pulse amplitude, bruits) • Pedal pulses (eg, pulse amplitude) • Extremities for peripheral edema and/or varicosities
Chest (Breasts)	
Gastrointestinal (Abdomen)	• Examination of abdomen with notation of presence of masses or tenderness • Examination of liver and spleen • Obtain stool sample for occult blood from patients who are being considered for thrombolytic or anticoagulant therapy
Genitourinary (Abdomen)	
Lymphatic	
Musculoskeletal	• Examination of the back with notation of kyphosis or scoliosis • Examination of gait with notation of ability to undergo exercise testing and/or participation in exercise programs • Assessment of muscle strength and tone (eg, flaccid, cog wheel, spastic) with notation of any atrophy and abnormal movements
Extremities	• Inspection and palpation of digits and nails (eg, clubbing, cyanosis, inflammation, petechiae, ischemia, infections, Osler's nodes)
Skin	• Inspection and/or palpation of skin and subcutaneous tissue (eg, stasis dermatitis, ulcers, scars, xanthomas)
Neurological/ Psychiatric	Brief assessment of mental status including • Orientation to time, place and person • Mood and affect (eg, depression, anxiety, agitation)

CONTENT AND DOCUMENTATION REQUIREMENTS

Level of Exam	*Perform and Document:*
Problem Focused	**One to five** elements identified by a bullet.
Expanded Problem Focused	**At least six** elements identified by a bullet.
Detailed	**At least twelve** elements identified by a bullet.
Comprehensive	Perform **all** elements identified by a bullet; document every element in each box with a shaded border and at least one element in each box with an unshaded border.

Ears, Nose and Throat Examination

System/Body Area	Elements of Examination
Constitutional	• Measurement of **any three of the following seven** vital signs: 1) sitting or standing blood pressure, 2) supine blood pressure, 3) pulse rate and regularity, 4) respiration, 5) temperature, 6) height, 7) weight (may be measured and recorded by ancillary staff) • General appearance of patient (eg, development, nutrition, body habitus, deformities, attention to grooming) • Assessment of ability to communicate (eg, use of sign language or other communication aids) and quality of voice
Head and Face	• Inspection of head and face (eg, overall appearance, scars, lesions and masses) • Palpation and/or percussion of face with notation of presence or absence of sinus tenderness • Examination of salivary glands • Assessment of facial strength
Eyes	• Test ocular motility including primary gaze alignment
Ears, Nose, Mouth and Throat	• Otoscopic examination of external auditory canals and tympanic membranes including pneumo-otoscopy with notation of mobility of membranes • Assessment of hearing with tuning forks and clinical speech reception thresholds (eg, whispered voice, finger rub) • External inspection of ears and nose (eg, overall appearance, scars, lesions and masses) • Inspection of nasal mucosa, septum and turbinates • Inspection of lips, teeth and gums • Examination of oropharynx: oral mucosa, hard and soft palates, tongue, tonsils and posterior pharynx (eg, asymmetry, lesions, hydration of mucosal surfaces) • Inspection of pharyngeal walls and pyriform sinuses (eg, pooling of saliva, asymmetry, lesions) • Examination by mirror of larynx including the condition of the epiglottis, false vocal cords, true vocal cords and mobility of larynx (use of mirror not required in children) • Examination by mirror of nasopharynx including appearance of the mucosa, adenoids, posterior choanae and eustachian tubes (use of mirror not required in children)
Neck	• Examination of neck (eg, masses, overall appearance, symmetry, tracheal position, crepitus) • Examination of thyroid (eg, enlargement, tenderness, mass)
Respiratory	• Inspection of chest including symmetry, expansion and/or assessment of respiratory effort (eg, intercostal retractions, use of accessory muscles, diaphragmatic movement) • Auscultation of lungs (eg, breath sounds, adventitious sounds, rubs)

Table continues on following page

Ears, Nose and Throat Examination *Continued*

System/Body Area	Elements of Examination
Cardiovascular	• Auscultation of heart with notation of abnormal sounds and murmurs • Examination of peripheral vascular system by observation (eg, swelling, varicosities) and palpation (eg, pulses, temperature, edema, tenderness)
Chest (Breasts)	
Gastrointestinal (Abdomen)	
Genitourinary	
Lymphatic	• Palpation of lymph nodes in neck, axillae, groin and/or other location
Musculoskeletal	
Extremities	
Skin	
Neurological/ Psychiatric	• Test cranial nerves with notation of any deficits Brief assessment of mental status including • Orientation to time, place and person • Mood and affect (eg, depression, anxiety, agitation)

CONTENT AND DOCUMENTATION REQUIREMENTS

Level of Exam	*Perform and Document:*
Problem Focused	**One to five** elements identified by a bullet.
Expanded Problem Focused	**At least six** elements identified by a bullet.
Detailed	**At least twelve** elements identified by a bullet.
Comprehensive	Perform **all** elements identified by a bullet; document every element in each box with a shaded border and at least one element in each box with an unshaded border.

Eye Examination

System/Body Area	Elements of Examination
Constitutional	
Head and Face	
Eyes	• Test visual acuity (does not include determination of refractive error) • Gross visual field testing by confrontation • Test ocular motility including primary gaze alignment • Inspection of bulbar and palpebral conjunctivae • Examination of ocular adnexae including lids (eg, ptosis or lagophthalmos), lacrimal glands, lacrimal drainage, orbits and preauricular lymph nodes • Examination of pupils and irises including shape, direct and consensual reaction (afferent pupil), size (eg, anisocoria) and morphology • Slit lamp examination of the corneas including epithelium, stroma, endothelium, and tear film • Slit lamp examination of the anterior chambers including depth, cells, and flare • Slit lamp examination of the lenses including clarity, anterior and posterior capsule, cortex, and nucleus • Measurement of intraocular pressures (except in children and patients with trauma or infectious disease)

Eye Examination *Continued*

System/Body Area	Elements of Examination
Eyes (*continued*)	Ophthalmoscopic examination through dilated pupils (unless contraindicated) of • Optic discs including size, C/D ratio, appearance (eg, atrophy, cupping, tumor elevation) and nerve fiber layer • Posterior segments including retina and vessels (eg, exudates and hemorrhages)
Ears, Nose, Mouth and Throat	
Neck	
Respiratory	
Cardiovascular	
Chest (Breasts)	
Gastrointestinal (Abdomen)	
Genitourinary	
Lymphatic	
Musculoskeletal	
Extremities	
Skin	
Neurological/ Psychiatric	Brief assessment of mental status including • Orientation to time, place and person • Mood and affect (eg, depression, anxiety, agitation)

CONTENT AND DOCUMENTATION REQUIREMENTS

Level of Exam	*Perform and Document:*
Problem Focused	**One to five** elements identified by a bullet.
Expanded Problem Focused	**At least six** elements identified by a bullet.
Detailed	**At least nine** elements identified by a bullet.
Comprehensive	Perform **all** elements identified by a bullet; document every element in each box with a shaded border and at least one element in each box with an unshaded border.

Genitourinary Examination

System/Body Area	Elements of Examination
Constitutional	• Measurement of **any three of the following seven** vital signs: 1) sitting or standing blood pressure, 2) supine blood pressure, 3) pulse rate and regularity, 4) respiration, 5) temperature, 6) height, 7) weight (may be measured and recorded by ancillary staff) • General appearance of patient (eg, development, nutrition, body habitus, deformities, attention to grooming)
Head and Face	
Eyes	
Ears, Nose, Mouth and Throat	

Table continues on following page

Genitourinary Examination *Continued*

System/Body Area	Elements of Examination
Neck	• Examination of neck (eg, masses, overall appearance, symmetry, tracheal position, crepitus) • Examination of thyroid (eg, enlargement, tenderness, mass)
Respiratory	• Assessment of respiratory effort (eg, intercostal retractions, use of accessory muscles, diaphragmatic movement) • Auscultation of lungs (eg, breath sounds, adventitious sounds, rubs)
Cardiovascular	• Auscultation of heart with notation of abnormal sounds and murmurs • Examination of peripheral vascular system by observation (eg, swelling, varicosities) and palpation (eg, pulses, temperature, edema, tenderness)
Chest (Breasts)	[See genitourinary (female).]
Gastrointestinal (Abdomen)	• Examination of abdomen with notation of presence of masses or tenderness • Examination for presence or absence of hernia • Examination of liver and spleen • Obtain stool sample for occult blood test when indicated
Genitourinary	**MALE:** • Inspection of anus and perineum Examination (with or without specimen collection for smears and cultures) of genitalia including: • Scrotum (eg, lesions, cysts, rashes) • Epididymides (eg, size, symmetry, masses) • Testes (eg, size, symmetry, masses) • Urethral meatus (eg, size, location, lesions, discharge) • Penis (eg, lesions, presence or absence of foreskin, foreskin retractability, plaque, masses, scarring, deformities) Digital rectal examination including: • Prostate gland (eg, size, symmetry, nodularity, tenderness) • Seminal vesicles (eg, symmetry, tenderness, masses, enlargement) • Sphincter tone, presence of hemorrhoids, rectal masses **FEMALE:** Includes **at least seven of the following** eleven elements identified by bullets: • Inspection and palpation of breasts (eg, masses or lumps, tenderness, symmetry, nipple discharge) • Digital rectal examination including sphincter tone, presence of hemorrhoids, rectal masses Pelvic examination (with or without specimen collection for smears and cultures) including: • External genitalia (eg, general appearance, hair distribution, lesions) • Urethral meatus (eg, size, location, lesions, prolapse) • Urethra (eg, masses, tenderness, scarring) • Bladder (eg, fullness, masses, tenderness) • Vagina (eg, general appearance, estrogen effect, discharge, lesions, pelvic support, cystocele, rectocele) • Cervix (eg, general appearance, lesions, discharge) • Uterus (eg, size, contour, position, mobility, tenderness, consistency, descent or support) • Adnexa/parametria (eg, masses, tenderness, organomegaly, nodularity) • Anus and perineum
Lymphatic	• Palpation of lymph nodes in neck, axillae, groin and/or other location
Musculoskeletal	
Extremities	
Skin	• Inspection and/or palpation of skin and subcutaneous tissue (eg, rashes, lesions, ulcers)
Neurological/ Psychiatric	Brief assessment of mental status including • Orientation (eg, time, place and person) and • Mood and affect (eg, depression, anxiety, agitation)

CONTENT AND DOCUMENTATION REQUIREMENTS

Level of Exam	*Perform and Document:*
Problem Focused	**One to five** elements identified by a bullet.
Expanded Problem Focused	**At least six** elements identified by a bullet.
Detailed	**At least twelve** elements identified by a bullet.
Comprehensive	Perform **all** elements identified by a bullet; document every element in each box with a shaded border and at least one element in each box with an unshaded border.

Hematologic/Lymphatic/Immunologic Examination

System/Body Area	Elements of Examination
Constitutional	• Measurement of **any three of the following seven** vital signs: 1) sitting or standing blood pressure, 2) supine blood pressure, 3) pulse rate and regularity, 4) respiration, 5) temperature, 6) height, 7) weight (may be measured and recorded by ancillary staff) • General appearance of patient (eg, development, nutrition, body habitus, deformities, attention to grooming)
Head and Face	• Palpation and/or percussion of face with notation of presence or absence of sinus tenderness
Eyes	• Inspection of conjunctivae and lids
Ears, Nose, Mouth and Throat	• Otoscopic examination of external auditory canals and tympanic membranes • Inspection of nasal mucosa, septum and turbinates • Inspection of teeth and gums • Examination of oropharynx (eg, oral mucosa, hard and soft palates, tongue, tonsils, posterior pharynx)
Neck	• Examination of neck (eg, masses, overall appearance, symmetry, tracheal position, crepitus) • Examination of thyroid (eg, enlargement, tenderness, mass)
Respiratory	• Assessment of respiratory effort (eg, intercostal retractions, use of accessory muscles, diaphragmatic movement) • Auscultation of lungs (eg, breath sounds, adventitious sounds, rubs)
Cardiovascular	• Auscultation of heart with notation of abnormal sounds and murmurs • Examination of peripheral vascular system by observation (eg, swelling, varicosities) and palpation (eg, pulses, temperature, edema, tenderness)
Chest (Breasts)	
Gastrointestinal (Abdomen)	• Examination of abdomen with notation of presence of masses or tenderness • Examination of liver and spleen
Genitourinary	
Lymphatic	• Palpation of lymph nodes in neck, axillae, groin, and/or other location
Musculoskeletal	
Extremities	• Inspection and palpation of digits and nails (eg, clubbing, cyanosis, inflammation, petechiae, ischemia, infections, nodes)
Skin	• Inspection and/or palpation of skin and subcutaneous tissue (eg, rashes, lesions, ulcers, ecchymoses, bruises)
Neurological/ Psychiatric	Brief assessment of mental status including • Orientation to time, place and person • Mood and affect (eg, depression, anxiety, agitation)

CONTENT AND DOCUMENTATION REQUIREMENTS

Level of Exam	*Perform and Document:*
Problem Focused	**One to five** elements identified by a bullet.
Expanded Problem Focused	**At least six** elements identified by a bullet.
Detailed	**At least twelve** elements identified by a bullet.
Comprehensive	Perform **all** elements identified by a bullet; document every element in each box with a shaded border and at least one element in each box with an unshaded border.

Musculoskeletal Examination

System/Body Area	Elements of Examination
Constitutional	• Measurement of **any three of the following seven** vital signs: 1) sitting or standing blood pressure, 2) supine blood pressure, 3) pulse rate and regularity, 4) respiration, 5) temperature, 6) height, 7) weight (may be measured and recorded by ancillary staff) • General appearance of patient (eg, development, nutrition, body habitus, deformities, attention to grooming)
Head and Face	
Eyes	
Ears, Nose, Mouth and Throat	
Neck	
Respiratory	
Cardiovascular	• Examination of peripheral vascular system by observation (eg, swelling, varicosities) and palpation (eg, pulses, temperature, edema, tenderness)
Chest (Breasts)	
Gastrointestinal (Abdomen)	
Genitourinary	
Lymphatic	• Palpation of lymph nodes in neck, axillae, groin and/or other location
Musculoskeletal	• Examination of gait and station Examination of joint(s), bone(s) and muscle(s)/ tendon(s) of **four of the following six** areas: 1) head and neck; 2) spine, ribs and pelvis; 3) right upper extremity; 4) left upper extremity; 5) right lower extremity; and 6) left lower extremity. The examination of a given area includes: • Inspection, percussion and/or palpation with notation of any misalignment, asymmetry, crepitation, defects, tenderness, masses or effusions • Assessment of range of motion with notation of any pain (eg, straight leg raising), crepitation or contracture • Assessment of stability with notation of any dislocation (luxation), subluxation or laxity • Assessment of muscle strength and tone (eg, flaccid, cog wheel, spastic) with notation of any atrophy or abnormal movements *Note:* For the comprehensive level of examination, all four of the elements identified by a bullet must be performed and documented for each of four anatomic areas. For the three lower levels of examination, each element is counted separately for each body area. For example, assessing range of motion in two extremities constitutes two elements.
Extremities	[See musculoskeletal and skin.]

Musculoskeletal Examination *Continued*

System/Body Area	Elements of Examination
Skin	• Inspection and/or palpation of skin and subcutaneous tissue (eg, scars, rashes, lesions, cafe-au-lait spots, ulcers) in **four of the following six** areas: 1) head and neck; 2) trunk; 3) right upper extremity; 4) left upper extremity; 5) right lower extremity; and 6) left lower extremity. *Note:* For the comprehensive level, the examination of all four anatomic areas must be performed and documented. For the three lower levels of examination, each body area is counted separately. For example, inspection and/or palpation of the skin and subcutaneous tissue of two extremities constitutes two elements.
Neurological/ Psychiatric	• Test coordination (eg, finger/nose, heel/ knee/shin, rapid alternating movements in the upper and lower extremities, evaluation of fine motor coordination in young children) • Examination of deep tendon reflexes and/or nerve stretch test with notation of pathological reflexes (eg, Babinski) • Examination of sensation (eg, by touch, pin, vibration, proprioception) Brief assessment of mental status including • Orientation to time, place and person • Mood and affect (eg, depression, anxiety, agitation)

CONTENT AND DOCUMENTATION REQUIREMENTS

Level of Exam	*Perform and Document:*
Problem Focused	**One to five** elements identified by a bullet.
Expanded Problem Focused	**At least six** elements identified by a bullet.
Detailed	**At least twelve** elements identified by a bullet.
Comprehensive	Perform **all** elements identified by a bullet; document every element in each box with a shaded border and at least one element in each box with an unshaded border.

Neurological Examination

System/Body Area	Elements of Examination
Constitutional	• Measurement of **any three of the following seven** vital signs: 1) sitting or standing blood pressure, 2) supine blood pressure, 3) pulse rate and regularity, 4) respiration, 5) temperature, 6) height, 7) weight (may be measured and recorded by ancillary staff) • General appearance of patient (eg, development, nutrition, body habitus, deformities, attention to grooming)
Head and Face	
Eyes	• Ophthalmoscopic examination of optic discs (eg, size, C/D ratio, appearance) and posterior segments (eg, vessel changes, exudates, hemorrhages)
Ears, Nose, Mouth and Throat	
Neck	
Respiratory	

Table continues on following page

Neurological Examination *Continued*

System/Body Area	Elements of Examination
Cardiovascular	• Examination of carotid arteries (eg, pulse amplitude, bruits) • Auscultation of heart with notation of abnormal sounds and murmurs • Examination of peripheral vascular system by observation (eg, swelling, varicosities) and palpation (eg, pulses, temperature, edema, tenderness)
Chest (Breasts)	
Gastrointestinal (Abdomen)	
Genitourinary	
Lymphatic	
Musculoskeletal	• Examination of gait and station Assessment of motor function including: • Muscle strength in upper and lower extremities • Muscle tone in upper and lower extremities (eg, flaccid, cog wheel, spastic) with notation of any atrophy or abnormal movements (eg, fasciculation, tardive dyskinesia)
Extremities	[See musculoskeletal.]
Skin	
Neurological	Evaluation of higher integrative functions including: • Orientation to time, place and person • Recent and remote memory • Attention span and concentration • Language (eg, naming objects, repeating phrases, spontaneous speech) • Fund of knowledge (eg, awareness of current events, past history, vocabulary) Test the following cranial nerves: • 2nd cranial nerve (eg, visual acuity, visual fields, fundi) • 3rd, 4th and 6th cranial nerves (eg, pupils, eye movements) • 5th cranial nerve (eg, facial sensation, corneal reflexes) • 7th cranial nerve (eg, facial symmetry, strength) • 8th cranial nerve (eg, hearing with tuning fork, whispered voice and/or finger rub) • 9th cranial nerve (eg, spontaneous or reflex palate movement) • 11th cranial nerve (eg, shoulder shrug strength) • 12th cranial nerve (eg, tongue protrusion) • Examination of sensation (eg, by touch, pin, vibration, proprioception) • Examination of deep tendon reflexes in upper and lower extremities with notation of pathological reflexes (eg, Babinski) • Test coordination (eg, finger/nose, heel/knee/shin, rapid alternating movements in the upper and lower extremities, evaluation of fine motor coordination in young children)
Psychiatric	

CONTENT AND DOCUMENTATION REQUIREMENTS

Level of Exam	*Perform and Document:*
Problem Focused	**One to five** elements identified by a bullet.
Expanded Problem Focused	**At least six** elements identified by a bullet.
Detailed	**At least twelve** elements identified by a bullet.
Comprehensive	Perform **all** elements identified by a bullet; document every element in each box with a shaded border and at least one element in each box with an unshaded border.

Psychiatric Examination

System/Body Area	Elements of Examination
Constitutional	• Measurement of **any three of the following seven** vital signs: 1) sitting or standing blood pressure, 2) supine blood pressure, 3) pulse rate and regularity, 4) respiration, 5) temperature, 6) height, 7) weight (may be measured and recorded by ancillary staff) • General appearance of patient (eg, development, nutrition, body habitus, deformities, attention to grooming)
Head and Face	
Eyes	
Ears, Nose, Mouth and Throat	
Neck	
Respiratory	
Cardiovascular	
Chest (Breasts)	
Gastrointestinal (Abdomen)	
Genitourinary	
Lymphatic	
Musculoskeletal	• Assessment of muscle strength and tone (eg, flaccid, cog wheel, spastic) with notation of any atrophy and abnormal movements • Examination of gait and station
Extremities	
Skin	
Neurological	
Psychiatric	• Description of speech including: rate; volume; articulation; coherence; and spontaneity with notation of abnormalities (eg, perseveration, paucity of language) • Description of thought processes including: rate of thoughts; content of thoughts (eg, logical vs. illogical, tangential); abstract reasoning; and computation • Description of associations (eg, loose, tangential, circumstantial, intact) • Description of abnormal or psychotic thoughts including: hallucinations; delusions; preoccupation with violence; homicidal or suicidal ideation; and obsessions • Description of the patient's judgment (eg, concerning everyday activities and social situations) and insight (eg, concerning psychiatric condition) Complete mental status examination including • Orientation to time, place and person • Recent and remote memory • Attention span and concentration • Language (eg, naming objects, repeating phrases) • Fund of knowledge (eg, awareness of current events, past history, vocabulary) • Mood and affect (eg, depression, anxiety, agitation, hypomania, lability)

CONTENT AND DOCUMENTATION REQUIREMENTS

Level of Exam	*Perform and Document:*
Problem Focused	**One to five** elements identified by a bullet.
Expanded Problem Focused	**At least six** elements identified by a bullet.
Detailed	**At least nine** elements identified by a bullet.

Comprehensive	Perform **all** elements identified by a bullet; document every element in each box with a shaded border and at least one element in each box with an unshaded border.

Respiratory Examination

System/Body Area	Elements of Examination
Constitutional	• Measurement of **any three of the following seven** vital signs: 1) sitting or standing blood pressure, 2) supine blood pressure, 3) pulse rate and regularity, 4) respiration, 5) temperature, 6) height, 7) weight (may be measured and recorded by ancillary staff) • General appearance of patient (eg, development, nutrition, body habitus, deformities, attention to grooming)
Head and Face	
Eyes	
Ears, Nose, Mouth and Throat	• Inspection of nasal mucosa, septum and turbinates • Inspection of teeth and gums • Examination of oropharynx (eg, oral mucosa, hard and soft palates, tongue, tonsils and posterior pharynx)
Neck	• Examination of neck (eg, masses, overall appearance, symmetry, tracheal position, crepitus) • Examination of thyroid (eg, enlargement, tenderness, mass) • Examination of jugular veins (eg, distension; a, v or cannon a waves)
Respiratory	• Inspection of chest with notation of symmetry and expansion • Assessment of respiratory effort (eg, intercostal retractions, use of accessory muscles, diaphragmatic movement) • Percussion of chest (eg, dullness, flatness, hyperresonance) • Palpation of chest (eg, tactile fremitus) • Auscultation of lungs (eg, breath sounds, adventitious sounds, rubs)
Cardiovascular	• Auscultation of heart including sounds, abnormal sounds and murmurs • Examination of peripheral vascular system by observation (eg, swelling, varicosities) and palpation (eg, pulses, temperature, edema, tenderness)
Chest (Breasts)	
Gastrointestinal (Abdomen)	• Examination of abdomen with notation of presence of masses or tenderness • Examination of liver and spleen
Genitourinary	
Lymphatic	• Palpation of lymph nodes in neck, axillae, groin and/or other location
Musculoskeletal	• Assessment of muscle strength and tone (eg, flaccid, cog wheel, spastic) with notation of any atrophy and abnormal movements • Examination of gait and station
Extremities	• Inspection and palpation of digits and nails (eg, clubbing, cyanosis, inflammation, petechiae, ischemia, infections, nodes)
Skin	• Inspection and/or palpation of skin and subcutaneous tissue (eg, rashes, lesions, ulcers)
Neurological/ Psychiatric	Brief assessment of mental status including • Orientation to time, place and person • Mood and affect (eg, depression, anxiety, agitation)

CONTENT AND DOCUMENTATION REQUIREMENTS

Level of Exam	*Perform and Document:*
Problem Focused	**One to five** elements identified by a bullet.
Expanded Problem Focused	**At least six** elements identified by a bullet.
Detailed	**At least twelve** elements identified by a bullet.

Comprehensive	Perform **all** elements identified by a bullet; document every element in each box with a shaded border and at least one element in each box with an unshaded border.

Skin Examination

System/Body Area	Elements of Examination
Constitutional	• Measurement of any **three of the following seven** vital signs: 1) sitting or standing blood pressure, 2) supine blood pressure, 3) pulse rate and regularity, 4) respiration, 5) temperature, 6) height, 7) weight (may be measured and recorded by ancillary staff) • General appearance of patient (eg, development, nutrition, body habitus, deformities, attention to grooming)
Head and Face	
Eyes	• Inspection of conjunctivae and lids
Ears, Nose, Mouth and Throat	• Inspection of lips, teeth and gums • Examination of oropharynx (eg, oral mucosa, hard and soft palates, tongue, tonsils, posterior pharynx)
Neck	• Examination of thyroid (eg, enlargement, tenderness, mass)
Respiratory	
Cardiovascular	• Examination of peripheral vascular system by observation (eg, swelling, varicosities) and palpation (eg, pulses, temperature, edema, tenderness)
Chest (Breasts)	
Gastrointestinal (Abdomen)	• Examination of liver and spleen • Examination of anus for condyloma and other lesions
Genitourinary	
Lymphatic	• Palpation of lymph nodes in neck, axillae, groin and/or other location
Musculoskeletal	
Extremities	• Inspection and palpation of digits and nails (eg, clubbing, cyanosis, inflammation, petechiae, ischemia, infections, nodes)
Skin	• Palpation of scalp and inspection of hair of scalp, eyebrows, face, chest, pubic area (when indicated) and extremities • Inspection and/or palpation of skin and subcutaneous tissue (eg, rashes, lesions, ulcers, susceptibility to and presence of photo damage) in **eight of the following ten** areas: • Head, including the face and • Neck • Chest, including breasts and axillae • Abdomen • Genitalia, groin, buttocks • Back • Right upper extremity • Left upper extremity • Right lower extremity • Left lower extremity *Note:* For the comprehensive level, the examination of at least eight anatomic areas must be performed and documented. For the three lower levels of examination, each body area is counted separately. For example, inspection and/or palpation of the skin and subcutaneous tissue of the right upper extremity and the left upper extremity constitutes two elements. • Inspection of eccrine and apocrine glands of skin and subcutaneous tissue with identification and location of any hyperhidrosis, chromhidroses or bromhidrosis
Neurological/ Psychiatric	Brief assessment of mental status including • Orientation to time, place and person • Mood and affect (eg, depression, anxiety, agitation)

CONTENT AND DOCUMENTATION REQUIREMENTS

Level of Exam	*Perform and Document:*
Problem Focused	**One to five** elements identified by a bullet.
Expanded Problem Focused	**At least six** elements identified by a bullet.
Detailed	**At least twelve** elements identified by a bullet.
Comprehensive	Perform **all** elements identified by a bullet; document every element in each box with a shaded border and at least one element in each box with an unshaded border.

C. Documentation of the Complexity of Medical Decision-Making

The levels of E/M services recognize four types of medical decision-making (straightforward, low complexity, moderate complexity and high complexity). Medical decision-making refers to the complexity of establishing a diagnosis and/or selecting a management option as measured by:

- the number of possible diagnoses and/or the number of management options that must be considered;
- the amount and/or complexity of medical records, diagnostic tests, and/or other information that must be obtained, reviewed and analyzed; and
- the risk of significant complications, morbidity and/or mortality, as well as comorbidities, associated with the patient's presenting problem(s), the diagnostic procedure(s) and/or the possible management options.

The following chart shows the progression of the elements required for each level of medical decision-making. To qualify for a given type of decision-making, **two of the three elements in the table must be either met or exceeded.**

Number of diagnoses or management options	Amount and/or complexity of data to be reviewed	Risk of complications and/or morbidity or mortality	Type of decision-making
Minimal	Minimal or None	Minimal	***Straight-forward***
Limited	Limited	Low	***Low Complexity***
Multiple	Moderate	Moderate	***Moderate Complexity***
Extensive	Extensive	High	***High Complexity***

Each of the elements of medical decision-making is described following.

Number of Diagnoses or Management Options

The number of possible diagnoses and/or the number of management options that must be considered is based on the number and types of problems addressed during the encounter, the complexity of establishing a diagnosis and the management decisions that are made by the physician.

Generally, decision-making with respect to a diagnosed problem is easier than that for an identified but undiagnosed problem. The number and type of diagnostic tests employed may be an indicator of the number of possible diagnoses. Problems which are improving or resolving are less complex than those which are worsening or failing to change as expected. The need to seek advice from others is another indicator of complexity of diagnostic or management problems.

- DG: For each encounter, an assessment, clinical impression, or diagnosis should be documented. It may be explicitly stated or implied in documented decisions regarding management plans and/or further evaluation.
  - For a presenting problem with an established diagnosis the record should reflect whether the problem is: a) improved, well controlled, resolving or resolved; or, b) inadequately controlled, worsening, or failing to change as expected.
  - For a presenting problem without an established diagnosis, the assessment or clinical impression may be stated in the form of differential diagnoses or as a "possible," "probable," or "rule out" (R/O) diagnosis.
- DG: The initiation of, or changes in, treatment should be documented. Treatment includes a wide range of management options including patient instructions, nursing instructions, therapies, and medications.
- DG: If referrals are made, consultations requested or advice sought, the record should indicate to whom or where the referral or consultation is made or from whom the advice is requested.

Amount and/or Complexity of Data to Be Reviewed

The amount and complexity of data to be reviewed is based on the types of diagnostic testing ordered or reviewed. A decision to obtain and review old medical records and/or obtain history from sources other than the patient increases the amount and complexity of data to be reviewed.

Discussion of contradictory or unexpected test results with the physician who performed or interpreted the test is an indication of the complexity of data being reviewed. On occasion the physician who ordered a test may personally review the image, tracing or specimen to supplement information from the physician who prepared the test report or interpretation; this is another indication of the complexity of data being reviewed.

- DG: If a diagnostic service (test or procedure) is ordered, planned, scheduled, or performed at the time of the E/M encounter, the type of service, eg, lab or x-ray, should be documented.
- DG: The review of lab, radiology and/or other diagnostic tests should be documented. A simple notation such as "WBC elevated" or "chest x-ray unremarkable" is acceptable. Alternatively, the review may be documented by initialing and dating the report containing the test results.
- DG: A decision to obtain old records or decision to obtain additional history from the family, caretaker or other source to supplement that obtained from the patient should be documented.
- DG: Relevant findings from the review of old records, and/or the receipt of additional history from the family, caretaker or other source to supplement that obtained from the patient should be documented. If there is no relevant information beyond that already obtained, that fact should be documented. A notation of "Old records reviewed" or "additional history obtained from family" without elaboration is insufficient.

- DG: The results of discussion of laboratory, radiology or other diagnostic tests with the physician who performed or interpreted the study should be documented.
- DG: The direct visualization and independent interpretation of an image, tracing or specimen previously or subsequently interpreted by another physician should be documented.

Risk of Significant Complications, Morbidity, and/or Mortality

The risk of significant complications, morbidity, and/or mortality is based on the risks associated with the presenting problem(s), the diagnostic procedure(s), and the possible management options.

- DG: Comorbidities/underlying diseases or other factors that increase the complexity of medical decision making by increasing the risk of complications, morbidity, and/or mortality should be documented.
- DG: If a surgical or invasive diagnostic procedure is ordered, planned or scheduled at the time of the E/M encounter, the type of procedure, eg, laparoscopy, should be documented.
- DG: If a surgical or invasive diagnostic procedure is performed at the time of the E/M encounter, the specific procedure should be documented.
- DG: The referral for or decision to perform a surgical or invasive diagnostic procedure on an urgent basis should be documented or implied.

The following table may be used to help determine whether the risk of significant complications, morbidity, and/or mortality is *minimal, low, moderate,* or *high*. Because the determination of risk is complex and not readily quantifiable, the table includes common clinical examples rather than absolute measures of risk. The assessment of risk of the presenting problem(s) is based on the risk related to the disease process anticipated between the present encounter and the next one. The assessment of risk of selecting diagnostic procedures and management options is based on the risk during and immediately following any procedures or treatment. **The highest level of risk in any one category (presenting problem(s), diagnostic procedure(s), or management options) determines the overall risk.**

Table of Risk

Level of Risk	Presenting Problem(s)	Diagnostic Procedure(s) Ordered	Management Options Selected
Minimal	• One self-limited or minor problem, eg, cold, insect bite, tinea corporis	• Laboratory tests requiring venipuncture • Chest x-rays • EKG/EEG • Urinalysis • Ultrasound, eg, echocardiography • KOH prep	• Rest • Gargles • Elastic bandages • Superficial dressings
Low	• Two or more self-limited or minor problems • One stable chronic illness, eg, well controlled hypertension, non-insulin dependent diabetes, cataract, BPH • Acute uncomplicated illness or injury, eg, cystitis, allergic rhinitis, simple sprain	• Physiologic tests not under stress, eg, pulmonary function tests • Non-cardiovascular imaging studies with contrast, eg, barium enema • Superficial needle biopsies • Clinical laboratory tests requiring arterial puncture • Skin biopsies	• Over-the-counter drugs • Minor surgery with no identified risk factors • Physical therapy • Occupational therapy • IV fluids without additives

Table of Risk *Continued*

Level of Risk	Presenting Problem(s)	Diagnostic Procedure(s) Ordered	Management Options Selected
Moderate	• One or more chronic illnesses with mild exacerbation, progression, or side effects of treatment • Two or more stable chronic illnesses • Undiagnosed new problem with uncertain prognosis, eg, lump in breast • Acute illness with systemic symptoms, eg, pyelonephritis, pneumonitis, colitis • Acute complicated injury, eg, head injury with brief loss of consciousness	• Physiologic tests under stress, eg, cardiac stress test, fetal contraction stress test • Diagnostic endoscopies with no identified risk factors • Deep needle or incisional biopsy • Cardiovascular imaging studies with contrast and no identified risk factors, eg, arteriogram, cardiac catheterization • Obtain fluid from body cavity, eg, lumbar puncture, thoracentesis, culdocentesis	• Minor surgery with identified risk factors • Elective major surgery (open, percutaneous or endoscopic) with no identified risk factors • Prescription drug management • Therapeutic nuclear medicine • IV fluids with additives • Closed treatment of fracture or dislocation without manipulation
High	• One or more chronic illnesses with severe exacerbation, progression, or side effects of treatment • Acute or chronic illnesses or injuries that pose a threat to life or bodily function, eg, multiple trauma, acute MI, pulmonary embolus, severe respiratory distress, progressive severe rheumatoid arthritis, psychiatric illness with potential threat to self or others, peritonitis, acute renal failure • An abrupt change in neurologic status, eg, seizure, TIA, weakness, sensory loss	• Cardiovascular imaging studies with contrast with identified risk factors • Cardiac electrophysiological tests • Diagnostic Endoscopies with identified risk factors • Discography	• Elective major surgery (open, percutaneous or endoscopic) with identified risk factors • Emergency major surgery (open, percutaneous or endoscopic) • Parenteral controlled substances • Drug therapy requiring intensive monitoring for toxicity • Decision not to resuscitate or to de-escalate care because of poor prognosis

D. Documentation of an Encounter Dominated by Counseling or Coordination of Care

In the case where counseling and/or coordination of care dominates (more than 50%) of the physician/patient and/or family encounter (face-to-face time in the office or other or outpatient setting, floor/unit time in the hospital or nursing facility), time is considered the key or controlling factor to qualify for a particular level of E/M services.

- DG: If the physician elects to report the level of service based on counseling and/or coordination of care, the total length of time of the encounter (face-to-face or floor time, as appropriate) should be documented and the record should describe the counseling and/or activities to coordinate care.

Glossary

A-mode: one-dimensional ultrasonic display reflecting the time it takes the sound wave to reach a structure and reflect back; maps the structure outline

abortion: termination of pregnancy

abscess: localized collection of pus that will result in the disintegration of tissue over time

abuse: misuse of substance

acquired: not genetic

actinotherapy: treatment of acne using ultraviolet rays

acute: of sudden onset and short duration

addiction: dependence on a drug

adrenal: glands, located on the top of the kidneys, that produce steroid hormones

AHA: American Hospital Association

AHIMA: American Health Information Management Association

allogenic: of the same species, but genetically different

allograft: tissue graft between individuals that are not of the same genotype

allotransplantation: transplantation between individuals that are not of the same genotype

amniocentesis: percutaneous aspiration of amniotic fluid

anastomosis: surgical connection of two tubular structures, such as two pieces of the intestine

aneurysm: sac of clotted blood or fluid formed in the circulatory system, ie, vein or artery

angiography: taking of x-ray films of vessels after injection of contrast material

angioplasty: surgical or percutaneous procedure on a vessel to dilate the vessel opening; used in the treatment of atherosclerotic disease

anomaly: abnormality

anomaloscope: instrument used to test color vision

anoscopy: procedure that uses a scope to examine the anus

antepartum: before childbirth

anterior (ventral): in front of

anterior segment: those parts of the eye in the front of and including the lens, orbit, extraocular muscles, and eyelid

anteroposterior: from front to back

antrotomy: cutting through the antrum wall to make an opening in the sinus

antrum: maxillary sinus

aortography: radiographic recording of the aorta

apexcardiography: recording of the movement of the chest wall

APGs (Ambulatory Patient Groups): a patient classification that provides a payment system for outpatients

aphakia: absence of the lens of the eye

apicectomy: excision of a portion of the temporal bone

Appendix A: located near the back of the CPT manual and lists all 30 modifiers with complete explanations for use

Appendix B: located near the back of the CPT manual and contains a complete list of additions, deletions, and revisions from previous editions

arteriovenous fistula: direct communication (passage) between an artery and vein

artery: vessel that carries oxygenated blood from the heart to body tissues

arthrodesis: surgical immobilization of a joint

arthrography: radiographic recording of joint

arthroplasty: reshaping or reconstructing a joint

aspiration: use of a needle and a syringe to withdraw fluid

assignment: Medicare's payment for the service, which participating physicians agree to accept as payment in full

astigmatism: condition in which the refractive surfaces of the eye are unequal

asymptomatic: not showing any of the typical symptoms of a disease or condition

atrium: chamber in the upper part of the heart

attending physician: physician with the primary responsibility for care of the patient

audi-: prefix meaning hearing

audiometry: hearing testing

aur-: prefix meaning ear

aural atresia: congenital absence of the external auditory canal

autogenous, autologous: from one's self

axillary nodes: lymph nodes located in the armpit

B-scan: two-dimensional display of tissues and organs

barium enema: radiographic contrast medium-enhanced examination of the colon

benign: not progressive or recurrent

benign hypertension: hypertensive condition with a continuous, mild blood pressure elevation

bifocal: two focuses in eyeglasses, one usually for

close work and the other for improvement of distance vision
bilateral: occurring on two sides
biofeedback: process of giving a person self information
biometry: application of a statistical measure to a biologic fact
biopsy: removal of a small piece of living tissue for diagnostic purposes
blephar/o-: prefix meaning eyelid
brachytherapy: therapy using radioactive sources that are placed inside the body
bronchography: radiographic recording of the lungs
bronchoscopy: inspection of the bronchial tree using a bronchoscope
bulbocavernosus: muscle that constricts the vagina in a female and the urethra in a male
bulbourethral gland: rounded mass of the urethra
bypass: to go around
calculus: concretion of mineral salts, also called a stone
calycoplasty: surgical reconstruction of a recess of the renal pelvis
calyx: recess of the renal pelvis
cannulation: insertion of a tube into a duct or cavity
cardiopulmonary: refers to the heart and lungs
cardiopulmonary bypass: blood bypasses the heart through a heart-lung machine during open heart surgery
cardioversion: electrical shock to the heart to restore normal rhythm
cardioverter-defibrillator: surgically placed device directs an electrical current shock to the heart to restore rhythm
cataract: opaque covering on or in the lens
catheter: tube placed into the body to put fluid in or take fluid out
caudal: same as inferior; also known as caudad; away from the head, or the lower part of the body
cavernosa-corpus spongiosum shunt: creation of a connection between a cavity of the penis and the urethra
cavernosa-glans penis fistulization: creation of a connection between a cavity of the penis and the glans penis, which overlaps the penis cavity
cavernosa-saphenous vein shunt: creation of a connection between the cavity of the penis and a vein
cavernosography: radiographic recording of a cavity, eg, pulmonary cavity or the main part of the penis
cavernosometry: measurement of the pressure in a cavity, ie, penis
-centesis: suffix meaning puncture of a cavity
central nervous system: brain and spinal cord
cervical: pertaining to the neck or cervix of the uterus
cervix uteri: rounded, cone-shaped neck of the uterus, part of it protruding into the vagina
cesarean: surgical opening through abdominal wall for delivery
CF (conversion factor): national dollar amount that is applied to all services paid on the Medicare Fee Schedule basis
cholangiography: radiographic recording of the bile ducts
cholangiopancreatography (ERCP): radiographic recording of the biliary system or pancreas
chole-: prefix meaning bile
cholecystectomy: surgical removal of the gallbladder
cholecystoenterostomy: creation of a connection between the gallbladder and intestine
cholecystography: radiographic recording of the gallbladder
chordee: condition resulting in the penis being bent downward
chorionic villus sampling: biopsy of the outermost part of the placenta
Cloquet's node: also called a gland; it is the highest of the deep groin lymph nodes
closed treatment: fracture site that is not surgically opened and visualized
colonoscopy: fibroscopic examination of the entire colon that may include part of the terminal ileum
colostomy: artificial opening between the colon and the abdominal wall
combination code: single five-digit code used to identify etiology and manifestations of a disease
communicable: disease that can be transmitted from one person to another or one species to another
comparative conditions: patient conditions that are documented as "either/or" in the patient record
computed axial tomography (CAT or CT): procedure by which selected planes of tissue are pinpointed through computer enhancement, and images may be reconstructed by analysis of variance in absorption of the tissue
concurrent care: provision of similar services (eg, hospital visits) to the same patient by more than one physician on the same day. Each physician provides services for a separate condition, not reasonably expected to be managed by the attending physician. When concurrent care is provided, the diagnosis must reflect the medical necessity of different specialties.
congenital: existing from birth
conjunctive: lining of the eyelids and covering of the sclera
consultation: includes those services rendered by a physician whose opinion or advice is requested by another physician or agency concerning the evaluation and/or treatment of a patient; a consultant is not an attending physician
contralateral: affecting the opposite side

cor/o-: prefix meaning pupil
cordocentesis: procedure to obtain a fetal blood sample; also called a percutaneous umbilical blood sampling
corneosclera: cornea and sclerea of the eye
corpora cavernosa: the two cavities of the penis
corpus uteri: uterus
counseling: discussion with a patient and/or family concerning one or more of the following areas: diagnostic results, impressions, and/or recommended diagnostic studies; prognosis; risks and benefits of treatment; instructions for treatment; importance of compliance with treatment; risk factor reduction; and patient and family education
CPT: Current Procedural Terminology, a coding system developed by the American Medical Association (AMA) to convert widely accepted, uniform descriptions of medical, surgical, and diagnostic services rendered by health care providers into five-digit numerical codes.
cranium: that part of the skeleton that encloses the brain
critical care: care of critically ill patients in medical emergencies that requires the constant attendance of the physician (eg, cardiac arrest, shock, bleeding, respiratory failure); critical care is usually, but not always, given in a critical care area, such as the coronary care unit (CCU) or the intensive care unit (ICU)
Crohn's disease: regional enteritis
cryosurgery: destruction of lesions using extreme cold
curettage: scraping of a cavity using a spoon-shaped instrument
cycl/o-: prefix meaning ciliary body or eye muscle
cyst: closed sac containing matter or fluid
cystic hygroma: congenital deformity or benign tumor of the lymphatic system
cystocele: herniation of the bladder into the vagina
cystography: radiographic recording of the urinary bladder
cystolithectomy: removal of a calculus (stone) from the urinary bladder
cystolithotomy: cystolithectomy
cystometrogram (CMG): measurement of the pressures and capacity of the urinary bladder
cystoplasty: surgical reconstruction of the bladder
cystorrhaphy: suture of the bladder
cystoscopy: use of a scope to view the bladder
cystostomy: surgical creation of an opening into the bladder
cystotomy: incision into the bladder
cystourethroplasty: surgical reconstruction of the bladder and urethra
cystourethroscopy: use of a scope to view the bladder and urethra
cytopathology: study of the diseases of cells
dacry/o-: prefix meaning tear/tear duct
dacryocyst/o-: prefix meaning pertaining to the lacrimal sac
dacryocystography: radiographic recording of the lacrimal sac or tear duct sac
debridement: cleansing of or removing dead tissue from a wound
delivery: childbirth
dermis: second layer of skin holding blood vessels, nerve endings, sweat glands, and hair follicles
destruction: killing of tissue, possible by electrocautery, laser, chemical, or other means
DHHS: Department of Health and Human Services
diaphragm: muscular wall that separates the thoracic and abdominal cavities
diaphragmatic hernia: hernia of the diaphragm
dilation: expansion (of the cervix)
diskography: radiographic recording of an intervertebral joint
dislocation: placement in a location other than the original location
distal: farther from the point of attachment or origin
Doppler: ultrasonic measure of blood movement
dosimetry: scientific calculation of radiation emitted from various radioactive sources
drainage: free flow or withdrawal of fluids from a wound or cavity
DRGs (Diagnosis-Related Groups): a disease classification system that relates the type of inpatients a hospital treats (case mix) to the costs incurred by the hospital
dual chamber pacemaker: electrodes of the pacemaker are placed in both the atria and the ventricles of the heart
duodenography: radiographic recording of the duodenum or first part of the small intestine
ear, parts of the external: auricle, pinna, external acoustic, and meatus
ear, parts of the inner: vestibule, semicircular canals, and cochlea
ear, parts of the middle: malleus, incus, and stapes
ECG: *see* electrocardiogram
echocardiography: radiographic recording of the heart or heart walls or surrounding tissues
echoencephalography: ultrasound of the brain
echography: ultrasound procedure in which sound waves are bounced off an internal organ and the resulting image is recorded
-ectomy: suffix meaning removal of part or all of an organ of the body
ectopic: pregnancy outside the uterus (ie, in the fallopian tube)
EEG: *see* electroencephalogram

electrocardiogram (ECG): written record of the electrical action of the heart
electrocochleography: test to measure the eighth cranial nerve (hearing test)
electrode: lead attached to a generator that carries the electric current from the generator to the atria or ventricles
electrodesiccation: destruction of a lesion by the use of electrical current radiated through a needle
electroencephalogram (EEG): written record of the electrical activity of the brain
electromyogram (EMG): written record of the electrical activity of the skeletal muscles
electromyography (EMG): recording of the electrical impulses of muscles
electro-oculogram (EOG): written record of the electrical activity of the eye
embolectomy: removal of blockage (embolism) from vessels
embolism: blockage of a blood vessel by a blood clot or other matter that has moved from another area of the body through the circulatory system
emergency care services: services that are provided by the physician in the emergency department for unplanned patient encounters; no distinction is made between new and established patients who are seen in the emergency department
encephalography: radiographic recording of the subarachnoid space and ventricles of the brain
endarterectomy: incision into an artery to remove the inner lining to remove disease or blockage
endomyocardial: pertaining to the inner and middle layers of the heart
endopyelotomy: procedure of the bladder and ureters with insertion of a stent
endoscopy: inspection of body organs or cavities using a lighted scope that may be placed through an existing opening or through a small incision
enterocystoplasty: surgical reconstruction of the small intestine after the removal of a cyst and usually including a bowel anastomosis
enucleation: removal of an organ(s) of a body cavity
epidermis: outer layer of skin
epididymectomy: surgical removal of the epididymis
epididymis: tube located on the top of the testes that stores sperm
epididymovasostomy: creation of a new connection between the vas deferens and epididymis
epididymography: radiographic recording of the epididymis
ESRD: end-stage renal disease
established patient: patient who has received professional services from the physician or another physician of the same specialty in the same group within the past 3 years
etiology: study of causes of diseases
evisceration: pulling the viscera outside the body through an incision
excision: cutting or taking away (in reference to lesion removal, it is full-thickness removal of a lesion that may include simple closure)
excisional: removal of an entire lesion for biopsy
Exclusive Provider Organization (EPO): similar to a Health Maintenance Organization except that the providers of the services are not prepaid, but rather are paid on a fee-for-service basis
exenteration: removal of an organ all in one piece
exostosis: bony growth
exstrophy: condition in which an organ is turned inside out
Federal Register: official publication of all "Presidential Documents," "Rules and Regulations," "Proposed Rules," and "Notices"; government-instituted national changes are published in the *Federal Register*
fenestration: creation of a new opening on the inner wall of the middle ear
fimbrioplasty: surgical repair of the fringe of the uterine tube
fistula: abnormal opening from one area to another area or to outside the body
fluoroscopy: procedure for viewing the interior of the body using x-rays and projecting the image onto a television screen
fracture: break in a bone
fulguration: use of electrical current to destroy tissue
fundoplasty: repair of the bottom on an organ or muscle
gastro-: prefix meaning stomach
gastrointestinal: pertaining to the stomach and intestine
gastroplasty: operation on the stomach for repair or reconfiguration
gastrostomy: artificial opening between the stomach and the abdominal wall
gloss-: prefix meaning tongue
gonioscopy: use of a scope to examine the angles of the eye
group practice model: an organization of physicians who contract with a Health Maintenance Organization to provide services to the enrollees of the HMO
grouper: computer used to input the principal diagnosis and other critical information about a patient and then provide the correct DRG code
Guidelines: provide specific instructions about coding for each section; the Guidelines contain definitions of terms, applicable modifiers, explanation of notes, subsection information, unlisted services, special reports information, and clinical examples
HCFA: Health Care Financing Administration

Health Maintenance Organization (HMO): a health care delivery system in which an enrollee is assigned a primary care physician who manages all the health care needs of the enrollee
hemodialysis: cleansing of the blood outside the body
hepat-: prefix meaning liver
hepatography: radiographic recording of the liver
hernia: organ or tissue protruding through the wall or cavity that usually contains it
histology: study of minute structures, composition, and function of tissues
Hodgkin's disease: malignant lymphoma
hydrocele: sac of fluid
hypertension, uncontrolled: untreated hypertension or hypertension that is not responding to the therapeutic regimen
hypertensive heart disease: secondary effects on the heart of prolonged, sustained systemic hypertension; the heart has to work against greatly increased resistance, causing increased blood pressure
hypogastric: lowest middle abdominal area
hyposensitization: decreased sensitivity
hypospadias: congenital deformity of the urethra in which the urethral opening is on the underside of the penis rather than the end
hypothermia: decreased body temperature
hysterectomy: surgical removal of the uterus
hysterorrhaphy: suturing of the uterus
hysterosalpingography: radiographic recording of the uterine cavity and fallopian tubes
hysteroscopy: visualization of the canal of the uterine cervix and cavity of the uterus using a scope placed through the vagina
hysterotomy: incision into the uterus
ileostomy: artificial opening between the ileum and the abdominal wall
imbrication: overlapping
immunotherapy: therapy to increase immunity
incarcerated: regarding hernias, a constricted, irreducible hernia that may cause obstruction of an intestine
incision: surgically cutting into
incision and drainage: to cut and withdraw fluid
incisional: *see* incision
Individual Practice Association (IPA): an organization of physicians who provide services for a set fee. Health Maintenance Organizations often contract with the IPA for services to their enrollees.
infectious disease carrier: person who has a communicable disease
infectious disease contact: encounter with a person who has a disease that can be communicated or transmitted
inferior: away from the head or the lower part of the body; also known as caudad or caudal
inguinofemoral: term that refers to the groin and thigh
injection: forcing of a fluid into a vessel or cavity
in situ: malignancy that is within the original site of development
internal/external fixation: application of pins, wires, screws, and so on to immobilize; these can be placed externally or internally
intramuscular: into a muscle
intravenous: into a vein
intravenous pyelography (IVP): radiographic recording of the urinary system
introitus: opening or entrance to the vagina from the uterus
iontophoresis: introduction of ions into the body
ischemia: deficient blood supply due to obstruction of the circulatory system
isthmus: connection of two regions or structures
isthmus, thyroid: tissue connection between right and left thyroid lobes
isthmusectomy: surgical removal of the isthmus
italicized code: an ICD-9-CM code that can never be sequenced as the principal diagnosis
jejunostomy: artificial opening between the jejunum and the abdominal wall
jugular nodes: lymph nodes located next to the large vein in the neck
kerat/o-: prefix meaning cornea
keratoplasty: surgical repair of the cornea
Kock pouch: surgical creation of a urinary bladder from a segment of the ileum
labyrinth: inner connecting cavities, such as the internal ear
laminectomy: surgical excision of the lamina
laparoscopy: exploration of the abdomen and pelvic cavities using a scope placed through a small incision in the abdominal wall
laryngo-: prefix meaning larynx
laryngography: radiographic recording of the larynx
late effect: residual effect (condition produced) after the acute phase of an illness or injury has terminated
lateral: away from the midline of the body (to the side)
lesion: abnormal or altered tissue, ie, wound, cyst, abscess, or boil
ligation: binding or tying off, as in constricting blood flow of a vessel or binding fallopian tubes for sterilization
litholapaxy: lithotripsy
lithotomy: incision into an organ or a duct for the purpose of removing a stone
lithotripsy: crushing of a gallbladder or urinary bladder stone followed by irrigation to wash the fragment out
lobectomy: excision of a lobe of the lung
lymph node: station along the lymphatic system

lymphadenectomy: excision of a lymph node(s)
lymphadenitis: inflammation of a lymph node
lymphangiography: radiographic recording of the lymphatic vessels and nodes
lymphangiotomy: incision into a lymphatic vessel
lysis: releasing
M-mode: one-dimensional display of movement of structures
MAAC (Maximum Actual Allowable Charge): limitation on the total amount that can be charged by physicians who are not participants in Medicare
magnetic resonance imaging (MRI): procedure that uses nonionizing radiation to view the body in a cross-sectional view
malignancy: used in reference to a cancerous tumor
malignant: used to describe a cancerous tumor that grows worse over time
malignant hypertension: accelerated, severe form of hypertension, manifested by headaches, blurred vision, dyspnea, and uremia; usually causes permanent organ damage
mammography: radiographic recording of the breasts
Managed Care Organization (MCO): a group that is responsible for the health care services offered to an enrolled group of persons
manifestation: sign of a disease
manipulation or reduction: words used interchangeably to mean the attempted restoration of a fracture or joint dislocation to its normal anatomic position
marsupialization: surgical procedure that creates an exterior pouch from an internal abscess
mast-: prefix meaning breast
mastoid-: prefix meaning posterior temporal bone
MDC (Major Diagnostic Categories): the division of all principal diagnoses into 25 mutually exclusive principal diagnosis areas within the DRG system
meatotomy: surgical enlargement of the opening of the urinary meatus
medial: toward the midline of the body
mediastinoscopy: use of an endoscope inserted through a small incision to view the mediastinum
mediastinotomy: cutting into the mediastinum
mediastinum: that area between the lungs that contains the heart, aorta, trachea, lymph nodes, thymus gland, esophagus, and bronchial tubes
Medicare risk HMO: a Medicare-funded alternative to the standard Medicare supplemental coverage
MEI (Medicare Economic Index): government-mandated index that ties increases in the Medicare prevailing charges to economic indicators
MeV: megaelectron volt
MFS (Medicare Fee Schedule): schedule that listed the allowable charges for Medicare services; was replaced by the Medicare reasonable charge payment system
modality: treatment method
modifiers: two- or five-digit numbers added to CPT codes to supply more specific information about the services provided to the patient
monofocal: eyeglasses with one vision correction
morbidity: condition of being diseased or morbid
morphology: study of neoplasms
mortality: death
MSLT: multiple sleep latency testing
multiple coding: use of more than one code to identify both etiology and manifestation of a disease, as contrasted with combination coding
MVPS (Medical Volume Performance Standards): government's estimate of how much growth is appropriate for nationwide physician expenditures paid by the Part B Medicare program
myasthenia gravis: syndrome characterized by muscle weakness
myelography: radiographic recording of the subarachnoid space of the spine
myocardial infarction (MI): necrosis of the myocardium resulting from interrupted blood supply
myring-: prefix meaning eardrum
nasopharyngoscopy: use of a scope to visualize the nose and pharynx
NCPAP: nasal continuous positive airway pressure
NEC: not elsewhere classified
neoplasm: new tumor growth that can be benign or malignant
nephrectomy, paraperitoneal: kidney transplant
nephro-: prefix meaning kidney
nephrocutaneous fistula: a channel from the kidney to the skin
nephrolithotomy: removal of a kidney stone through an incision made into the kidney
nephrorrhaphy: suturing of the kidney
nephrostolithotomy: creation of an artificial channel to the kidney
nephrostolithotomy, percutaneous: procedure to establish an artificial channel between the skin and the kidney
nephrostomy: creation of a channel into the renal pelvis of the kidney
nephrostomy, percutaneous: creation of a channel from the skin to the renal pelvis
nephrotomy: incision into the kidney
new patient: patient who has not received any professional services from the physician or another physician of the same specialty in the same group within the past 3 years
NOS: not otherwise specified
nystagmus: rapid involuntary eye movements
OBRA (Omnibus Budget Reconciliation Act of 1989): act that established new rules for Medicare reimbursement

ocul/o-: prefix meaning eye
ocular adnexa: orbit, extraocular muscles, and eyelid
Official Coding and Reporting Guidelines: rules of coding diagnosis codes (ICD-9-CM) published by the Editorial Advisory Board of Coding Clinic
omentum: peritoneal connection between the stomach and other internal organs
oophor-: prefix meaning ovary
oophorectomy: surgical removal of the ovary(ies)
opacification: area that has become opaque (milky)
open treatment: fracture site that is surgically opened and visualized
ophthalmodynamometry: test of the blood pressure of the eye
ophthalmology: body of knowledge regarding the eyes
optokinetic: movement of the eyes to objects moving in the visual field
orchiectomy: castration
orchiopexy: surgical procedure to release undescended testis
orthoptic: corrective; in the correct place
ostomy: artificial opening
oto-: prefix meaning ear
-otomy: suffix meaning incision into
outpatient: a patient who receives services in an ambulatory health care facility and is currently not an inpatient
overdose: excessive dose
oviduct: fallopian tube
pacemaker: electrical device that controls the beating of the heart by electrical impulses
paraesophageal hiatus hernia: hernia that is near the esophagus
parathyroid: produces a hormone to mobilize calcium from the bones to the blood
paring: removal of thin layers of skin by peeling or scraping
Part A: Medicare's Hospital Insurance; covers hospital/facility care
Part B: Medicare's Supplemental Medical Insurance; covers physician services and durable medical equipment that are not paid for under Part A
participating provider program: Medicare providers who have agreed in advance to accept assignment on all Medicare claims
pelviolithotomy: pyeloplasty
penoscrotal: referring to the penis and scrotum
percutaneous: through the skin
percutaneous skeletal fixation: considered neither open nor closed; the fracture is not visualized, but fixation is placed across the fracture site under x-ray imaging
pericarditis: swelling of the sac surrounding the great vessels and the heart
pericardium: membranous sac enclosing the heart and ends of the great vessels
perineal approach: surgical approach in the area between the thighs
perinephric cyst: cyst in the tissue around the kidney
perineum: area between the vulva and anus; also known as the pelvic floor
peripheral nerves: 12 pairs of cranial nerves, 31 pairs of spinal nerves, and autonomic nervous system; connects peripheral receptors to the brain and spinal cord
perirenal: around the kidney
peritoneal: within the lining of the abdominal cavity
peritoneoscopy: visualization of the abdominal cavity using one scope placed through a small incision in the abdominal wall and another scope placed in the vagina
perivesical: around the bladder
perivisceral: around an organ
phlebotomy: cutting into a vein
phonocardiogram: recording of heart sounds
photochemotherapy: treatment by means of drugs that react to ultraviolet radiation or sunlight
physics: scientific study of energy
-plasty: suffix meaning technique involving molding or surgically forming
plethysmography: determining the changes in volume of an organ part or body
pleura: covering of the lungs and thoracic cavity that is moistened with serous fluid to reduce friction during respiratory movements of the lungs
pneumo-: prefix meaning lung or air
pneumoplethysmography: determining the changes in the volume of the lung
polyp: tumor on a pedicle that bleeds easily and may become malignant
posterior (dorsal): in back of
posterior segment: those parts of the eye behind the lens
posteroanterior: from back to front
postpartum: after childbirth
Preferred Provider Organization (PPO): a group of providers who form a network and who have agreed to provide services to enrollees at a discounted rate
priapism: painful condition in which the penis is consistently erect
primary site: site of origin or where the tumor originated
principal diagnosis: defined in the Uniform Hospital Discharge Data Set (UHDDS) as "that condition established after study to be chiefly responsible for occasioning the admission of the patient to the hospital for care"; the principal diagnosis is sequenced first

proctosigmoidoscopy: fibroscopic examination of the sigmoid colon and rectum

prognosis: probable outcome of an illness

prophylactic: substance or agent that offers some protection from disease

PROs (Peer Review Organizations): group established to review hospital admission and care

prostatotomy: incision into the prostate

PSRO (Professional Standards Review Organization): voluntary physicians' organization designed to monitor the necessity of hospital admissions, treatment costs, and medical records of hospitals

punch: use of small hollow instrument to puncture a lesion

pyelo-: prefix meaning renal pelvis

pyelocutaneous: from the renal pelvis to the skin

pyelography: radiographic recording of the kidneys, renal pelvis, ureters, and bladder

pyelolithotomy: surgical removal of a kidney stone from the renal pelvis

pyeloplasty: surgical reconstruction of the renal pelvis

pyeloscopy: viewing of the renal pelvis using a fluoroscope after injection of contrast material

pyelostolithotomy: removal of a kidney stone and establishment of a stoma

pyelostomy: surgical creation of a temporary diversion around the ureter

pyelotomy: incision into the renal pelvis

pyloroplasty: incision and repair of the pyloric channel

qualitative: measuring the presence or absence of

quantitative: measuring the presence or absence and amount of

radiation oncology: branch of medicine concerned with the application of radiation to a tumor site for treatment (destruction) of cancerous tumors

radiograph: film on which an image is produced through exposure to x-radiation

radiologist: physician who specializes in the use of radioactive materials in the diagnosis and treatment of diseases and illnesses

radiology: branch of medicine concerned with the use of radioactive substances for diagnosis and therapy

RBRVS (Resource-Based Relative Value Scale): scale designed to decrease Medicare expenditures, redistribute physician payment, and ensure quality health care at a reasonable rate

real time: two-dimensional display of both the structures and the motion of tissues and organs

reanastomosis: reconnection of a previous connection between two places, organs, or spaces

rectocele: herniation of the rectal wall through the posterior wall of the vagina

reducible: able to be corrected or put back into a normal position

referral: transfer of the total or a specific portion of care of a patient from one physician to another that does not constitute a consultation

renal pelvis: funnel-shaped sac in the kidney where urine is received

repair: to remedy, replace, or heal (in the Integumentary subsection pertains to suturing a wound)

residual: that which is left behind or remains

resource intensity: refers to the relative volume and type of diagnostic, therapeutic, and bed services used in the management of a particular illness

retrograde: moving backward or against the usual direction of flow

retroperitoneal: behind the sac holding the abdominal organs and viscera (peritoneum)

rhino-: prefix meaning nose

-rrhaphy: suffix meaning suturing

rubric: heading used as a direction or explanation as to what follows and the way in which the information is to be used. In ICD-9-CM coding, the rubric is the three-digit code that precedes the fourth- and fifth-digit codes

rule of nines: rule used to estimate burned body surface in burn patients

RUQ: right upper quadrant

RVU (Relative Value Unit): unit value that has been assigned for each service

staff model: a Health Maintenance Organization that directly employs the physicians who provide services to enrollees

salpingectomy: surgical removal of the uterine tube

salpingo-: prefix meaning tube

salpingostomy: creation of a fistula into the uterine tube

scan: mapping of emissions of radioactive substances after they have been introduced into the body; the density can determine normal or abnormal conditions

sclera: outer covering of the eye

secondary site: place to which a malignant tumor has spread, metastatic site

sections: six major areas into which all CPT codes and descriptions are categorized

"See" or "See Also": cross-reference system within the index of the CPT manual used to direct the coder to another term or other terms. The "See" indicates that the correct code will be found elsewhere. The "See Also" indicates that a more specific code may be found in a different location.

seminal vesicle: gland that secretes fluid into the vas deferens

separate procedures: minor procedures that when done by themselves are coded as a procedure, but when performed with another major procedure are considered incidental and not coded separately

sequela: condition that follows an illness

severity of illness: refers to the levels of loss of function and mortality that may be experienced by patients with a particular disease

shaving: horizontal or transverse removal of dermal or epidermal lesions, without full-thickness excision

shunt: divert or make an artificial passage

sialography: radiographic recording of the salivary duct and branches

sigmoidoscopy: fibroscopic examination of the entire rectum and sigmoid colon that may include a portion of the descending colon

single chamber pacemaker: the electrode of the pacemaker is placed only in the atrium or only in the ventricle, but not in both places

sinography: radiographic recording of the sinus or sinus tract

sinuses: cavities within the nasal bones

skin graft: transplantation of tissue to repair a defect

skull: entire skeletal framework of the head

slanted brackets: indicate that the ICD-9-CM code can never be sequenced as the principal diagnosis

soft tissue: tissues (fascia, connective tissue, muscle, etc) surrounding a bone

somatic nerve: sensory or motor nerve

special reports: detailed reports that include adequate definitions or descriptions of the nature, extent, and need for the procedure and the time, effort, and equipment necessary to provide the services

spermatocele: cyst filled with spermatozoa

spirometry: measurement of breathing capacity

splenectomy: excision of the spleen

splenography: radiographic recording of the spleen

splenoportography: radiographic procedure to allow visualization of the splenic and portal veins of the spleen

starred procedures: indicates procedures and services that do not include variable preoperative or postoperative services

stem cell: immature blood cell

stent: mold that holds a surgically placed graft in place

stereotaxis: method of identifying a specific area or point in the brain

strabismus: extraocular muscle deviation resulting in unequal visual axes

subcutaneous: tissue below dermis, primarily fat cells that insulate the body

subsections: further division of sections into smaller units, usually by body systems

superior: toward the head or the upper part of the body, also known as cephalad or cephalic

supine: lying on the back

surgery package: bundling together of time, effort, and services for a specific procedure into one code instead of billing separately for each component

suture: to unite parts by stitching them together

symbols: special guides that help the coder compare codes and descriptors with previous editions. A bullet (●) is used to indicate a new procedure or service code added from the last edition of the CPT manual. A solid triangle (▲) placed in front of a code number indicates that the code has been changed or modified since the last edition. A star (✱) placed after a code number indicates a minor procedure not subject to the surgery package.

sympathetic nerve: part of the peripheral nervous system that controls automatic body function and sympathetic nerves activated under stress

symphysiotomy: cutting of the pubis cartilage to help in birthing

systemic: affecting the entire body

tarsorrhaphy: suturing together of the eyelids

TEFRA (Tax Equity and Fiscal Responsibility Act): act that contains language to reward cost-conscious health care providers

term location methods: service/procedure, anatomic site/body organ, condition/disease, synonym, eponym, and abbreviation

thermogram: written record of temperature variation

thoracentesis: surgical puncture of the thoracic cavity, usually using a needle, to remove fluids

thoracic duct: collection and distribution point for lymph, and the largest lymph vessel located in the chest

thoracoscopy: use of a lighted endoscope to view the pleural spaces and thoracic cavity or perform surgical procedures

thoracostomy: cutting the thoracic cavity to allow for enlargement of the heart or for drainage

thoracotomy: surgical incision into the thoracic cavity

thrombosis: blood clot

thymectomy: surgical removal of the thymus

thymus: produces hormones important to the immune response

thyroglossal duct: connection of the thyroid and the pharynx and continuation with the endodermal floor of the mouth

thyroid: part of the endocrine system that produces hormones that regulate metabolism

thyroidectomy: surgical removal of the thyroid

thyroiditis: a thyroid gland inflammation

tissue transfer: piece of skin for grafting that is still partially attached to the original blood supply and is used to cover an adjacent wound area

tocolysis: repression of uterine contractions

tomography: procedure that allows viewing of a single plane of the body by blurring out all but that particular level
tonography: recording of changes in intraocular pressure in response to sustained pressure on the eyeball
tonometry: measurement of pressure or tension
traction: application of force to a limb
transabdominal: across the abdomen
transcutaneous: entering by way of the skin
transesophageal echocardiogram (TEE): echocardiogram performed by placing a probe down the esophagus and sending out sound waves to obtain images of the heart and its movement
transhepatic: across the liver
transmastoid antrostomy: called a simple mastoidectomy, it creates an opening in the mastoid for drainage
transplantation: grafting of tissue from one source to another
transsseptal: through the septum
transthoracic: across the thorax
transverse: horizontal
transureteroureterostomy: surgical connection of one ureter to the other ureter
transurethral resection, prostate: procedure performed through the urethra by means of a cystoscopy to remove part or all of the prostate
transvesical ureterolithotomy: removal of ureter stone(calculus) through the bladder
trocar needle: needle with a tube on the end, used to puncture and withdraw fluid from a cavity
tumescence: state of being swollen
tumor: swelling or enlargement; a spontaneous growth of tissue that forms an abnormal mass
tunica vaginalis: covering of the testes
tympanic neurectomy: excision of the tympanic nerve
tympanometry: test of the inner ear using air pressure
UHDDS: Uniform Hospital Discharge Data Set
ultrasound: technique using sound waves to determine the density of the outline of tissue
uncertain behavior: refers to the behavior of a neoplasm as neither malignant nor benign but having characteristics of both malignant and benign
uncertain diagnosis: diagnosis documented at the time of discharge as "probable," "suspected," "likely," "questionable," "possible," or "rule out"
unilateral: occurring on one side
unlisted procedures: procedures that are considered unusual, experimental, or new and do not have a specific code number assigned; unlisted procedure codes are located at the end of the subsections or subheadings and may be used to identify any procedure without a specific code
unspecified hypertension: hypertensive condition that has not been specified as either benign or malignant hypertension
unspecified nature: when the behavior or histology of a neoplasm is not known or is not specified
uptake: absorption of a radioactive substance by body tissues; recorded for diagnostic purposes in conditions such as thyroid disease
ureterectomy: surgical removal of ureter, either totally or partially
ureterocolon: pertaining to the ureter and colon
ureterocutaneous fistula: the channel from the ureter to the exterior skin
ureteroenterostomy: creation of a connection between the intestine and the ureter
ureterolithotomy: removal of a stone from the ureter
ureterolysis: freeing of the adhesions of the ureter
ureteroneocystostomy: surgical connection of the ureter to a new site on the bladder
ureteroplasty: surgical repair of the ureter
ureteropyelography: ureter and bladder radiography
ureteropyelonephrostomy: surgical connection of the ureter to a new site on the kidney
ureteropyelostomy: ureteropyelonephrostomy
ureterosigmoidostomy: surgical connection of the ureter into the sigmoid colon
ureterotomy: incision into the ureter
ureterovisceral fistula: surgical formation of a connection between the ureter and the skin
urethrocutaneous fistula: surgically created channel from the urethra to the skin surface
urethrocystography: radiography of the bladder and urethra
urethromeatoplasty: surgical repair of the urethra and meatus
urethroplasty: surgical repair of the urethra
urethrorrhaphy: suturing of the urethra
urethroscopy: use of a scope to view the urethra
urography: same as pyelography; radiographic recording of the kidneys, renal pelvis, ureters, and bladder
uveal: vascular tissue of the choroid, ciliary body, and iris
V codes: numerical designations preceded by the letter "V" used to classify persons who are not currently sick when they encounter health services
vagina: canal from the external female genitalia to the uterus
vagotomy: surgical separation of the vagus nerve
varicocele: swelling of a scrotal vein
vas deferens: tube that carries sperm from the epididymis to the urethra
vasogram: recording of the flow in the vas deferens
vasotomy: creation of an opening in the vas deferens

vasovasorrhaphy: suturing of the vas deferens
vasovasostomy: reversal of a vasectomy
VBAC: vaginal delivery after a previous cesarean delivery
vectorcardiogram (VCG): continuous recording of electrical direction and magnitude of the heart
vein: vessel that carries unoxygenated blood to the heart from body tissues
vena canal thrombectomy: removal of a blood clot from the blood vessel (inferior vena cava, which is the vein trunk for the pelvic and abdominal area)
venography: radiographic recording of the veins and tributaries
ventricle: chamber in the lower part of the heart
version: turning of the fetus from a presentation other than cephalic (head down) to cephalic for ease of birth
vesicostomy: surgical creation of a connection of the viscera of the bladder to the skin
vesicovaginal fistula: creation of a tube between the vagina and bladder
vesiculectomy: excision of the seminal vesicle
vesiculography: radiographic recording of the seminal vesicles
vesiculotomy: incision into the seminal vesicle
vitre/o-: prefix meaning pertaining to the vitreous body of the eye
vulva: external female genitalia including the labia majora, labia minora, clitoris, and vaginal opening
World Health Organization (WHO): group that deals with health care issues on a global basis
wound repair, complex: involves complicated wound closure including revision, debridement, extensive undermining, and more than layered closure
wound repair, intermediate: requires closure of one or more subcutaneous tissue and superficial fascia, in addition to the skin closure
wound repair, simple: superficial wound repair, involving epidermis, dermis, and subcutaneous tissue, requiring only simple one-layer suturing
xeroradiography: photoelectric process of radiographs

Index

Note: Page numbers in *italics* refer to illustrations; those followed by t refer to tables.

B

C

Q

R